Jesus *Is* One of Us

Jesus *Is* One of Us

Recovering God's Firstborn, Glorified, and Completed Human

RON SIMKINS

RESOURCE *Publications* · Eugene, Oregon

JESUS IS ONE OF US
Recovering God's Firstborn, Glorified, and Completed Human

Copyright © 2021 Ron Simkins. All rights reserved. Except for brief quotations in critical publications or reviews, no part of this book may be reproduced in any manner without prior written permission from the publisher. Write: Permissions, Wipf and Stock Publishers, 199 W. 8th Ave., Suite 3, Eugene, OR 97401.

Resource Publications
An Imprint of Wipf and Stock Publishers
199 W. 8th Ave., Suite 3
Eugene, OR 97401

www.wipfandstock.com

PAPERBACK ISBN: 978-1-7252-6311-6
HARDCOVER ISBN: 978-1-7252-6310-9
EBOOK ISBN: 978-1-7252-6312-3

All Scripture quotations, unless otherwise indicated, are taken from the Holy Bible, New International Version®, NIV®. Copyright ©1973, 1978, 1984, 2011 by Biblica, Inc.™ Used by permission of Zondervan. All rights reserved worldwide. www.zondervan.com.

The "NIV" and "New International Version" are trademarks registered in the United States Patent and Trademark Office by Biblica, Inc.™

08/06/21

Contents

Acknowledgments		vii
Introduction		1
1	The God and Father of Our Lord Jesus the Messiah	21
2	God's Purpose: Male and Female in the Image of God	32
3	Jesus: God's Definition of Human Potential	65
4	Jesus Was One of Us	70
5	Jesus Is One of Us—Now and Forever	94
6	Jesus: God's Exalted Human	112
7	Personal Trust and Debt to Jesus	136
8	Jesus's Role as Messiah	151
9	Jesus's Role as Son of God	162
10	Jesus's Role as Savior	173
11	Jesus's Role as Burden-bearer	183
12	Jesus's Faith and Faithfulness	197
13	Jesus's Cross and Resurrection	216
14	Jesus: Spirit-filled and Spirit-led Human	267
15	Jesus's Jewishness	287
16	Jesus's Other Roles	303
17	The God and Father of Our Lord Jesus the Messiah: Revisited	347
Conclusion		386
Bibliography		389
Index		393

Acknowledgments

The time and expertise freely given by people who read this book at various stages of development have been priceless gifts. Martin Shupack read all my early drafts and helped me decide where to focus. Marty brought his perspective as a Harvard lawyer committed to advocating for God's justice for everyone, as well as his Mennonite theological perspective. Judy Checker, whom I first met when we were both graduate students in the Philosophy Department at the University of Illinois, shared her insights and encouragement from the point of view of a Jewish follower of Jesus. Walter Zorn, a friend since seminary, who shares my Restoration Movement church background, gave freely from his expertise with Hebrew, Greek, theology, and bibliographical resources. Always an encourager, Walt read every page of my later drafts and made the book immeasurably better.

Friends—Thomas Ewald, from his background that weds psychology and theology, Paige Weston, from her editing experience, and Adey Wassink, from her perspective as a pastor, offered helpful insights on specific chapters. Family members—David Simkins, Karyn Hunt, Mari Hunt Wassink, and Mary Ann Simkins—each added insights on specific chapters as well.

The fact that it is a cliché doesn't change the need to say that none of these dear people are responsible for any errors or weaknesses in the book. Those are mine. Neither does their generosity mean they agree with everything I have written.

This is the second book Rob Siedenburg has edited for me. His expertise with the English language, and his experience from the many books he has edited for others, have been a wonderful gift. Rob seems to know something interesting about everything. He also became a personal encourager. Samuel Carroll also contributed important editing and insights throughout the book. I am grateful for the personnel I have worked with at Wipf & Stock Publishers. Throughout the process with two books now, I have found every person a pleasure to interact with.

Finally, I honor Donna Simkins who, next only to Jesus, is more responsible than anyone else for the relationship I have with God. She passed into God's next age as I was nearing the completion of this book. We were kids when we married, but we not only completed more than fifty-seven years of marriage, we grew more in love and more faithful to God as the years passed. She loved and encouraged me

Acknowledgments

in life beyond my wildest expectations, and certainly beyond anything I deserved. Perhaps the following poem will help you understand that her influence touches every page of the book you are preparing to read.

CELEBRATING DONNA

I could say we fell deeply in love—if it hadn't occurred before we knew it.

I could say you are a serious woman—if not for your lively dancing eyes.

I could say you are a solemn woman—if you didn't delight so in laughing.

I could say you are an independent woman—if not for your never-ending giving.

I could say you are a calm woman—if not for your fierce passion.

I could say you are a hard-working woman—if not for your many playful ways.

I could say you are a quiet woman—if not for the thunder of your truths.

I could say you loved from the first—if not for the depths learned since.

I could say you are my wife—but really, you are my life.

I could say you saved me— but really, you did let Jesus help.

I could say I will love you until I die—but really, forever is as far as we go.

Introduction

AN INVITATION TO SHARE A JOURNEY WITH ME.

When we are asked to follow Jesus, we are being invited to take part in a journey toward becoming more fully human than we usually dare to imagine. It's not so much that we sell ourselves short; it's that we sell the God who created humans short. I am inviting you to explore this journey with what might be a new pair of theological eyeglasses for you. At least it seems to be so for many people I know.

As they wrote, the writers of the New Testament were still overwhelmed with this Jesus they had come to trust. None of them thought they had arrived on their journey with Jesus. In fact, they often spoke of "following" Jesus as "a way" of life, as a "walk," and as choosing the best "road." They challenged fellow travelers, and themselves, to "press on" and "persevere." They also invited others to join them on this journey of great joy and deep heartbreak just as Jesus had invited them to join him on the journey.

You are being invited to reread the New Testament with a lens that allows Jesus to be fully embedded in our humanity. I encourage you to experience Jesus as the writer of the second chapter of Hebrews describes him—the first human to be "crowned" with the fullness of God's "glory and honor." He (or she, as a few scholars suggest) also identifies Jesus as our human brother whom God "made perfect" or "made complete" (*teleioō* in Greek). The writer of Hebrews joined Paul and the writer of Revelation in describing Jesus as the "firstborn" of God's forever human family. Encountering Jesus as fully and genuinely *one of us* has been, and continues to be, a very exciting adventure and a growth-filled experience for me. I think that it can be a delightful journey for you as well.

I have found that it is a somewhat risky journey—risky because it challenges us to be more human than we typically dare to be. We are challenged to keep growing so that, more and more, we think and act as Jesus did (Phil 2:5). The goal of this Jesus-road arrives when God is able to complete us as humans, and "we shall be like him, for we shall see him as he is" (1 John 3:2). Becoming fully human then becomes our highest and ultimate goal, rather than our excuse for our failures. Being "completed" and "glorified" humans is something God wants to "crown" us with as a gift, just has God has already done for Jesus (Heb 2:6–18).

The journey into a fuller recognition of Jesus's humanness is also risky because it seems to raise anxious feelings and thoughts in quite a few fellow Christians. This is especially true when the implications begin to become clear. We all tend to become uneasy when Jesus is suddenly not content to stay in the pigeonholes where we have attempted to stick him. Sometimes, brothers and sisters who are feeling this anxiety would prefer that you just go away if you begin to speak of God's relationship with Jesus in ways they are not accustomed to hearing.

I hope you will go with me on this journey focused on Jesus's humanity and ours. If, as often occurs with a new pair of glasses, you find things a bit out of focus at first, please stick with it. At least entertain the possibility that the main message in the New Testament concerning what God is revealing through God's relationship with Jesus is an overwhelming new step in God's creation project—humans in the image of God as God's forever family. What if Jesus, the "firstborn," really is God's first completed and glorified human? What if the entire creation is waiting in frustration until God is able to complete this glorious purpose for many other humans in addition to Jesus (Rom 8:22–24, 28–30)?

SOME PREPARATION FOR THE JOURNEY MIGHT BE IMPORTANT TO YOU.

For many years it has seemed to me that writers, teachers, pastors, and professors should tell their audience a bit about their own experiences and basic belief framework. After all, everything we say and do is shaped by them. To that end, I will use this Introduction to orient you as reader to the person who is inviting you to walk together through this book.

A rather substantial portion of the book is about what Christians often call biblical doctrine. It is important that you know at least three things as we begin. First, for those of you who think that sounds boring, I will do my best not to make it a boring journey. Second, I do not think that I have arrived at a complete understanding of the relationship between God, Jesus, and the rest of us. I fully expect to stand before God and Jesus someday very surprised about many things that I only partially understood. I also fully expect the same will be true about you.

Third, by nature, I seem to be a questioner and somewhat cynical. Friends have often talked about people who have "the gift of faith," to which I respond "God gave me the gift of questioning." Certainly, no one who knows me has ever accused me of failing to see how evil, corrupt, self-centered, broken, and destructive we humans can be. I know it about myself, and I know it about you. Nonetheless, I find myself writing a book celebrating God's invitation for us to become more fully human, more wonderful than we can imagine. If that is doctrine, then I do not find it boring! This is a book that I have been wishing to write for more than thirty years.

I hope what follows will provide enough initial information about the framework I am working from to orient you to the rest of the book.

Journeying Together Does Not Depend on Discovering Previously Unavailable Data, but Rather on Risking a Different Lens.

Nothing can possibly appear in this book that someone hasn't been working with, and thinking about in some way, long before we were born. But we can adjust our eyes and tilt our hearts to see whether there is a better view of claims and information that have been available for millennia. The fact that there is no new data has two important implications: First, successful or not, what I am attempting to do is focus on a theme that I find emerging throughout the Bible in various ways. So, the raw data is at least 2000 years old, often much older. Nothing new about that!

Second, I try to footnote enough to give credit when I am directly interacting with someone else's material. I have no desire to claim someone else's work. On the other hand, I have limited footnoting because I want this book to be easily accessible to anyone who is interested in the theme "Jesus *Is* One of Us." If, as you read, you find yourself thinking you remember a similar insight or perspective from reading C. S. Lewis, Brenda Salter McNeil, Paul Tournier, N. T. Wright, Soren Kierkegaard, Austin Channing Brown, Jacques Ellul, F. F. Bruce, Phyliss Tribble, Thomas Kuhn, Daily Bread Meditations, or whoever else might come to your mind, please know that you could be right.

I gladly give them, and hundreds of others, credit for helping form my perspectives on life. I am a synthesizer by nature, one who is always looking for the bigger picture. It is also possible that I read something one of these or another author wrote and thought, "Yes, that is what I think too!" Which likely means that at an earlier time someone else started me down that same path. I gladly credit every author, teacher, friend, family member, fellow church member, and even some who consider me an enemy, with teaching me everything I know. After all, like you, I came into this world knowing nothing. Everything I know, or think I know, began with someone else's influence. My goal as we journey together is to encourage you to take a new look at what is available in the Scriptures for all of us to see.

Journeying Together Does Not Depend on Our Agreeing about Theories of Dating, Interpretation, Inspiration, or Authorship of the Bible.

I decided not to expend space on theories of inspiration, interpretation, biblical authorship, editing, and dating. These are all very important, but they are not the subject of this book. I think the main themes of this book stand, regardless of whether as a reader you sort these controversial issues in the more progressive and insightful manner of the late Rachel Held Evans[1], or in the somewhat more conservative and perceptive manner of the prolific N. T. Wright.[2] For example, I am going to designate the writer(s) of the Gospel of John, the Epistles of John, and the book of Revelation as "John." It does not matter for my point in this book whether "John" refers to one John, two different Johns, or three different Johns. My personal opinion is there was likely one author at different stages of life, but it does not matter for the theme of this book. Whoever wrote the materials, I am grateful that we have them.

Since I was a young adult—long ago—I have been intrigued with how we humans interpret reality (hermeneutics) and with what it means for us to claim that we know something (epistemology). My son came home from college wearing a T-shirt he and his philosophy classmates designed, asking, "What part of *know* don't you understand?" He was sure (knew?) that I would love it. Having pursued these interests in how we "know" and "interpret" for years, experience has taught me that many sisters and brothers will reflexively disagree with how I respond to the Bible.

For some, the way I relate to God through the Bible—the book I love above all other books—might seem not nearly reverent enough. Long ago, I realized the often-well-meaning Christians in my conservative evangelical background who taught me that every sentence in the Bible had to be woodenly inerrant were espousing a modern philosophy, not reflecting the Bible itself. To claim that authors two or three thousand years ago had to be inerrant about every statement that touches on what we have learned since about creation (nature), history, geography, psychology, sociology, or the cosmos is to remove humanity from the writing of the biblical materials.

I sadly watched quite a few young university students lose their faith in God over that doctrine during their first religious studies class or first biology class. They thought they could no longer believe in God, if the Bible had even one *mistake* in it. I experience the Bible as a gift from God to us. I also trust that the Bible can do everything that God wants it to do when we allow God to speak and act through it. I suppose that is a form of inerrancy, but the "when we allow God" is a huge caveat as is "everything that God wants it to." Why do we want to construct theories of inerrancy that essentially remove the Bible from its main claim: God is at work in the lives of real humans in the real world—people like us, people who make mistakes?

Equally, or perhaps more importantly, as I allowed the Bible to correct my earlier understanding of the Bible, it became clear that the truest truth about God in the Bible is true only when we find the right context for it. In fact, few falsehoods are more deadly than scriptural truths, or any other truths, in the wrong context. Truths that become lies when the context is blurred are often spiritually deadly. Isn't that the crux

---

1. Evans, *Inspired*.
2. Wright, *Victory of God*, and *Broken Signposts*.

of Jesus's experience in the wilderness? Matthew and Luke describe quoting Scriptures in the wrong context as a primary tool of evil.

So much damage has been done in Christian circles by quoting verses of the Bible into situations where they do not belong. One quick example: I believe it is true that even in the worst situations, God will work toward the good of making humans who love God more into the image of God (Rom 8:28–30; Heb 5:8–9). But it would have been wrong for one of Jesus's friends to say during the brutal Roman crucifixion, "Don't fret; it will all turn out for the good." It would not have been helpful to *encourage* Jesus by saying, "Now Jesus, you know the psalmist says you cannot get away from God's presence," while he was lamenting experiencing God's apparent absence. The only right thing to do was to be with him, cry with him, and hurt with him. To attempt to put a happy face on Jesus's experience at Golgotha by quoting an up-beat Bible verse would have been exceedingly cruel, no matter how well-intended.

Similarly, Bible quotations meant to put a happy face on reality did not help my dear friends who watched their wonderful daughter die, inch by inch, in excruciating pain, due to lung cancer. Neither did they help me as my wife lost a bit more of herself every month with Parkinson's Brain Disease, and then finally passed out of this age looking like a holocaust victim.

For another example of the damage easy theological answers can do to a person willing to risk loving in the real world, I encourage you to read Jeremy Courtney's *Love Anyway*. Throughout the book, he documents how deeply he and his wife were hurt and betrayed by the easy answers and Bible quotations coming from back home in Texas. Back home, a form of "we Christians are the elite" theology seemed to be working for people. But when the chips are down, and life is hell, they don't really work. In Iraq—in conditions much more like those Jesus lived in—they were truths in completely the wrong context.[3] Even the truest truth needs the right context in order to be true.

Others might find my acceptance of the Bible as a God-given gift that is grounded in real historical human experiences with God far too naïve. I do not think it is a book filled with made-up history; I think it is filled with real people's real experiences with a very real God. I also trust that God continues to speak through the Bible to people with open hearts. I do not think that you need to be a theological or biblical scholar in order for God to speak to you through the Bible.

As my relationship with Jesus grew, I learned to let experts—conservative, moderate, and liberal alike—help inform me about all they have learned, and all they think they have learned. This includes the areas of theology, languages, history, cultures, anthropology, DNA/RNA science, the age of the earth, adaptation (evolution), sociology, psychology, and archaeology, but I do not allow them to tell me what God could and couldn't do in the past. They are not necessarily specialists in knowing what God can and cannot do today either. The smartest biblical scholar does not necessarily

---

3. Courtney, *Love Anyway*, 61–62, 93–97.

know more—he or she might know a lot less than others—about how God has or has not interacted with humans in the past or in the present.

The real experts in this area are the sisters and brothers who humbly relate to God, seek God with their whole hearts, and genuinely experience God working in their daily lives to transform them more and more into the image of God. Of course, they can be wrong about some things too, but I have learned as much about what God does and does not do from brothers and sisters who never graduated from college as I have from people with several advanced degrees hanging on their office walls. God seems to love to relate to humans who really want to relate to God. That includes God's choice to speak to children of God with open hearts and to act through the Scriptures on their behalf.

Experience also tells me there will be disagreements with the way I understand events recorded in the Bible, especially those maintaining that God was involved in horrible occurrences. Some of you might disagree because you are sure God couldn't have been involved in these horrors. Others might disagree because you are sure that, if God was involved, they can't be horrible and sinful events. As I will explore with you throughout the book, I think God has often accommodated to be present in our world as it is. This is not because God approves of how it is. God often accommodates to where we are because God couldn't work in the world at all if God did not choose to be involved with us in the tragedies we create for ourselves and for one another.

Here is a modern-day example of what I mean about God's apparent willingness to be involved in the broken and tragic situations we humans create. I am pretty sure that God heard and answered prayers for Pastor Helmut Thielicke (an active opponent of Hitler and Nazism) and the German soldiers he loved and counseled, as they asked whether he really believed in resurrection. Many of them knew they would die the next day, as they battled to protect their homeland and families by killing American soldiers.

I also remember, as a young adult, hearing American WWII veterans talk about how God, at the same time these German soldiers were praying, answered their prayers and changed their lives. God heard their prayers and transformed their lives during those days when they battled and killed German soldiers.

Does that mean God fully approved of the hellish mess we humans placed those prayerful German and American brothers and sisters in—young people who shared the same faith in God and Jesus? Did God want these Christians to see who could kill the other first? Or, to slightly turn the lens, do you think God fully approved of thousands of Christians, many singing the same hymns of faith, killing one another in the American Civil War? Did God hear and respond only to the prayers of the many Christians in Nagasaki or only to those of the Christians who sent and flew the American bomber? On the other hand, are all the experiences with God from people on both sides of these horrendous wars just wishful thinking? God seems to do a lot of accommodating in our world.

Why wouldn't it be the same with events in the Bible? Especially, those that reflect cultures filled with misogyny, patriarchy, genocidal wars, monarchy, despotism, and slavery? It appears to me that this is precisely the way Jesus responded to the Old Testament records. He believed that God was with David, and he believed that he was definitely not supposed to act as David did when it came to war, political intrigue, lying, kingship, treatment of women, revenge, or harems.

Whether you agree with the way I relate to the Bible or not, I hope you will consider my primary claim that most, perhaps all, of the New Testament writers explicitly and implicitly see Jesus as fully embedded in humanity in the past, in the present, and in the future. He *is* one of us.

To be clear, claiming there is an overarching master story in the Bible concerning how much God values humanness is not a claim for which the Bible provides a nice little three-point outline of the master narrative. Outlining does not seem to have been a big concern for the writers of our Scriptures. They preferred recording human experiences, stories, and parables.

Neither am I claiming that everything in the New Testament is fully complementary and consistent. The recounting of events by observers and participants in an automobile accident are never fully complementary and consistent. That doesn't mean a real wreck, real injuries, and real fault never occurred. Why would we expect the recounting of the electrifying events of Jesus's ministry, miracles, healings, arrest, execution, and resurrection appearances to be without inconsistencies? They aren't!

That does not mean that Jesus did not do miracles and healings, nor does it mean that he was not arrested, tortured, executed, buried, and raised from death. It just means that real humans related the events from the perspectives, advantages, and limitations they had. Why would we think that a liberal Jew like Philip, a Hellenistic Jewish Roman citizen like Paul, a moderate Galilean Jew like Peter, and a conservative Galilean Jew like James would experience following Jesus the same way? What we are told about them, and by them, seems to indicate they did not.

It is also true that the biblical records are so sparse that we should never think that two thousand years later we can put all of the unorganized fragments together in a nice smooth consistent picture. Willie James Jennings is right to remind us that, though we have some words from Jesus and from various prophets:

> . . . *everything is in slices and slivers, pieces and shards.* We have no whole here—no whole picture of ancient Israel, or the prophets, or their families, or Jesus, or his family. . . . All of it is merely fragments, large and small.[4]

The same Gospels that tell us Jesus taught and ministered for about three and a half years, that would be about 1300 days, describe what we know about Jesus's words and actions in material that can easily be read in about 13 hours. That is indeed a very small slice of Jesus's words and actions! Even the little bit we do have of what Jesus did

---

4. Jennings. *After Whiteness*, 32.

and said—of course, scholars argue vehemently about how much we have—is presented in a manner such that no two writers of the four Gospels agree on exactly how the content should be organized chronologically or outlined topically. This lack of organization seemed to bother Luke a bit (Luke 1:1–4), but the church still saved four Gospels, not just Luke's. Similarly, we can't figure out for sure how many letters Paul wrote to the Corinthian church, or why only two of them were saved for us.

What I am claiming is that, among all the slices and slivers the Bible offers us, there is a theme that appears as a central claim on the first page of Genesis and reappears throughout the New Testament in relationship to Jesus. It is a theme that should be taken far more seriously than we often do. That claim? God's goal for creating us humans, and God's goal for humans as it comes to fruition in Jesus, is humans *in the image of God*. In that sense, God is the original *humanist* who highly values human potential. In fact, as a whole, though certainly not in every part, the Bible celebrates God's passionate love for humans.

Taking This Journey Together Does Not Depend upon Resolving Theological Issues Involving Other Religions, the Trinity, Preexistence, or Sovereignty.

God sent God's Son into the world to redeem us (Gal 4:4–5) because "God so loved the world [not just us and not just me]" (John 3:16). I trust my life to that promise. I also unequivocally trust that the relationship between God and Jesus is the only reality that could save me from being prone to act in ways filled with destruction of others and self. Praying for God to save others from me, and to save me from myself, is a meaningful prayer. It is a prayer that I definitely pray "in Jesus's name."

Having said that, I am less confident when it comes to the various constructs we Christians have created in our attempts to explain Jesus's relationship with God. As I mentioned, I do not think for a minute that either you, I, or anyone else has arrived at a complete understanding of God or of what God is doing in our world. For this reason, I will not attempt to try to harmonize the biblical theme "Jesus *is* one of us" with any, or all, of the different theories Christians hold concerning how God responds to people in other religions and cultures, the Trinity, or Jesus's preexistence. To be transparent, I admit that I attempt to do a little more harmonizing where the biblical teachings about God's sovereignty are concerned. But I am certain that neither you nor I have that all worked out either.

Concerning people in *other religions*, the framework I live and work from is one that I think reflects the overall biblical framework: *God has an inclusive heart and an exclusive purpose.* The inclusive heart means God is looking anywhere and everywhere for humans who are thankful for God's gifts and who seek goodness, righteousness, and justice for their fellow humans. The exclusive purpose means God has relentlessly pursued through human history God's goal of creating a forever human family made up of women and men in the image of God. This exclusive purpose has been moved forward through God's covenant with Abraham, and then again through God's covenant through Jesus. I see the covenant relationship shared by God and Jesus as the clearest and deepest revelation of both the inclusiveness of God's heart and the exclusiveness of God's purpose in history.

Surely God is never awed by our religious institutions—Christian or other. God is looking for hearts turned toward God, seeking for God, and loving fellow humans—a way of life. That does not mean I think all religions are equally valid. They certainly are not. Neither do I think any religion rivals the awesome reality that God has revealed in Jesus. Surely God's inclusive heart and exclusive purpose transcend all of the structures we have created.

One reason for the decision not to attempt to reconcile the biblical theme of Jesus's full humanity with *various church doctrines of the Trinity* is that even the most brilliant scholars have never been able to agree on exactly how the Bible and the doctrine of the Trinity fit together. I have enjoyed, benefitted from, and learned a lot from reading the ongoing dialogue concerning different views of how the New Testament writers understood the relationship between Jesus and God, by four brilliant and careful Christian scholars of the British academic world—Richard Bauckham,[5] the late James D. G. Dunn,[6] the late Larry Hurtado,[7] and N. T. Wright.[8]

All four of these scholars contributed greatly to my study of the New Testament for many years. If these four erudite scholars could not even convince one another of the right way to understand how the New Testament's description of the relationship between God and Jesus squares with the development of trinitarian doctrine, I lack the arrogance to claim that I could possibly resolve the questions to any reader's satisfaction. As my son-in-law likes to say, as he and others wrestle with important corporate decisions, "That one is above my pay grade." Or, to use the language of my charismatic sisters and brothers, "Stay with your gifts" (Rom 12:3). Or, following Paul, let's remember we see only a poor reflection of God right now (1 Cor 13:12).

Looking at the relationship between God and Jesus becomes even more intriguing in the light of the background materials from near Jesus's time, provided by non-Christian scholars, such as Daniel Boyarian[9] and Bart Ehrman.[10] My intrigue is ratcheted even higher by Marilynne Robinson, a staunch Calvinist trinitarian, who presents yet another fascinating understanding of the Trinity, linking our humanity

---

5. Bauckham, *Jesus and the God*.
6. Dunn, *First Christians Worship*.
7. Hurtado, *How on Earth?*
8. Wright, *Paul and the Faithfulness*.
9. Boyarin, *Jewish Gospel*.
10. Ehrman, *Jesus Became God*.

to what she believes is the preexistent humanity of the trinitarian Christ as Creator.[11] Then, just as I am finishing this book, I hear about a book by an author I had never heard of. This self-proclaimed former Calvinist and former Evangelical has written from a strange but interesting stance, a book that on every page stresses the importance of the Trinity and the importance of understanding that Jesus is still human.[12]

No two of the authors I have just referenced agree on exactly how to synchronize what the New Testament writers say about the relationship between God and Jesus with the later credal understanding of the Trinity. What is important here is that nothing any of these scholars say negates our theme—the New Testament claim that Jesus *is* one of us.

Neither will I attempt to resolve the related arguments raised in many commentaries and translations concerning whether or not various New Testament passages refer directly to Jesus as God.[13] If you read these Scriptures in various translations, you will find that often translators and translation committees do not agree on how to best translate a passage. The same is true among commentators.

Several of the questions revolve around what the function of the "and" (*kai* in Greek) is in a sentence. We have this same issue in English. If you read, "They saw an athlete and a trainer," you must decide whether this means one person who fills both roles—a very athletic trainer—or two people, each filling one of the roles—an athlete with her trainer. Sometimes the context makes this easy, and sometimes it does not.

Other discussions revolve around when forms of the Greek word *theos* mean what we mean in English when we translate *God* with a capital *G*, or what we mean in English when we translate *theos* as *god* with a small *g* or as *divine*. *Elohim* in Hebrew was used for what we translate as *God*, and *god(s)*, *champion*, and *person of great status*. *Theos* was used the same way. In fact, in John 10:33–37, Jesus used what we would call the small *g* argument from a psalm to rebut the accusation that he was too arrogant (Ps 82:1, 6). He identifies himself with those agents of God whom "God [*elohim*]" called "god(s) [*elohim*]." Then in John 20:17, Jesus speaks of "my God and your God" and "my Father and your Father" in what we clearly see as our capital *G* manner. In that statement, he distinguishes himself from "God" and identifies himself with the relationship his disciples have with "God." So, some commentators and translators ask, which are we to understand as Thomas's meaning in John 20:28?

Among the Christian scholars mentioned earlier, Wright and Bauckham argue extensively that New Testament writers wanted to convey unequivocally that "Jesus is God." Dunn argues that—with the possible exception of Revelation—they did not

---

11. Robinson, *Giveness*, 188–225.
12. Kruger, *Jesus Undoing Adam*, 8.
13. The most discussed passages are John 1:1, 18; 20:28; Rom 9:5; Titus 2:13; 3:4; Heb 1:8; 2 Pet 1:1; 1 John 5:20; and sometimes 1 Cor 12:6.

intend to identify "Jesus as God," but rather to say that Jesus uniquely participates in God through their [Jesus's and God's] relationship.[14]

My goal is not to attempt to improve on what these amazing scholars have done for us. I do find it intriguing that various New Testament writers often refer to Jesus as "Our Savior," "Our Lord," and "Our Messiah" in completely unambiguous ways, but seem to have been reticent to ever refer to Jesus simply as "Jesus Our God." I also find it intriguing that both the Gospel of John and 1 John continue to insist that humans have seen and touched Jesus, but "No one has ever seen God." Clearly, they are attempting to make some important distinction between Jesus and God, while also linking them inextricably. However you sort all of this out, your solution needs to include the theme of this book. New Testament writers followed a Jesus they trusted was, is, and always will be one of us humans. And, they also believed that you could never find the words to exhaust all the wonder of what God has done for us through Jesus.

As for Jesus and *preexistence*, there are a dozen passages—or perhaps several dozen, depending on how some passages are understood—that indicate some form of preexistence for "the Son." Some theologians and commentators think these passages indicate that the Son preexisted as God-the-Son, some as an archangel, some as the Christ but not as Jesus, some as the preexistent firstborn human, some as the Creative Word of God or the Wisdom of God, and some as the future intended purpose in the mind and heart of God. Others think that time means nothing to God because all time is present to God at the same time; so in some sense preexistence is a meaningless concept—except for the 33 or so years the Son spent as the human Jesus in Israel. If erudite scholars of biblical languages, cultures, and theologies cannot resolve to one another's satisfaction how the different biblical statements—even in the same book or letter—can fit together, I know better than to think I can do so satisfactorily in this book. It is not my topic anyway. And, no matter which of these understandings you hold concerning preexistence, the theme of this book still holds—Jesus *is* one of us.

Theological and doctrinal views of *sovereignty* are the source of many disagreements among Christian scholars and nonscholars. As a reader, you might vehemently disagree with some of my views on God's sovereignty and with how I think most, perhaps all, biblical writers viewed God's sovereignty. The Old Testament is filled with statements ascribing causality to God, even when they are speaking of some devastating judgments on various cultures and on Israel. Often in the same book, a prophet will attribute causality to an enemy's military might, to the conqueror's greed, to the failures of Israel's leaders (priests, prophets, kings, and elders), to the sins of the current generation, to the sins of past generations, and to the judgment of God.

And, to further complicate the sovereignty issue, in that same section of the book, there will be a declaration that only goodness and love, never evil and hate, originate with YHWH. Some think this clearly illustrates a lack of even a basic level of logic. Given how scholars are increasingly recognizing the intricate brilliance of the

---

14. Dunn, *First Christian Worship*, 132–144.

writing style of many of the biblical writers, the claim that they ignore all basic logic is increasingly untenable. We have a record of a logic that wrestles openly with all of these causalities, while refusing to let go of the Oneness of God, the involvement of God at some level in all events, and the goodness of the God who would never approve of the horrible things we do to one another and to the creation. We will return to the tension this created in their faith, and creates in ours, throughout the book.

As you read, it will become obvious that I have some strong opinions concerning how I think the dynamic tension between God's sovereignty and human choices is best understood. If you strongly disagree with how I understand the relationship between God's sovereignty and human choices, please do not let that keep you from seeing what is clearly a New Testament stance—the faithful Jesus is our firstborn human brother through whom the sovereign God is creating God's future human family and culture (kingdom). Jesus *was*, *is*, and always *will be* one of us.

Journeying Together Does Not Depend upon This Book Being Without Errors.

Undoubtedly, you will find things in this book that you disagree with. Despite my efforts to be accurate, you might find mistakes or errors along the way. Perhaps you have already, and you have not yet even finished the Introduction! Probably by the time this book is in print, I will have learned something that causes me to wish that I could tweak a sentence or a claim just a bit—perhaps even more than a bit. Many of us find something we think is wrong or misguided in almost every nonfiction book we read, even when the author is extremely well-versed, or even if we are reading one of our favorite authors.

It is always tempting, but never smart, to allow a disagreement or a mistake to become our excuse for not permitting ourselves to be stretched. The temptation is doubly powerful when the challenge confronts something *we already know*. My past experience indicates that some readers might be sure that they already know that the New Testament cannot possibly view Jesus as still human. I beg you to not allow any errors I have made, or you think I have made, in exegesis, application, or anything else, to become an excuse for ignoring that there is a lot of data from the New Testament to indicate that Jesus's continuing humanity was definitely the writers' understanding of who he is. His exalted status and roles do not separate him from our humanity, but rather embed him deeply in our humanity.

INTRODUCTION

Translation Issues Posed Difficult Decisions for Me as I Planned for This Journey with You.

I was once far more proficient in reading and translating Hebrew and Greek than I am now. Even back then, I was more focused on theology and philosophy than on languages, but turning down the opportunities to go the academic route and choosing to pastor took me further from the daily practice of original languages. However, I knew then, and I know now, to deeply appreciate those who have made it their lifework to translate well for the rest of us. It is difficult and complicated work. Without hesitation, I often turned to the expertise of translators and scholarly commentators for help as I wrote this book, just as I always have in every facet of my Bible reading, teaching, and preaching.

On the other hand, like all of us, translators and even translation committees have their biases. One bias that appears in most English translations is the insistence on translating—actually transliterating—the Greek *christos* as "Christ." In the early drafts of this book, I changed the transliteration of the Greek *christos* ("Christ") to "Messiah" or "Anointed One" in every passage. Finally, I decided that it was too cumbersome and often distracted from the main reason for giving a quotation. However, when I do my own translating, I use either "Anointed One" or "Messiah" instead of "Christ." For reasons I will explain later, if I had my way all translations would always use "Anointed One."[15]

I also think God might approve if we put a note at the beginning of every Bible translation explaining that, as often as can possibly be done without destroying the English style or destroying a clear intentional allusion, we will use "God" in place of "He," "brothers and sisters" in place of "brothers," "sons and daughters" or "children" in place of "sons," and "human" in place of "man." Of course, that choice would have to include an acknowledgement that this does not represent the literal translation from the Hebrew and Greek texts. Those texts reflect the cultures in which they were written, and they are heavily male gendered when referring to God and to humans in general. But perhaps I am wrong about suggesting such a change.

Though I am confident we would be better off if all translations translated *christos* as "Anointed One" or "Messiah," I am less confident about the suggestion concerning gender. Perhaps it really is better to reproduce accurately the original cultural background that is reflected in the more literal translations. After all, it is very important that we not forget that the biblical materials reflect very different cultural times. The problem is that so many readings, sermons, and books use the more literal translations, but do not take the time to remind the listener or reader that our Bible was written in cultures of patriarchy, monarchy, violent warfare, and slavery—cultures not to be emulated, but cultures that were broken, bent, and sinful. In Peter's words describing the cultures of his time—they were "corrupt" and "futile" cultures (Acts 2:40;

---

15. *See* chapter 8.

1 Pet 1:18). As Peter also said in these same contexts, the cultures in which the biblical materials were written were cultures from which people needed to be "saved" and "redeemed." They were not cultures followers of Jesus needed to reproduce. Neither is the one we live in today. Paul was definitely right when he maintained that our cultures, and sub-cultures, become our automatic default and conform us to their patterns. They always will conform us, unless we present ourselves daily for God's miraculous transformation into a different way of seeing reality and actively responding to this new way of seeing (Rom 12:1–2).

I am not certain what is the better trade-off. The emotional pain caused by language that seems to us to identify God and humanity as paradigmatically male, or downplaying the reality that our Scriptures come to us reflecting "givens" in cultures that were far from God's ideals. I decided to stay with the more literal translation in this book, even though I am confident God is delighted with the degree to which we have moved beyond the ancient forms of patriarchy that saw women as property and second-class. I love the look in women's eyes when they are clearly included in our readings of the Bible and when they are recognized as the equals they truly are in our churches and our world. We need a way of hearing God speaking to us today through the language of both "then" and "now." Perhaps there is no perfect single solution when it comes to Bible translations, but I pray that we continue looking for ways to do better.

Pursuing This Journey Together Does Not Depend on Labels—Yours or Mine.

As I mentioned, I have long thought that authors (and all teachers and leaders) should be upfront about their personal beliefs and worldviews. I attempted to do that as a teaching assistant at the University years ago, in every class I taught for various church-supported colleges, and in my tenure as pastor. That is my reason for the personal nature of parts of this Introduction, and it is the reason why you will see occasional glimpses of my personal journey as you continue reading.

Having said that, I am honestly not certain what label to give you so you can slot me on the theological continuum. I find that I do not wish to self-identify as Progressive, Fundamentalist, Conservative, Liberal, Evangelical, Protestant, Catholic, or Ecumenical—I just want to be one of many members of the community of Jesus followers. If you belong to that community, I consider you my sister or brother. I suppose that fits some people's definition of *small c* catholic. If you do not belong to that community, I consider you to be a valuable human whom God loves and whom I would be delighted to have the opportunity to know.

I realize that pushing away from all of these labels can be an attempt to hide an arrogant "I am above it all" attitude. I do not think I am better than those who identify comfortably with the various labels I just listed. I have met people wearing each of those labels who live more Christ-like lives—in some ways or in many ways—than I have ever managed. Perhaps I just don't know myself well enough, but it seems none of the labels quite fits. If you want to put me in a slot, you will have to choose it yourself. I am no help. If you have read this far, it will probably come as no surprise to you that some sisters and brothers think I am far too progressive and others that I am far too conservative.

In the interest of further transparency, I acknowledge that I have used the label "Christian" far more often in this book than I am comfortable with. This ambivalence has nothing to do with Jesus—I am unashamedly a Jesus follower. There are two reasons for my reticence, and for my determination, to use the label "Christian."

First, is the matter of authenticity. The word Christian has come to be so laden with our evils and our mistakes that I find it difficult to use. This is true of church history, and it is true today in America and around the world. As will be obvious throughout this book, I find Christian history and Church history (how much do they overlap?) in need of very serious critiquing. And yet, it is that corporate history that provided a place for me to meet God through Jesus. As frustrating as the church is as a corporate entity, it is also the only thread I have found providing a down payment on the promise of the kind of future the New Testament writers say Jesus promises.

I find it inauthentic to attempt to disassociate myself from Church history or from the label Christian, even though I almost daily find many reasons to wish to do so. To be authentic, I must pray "forgive us *our* sins" as Jesus teaches us to do, rather than pretend that I can fully disassociate from the tragic side of Christian history.

Still, I am glad that the New Testament authors did not choose to use the word Christian very much (three times in all, and only once that is clearly positive). Instead, they chose to identify with terms such as "disciples"—apprenticed to learn, "the faithful"/those who trust, "servants of Jesus the Messiah," "followers of Jesus," "saints"—made holy by God, "the called," "body of the Messiah," "aliens and sojourners in the world," "children of God," "sons of God," "brothers in Jesus the Messiah," and "the assembly" (church). To me this means that it is not my desire to be biblical that makes me use the word Christian; it is the fact that I cannot deny some continuity with later church history—both its gifts and its sins. Personally, being called a faltering, but trying to be trusting and trustworthy, follower of Jesus works fine for me.

The second reason for my ambivalence about the label *Christian* is much more personal. It flows from my lifelong experiences with Christians. No one has disappointed and hurt me as deeply as Christians have throughout my life. This began as a child, continued through my teens, and has never stopped. Some of the disappointments have been brutal and inexcusable. The depth of the disappointment is not because individual Christians have been worse than other people in my life experiences; it is because we are supposed to be moving toward becoming more like Jesus. I also have no doubt that there are sisters and brothers who have good reasons for having been very disappointed in, and hurt by, me as well.

Equally important to acknowledge, no one in my life experience has even come close to my fellow Jesus followers when it comes to loving me, caring about me, and amazing me with choices that allow me to see the Spirit of Jesus incarnate among us in very practical and meaningful ways. I love being with, praying with, serving others with, playing with, worshiping with, crying with, and laughing with my sisters and brothers. My life at every level would be so much poorer if it were not for the many gifts of God's Spirit that I have experienced as they have flowed through the lives of sisters and brothers who share the quest to be followers of Jesus.

Finally, when it comes to labels, I will write things that might tempt you to slot me as a Republican or a Democrat. I am neither. I don't like how either party operates or how easily each breaks its promises.

What label to help you understand this book? Obviously, the *label* I prefer is "follower of Jesus." The label I must not attempt to completely avoid is "Christian." So, I chose to use the term a lot throughout the book. "Christian" with all the warts, ambivalence, and reticence—that is who I am. Proud of it. Ashamed of it. But, not ashamed of Jesus. I hope that shows throughout the book.

MY PURPOSE FOR THE JOURNEY I INVITE YOU TO JOIN IS TO HONOR THE FULL HUMANITY OF JESUS.

I think our journey can arrive at a place that most, perhaps all, of the New Testament writers shared. It seems clear to me that many parts of the New Testament reflect the understanding that Jesus was fully human, continues to be fully human, and will be fully human forever as the firstborn of God's forever human family. For all, or most, New Testament writers, Jesus is fully embedded in what it means to be human and is God's revealed definition of what it means to be completed as a human in the image of God.

Perhaps you will find it ironic, as I do, that the understanding of human potential revealed in New Testament claims about Jesus is in some ways more compatible with twenty-first century understandings of human nature than it is with a lot of our Christian theology. From the second century AD forward, much of our theology was more deeply influenced by Greek philosophy than it was by our Old Testament roots. We will explore this irony throughout the book.

Of course, I am not maintaining that God raising Jesus from death and exalting him to God's right hand sits easily within most twenty-first century worldviews. It clearly does not! However, I do think that our current scientific, psychological, and sociological understanding of what it means to be human has been moving increasingly toward an understanding of humans as *wholes*. We are less and less inclined to understand humans as neatly divided souls with bodies, and instead more inclined to understand ourselves as single living units, existing in a deeply related web of relationships. We are also often told that we have not even begun to activate the vast amount of untapped potential embedded in human nature.

Increasingly we see that our personality, our mind, our brain, and our body chemistry are completely interrelated. Though the modern view of our potential and our organic unity as humans might prove to be arrogant and very deadly without God, with God it is not so far from the view of humanness that Paul voiced in a Jewish blessing. He prayed that God would finally make his readers abundantly and completely whole humans with spirit, soul, and body intact forever (1 Thess 5:23).

With God, this understanding of human potential as an integrated whole, designed to be in relationship with an integrated communal wholeness, seems to be almost beyond our ability to imagine, and yet many of us long for it. The New Testament writers claim that it was exactly this kind of completely integrated whole and completed human that they encountered in the risen Jesus. They say they saw revealed before their eyes and touched with their hands what before had been beyond imaging—a glorified and completed/perfected human (1 John 1:1; 1 Cor 2:7–9; Heb 2:9).

What if human potential for goodness, beauty, justice, truth, creating, belonging, caring, and loving exceeds our wildest imaginings? Suppose that a—perhaps the—primary revelation from God in God's relationship with Jesus is to manifest for us this human potential and to make clear God's joy when this potential can be brought to completion. What if a—perhaps the—primary revelation is not so much focused on the fact that God can come and spend 33 years on earth and then go back to being God in heaven, but is rather the revelation of God completing God's purpose for creating humans—"male and female in the image of God?" What if being and becoming more and more like Jesus was, and truly is, God's forever goal for your life and the lives of the people around you? In short, what if Jesus was one of us, is one of us, will forever be one of us—God's firstborn among many brothers and sisters who are yet to be fully completed and glorified?

And, to highlight an irony that appears on almost every page of the New Testament, what if the only way we humans can allow God to fulfill this extraordinarily high vision of human potential is to never become fixated on how great and gifted we are? What if Jesus is right that God has given us power that can be expressed rightly only through the vulnerability of loving and serving our fellow humans? Jesus said it, and lived it, this way:

> [43] Instead, whoever wants to become great among you must be your servant, [44] and whoever wants to be first must be slave of all. [45] For even the Son of Man did not come to be served, but to serve, and to give his life as a ransom for many" (Mark 10:43–45).
>
> [13] You call me "Teacher" and "Lord," and rightly so, for that is what I am. [14] Now that I, your Lord and Teacher, have washed your feet, you also should

wash one another's feet. ¹⁵ I have set you an example that you should do as I have done for you (John 13:13–15).

Can it be that we have more potential than we can imagine, and at the same time, that the only way to reach this potential is to humbly give ourselves away? Note Jesus's confidence that it was absolutely right for him to identify himself as "Teacher" and "Lord," and to use those roles and gifts to humbly serve others. Can it be that the only way to become the individual God can exalt and glorify is to quit attempting to be the self-made, self-sufficient human who has been glorified in the Western world from the time of the ancient Greeks and Romans through the modern American era?

To more fully reach human potential, must we learn to see ourselves as part of a community in which our goal is to serve others? Can it really be that the irony is actually the reality: humans who want to save their lives lose who they really are, and humans who follow the Jesus way have to live in a manner that makes all of their gifts and abilities vulnerable? And amazingly, through humbly sharing our gifts and roles, we become who God meant for us to become (Mark 8:35)?

But we need to know the value and potential of what we are being asked to risk and give away. There is no honor in giving away what is worthless anyway. The Westminster Shorter Catechism begins by declaring that the highest calling for humans is to glorify God. To my knowledge, none of our credal statements or catechisms emphasize the equally important claim in Scriptures that God's goal in relating to humans is to glorify us. *Nonetheless, various biblical authors do seem convinced that the reason we exist—the reason you exist—is because God wants to glorify and honor us humans.* Psalm 8:4–9 explicitly makes this claim about God's goal for humans, and the writer of Hebrews claims that Jesus is evidence that God has taken a huge step forward in this project (Heb 2:5–18). The creation project of a loving, personal, purposeful, and responsive God who desires "male and female in the image of God" is just begun, rather than being completed, in Genesis 1:26–31. As John Walton says, the building of God's Temple is completed in the narrative of Genesis 1:1–2:4; then the work of the Temple was ready to begin.¹⁶ As we work our way through the Scriptures, it turns out that the place God most wants to dwell in this wonderful creation is in the lives of humans. Once again, Jesus is the first human Temple of God to be completed; because of his faithful relationship with God, he will not be the last.

The itinerary for our journey is to explore more deeply the relationship between God and Jesus, as it is presented in the New Testament and to experience more of the profound promises and challenges that it includes for the rest of us humans. The method is partly pastoral, partly personal, and partly a parsing of biblical passages, the implications of which I think have often been ignored. Though I certainly make no claim to be a prophet, I hope that the book has a bit of a prophetic edge to it as well.

---

16. Walton, *Lost World*, 86–91.

FOR ME, THE JOURNEY IS A TRIBUTE IN HONOR OF BOTH OF MY FATHERS.

I hope and pray that God has sent me on this journey. I think it was "the God and Father of our Lord Jesus the Messiah" (Eph 1:3, 17) who, for decades, nudged me in the directions reflected in this book. That is certainly not a claim to infallibility. It is an acknowledgment that I take God seriously and take the Bible seriously as a gift from God. It is also an acknowledgment that I have been wrong about things I once held firmly. Or, to say it more positively, I have found it very important to keep growing and learning in my relationship with God through Jesus. I want that need to grow to always include how I understand and respond to what I read in the Bible and how I allow the Spirit of God to work through that reading. Of course, this Bible reading needs to be in a broad context. We allow God's Spirit to work best when we read the Scriptures with the spiritual power that comes through personal relationships, community, intuition, experience, choices, reflection, action, memory, reason, the spiritual gifts God has given us, and sound theology.

I know for certain that my earthly father sent me on this journey. So much of how I understand God, Jesus, and life came from long discussions with him. It would be dishonoring to him, and to Jesus in his life, not to acknowledge his many contributions to this book. Cyril Simkins loved Jesus and loved the Bible as much as or more than anyone else I have ever known. He taught in relatively Conservative Evangelical seminaries and Bible colleges. He founded a pastor-training college in Accra, Ghana, and he taught pastors in Zimbabwe as well as in the United States. He was theologically, doctrinally, socially, and politically conservative in many ways, and he was simultaneously an intelligent freethinker and often an astute social critic as well. He had four graduate degrees, including a doctorate earned after the age of sixty. When I would visit him in his seventies, he would often quote John 1:1–18 from memory in New Testament *Koine* Greek and then again in King James English, just to stay in practice.

Even though in some ways Dad often saw the world, the church, and the Bible through eyes different from those I see through, I constantly stand in awe of his wisdom. Some of that wisdom bears directly on the content of this book. In various forms, he frequently repeated the following four comments to me:

1. Human knowledge is wonderful, and we should thank God for it. We should also always remember that it is "human" knowledge with all the limitations and provisional nature the word "human" currently implies. This applies to our knowledge of science, theology, sociology, psychology, human nature, creation, biblical interpretation, doctrine, and everything else we "know."

2. With wry irony: For most of us, the main problem with faith (trust) is that it requires faith (trust).

3. There is a lot we can know and experience about God, and a lot we do not know and have not experienced. The main thing to remember is that we are not God—not individually and not corporately.

4. Most Christians have no idea how wonderful the human Jesus was and is. They think they do, but they don't; and many don't really want to know.

Now, after fifty-five years as a pastor, fifty of them in a major university community, I am aware of how right he was—and is—concerning these guidelines for better understanding our relationship to God and to one another. They pointed me in the direction this book has taken.

Dad had no qualms about saying, "Jesus saved me." For him, this was not a politically correct expression of his relatively conservative evangelical theology; it was just a fact of life. His father, who was a well-educated engineer for the time, and an alcoholic, murdered a woman in front of my ten-year-old father and his siblings. He then walked out of his children's lives forever, leaving them alone in the house with a dead body. This occurred while their mother was in the hospital giving birth to another child. Dad's large, blended family of origin was a train wreck prior to that event; imagine what it was like afterward! Dad grew up unsupervised and unloved on the streets of early twentieth-century metropolitan Chicago. He was very clear that God, through Jesus and through the church community, had saved his life—at many different levels of "life."

Though I have come to love Jesus as God's wonderful gift to us humans, much as Dad did, I imagine a few things I say in this book would bother him. Perhaps an occasional conclusion in this book might even disappoint him. Nevertheless, he would passionately affirm the main claims in this book. He would say even more fervently than I do that we cannot praise Jesus enough because our language cannot stretch as far as the reality of what God has done through Jesus. He would loudly *amen* that Jesus was, is, and always will be human—God's first completed and glorified human who truly is one of us. He would agree that God is a risk-taking God. He would also affirm that we have not even begun to imagine what Jesus's humanity means, concerning the value and potential of every other human.

God, please allow my father to hear these words that I wish I had spoken to him more clearly while he was here: Dad, thanks for setting me on this journey with God and with Jesus. I owe them, and in several ways, I owe you, my life. I hope some of our sisters and brothers in the church, and our fellow humans who are understandably repulsed by the words and actions of many of us Christians past and present, hear what you always wanted them to hear—"Jesus truly is one of us, and he loves you."

1

The God and Father of Our Lord Jesus the Messiah

GOD WAS JESUS'S GOD—THEN.

I find the New Testament's presentation of Jesus as fully human to be gracious, wonderful, exhilarating, frightening, and very challenging. Sometimes it is easier to believe that Jesus was not, and is not, really one of us in his relationship with God. If he was, if he is, the implications about who we humans are in relationship to the One True God are astounding. Equally astounding is what this means concerning who God is.

Most of this book will be focused on Jesus and his humanity. But it would be foolish to explore who Jesus was and is without beginning where Jesus began. Jesus saw the meaning of life as summed up in how a human relates to God and to fellow humans. Who was Jesus's God? Jesus comes to us through the pages of the New Testament as a Jewish human who saw everything that he did and said as related to the God of Israel who was also God over all nations. From his earliest recorded words—"Didn't you know I had to be in my Father's house?"—to his final dying breath—"Father, into your hands I commit my spirit"—Jesus lived in a trusting relationship with God, who he also knew as Father (Luke 2:49, 23:46). Jesus talked about God, and to God, when resisting temptations (Matt 4:4–10, 26:38–42). He talked about God's kingdom when challenging others to repent and to follow him (Mark 1:14–17). He taught about God regularly (Mark 12:28–34). Then he talked to God as he took his final breaths before dying (Luke 23:46; John 19:30). How else could life be lived by this radically faithful Jew?

Jesus claimed to know what God was like. He often began parables with "the Kingdom of Heaven is like. . . ." Not only did he trust that he knew what God's reign on earth looks like, he claimed to be joining in with God's work, knowing what to do by looking and seeing what God was doing (John 5:19). What a bold claim! *If you want to know what God is like, look at what I am doing. What I am doing is a direct reflection of what God is doing.*

What is Jesus's God like? Jesus related to God knowing he was loved; therefore he could risk loving and serving other humans. We are told that Jesus's joining into what he saw his Father doing meant sharing gracious love with other humans—especially those who experienced little of it. It also involved confronting people with truth. And truth included exhorting people to grow and to behave in a godly manner toward others. Truth meant challenging people to allow God to transform their understanding of themselves, others, and the systems they lived in. Jesus knew God valued every human he encountered, even those who saw Jesus as their enemy. People who saw Jesus as their enemy would often have included idolatrous Romans, heretical Samaritans, arrogant church leaders, the oppressive and wealthy 1%, and Jewish revolutionaries. Jesus touched despised and sometimes contagious lepers, hung out with tax collectors who most contemporaries loathed, and ministered with women who most religious leaders ignored. Why? Because he believed they were valuable to God, and God wanted to be with them. Knowing God was seeking a relationship with these people was far more important to Jesus than whatever might happen to his reputation.

What is Jesus's God like? Jesus taught that God seeks a relationship with us like a poor woman seeks for a lost coin and like a father seeks for a wayward son (Luke 15:8–31). He tells a religious leader that sometimes God is happier with a prostitute who is learning to love than with a preacher who is hedging his bets (Luke 7:36–50). What is Jesus's God like? God is a God who wants humans to be faithful and obedient. God wants this, not because God is a rule-bound dictator, but because God is "Abba" who wants his children to mature and become more fully human. Various New Testament writers emphasize Jesus's faithfulness to God as listening to God, obeying God, keeping God's commandments, serving God, loving God, and ministering for God. Each Gospel writer, as well as the writer of Hebrews, emphasizes that Jesus prayed intensely and consistently, then acted on what he saw and heard the Father showing him.

As we will soon explore, God was so central to who Jesus was that several New Testament writers began to speak of God as *The God and Father of our Lord Jesus the Messiah*.

All the ways Jesus related to God are ways the New Testament challenges the rest of us humans to relate to God as well. Some Christians teach that Jesus's challenge for us to live as he lived before God was primarily designed to show us how sinful we are. That is not true. Jesus's goal was to encourage his followers to live like children of a great and loving God. Seeing how far we fall short of who we should be in God's design can be a result of seeing how Jesus lived. That is not, however, God's primary revelation through Jesus's faithfulness. Jesus modeled for us the relationship between God and humans that God wants. The primary revelation is that we can now see human potential in its completeness. We can now see what being a "completed" child of God looks like. Even the forgiveness the New Testament proclaims as a wonderful part of the "Good News" is made possible because of Jesus's faithfulness in his relationship to

God (John 17:19). Forgiveness is God's means for moving humans toward God's end goal for humanity—God's forever human family made up of humans in the image and likeness of God. To say it a bit differently, *Jesus's God decided before creation began that it would someday be necessary, and a joy, to renew Creation, Community, and Character. Jesus's relationship with God was the "firstfruits" of a human in the right relationship with God* (1 Cor 15:20–23).

GOD IS JESUS'S GOD—NOW.

After the resurrection-ascension-exaltation event, Jesus's relationship with God is still described as a relationship with "the *God* and Father of our Lord Jesus the Messiah." I found this surprising when I first began to pay attention. In my church background, people did not speak of God as Jesus's God now. I suspect the same is likely to have been true for you if you grew up in church settings.

I wondered why the fact that several New Testament authors indicate God continues into eternity to be Jesus's God had so completely eluded me. It had apparently eluded most of my mentors as well. Surprising or not, it is this relationship shared by God and the risen and exalted Jesus that we are invited to participate in by the writers of the following passages.

> [5] *May the God who gives endurance and encouragement* give you a spirit of unity among yourselves as you follow Christ Jesus, [6] so that with one heart and mouth you may glorify *the God and Father of our Lord Jesus Christ* (Rom 15:5–6, *emphasis mine*).
>
> Praise be *to the God and Father of our Lord Jesus Christ*, the Father of compassion and the God of all comfort. . . . (2 Cor 1:3, *emphasis mine*).
>
> Praise be *to the God and Father of our Lord Jesus Christ*, who has blessed us in the heavenly realms with every spiritual blessing in Christ (Eph 1:3, *emphasis mine*).
>
> I keep asking that *the God of our Lord Jesus Christ, the glorious Father*, may give you the Spirit of wisdom and revelation, so that you may know him better (Eph 1:17, *emphasis mine*).
>
> We always thank *God, the Father of our Lord Jesus Christ*, when we pray for you. . . . (Col 1:3, *emphasis mine*).
>
> And again he says, "Here am I, and the children *God has given me*" (Heb 2:13, *emphasis mine*).
>
> Praise be *to the God and Father of our Lord Jesus Christ*! In his great mercy he has given us new birth into a living hope through the resurrection of Jesus Christ from the dead (1 Pet 1:3, *emphasis mine*).
>
> [5] . . . and from Jesus Christ, who is the faithful witness, *the firstborn from the dead*, and the ruler of the kings of the earth. To him who loves us and has freed

us from our sins by his blood, ⁶ and has made us to be a kingdom and priests *to serve his God and Father*—to him be glory and power for ever and ever! Amen (Rev 1:5–6, *emphasis mine*).

² Wake up! Strengthen what remains and is about to die, for I [the exalted Jesus] have not found your deeds complete *in the sight of my God*.... ¹² Him [the person] who overcomes I will make *a pillar in the temple of my God*. Never again will *that one* leave it. I will write on him [that person] *the name of my God* and the name of *the city of my God*, the new Jerusalem, which is coming down out of heaven *from my God*; and I will also write on him my new name (Rev 3:2, 12, *emphasis mine*).

¹⁷ Jesus said, "Do not hold on to me, for I have not yet returned to the Father. Go instead to my brothers and tell them, *"I am returning to my Father and your Father, to my God and your God."* ¹⁸ Mary Magdalene went to the disciples with the news: "I have seen the Lord!" And she told them that he had said these things to her (John 20:17–18, *emphasis mine*).

Except for the final quotation from the Gospel of John, which is post-resurrection and pre-ascension, each of the ten passages just quoted describes Jesus's relationship with God *after* Jesus was raised from death, ascended to be with God in heaven, and was exalted to the right hand of God. In each case, the relationship is that *God continues to be Jesus's God.*

It seems likely that the authors of these ten passages believed the relationship between God and Jesus provides us with *a new name for God.* Much as the covenant with humanity through Abraham led to God often being identified as "the God of Abraham," now God's new covenant with humans through Jesus leads to God being identified as "the God of Jesus." Whether or not you believe this constitutes a new name for God, what is clear is that these authors believed the relationship between Jesus and God continues to be a relationship in which God *is* Jesus's God.

Let's reclaim what this ongoing relationship between Jesus and the "One God of Israel" who is "The God and Father of our Lord Jesus the Messiah" means concerning Jesus's humanity and our humanity.

GOD WAS JESUS'S FATHER THEN. GOD IS JESUS'S FATHER NOW.

New Testament authors also believed that Jesus's relationship with God provided new depth for an older name for God. God was and is the God and *Father* of our Lord Jesus the Messiah. Jesus's use of "Father" in describing God's relationship with him and with others was not new. Several Old Testament texts, and other ancient Jewish texts as well, refer to God as "Father." This meant that both Abraham's and David's descendants could be identified as "sons" of God.

In Exodus 4:22–23, God tells Moses to identify Israel to Pharaoh as "*my firstborn son.*" The following quotations provide several further instances in which God's role and/or name is "Father," in relationship either to the nation of Israel, to the faithful, to the oppressed, or to the royal lineage of King David.

> *I will be his father, and he will be my son. When he does wrong*, I will punish him with the rod of men, with floggings inflicted by men. (2 Sam 7:14, *emphasis mine*).

> *A father to the fatherless, a defender of widows, is God* in his holy dwelling (Ps 68:5, *emphasis mine*).

> *As a father has compassion on his children, so the LORD* has compassion on those who fear him (Ps 103:13, *emphasis mine*).

> Yet, O LORD, *you are our Father*. We are the clay, you are the potter; we are all the work of your hand (Isa 64:8, *emphasis mine*).

> Hear, O heavens! Listen, O earth! For *the LORD has spoken: "I reared children and brought them up*, but they have rebelled against me" (Mal 1:6, *emphasis mine*).

> "*A son honors his father*, and a servant his master. *If I am a father, where is the honor* due me? If I am a master, where is the respect due me?" says the LORD Almighty (Mal 2:10, *emphasis mine*).

> (*See also* Isa 9:6–7, 63:16; Jer 3:4, 3:19, 31:9; 1 Chron 22:10, 28:6; Ps 89:26; Prov 3:12.)

The Father–Son relationship was understood to be a covenant relationship in Old Testament times. That understanding continues to be reflected in both Jesus's relationship, and our relationship, with the Father as well.

On the other hand, although relating to God as Father is not a new revelation, the New Testament writers do indicate that Jesus's way of relating to God as "Father" expressed a new and deeper intimacy with God than anyone ever had before. This expressed intimacy impressed his disciples and angered his enemies (Mark 14:36; John 5:17–18). Although "Father" (*ab* in Hebrew) was not a "new name" for God, Jesus's use of "Abba" was so intimate that both Mark and Paul choose at points to leave it untranslated. Paul also indicates that through Jesus, God is extending this offer of intimacy to the rest of us humans as well—whether Jewish or Greek, slave or free, male and female (Gal 3:25–4:6; Rom 8:15).[1] Though "Abba" is not used in either Matthew or Luke's Greek version of Jesus's model prayer that we have labelled "The Lord's Prayer" or the "Our Father," the prayer has the same implication of both intimacy and authority that "Father" always carried for Jesus (Matt 6:9).

---

1. Thanks to Tom Ewald for reminding me that the shift from "or" to "and" (*kai* in Greek) in Gal 3:28 seems to imply extra equivalency between male and female in the realm where the Messiah is Lord. Some translations indicate the shift.

The new name for God—"The God and Father of our Lord Jesus the Messiah"—and the renewed and deepened focus on God as "Abba" embed Jesus deeply in our humanity and in the relationship that God wants to have with us as humans. Both the new name and the renewed name reveal more fully than ever before the relationship God is pursuing with humans. In Jesus, God finally has the human who genuinely and consistently relates to God as "Father." Rather than being separated from our humanity, this "Son" invites the rest of us into this relationship as God's children: "*Our* Father in Heaven; may your name be made holy."

If you allow it to sink in, the claim is audacious. We are being invited to join Jesus in relating to the Creator of our universe, who is also the One God over all peoples from all eras of history as "Our Abba/Father."

But what exactly is meant by describing the relationship we are being invited to accept as a Father–Child relationship? As various scholars correctly point out, the designation "Father" in the cultures of the ancient world in which the biblical materials were written did not automatically focus on intimacy and tenderness. It designated a role with ultimate family authority and often described a person who could be quite distant from his children and family in terms of both time and intimacy.

Jesus's use of "Father" never moves away from fully recognizing the ultimate authority that God has over God's human family. Jesus's use of "Father," as well as all his words and actions, demonstrate that the God who is Father is the ultimate authority in his own life too. "Father" also always includes intimacy for Jesus. I grew up in the South, and it was possible for the title "Papa" to have a strong emphasis on both authority and intimacy. I understand the word "Ab" in Arabic, as well as "Baba" in India, often has that same dual emphasis today.

Jesus demonstrated an interpersonal trust and intimacy toward God who is his Father that was often not what sons experienced from their fathers in the ancient world. It was also a level of intimacy that many who worshiped YHWH felt inappropriate.

"*Abba*, Father," Jesus said to God, "everything is possible for you. Take this cup from me. Yet not what I will, but what you will" (Mark 14:36). This level of intimacy in the relationship between Jesus and God is breath-taking when we focus on what God was asking Jesus to do. It is equally breath-taking to focus on the freedom Jesus felt in making the request. Just as astounding, perhaps more so in some ways, is the fact that Paul and John claim that this intimate relationship is available to the rest of us as well. "For you did not receive a spirit that makes you a slave again to fear, but you received the Spirit of sonship. *And by the Spirit we cry, 'Abba, Father'*" (Rom 8:15, *emphasis mine; see also* Gal 4:6). "How great is the love the Father has lavished on us, that we should be called children of God! And that is what we are" (1 John 3:1)! No matter how tough and rotten life can be—and at times it is—through God's relationship with Jesus, we are being offered a relationship that guarantees that the final authority in our universe is also the source of stubborn intimate love for us—our "Abba."

My goal throughout this book is to encourage us to pursue and deepen this relationship that has been made available to us through the relationship God and Jesus share. God loved and supported Jesus through life, through death, and through resurrected life so powerfully that this God can now be known as *The God and Father of the Lord Jesus the Messiah.*

The rest of us humans are invited to accept the invitation to be adopted into this renewed human family that began through the relationship between God and Jesus, God's "Firstborn" in the renewal of the human family. God graciously wants each of us to be God's heir to the beautiful family name being created through God's relationship with Jesus. No matter what your current social and economic status are in the culture you live in, the Father who wants to adopt you into the future forever family is the most loving, the most powerful, and—far less important but nice—the Father with the greatest wealth of resources available! Not a bad family to be adopted into!

JESUS'S GOD IS A RELATIONAL, PURPOSEFUL, RESPONSIVE, AND PERSONAL COMMUNICATOR.

The Biblical Writers Claim That God Is the Personal Communicator par Excellence.

The God described in biblical writings is creative, good, relational, purposeful, responsive, and personal. God is the God who speaks things into existence and who is the source of the spiritually energized "word." Complicated, confusing, and even easily misunderstood at times from our human perspective? Yes! Silent sometimes when we want to hear—right now? Yes! But still always a relational God, bent on communicating with us humans.

If we take the biblical claims about the One God seriously, we humans are invited to enter a great adventure with God. Austin Channing Brown calls this adventure a call to live "wildly holy and free." We are encouraged to risk all on our relationship with the God who loves, chooses, values, becomes deeply involved in, and delights in positive relationships with humans—a God who wants to communicate with us about God and about ourselves.

It is not because God must, or because it is written in the stars, that God chooses to relate to us in this interpersonal manner. Rather, the God of the Old Testament (*Elohim* who is *YHWH*) chooses to create humans and to love humans because God desires to. This means God is more committed to good for us than God is committed to avoiding personal hurt and pain. As Ben Witherington III remarks, "to say God 'is love' is to say that God is the most self-sacrificial being in the universe, and as such he was prepared to go to incredible lengths to set humankind right."[2]

---

2. Witherington, "God is Love," 60.

When the relationship with God is healthy, our relationship with God "delights" and "pleases" God. David's praise hymn said it this way: "He [YHWH] brought me out into a spacious place; the LORD rescued me because *the LORD delighted in me*" (2 Sam 22:20, *emphasis mine*).

My friend Robert Husband, retired faculty member in the Department of Communication at the University of Illinois and founder of The Aslan Group, tells me that studies indicate communication is not just an important part of relationships, but to a great extent communication *is* the relationship. When you watch people communicating, you are looking at the relationship as it is being created and enacted. Isn't this true when we watch parents communicating with their children? Isn't this also true when someone shows how delighted she or he is to be communicating with you? I remember reading a text from a dear friend to my wife while she was in home-hospice. The friend's text said that he was praying for her, valued her friendship extended so freely through the years, and loved her. Her eyes lit up, and she responded, "Tell him that means so much to me." Communication *is* the relationship happening. In addition to the specific verbal content of the communication, the event itself increases the depths of the relationship.

Our Bible begins in Genesis 1 with the claim that everything in the creation, including humans, exists as an expression of God's word— "And God said . . ." The creation, the patriarchs, the history of Israel, the prophets, and then finally the birth of Jesus are all God's "word" to us. Remember my friend's point—communication isn't just about the relationship; it *is* the relationship in action.

If we take seriously that the God presented in the Bible is real, then it is always right to be asking ourselves questions such as the following:

1. What is God attempting to communicate to us, to me, in this situation?

2. What is the Creator communicating through the "creation" that we label "nature"? Was the Psalmist (Ps 19) right in saying that when the sun shines God is speaking to us?

3. What is God saying to us through church history and through current expressions of church?

4. What is God saying through our relationships with friends, family, immigrants, the poor, strangers, and people who are not similar to us in various important ways?

5. What is God saying to us through the people who do not like us very much or through the people we do not like very much?

6. What is God speaking today through the Scriptures and through modern-day spirit-filled people as well?

7. What is God saying to us through our most recent scientific discoveries?

8. What is God attempting to say to us today through God's Son Jesus about what it means to be human and to walk with God?

9. What is God attempting to tell us about our humanity, if, as chapters 2 through 4 will demonstrate, Jesus is God's firstborn "glorified" and "perfected/completed" human—a glorified human who continues to be human now, and will be human in God's future age-to-come?

The biblical writers claim again and again that God is speaking. Is anyone listening for God's answer to these questions? Am I? Are you listening and looking for a communication from God today? Are we listening and looking in any of the right places? If God is as personal and communicative as Jesus and the writers of the Old and New Testaments believed, all the previous questions are important ones.

The Central Scriptural Revelation is God's Desire for Interpersonal Relationships.

The Old Testament writers emphasize in many ways that the goal dominating God's process of self-revelation to us is God's desire for wholesome interactive relationships with humans. Here are four of many possible examples:

1. God "chooses" to relate to Abraham and the nation of Israel, and God promises that this choice is ultimately intended to bless the humans of all nations (Gen 12, 15, 22).

2. God chooses to be present in the midst of the community both through the tabernacle and the cloud. In the tabernacle we learn that sometimes we must work hard and bring our gifts to make a place for God to come dwell among us. In the cloud we learn that sometimes God is completely beyond our control and we must just follow this unpredictable God. In both, we learn that God is willing to be with us as God's community even when we wander around in the wildernesses of daily life and of human history (Exod 40:34–36)

3. God wants God's "children" to return to healthy ways of relating to God (Isa 1:2–3).

4. Hosea's pained relationship with an adulteress mirrors the hurt God experiences in relating to the people of God (Hos 3:1–3).

The remaining chapters of this book will explore various facets of the claim that the central focus of the New Testament is on God communicating anew who God is through the relationship that God and the human Jesus shared and continue sharing. We will also explore some of the many tensions this claim causes in the lives of those of us who attempt to take this claim seriously. What do I mean by tension? If God is a communicating God, why do we only find records of God speaking to Abraham seven times over the period of a hundred years (Genesis 12–25)? If God can show up in a vision when Jacob doesn't even know God is present and isn't looking for God (Gen 28), why does God let Jacob go for decades weeping the death of his son Joseph who isn't dead (Gen 37–45)? Since Jesus seems to have been in regular daily communication with God, why does God remain silent when Jesus most wants to hear God speak (Matt 27:46). Surely these times of silence create tension in your life and relationship with God too!

I will also be attempting to show that the New Testament writers' understanding of Jesus remained within the earlier Old Testament emphasis on God's Creation goal—human in the image of God. The New Testament understanding of God's relationship with Jesus is fully embedded in God's desire to have a forever human family related to God as the "children of God," living within the "reign (kingdom) of God," fully experiencing the "love of God."

JESUS'S GOD IS THE GOD OF THE OLD TESTAMENT.

As I mentioned at the beginning of this chapter, Jesus's God is the God revealed in the Old Testament as "the God of Abraham, Isaac, and Jacob" and as YHWH. Many Christians of the past and today seem to wish to separate Jesus from the God of the Old Testament, but it is extremely important that we not take this dishonest step in order to resolve the tension we experience as we attempt to reconcile Jesus and the Old Testament. Even a casual reading of the Gospels, not to mention the rest of the New Testament, makes it clear that the Jesus of the New Testament is fully embedded in the narratives, the wisdom for daily living, the poetry, and the prophetic messages of the Old Testament. The same casual reading also makes it abundantly clear that Jesus consistently makes choices in serving God that differ drastically from those made by his forefathers and foremothers in the faith.

If you do not like the fact that Jesus fully embraced the God of his fathers, admit that, but do not pretend Jesus covertly or inadvertently attempted to redesign, worship, and serve a different God. Jesus had no intention of starting a new religion. Did Jesus's relationship with God reveal the God of the Old Testament more fully and more deeply? Yes! Was Jesus's God a different God? Absolutely not! Jesus is presented as living openly with the tension between his words and actions and the Old Testament revelation of God. If we wish to follow Jesus, we should practice doing the same. How does one fully embrace God's relationship with David and Joshua and fully resist the temptation to use that relationship as an excuse for shedding the lifeblood of others in the name of God as they did? How did Jesus handle this tension and justify his choices?

It is foolish to pretend that resolving the tension between the Old Testament and how Jesus lived is easy. It is equally foolish to think it was always easy for Jesus. Jesus went away quite often to pray about next steps! I will suggest throughout this book that much of the resolution is to be found in the way Jesus viewed God's willingness to accommodate to where we are in history while pursing where God wants to go in history. The legacy of the Old Testament concerning God's purpose in creating humans, as well as the revelation that God is a personal, purposeful, and relational communicator, provide much of the content of Jesus's relationship with God. This personal God is presented as pursuing a real purpose in history, which progresses through the ups and downs of our human relationships with God. The journey takes many detours, but God's goal will not ultimately be thwarted. This legacy from the Old Testament makes it possible to understand God's relationship with the human Jesus the way it was intended to be understood—he was, he is, and he will always be one of us humans, embedded fully in God's goal for human history.

True, in God's relationship with Jesus, God overwhelmingly exceeds the wildest expectations and hopes generated in God's previous self-revelation to and through humans. But in overwhelmingly exceeding expectations, God did not change the narrative or the goal, and God certainly did not take on a new identity. God deepened and broadened the narrative and clarified the goal. It is in focusing on the relationship shared between God and Jesus that we learn far more about who God is and how "Abba" wishes to relate to us humans. It is in focusing on the relationship shared between God and the human Jesus that we learn what God is communicating to us about being "completed" (*telos*) and "glorified" as humans; or, to say it another way, it is in Jesus that we see God's "end goal" (*telos*) for what it means to be human.

Sometimes Jesus's relationship to God is portrayed as the new and overwhelming fulfillment of an Old Testament pattern. For example, the exodus from slavery in Egypt was a wonderful gift, and now God is providing an even deeper liberation from an even more deadly slavery. At other times, Jesus's relationship to God is portrayed as a contrasting step, moving beyond God's previous accommodation to past human weaknesses toward a much godlier human response to similar situations in Jesus's life. For example, God was with David in his violent wars, despite the blood on David's hands, but now God is with Jesus as he rejects violence and takes the bloody violence of the world upon himself.

Whether God's next step in God's relationship with Jesus emphasizes the similarity or the contrast with earlier revelation, it is always a continuation of "God with us." It is also always another step toward the fulfillment of God's creation goal—"male and female in the image of God." These realities informed all of Jesus's words and actions.

SUMMARY

If we understand that (1) God was and is *The God and the Father of our Lord Jesus the Messiah,* (2) God is a very personal and purposeful communicator, and (3) the content of God's communication through the Old and New Testaments reveals God's pursuit of a relationship that creates a forever human family, then we can ask God to deepen our experience of what it means to be human. In doing so, we are placing ourselves within a framework for understanding the New Testament claim that the human Jesus is God's first completed and glorified human. I find wrestling with this reality to be exciting, humbling, liberating—and challenging at many levels. I think you will as well.

2

God's Purpose: Male and Female in the Image of God

WE HAVE AN IMPORTANT OPPORTUNITY.

Those of us who are followers of Jesus might well be missing one of the greatest opportunities we have for speaking to the twenty-first century world. We need to be much more focused on what God revealed about human potential through God's relationship with Jesus. Jesus's first followers saw their obviously human friend Jesus die and then be raised, not just from death, but into an entirely new level of human existence. They were astounded. No matter the cost to God and to Jesus, no matter how broken some of our political and religious systems, no matter the power of death, God showed a determination to achieve God's purpose—humans in the image and likeness of God. This revelation made sharing the "Good News" about God's commitment to us humans an adventure worth what it often cost those early followers. They were overwhelmed and passionate about what they had experienced in their empirical world:

> That which was from the beginning, which we have heard, which we have seen with our eyes, which we have looked at and our hands have touched—this we proclaim concerning the Word of life (1 John 1:1).

By the second century AD, Christian leaders were beginning to move toward a more abstract understanding of Jesus both before and after his death and resurrection. They began portraying Jesus less as Jewish man and more as universal human. He began to be viewed as less genuinely one of us and more distantly divine. It is easy to see how their predominantly Greek worldview that divided body (not good) and soul (a separate essence) moved them this direction. It is equally easy to see that their Gentile anti-Semitism encouraged this movement toward redefining Jesus. Still, it seems ironic that a central, and wondrously hopeful, emphasis in God's Good News slipped away so soon. We have never recovered from the loss, and the price we have paid is enormous!

The movement away from the importance of Jesus's particularity as an embodied Jewish person, through whom God opened the covenant with Abraham to Gentiles, and toward a theology that saw Jesus as an abstractly universal human was sad in many ways. One of the sad results was that it laid the groundwork that later allowed the church to become "Roman" and "Byzantine." Later the church also became over-identified with Spanish, Swedish, German, Dutch, French, English, and American. Views of Jesus became centered in Gentile theology, and the deep roots of the "Good News of Jesus" as a faithful Jew were greatly diminished. Once the church chose to center itself around Empire, the church had paved the way for the following centuries that were filled with the development of theologies that have also rationalized Western Euro-American exceptionalism and then White supremacy. These became the dominant context for interpreting "the Good News."[1]

The losses are increasingly costly to the "Good News" as the twenty-first century world becomes more and more focused on multiethnicity, the relationship among people of all nations, the deep relationship between humans and the rest of "nature" (creation), and human potential. In this chapter, we will explore how our abstract theology of Jesus as universal human and our overemphasis upon Jesus's divinity as something separate from his humanness are diminishing our witness to God's Good News. It is very costly.

As I mentioned in the Introduction, in many ways the current understanding of what it means to be human is often closer to what the first-century followers of Jesus claim they saw God do in Jesus's life than is the understanding of Jesus's humanity that has dominated Christian theology for almost two millennia. But this current understanding of "human" can very easily become horribly destructive, frightfully arrogant, or hopeless and depressing apart from the additional understanding that this must all be submitted to "The God and Father of our Lord Jesus the Messiah."

THE DESCRIPTION OF HUMAN NATURE IN THE BIBLICAL MATERIALS IS COMPLEX.

What if to understand the relationship between God and the human Jesus is to also understand the relationship God wants to pursue with every human? What if God really does have an incredibly exalted purpose for why you are here? What if you and I are more important to God than we can imagine? What if human potential is being defined by God when we realize that Jesus has been crowned with the glory and honor that God always intended for humans (Heb 2:9 meditating on Ps 8)?

---

1. Gushee, *White American Christianity*, and Swanson, *Rediscipling White Church*, 136–142.

To fully understand how the New Testament authors address these questions, we must see how they grounded their answers in the Old Testament context. I think the writer of Hebrews represents the overall New Testament understanding of what God has done in Jesus when he presents Jesus as God's first completed human, or as many English translations have it—the first human God has "made perfect" (Heb 2:10; 5:9). Everything God was doing through Jesus is a part of the continuing story of God's original reason for creating humans. Jesus is not other than us, but one of us—God's first glorified and completed human. We will pursue various aspects of this New Testament theme throughout this book, but first it is important to revisit the Old Testament context in which it is rooted.

Humans are Chemicals, Animal, and Spirit.

The biblical claim concerning God's purpose for creating humans is obvious at two levels and audacious in its third aspect. The Hebrew Bible begins in Genesis 1–2 by saying that we humans (*Adam* = human in Hebrew) are made from dust. We would now say we are made up of many basic chemicals that return to dust and into the environment when we die. Robert Alter brilliantly translates the wordplay in Genesis 2:7 that clearly roots human nature in the ground, saying that *adam* comes from *adamah*, or as Alter translates into English, "human" is made from "humus."[2] A reality that takes a sad turn a bit later when the consequences of alienating ourselves from God, creation, ourselves, and other humans means our observable destiny is reduced to humus/*adamah*/dirt (Gen 3:19).

We are also identified as being in continuity with animals—humans are "living souls" just as the animals are (Gen 1:20, 24, 30, 2:7, each using the Hebrew word *nephesh*). In the Bible, "soul" describes what is living and animated. This identification of humans as "souls" includes Jesus in the Greek of 1 John 3:16 which says Jesus laid down his soul (*psyche*) for us (*see also* Mark 14:34).

Regardless of how you personally understand the genre of Genesis 1–11, it reflects the foundational biblical understanding of "humans" in relationship to God. Identifying us as ground/chemical and as animal should not be controversial because people all over the world have made this observation for centuries. As the author of Ecclesiastes insisted millennia ago, real "wisdom" means facing squarely how much we humans have in common with the rest of the animal world and how easily we become "dust" (*aphar* in Hebrew). He further notes how we cannot empirically prove that our "spirit" (*ruach* in Hebrew) has a destiny that differs from that of our cow, sheep, or pet (Eccl 3:19–21). Our modern scientific studies make it only more evident that we humans are deeply connected to both the nonliving material world and the animal world.

---

2. Alter, *Genesis: Translation*, 8.

The "Breath of God" is the Controversial Biblical Claim Concerning Humans.

What makes the biblical claim concerning human nature controversial is the further claim that these beings who are a bundle of earth chemicals and animal life were also created with the breath of God. Even more controversial is the further claim that this breath of God stamps us with the image and likeness of God (Gen 1–2, Ps 8). The writer of Ecclesiastes is correct in saying we cannot prove it, but other biblical writers are adamant in maintaining that God did add something unique when humans were created. As controversial as this claim can be, still more controversial is the further claim that, if we allow God to do so, God will someday choose to complete human life by making it spirit-filled eternal human life. There were hints of this claim in a few Old Testament prophetic writings, but it becomes a central part of the "Good News" concerning God raising Jesus from death. In the biblical writings, this "*and Spirit*" reality is not viewed as a God-spark held captive by humanness, but rather as an integrated part of the whole human.

The Hebrew Bible often claims that the "One God" who is Creator so highly values a relationship with humans that God wants to be, and often is, "with us" humans. In fact, we are God's most prized treasure.[3] What a daring claim—God, who created the universe, chooses to be personal, responsive, and caring for humans who are clearly dust, obviously animal, but who in God's eyes are made for a unique forever relationship with the God of the universe. In the biblical paradigm, this goal comes to its first fulfillment in Jesus. The accompanying claim is that every step of human history, before and after Jesus, involves God's continuing movement toward the completion of this creation project.

Jesus and Other Humans are Designated as "Completed" and "Glorified" Humans.

I think the clearest claims in the New Testament that Jesus is the completion of God's creation project occur in the letter to the Hebrews, but other authors reflect a similar understanding of Jesus's continuing humanity. Several also speak of the ongoing importance of Jesus's continuing humanity and our humanity. After experiencing the resurrection of Jesus, the early followers of Jesus make the astounding claim that the human Jesus ascended into the direct presence of God and was exalted and glorified by God as Lord and Messiah over the rest of human history (Acts 2:36). Because of what God has done for Jesus, and through Jesus for other humans, they now understand that God can and will make every single human capacity gloriously whole and holy for those who allow God to do so (1 Thess 5:23–24; Heb 2:5–18; 1 Cor 15:40–58; Phil 3:12, 3:20–21; John 17:22; Rev 21:1–4).

3. Zorn, "Segullah."

As we will see later in this chapter and in the next, these writers begin to speak anew and quite boldly of God's goal for humanity as humans in the image of God. They maintain that God's relationship with Jesus is the evidence that God can reach God's creation goal for humanity. God's relationship with Jesus is not just the model, but also the means, through which God intends to do this for others. Isn't this the most likely way to understand Paul's admonition that "all things belong to you . . . and you belong to the Messiah, and the Messiah belongs to God" (1 Cor 3:21–23, my translation)?

I do believe the claim that the relationship between God and Jesus is how God is moving toward God's purpose in creating us humans. Whether you believe that to be true or not, I encourage you to entertain the fact that this is the master story of the New Testament. The link between us humans as created to be "in the image of God" and Jesus as the revelation of a human fully "in the image of God" has been vastly underemphasized for centuries in many strands of Christian theology. This has been especially true in our lack of emphasis on the centrality of God's relationship with Jesus as the first glorified, completed, and mature human who now demonstrates God's end goal for humanity. In the New Testament master story, Jesus *was*, and Jesus *is*, one of us.

In Hebrews, the theme of "perfection" or "completion" or "maturity" is one of the primary themes describing what God has done in Jesus and what God is doing in other humans as well. The Greek word group *teleioō* which many English translations translate with various forms of "perfect," is probably better translated into English with forms of "complete" or "mature" or "goal reached." We do not tend to use "perfect" to designate *process* as the author of Hebrews and several other New Testament authors clearly do. In fact, Hebrews consistently uses the word to describe an act of God that brings someone or something to a new level of completion. Jesus "was made perfect" is used this way to describe what God has done in the relationship between God and Jesus (Heb 2:10, 5:9, 7:28). Each of these statements is a claim that God brought Jesus to a new level of "completion" as a human servant of God.

I find it intriguing that Jesus died without completing any of his ultimate ministry goals. Followers who stuck it out to the end seem to have numbered only a few hundred at most, even if we add some Galileans to the count of the reported 120 (Acts 1:15). Just before his arrest, even his closest disciples still thought they could resolve Jesus's problems with swords (Luke 22:38, 49). His inner circle of friends slept when he asked them to pray, and then ran when he most needed their support. Without question, he had not yet become the "blessing to all nations on earth" that the covenant with Abraham promised. During the last supper, Jesus told the disciples that he had much more to teach them, but that they couldn't handle it. The Holy Spirit would have to complete Jesus's teaching later (John 16:12–13). You could add other examples. I find it fascinating that, like most of us, Jesus died with few, if any, of his major goals in life completed.

There is one exception to the "unfinished" business in Jesus's life, an exception none of us will experience this side of death. Jesus did complete a life and death filled with unrelenting faithfulness to God, and that, it turns out, was his real mission. Everything else had to flow from that. For this reason, he could say that he was doing "the very work that the Father has given me to finish" (John 5:36), and then say, with one of his last breaths on the cross, "It is finished" (John 19:30). God would see to bringing the rest to completion after Jesus's death.

In fact, God and Jesus are still at work completing that mission. And the mission they are still working to complete involves those who follow Jesus. The writer of Hebrews boldly claims that the "completing" of the relationship between God and Jesus has opened the way for God to *bring to completion (or, bring to maturity) other humans* as well (Heb 6:1, 10:1, 10:14, 11:40, 12:23). If you prefer the more common English translations that describe Jesus, and then others, as "made perfect," it does not diminish, but in fact enhances my point—this writer believed the relationship between Jesus and God was a process that brought God's creation goal to its first completion or perfection. Jesus was and is one of us.

A similar thought seems to occur in Ephesians 4:13 where God's desire to bring us into a "completed [*teleion* from *telos*] adulthood" or "completed humanness" means that we also attain to the fullness of the maturity (*helikia*) of the Messiah. Learning to live with faithfulness as Jesus did allows a community of Jesus followers to begin to approximate the presence of "the Messiah, the completed [*teleion*] human."[4] In John 17:23, Jesus prays that his followers might "become completed [*teteleiōmenoi*] into one [oneness]"—the holy human community God desires. Paul makes it very personal when he expresses that he is not yet a completed/perfected human, but that he expects to be someday (Phil 3:12, *teteleiōmai* from *teleioō*). James assures his readers that the invasion of God's goal for humans in God's new age is already well underway in this age as the new penetrates the old through our learning to trust: "Now hold on to endurance [for] a complete (*teleion*) work [in you], in order that you may be complete (*teleioi*) and lacking nothing [or, preserved completely] with no one left behind" (Jas 1:4, my translation).

One of my favorite passages concerning God's desire to complete us as human beings is probably a later reflection on one of the most difficult challenges in the New Testament—"love your enemies." It occurs in 1 John. I love *the promise* that God will complete the community of Jesus followers as a community of love. I find *the challenge* to love those who consider me an enemy and those I consider enemies to be daunting. Of course, my experience in churches, and perhaps yours as well, has taught me that, sadly, the opportunity to learn to love our enemies can become very challenging in the communities of faith. It appears that might have been true for John's original audience, too.

---

4. Barth, *Ephesians 4–6*, 484, and *see Ephesians 1–3*, 224–225.

Listen to what the author of 1 John says can happen if we let God reach his goal in our lives: "No one has ever seen God; *but if we love* one another, *God lives in us and his love is made complete* [*teteleiōmena* from *teleioō* in Greek] *in us*" (1 John 4:12, *emphasis mine*, compare 4:17). Whether John had Jesus's teaching from the Sermon on the Mount in mind or not, he is making a similar promise. Jesus ends his challenge to "love your enemies" with "be perfect [*teleioi*] as your Father in Heaven is perfect [*teleios*]" (Matt 5:48). Both 1 John and Matthew see Jesus's teaching as a promise that God is at work in the lives of Jesus's followers to "complete" us by "reaching the goal"— both nuances of *teleios*—God has for humans. What is that goal? The audacious claim is that God's goal is to live in us and increasingly empower us to love our fellow humans just as our Father God loves them.

COMPARING CLAIMS ABOUT WHAT IT MEANS TO BE HUMAN BRINGS INSIGHT.

There Have Been Many Definitions of "Human."

There have been and continue to be numerous claims and speculations about what it means to be human, and they cover a wide range of constructs. Most of the following examples have been influential in human history. Some are quite ancient, though others are relatively modern.

There have been many forms of mind–body dualism, such as ancient Hinduism, the Buddhist principle that the goal of life is to achieve enlightenment and escape suffering, Plato's realm of the ideal mind versus the current shadowy world that is limited by matter, and Descartes's "I think therefore I am." There have also been both ancient and modern views of what it means to be human that are thoroughgoing materialistic constructions. These materialistic philosophies see humans as "nothing but" an accidental or lucky chemical development in the backwaters, or the deep waters, of an essentially meaningless universe.

Fredrich Nietzsche, who saw both the greatness and the smallness of humans, described us: "Man is a rope stretched between the animal and the Superman—a rope over an abyss."[5] Soren Kierkegaard had a view of human life similar to Nietzsche in many ways, except he believed that God really was on the other side of the abyss waiting for us to leap into God's arms.

There is also the long-ignored understanding of what it means to be human that was held by many Native American tribes. The Potawatomi and the Haudenosaunee Confederacy are examples of tribes who believed the Creator (or a lower god and/or goddess) created this world as a web of mutual gift-givers, with mutual responsibility toward one another, including sustainability and thankfulness.[6] The spiritism of the

---

5. Nietzsche, *Thus Spoke*, sec 4, 10.
6. Kimmerer, *Braiding Sweetgrass*, 23, 106, 128–140.

Native Americans differs from the "One God" insistence of the Bible. But in other ways, this view has much in common with some of the stewardship of the earth commands of the Old Testament—commands that many Western Christians have sadly turned into permission to abuse and rape the earth. The Native American call to be grateful for every gift of creation also resonates with Jesus's thankfulness as he blessed YHWH for every piece of bread and cup of wine.

A more recent construction by "deep ecologists" of what it means to be human is often rooted in the recovery of Native American understandings. However, this "radical green movement" has usually been without the Native American thankfulness to the Creator, and therefore tends to see human life as no more important than any other part of the web of existence. Many in this movement encourage us to begin acting as though we humans are no more important than a cat.

Political systems such as radical capitalism and radical communism have their own narrow claims about the meaning of human life and society as being defined primarily in terms of economics. Interestingly, though each system claims to be radically different from the other, they both define human society and culture by how it relates to money and property. Mammon is the god that explains and defines both systems.

The New Testament Definition of "Human" is the Most Audacious Ever.

What becomes clear, if we allow the biblical writers—especially the Jewish writers of the New Testament—to tell their own story, is that even when we grant all systems their best claims and their highest hopes, no religion, no political promise, no philosophy, and no other assertion about the meaning of being human comes close to these authors' lofty claims about human potential. How can you exceed the claim that humans were meant to image and mirror the creativity and goodness of the One God who created our world? To claim that God's purpose for humans is to complete God's original project of making humans into the image of God so that they can live forever as one family in the presence of this One God is either ludicrous or wonderfully daring! It is either true revelation or it is utter foolishness!

It is important that we followers of Jesus give our generation the opportunity to see just how amazing the claim is—"male and female, in the image of God" as God's forever family. It is within this primary biblical paradigm that we should be assessing the New Testament writers' declarations about the relationship between God and Jesus. Then we can allow people to decide whether they want to participate in this extraordinary "God story" or not. But we will not understand the importance of Jesus's ongoing humanity if we do not permit his relationship with God to be fully situated within God's purpose and desire for all humans.

God's Revelation of "Human in the Image of God" Unfolds Progressively in the Biblical Materials.

Certainly, there is a historical progression in this unfolding biblical narrative. I am not implying that the early Old Testament materials envision human nature in the same bright light that the New Testament writers do after the life, death, resurrection, and exaltation of Jesus. They do not. The New Testament provides a new definition of what it means to be "the Son of Man (Adam/Humanity)." However, from the beginning, the biblical materials include a high and unique perspective on what it means to be human and a very high and unique understanding of just how much God values human personality and potential.

It is true that the emphases vary within the materials in the Bible—sometimes greatly. At times, there is a somewhat unresolved tension between one author and another, but I think it is fair to say the dominant biblical paradigm concerning humans is God's relentless, should we say reckless, pursuit of a wholesome covenant relationship with humans. God wants to "be with" us humans. Far more than humans seek a relationship with God, God seeks a relationship with us.[7]

The Irony of "Nothing but a Worm" Theology is Tragic.

Some of my fellow Christians drive me crazy! In what they think is humility, they insist that we should know that "we are worth nothing—but God loves us anyway." I know they mean well, and it is true that, at times, people like me need to be called out for our arrogance and lack of humility. However, this "worth nothing" doctrine is an insult to God who created us, and it is an insult to us as God's creation. Many accuse Christians of holding a very low opinion of human nature, sadly an accusation many of our sermons and books deserve. Tragically, Christians are known world-wide for a faith that is defined primarily by its insistence that we humans are lost and degraded sinners who are of little to no value—unless we "get saved."

I maintain that this degrading message is both ironic and disastrous. How tragic that the Christian "Good News" concerning God and humans is often as negative a view of *human* as is the most thoroughgoing materialistic view of what it means to be human! How unfair we Christians have been to our biblical heritage! We are our own worst enemies, and we are far more dangerous to God's Good News than the brightest and most antagonistic atheists.

The biblical understanding of humans does not begin with, "Repent, you worthless sinner." It begins quite clearly with humanity as "very good" and in "the image of God" (Gen 1:26–31). The biblical understanding of humans does not climax with God helping us escape our humanity with all of its passions, desires, talents, social ability,

---

7. Heschel, *God in Search*, 412.

and physicality. To the contrary, it climaxes with God bringing every human capacity to completion and wholeness and goodness (1 Thess 5:23–24).

That we are sinners who continually fall short of living life in "the image of God," the biblical writers do not doubt (Ps 53:3; Rom 3:23; 1 John 1:8). Neither do I. Personal, as well as worldwide experience, is quite convincing concerning our propensity to fall far short of who we should and could be. The biblical narrative, however, does not start with our brokenness. The biblical view of what it means to be human is first established upon the foundational wonder of humanness in the image of God. To put it in terms of a modern theological argument, if being a *humanist* means highly valuing human potential when it is lived out in a positive relationship with God and with our fellow humans, then the *God of the Bible* is certainly presented by the writers as *the first Humanist*. Granting that the Bible leaves many of us frustrated with its accommodation to the patriarchal world in which it was written (more about that later), it is also important to note we have never found any other ancient source with the high view of women that is recorded on the first page of our Bible: male and female are equally in the image of God. How much higher can language go than declaring that "male and female in the image of God" is evaluated by God, not just as "good," but as "very good" (Gen 1:31)?

But, perhaps the Old Testament writers did attempt to go even higher, according to a fascinating article by Walter Zorn. The Hebrew word *segullah* was used several times in the Old Testament to describe a King's most prized treasures. Zorn shows that it is also used to describe God's most prized personal treasure—God's people (Exod 19:5; Deut 7:6). He then demonstrates that *segullah* is almost certainly the content from the Old Testament that is carried over into the New Testament passages using the Greek word group *periousios* which had been used to translate segullah in the Greek Old Testament [LXX]. Think about the wonder of these New Testament authors claiming that *following Jesus allows us to be renewed as God's most prized personal treasure* (1 Pet 2:9; Eph 1:14; Heb 10:39; Titus 2:14).[8] About as far from "nothing but a worm" theology as one could imagine!

The Biblical Theology of Humans as "Glorified" and "Perfected [Completed]" is Audacious.

Abraham Heschel made an unusual, but I think in many ways correct, observation about the Old Testament when he said,

> The decisive thought in the message of the prophets is not the presence of God to man but rather the presence of man to God. This is why the Bible is God's

---

8. Zorn, "Segullah," 6–9.

anthropology, rather than man's theology. The prophets speak not so much of man's concern for God as of God's concern for man.[9]

So, if it is true that the Old Testament is less about helping humans fully understand God in our presence, and more about helping us humans understand who we are in God's presence, how does that theme move into the New Testament? In a rising crescendo! If we reflected more accurately the further step taken in the New Testament through God's relationship with Jesus, we would be accused of holding far too high an opinion of human nature. Something like the following is the accusation Christians should be hearing from others:

> Audacious! In fact, ludicrous! You believe human potential is that great? You believe God values humans that much? What self-centered foolishness to think the God of the universe—if there is such a God—cares about the daily life of individual human beings! What overblown wishful thinking to believe that such finite and death-bound beings, who are little more than the rest of the animal kingdom, can be transformed into immortal beings who will always choose good, right, and life! What absolute nonsense given what we know of ourselves from the history of the universe and the history of humanity!

Occasionally, one sees the Judeo-Christian narrative critiqued for its hubris concerning human nature and the supposed arrogance—not to mention "wishful thinking"—of those who claim there is a God who cares personally about and responds to us humans. Our assertions about how valuable we humans are to God appear to them to be naïve avoidance of reality. Isn't it clear that humans just happened to appear by luck on a little speck in an ever-expanding universe? Of course, that claim is not the result of scientific observation. It is every bit as much a faith statement flowing from a chosen master narrative of reality as is the one we are offered in the New Testament. We humans were created to be God's most prized treasure—either the height of arrogance or the reason we exist.

Much more often, we Christians are rightly criticized for the way we demean people by demanding that they accept a very low view of humanity. We demand that they confess their own personal worthlessness. How sad that many of these critics think this demeaning view of "human" represents the heritage we have from the writers of the Bible. Not so! Even the most negative critiques of humanity by biblical writers are critiques that see us humans as being less than we should be and less than we could be. It is heartbreaking that much of Christianity has deviated from the basic biblical master story. Our claim should be that humans in the presence of God, with empowering from God, have potential beyond our wildest imagination! Just look at Jesus (Heb 2:9)!

---

9. Heschel, *God in Search*, 412.

HUMANS ARE STAMPED WITH A "GODLIKENESS" THAT NEEDS TO BE BROUGHT TO COMPLETION.

Humans, including many Christians, do and say a lot of things that justify a severe critique of how the claim that we are in the image of God has been practiced. We have also done and said numerous things that justify the negative critiquing of our misuse of the "subdue" passages that identify us humans as intended to corule with God in God's creation (Gen 1; Ps 8; Heb 2). As I write, many Christians in the United States still see these passages as permission to rape the earth's environment or to ignore environmental and social concerns because "this world won't last long." Such attitudes are tragic, coming from the heirs of writers who taught that the Creation rings with praises for God every day and every night (Pss 19, 148).

Still, for good or ill, we have no choice but to relate to the earth with a certain godlikeness. Every choice we make affects the complex systems that sustain our earth—a truth many environmentalists are attempting to get the rest of us to understand. We humans will structure and restructure creation. The question is whether we will do it thankfully and well in a mutual covenant relationship with God, or arrogantly in a spiral of destruction. Either way, we will continue restructuring the gift either by renewal or by further damaging it. As advertisers like to say, "That is what we do!" It is who we humans are.

We might play out our godlikeness in ways that are arrogant and manipulative and even demonic, perhaps even blasting ourselves back to the stone age, or even into annihilation. Many movies, books, and games envision such a negative apocalypse. Quite a few scientific documentaries do as well. At least one passage in the New Testament sounds eerily similar in suggesting that choices we humans make will determine how long this current age continues (2 Pet 3:7–12). Alternatively, we might live out our godlikeness in ways that honor the Creator and appreciatively share the Creator's gifts and blessings with other humans and with the rest of the amazing web of life called creation (nature).

Either way, our godlikeness will deeply impact every part of the creation we touch. Almost every month I watch yet another nature documentary that ends with some form of the statement, "And, whether this incredible system of nature continues to function well or not is now, in many ways, up to humans. We now impact every aspect of the global system." Although it is almost never acknowledged in these documentaries, each of these concluding statements is a validation of the biblical descriptions of humans as creatures imaging God. We are creatures destined to co-create ("subdue") the earth for good or ill (Gen 1; Ps 8).

GOD RELENTLESSLY PURSUES A RELATIONSHIP WITH THESE GOD-STAMPED BEINGS.

Occasionally, a song is written that captures the biblical emphasis on God's relentless pursuit of humans. A generation ago, Don Francisco's *Adam, Where Are You?* expressed with haunting words and melody God's search for us humans. More recently, Gungor's *Beautiful Things* expressed God's purpose in creation and the amazing promise that God can bring overwhelming newness where we see only dust. Similarly, an occasional book such as Abraham Joshua Heschel's *God in Search of Man: A Philosophy of Judaism* or Helmut Thielicke's *The Waiting Father* appears that emphasize God's relentless pursuit of relationships with us humans.

The New Testament authors proclaim God's passionate and relentless pursuit of God's creation project. We need to begin our quest for understanding the relationship between God and Jesus in this context just as they did. By the second and third centuries AD, the emphasis in Christian theology had shifted toward attempting to convince people that Jesus is God. That was not the question that was uppermost in the minds of New Testament writers. They were much more focused on the question raised much earlier by a psalmist: "What is man that you [God] are mindful of him, and the son of man [*adam*] that you care for him" (Ps 8:4). The psalmist followed that question with an amazing assertion concerning the relationship God desires with us humans:

> [5] You made him a little lower than the heavenly beings and *crowned him with glory and honor.* [6] You made him *ruler over the works of your hands*; you put *everything under his feet* (Ps 8:5–6, *emphasis mine*, also note how Heb 2:5–18; Rom 5:12–21; 1 Cor 15:20–28; apply this psalm to Jesus and to other humans as well).

The psalmist wondered, given what he knew about the universe and about humanity, how it could be that God cares what happens to us. Nonetheless, he trusted that God not only cares, but will succeed in the adventure of making humans into the image of God, crowned with the glory and honor of God. The writer of Daniel 7 predicted that someday God would enthrone one "like the Son of Man," who would then make it possible for God to achieve God's original goal for many other humans as well: "Then the *sovereignty, power, and greatness of the kingdoms* under the whole heaven will be *handed over to the saints, the people of the Most High*" (Dan 7:27, *emphasis mine*).

As we will explore in the next chapter, the New Testament writer of Hebrews 2 reengages the psalmist's "How can it be?" and "What is human?" questions, as well as Daniel 7's claim that "one like the son of man" would be God's way of including "many holy ones" in God's reign. The writer suggests that God's relationship with Jesus is God's next major step toward answering those questions by giving clear evidence that God wants to "glorify" us humans.

However, the New Testament writer's claim that God wants to glorify humans is not a novel assertion. It is presented in the context of a long biblical history claiming that God wants to glorify, exalt, and honor humans.

GOD'S DESIRE TO GLORIFY, EXALT, AND HONOR HUMANS IS FUNDAMENTAL.

The credal statement "Man's highest goal is to glorify God," is biblically sound only if it is placed in a larger biblical context. The larger context is the claim that God's highest goal for this creation and for human history is to glorify humans. Apart from this larger context, the credal statement makes God sound like the ultimate egoist. However, within the context of God's great desire to exalt and glorify (honor) humans, the only proper response is an overwhelmingly grateful desire to honor, glorify, and exalt the God who amazingly chooses to want, love, and honor us. "Thank you, Father! You are wonderful beyond words!" How else would you want to respond?

God's Desire to Glorify Humans is an Old Testament Theme.

Interestingly, the Old Testament moves away from using the phrase "image of God" positively after Genesis 5:1–3 and 9:6. On the other hand, Old Testament writers did not move away from trusting that God's desire is to elevate human potential so we can increasingly reflect our glorious Creator.

One way the Hebrew Bible speaks of God's goal is God's desire to share God's glory with humans, sometimes using the Hebrew word group *kavad* and sometimes *yikar*. The biblical concept of "glorify" might be more than, but is never less than, the action of honoring appropriately in a *weighty* manner. In the 1970s, many of my friends from the Counterculture captured the nuance of the Hebrew *kavad* with a "that's heavy" description of weighty events.

Throughout the Old Testament, the theme that humans need to glorify God is presented as the proper response to God's desire to glorify humans. Of course, God's desire to glorify and exalt us is not to be equated with our arrogant ways of attempting to glorify and exalt ourselves. Our arrogant self-glorification always leads to self-destruction as well as to the destruction of others. The glory God wants for us is glory that comes from deepening our relationship with God and our willingness to love and serve our fellow humans.

Although no statement of God's desire to glorify humans is stronger than Psalm 8:4–5, there are other examples in the Old Testament portraying God's desire to glorify and exalt humans. (*See* Josh 3:7, 4:14; 1 Sam 2:10; 2 Sam 22:47–49; Jer 30:18–19; Pss 62:7, 91:14–16; Isa 62:1–3.)

God's Desire to Glorify Humans Is an Emphatic New Testament Theme.

The New Testament writers also see the covenant relationship between God and humans as one in which God wishes to honor, glorify, and exalt humans. As the writers of the New Testament transitioned to Greek, they used the word group *doxa* that earlier Jewish translators of the Old Testament had used. They never completely abandoned the Hebrew idea of "weightiness" (2 Cor 4:17), but this translation emphasized concepts such as splendor, light, and brightness, much as our current English word *glory* tends to do. The combination of the Hebrew word and its Greek translation reflected an Old Testament pattern that often presented God's special presence as both weighty and bright.

Other than perhaps Psalm 8 and Hebrews 2, no chapter in the Bible emphasizes God's desire to "glorify" humans, and God's desire that we humans glorify God, as strongly as John 17. The Greek version of what is often termed Jesus's High Priestly prayer uses various forms of the word group *doxazo/doxa* (glorify/glory) throughout. Jesus prays that God will fulfill the purpose God has planned for humans since before this creation began. He begins by twice asking the Father to glorify him (John 17:1, 5). Jesus also prays that God's desire to glorify Jesus will have an important result— "Glorify your Son, that [Greek *hina*, 'in order that'] your Son may glorify you" (John 17:1, *see also* John 13:31–32).

As the prayer continues, it becomes even clearer that Jesus does not see being glorified by God as something that will separate him from humanity. He ends the prayer by thanking God that he could share the glory the Father has given him with other humans—"I have *given them the glory that you gave me*, that they may be one as we are one" (John 17:22, *emphasis mine*). The entire prayer exhibits Jesus's confident self-identification with God's purpose and goal for relating to humans—we humans were created because God wants to glorify us along with and through Jesus. This results in our desire and ability to glorify God in response.

As for Paul's letters, the rarely-referred-to letter of 2 Thessalonians, as well as the often-referred-to letters of Romans, 2 Corinthians, and Philippians, declare that God's goal is to share God's glory with Jesus and with other humans.

> [18] I consider that our present sufferings are *not worth comparing with the glory that will be revealed in us*. [19] The creation waits in eager expectation *for the sons* [and daughters] *of God to be revealed*. . . . (Rom 8:18–19, *emphasis mine*).

Later in the same chapter of Romans, Paul returns to his theme of God's desire to glorify us.

> [28] And we know that in all things God works for [*eis* in Greek often implies moving "toward"] the good of those who love him [God], who have been called according to his purpose. [29] For those God foreknew he also predestined to be *conformed to the likeness of his Son*, that he might be *the firstborn among*

many brothers and sisters. ³⁰ And those he predestined, he also called; those he called, he also justified [put into a right and just relationship]; those he justified, *he also glorified. . . .* (Rom 8:28–30, *emphasis mine*).

God's desire to glorify and honor, not only Jesus as firstborn, but other humans through what God has done in Jesus is affirmed in the following passages as well:

> And we, who with unveiled faces *all reflect the Lord's glory, are being transformed into his likeness with ever-increasing glory,* which comes from the Lord, who is the Spirit (2 Cor 3:18, *emphasis mine*).
>
> ²⁰ But our citizenship is in heaven. And we eagerly await a Savior from there, the Lord Jesus Christ, ²¹ who, by the power that enables him to bring everything under his control, *will transform our lowly bodies so that they will be like his glorious body* (Phil 3:20–21, *emphasis mine*).
>
> To this he called you through our gospel *so that you may be a glorious treasure of our Lord Jesus* the Messiah" (2 Thess 2:14; Zorn translation, *emphasis mine*).[10]

Peter agrees with Paul that it is the work of the Spirit of God to bring the glory of God into the lives of humans: "You are blessed, for the Spirit of glory and of God rests on you" (1 Pet 4:14). (*See* for further New Testament examples of God's desire to glorify humans: Rom 2:10, 3:23–24; 1 Cor 2:7, 12:24–25; 2 Cor 4:17; Col 1:27, 3:4; 2 Thess 1:11–12, 2:14; Heb 2:5–10; Jas 4:10; 1 Pet 1:6–7, 5:1–4.)

More clearly than many of his contemporaries, Irenaeus, one of the second-century church fathers, seems to have grasped the value God has for humanness. His phrase "The glory of God is man fully alive, . . ." or as others translate it "The glory of God is living man. . . ." emphasizes that a right relationship between humans and God leads to "the glory of God" flowing into our human lives.[11]

"IMAGE OF GOD" IS A RENEWED THEME IN THE NEW TESTAMENT WRITINGS.

The Old Testament writers let the "image of God" phrase drop away. The almost reluctant usage in Genesis 9 marks the end of referring to humans as "in the image of God" in Old Testament canon. From that point on, the concept of an "image" relating to God is negative and used to describe idols. Even the very hopeful language of Psalm 8 avoids using the phrase. Paul's writings, plus a reference in both Hebrews and in James, bring back this description of God's original project in the New Testament. As the following passages illustrate, this renewed usage is clearly embedded in an understanding of Jesus's humanity.

---

10. Zorn, "Segullah," 9.
11. Irenaeus, *Against Heresies*, Lib. 4, 20, 5–7; SC 644–648.

Image of God is Used to Describe Jesus.

Jesus is described as reflecting and imaging God. Because of Jesus's relationship with God, the New Testament writers renew language that had been dropped by Old Testament writers. In doing so, they clearly link Jesus to God's original creation project as it is described in Genesis 1–2. Here are a few examples:

> The god of this age has blinded the minds of unbelievers, so that they cannot see the light of *the gospel [good news] of the glory Christ who is the image of God* (2 Cor 4:4, *emphasis mine*).

> ⁵ Your attitude should be *the same as* that of Christ Jesus: ⁶ Who, being in *very nature God* [*en morphē theo*, perhaps best "the form of God"], did not consider *equality with God* something to be grasped (Phil 2:5–6, which will be discussed more extensively later, *emphasis mine*).

> He [the Son God loves] is *the image of the invisible God*, the *firstborn* over all creation (Col 1:15, *emphasis mine*).

> *The Son is the radiance of God's glory* and the *exact representation of his being*, sustaining all things by his powerful word (Heb 1:3, *emphasis mine*).

Image of God is also Used to Describe Other Humans as God's Children.

Passages such as those just referenced are often understood as though they separated Jesus from our humanity—and his. However, the claim that through God's relationship with Jesus it is now possible for other humans to be renewed into the image of God points in a very different direction. Jesus, and others in relationship to him, are being moved toward the same completion of God's original creation goal—into the image of God. Sharing this gift from God embeds Jesus in our humanity and embeds us in Jesus's humanity.

Paul sees Jesus's imaging God as the source of other humans being able to image God in Romans 8:28–30. The "good" toward which God can work in even the worst situations is the good of making us more fully into the image of Jesus, who is the "firstborn" of God's future forever human family. We choose to be lovers of God; God has chosen and planned from the beginning to do more for us than we can even imagine (1 Cor 2:9)! "For those God foreknew he also predestined [decided ahead of time] to be *conformed to the likeness of his Son*, that he might be *the firstborn among many brothers*" (Rom 8:29, *emphasis mine*).

If it is possible to be even more explicit about the connection between Jesus and other humans being in the image of God than Romans 8, Paul manages to do so in the following statements:

> And *just as we have borne the likeness of the earthly man* [human], so shall *we bear the likeness of the man* [human] *from heaven* (1 Cor 15:49, *emphasis mine*).

> And we, who with unveiled faces *all reflect the Lord's glory*, are being *transformed into his likeness with ever-increasing glory*, which comes from the Lord, who is the Spirit (2 Cor 3:18, *emphasis mine*).

> ¹ Be *imitators of God*, therefore, as dearly loved children ² and *live a life of love, just as Christ* loved us and gave himself up for us as a fragrant offering and sacrifice to God (Eph 5:1–2, *emphasis mine*).

> And [you] have put on the *new self*, which is being *renewed* in knowledge in the *image of its Creator* (Col 3:10, *emphasis mine*).

The author of 1 John maintains that reflecting the image of God is the goal of daily living for those who follow Jesus. He also tells us that Jesus currently mediates between us and God in order that this goal might be accomplished. Moreover, God plans yet another intervention into human history that will bring this goal to completion for God's human family.

> ¹⁶ᵇ God is love. Whoever lives in love *lives in God, and God in him.* ¹⁷ In this way, love is *made complete* [form of *teleioō* among us so that we will have confidence on the day of judgment, *because in this world we are like him* [God] (1 John 4:16b–17, *emphasis mine*).

> ¹ How great is the love the Father has lavished on us, that we should be *called children of God! And that is what we are!* The reason the world does not know us is that it did not know him [Jesus]. ² Dear friends, now we are children of God, and what we will be has not yet been made known. But we know that *when he* [Jesus] *appears, we shall be like him*, for we shall see him as he is (1 John 3:1–2, *emphasis mine*).

Scattered throughout the New Testament, there is an understanding that the relationship between God and Jesus has allowed God to renew and continue moving toward the completion of God's creation adventure. One passage that does not use the words "likeness," "image" or "heaven," but clearly agrees with this understanding of what God is doing, appears in 2 Peter. There God's involvement in bringing about the fruit of the spirit in our daily life is described as God's "divine power" (*theias* in Greek) that empowers us to be participators "in the divine [*theias* in Greek] nature" (2 Pet 1:3–4). Peter clearly believed that, through God's relationship with Jesus, God is continuing toward the goal of creating other humans who will be forever in the image of God, sharers in the divine, just as Jesus already is. Jesus *is* one of us, and we will be like him in God's presence forever!

(*See* for further examples of "image" of God or Jesus applied to us humans: 1 Cor 11:7; Eph 4:24; 1 Thess 5:23–24; Jas 3:9; and each of the "perfection/completion" passages noted earlier.)

Sometimes We See the Image of God Enacted in the Goodness of Fellow Humans.

The challenge for us humans is to honor and glorify God by living in the image of God. This challenge, however, needs to remain within the context of God's determination to sustain a covenant relationship with us that allows God to glorify and honor humans who were created to mirror and image God.

Do we humans actually image God in positive ways? If you spend time as I do with fellow followers of Jesus in settings where you have the opportunity to see some of what goes on behind the scenes, surely you, too, have seen humans imaging and mirroring God. If a member of my relatively small church or very small Bible study group cannot find a job, others often step up with money, food, and contacts. Sometimes they do this personally and directly, and sometimes through a "Family Fund" that is available when needed.

If someone in the community has a family member who is developing Alzheimer's, others step up with visits, reading books that still resonate, and buying two new pianos because music still speaks to several clients in the Memory Home. If a hurricane hits Houston or Puerto Rico, people of all races and every economic status rush to save one another. Meanwhile, those of us in a small group in Illinois pray for them and send money so hungry people in Houston and Puerto Rico, people we will never meet, can eat. Brothers and sisters sustained me and my family with love, prayers, food, and running errands, as my wife lay dying while we were all quarantined due to distancing for Covid-19. No, I am not glorifying my church or Christians in general: our failures are abundant, and they will be acknowledged over and over throughout this book. I am instead suggesting that imaging God *does* occur sometimes, and that, when it does, it is an expression of genuine human potential.

Members and family members of the small Bible study group I participate in spend their energies working for racial reconciliation, justice for immigrants, better living conditions for the homeless, clean water for all, justice for prisoners, and helping teens in California escape their addictions. If a member has great new success in her vocation, another is publishing one more book, and another is blessed financially, others honestly rejoice without jealousy or behind-the-back comments. If one member receives a rather miraculous healing, while others do not, there is joy for the one who does. Are we far from perfect in imaging Jesus, who images God for us? Yes! But can we see the potential in our humanity for reflecting the image of God as Jesus does? At least sometimes—Yes!

I have just catalogued a few personal experiences that I have seen with my own eyes, but I know that similar things go on all over the world in communities of people who follow Jesus. We are all far from perfect, but the image of God does show vividly at times in human lives.

Does this imaging of God occur outside of churches and outside of Christianity? Are similar "godly" characteristics shown by people who are not followers of Jesus? Do some atheists or participants in other religions of the world also respond to their fellow humans similarly, sometimes in even more godly ways? Certainly! We humans are deeply stamped with the Creator's image, and, thankfully, that reality is often expressed all over the world in kind-hearted acts of goodness, mercy, and justice. Isn't that one of the central implications of Jesus's famous parable of *The Good Samaritan*, a short story about an "outsider" who images God's compassion for the hurting far better than the church "insiders" of the time (Luke 10:25–37)? This is a reality I have often seen. Haven't you? Apparently, Jesus saw it too, even in a Roman officer—"I tell you the truth, I have not found anyone in Israel with such great faith" (Matt 8:10).

My wife and I recently watched a *60 Minutes* segment that touched our hearts so deeply that we responded the only way we knew how and wrote another check to Doctors Without Borders. What was it that was so amazing? It was the account of two doctors who give away cataract surgeries and contact lenses in economically poor areas of the Himalayas. Neither doctor ever mentions God or faith.

These two exceptionally creative and gifted doctors could have easily made millions of dollars of extra income for the time and expertise they have been giving away since 1994. Why give so freely? Because doctors Sanduk Ruit (Nepalese) and Geoff Tabin (American) have dedicated themselves to eradicating as much unnecessary blindness as they possibly can in their lifetimes. They are motivated to respond to the systemic injustice that allows people who are poor to go blind, when a simple operation could save their sight and perhaps even their lives. Regardless of how each doctor would describe what he is doing, I am sure these gifts "image" God's compassionate concern that humans work for justice and goodness in our world, including specifically "recovery of sight for the blind" (Luke 4:19; Isa 61:1–2).

I do not know how either of these doctors relates to God, but I don't have to know that to know that they are imaging God in their expressions of compassion. Jesus does not bother to tell the theologian of his time, or us today as listeners, what the compassionate Samaritan did or did not believe about God when he became an example for us to "go and keep doing likewise." The Greek tenses in the story indicate the Bible scholar wanted an answer that would give him a one-time action that would ensure that he was right with God (Greek *aorist* in Luke 10:25, 37a). In contrast, Jesus asks for a lifestyle that models the compassion this outsider showed for a fellow human (Jesus's present tense in Luke 10:28, 37b). Keeping on keeping on with compassion for those we might not even have a close relationship with is what most images God—not a one-time event.

HUMANS ARE MARRED WITH BROKENNESS AND BENTNESS. YES, BUT.

In case you are wondering, I am not downplaying sin and brokenness. Skepticism about humans, and about Christians including myself, comes easily for me. From my youth, I have been around churches, church schools, and Christian institutions. Nothing I have experienced has ever inclined me toward Pollyanna attitudes concerning Christians. There is no proper response to our constant failures as humans, and as people who claim to follow Jesus, that does not include our need for Truth (confession), Tears, (lamentation), Turning (repentance—always turning from and turning toward), and Trusting that God will respond (faith).[12] These responses are constantly called for in my life, the life of every follower of Jesus, and of every human I know.

Because I just mentioned *60 Minutes*, let me acknowledge that my unscientific estimate is that more than 60% of their airtime is spent exposing the "dark" side of human endeavors, and if you listen to, read, or watch the daily news, the percentage of "darkness" reported there tends to be far higher. Only recently has it become fashionable in the daily television network news to be sure to conclude with one short two-to-four-minute bright spot at the end of a barrage of darkness and destruction.

I am not glossing over the brokenness of humans, Christians, Church, followers of Jesus, or myself. I am maintaining that we need to see the bentness and brokenness in human affairs from the perspective of the master story in the Bible. If God's goal for us is that we become humans who use all of our God-given gifts to love and honor God 24/7, and to love our neighbor 24/7, and to love our selves appropriately 24/7, then there is no question that we "have all sinned and are consistently falling short of the glory of God" (Rom 3:23). But unlike many who have quoted him since, Paul's starting assumption was that we humans do in fact have the potential to reflect God's glory because we were created to be in the image of God. It is this potential God placed in us at creation that we are constantly falling short of. Still, God has never forsaken the goal. Earlier in Romans, Paul made this point strongly: [10] *. . . but glory, honor and peace for everyone who does good: first for the Jew, then for the Gentile.* [11]*For God does not show favoritism* (Rom 2:10–11, *emphasis mine*).

I am aware that what appears to be the obvious meaning of the statement just quoted is often explained away by theologians and pastors, but Paul never explains it away. We can honestly thank God for those who seek good and peace, whoever they are and wherever they are, and we can at the same time honestly acknowledge that, as individuals and as societies, our actions reveal the constant falling short of the wonderful potential God gave us humans. In that context, I have no problem also insisting that every human, including "everyone who does good," would be better off knowing and following Jesus, just as Paul maintains later in Romans.

---

12. Simkins, *Truth, Tears*.

One does not have to turn to the Bible to find the assessment that we constantly fall short of our human potential. We experience this falling short of our potential daily. It is the tragic theme of many of our great literary works, songs, plays, and motion pictures. Isn't this also the sad admission that many of us parents make to our older children when we admit that we meant to be better parents than we were? We could have been, we wanted to be, we meant to be, we even tried to be, but somehow, we didn't manage to be. That is also the confession I often made to my wife of 57 years whom I deeply loved from the beginning of our relationship—I could have been, I wanted to be, I meant to be, I even tried to be a better husband, but somehow I often did not manage to be.

We experience this same reality at the more systemic level. Many of us want the environment to be healthier, safer, and better; yet as a culture we continue making decisions that do not further that goal. Decisions that make the environment worse, and those that do not make it better, are not made only by people who don't care or who deny the importance of good decisions. Sadly, they are made by all of us at times.

Perhaps nowhere do we see the difference between intentions and actions at the corporate level more clearly than the difference between the good intentions we are promised prior to every election, and the outcomes we see during the following four years. I am not talking about the false promises, of which there are far too many, but rather about the genuine intentions that are almost never completely enacted. Politics becomes "business as usual." The prospectus of almost every new business raises again the specter of hopeful potential for how wonderful we could be as human societies. This only works because we all sense the truth that our potential exceeds our current reality. Then invariably the new corporation reveals yet again the enormous power of "business as usual," as the poor get poorer and the rich get richer. As Hobbes sadly shares with Calvin while they ruminate about New Year's resolutions, "The problem with the future is that it keeps turning into the present."[13]

In this sense, the claim we are all sinners (that is, that we all "miss the mark" of fulfilling our God-given potential) isn't a very controversial claim. In fact, it is the tension we all live in. We never reach our full potential, not only in a lifetime, but even within a 24-hour day. We know there is more to us than we seem to be able to sustain. We make and break our resolutions to do better, not just annually but daily, often hourly. Somehow, we know that Bryan Stevenson of *The Equal Justice Initiative* is correct when he maintains that "Each of us is more than the worst thing we've ever done."[14] We can also say, "Each of us is less than the best thing we have ever done." And, if a primary definition of "sin" is failing to trust God 24/7 and failing to love God with the whole mind, heart, body, and possessions 24/7, who can claim not to be constantly falling short? That dynamic tension between what we know we should and

---

13. Watterson, *Calvin*, 12.30.1990.
14. Stevenson, *Just Mercy*, 290.

could be, and what we so often are not, is the human dilemma described on almost every page of the Bible.

In the biblical master story context, it is "Good News" to own up to this reality and to allow the wonderful, yet bent and broken, dynamic to explain the severe tension we all experience in our more honest moments. We experience a powerful tension between our sense of potential and our sense of failure at living up to that potential. The individual and corporate potential is real, not just imagined. Likewise, the falling short of both is very real, and not just the imagination of Christian evangelists. There are plenty of reasons for truth (confession), tears (lamentation), and turning (repentance) as we choose trusting (faith) that God will continue to pursue God's end goal of a forever human family made up of females and males in the image of God. But let's be sure we remember the goal.

GOD'S GOOD NEWS FOR HUMANS IS TRULY GOOD NEWS ABOUT OUR VALUE TO GOD.

As real as individual and corporate sin is, it is neither the first nor the last word about human nature, according to the biblical writers. The Good News is much larger than the common summary offered by many Christian evangelists: "We humans can be forgiven for failing."

The following summarizes the overall biblical understanding of human nature:

1. Every individual and corporate human capacity is good by God's origin and intent. We were created to be in the image of God and to mirror and reflect God.

2. Every individual and corporate human capacity has become broken and bent back upon itself; we are constantly falling short of our God-given potential. Sometimes we actively choose evil, and sometimes we choose not to do good; we are sinful individuals living in sinful societies.

3. Every individual and corporate human capacity can yet be made whole by God's grace. God's ultimate purpose is not forgiveness for our failings—that gift is just a gracious means to a much higher end. God's ultimate purpose is the transformation of humans and a final fulfillment (wholeness/completion/salvation) of our God-given potential.

To be truly biblical, these three aspects of human nature must be emphasized in the right order. Though it is important to know the truth about ourselves, it is also important to know that the *first word* of the Good News is not, "We are sinful and broken." Nor is the first word of the Good News that we need to be and can be "saved." That God can "heal," "make whole," "redeem," and "rescue," us humans is certainly a part of the concept of "saved" or "salvation," and that is definitely Good News.

Every day, events make it clear that we need to be saved, including every nuance of that powerful word. Still, the gracious news that salvation and transformation are possible, as incredibly important as that is, is not the first word in God's Good News for humans. The first word is that being human is a "very good" thing in God's eyes. God created something of such great value to God that we humans are called God's most prized treasure. God sees us as valuable and worth saving at great cost to God.

It is this first word that makes the second and third words of the good news concerning God's relationship with Jesus so wonderful. When we fail to save a teenager who is wasting herself on drugs, we do not cry because she is worth nothing unless we save her; we cry because someone worth so much is in danger of being lost to us. When we see that American society has wasted so much of the potential and giftedness of our Black, Hispanic, Native American, Immigrant, and Female population for centuries, the sadness is not because those groups that have been marginalized by a White- and Male-dominated society had nothing to offer, but because as a society we have wasted so much God-given talent and beauty. Sadly, we still do!

When culture after culture falls short of its potential, we do not weep because a culture wasn't of much value anyway; we weep because so much potential has been lost to humanity. Often magnificent potential is senselessly wasted and trashed by arrogant, greedy, and corrupt leaders—and clueless followers. When we take seriously the first word of the Good News, humans are incredibly valued by God, then the promise that God's relationship with Jesus provides a way to salvage us—both as individuals and as community—finds its rightful context.

Jesus illustrated this perspective as the primary emphasis in one of his most famous stories (Luke 15:11–32). Both the prodigal younger brother and the judgmental older brother thought the younger brother wasn't worth much because he had failed so miserably as a son. The father on the other hand—the God-figure in the parable—waited and watched every day, hoping the son would return and renew the relationship. The waiting father constantly watched, not because the son could become valuable if he returned home, but because the son was already so valuable and loved by the father. It wasn't that the Father didn't love the son when he was away wasting himself. The reality was that the son wasn't choosing to be close enough to experience the love the Father had for him every minute of every day.

The younger son tried to come up with a new way to become valuable—"make me like one of your hired men." His big brother was convinced that he could no longer be of any value—"this son of yours has squandered your property with prostitutes." On the other hand, the father, just like the shepherd who finds the lost sheep and the peasant woman who finds the lost coin, calls for a party. Why? Because a son who was always valuable is home again. Never once did that son lose his value to the waiting father.

GOOD NEWS CONCERNING HUMAN POTENTIAL IS A PROMISE YET TO BE FULFILLED—TODAY WE ONLY SEE DOWN PAYMENTS.

The third aspect of the Good News about God's purpose for humanity is what some skeptics call "pie in the sky by and by when you die." Of course, it could logically be wishful thinking, but it is also logically consistent to claim what the New Testament writers assert God has now revealed. They claim to have seen with their own eyes that God intends to use our experience of the enormous gap between our obvious potential and our consistent falling short to educate us and prepare us for the future God has opened up before us. Through God's relationship with the human Jesus, a way forward has been prepared. God's "way" toward this future begins now.

God's work in our lives now through the Holy Spirit is only a "down payment" on God's future for those of us who are God's most prized special treasure (Eph 1:14). But the future is not "pie in the sky by and by." God fully intends for the transformation into the image and likeness of God to begin in our lives right now (Eph 4:23–24, 5:1). I suggest that the biblical writers are far more in touch with reality concerning human potential than are the skeptics.

I have been privileged to see God work amazing changes in the lives of people who have chosen to ask God to help them "image God" more fully by modeling Jesus as best they can. I have seen women who had been sexually abused by their church-going fathers, and others by their pastors, become giving, prayerful, caring individuals who genuinely bless those around them. Scars? Surely! But growth that they once thought unimaginable.

I have seen alcoholics become some of the most passionately generous people I have ever known. I have seen people who were struggling with their mental health become level-headed and big-hearted brothers and sisters, filled with wisdom for others. I have seen people bored to death with the meaninglessness of life become highly motivated lovers of others. I have seen marriages that looked hopelessly broken healed by Jesus's presence and turned into homes of joy and love.

Transformations can be truly miraculous. As a ten-year-old, my father saw his father murder a woman in cold blood and then lock my father (and his siblings) in the house with the dead body and abandon them permanently. But what I experienced was a father who learned to love his children. He loved us with an abundance of grace and freedom that were amazing. I grew up being loved and nurtured by a prayerful, gentle, strong, and caring mother who herself grew up with an overbearing authoritarian father and a distant mother. I have personally experienced myself being slowly moved from an almost totally self-centered and deeply prejudiced young adult to someone who sometimes completely forgets myself for a few minutes in my desire to serve God and love a fellow human. Sporadic? Surely so in my case, but nonetheless, miraculous in the transformation I have experienced, and my transformation has been small compared to the changes I have seen in many others.

Still, the current transformations are never enough! They are tastes of a future intended to make us hunger for more goodness, righteousness, and justice (Matt 5:6). They are truly meant to be "down payments," not the final outcome of a relationship with God made possible by what God has done through Jesus. Wishful thinking? Having seen a lot of wishful thinking among Christians in my lifetime, I understand the argument well, but I don't think this is wishful thinking. I think, and I trust, we are experiencing a step toward the future God has guaranteed through bringing Jesus's humanity to completion as the "firstborn" of God's forever family.

And what a vision of God's future the New Testament gives us. The goal is not to escape our humanity; rather, it is fulfillment of all that it means to be human! Our existence has real meaning in the universe. Our capacities and potentials, both individually and corporately, are not gratuitous accidents, but gifts yet to be fulfilled when God reaches the end goal (*telos*) planned from the beginning for humans who were created with the potential to be *completed* and *glorified* forever in God's forever human family.

True, this age of the universe will not and cannot last. Physicist (fellow of Britain's Royal Society of scientists)) and Anglican theologian John Polkinghorne maintains that all of our scientific inquiry indicates the world as we know it cannot last. Polkinghorne also reminds us that the New Testament writers were certain the world as we know it now was never meant to last! Rather, it is an important step toward God's plan for fulfillment in "the age to come," and that age to come will be a world that can last.[15]

As C. S. Lewis suggested several times, a human who allows the image of God to shine through empowered him or her in life will never be fully at home in this age because we were created for an age that is yet to come. We will always long for a future age of fulfillment because that is what we were made for. That is the potential we sense and sometimes see. It isn't that we want to escape this wonderful creation; it is rather that God always meant for it to lead to much more—not toward escape, but toward fulfillment! Eugene Peterson said it this way:

> Heaven is also more, far more. But the "more" is the completion of what is, not an escape from it. It is the wholeness of what we now see in part, not the repudiation of it.... Heaven is an intricate system of completions.[16]

Of course, being logically possible and consistent is not proof that a possibility is going to occur. Only an act of God that brings God's future to a climax in human history can "prove" that this intended fulfillment is why we humans exist. At the level of logic alone, one possibility is that the claim God has humanity in a ripening process with the final mature goal yet to be accomplished is just wishful thinking. Over a century and a half ago, Ludwig Feuerbach inspired Karl Marx's desire for a state and world without God or religion with precisely this assertion. Feuerbach

---

15. Polkinghorne, *God of Hope*.
16. Peterson, *Reversed*, 173, 177.

argued that "God" is nothing but human abilities, fears, and wishes projected onto the large screen of history.[17]

That is a powerful argument because we humans do project a lot of our fears and wishes upon reality, and we certainly project many of our fears and wishes upon God. Our projections that turn God into gods imaging our wishes, fears, and wants is called idolatry in the Bible. Like the Jeroboam of the Northern Kingdom, we might name our golden calf YHWH, but even when we attempt to name it "God" it remains an idol—a projection of our own brokenness. However, I trust, and sometimes I see strong evidence as well, that "the God and Father of our Lord Jesus the Messiah" will have the last word (Eph 1:3–23).

Obviously, no one we know has completely reached God's goal for humans before reaching death—that includes Jesus, who died a death intended to reduce him to shame and disgrace. As the writer of Hebrews states clearly, even for Jesus the "completion" of his "life" came after his death (Heb 5:7–9, 8:4).

The coming fulfillment that can only come as God's gift of life after death is very important to the Good News. If Jesus had to trust God to do what no one can prove will occur, you and I will have to do the same. Only God can ultimately make the possible become reality; human logic can never prove it will happen.

Having said that, I maintain that our corporate and individual experience of an intense dynamic tension between our potential and our performance is, in fact, logically consistent and coherent with the biblical claim that God is in the middle of a great project that is incomplete, but is continuing toward God's goal for human history. This possibility makes sense of the tension we all experience between who we are and who we sense we can be as humans—both individually and corporately. If we understood this assertion, we might understand much better the claims concerning God's relationship to Jesus and Jesus's relationship to God, which we will begin exploring in the next chapter.

For now, let's at least allow the audacious expectation of fulfillment that the New Testament writers present as God's goal for Jesus and other humans to stretch our imagination. Although it is tempting to write many pages about it, I'll note here only a few biblical passages concerning this "good news" about the promised fulfillment of human potential yet to come.

Fulfillment is Promised Concerning Individual Human Potential.

The fulfillment of human purpose and potential will be fully seen only when, in God's age to come, God gives to other humans the gift God has already given to the resurrected and exalted human Jesus—immortality and imperishability (1 Cor 15:42–44,

---

17. Feuerbach, *Essence of Christianity*, 29–30, 181.

50–54). Paul claims that God will give to other humans the gift of being humans "of heaven" who will then be fully in the image of Jesus, the first human "of heaven."

> [48] As was the earthly man, so are those who are of the earth; and *as is the man from heaven, so also are those who are of heaven.* [49] And *just as we have borne the likeness of the earthly man, so shall we bear the likeness of the man from heaven* (1 Cor 15:48–49, *emphasis mine*).

It seems obvious in both the previous quotation and in the one that follows that Paul did not think we humans inherently possess an immortal soul. He saw immortality as a gift God can give us in the future, if and when God chooses to do so.

> [9] For God did not appoint us to suffer wrath but to *receive salvation* through our Lord Jesus Christ. [10] He died for us so that, whether we are awake or asleep, we may *live together with him*. . . . [23] May God himself, the God of peace, *sanctify you through and through*. May *your whole spirit, soul and body* be kept blameless at the coming of our Lord Jesus Christ. [24] The one who calls you is faithful and *He* [God] *will do it* (I Thess 5:9–10, 23–24, *emphasis mine*)

According to these early letters from Paul, the goal is not to escape our humanity, but finally to become entirely and completely human—spirit, soul, and body. Every capacity we have as humans is to be brought to wholeness and fulfilment. God does not want to just save a soul or a spirit or a mind; God wants to make each of us holy and wholly human forever, and Jesus is God's means, method, and model for this next big step toward getting us there! Through being included in God's relationship with Jesus, we too can finally become mature, completed humans. Isn't it ironic that Paul, the writer who is so often accused of having a very low and demeaning view of human nature, thought we humans—male and female—could be made completely *whole and holy in every human capacity*?

Fulfillment is Promised Concerning Corporate Human Potential.

Because modern Western thinking is so individualistic, it is important to note the corporate nature of God's Good News in the Scriptures. "The kingdom of God," a very corporate image, is what Jesus heralded as God's desire for the present and the future. God's people are also often designated as "the household of God," another corporate image. We are reminded that God decided from the beginning to have a forever human family made up of "children of God." One New Testament image is that individuals can be "born" into that family by accepting God's offer of "new birth" or "birth from above." Another image is that God "adopts" us into that family as individuals. Yet another image is that God restarts the human race through the "second Adam/human" or "last Adam/human," and then God invites us to join this new family of God as brothers and sisters of Jesus.

Whatever image we focus on, God's gift of future wholeness for humans is corporate first and individual second. Contrary to much of our preaching and singing in church today, it is accurate to say that the biblical writers emphasize the corporate side of salvation more than they emphasize the individual side of salvation. There are many more plural "yous," many more "family"—brother, sister, son, daughter, household—statements, and many more "kingdom," "priesthood," and "fellowship" statements, in the New Testament describing God's purpose for humans than there are statements in the singular concerning individuals.

Nonetheless, many—probably most—of us have been trained to read the corporate statements as though they were about individuals rather than communities. The culture of the modern Western world is a predominantly individualistic culture, and American Christianity is predominantly built within individualistic theology; we tend to read our Bibles from the water we swim in. This problem is exacerbated by the fact that in modern English—unlike Hebrew and Greek—the plural and the singular "you" are indistinguishable.

Isaiah envisioned fulfillment in the following corporate terms:

> *He* [YHWH] *will swallow up death forever*. The Sovereign LORD will wipe away the tears from all faces; he will remove the disgrace of his people from all the earth. The LORD has spoken (Isa 25:8, *emphasis mine*).

> [17] Behold, *I will create new heavens and a new earth*. The former things will not be remembered, nor will they come to mind. [18] But be *glad and rejoice forever in what I will create*, for I will create Jerusalem to be a delight and *its people a joy* (Isa 65:17–18, *emphasis mine*).

The corporate nature of Isaiah 65 is broader in that it involves the entire creation. The corporate nature of Isaiah 25 is broader in that it involves people from all the earth as did the original covenant with Abraham. Both passages are alluded to several times by New Testament authors.

The New Testament letter to the seven churches (Revelation) carries this Old Testament claim of corporate fulfillment to even grander heights. Granting the book of Revelation is filled with imagery that is often unfamiliar to those of us living in the twenty-first century, the following passages are fairly straightforward in terms of the expectation that human capacities, and the capacities of the entire creation, will someday fulfill their potential. When we then add to this the fact that lawyer-like Paul holds the same view of God's coming age, we can be certain it reflects a widespread understanding among the early followers of Jesus.

In Revelation, the expectation is that *character*, *community*, and *creation* are all to be renewed forever by God.

> [1] Then I saw *a new heaven and a new earth*, for the first heaven and the first earth had passed away, and there was no longer any sea. [2] I saw the Holy City, the new Jerusalem, *coming down out of heaven from God*, prepared as

a bride beautifully dressed for her husband. ³ And I heard a loud voice from the throne saying, "*Now the dwelling of God is with men, and he will live with them.* They will be *his people*, and *God himself will be with them* and be their God. ⁴ He will wipe every tear from their eyes. There will be no more death or mourning or crying or pain, for *the old order of things has passed away*" (Rev 21:1–4, *emphasis mine*).

In this great promise, the goal God initiated at the creation comes to fruition. The cosmos, and especially the earth, becomes the Temple of God. No other temple is needed because God's renewed human family is God's dwelling place, and the renewed earth, as well as the renewed universe, is truly home for both humans and God.

The Scriptures as they come to us not only begin with God, focusing attention and purpose on humans who live on the earth—they end the same way. God cares about, wants to be with, and relentlessly pursues a permanent relationship with humans as God's *forever family* and intends to provide for us a *forever home*. The nicest homes envisioned by HGTV do not compare. The Bible begins with God, pursuing a purpose and project—a relationship with humans; and the New Testament ends by saying that God will complete this goal by incorporating other humans into the covenant relationship between God and Jesus. What God always intended for humanity is now guaranteed because of Jesus's relationship with God, which guarantees it is as good as done (Rev 21:6).

I have no idea how many cultures with special insights and gifts have existed in human history. The ones I am aware of cause the promise I am about to quote to bring me to tears of joy and amazement. If I understand correctly the promise quoted here, we are being promised that the best gifts of every culture throughout human history will become a part of God's great new future human culture called the "Kingdom of God." Every culture is pictured as represented by a leader who brings the best gifts of that culture to the feet of Jesus, to be incorporated into the future reign of God. Only destructive things, or people determined to remain destructive and to mess up God's future for others, will be banned from participation in God's goal for humanity.

> ²³ The city does not need the sun or the moon to shine on it, for the glory of God gives it light, and the Lamb is its lamp. ²⁴ The *nations* will walk by its light, and the *kings of the earth will bring their splendor into it*.... ²⁶ The *glory and honor of the nations* will be brought into it. ²⁷ *Nothing impure* will ever enter it, nor will anyone who does what is shameful or deceitful, but only those whose names are written in the Lamb's book of life (Rev 21:23–24, 26–27, *emphasis mine*).

If attempting to envision this great promise involving all human history is too much for us, we can at least envision an example from the American experience. What if Euro-American culture had incorporated, rather than oppressed, the gifts of various Native American tribes, the cultural and individual gifts of Black Americans, and the delightful differences of Mexicans, Jews, and Asians through the centuries? Even more stretching is the attempt to envision what cultural history might look like if the European Christians who arrived in the Americas had chosen to bring what was best from European culture and shared as equals with the people already here in the establishment of a new culture filled with the gifts of both? Now extrapolate that vision to thousands of tribes, nations, and cultures in human history. Talk about fulfillment of corporate human potential!

There should be no mistaking that this is the future the writer of Revelation expected because he celebrates it in various ways.

> [9] And they sang a new song: "You are worthy to take the scroll and to open its seals, because you were slain, and with your blood you purchased men for God *from every tribe and language and people and nation.* [10] You have made them to be a kingdom and priests to serve our God, and *they will reign on the earth*" (Rev 5:9–10, *emphasis mine*).

The writer is not envisioning that suddenly these people become abstract universal humans. They are still people "from every nation, tribe, people and language, standing before the throne and in front of the Lamb" experiencing God's salvation (Rev 7:9–10). It is as tribal members of hundreds of human kingdoms that this great multitude receives the hope for a coming fulfillment of human capacities as "*The kingdom of the world has become the kingdom of our Lord and of his Christ*, and he will reign for ever and ever" (Rev. 11:15, *emphasis mine*).

We Christians have often turned words such as those just quoted into an escapist vision that expresses a desire to flee this world, rather than to see its fulfillment. However, throughout Revelation the writer is clear that he does not envision escape from earth or from human history, but rather the fulfillment of human corporate capacities on earth through a renewal of the creation, a renewal of community, and a renewal of character.

Revelation 21–22 tells us that somehow *the City of God will also be the Garden of God, and the Garden of God will somehow also be the City of God.* We humans have never figured out how to do city-civilization and garden-environment as mutually supportive. John the Seer maintains that God does know how and will do what we have again and again failed to accomplish. We humans started in the Garden and have built the City that is rapidly destroying the Garden. God does not intend to take us backward, but rather to move us forward to a future we have never yet seen—a future we can only barely imagine and a home where we have never yet lived (1 Cor 2:9, Rev 21:3). A future city (civilization) where God's home and human's home is the same home, and a city that is also a garden, and every part of the new creation brings constant and complete healing to humanity. You might or might not believe the promises implied with this amazing imagery—but you will not find any human philosophy or theology with a hope that exceeds them. These claims are either audaciously absurd or are the fulfillment of every potential we humans have ever imagined we could be at our best—and more!

It is not only the final and highly symbolic book of Revelation, but also writers such as Matthew and Paul, who look forward to the day when God fulfills God's purpose for humans corporately. Matthew 5:5 has Jesus expressing this future corporate hope in words borrowed from Psalm 37:22, 29, when he says "Blessed are the meek" for *they will inherit the earth* (emphasis mine). The Greek *praeis* is perhaps better translated "the tamed" because God wants tamed passions, not broken spirits—and a closely related word was used for taming animals.[18]

Paul shares the same hope for a corporate fulfillment of human potential as the visionary author of Revelation, but in a more matter-of-fact manner. Paul too speaks of a final transformation of creation, character, and community. With a bit of realistic irony, he claims that it will be much easier for God to renew creation than it will be to complete the transformation of human character and community.

> [19] The *creation waits in eager expectation for the sons* [and daughters] of God to be revealed. [20] For the creation was subjected to frustration, not by its own choice, but by the will of the one who subjected it, in hope [21] that *the creation itself will be liberated* from its bondage to decay and brought *into the glorious freedom of the children of God*. . . . [23] Not only so, but we ourselves, who have the firstfruits of the Spirit, groan inwardly as we wait eagerly for our *adoption as sons* [and daughters], *the redemption of our bodies* (Rom 8:19–21; 23, emphasis mine; 2 Pet 3 makes much the same point).

A bit later in the same chapter, Paul asserts that the goal of bringing humans fully into the image of God is the one goal that God never stops pursuing. True, this is an age of history when things can be so confusing we don't even know what to pray (Rom 8:26–27). But God wastes nothing that we get into God's hands. Even in the worst situations, just as he did for Jesus, God will continue working toward good for those who love God. What is that good? The "good" of making us into a family of brothers and sisters who are "glorified" humans in the image of Jesus!

> [28] And we know that in all things God works for [toward—*eis* in Greek] the good of *those* who love him, who have been called according to his purpose. [29] For *those* God foreknew he also *predestined to be conformed to the likeness of his Son*, that he might *be the firstborn among many brothers*. [30] And *those he* predestined, *he* also called; *those he* called, *he* also justified; *those he* justified, *he also glorified*. (Rom 8:28–30, emphasis mine).

It is important to note that Paul (contrary to the way he is often interpreted) was not speaking in individualistic terms in this passage that mentions what God decided ahead of time ("predestination"). All the language Paul used is plural, and it reflects

---

18. Barclay, *Flesh and Spirit*, 113–114.

the Old Testament understanding of God's choice of Israel. God chose Israel corporately as "the people of God," whereas individuals had to choose how they would respond to that choice individually. In other words, God has chosen us, but a real relationship involves our choosing God back. Isn't that true of all genuine relationships? Relationships are real, mature relationships only when they are relationships mutually chosen. Maintaining that *predestination to salvation* is God choosing one individual and not choosing another individual is a denial that the relationship between God and humans is a genuinely mutual relationship—a real interpersonal relationship.

Predestination in Paul's usage is God working toward a pre-decided corporate goal. Even Paul's description of how God worked with Pharaoh and Moses involved God working toward fulfilling a corporate promise to Abraham's descendants. God worked through one man who had long wanted to see Israel freed, and through another man who never had any intention of freeing Israel. All God had to do to "harden" this stubborn man's heart was to have someone tell him he should do something he didn't want to do (Romans 9). Ever see a leader like that? God always prefers working through the cooperative—but God will not be stopped by the stubborn.

Paul writes of a God who is relentlessly pursuing a final fulfillment of our God-given human potential. The relationship between God and Jesus has made this possible for other humans as well. Thankfully, no power on earth or in the heavens can stop God from reaching the goal (Rom 8:31–39).

SUMMARY

As we have noted throughout this chapter, the New Testament writers understood the covenant relationship between God and humanity to be God's primary concern throughout the Old Testament narrative. The focusing of God's covenant relationship through Abraham is not to limit God's goal ethnically, but rather to allow God to pursue God's desire to bless all peoples of the earth. Likewise, the focusing of God's covenant relationship with humanity through Jesus is not to reduce the scope of the covenant, but to open up God's next step of creation so that every culture, language, tribe, and nation will be included in the people of God who will someday reign with Jesus on earth as humans in the image of God (Gen 12:1–3; Matt 5:5; Rev 5:9–10).

The narrative is honest about the fact that we are sinful, fall short, and experience the effects of brokenness and bentness. But nothing will be wasted. God will have a forever family, male and female, in the image of God. Now that is a goal worthy of a great God!

3

Jesus: God's Definition of Human Potential

HUMAN POTENTIAL—WHO DEFINES IT?

I often hear friends respond to their failures and sins with, "Well, I am only human." Although I certainly identify with the feeling behind those words, the New Testament understanding of "human" urges us to view ourselves quite differently. If we trust that the writers of the New Testament represented honestly what they saw God do, then God defines human potential for us through Jesus's relationship with God. The writers see the actions we tend to refer to as "only human" as behaviors that are less than fully human.

The phrase Brenda Salter McNeil coined as a mantra for evaluating racism in our systems—"on whose terms?"[1]—is a good litmus test for our topic as well. We will decide the ultimate meaning of being "human" by "on whose terms" we base our answer. Basing our answer on the relationship shared by God and Jesus will produce a very different outcome from basing our definition on human brokenness. If we allow the New Testament claim that Jesus's human life was, and is, without sin—a life of always trusting God—the conclusion is not that we sin because we are humans, but rather that we sin because we are not yet fully completed humans.

JESUS WAS HUMAN, IS HUMAN, AND WILL ALWAYS BE HUMAN IN HIS RELATIONSHIP WITH GOD.

As mentioned in the previous chapter, and as will be explored more fully in the next two chapters, Jesus's initial followers experienced a human who lived each stage of his life in a manner that allowed God to reach the end goal (*telos*) by "completing" (*teleioō*) Jesus. Step by step God's purpose in creating humans is revealed through

---

1. McNeil, Swanson Book Launch, FB, May 21, 2020.

Jesus's faithfulness. Finally, God has the "firstborn" of God's future family of humans—humans "in the image of God." The New Testament writers then claim God is providing a way through Jesus for other humans to become fully human as well.

Several New Testament writers explicitly treat Jesus's continuing humanity as a central part of his relationship with God.[2] They see Jesus as God's revelation of human potential fully in the hands of God. Doesn't this view of Jesus as God's definition of *completed human* make sense of the recurring claim in the New Testament that God wants the rest of us humans to become more and more like Jesus? We are challenged to allow God to transform us by empowering us to increasingly become like Jesus in relating to God and to our neighbor. We are also promised that God will complete the project as God takes us into God's future age. God intends to take us into that age as children of God who are in the image of God.

You might be thinking that controversy arises among Christians only around the second and third parts of the claim that Jesus *was*, *is*, and *will always be* human. However, as I intend to demonstrate in the following chapter, I think Christians have drastically underemphasized Jesus's humanity during his 30-plus years living in ancient Israel, as well.

As we are prone to do, Christians quickly began revising the New Testament paradigm in ways that felt more comfortable and culturally acceptable. By the second century AD, Christian leaders began shifting the focus away from what amazed the first followers of Jesus—how could someone so obviously human be so close to God? The new leading question became—how could someone who was obviously God be genuinely human? Whether in theology, politics, or science, when we make the wrong question primary, we are bound to skew our results. As is often noted—though far less often remembered by any of us in practice—it is those who are privileged to frame the initial questions who heavily influence the answers we find.

No New Testament writer wrestles with essences, substances, or second natures as later Church councils did. Whether they wondered about such things, they never tell us. What is clear is that they had a different primary concern. The New Testament focuses on the unique relationship of mutual faithfulness between Jesus and God. Various Old Testament authors describe God as communicative, personal, purposeful, and relational. Each of these characteristics is foundational for understanding God's relationship with Jesus. The question raised again and again in the Old Testament concerns whether God will prove to be faithful in God's relationship with humans—or not. The New Testament claim is that Jesus's life, death, resurrection, and exaltation are God's resounding *Yes, I am faithful in my relationship with humans—look at Jesus!*

True, in God's relationship with Jesus, God overwhelmingly exceeded the wildest hopes generated in God's previous self-revelation. However, this overwhelming excess did not change the narrative. God deepened it. Throughout this book, we will see that, by focusing on the relationship shared between God and Jesus, we can learn far more

2. *See* chapter 5.

about who God is. In Jesus's relationship with God, we learn more fully than anywhere else how "Abba" wishes to relate to us humans. Focus on that relationship also teaches us far more about who we are.

We will also explore God-with-us (*Immanuel*) as a relational claim with many precedents in the Old Testament and many further examples in the lives of Jesus's followers. Likewise, "oneness" with God is a relational term with which Jesus wants his followers to be blessed. It is when we focus on these and other aspects of the relationship shared between God and the human Jesus that we learn what it means for us to be promised that we, too, will someday be "completed" as humans. This definition of human potential, seen on God's terms, makes it clear that Jesus is fully rooted and embedded in humanity.

MISSING THE REVELATION OF JESUS'S GENUINE FOREVER HUMANNESS HAS BEEN COSTLY.

Our failure as followers of Jesus to emphasize the original biblical paradigm has led to several sad outcomes in how we look at Jesus's 30-some years in Israel. It has also caused us to diminish the importance of his role as *human* mediator after God raised him from death and exalted him to the "right hand of God." We have, for centuries, underemphasized Jesus's humanity. It is not that most Christians do not say Jesus was human, but for many, the words do not mean what they seem to imply.

Many Christians blanch at the thought that Jesus needed to grow in his relationship with God, had to stop for a bathroom break, might have related to his parents with a teenage lack of awareness, needed to learn the scriptures from a local rabbi and his mother, seems to have misquoted a scripture from memory, took much needed vacations, prayed regularly for guidance, and at times assigned "the twelve" the job of keeping people away from him. Surely, he mis-measured a few boards in the carpentry shop. Was he bothered by the fact that girls were not allowed in Hebrew school? Did he notice that one of the women who adored him was particularly sexually attractive? Not one of these possibilities implies sin; and yet many of us tend to avoid thinking about them.

Why do so many of us have so much reticence about these human realities and possibilities? It's a good question, given that every New Testament writer insists that Jesus was profoundly human. One even insists that Jesus was *tempted in every way* we are (Heb 4:15). Another insists we cannot honor Jesus at all properly unless we focus on the fact that Jesus was fully embedded in human "flesh" (1 John 4:2). Jesus did not just participate in humanness, he participated in the humanness we all experience, but without choosing to sin—to break trust with God (Heb 3:2; Rom 8:3). He shared in "the flesh" that is sometimes vulnerable, weak, and easily drawn away from God and good; yet he refused to be drawn away.

Several New Testament writers explicitly state that in God's relationship with Jesus, God has taken a new step in human history. Others imply the same. God now has a faithful human who fulfills what it means to be "in the image and likeness of God." Finally, God has a human who can reign as Lord over God's creation without destroying the creation in the process. At last, God has a human who can be entrusted with authority and power, without this leading to oppressing, using, abusing, and discarding other humans. At last, God has a human who can faithfully fill the role of "firstborn" brother in God's forever human family. Eugene Peterson captured the importance of understanding that emphasizing Jesus's humanness allows us to begin to grasp God's view of human potential:

> Heaven shows the conditions sufficient to our creation, conditions under which we get what we need to be who we are. Our need for the basics is endless—far more extensive than we ever realize, for we have hardly begun to realize what it means to be human, human as Adam and Eve were human, human the way our Lord was human. None of us has laid eyes on a person fully human.[3]

The roles that God bestows upon the exalted human Jesus flow from Jesus's faithfulness to God while living as a human under the trying conditions of a Jewish believer. Jesus consistently experienced the brutal Roman occupation of his homeland, worshiping in a Temple controlled by a deeply compromised High Priestly clan and worshiping in synagogues overseen by Pharisees—some of whom were as arrogantly pious as many of us ministers and priests tend to be today. Whatever trials and suffering you have experienced at the hands of your nation and church, Jesus understands from personal experience. To these trials were added the questioning and doubting that came from his inner circle of disciples on an almost daily basis and the questioning and doubting from his family of origin and his best friends. God did not make it easy for Jesus to choose to be faithfully trusting in every situation!

Demeaning Jesus's humanness leads to diminishing his amazing faithfulness. Demeaning Jesus's continuing humanity after his resurrection and exaltation causes us to diminish God's goal for other humans as well. When we see Jesus's resurrection and exaltation as Jesus escaping his humanity, we see whatever future God has for the rest of us as our need to escape our humanity. When we understand Jesus's resurrection, ascension, and exaltation as God's next step in completing and fully maturing Jesus's human relationship with God, we begin to understand God's purpose for the rest of us humans as bringing wholeness to our full human potential.

When the New Testament writers present Jesus as God's revelation of God's end goal for completing humans, they are claiming that God demonstrates the end goal right in the middle of history. God has defined human potential for us when "we see Jesus," who completely reflects the image of God (Heb 2:5–9). This gives substance

---

3. Peterson, *Reversed*, 181.

and context to "For God so loved the world" and to "Good News of great joy for all peoples!" *"Salvation" defined as needing to escape our humanity and our world is not good news if you value being human and you value the creation God has given us.*

Perhaps as sad as any result that flows from demeaning Jesus's genuine humanity is the diminishing of the risky and wondrous relationship between God and Jesus described in the New Testament. It is a relationship that brings to a climax God's risky choice to love, to be faithful to, and to remain responsive to humans, no matter the cost. Likewise, it simultaneously brings to a crescendo Jesus's risky human choice to be faithful, obedient, and responsive to God, no matter the cost.

There are many other consequences flowing from our centuries-old underemphasis on Jesus's genuine humanity. Sadly, we Christians have diminished the importance of Jesus's Jewishness as part of his humanity and consequently justified our horrendous anti-Semitism and anti-Judaism. We have also failed to see how central the theme of fulfillment is as a connection between the human experiences with God, recorded in the Old Testament, and Jesus's human experiences with God.

With these thoughts in mind, let's explore further the New Testament claims about Jesus's humanity then, now, and forever. Let's also allow this exploration to have the impact it should have on our understanding of human potential in the hands of God.

4

Jesus was One of Us

WHAT DO WE ACTUALLY BELIEVE ABOUT JESUS'S HUMANITY?

Do Our Actions Reflect What We Claim to Believe?

This chapter might initially seem to be an exercise in the obvious. However, my experiences as a teacher and a pastor have convinced me that what sounds obvious in theory is far from obvious in practice.

Was Jesus human? I am certain nearly every reader or potential reader—atheist, agnostic, Jewish, Muslim, staunch traditional Christian Trinitarian, and others—will respond, "Yes." The Christian creeds insist that it is so, and today most scholars and historians agree that a man named Jesus lived, taught, developed a following, and was executed during the early first century AD. However, if you pay attention to what is said, and to what is not said, in the average Bible study and sermon, or if you pay attention to Christian art, Christian songs, and books about Christian doctrine through the past seventeen centuries, you would likely conclude that many Christians think Jesus was not authentically human—not really one of us.

It is rather easy to see that longstanding theological practice has led to a de facto dehumanization of Jesus. Quite early, Christian theology and apologetics began to be mainly about "Jesus is God," with an occasional nod to his humanity. Not too much later, Christian art began to introduce halos and ethereal faces. Jesus wears a halo in famous depictions of him teaching, serving the Passover to his disciples, and sometimes even in the manger. A more recent popular public domain Christmas song (*Away in a Manger*) proclaims, "The cattle are lowing, the Baby awakes / But little Lord Jesus, *no crying He makes*." What healthy human baby does not cry? That baby would not be one of us. And to press the point, what genuinely human baby has a mother who wears a halo by his bedside, as Mary often does in Christian art?

In Bible study after Bible study, I have heard fellow Christians say "Of course Jesus knew what everyone else was thinking; 'He was God.'" Some of us even demand that Jesus's mother Mary be viewed as a perpetual virgin who is worthy of being "the Mother of God." We do this by assigning the other six or more of Mary's children (Mark 6:3) to Joseph's completely fabricated earlier marriage or dismissing them as cousins. Of course, this also causes us to ignore Luke's statement that Mary went to the Temple to be declared "pure" for sexual activity by a priest after the birth of her son (Luke 2:22–24; Lev 12:1–8). We are a determined bunch, aren't we?

Partially in reaction to all of this dehumanizing and mythologizing of Jesus, his family, and his followers, many scholars and pastors have reconstructed the telling of the Jesus story to indicate that Jesus was "just" another human who tried hard to teach good things and do good things but who, in the end, failed to do much to change the real world. Some current historians, such as John Dominic Crossan, assert that we know little about Jesus other than that he was an itinerant peasant Jewish teacher, with a ragtag following, who managed to get himself crucified by the Romans, after which the dogs ate his body.[1] Even a scholar who is this skeptical about New Testament claims agrees that Jesus was a genuine human who generated some sort of religious following, as well as a good bit of high-priestly and Roman angst. So why is it so difficult to find this fully human Jesus in so much of our theology, doctrine, preaching, teaching, art, and worship?

Diminishing Jesus's Humanity Eliminates God's Gift of a Model for Human Living.

Our underemphasis on Jesus's genuine humanity does not determine only what we believe about Jesus's relationship with God; it *also determines what most of us do not believe about God, Jesus, and ourselves as humans*. At least in this area, the stakes are high. Why?

One reason is that it leads a large percentage of Christians to diminish the power of a central New Testament commandment. That commandment can be summarized thus: You are called to follow (mirror/image) Jesus as your model for living daily life before God. No matter how much we try not to do so, if we *overemphasize that Jesus was God*, we tend to *simultaneously underemphasize that Jesus was human*. This quite often leads to *the next step of excusing ourselves for not living faithfully as Jesus did* by saying (or thinking), "But Jesus was God. How can I live like he did?"

Taking this step has frequently led to yet another step away from what would appear to be the obvious meaning of New Testament commandments that tell us to

---

1. Crossan, *Jesus a Revolutionary*, 124–127.

reflect God in our daily lives by living as Jesus lived. An entire branch of Christian theology has repurposed these commandments by claiming that their primary objective is to teach us how sinful we are and how incapable of obedience we are. This theological gymnastic turns God into a very bad parent. What happens when human parents raise their children by constantly demanding that the children do what is impossible for them to do? These children usually develop into people who live in denial, develop low self-esteem, suffer anxiety neuroses, or choose to rebel. Why would we think it any different if this was the real goal of the commandments to obey God and to live like Jesus?

Seeing commandments, like those in the Sermon on the Mount for example, as primarily meant to show us we are incapable of obeying them is to also ignore the clear intention of the writers. They consistently see our less-than-perfect obedience as taking genuine steps toward God's goal that we humans grow in faithfulness. Our obedience is our growing reflection of the way Jesus lived as a human in the image of God. Representing Paul as the champion of the view that commandments are mainly to show we cannot do them ignores the fact that he is just as strident about our need to be faithful, obedient, "mind of Christ" people in our behaviors as he is about our "continual falling short of the glory of God" (Rom 1:5, 3:23, 16:19).

In a book that emphasizes the often endearing ways St. Francis of Assisi attempted to model Jesus, Murray Bodo captures what we have done to Jesus as God's model for daily living.

> It is impossible to feel a kinship with Saint Francis without looking at one's own life and changing something. It is easier to rationalize and dismiss Jesus than Francis, because Jesus, after all, is divine and so far above us. But Francis is only human like us.[2]

So much for Jesus as our model! I believe deeply in our need for grace, and I observe daily how we all keep falling short of the glorious humanness God wants for us (Rom 3:23). However, we lose the key New Testament claim concerning God's revelation if we think that we can dismiss Jesus as being the central model, as well as being the means, God has given us for how we can become more fully human.

This common diminishing of Jesus as our model for being human also means subverting the New Testament challenge captured in Paul's admonition "Your attitude should be the same as that of Jesus Christ" (Phil 2:5) or John's "We know love by this, that he laid down his life for us—and we ought to lay down our lives for one another" (1 John 3:16). Bodo is right: it seems very easy for us to see "Jesus was God" as a way out of taking these instructions seriously.

Another effect of our tendency to diminish Jesus's humanity can be seen in the fact that many Christians often say, implicitly or explicitly, that the four Gospels are mainly about the cross and resurrection. Each Gospel climaxes with the death and

---

2. Bodo, *Francis*, 89.

resurrection of Jesus, but each actually focuses approximately three-fourths of its material on how Jesus lives daily human life before God. Three-fourths of each Gospel is about Jesus's teaching, healing, praying, loving his enemies as well as his friends, and confronting the principalities and powers entrenched in religious and political institutions that oppressed his fellow humans.

It is Jesus's faithfulness in daily life as a human that is God's revelation of what a human relationship with God can and should look like. It is this daily faithful human living throughout his thirty-plus years of life that gives Jesus's faithfulness in the face of an unjust execution its deep meaning. The cross is one further step in a life of faithfulness, and it is a step that exhibits full dependence on God's faithfulness to do for humans what we cannot do for ourselves (Heb 5:7–10). It is important to remember that it is also these thirty-three years of living faithfully that are the cause of Jesus being executed by church and empire. Those same thirty-three years of faithfulness are why God was pleased to raise Jesus from death.

What have we done to God's central self-revelation? True, Jesus is the *means* God provides for a renewed relationship between God and other humans. Just as clearly in the New Testament, Jesus is also the *model* for expressing a faithful relationship between God and humans. Why have we so diminished Jesus as God's firstborn of God's renewed human family? What a loss in honoring Jesus! What a loss in understanding how God views human potential when it is brought to "completion" in a full relationship with God!

THE NEW TESTAMENT STRESSES JESUS'S GENUINE HUMANITY.

The Question Raised by the New Testament Writings is How Can Someone So Clearly Human Be So Close to God?

The Gospel writers claim that people who encountered Jesus in Israel many years ago experienced an amazing dynamic. They experienced a human standing confidently in the presence of God. Simultaneously they experienced themselves as being uniquely in the presence of God through being in the presence of this specific human. How could this be? This experience flowed from the covenant relationship God and Jesus shared. It was God's relationship with the human Jesus that both puzzled and awed (and sometimes infuriated) those around Jesus.

The New Testament writers present Jesus as the human through whom heaven and earth meet. The thin places in the veil between heaven and earth were torn open as never before in Jesus's relationship with God. Nevertheless, the reality of "God-with-us" in Jesus is described in the New Testament as part of the great Jewish narrative of humans who are created "in the image" of the One God and as part of God's desire to "be with us" (*Immanuel*) in our humanity. God's Good News through Jesus is that God is moving this great godly purpose forward in ways that were promised, and yet were also very unexpected.

Despite good intentions, we Christians tend to do to Jesus's humanity what humans have done in many of our religions and philosophies throughout the ages: we separate the world into the sacred and the secular or profane.[3] For the most part, we see every-day human life as secular. Humans might contain a sacred God-spark, immortal soul, spirit, or Atman, but what do eating, working, sex, sleep, and play have to do with the holiness? If we take this view, we find it almost impossible to think Jesus could really have been embedded in our humanity—Jesus must have been more than human. And, if more than human, also something other than human.

In contrast, the Biblical paradigm is that everything in the entire creation was by intent and origin meant to be holy. There is no secular area of life. There is no neutral area of life. There are only the areas that welcome God's presence, goodness, and righteousness, and the areas where God's gifts to us have become bent, broken, and desecrated by us humans. As the ending of Zechariah says, when humans are in a right relationship with God, even the dishes on the table (the black Pfaltzgraff cup I am drinking from?) and the bells on the horses' bridles (the steering wheels in our cars?) are stamped as "belonging to YHWH (LORD)" (Zech 14:20–21).

This certainly included humans who were to relate to God as God's holy people (for examples, *see* Exod 22:31; Lev 11:44; Deut 7:6, and the Hebrew and Greek behind most of the appearances of "saint" and "saints" in translations of the Old and New Testament). If this perspective is true, why do so many Christian books, sermons, and Bible study comments indicate that Jesus can be "the Holy One of God" only if he was something more than "just" human? If so, does that mean for us to be the "holy ones" of God addressed regularly in the introductions to Paul's letters, we have to be something other than human? Good luck!

In the New Testament, Jesus being "more than" the rest of us is not assigned to Jesus being something more than or other than human. Jesus's uniqueness is Jesus's complete faithfulness, trust, and obedience in relating to God. This faithfulness to God is then coupled with his complete stubborn commitment toward doing what is good for fellow humans ("love/agape"). His faithfulness is described as his being tempted like all of us humans, but never choosing not to trust God—never choosing to sin (John 17:19; Heb 4:15). In the New Testament narratives, Jesus invariably chooses to live a fully human life that is fully stamped "belonging to YHWH." Jesus identifies himself as a human steward of God's great gifts (Mark 10:45; Matt 4:10), and he encourages the rest of us humans to do the same.

When a scribe and theologian asked Jesus for the primary paradigm of human faithfulness and obedience, Jesus responded with what Scot McKnight delightfully

---

3. Eliade, *Sacred and Profane*, 20.

designates as *The Jesus Creed*.[4] Mark and Luke indicate that this credal summary was shared by some other Jewish teachers of the time as well.

> [29] "The most important one," answered Jesus, "is this: 'Hear, O Israel, the Lord our God, the Lord is one. [30] Love the Lord your God with all your heart and with all your soul and with all your mind and with all your strength.' [31] The second is this: 'Love your neighbor as yourself.' There is no commandment greater than these." [32a] "Well said, teacher," the man replied" (Mark 12:29–32a; see also Luke 10:26–28).

Jesus didn't *teach* just that we were to love God and love our neighbor; he fully *lived* it. We need to recognize in Jesus a human who is relating to God and to other humans as we humans are meant to. He did this even when it was very costly to do so in this broken and desecrated world. Jesus was the human who was completely holy, living a fully human life that was not desecrated, broken, or bent. He was one of us—really! *In fact, he is God's definition of God's end goal for what it means to be human—of human potential in the hands of God.*

Specific Descriptions of Jesus's Genuine Humanness Abound. Jesus Was One of Us.

It is not just the general presentation of Jesus in the New Testament, but also the specifics that emphasize Jesus's genuine humanness. Below are some of the many passages that emphasize Jesus's real, wondrous, and sometimes frail humanity—you could add quite a few others. I risk belaboring what should be an obvious point because I have so often been in discussions about the Bible with very thoughtful, intelligent, and well-educated Christians, who have been astounded when they focused on the implications of the following biblical descriptions of Jesus. Quite often, I hear, "I didn't know the Bible said that," or, from those more familiar with the Bible, "I never really thought about what that passage was saying and implying." Sadly, the hundreds of commentaries on my shelves indicate that many Christian scholars also slide past the implications of the texts that follow.

1. Jesus Had to Grow and Learn. He Was a Human-in-process with God.

Jesus was a human who had to grow and learn not only in his relationship with other humans (including his parents) but also in his relationship with God.

> [51] Then he went down to Nazareth with them and was obedient to them. But his mother treasured all these things in her heart. [52] And *Jesus grew* in wisdom and stature, *and in favor with God and humans* (Luke 2:51–52, *emphasis mine*).

---

4. McKnight, *Jesus Creed*, 8.

Luke's understanding of Jesus growth process is far from static. The process of change and growth includes Jesus's relationship with his parents as well as his social, intellectual, and physical growth. But what most often surprises many Christians when they stop and focus on it is Luke's claim that the relationship between God and Jesus was not static, but rather a process of growth. Luke describes the relationship as one in which Jesus continually needed to grow to remain pleasing to God.

If you disagree with the way I am about to explain how I hear Luke's narrative, please do not use that as an excuse for ignoring what Luke's text clearly states—Jesus's life was a growth process in his relationship with God. Like the writer of Hebrews, Luke believed that Jesus's life was a genuine maturing process, including his relationship with God. Having said that, I personally think the summary statement Luke gives us concerning Jesus's maturation should be seen in the context where he placed it. Jesus is described as a faithful, mature-for-his-age, intelligent, inquisitive, and insightful twelve-year-old. Even at this age, Jesus is putting his relationship with God above his relationship with his parents—something he later says we all must do. Still, it is important to see that this occurs during a very human situation in which parent and child find it impossible to communicate in a manner that fully resolves their tensions with one another. Apparently, by the age of twelve Jesus was already getting into what John Lewis called "good trouble, necessary trouble"—at least with his mother.

As I read Mary's reaction to Jesus, I think of my mother (also Mary, and also a loving and concerned parent) reacting to my brother's and my behavior when we were just a little older than Jesus was in this narrative. Obviously, my brother and I did not have Jesus's high spiritual values in mind, but the interfamily tussle was similar. My mother could never understand why, as a teenager, I insisted on playing an away basketball game, even when I had passed out from the flu earlier that day. Neither could she understand why my brother insisted on playing football with his broken nose. Why, she wondered, couldn't we understand that she was just concerned about our well-being?

Neither my brother nor I could ever understand why our mother could not understand that "we have to do this; it is who we are." And much like Joseph in Luke's Gospel, our father often stood by quietly during these arguments, probably both fathers realizing that attempting to moderate such situations was certain to be no-win. I think Luke's narrative assumes that Jesus grew up as a genuinely human son in a family filled with genuinely human family dynamics. Other Gospel accounts make it clear that family tensions with both his mother and his siblings only heightened in later years (Mark 3:31–35; John 2:1–5; 7:1–8).

Like Luke, the writer of Hebrews understood Jesus's relationship with God to be a growth process. He does not describe Jesus as "perfect," but as "made perfect," and he describes Jesus as having "learned obedience" through hard times. Further, he maintains that Jesus had to go through this learning and maturing process in order to *become the source* of God's salvation for other humans.

> ⁸ Although he was a son, he [Jesus] *learned obedience* from what he suffered
> ⁹ and, once *made perfect* [mature/complete], he *became the source* of eternal salvation for all who obey him (Heb 5:8–9, *emphasis mine*).

The life-long process of becoming completed as a human in relationship to God is central to this writer's understanding of Jesus. It is also central to the writer's understanding of why Jesus is God's means of salvation for the rest of us humans.

The Hebraic rather than the Greek understanding of *perfection* is important. The Greek philosophers (and thus many of our early church fathers and many Christians today) saw "perfect" as a static and necessarily unchangeable state. How can something or someone be perfect and simultaneously in a process that involves change? How can anything or anyone who is perfect be made more perfect? The Jewish paradigm of *perfection* (Hebrew words such as *tiklah*, *tamam*, *tom*, and *tam*) makes these statements more intelligible. *Being perfect is being appropriate, blameless, and mature (complete) for the current situation.*

A psalmist indicates that he has never seen anyone's maturity that wasn't limited compared to what God wanted the person to be like (Ps 119:96). New Testament writers agree, except they claim that now there is one such human. *The kind of perfection they claim for Jesus must transition and change to remain perfect (complete and mature) in the next situation.* Like Luke, the writer of Hebrews saw Jesus's perfection as a process of appropriate change and growth through each stage of life, each new situation, and each new context. In the constantly fluctuating situations of life, as he grows and adapts to each new situation, Jesus consistently chooses to faithfully trust God. That is what it means to be "without sin" (Heb 3:2, 4:15).

Equally important, Hebrews presents this growth process as a necessary part of Jesus becoming the kind of person through whom God could save the rest of us humans from the consequences of our bent and broken world.

> *In bringing many* sons [and daughters] to glory, it was fitting that God, for whom and through whom everything exists, should *make* the author of their salvation *perfect* [complete/mature] through suffering (Heb 2:10, *emphasis mine*).

The relationship between God and Jesus is described as a developing process. Jesus's faithfulness, as he experienced the hard and often unjust realities of human life allowed Jesus's relationship with God to continually grow. It also allowed God to "make" Jesus "perfect" (complete and mature). And, being "completed" as a human allows Jesus to be the agent of God's determination to save humans from our rampant self-destruction and others-destruction. Jesus is the first human God has brought to the "end goal [*telos*]," but he will not be the last "completed" human. God now has an experienced human who has chosen faithfulness in each phase of living his life in this rough and tumble world. This was always God's "end goal" or *telos* for creating humans. Jesus has now reached that goal, and followers of Jesus are called to "press on" toward this same outcome or goal/maturity/completion (Heb 6:1 using teleiotēta and 6:11 using *telous*).

2. Jesus Needed and Enjoyed Food.

I once began this section, "And now for the more mundane." Then I remembered that Jesus never treated food as something to be taken for granted. He always treated it as a precious gift from God. For Jesus, eating was a holy event.

Jesus not only needed, but apparently really enjoyed, food (Luke 4:2, 7:34–36, 14:1). In fact, the Gospels stress his enjoyment of food more than his need of it. Humorously, and somewhat "in your face," Jesus responds to the criticism of some religious leaders who complained that Jesus liked to eat and drink too much by immediately accepting another invitation to a banquet at the home of one of their fellow religious leaders (Luke 7:33–36).

Jesus often took time to thank and bless God for providing food. He did so even as he faced imminent torture and death (Luke 22:19–22). Jesus seems to have existed in a temporary and somewhat strange in-between state from the cross-resurrection event to the ascension-exaltation event. Luke indicates that during that period, Jesus's way of being thankful to God for providing food was so powerful, and so uniquely his own, that it allowed his followers to recognize him during this forty-day in-between state. They did not recognize his looks, his talk, his teaching, his way of walking, or his interpreting of scriptures, but when he thanked God for food, "Jesus was recognized by them when he broke the bread" (Luke 24:35).

I find it fascinating, and perhaps also telling, that we seem inclined to emphasize the two times we are told Jesus temporarily went without food (the intense forty-day fast at the beginning of his ministry and the statement in John 4:32—"I have bread you do not know about") while we tend to deemphasize the many times we find Jesus enjoying food and table fellowship. We tend to do this even though we are told detractors accused Jesus of gluttony (Matt 11:19).

Jesus, like the Jewish writers before him (Lev 25:18–28; 1 Chron 29:14–16; 2 Chron 36:21), and much like the Potawatomi tribes of America, saw life as a stewardship of gifts given freely by the Creator, for which we can only respond appropriately with celebrative thanksgiving.[5] Eating, drinking, and socializing with others were "stamped holy" through the relationship God and Jesus shared. Certainly, in Jesus's life, and in ours as followers of Jesus, there are times for fasting. On the other hand, Jesus's model makes it clear that these times are no more godly in a human's relationship with God than are the times of celebration and thanksgiving to God for the gifts of food, friends, and fellowship (Matt 9:14–15). I for one am thankful that Jesus (like the prophets before him) regularly described God's future for God's forever family as a banquet, rather than as a fast.

---

5. Kimmerer, *Braiding Sweetgrass*, 30–31.

3. Jesus Was at Times Fatigued and Worn Out.

Jesus often became fatigued and worn down. In John 4:6, he was so tired that he sent the disciples into town for food and supplies, while he just sat, waited, and intended to rest. Once Jesus was so tired and worn out that he didn't wake during a huge thunderstorm, even though he was in an open boat—that is deep fatigue (Mark 4:35–41)! Another time, Jesus was so exhausted that he attempted to escape the crowds for a short vacation near the Mediterranean Sea. The vacation was cut short by his encounter with the relentlessness of a mother's love for her tormented daughter, but the narrative makes it clear that Jesus was not easily convinced to allow this invasion of his down time (Matt 15:21–29). After his trial, Jesus was so weak, beaten, and abused that he could not carry his cross without the help of a fellow human (Matt 27:32).

The failure to attend to Jesus's full humanity has often led Christian leaders to ignore their own human limitations as well. I remember hearing a Father's Day sermon that included the admonition, "You men all need to take a day off every week in order to be healthy, rested, and with your families. I cannot; I just have too much of God's work to do as a minister." Perhaps not too surprisingly, the preacher of that sermon shipwrecked his family life, as well as seriously damaging several churches, due to his affairs. He would have done well to recognize the limitations his humanity demanded, as Jesus so wisely did.

In the early years of my ministry, I often overcommitted myself and ended up being away from my wife and young children for sixty, sometimes even eighty, hours a week. What I convinced myself was that commitment to God was actually participation in the sinful American ego-building busyness that fails to respect our human need for "Sabbath rest." My daughter tells me that she used to stand at the window and watch for me to come home. She remembers, "You often didn't come home when you were expected." Did God still use those years to bless people? Yes, but that is God's mercy for me and for others, not approval. Such behavior does not strengthen, but rather weakens, our relationship with God and with our fellow humans. I have since asked each member of my family to forgive me, and thankfully, they have graciously and willingly done so.

In contrast to the way the pastor preached and lived who thought he needed no time off, to the way I chose to live for several years, and to the way I see many other brothers and sisters living now, Jesus knew downtime was an important part of being a mature human. Except for his last ride into Jerusalem, he seems to have walked everywhere. He took time to pray, to regroup, to spend time with friends, and to get away.

4. At Times Jesus "Could Not" Do What He Wanted to Do.

It is not uncommon to hear Christians say, "Jesus could do anything he wanted to; he was God." Mark, on the other hand, gives us a different picture. Like all of us humans, sometimes Jesus was "not able" to carry out his plans and wishes. Four times the Gospel of Mark tells us that Jesus "could not" do what he wanted to do. In fact, the Greek *dunamai* Mark uses in each instance might be better translated as "*did not have the power to do*" what he wanted to do.

We are told that Jesus *could not* any longer carry out his ministry in towns and had to resort to the countryside (1:45). Jesus *could not* make time for his newly chosen disciples and himself to eat. The crowd overwhelmed his planning (Mark 3:20). The event I find most stunning is when Jesus *could not* heal very many people because of the environment of unbelief (6:5). Jesus wanted to keep his whereabouts a secret, but he *could not* escape being noticed (7:24). Mark uses a different phrase to describe yet another time when Jesus and his disciples "could not even find a good time to eat" (6:31, my translation).

5. Jesus was Rooted in Human History.

Jesus was rooted in history, community, and human genealogy. The genealogy of Matthew focuses on Jesus as a genuine Jewish human, living in a definite time and place and rooted in a specific family lineage—a lineage with several less-than-sterling moral and ethnic origins. Galatians 4:4–5 emphasizes that Jesus is "born of a woman." Hebrews 2:10–13 stresses Jesus's familial relationship to God's other human children.

The first two chapters of Luke stress that Jesus is embedded in real human history. The names and titles of important contemporary people are noted. The existence of various biographical documents about Jesus are referred to in the introduction. Basic Jewish obedience to specific Temple requirements for the "circumcision" of a son and the "cleansing" of the mother for future sexual activity are described. Luke then follows these historical markers with a genealogy (Luke 3:21–38) identifying Jesus as legally in the line of David because he is "assumed to be son of Joseph." Luke's genealogy roots Jesus fully in humanity when it concludes by identifying Adam as "(son) of God." The many New Testament references to Jesus as "Son of David" also serve to root Jesus in his Jewish humanity and in Jewish history.

Long before the cross, Jesus is exhibiting the willingness to bear in his own body the sins of the rest of us humans. An early example occurs when Jesus refuses John's encouragement to recognize himself as *too good,* or *too close to God,* to need the baptism of repentance.

> [14] But John tried to deter him, saying, "I need to be baptized by you, and do you come to me?" [15] Jesus replied, "Let it be so now; it is proper for us to do this *to fulfill all righteousness*" (Matt 3:14–15, *emphasis mine*).

It seems to me that Jesus is presented as taking his place in the human community, in which no individuals can be righteous before God without repenting of the corporate guilt of the community to which they belong. Like Ezra, Daniel, Moses,

Nehemiah, and various psalmists, Jesus understands that corporate sins must be addressed as "our sins," not just "their sins," even when we would never, or at least many of us like to think we would never, individually choose to participate in them.

When Jesus taught his disciples to pray "forgive us *our* sins," I believe he was teaching his followers to think about their relationship to God and to their fellow humans as he thought about those relationships. How I wish those of us who are White Christians in the USA would understand this truth about the corporate sins of America, and of the White American church, with regard to the enslavement of African Americans, ongoing racism, wars in the Middle East designed to keep oil cheap, and the genocide of Native Americans. If we did, we would confess and lament, rather than attempt to justify or distance ourselves from the sins that continue to privilege us and oppress others. I am humbled by Jesus's willingness to walk ninety miles in order to acknowledge that a call for the children of Abraham to "repent" is a call for him individually to respond without self-justifying protest. Instead, it is John who protests, and Jesus who insists that he must participate in God's call for corporate repentance *in order to fulfill all righteousness* (Matt 3:13–15).

Whether you agree or disagree with what I see as the implications of Jesus's insistence on being baptized, what is clear is that he sees himself as embedded in the call to "the children of Abraham," and he insists on personally responding to the prophetic call for God's people to "repent."

6. Jesus Displayed Limited Knowledge.

Nothing I am about to say is a denial that sometimes Jesus displayed amazing pre-knowledge that expressed a direct gift of the fullness of the indwelling Spirit of God. Sometimes this prescience seems to be a deduction from knowing the Scriptures so well, sometimes the wisdom that sees through our pretenses as societies, churches, and individuals, and sometimes what Paul calls a "gift of knowledge." Having personally seen glimpses of this gift of preknowing in my grandmother, my mother, my wife, my sister, my daughter, and my granddaughter, as well as in a several friends, I see no reason to think that it somehow separates Jesus from our humanity. Jesus exercised this gift more fully than anyone else I have known, but he did so on the continuum the New Testament credits to others as well as to Jesus.

Having said that, the Gospels indicate Jesus did not know everything that was about to occur ahead of time. Jesus was at times surprised, amazed, stunned, startled, and filled with wonder. Each of these reactions indicates a limitation of knowledge. No one is genuinely surprised or amazed by what she or he already knows is going to happen. Jesus was amazed by the trust and insight of a pagan warrior (Luke 7:9; Matt 8:10). In contrast, Jesus was stunned by the lack of faith and the hard-heartedness of some members of his hometown faith community (Mark 6:1–6). "Who touched me?" presents a straightforward statement of limited knowledge (Luke 8:45). Implicitly, amazement also seemed to be Jesus's inner reaction when he was apparently so overwhelmed by the persistent motherly love of a pagan Canaanite that he temporarily circumvented his own God-given boundary rules for his ministry (Matt 15:21–28; Mark 7:24–30). Responding to her fierce love for her dying daughter, he crossed the "right/good" (*kalos* in Greek) boundaries God has given him for this period of his ministry. We have here the only record of someone winning a theological argument with Jesus. Perhaps this stunned Jesus too especially since she was ethnically Phoenician-Canaanite and female.

Jesus also stated that he had no knowledge concerning when the final judgment will occur—"But about that day and hour no one knows, neither the angels of heaven, *nor the Son*, but only the Father" (Matt 24:36, *emphasis mine, compare with* Matt 20:23). In John 5:6, some translations describe Jesus as having to learn or "come to know" how long the man had been paralyzed, whereas other translators prefer "knew" and imply prescient knowledge. Either could be the meaning because both kinds of "knowing" by Jesus are illustrated throughout the Gospels—much as they are by several of the prophets in the Old Testament literature.

Jesus's limited knowledge is described in other ways. In Mark 5:32, a verb is used that can well be translated as Jesus "kept looking in order to see who it was." In Luke 2:46 and 52, we see a young Jesus who needs to learn and grow, both in knowledge and in relationships, just as all humans do. Even a somewhat prescient statement such as Mark 11:3, where Jesus tells the disciples to go find a colt for him to ride into Jerusalem frames part of the instructions in terms of "if" this occurs, "then" do this.

Asking difficult and pointed questions that students are expected to answer is a typical Rabbinic school process for bright students. It is also a tool that Jesus used freely as a part of his teaching style. In this light, I suggest that the narrative in Luke 2:41–52 is not claiming that the 12-year-old Jesus was more knowledgeable than the rabbis. Rather, he is presented as an amazing and remarkable young student, one whom the rabbis of Jerusalem would find particularly remarkable because he would have been trained by small-town Galilean rabbis (and probably by his mother, though the theologians likely never entertained that possibility), not in their elite schools in Babylon and Jerusalem.

Jesus knew the Hebrew Scriptures very well and quoted them freely from memory, just as his mother had, but there is no indication that he would have had the monetary resources to own his own scrolls during the first 30 years of his life. During the three years of his ministry, even if some well-funded friends did purchase scrolls for him, he was on the move so much that most of his quoting of the Old Testament would certainly have been from memory. It seems to have been an amazing memory.

Nevertheless, at least two examples of what appear to be memory slips by Jesus occur in the Gospels. If Mark 2:25–28 represents Jesus accurately, Jesus misremembers an Old Testament narrative. I Samuel 21:2–7 indicates that Ahimelech, not Abiathar, who befriended David much later, was the high priest on duty at the time of the event Jesus references. In Matthew 23:35, Jesus apparently confuses or conflates two different Zechariahs. It was the son of Jehoida (not the son of Berekiah, who lived 300 years later) who was killed in the temple (II Chron 24:20–24; Zech 1:1).

Of course, both memory slips might be the work of Mark and Matthew or the work of earlier note-takers they used as sources. But they might go back to rather accurate notes taken by those who kept track of Jesus's teachings as they occurred. We are finding that more people in Jesus's time, and long before, were able to read, write, and speak several languages than was once believed to be true about the ancient world. So, there is no reason to deny that, in addition to oral accounts, there might have been quite a few written accounts of Jesus's teachings and actions long before the final versions of the Gospels that have come down to us. In fact, Luke states that he "investigated many" sources as he wrote his Gospel (Luke 1:1–3).

7. Jesus Wanted to be Spared the Horror of a Roman Execution.

If it was at all possible from God's viewpoint, Jesus wanted God to spare him from the painful injustice of Roman execution. Although Jesus understood that God had been leading him toward arrest and execution, he prayed for a last-minute reprieve. Jesus knew full well the natural course and consequences that often flow from confronting political and religious systems. Not only was his Bible filled with accounts of prophets who were hated and persecuted by the established leadership, he also knew that thousands of Jews had been executed in the two centuries before his birth by the Seleucid king Antiochus III and by the Jewish king Alexander Jannaeus. More importantly, the Romans had crucified thousands of Jews before they crucified Jesus. What human would not want to avoid the horrendous execution that thousands of Jews and many thousands more non-Romans across the Empire experienced at the hands of the Roman occupying forces?

To the brutality of crucifixion is added Jesus's expectation that his closest friends would misunderstand what he was doing and would forsake him. Jesus also foresaw that the leaders of his faith community and his nation would designate him a blasphemer against his God. And he certainly had no doubt that the representative of the most powerful empire in the world would flick him off like a bothersome fly. Knowing that in these, and many other ways, he would bear the weight of the sins of humanity on his shoulders, what human would not experience horror and agony concerning what was about to occur?

Mark uses highly emotional phrases to describe Jesus's deep feelings as the hour of arrest draws near. Ched Myers argues that even the most graphic English translations of Mark 14:34 tend to be too tame in reflecting Jesus's horror, terror, anguish, overwhelming anxiety, shuddering distress, emotional upheaval, and dreadful broken-heartedness.[6] Luke, too, presents Jesus as deeply emotional in the Garden experience with his use of "anguish" [*agonia*] in Luke 22:44.

Why do we—unlike Mark—find it so difficult to view Jesus as overwhelmed and horrified as he faces the biggest challenge of his life, both to his faith and his faithfulness? And why do we—unlike Luke—find it so difficult to think that, even with the comforting presence of an angel, Jesus still experienced stress so intense that it caused him to perspire like someone in the throes of death? The word "anguish" (*agonia*) was used at times to describe a gladiator or warrior preparing to fight to the death. Jesus, who was named after Joshua the great warrior, prepares himself to fight to the death as God's warrior (one might also accurately say "antiwarrior"). He was pitting his trust and faithfulness, his way of peace, against the evil, violence, and injustice of our world powers. The power structures of a world empire, of his own nation, and of his faith community were all prepared to defeat and destroy him. No wise warrior, just like no wise pro athlete, ever enters a contest without taking seriously the fact that he will lose if he is not completely prepared and focused. At every level this was a life-and-death event.

8. Jesus's Experience of Dying and Death was an Authentically Human Experience. He had Only God's Promise to Rely On.

Having recently experienced the brutal dying process of my beloved wife due to Parkinson's Brain Disease and a fractured back, I have no doubt that any healthy-minded human would prefer not to go through what she went through during her final months in this world. Likewise, any genuine and healthy-minded human would wish to be spared the kind of dying that Jesus endured. The Gospels describe Jesus as experiencing the hatred of enemies, the abandonment of friends, and the silence of God (Mark 14:34, 15:34). Obviously, it was not just the physical pain involved in a brutal death, but also the spiritual, psychological, and social pain that accompanies a dying process filled with the experience of abandonment. In addition to the Gospels, other passages make it clear that Jesus's dying process was deeply embedded in intense human suffering (1 Pet 2:21–25; Heb 5:7–10; *see also* the many allusions to Isa 53).

But most importantly, like all humans, Jesus faced death with only God's promise that death would not win. Philippians 2:1–13, a passage we will return to repeatedly, is often treated as though Paul's main emphasis is Jesus's divinity. There are several important reasons for this interpretation including the exalted language Paul uses to describe Jesus's coreign with God. However, this passage is contextually focused on challenging the very human readers of the letter to imitate Jesus's human faithfulness to God, no matter the cost ("even unto death"), as well as to imitate Jesus's concern for other humans. Emphasizing Jesus's humanity throughout is a controversial way of viewing the passage, as you will see if you contrast the exegesis of the passage by

---

6. Myers, *Binding*, 366.

New Testament scholars N.T. Wright (emphasizing divinity)[7] and James D. G. Dunn[8] (emphasizing humanity and contrast with Adam). Even though my theology and understanding of the New Testament is much closer to Wright's—to whom I owe many precious insights—in this case I think Dunn's exegesis honors Paul's context more fully. Here are five of the many reasons I think Paul was stressing Jesus's humanity throughout the passage.

1. Paul is emphasizing how costly faithfulness was to Jesus. It led him into a real human death experience.

2. Contextually this passage is explicitly presented as a motivation for Paul's readers to live like Jesus lived and think like Jesus thought about daily life in community—"Let your thinking be just like that of Jesus the Messiah" (Phil 2:5). It also ends with the same emphasis on human obedience empowered by God's Spirit in us (Phil 2:12–13). In other words, the entire section about Jesus' faithfulness is bracketed with the challenge to model his costly faithfulness in our lives.

3. Paul does use an unusual word to describe Jesus being in the "image" and "likeness" of God (*morphē* in the Greek of 2:6), but the context still indicates he is asking his readers to image Jesus, just as Jesus images God. Some scholars also point out that Greek words related to *morphē* are used in Galatians 4:19 by Paul and in 2 Timothy 3:5 (scholars argue authorship). In both passages, *morphē* clearly means "similar" or "like," not "the same as," indicating that Paul's usage here fits more easily into the Genesis 1–2 "image of God" context than into an interpretation emphasizing divinity.

4. The phrase "being found in appearance as a man" uses the Greek word *schemati*, which is used only one other time in the New Testament, and that is also by Paul. In 1 Corinthians 7:31, he applies it to the very real though nonpermanent material world of this age. It would seem most likely that here, too, Paul is emphasizing Jesus's materiality as a human and perhaps the impermanence of Jesus's human body—and ours as well.

5. In Philippians 2:8–9, right at the point where one might expect a "Jesus is God" statement, if emphasizing divinity were the purpose of this passage, we instead find a stress on God's gracious gift to the trusting and faithful human Jesus. It is *because* of Jesus's willingness to experience a very real and very horrible, fully human, death process, in order to remain faithful to God, that God exalts Jesus. This seems clear because the description of the exaltation by God begins with "therefore"—"*Therefore God* also highly *exalted him and gave him* the name that is above every name" (*emphasis mine*).

---

7. Wright, Paul and Faithfulness, 680–689.
8. Dunn, Worship Jesus? 137.

The risk for Jesus as a human who trusted that death could not hold him because of his relationship with God and God's faithfulness was great (Heb 5:7–8; 2 Cor 13.4). Like us, Jesus had a promise from God. Like us, that meant he must trust God to do what only God can do. It is that risky faithfulness in facing a very real death that God honored, and it is that human faithfulness of Jesus that Paul asks his readers to imitate. Because I, and I think most of us who are honest, experience trusting God with life, resources, and death as a risk, I do not think we can "have the mind of Christ" unless he too experienced choosing to trust God with life and death as risking everything on God's promises.[9]

Jesus lived his life aware he was a person who could and would die. And he did die—really die. For Jesus, just as for the rest of us, it is up to God to decide whether death is the end of Jesus of Nazareth, or the next step in the relationship between Jesus of Nazareth and God. Isn't this the implication of Jesus's dying words from the cross: "Father, into your hands I commend my spirit" (Luke 23:46)? On Pentecost, Peter framed Jesus's trust and God's response in these words:

> [24] But *God raised him* from the dead, *freeing him* from *the agony of death*, because it was impossible for death to keep its hold on him.... 36 *God has made this Jesus*, whom you crucified, *both Lord and Christ* (Acts 2:24, 36, *emphasis mine*).

Death had no power to retain a hold on a human who remained faithful to God, because God would not allow death to win. We are called to the same trust. But trusting is not easy because we are very aware that we cannot make it happen ourselves. It is up to God. Jesus faced the coming suffering and execution with more trust than most of us are ever able to muster, believing that death could not hold him because of God's faithfulness and his own faithfulness. Still, Jesus did have to faithfully trust that God would keep God's promises because Jesus's death was real death. That trust in God is why he is designated the pioneer and the perfecter of human faithfulness (Heb 5:7, 12:2).

9. Jesus Saw His "Lordship" as Embedded in God's Human Project.

In the midst of one of his early and pivotal controversies with some Pharisees, Jesus's theological argument fully roots his personal authority in God's view of humanity.

> [27] Then he [Jesus] said to them, "The *Sabbath was made for man* [human], *not man* [humans] *for the Sabbath*.[28] *So* [hoste] *the Son of Man* [Humanity] *is Lord even of the Sabbath*" (Mark 2:27–28, *emphasis mine*).

According to Greek scholars, *hoste* often means "consequently" or "resulting in." Jesus sees his Lordship over the Sabbath as derived from his fulfillment of God's

---

9. See chapter 16 for a more extended look at Phil 2:1–13.

original intentions in Creation. Even the Sabbath was to be "subject" to humans "in the image of God," who are themselves "subject" to God.

This is consistent with how the writer of Genesis 1–2, the writer of Psalm 8, and Jesus himself understood all of God's gifts to humans. Paul maintains that this process of human lordship will not be brought to complete fulfillment, even in Jesus's life, until the *age to come* (1 Cor 15:24–28). Importantly, in both the Old Testament and the New Testament, "subject" did not mean "do with as you please," but rather to have the freedom to interact creatively and gratefully as stewards of God's gifts who are living in the presence of God. Jesus was an observant Sabbath keeper, but he saw the Sabbath as a gift to be creatively engaged in God's presence with gratitude. He treated all of the structures of creation this way.

10. Other Descriptions Also Deeply Embed Jesus in the Human Experience.

1. Mary carried Jesus in the womb the normal nine months of human pregnancy, presumably with morning sickness and bouncing hormones included (Luke 1–2).

2. John the Baptist's prophetic prediction includes a "coming male" (John 1:30).

3. Jesus craved water (John 4:4–10, 19:2–8).

4. Jesus was not enslaved by, but seems to have needed, and certainly used, money (Luke 8:1–3, 10:38–42; Mark 14:1–11; Matt 17:27).

5. Jesus worked with his hands as Joseph's apprentice and then on his own (Mark 6:3). As "firstborn son" in his family, Jesus was probably the primary bread winner and "the boss" of the family carpentry business after his father's death. If he was really tempted like the rest of us, I assume this included dealing with his own mistakes, even if he did always remember to measure twice before cutting once. I have known several expert woodworkers, and not one of them has been exempt from the frustration of having to redo things due to mistakes. Neither have any of them been exempt from the added frustration of lost time and income due to those mistakes. Like my friends today, Jesus would have had to decide how much to charge the widow Sarah down the street and how much to charge the wealthiest merchant in town for a similar table and chair. What is justice in setting prices in a situation like that? If Jesus was a stonemason, as some scholars think, or was a versatile craftsman, all of the same kinds of practical daily-life situations would have been faced.[10]

6. Jesus needed and often worked hard to create and protect alone-time (Luke 5:15–16; Matt 14:22–23).

---

10. France, *Mark*, 243.

7. Jesus needed to pray to God, whom he often addressed as Father, with an intimacy that impressed his followers and became a model for them (Luke 5:16, 6:12–19, 9:28–29, 11:1–4; Mark 14:32–35; Matt 26:36–41).

8. Jesus saw it as very important to set strong boundaries around himself in order to minister effectively. The disciples were given the responsibility of enforcing these boundaries, and they often showed frustration with Jesus as they struggled to determine when Jesus wanted them to enforce these boundaries and when he did not (Luke 18:15–17; Matt 15:21–28).

9. Jesus exhibited a deeply emotional life.

    a. Jesus was often joyful (Luke 10:17–21; John 15:9–17, 17:3; Heb 12:1–2).

    b. Jesus could become very angry (Mark 1:40–45, 3:1–6, 10:14; Matt 9:30, 12:16, 16:23; Luke 18:15–18; John 11:33, 11:38). Translators tend to resist portraying Jesus as extremely angry, but the New Testament writers did not hesitate to do so. Once Jesus was so frustrated and angry at Peter that he labeled him "Satan's" pawn (Matt 16:23). In Mark 1:43, the Greek wording indicates that something the man did or said made Jesus so "furious" that Jesus "threw him out" right after healing him from leprosy. In John 11:33 and 11:38, Jesus seems to have been "enraged" at the pain and confusion death caused the friends he loved. Mark 11 indicates that Jesus was very angry with the blasphemous ways the Temple was being run, and he expressed this anger by overturning the money-changing tables, blocking the entrance to the area, and carrying a whip as he did so. Doesn't Jesus's symbolic destruction of a fig tree seem like a safe way to vent some of that anger toward the religious and political leaders, while also teaching his disciples a lesson?

    c. Jesus was compassionate (Matt 9:35–38, 14:3–14, 15:29–39, 20:29–34; Mark 1:41; Luke 17:11–17).

    d. Jesus could be both humorous and ironic (Matthew 7:3–5, 23:16, 23:19, 23:23–36, 26:55; Mark 3:12; Luke 7:31–35).

    e. Jesus sometimes wept and sometimes wailed (Luke 19:41–44; John 11:33, 11:35, 13:18–22; Matt 23:37–39, 27:50).

    f. Jesus sometimes sighed deeply in frustration (Mark 7:33–35, 8:11–13).

    g. Jesus experienced deep feelings of friendship (Matt 26:36–41; Luke 22:14–16; Mark 10:17–31; John 11:11, 11:16, 11:35–36, 15:9–17).

    h. Jesus describes himself, and is described in 1 John, as "soul" (Greek *psyke*, "unique personality/self"), a word used of all other humans as well (Mark 14:34; 1 John 3:16).

10. Jesus was genuinely tempted to sin and fail God's calling (Matt 4:1ff, 16:22–23; John 12:20–33; Heb 2:17–18, 4:15–16, 5:7). As a male with testosterone flowing through his body, and with many women around who adored him, surely some of these temptations were sexual, and many of them involved money, power, and fame. Perhaps one of the greatest temptations was to despise his enemies rather than love them.

11. With gifts that most of us find it difficult to discipline, he consistently resisted the magnetic draw to misuse power, money, sex, and fame. I have often said that even if I had resisted all other temptations as Jesus did (a pipe dream for sure), I could not have resisted the taunt "If you are the Son of God, come down from the cross." That would have been the last straw. I would have been off that cross with the twelve legions of angels in tow saying, "See how wrong you are!" Resisting the misuse of power and ego is impressive only if Jesus is truly and completely human and, therefore, at risk as he navigates his relationship with God and with the fellow humans around him. It is amazing to see a human with so much power again and again choose to make himself vulnerable and choose to take his stand with the most vulnerable people around him.

JESUS'S TEACHINGS AND ACTIONS FLOW OUT OF HIS HUMAN CONTEXT.

The writer of 1 John thought it was so important to relate to Jesus as a real human that he said to fail to do so was to be antichrist.

> ² This is how you can recognize the Spirit of God: Every spirit that acknowledges that Jesus Christ has *come in the flesh* is from God, ³ but every spirit that does not acknowledge Jesus is not from God. This is the *spirit of the antichrist*, which you have heard is coming and even now is already in the world (1 John 4:2–3, *emphasis mine*).

If Jesus was authentically human in that earthy sense that John describes as "flesh," isn't it important to try to think about how his environment affected him? All humans grow up deeply influenced by their experiences in their family and their hometown, as well as by their experiences that come from being a part of a "people."

We know a bit about some of the positive influences of various individuals in Jesus's more immediate environment. We know that Jesus grew up in an extended family with a deep faith in a personal and active God, informed by their charismatic and prophetic Jewish faithfulness (Luke 1). We also know his parents instilled in him a strong sense that God was his "Father" (Luke 2:49). It is a guess, but my guess is that he was influenced by a thoughtful and insightful local rabbi who taught him how to respond thoughtfully to the question-and-answer format of Jewish education (Luke 2:46–47). We are told that Jesus matured well, including in his relationship with God and his fellow humans (Luke 2:50–52). How much did his parents share with him the stories surrounding his conception? We are never told. How did they, or could they, protect him from local gossip about his mother's pregnancy prior to marriage? We are never told.

Even at the micro-level, it wasn't all positive. We are told that he grew up in a family that knew the hardships of having to leave their homeland fearing for the life of their child. This means some of Jesus's earliest years were spent as part of an immigrant family in a foreign land (Matt 2:14–23). We are also told implicitly that somewhere between the age of thirteen and thirty, the family lost their father to death, and that Jesus, as firstborn son, inherited the vocation and the role of his missing father (Mark 6:3).

We are told that Jesus's brothers, and even his mother at times, did not approve of the way Jesus went about his ministry. They made their opinions quite clear (Mark 3:21, 31–35; John 7:3–5). The same was true of quite a few people in his hometown of Nazareth (Luke 4:24–30). In other words, he was criticized by both family and neighbors for the way he understood God. This, despite the fact that he knew the Old Testament well, was regularly present for Sabbath worship (Luke 4:16), and wore the "fringes" that Torah demanded (Luke 8:44).

Economically, his family was relatively poor, though not destitute. He grew up surrounded by fear and stories of fear. His family had personal stories of harrowing family experiences involving violence perpetrated by the police-soldiers of his country's rulers (Matt 2:16). Beyond that, he grew up in a town and a region of the country that would have constantly been relating fearful accounts that came from being threatened with violence by the powers that ruled their nation—more on that when we examine the corporate setting of Jesus's life.

How much fear did Joseph and Mary carry from having to flee to Egypt, and how many worries did Mary have once Joseph passed and she was left to finish raising five boys and at least two girls (Mark 6:3)? As a young child, Jesus grew up around the fears that come from being an immigrant and sojourner in a foreign land. Did Jesus have to struggle against fear when he suddenly inherited more responsibilities than any young man wants when his father passed?

So, although we do not know as much as we wish we did about the environment that surrounded Jesus as a maturing human individual, we know enough to make most of those of us who are White Middle-Class American Christians do a double-take. Especially if we also work at remembering that he did not look like a European or an American, but like a brown-skinned Jewish person born of a brown-skinned Jewish mother.

At least as important was the corporate environment in which the human Jesus grew up. We all grow up swimming in the water of a social, political, religious, and cultural environment. From both Roman and Jewish sources, as well as from the mostly Jewish writers of the New Testament, we know quite a bit about what that environment was like for the maturing Jesus.

He grew up as a member of an ethnic community that was occupied and oppressed by invaders from a first century superpower. The Romans brought a different culture, ethnicity, and religious atmosphere to the countries they occupied. Jesus grew up with stories about how, just before he was born the Roman soldier-police had crucified 2000 innocent Jewish men on the roads near his hometown because no one would turn informer on the few guilty Jewish men who had killed a few Roman soldier-police. This was Rome's way of reminding the nations where their soldiers were stationed: "We are in charge; never question that reality!" He would have heard many times how the Romans had destroyed the thriving Jewish city of Sepphoris about the time he was born. Since Sepphoris was only about 4 miles from Nazareth, during his young adult years, Jesus might have used his carpentry and/or stone masonry skills to earn a living for his family, as the Romans rebuilt the city that would now serve as an important Roman center.[11]

He grew up knowing that at any moment a Roman policeman-soldier could stop him without cause and make him carry his heavy pack. He grew up in a faith and an ethnicity that many influential people in the dominant colonial culture—Cicero and Tacitus, for example—looked down upon as obnoxious, naïve, and dangerous to the stability of the Empire. He also grew up being taught that many of the Jewish people who were doing well economically, such as the High Priestly clan, the Herods, some tax-collectors, and a few landowners and businessmen, were doing well because they had sold out to the Roman occupiers.

To all of this, we can add that, being a Galilean, he was also looked down upon by the Jewish power structure to the south in Jerusalem. And, perhaps especially important to Jesus, the Jerusalem theological elite viewed a rabbi who was not trained in either Jerusalem or Babylon as clearly of lesser status than they were. Paul gives us a taste of what that elitism looked like (Phil 3:3–6), as does John's Gospel (7:41–50).

So Jesus grew up knowing that violence could be perpetrated upon his person at any moment. He grew up being looked down upon by the Roman occupiers and by the elite of his own people. He was never really politically a "free man," nor was he ever socially empowered by the state or by his religious leaders. He grew up politically, socially, economically, and religiously among those disenfranchised and underprivileged by the Roman Colonial Empire of his day. He and his family might not have remained as poor economically as his parents were when they could only offer the two doves while presenting the new-born Jesus at the Temple (Luke 2:24), but craftsmen in Israel were certainly not becoming wealthy. He grew up among a people who lived constantly in fear of what the Romans could do to them as a people. Not an unfounded fear, because between AD 70 and 135, the Romans slaughtered myriads of Jews.

---

11. Sarna, *Story of Jews*, 109, 192–201.

To make it somewhat understandable in our current environment, Jesus grew up much like many African Americans and Native Americans have grown up in the United States over the past few centuries. He grew up as a human among the poorer people of the land, the often abused, always threatened, and underprivileged.

If you wish to think more carefully and fully about the impact that his environment must have had on Jesus and on his teachings, I highly recommend a prayerful reading of Howard Thurman's amazing and brilliant book on the topic.[12] It's a book only an African American could ever have the right to write.

Think about the struggle a human growing up as Jesus grew up has in developing a strong sense of self as a child of God—yet Jesus does have that self-confidence. Think about how difficult it is not to always be afraid of those who can bring violence and even death upon you whenever they choose, and then remember how many times Jesus taught about living in trust not terror, in faith not fear. And he not only taught it, he lived it as almost every page of all four Gospels makes clear. As Thurman pointed out, Jesus's challenges to choose loving enemies rather than hating, to be truthful in a society where truthfulness could get you convicted in court, and to not take up arms in a society that was constantly threatened by armed Romans, each take on an entirely new and radical level of meaning and courage when we understand his environment. Jesus was teaching what the maturing Son of God was living every day of his life.

Only when we focus on Jesus as a real human, growing up in conditions that often succeed in deeply wounding, or even destroying, the humanity of a person, do we begin to realize what an amazing and courageous faithfulness to God Jesus showed in his teaching and in his day-to-day living. Only when we realize how destructive the conditions he grew up in often are for humans, can we begin to appreciate what it means that God managed to "complete" this human Son of God in such circumstances. It was faithfulness in the real world that allowed God to make Jesus the Savior for the rest of us humans (Heb 5:7–10).

Growing up and living in an Empire that makes it clear the world is their kingdom means there is nothing abstract about Jesus's message that the Kingdom of God is among us. Neither was there anything abstract about his promises that God will take care of you even if they kill you. Jesus did not float around like a mystical flower child, spouting cliches, though he has often been portrayed that way in movies. Rather, as a person growing up and living among the disinherited of the world, he tells us we are heirs of God. Growing up as a rather poor person, he tells us our Father owns everything, and we are richly blessed. Living daily as a person under the threat of violence, he tells us not to fear. As a person about to face a cross, he tells us to take up our cross and follow him—and we will find real life!

When we underemphasize the power of the realities in which Jesus grew up, we make abstract what was not at all abstract—Jesus's empathy and love that flow into forgiveness and brotherhood for those of us who live in this world. Jesus loves and

---

12. Thurman, *Jesus and Disinherited*, 1–25.

challenges us to follow him in a world where it can be very difficult to allow the Spirit of God to keep us maturing into godliness (Heb 2:11, 4:15–16; Matt 9:26). But it is a world he knows by experience. When we underemphasize Jesus's humanness, we also steal from him the amazing wonder of his godliness as a human—as "flesh." We diminish the human who allowed the fullness of God's Spirit to mature within him step by step into a faithfulness God was preparing to use to transform and save the world (1 John 4:14).

SUMMARY

Unlike what many of our songs, sermons, comments in Bible studies, pictures, and even scholarly tomes say, the New Testament writers describe Jesus as genuinely and completely human during his approximately 33 years in Israel. He is presented as an always-faithful human in a learning and maturing relationship with God and the other humans around him. Jesus *was* human! Jesus *was* one of us! Really! Does the New Testament also tell us that he *is* and *will be* human?

5

Jesus is One of Us—Now and Forever

**JESUS IS NOT A COURAGEOUS DEAD HERO,
BUT A LIVING FELLOW HUMAN.**

In a recent conversation, my daughter reminded me how easily those of us who claim to follow Jesus slide into thinking *about* Jesus rather than presenting ourselves, daily ready to live *with* Jesus. The following Sunday, my pastor preached about how often we treat Jesus as another dead hero. Dead heroes are the source of great wisdom, courage, and modelling, but they are not a living, communicating, loving presence. Both women made me very sad because they were absolutely right about my personal tendencies. I attempt to resist, but I fall into this temptation again and again in life. Even as I write this book about Jesus, I must regularly repent for not remembering I am constantly in his presence.

Both my daughter and pastor also made me happy, because they reminded me of the many blessed experiences I have had when I do remember to live in Jesus's presence and empowering. Of course, I was further blessed by the fact that these two young women I have had the opportunity to mentor have now become my mentors! I am thrilled to call these *daughters* my *sisters*, my *colaborers*, and my *instructors* in the family of God.

This blessed relationship all flows from our "firstborn" brother—Jesus. My joy in Jesus's presence moves higher and deeper when I remember that Jesus is with me as a fellow human. On the Father's behalf, Jesus is delighted to relate to me as his *brother*, and to these two wonderful young women as *sisters*. We are all invited into the "same family," sharing the "same Father." Each of us knows we have some very real weaknesses, but we are assured that Jesus is "not ashamed" to identify with us as a part of his forever human family, despite our weaknesses and temptations (Heb 2:11–17). Amazing!

JESUS IS STILL HUMAN—A CONTROVERSIAL CLAIM.

That Jesus *was* human is not controversial in Christian doctrine and theology, although his humanity is severely diminished, and often does become controversial in the thinking, teaching, and practice of many Christians. I hope this is adequately illustrated in the previous chapter.

On the other hand, the New Testament affirmations that Jesus continues to be fully human now and forever have often been ignored by Christian scholars, pastors, and laypersons. In a recent conversation with a very knowledgeable Christian friend, who has been in church since birth, I mentioned that several New Testament writers explicitly speak of Jesus as continuing to be human. My friend's response was, "I have never heard anyone say that."

I have raised this fact in sermons and in discussions with various friends during the past three decades, and my experience has been that often those listening did not even hear what I was saying. We humans tend to be so sure of what we think we already know that we do not even register data to the contrary. These bright, intelligent friends were so sure of what they thought they already knew, and of what they were certain I already knew, that they were positive I was not saying what I was saying!

So, I will say it as clearly as I can here. New Testament writers, several and perhaps all, thought Jesus continued to be human as they wrote, and they believed that he would be human forever. They write from the perspective that Jesus *is* one of us. As we will see later in this chapter, some say so explicitly. Others imply the same.

Whether you find this claim disconcerting, controversial, intriguing, or exciting, please keep an open mind, and test the assertion that this is a view explicitly stated by several New Testament authors. Perhaps if we emphasized that the master narrative of the Bible is God's desire to create humans in the image of God, we would not find it strange that Jesus is God's next great step in the creation project. According to the broad New Testament narrative, Jesus now stands as a human in the presence of God. Prior to Jesus, this was impossible for a human, but it is a status God always intended for humans.

In addition to the explicit statements we will look at shortly, there is also a general framework in the New Testament that reflects this understanding of Jesus's continuing humanity. One example of this general framework is the presentation of Jesus as "the human" who is the faithful trailblazer and pioneer for the rest of us humans on the path into God's future for humanity (Heb 2: 11–12; 11:39–12:3).

Another example of how this perspective can be implicit is illustrated by the way Paul and the writer of Hebrews both identify Jesus as the "firstborn" of the new human family of God (Rom 8:29; Heb 1:6, 12:23). Paul also sees Jesus as the "firstfruits" of God's new humanity (1 Cor 15:23). Despite many attempts in commentaries to skirt the implications of passages such as these, I suggest there is no proper alternative way to understand these descriptions of Jesus, other than his continuing humanity.

Further, throughout the New Testament, Jesus is the epitome of the faithfulness that fulfills the credal statement "man's highest goal is to glorify God." Just as importantly, Jesus is the epitome of the claim that runs through the Old Testament writings and is overwhelmingly enhanced in the New Testament writings—God's highest goal in creation and in human history is to glorify humans. In amazing ways, through Jesus, God moves forward the goal of glorifying and completing humans. Wouldn't it be great to have this included in our credal statements?

GOD'S GOAL FOR JESUS—AND FOR THE REST OF US—IS NOT TO ESCAPE, BUT TO FULFILL GENUINE HUMANNESS.

The New Testament writers never thought the goal for a human relationship with God was escaping earth or escaping humanness. They did not see Jesus's resurrection, ascension, and exaltation as his escape from humanness. Neither did they see his ascension as his escape from God's creation we call "Earth." After all, the writers keep saying that Jesus is coming back to reign over the earth someday. Unlike a lot of escapist Christian theologies that present the intended future for humanity as an escape from the "bondage" of the human body, the human mind, and the earth, the earliest followers of Jesus understood God's goal to be the fulfillment of what it means to be a human.

They also thought this fulfillment meant a renewal of all creation, as well as of humanity. Jesus was God's illustration of fulfillment and completion, not of escape. They believed that Jesus was the first, but by God's grace would not be the last, to enter God's future age for humans. Jesus is the first "completed" human, the firstborn of the new forever family of God, the firstfruit of God's new creation, and the trailblazer into God's future human society. In the relationship shared by God and Jesus, God is moving toward *the completion of the reality that makes us human—the completion of character, community, and creation.*

THERE ARE EXPLICIT STATEMENTS IN THE NEW TESTAMENT ABOUT JESUS'S CONTINUING HUMANITY.

Jesus's Continuing Humanity is Explicit in Acts.

Luke tells us in Acts that Paul ended his debate with the pagan philosophers in Athens with this statement concerning Jesus's continuing and future humanity:

> For he [God] has set a day when he will *judge* the world with *justice* [or, righteousness] *by the man* [*andri* in Greek] he has *appointed*. He has given *proof* of this to all men *by raising him* from the dead (Acts 17:31, *emphasis mine*).

Though it was bound to sound a bit crazy to many of the Athenian intellectuals, Paul sees it as an essential part of his witness to insist that the risen, exalted, and yet-to-return-as-judge Jesus is still, and will continue to be, human. In fact, it is because Jesus continues in his humanity that God has "appointed" him to be the rightful authoritative agent for exercising God's judging of all humanity. The fact that Jesus was, is, and will be human allows God's judgment of other humans to be righteous and just at a deeper level.

Given the fact that "judging" has become a negative word to many of us, it is important to remind ourselves that judgment in the biblical paradigm was God reordering society in a manner that brought justice for the oppressed and righteous relationships for all. It was negative only for those humans who did not want the broken social order to be healed and renewed in justice and righteousness. Resisting "justice" turns "judgment" into a negative experience. The "judges" often failed, but they were chosen by God as agents tasked with bringing a more just and less oppressive social order out of chaos and subjugation. Reordering society would have been the primary paradigm in Paul's mind when he claimed that God intends the human Jesus to be the judge at the end of this age.

When Paul maintains God will judge the world through the human Jesus, he might have had in mind an earlier claim along the same lines made by Jesus (John 5:27). This understanding that God's justice needs to be carried out through a human might also be the paradigm Paul had in mind when he argues that it is Jesus's faithfulness that allows God to be just and to judge us justly (Rom 3:26). It seems God is appointing Jesus as judge over human history for at least three important reasons. First, as a fellow human, Jesus consistently chose justice and righteousness in his relationships with God and with fellow humans; therefore, he is God's rightful agent for judging us humans justly.

Second, Jesus's human faithfulness, even when tempted as we all are to be unfaithful, means that we cannot stand before God, saying, "But you are God; you cannot understand how difficult it is to deal with what we humans have to deal with." Third, having lived in this tough and broken world, Jesus is sympathetic with how difficult faithfulness is for us. For these reasons, my trust is in Jesus's faithfulness to God and his love for us. My trust is not that I am getting enough right, or have enough faith, to qualify for God's future. We miss this powerful New Testament paradigm concerning God's justice when we fail to emphasize that Jesus was, Jesus is, and Jesus always will be truly human.

In Acts 2, Luke presents Peter's sermon with a persistent thread throughout. The very "same Jesus of Nazareth" (1) preached and healed; (2) was unjustly executed; (3) is the son of David; (4) is the one David prophesied in Psalm 110:1 would be called "Lord" (*adoniah* in Hebrew) by "the Lord" (*YHWH* in Hebrew); (5) was raised out of death by God; (6) was "appointed Lord and Messiah" by God; and (7) is the one pouring out the Spirit of God upon his followers, as Joel promised. It is essential to Peter's argument that all of these great realities are true of "*this same Jesus of Nazareth*" (Acts 2:22, 36).

Finally, in Acts 7:56. as Stephen is about to be executed, he experiences a vision of the exalted Jesus who is ready to receive him as he passes over into God's next age. His vision of Jesus is a vision of "the *Son of Man* [*anthrōpou* in Greek] standing at the right hand of God." (*see also* Acts 25:19 where Festus understands Paul's claim to be that "someone" died, but is now alive, not that the "someone" who died proved to be God.)

Jesus's Continuing Humanity is Expressed in 1 Timothy.

Jesus's continuing humanity is a theme that runs through other New Testament passages as well. A very explicit statement occurs in 1 Timothy[1] where Jesus's role as mediator is said to be possible because of Jesus's continuing humanness. Note how the author uses the same word to describe Jesus's continuing humanity and the humanity of the readers.

> [3] This is good, and pleases God our Savior, [4] who *wants all men* [*anthrōpous* = humans] to be *saved* and to come to a knowledge of the truth. [5] For there is one God and *one mediator between God and men* [*anthrōpon* = humans], *the man* [*anthrōpos* = human] Jesus Christ, [6] who gave himself as a ransom *for all* men—the testimony given in its proper time (1 Tim 2:3–6, *emphasis mine*).

Not only was Jesus human when he "gave himself" as a ransom for all other humans, but his continuing humanity is fundamental to his ongoing ministry as mediator of the relationship between God and the rest of us humans.

Jesus's Continuing Humanity is Essential to the Understanding of Jesus Expressed in Hebrews.

In addition to the previous simple and short statements, there are entire theological contexts in the New Testament that depend upon the reality of Jesus's continuing humanity. The relevant passages in the letter of Hebrews are too numerous to quote them all here. The theme runs throughout the book as the following summaries demonstrate.

In the first chapter of Hebrews, the writer argues that Jesus is the fulfillment of God's purpose in creating humans because he is the "*reflection of God*." He mirrors God perfectly. That was God's goal for humans from creation forward (Gen 1:26–31). God previously "spoke" through many humans in many ways, and now God has "spoken" by means of God's Son. This chapter also celebrates Jesus as the "*Son of David*," who was promised the throne that belonged to both God and David (2 Sam 7). In

---

1. Some scholars think Paul could not have written 1 Timothy. Although I do not find the arguments against Paul's authorship compelling, I am not placing this quotation under Paul's letters. My point here does not depend upon who wrote the letter. In fact, the "not Paul" argument adds an additional source to the evidence.

chapter 2, the writer argues that Jesus is the *first of many brothers and sisters* who will fulfill God's human creation project as it had been described in Psalm 8 (itself a mediation on Gen 1). The promise is that humanity is so valued by God that *glorified and completed humans will yet reign as Jesus's brothers and sisters* in God's creation. In Hebrews 3–4, Jesus is the human leader of God's people, who is *even more faithful* than Moses and Joshua as he leads other humans toward God's promises and further establishes God's household. Hebrews 5:8–10 then claims that Jesus "*learned obedience*" and "*was perfected/completed.*" Once completed, he "*became*" the source of God's salvation for the rest of us humans (compare John 17:19 where Jesus says he lived a holy life *so that* his followers could be made holy).

In Hebrews 2, 4, and 5, Jesus is presented as the *empathetic high priest* who, because he was tempted as all humans are but did not sin, and because he "learned obedience," was "perfected" by God (Heb 4:14–16, 5:8–9). In this "completed" state, he can now *mediate* the gulf between God and humans with far more depth and breadth than the Aaronic priesthood had been able to do. The writer makes it clear that the limitation of the Aaronic priesthood was not their humanity, but their sinfulness, their weaknesses, and their inability to continue serving because of death (Heb 7–10).

Particularly noteworthy is Hebrews 2:5–18, in which the author focuses completely upon Jesus's continuing real and genuine humanity as evidence that God is still moving toward God's *original goal for the human race* ("but we do see Jesus," present tense in 2:9). The author argues that so far, Jesus is the only human to have fulfilled God's great purpose for humanity as it was celebrated in Psalm 8. Jesus is now crowned with the glory and honor God purposed for humanity. We can now look at Jesus—the Greek verb is present tense, even though this letter was written some 30 to 50 years after Jesus's crucifixion/resurrection/exaltation—and when we look at Jesus, we can "see" the future God intends for us humans. It is the future Psalm 8 contemplated. God's goal for humans in the coming age has begun to be revealed in the middle of the current age through the relationship shared by God and Jesus.

This future which God is planning includes us receiving the gift of "glory and honor" that God always intended for humans. We receive this gift as Jesus's brothers and sisters. Why is Jesus "not ashamed to call us his brothers and sisters"? "For this reason . . . Jesus and we have the same Father" (Heb 2:11). The entire section is predicated on Jesus's continuing humanity, as the first of many to receive God's promised purpose for humanity—"crowned with glory and honor." Far from no longer being human, Jesus is presented as the first, but not the last, completed human! Jesus *is* one of us.

The sustained message of Hebrews presents Jesus's *pioneering role as the first fully faithful human* and the first completed human. This message draws toward its finale with the following statement:

> [1] Therefore, since we are surrounded by such a great cloud of [faithful] witnesses, let us throw off everything that hinders and the sin that so easily entangles, and let us run with perseverance the race marked out for us. Let us fix

our eyes on *Jesus, the author* [or, trailblazer] *and perfecter* [the one who brings to completion, to the end goal] *of our faith* [or, "faithfulness"],[2] who for the joy set before him endured the cross, scorning its shame, and sat down at the right hand of the throne of God (Heb 12:1–2, *emphasis mine*).

In addition to the overall flow of the book of Hebrews, which depends upon Jesus's continuing humanity, the writer speaks explicitly of Jesus as *the first, but not the last, "completed" or "perfected" human*. Hebrews 2:10 says that God brought Jesus to completion as the first fully glorified human through the process of faithful obedience in a tough world. Hebrews 5:9 reiterates the same claim. Hebrews 7:28 maintains that this completion (perfection/maturity) of the Son is going to last forever because God made an oath that the human Jesus would be the mediating priest between God and the rest of us humans forever (7:22–28).

It is this "completing" of the Son that is allowing God to promise to "complete" the rest of us, based on the intercession of our fellow human Jesus (7:25). Once again, this "completion" does not separate Jesus from our humanity, but provides the means through which God can also complete other humans forever, just as God completed Jesus (Heb 6:1, 10:14, 11:40, 12:23). Jesus *is* still one of us—really.

Jesus's Continuing Humanity is Implicit in John and Luke.

Like the writer of Hebrews, both the writers of John and Luke understood God raising Jesus from death and exalting him to the right hand of God as God crowning Jesus with the glory God had always intended to give humans. In John 17, Jesus prays for God to glorify him in the cross–resurrection event about to unfold, and then he asks God to share this same glory with Jesus's followers (see the earlier discussion of "glory" as God's goal for humans in chapter 2). In Luke 24:26, Jesus says: "Did not the Christ have to suffer these things and *then enter his glory*?" (*emphasis mine*).

Jesus's Continuing Humanity is Important in Paul's Letters.

Another New Testament author shares this understanding of the "glorifying" experienced by Jesus after the resurrection as the gift God also wants for other humans. In fact, Paul regularly describes the exalted Jesus's ongoing humanity as "glorified," "firstborn," "second Adam," "the last Adam/human," "firstfruits," and "the human of heaven."

In Romans 8:17–30, Paul presents Jesus as the "firstborn" of God's future glory for humanity—a "glory" other children of God will someday inherit. Being the "firstborn" of the future "glorified" human community makes sense only if Jesus continues to be human (*see also* Col 1:15; 18; Heb 1:6, 12:23; Rev 1:5).

In Romans 5, Paul provides yet another explicit understanding of Jesus's continuing humanity by identifying him as the new Adam (human). The following quotation makes clear how important it was to Paul that God's gift through Jesus be seen as the fulfillment of what God began with the creation of humans. The difference between Adam and Jesus the Messiah is not a contrast between "Jesus who is God" and Adam "who is only human." Instead, the difference is that the human Jesus is a fully faithful and obedient human, whereas Adam (along with the rest of us humans) is not. Therefore, the rest of us are dependent upon what has occurred in the relationship between God and "the one human Jesus the Messiah."

> [12] Therefore, just as sin entered the world *through one man [anthrōpos]*, and death through sin, and in this way death came *to all* men [*anthrōpous*], because all sinned.... [15] But the gift is not like the trespass. For if the many died by the trespass of the one man, how *much more did God's grace and the gift that came by the grace of the one man [anthrōpou], Jesus Christ,* overflow to the many (Rom 5:12, 15, *emphasis mine*).

Please note that at this important juncture in Paul's letter, where he celebrates the outcome of God's love for us as it has been expressed in God's relationship with Jesus, Paul celebrates the fact that Jesus was "the one *human*" through whom God has moved forward God's purpose for "many humans" to "reign in life."

1 Corinthians also identifies Jesus as continuing to be human. First, Paul argues that the Messiah's resurrection is fully embedded in God's intention to raise other humans. He even goes so far as to say, if God is not planning to raise humans from death, then Jesus the Messiah is also still dead—that is how embedded in humanity Paul understands Jesus to be! The logic depends completely upon Jesus's continuing to be fully rooted in our humanity. This connection between the resurrection of the human Jesus and the resurrection of other humans is so important to Paul that he repeats it three times in a very short portion of chapter 15.

> [13] *If* there is *no resurrection of the dead, then not even Christ has been raised...* . [15b] But *he* did not raise him *if in fact the dead are not raised*. [16] For if the dead are not raised, *then Christ has not been raised either* (1 Cor 15:13, 15b–16, *emphasis mine*).

Throughout this section of his letter, Paul claims that the Messiah is now and will always be the fulfillment of God's creative purpose that humans corule with God in God's creation. In the Messiah, we see what God intended when God "subjected" creation to humans under God's reign (Gen 1:26–31; Ps 8; and *see* Heb 2:5–18). As he pursues this line of thought, Paul insists that the Messiah continues to be embedded in humanity as the firstfruit of renewed humanity. He is the "human/man" through whom resurrection comes to other humans. He is the human who will finally bring creation into subjection without harming it, and he is the human who will finally fully subject himself and the entire creation to God. Finally, God has a human who can be given power, authority, and ongoing life without turning it into oppression, greed, arrogance, and death, but he is the "firstfruits." He is the first human, not the only human, God intends to bring to completion. This will allow all creation to be subject to humans—responding to our will without us causing destruction and perversion.

> [20] But Christ has indeed been raised from the dead, *the firstfruits of those who have fallen asleep.* [21] For since death came through a man [*anthrōpou*], the resurrection of the dead comes also *through a man* [*anthrōpou*]. . . . [27] For he [God] "has put everything under his feet." Now when it says that "everything" has been put under him, it is clear that *this does not include God himself,* who put everything under Christ. [28] When he [God] has done this, then *the Son himself will be made subject to him* [God] who put everything under him, so that God may be all in all (1 Cor 15:20-21, 27-28, *emphasis mine*).

After all of this, Paul is still not finished emphasizing Jesus's continuing humanity. He continues to emphasize the continuity between God's purpose in resurrecting Jesus and God's plans for resurrecting other humans. Jesus is the "last" and the "second" Adam (human), through whom God is defeating the death that the "first" Adam (humanity) unleashed (1 Cor 15:45-54). The Messiah is doing this not just for himself, but also for other trusting humans, who will "be made like" the Messiah in the resurrection. In the following quotation, coming to bear the likeness of Jesus is not a prediction that we will become nonhuman but that we will become as Jesus—"the human of heaven"—already is. We too will be "humans of heaven."

> [47] The first man [human] was of the dust of the earth, *the second man* [human] *from heaven.* [48] As was the earthly *man* [human], so are those who are of the earth; and as is *the man* [human] *from heaven,* so also are *those who are of heaven.* [49] And *just as we have borne the likeness of the earthly man* [human], *so shall we bear the likeness of the man* [human] *from heaven* (1 Cor 15:47-49, *emphasis mine*).

In Paul's thinking, being the human of heaven does not separate Jesus from our humanity, but rather explicitly connects him to God's intended future for our humanity.

Paul reflects this same understanding of God's master story of history in another letter. He assures his readers that God will someday give them a "glorious body" just like God has already given Jesus.

> [20] But *our citizenship is in heaven.* And we eagerly await a Savior from there, the Lord Jesus Christ, [21] who, by the power that enables him to bring everything under his control, *will transform our lowly bodies so that they will be like his glorious body* (Phil 3:20-21, *emphasis mine*).

Perhaps the most explicit statement in the letters reflecting Jesus's continuing humanity is in Colossians:[2] "For in Christ all the fullness of the Deity *lives in bodily*

---

2. I left Colossians until last because some scholars say it was not written by Paul. I do not agree with them, but if it wasn't, we have an additional source affirming Jesus's ongoing humanity.

form" (Col 2:9, *emphasis mine*). There are three important things to note in this brief quotation:

1. The verb "lives" or "inhabits" is present tense, meaning as he writes somewhere between AD 60 and AD 90, the author sees the risen and exalted Messiah as continuing to be in "bodily form" (*somatikos* in Greek from *soma* which has a strong emphasis on physicality).[3]

2. The Greek verb *katoikei* is not only present tense, it is also a strong word for "inhabit," "dwell in," or "take up residence in." Jesus is understood to continue to be the bodily incarnation of deity. (The author of 2 Pet 1:3–4 twice uses a slightly different form of this Greek word for "deity" and says it is the character of God that is being created in those humans who follow Jesus.)

3. The following sentence (Col 2:10) describes this same "fullness" from God as currently incarnating Jesus's followers as well—though importantly without the addition of "all." Incarnation does not separate the risen Jesus from other humans. Because of God's fullness that continues to incarnate the human Jesus, God is now free to move other humans toward that same incarnation with the fullness of God—except, as always, it is *more so* ("all") in Jesus.

Jesus's Continuing Humanity as Expressed in 1 John.

The author of 1 John maintains that the readers will someday come into the fullness of what it means to be "children of God" by becoming as Jesus is now.

> [1] How great is the love the Father has lavished on us, that we should be called children of God! And that is what we are! The reason the world does not know us is that it did not know him. [2] Dear friends, now *we are children of God,* and what we will be has not yet been made known. But we know that *when he appears we shall be like him, for we shall see him as he is.* [3] Everyone who has this hope in him purifies himself, *just as he is* pure (1 John 3:1–3, *emphasis mine*).

This future is possible because of the continuing faithful ministry of the human Jesus, serving as mediator between the rest of us humans and God (*see* 1 John 2:1–2; 1 Tim 2:3–7).

---

3. Tom Ewald, in a personal note, maintains that *soma* in the New Testament connects body and personhood—behavior, thought, and personality—far more than Western thought has tended to.

Jesus Is One of Us

OLD TESTAMENT PROMISES DEMAND JESUS'S CONTINUING HUMANITY IN ORDER TO BE TRULY FULFILLED BY GOD.

Perhaps you will find the following suggestions less compelling than the explicit statements referred to above. Or perhaps, as I have, you will find these descriptions of Jesus to suddenly take on new depth and meaning.

"Son of Man" Implies Continuing Humanity.

The term "Son of Man" was being used in some Jewish apocalyptic literature around Jesus's time to describe an exalted agent of God.[4] These were usually imaginative interpretations of Daniel 7. However, it is important to remember earlier uses of the phrase were poetic and decidedly human. The book of Ezekiel uses "son of man" frequently to emphasize the gap between God and the prophet Ezekiel. The writer of Psalm 8 uses the phrase "son of man" to designate humans who are meant to reign in God's creation, but who currently provide little evidence of how God will be able to fulfill this great goal. I see no reason to think this background was absent in Daniel 7 when "one like the Son of Man" was presented before God, was granted great authority by God, and then shared his new reign with other human "holy ones."

Like R. T. France, I think "the one like the Son of Man" in Daniel is deeply embedded in humanity.[5] That is why the dominion God gives to him (Dan 7:13) is also shared with "all the Holy Ones of God" (Dan 7:18, 27). Building on this prophecy in Daniel, we are told throughout the synoptic Gospels that Jesus taught that his reign (dominion) as "the Son of Man" would be shared freely with his human followers (*see* for examples: Matt 19:28, 20:21–23).

The Promised Seed of Eve Implies Continuing Humanity.

If one thinks, as I do, that God's threat against evil recorded in Genesis 3:15 constitutes a theological promise that should be taken seriously, then we have a promise of redemption that includes the final destruction of evil, coming through the actions of "your [Eve's] seed." The blow that brings the end to the damage caused by alienation from God, from one another, from self, and from the creation will be struck by a genuine human. Is there any reason to think that Jesus is not still "Eve's seed?" This same promise is likely the passage in Paul's mind when he identifies Jesus as "born of a woman" (Gal 4:4).

Although the imagery is certainly complex, I suggest that the Genesis promise is also in mind in the visionary drama of Revelation 12, where the "woman" seems

---

4. Ehrman, *How Jesus Became God*, 64–69, Boyarin, *The Jewish Gospels*, 35–52.

5. France, *Jesus and Old Testament*, 136–148. He also makes a strong case for the term "Son of Man" in the Gospels, reflecting Jesus's actual usage.

to represent Eve, Israel, Mary, and the Church, each of whom in their own way birth Jesus into the world as God's agent for destroying the dark side of the structures we humans have created. These evil structures take on a diabolical life of their own, attempt to destroy all God is doing, but will be destroyed by the "child" of "the woman."

The Promise to "Abraham's Seed" Implies Continuing Humanity.

Similarly, the promise that the seed of Abraham and Sarah will be God's covenant for blessing the nations is fully fulfilled if Jesus remains their "seed" forever. The "forever" promises occurring throughout the Bible in relationship to "Father Abraham," "the seed of Abraham," "Israel," and "the Jerusalem above who is our mother" (Gal 4:21–31), take on a much richer level of fulfillment if Jesus remains human forever.

The Promise to David and David's Son(s) Imply, Sometimes Explicitly State, Continuing Humanity.

The promise to David and to Israel that the "son of David will reign forever on God's throne" is very explicit in Isaiah 9:6–7 and is implied many times in the Old Testament. Throughout the New Testament, this promise is associated with Jesus in various forms. The New Testament writers understood the risen Jesus as remaining human forever as David's human descendant (Acts 13:34; Rom 1:3–4; 2 Tim 2:8; Rev 5:5, 22:16). After all, only if Jesus is still human is it true that a Son of David reigns with God forever.

The "Vine" Analogy of John 15 Implies Jesus's Continuing Humanity.

One final example rooting (pun intended) Jesus firmly in God's great promises to the very human community of Israel is Jesus's self-identification: "I am the vine." Several times Old Testament authors describe God's relationship with Israel as the vine grower and the vineyard owner. In that context, I think Jesus understood himself to embody in his humanity God's renewal of Israel as it had been promised by the Jewish prophets of old.

> ¹ *I am the true vine*, and my Father is the gardener [vine grower].... ⁴ *Remain in me, and I will remain in you*. No branch can bear fruit by itself; it must *remain in the vine*. Neither can you bear fruit unless you remain in me. ⁵ *I am the vine; you are the branches* (John 15:1, 4–5, *emphasis mine*).

This imagery implies Jesus's continuing humanity as the embodiment of God's renewed Israel. (*See* Pss 80:8, 8:14; Jer 2:21, 6:9, 8:13; Ezek 15:2–6, 17:6–10, 19:10; Hos 10:1, 14:7).

CLAIMING THE HUMAN JESUS IS INVISIBLY PRESENT IN OUR CURRENT WORLD IS NOT AS OUTLANDISH AS WE MIGHT THINK.

If this section seems a bit *too much* for you, please do remember that what we have been examining from the New Testament stands with or without my musings here. On the other hand, I find it stimulating to think about possibilities for better understanding Jesus's invisible presence today in the light of what we have been learning in the modern world. For years now, we humans have been learning there are many powerful realities all around us that are unavailable to our normal sensory capabilities.

As I write these sentences, I sit in an outdoor coffee area, wearing a mask, hopefully preventing the spread of the Covid-19 virus—definitely invisible to my eyes. Not many miles away in the University of Illinois labs, scientists are using high-powered equipment to make this invisible virus visible, as they invent reliable tests designed to slow or stop the spread. Perhaps biblical narratives that describe temporarily enhanced sensory capabilities that allowed someone to *see* what cannot normally be seen are not really as weird as we often seem to think.

Each time a New Testament writer claims that someone encountered the ascended and exalted Jesus, the description of Jesus is of a person who radiates incredible light (glory) and energy. They also describe a person who can be present wherever he chooses to be present and appear wherever he chooses to appear. This occurs in Acts 7 as Stephen is being executed, in Acts 9 as Paul encounters the exalted Lord, who turns out to be Jesus, and in the visionary experiences of the book of Revelation. Jesus appears to different people in different places—Jerusalem, Damascus Road, the Island of Patmos.

In each case, Jesus has not become a nonhuman Christ-Spirit, but rather is experienced as Jesus of Nazareth. He is still alive as Jesus of Nazareth, but he exists in a new dimension of "glory." He is still "the Son of Man" and "the Son of David," even though he now lives at "the right hand of God." In this exalted state, he is able to be present all around us, even though he is usually unavailable to our normally limited sensory abilities.

Perhaps these New Testament descriptions of the risen Jesus as invisible, but always able to be present, as well as occasionally visible, and enwrapped in glorious light, sound a bit like science fiction talk to you. Nevertheless, they are somewhat in harmony with descriptions of the universe we are coming to know.

One theme describes Jesus as reflecting the glory and light of God. His continuing experience seems to amplify the "transfiguration" that can occur when humans are allowed to be closer than we usually are to God's immediate presence (Exod 34:33–35; Matt 17:2). You might even find yourself thinking about the times you have seen people shine and "light up" with love in the presence of God or shine and "light up" with love for another human. I sit here remembering the glow in my granddaughter's eyes and on her face during her wedding a few years ago. All appearances of Jesus after his ascension and exaltation speak of him in terms of a high energy field that can knock you off your feet, or your horse. He is experienced as standing in the glory of God (Acts 7:56), as appearing in light so much brighter than the sun that it blinds (Acts 9:3–7, 26:13), and with a face shining like the sun (Rev 1:16).

Why don't we always see him if he is that bright and overwhelming? Perhaps you might consider "all the light we cannot see" on the light spectrum. The most recent scientific estimate I have seen is that your senses allow you to see only 0.0035% of the light that is all around you as you read this sentence. That seems a little weird, don't you think? But it also makes it less extraordinary that Jesus in all his glorious brightness might be present whenever he chooses to be, without my senses being adequate to perceive his bright presence.

The descriptions of the risen Jesus as able to be present all around us are also in harmony with other biblical descriptions of times when God drew back the veil between the dimensions of heaven and earth. Occasionally, humans were briefly allowed to "see" into the dimension of reality that is usually veiled to our limited senses. For example, Elisha's servant is permitted to see the angels who were always there, but who were not visible to his limited sensory abilities (2 Kgs 6:16–17). Israel follows the "bright cloud" of God's presence in the wilderness (Exod 40:34–38). Jacob's vision of angels descending from the realm of God to earth and then back to God is a related example—"God was here and I did not know it" (Gen 28:16–17). King Saul sees and hears the "dead" Samuel (1 Sam 28). Peter, James, and John, along with Jesus, briefly "see" Moses and Elijah, even though centuries earlier they had passed into a different sphere (Matt 17).

As our Irish brothers and sisters remind us, at some times and in some places, the veil between heaven and earth becomes quite thin. The heavenly sphere always surrounds us, but becomes available to our senses only at these special moments. The New Testament writers believed that the "glorified Jesus" is God's mediating human agent, who is operating in that space where the realms of heaven and earth meet within human history. The veil between heaven and earth is not just thin, but finally torn, where Jesus's relationship with God is concerned (Matt 27:50; Heb 10:19–20).

Is Paul's argument that the "unseen" is more real than the "seen" (2 Cor 4:16) really that different from our modern worldview? We claim that unseen energy is in some sense more basic to our reality than the chair I saw and took a seat on a few hours ago. Still sitting here, I do not see the atomic energy structure of the table I placed my computer on, the computer I am typing on, or the concrete my feet are resting on as I type this sentence. Their invisibility does not seem to hinder their very real presence.

We have come to live in a world that was the domain of science fiction only a few decades ago. We are becoming accustomed to the idea that something can exist all around us, and yet not be available to our unaided senses. All kinds of things that we cannot see are with us and in us. The subatomic world of electrons, quarks, and other subatomic particles is real, but not available to our unaided senses. Because of that invisibility, the fact that they exist never entered the minds of humans until about a century ago. Even as recently as my public school days, we were taught that the only parts of the atom that existed were electrons, protons, and neutrons. And even these three parts had only begun to be discovered in the 1930s. Did the fact that they were unseen for millennia mean that they did not exist all around every human on earth? Of course not. They did not come into existence when we learned how to develop techniques for "seeing" them. Likewise, the millions of neutrinos that flow through human bodies from explosions on the sun are real; and yet they were undetected until a few decades ago. It even seems that such things as "dark matter" and "black holes," which are not yet directly observable, might be the mechanisms that are holding everything together in the macro universe.

As I wrote an early draft of this chapter, a computer-generated image of a black hole based on evidence provided by many telescopes scattered around the world, and on mathematical calculations, was made public. Is the black hole now "visible?" Certainly not directly to my senses, but perhaps fairly accurately to my sensory experience as enhanced by computer generated replicas! Why then do some think it unquestionably impossible that God, Jesus, angels, and spirits exist throughout our universe, even though invisible to our normal, limited sensory abilities, unless those senses are enhanced?

Whatever argument someone wishes to make concerning God's nonexistence today, invisibility is no longer a good one. Not in our world, where most of what turns out to be "real" cannot be "seen" with our normal sensory abilities.

Let's press the point a bit further. The DNA codes (and now the accompanying importance of RNA) that we have recently discovered have not only been operating throughout our bodies every moment of every day since our conception, but we are certain that they have been operating undetected in the lives of our ancestors for millennia. The existence of what is "invisible" to our unenhanced senses as essential to sustaining life itself is becoming a commonplace component of our human knowledge.

And then I add the fact that scientists tell me that the way I am sitting, my weight, the speed my heart is beating, my needed glasses, my love of coffee, and even some of my current interests probably reflect my—invisible to me—inherited DNA/RNA. They even tell me, and seem to be able to demonstrate, that this DNA/RNA complex influenced many of the choices I have made in life.

As I write these words, I am again sitting in a coffee shop—my favorite office. It is impossible for me even to guess how many unseen waves are flowing all around and through me, from cell phones, wireless computers, internet modems, TV towers, satellite emissions, computer emissions, radio waves, radar units, sunspot explosions.... What if I could see all these waves bombarding my body? Does the fact that I cannot see them or feel them mean they are not real? Someone seems to think they are real, as they ring my cell phone to get my attention.

Still sitting here in the coffee shop, the multimillions of bacteria, viruses, germs, and other microbes on my skin, on my computer keys, on the coffee shop table, probably on many machines behind the counters, and undoubtedly in my coffee cup, boggles my mind. Even more impossible for me to comprehend is the fact that millions and millions of bacteria, microbes, germs, and viruses, all invisible to natural human senses, are living inside my body and on my tongue at this very moment. Ugh! But thank God, given that this invisible universe inside my body also sustains my life!

Despite this recent knowledge of the unseen all around and in me, I drink from my recently refilled coffee cup, bothered more by the one fly I can see than by the millions of germs and bacteria just beyond my sensory ability. And now I think of the fact that this was just as true for my coffee-loving father who shared his DNA with me as it is also of my coffee-loving daughter, son, and sister who share the same love. In the midst of all these previously unseen realities, like most followers of Jesus, I ponder and wrestle with the questions, "Is Jesus really here with me, just beyond my ability to see?" "Do I really believe in angels ready to serve us at God's command, as my wife always did?" And, "Do I really believe that the empowering I experience at times, or the amazing healings I occasionally see, are the actions of God's Spirit in our lives?"

Obviously, I can get carried away thinking about the presence of the invisible. The following sum up my thoughts.

1. The idea that a still human Jesus, as well as "the God and Father of the Lord Jesus our Messiah," and even angelic beings, can be present and active all around us without our sensory perception registering this reality is not so far-fetched after all in our modern world. I certainly am not claiming that our modern science *proves* the New Testament claims are true. Neither do I wish to inextricably link the biblical claims to our current scientific understanding—a mistake Christians have made far too often. What I do want to maintain is that there is nothing incoherent or inconsistent in the biblical claims that invisibility can be caused by our sensory limitations rather than being a proof of nonexistence. In fact, just a few centuries ago, almost every current scientific claim referenced in this chapter would have sounded just as weird, perhaps weirder, than anything described in the Bible.

2. We humans have learned to create ways to expand our sensory abilities with mechanisms that allow us to "see" the invisible. A somewhat parallel challenge occurs in the Bible. We are told that our spiritual practices can help us expand our spiritual sensibilities so that we see more of what is real and good. Here are three of many possible examples. Jesus tells us if we keep seeking and asking to see more of God's love for us, God will give us more and more of the Holy Spirit so we can (Luke 11:9–13). Paul tells us if we present ourselves daily before God, we will allow a transformation that will allow us to see more and more what is good and pleases God (Rom 12:1–2). In the letter to the seven churches, Jesus

tells a community to seek God's treasures and God's righteousness, and their eyes will be healed so they can see spiritual truths more freely (Rev 3:18).

3. At several points, New Testament writers indicate that a human being can, and does, exist as a real completed human in the "heavenly realms" with God. They also claim that this completed human is at work all around us in the unseen. It is not his reality, but our sensory limitations, that make this invisible to us most of the time. They did not think that Jesus had become something other than human when he ascended and was exalted to the right hand of God. They did believe, and claim to have experienced, that Jesus was still present with them, and he had been given the authority and responsibility to serve God as God's new firstborn human of God's forever family. The fact that he was now living in a dimension of human existence beyond their sensory ability to perceive did not mean he was not really alive as Jesus of Nazareth; it meant only that our senses are not equipped to see everything that is real

SUMMARY: JESUS WAS HUMAN—IS HUMAN— AND WILL CONTINUE TO BE HUMAN.

God's great master story of history is filled with promises that are kept, or at least that are far more fully kept by God, only if they are concretely fulfilled in a person who continues to be human forever. The New Testament understanding of Jesus is in continuity with the expectations generated by the Old Testament and with the early followers' personal experiences with Jesus. They believed Jesus to be the first fulfillment of God's purpose for humanity, and that he is also the source through whom God's promise to humanity is being passed on. "Completed humanity" and "renewed humanity" is what God's relationship with Jesus is accomplishing.

As we have been seeing throughout this and previous chapters, New Testament writers both explicitly and implicitly stress Jesus's humanity in the following ways.

1. Jesus was fully and obviously human throughout his life in Israel.
2. Jesus continued to be Jesus of Nazareth when God appointed him to be Lord and Messiah on David's throne.
3. Jesus continued to be human as they wrote.
4. Jesus continues to be human as he mediates between us humans and God throughout this age of history.
5. Jesus will continue to be human when he judges humanity as God's agent at the end of this age.

6. Jesus will continue to be human when, as the representative of renewed humanity, he presents the creation that has been made subject to him back to God as our gift.

7. Jesus will continue to be human when Jesus presents his sisters and brothers to God as the forever human family God always intended.

8. Jesus continues to be the human through whom God will make other humans into the image of God by making them like Jesus forever.

Shouldn't we followers of Jesus begin our understanding of Jesus's identity where the New Testament writers both began and ended? The claim is that Jesus was—is—and always will be—human! I find this celebration of human potential in the hands of God electrifying. Yes, it exceeds our wildest attempts to fully comprehend (1 Cor 2:9), and yet it also somehow makes sense of the dynamic tension we experience between human potential and human failure. God's "Good News" for humans is that Jesus still *is* and *always will be one of us*!

6

Jesus: God's Exalted Human

MY GOAL IS TO EXALT JESUS.

Perhaps, after reading this far, you fear that emphasizing Jesus's humanity demeans Jesus's status as God's Son. I do not think it does. I know that I would never intentionally do so. When people ask me about my wife, my children and their mates, and my grandchildren and their mates, I always answer that, no matter how much I tell you about how wonderful they are, they are much more wonderful. Having said that, I also think that Clarence Jordan, as quoted by Shane Claiborne, was correct when he wrote this:

> Jesus has been so zealously worshiped, his deity vehemently affirmed, his halo so brightly illumined, and his cross so beautifully polished, that *in the minds of many he no longer exists as a man. By thus glorifying him, we more effectively rid ourselves of him* than did those who tried to do so by crudely crucifying him[1] (*emphasis mine*).

My goal in emphasizing Jesus's humanity is to praise what God has done, and is doing, through God's relationship with Jesus. I will do so as much as my command of the English language (and lack thereof) allows. I also think that is what the New Testament writers were attempting to do in the Greek language. Never would I wish to diminish any of the grandeur and honor God has granted, and intends to grant, to Jesus.

The New Testament presents Jesus as self-aware that he is uniquely expressing the character of God. He is aware that he is engaging in actions that the Old Testament said only God would—or could—enact. Jesus is also conscientiously accomplishing

---

1. Claiborne, *Common Prayer*, 496.

God's purpose for humanity under God's direction as the Spirit-filled Son of God. Jesus is clearly mindful that God's self-giving love that created the universe saturates his being. All of this connects Jesus with God.

I think the many passages referred to later in this chapter and throughout the book indicate that this connection with God in the New Testament is consistently understood as God's revelation through the relationship God and the human Jesus share. Understanding Jesus's relationship with God in this manner explains why the New Testament writers feel so free to extend so many of the same descriptors to Jesus's followers as well.

Any emphasis that makes Jesus essentially different from us as humans diminishes the comfort this statement intended to convey: "For we do not have a high priest who is unable to *sympathize with our weaknesses*, but we have one who has been *tempted in every way, just as we are—yet was without sin*" (Heb 4:15, *emphasis mine*).

Instead of taking seriously the implications concerning "completed" human potential that the writer of Hebrews emphasizes again and again, many of us continue to whine, "But I am only human; he was God." Jesus's exaltation means it is Jesus's faithfulness, not our sinfulness, that defines human potential in God's hands. To be fully human is to love God and love our fellow humans the way the human Jesus loved (and loves) God and his fellow humans. Before examining some of what the New Testament emphasizes concerning God's exaltation of Jesus, it is important to remind ourselves how important it was to those early followers of Jesus to be faithful to "the One God" of Israel.

JEWISH WRITERS WHO SEE THEMSELVES AS FAITHFUL TO THE ONE GOD OF ISRAEL EXALT JESUS AS GOD'S SELF-REVELATION OF GOD'S PURPOSE IN CREATING HUMANS.

One implication of the previous chapters is that we do not diminish, but rather exalt Jesus when we see him as God's first expression of God's future purpose for humans. In Jesus, God shows us that we are amazing creatures when we allow God to bring us to our full potential as completed beings in the image of God.

The relationship between God and Jesus is both so powerful and so intimate that Paul says the rest of us humans can experience the glory of God by focusing our lives on Jesus the Messiah (2 Cor 4:6). The New Testament passages cited later in this chapter illustrate how exalted and audacious the New Testament claims are concerning the relationship between God and Jesus. As Larry Hurtado maintains from a Christian perspective[2] and Pinchas Lapide maintains from a non-Christian perspective,[3] these claims appear in the earliest New Testament writings and were made by very devout

---

2. Hurtado, *How on Earth*.
3. Lapide, *Resurrection of Jesus*.

Jews, who explicitly and implicitly continued to identify as faithful Jews. It is as faithful, God-fearing, God-serving Jews that they exalt Jesus in language previously reserved only for God. As both Hurtado and Lapide maintain, *these faithful Jews would have made these claims only if* they believed that doing so pleased the One God of Israel.

THE NEW TESTAMENT EXPRESSES GOD'S EXALTATION OF JESUS IN MANY WAYS.

The New Testament writers found numerous ways to tell us that God has exalted Jesus far beyond anything anyone ever imagined (1 Cor 2:9). This chapter examines a few of those claims.

Being Lifted Up on the Cross Expresses God's Exaltation of Jesus.

"Being lifted up" on the cross is at first glance the strangest exaltation theme in the New Testament. Nothing in the first century Roman world was meant to be as shaming and debasing as execution on a Roman cross. It was a symbol of Roman power that was designed to terrify and disempower anyone entertaining even the possibility of challenging that Roman power. It operated the same way the lynching and the mass incarceration of black and brown people has in American culture. In the ironic wisdom of God, this event that was meant for shaming is transformed into God's exaltation of the faithful Jesus. "But I, when I am lifted up from the earth, will draw all humans to myself" (John 12:32, *see* 3:14, as well).

According to Colossians 2:14–15, it is the attempt by the powers of Empire and Church to destroy Jesus that God has used to *disarm* those powers so that we need not fear them. The threat that demands complete allegiance is sometimes "death by a thousand cuts," but it is often ultimately the threat of arrest or even execution. This power has been shown not to have the final word concerning our lives since God raised Jesus out of death. Even a cursory reading of Colossians makes it clear that Paul is not celebrating anarchy, but is rather providing a clear-headed recognition that our human institutions have a dark side: they tend to develop in a manner that increasingly demands our ultimate allegiance.

Our institutions—nations, employers, professions, courts, police, churches, military, and as Jesus noted, even families (Mark 10:35–37)—often make sure those who refuse to acknowledge them with ultimate allegiance and submission pay the consequences. God's grace and mercy through Jesus have included us in the indestructible "life" that God gave to Jesus the Messiah when God raised him from death. In doing this, God shattered all other claims to ultimate power over our life and death.

We can be grateful for the good done by the institutions in our lives, but we do not "owe" them the allegiance they often demand. Neither do we "owe" them the fear that they often attempt to generate by threatening our livelihood or even our life. They want us to believe that our "survival" is up to them. The truth is that no one survives this life. If there is survival, it is not up to the powers and principalities that demand our allegiance. Survival can come only as a gift from the God who actually deserves allegiance. Jesus's death and resurrection are God's demonstration of who is "owed" allegiance and who is not.

In Jesus's time, as in ours, both the church and the nation are capable of morphing away from being structures that facilitate relationships with God and with one another, into structures that demand our final allegiance. This is certainly the message of Revelation 11–18, in which the author describes both as capable of being demonic and bestial. It is not anachronistic to use the word "church" to describe this dark side of the institution that cooperated in executing Jesus. It reflects the fact that the Old Testament word for assembled Israel was *qahal*, which was translated *ekklesia* in the Greek Old Testament. The New Testament then uses *ekklesia* to describe the "assembly" of Jesus followers that is translated into English as "church." It was a translation decision that chose not to use "church" for *qahal* (*ekklesia*) in the Old Testament. It probably would have been best to use "assembly" for *ekklesia* in the New Testament as well as for *qahal* in the Old Testament in order to stress the continuity. Perhaps a bit of our chronic anti-Semitism and anti-Judaism was showing when the decision was made to downplay the continuity? Whatever the reason, it makes it far too easy for us to apply these passages in anti-Semitic and anti-Judaism ways while ignoring the proper application to ourselves and our history as "church."

Neither is it historically anachronistic to claim the systems we have created in the "church" have often since the fourth century wed us to the world Empires in a manner that threatened not only the lives of non-Christians, but often the lives of fellow Christians, too. Between the fifth and sixteenth centuries, Trinitarians and non-Trinitarians learned to kill one another in various parts of the world. The Crusades and the Inquisition killed Jews and Muslims as well as fellow Christians. Protestants killed Catholics, and Catholics killed Protestants. Protestants and Catholics killed Anabaptists. And European Christians were credentialed by the church through "the Doctrine of Discovery" to enslave or kill anyone in the "new world" who was not "Christian" and would not convert.[4]

Of course, pillaging conquerors did not limit the slaughter to non-Christians, and a Papal commendation was given to the officer who led the AD 1565 slaughter of French Huguenot settlers—men, women, and children—in what is now either Florida or Georgia.[5] In order to legitimize these church-mandated grabs for power, wealth, land, and slaves, the Church created a racist theology that still haunts us today. Here in America, the economic advantages of Whiteness trumped brotherhood in Jesus. In section 34 of the Virginia Slave Act of 1705, a White Christian slave master was legally

---

4. Charles and Rah, *Unsettling Truths*, 14–23.
5. Spanish Massacre, AD 1565.

empowered to torture and even kill a black Christian he thought needed "correction." Even if the slave was disabled or killed by the "correction," the White slave owner "shall be free and acquitted of all punishment."

I am not being anti-institutional. I have dedicated my adult life to serving God through the church. I also benefit greatly from being American. However, it is crucial that we acknowledge the dark and idolatrous side of all our human institutions, lest we find ourselves giving our allegiance where it should never belong.

If we do not recognize and confess the dark side of our institutions, we will not exalt Jesus the way God has. In fact, we will find ourselves attempting to redefine Jesus into a "Jesus" who fits our institutional sins. In the past, it was a redefined Jesus who could support Emperor Constantine's murders and conquests, bless military Crusades, torture bodies in order to save souls, and grant us the privilege of stealing the land of Native Americans and the labor of black Africans in order to build "the new Israel." How are we redefining Jesus as "our Jesus" today, instead of allowing God's Jesus to be our Lord and Savior?

Seeing that "church" is often a part of the principalities and powers that war against God's ways, just as "Israel" was at times determined to be a nation like all other nations, allows us to grapple, as we should, with Jesus being "lifted up" in both meanings of that phrase. We should celebrate the continuity of faithfulness between those prior to Jesus and those who follow after him—the "church." If we wish to exalt the Jesus who was "lifted up," we must also see the continuity of unfaithfulness in church history that is just as clear as—perhaps even clearer than—it ever was in Israel's history.

Empire and Church have cooperated in attempts to subvert everything Jesus stood for, and stands for, many times during the past 17 centuries. We have often lifted up the cross of Jesus in ways that have far more in common with trying to execute him again than with exalting him as God's faithful suffering servant.

This ambiguity of "lifted up" not only intrigued John, it undergirds the Colossians view of principalities and powers, and it also appears in a different form in Philippians 2:1–13. There, Paul maintains that it was because Jesus lived a completely faithful life that his life was taken on the cross (Phil 2:8). And it was "because" of his completely faithful life that God exalted him above all "names"—another way of referring to the principalities and powers (2:9). Obviously, it is not just being crucified, because tens of thousands of humans were crucified by the Romans, some more brutally than Jesus. Jesus's uniqueness that led to exaltation was his faithfulness in all things, at all times, no matter the circumstances or consequences.

And it is through this faithful human, not through the broken and bent side of our institutions, that God can save the rest of us and allow us to share in the glorious future God has given Jesus. In Philippians 2:1–13, Jesus's faithfulness as a human not only allows God to exalt Jesus above all of creation, including all other humans, it also means that every knee will bow to the exalted person God has given a status "above every other name [authority]."

Seeing what God has done to lift up and exalt the faithful servant whom both State and Church attempted to shame and destroy should free us to "have the mind of Christ." Perhaps to our chagrin, many New Testament writers tell us that being faithful as Jesus was faithful might at times cost us dearly. This is especially true when that faithfulness threatens the very institutions we need and love.

Sadly, experience has taught me that the New Testament writers were correct. At times, my attempts to be faithful to what God has revealed through Jesus have led some of my fellow Christians to condemn me as insufficiently loyal to Church and Nation. Of course, my experiences of suffering condemnation by fellow Christians are dwarfed by the unjust accusations heaped upon other followers of Jesus in church history. I repeat: I have served the church most of my adult life, and I depend on the church as "the body of the Messiah." I am American in more ways than I even recognize, and I have been blessed to live here. I also know that if I shift my primary allegiance to Church and Nation instead of to the Jesus they executed, I will participate in the wrong side of Jesus being "lifted up."

Jesus's Four Inaugurations as King and Messiah Reveal a Human Endowed with the Authority of God.

Jesus becomes the first human whom God can entrust with the full authority and power that God always intended to give humans (Gen 1:26–31). Never before or since has a human had so much power and used it only for the good of God and for the good of other humans. Because of his faithfulness with the authority and power he had—the way he used it and the way he didn't use it (Phil 2:6–8)—God has given him even more authority and power (Phil 2:9–11; Acts 2:33–36).

Much like David in the Old Testament, Jesus was proclaimed King many years before he was exalted to reign on God's throne. Like David's first inauguration, when he was an unknown and seemingly unlikely figure, Jesus's first inauguration was prophetic of a coming future that seemed highly unlikely at the time. In both cases, the initial proclamation of a future kingship remained mostly secret for several years. In Luke 2, the angels proclaimed to outcast shepherds that the future king of God's people was being born (compare Heb 1:6), much as Samuel secretly proclaimed David's seemingly unlikely future kingship to a relatively unknown rural family (1 Sam 16:1–13).

In Matthew 2, the Gentile Magi who studied the astrological signs came to bow before the new king of the Jews, whose birth had been announced by the stars and planets, but they had to leave in secret to keep him from being killed. Then years went by. David passed those years first as an unknown shepherd boy and then as a young warrior; Jesus passed his early years as an immigrant refugee in Egypt, as a young boy in Nazareth, and then as an unknown carpenter caring for his family.

Jesus's second inauguration occurred during the event often called "the Triumphal Entry" (Mark 11:1–11). It too was a strange inauguration. On the one hand, the crowds coming down from Galilee, and out from Jerusalem, were proclaiming Jesus to be the rightful king, the heir to the kingdom of David. On the other hand, Jesus was boldly confronting the political claims of the High Priestly clan of Maccabean descendants, of Herod who ruled Jews at the pleasure of Rome, and of the Roman occupiers.

He rode into town reenacting Solomon's ride into Jerusalem, when Solomon was proclaimed the rightful heir to the throne among competing claims for the role as "Son of David" (1 Kgs 1:28–52). Jesus was quite aware that by accepting the proclamation of kingship, along with his subsequent overturning of the money tables in the temple, he was crossing two lines that could not and would not be tolerated by the principalities and powers (Church and State), who saw themselves as fully in charge.

Jesus's third inauguration occurred at his ascension, when Jesus was "exalted to the right hand of God" (Acts 2:33, 36; Heb 7:26, 12:2). The claim that Jesus now coreigns with God appears as a regular theme throughout the New Testament. He is "now crowned with glory and honor" by God (Heb 2:9), and he has been exalted by God to reign above every other name throughout the creation (Phil 2:9–11). God has appointed him "both Lord and Messiah" (Acts 2:36).

This third inauguration led to the "now" and "not yet" theme that guarantees Jesus's fourth inaugural experience. When God decides it is time, the final exaltation will begin, and it will then be said that "the kingdom of the world has become the kingdom of our Lord" (Rev 11:15). On that day, responding to Jesus's kingship will no longer be a matter of trust; it will be a reality for everyone who is thrilled—and for everyone who is not thrilled. Every knee will bow (Phil 2:9–11).

I have lived through four presidential inaugurations in the United States which led to huge celebrations by supporters who believed that that particular election was changing everything. I do not remember the first (I was a baby), but it can certainly be argued that Franklin Roosevelt's fourth election solidified major changes in the world and in the United States.

The second inauguration during my life that was heralded as a sea change was that of Ronald Reagan, openly committed to reversing many of FDR's changes. The third was for Barack Obama, elected by a populous swell hoping to reverse many of the policies instituted in the Reagan years. The fourth was for Donald Trump, elected by a populous swell openly committed to reversing many of Obama's changes. In each instance, for good or ill, major change was occurring. Each of these four inaugurations was celebrated by many—and dreaded by many.

Of course, world history is filled with similar moments of change in other nations and at other times. Two examples of leaders paying with their lives for the changes they were determined to make were Julius Caesar and Abraham Lincoln. Perhaps few inaugurations in history were any more unexpected and, in my view, as wonderful, as the inauguration of Nelson Mandela in South Africa. It too was heralded by many, inside and outside South Africa, and it too was fought against by many, inside and outside South Africa.

The New Testament is quite clear in maintaining that the great moments of American and South African celebration, and the promised changes that accompanied them, never begin to approach the level of change God is planning to bring about at the final inauguration of Jesus as Lord of all and King of kings. It is in the context of my personal conviction that Jesus deserves more adoration, praise, and exaltation than either you or I know how to put into words or actions that I attempt to describe how the New Testament writers celebrate what God has done for us through Jesus. God has chosen to give Jesus the role of "king" and "authority," codirecting with God the outcome of human history.

The reason I insist throughout this book that the Greek *christos* should be translated "Messiah," rather than transliterating it as "Christ," is because no first or second century Jew or Roman could forget that "Messiah" was a title that implied power and authority. It was a title Rome would never tolerate. Rome's refusal to tolerate a Jewish Messianic claim was made clear several times. If the Roman historian Cassius Dio is to be believed, Rome finished the lesson for ancient Jewish culture by killing "Messiah" Bar-Kokhba and by slaughtering as many as half a million of his fellow Jews in 132–135 AD.[6] That same mindset led Roman politicians and military leaders to begin persecuting the early followers of Jesus when Rome realized that they really meant "Jesus is Lord," which always has the inherent corollary, "Caesar is not."

Despite some scholarly claims to the contrary, I am certain no New Testament writer could have ever thought that adding "the Messiah" in identifying Jesus was just giving Jesus a second name. The hundreds of uses of "the Messiah" in the New Testament were a constant encouragement to the band of Jesus followers to never forget that they were the society of the future, following a king God had already anointed and exalted in anticipation of an almost unimaginable—to us—future reign.

Every use of "the Messiah" describing the risen Jesus was an in-your-face confrontation with Imperial Rome and with the Jewish High Priestly clan. Each use was a claim that a human they conspired to publicly shame and execute had been appointed by God, anointed by God, exalted by God, and empowered by God to continue to rule in God's kingdom when they and their kingdom would be long gone! Each use of "Messiah" was an assertion that the final inauguration of Jesus was already guaranteed by the authority of the God of the Universe.

(*See also* Matt 28:18–20, 7:28–29, 9:6, 9:8, 20:23; Mark 10:37–40; John 5:18–27; Acts 17:30–31; Rev 17:13–14; and the many uses of "Lord" designating Jesus's God-given authoritative role.)

---

6. Dio Cassius, *Roman History*, VIII, 69.14.1.

Jesus Is the Temple of God.

John Walton maintains that, from the first pages of the Bible forward, the entire creation is being described as the temple God built and intended to dwell in. It was also to be the place from which God would then continue the ongoing work of creation with humans as co-workers.[7] In that light, the New Testament claims that first Jesus, and then other humans through Jesus, are the temple of God and are to be seen as God's continuing fulfillment of God's purpose in creation. In the Gospel of John, the emphasis on the incarnation of Jesus as the temple of God begins in the Prologue.

> The Word became flesh and made *his dwelling among us. We have seen his glory,* the glory of the One and Only, who came from the Father, full of grace and truth (John 1:14, *emphasis mine*).

The word translated as "dwelling" conveys the idea of pitching one's tent, or setting up God's tabernacle—a place for God to dwell "among" humans. This emphasis becomes explicit a few paragraphs later, when Jesus's body is identified as "the temple" of God:

> [19]Jesus answered them, "Destroy this temple, and I will raise it again in three days." [20]The Jews [often used by John to designate religious leaders] replied, "It has taken forty-six years to build this temple, and you are going to raise it in three days?" [21]But *the temple he had spoken of was his body* (John 2:19–21, *emphasis mine*).

Throughout the Gospel of John, Jesus enacts (incarnates), in word and deed, the role of God's temple. Wherever Jesus is, God is present in a special way.

The claim that Jesus is uniquely God's temple on earth is not limited to John's Gospel. Matthew and Mark directly connect Jesus's self-identification as the "temple of God" with the confused testimonies of witnesses at his trial prior to his execution. The claim that Jesus is God's temple also appears in various ways in the letter to the Hebrews, where, among other claims, the rending of the temple veil and the rending of Jesus's flesh on the cross are presented as two dimensions of the same event. Both signify that God is offering greater access to God's presence through Jesus:

> [19] Therefore, brothers, since we have *confidence to enter the Most Holy Place* by the blood of Jesus, [20] by *a new and living way* opened for us through the curtain, that is, *his body*. . . . (Heb 10:19–20, *emphasis mine; see also* Matt 27:50–51).

Revelation 21:22 identifies both God and Jesus (the Lamb) as "the temple" of God's future kingdom. No other temple will be needed.

In fact, when you look for it, you see that the New Testament writers see Jesus as the fulfillment of everything the temple was about and of all the sacrifices and

---

7. Walton, *Lost World*, 86–91.

feasts that took part there. Jesus is the High Priest, his flesh is the torn veil that opens entrance into the Holy of Holies, he is the mercy seat, he is the bread of heaven placed in the Holy of Holies, he is the new Law placed in the Holy of Holies, he is the atoning life-blood sacrifice, he is the cleansing water, he is the Jubilee, he is the Passover Lamb, and he is the glorious light of God's presence that illuminated the tabernacle and temple.

These passages raise many interpretive issues, but the point for our purposes is clear. The New Testament writers claim that Jesus in his human body was and is the person through whom God's presence on earth is most clearly and overwhelmingly seen and experienced. He is the human temple of God, through whom God can dwell among us. He is Immanuel. New Testament writers indicate in multifaceted ways that, when people stood in the presence of Jesus, they stood in the presence of the human whose relationship with God allowed him to live fully in the presence of God. At the same time, when people stood in the presence of Jesus, they also stood in the presence of "God-with-us" because of God's unique relationship with the human Jesus. In all of this, Jesus was and is uniquely the "temple of God."

And yet he is also not unique, because he is the model and means by which those who form the community of Jesus followers also come to be called "the temple of God." In other words, this imagery, too, embeds Jesus deeply in our humanity.

In his letters, especially in the Corinthian correspondence, Paul uses the phrases "God's temple," "temple of the Holy Spirit," and "temple of the living God" to describe the *community* of people following Jesus, as well as the *individuals* who are following Jesus (1 Cor 3:16–17, 6:19; 2 Cor 6:16). These, along with the following passage, serve as a clear indication that, for Paul, the "shekinah glory" (God's bright presence) and the "temple of God" imagery could be applied freely to Jesus and to other "humans" as well.

> [17] Now the Lord is the Spirit, and where the Spirit of the Lord is, there is freedom. [18] And *we*, who with unveiled faces *all reflect the Lord's glory*, are *being transformed into his likeness with ever-increasing glory*, which comes from the Lord, who is the Spirit (2 Cor 3:17–18, *emphasis mine*; *see also* 2 Cor 4:6).

This intimate, two-way, in-one-another relationship between God and the followers of Messiah Jesus is also described in phrases such as those used in Romans 8:9–10: "God's Spirit lives *in* you" and "the Messiah lives *in* you." The relationship can also be described in the inverted phraseology of Romans 6:11: "You are living *for* God *in* Jesus the Messiah."

The claim that God's "word" incarnates Jesus, and then through "tabernacling" in Jesus, allows God to be more fully present among other humans, occurs in the Gospel of John as well. A vivid example would be, "Do you not believe that I am *in* the Father and the Father is *in* me?" from John 14:10, followed by John 17:17–26, where Jesus prays that God's word will make his followers holy, and in doing so, will let God dwell *in* them as God dwells *in* Jesus. The letter of 1 John also speaks of this incarnating presence of God in the followers of Jesus: "No one has ever seen God, but if we love one another, *God lives in us* and his love is made complete *in us*" (4:12, *emphasis mine*). Because Jesus is the temple of God, we who trust what God has done through Jesus are also called to be the temple of God—the place where God can dwell.

Jesus Is the Prophetically Promised Coming of God and Return of God.

The coming(s) of God promised in the prophets was sometimes a promise of great comfort, sometimes a warning of impending judgment, and sometimes both. The New Testament writers see Jesus as the overflowing or *filling full* ("fulfillment") of these Old Testament promises. Jesus is the new unique coming of God—the return of God—to Israel and to the world. He is the coming of God to bless, comfort, and enlighten. He is also the coming of God that will cause some to react in ways that show that they love darkness rather than light (John 3:16–19). This dual aspect of Jesus as the coming of God is particularly a focus of what is often designated the *realized eschatology* (the promised future being partially fulfilled now) of John's Gospel, as well as of the futuristic eschatology of Revelation.

The prophet Jeremiah had prophesied that God would come to the temple to destroy it (Jer 7:11–20). The reason? "Has this house, which bears my Name, become a den of robbers to you? But I have been watching! declares the LORD" (Jer 7:11). Jesus referenced these prophetic words of Jeremiah as he kicked over the money-changing tables (Matt 21:13). In Ezekiel 10:1–21, the "glory of the Lord" filled the temple, but this glorious sign of God's presence was a coming of God that preceded God choosing to leave the temple. Ezekiel portrays YHWH as coming in order to declare that YHWH is leaving because YHWH cannot live here anymore. Passages such as these seem to influence Jesus's words and actions as they are variously recorded in each of the Gospels (John 2:12–21; Mark 11:12–19, 12:9–12, 13:1–2, and parallels).

More in tune with positive Old Testament promises of YHWH coming to renew the temple are the positive presentations in Revelation (3:12, 21:1–4, 21:22, *see* Ezek 43; Isaiah 52). This final book in the New Testament canon celebrates the presence of God and Jesus with humans as the ultimate renewal of the temple of God.

Current scholarship indicates that quite a few Jewish groups in Jesus's time believed that, at least in some sense, the "exile" that began with the Babylonian conquest of Jerusalem still continued. Why? Because the great promises of God's glorious return in a manner that would leave his people free and holy, end their constant wars, cause all nations to be amazed, and draw all nations to worship the God of the temple mount had yet to be fulfilled (Isa 2:2–5).[8] Perhaps they felt a lot like the way many African Americans feel about the gains from, but very partial fulfillment of, the

---

8. Wright, *Jesus: The Victory*, 126–128.

promises made in the Emancipation Act, the Civil Rights Act, and the election of Barack Obama. Though various prophets, such as Zechariah, Haggai, Malachi, Ezra, and Nehemiah, were participants in the "coming" or "returning" of God to Jerusalem, it was clearly not enough to match the promises. Another "coming of God" was needed to bring liberation.

The New Testament writers claimed that Jesus's words and actions repeated, and filled full of new meaning, the actions and words of great prophets of Israel. They had predicted, and sometimes enacted, judgment on the temple and renewal of the temple as a coming of God. Just as it caused a lot of trouble for the prophets who claimed that the coming of God into the temple would be an act of judgment, the synoptic Gospels tell us that when Jesus enacted the coming of God into the temple as God's judgment, it led directly to Jesus's arrest and execution.

John 3:19 describes Jesus as God's "light *come* into the world." John 3:31 and 6:38 describe Jesus as "the one who comes from above" and the "one who has come down from heaven." In John 5:43, Jesus is "the one who *comes* in the Father's name." In John 8:42, Jesus says, "I *came* from God." In John 8:39, he comes to bring God's judgment into the world. Clearly, John had many ways of describing Jesus as coming from God, or as the coming of God. (In chapter 16, I will revisit many of these descriptive phrases as embedding Jesus in our humanity.)

The claim that Jesus is the coming of God is by no means limited to the Gospels and the book of Revelation. The Pentecost sermon in Acts 2 identifies Jesus of Nazareth, and Jesus's outpouring of the Spirit of God upon the gathered community of faith, with the prophet Joel's promise that God would "come" to pour out God's Spirit on all flesh—"this is that," says Peter. Matthew 28:18–20 records Jesus's last words in the Gospel as a fulfillment of God's great promise "to be with you always," recorded throughout the Old Testament writings. One of the most audacious statements of Jesus's self-understanding describes his coming as *the coming of a new fullness of God's salvation*, "For the *Son of Man came* to seek out and to save the lost" (Luke 19:10, *emphasis mine*). The great promises that God is always seeking a relationship with us humans, and the great prophecies that God was coming to save humans, were being fulfilled at this very moment!

A somewhat related thought about Jesus as the "coming" of God occurs in Galatians 3:19, where Jesus is described as the coming of God's promise in the following words: "Until the seed who was promised had *come*." In some sense he is both the coming of the life ("seed") of Abraham passed from human generation to generation and the coming of God's promise to Abraham.

Jesus Is the One Who Knows the Father.

For decades, I read the passages that follow as if "know" were being used primarily as a rational and intellectual knowledge—that Jesus was claiming to "know" more about

God than the rest of us humans. One day as I listened to someone else's sermon, I suddenly realized that this thinking did not take into account how often both the Old Testament and the New Testament use "know" as "knowing by personally experiencing." Of course, the Hebrew word group *yada* and the *koine* Greek word group *ginōskō* can describe, and often include, intellectual and rational knowing; however, the writers also often include a dimension of personal relational experience that goes far beyond the intellectual. This emphasis on more than just intellectual is obvious when these words are used to describe sexual intercourse as "knowing" the other person. It can also be quite clear in other passages, too, that a deep experience is being described.

(For a few of the many examples in the Old Testament, *see* Exod 7:17, 8:10; Isa 43:10; Jer 31:34; and Ezek 7:4. For some New Testaments examples that I think emphasize relational and/or experiential knowledge, rather than just intellectual "knowing about," *see* Matt 25:12, 26:72, 26:74; Mark 2:10, 14:71; Luke 13:26–27; John 1:48, 6:69, 13:35, 17:7, 21:15–17, 21:24; Acts 12:11, 15:8; Rom 8:22, 8:27; 1 Cor 13:12; 2 Cor 5:11; Gal 4:8–9; Eph 1:18; and Phil 3:10.)

Both Jesus's claim to be the only one who "knows the Father," and the claim that the Son is "known" only by the Father, are focused on experienced relationships, not just on intellectualized knowledge of a fact. Jesus is claiming a unique, shared intimacy of relationship that creates for him a unique experience of God as Father and that creates for God a unique experience of Jesus as God's Son. John 17:25–26 (*see also* 8:19, 8:55) seems to describe the same depth of knowing that is far deeper than just intellectual ideas about God as Father. Jesus experiences a relationship with God that the "world" cannot experience. However, the disciples are beginning to enter into this experience. It is an intimate experience of "knowing" that can come only by revelation and trust, not by just figuring things out intellectually (Matt 11:25–30).

Understanding the repeated use of various forms of *ginōskō* in John 14:4–9, as focused on relationally experienced knowing, allows the passage to be loaded with the heavy content that the context demands. The disciples have experienced so much of the relationship between Jesus and the Father that a deeper understanding of the intimacy of the relationship should be obvious to them. However, quite demonstrably, and very frustratingly to Jesus, they have not yet grasped the deeper implications of their experiences of Jesus's relationship with the Father.

He wants them to obtain this blessing of "knowing" the "way" to experience God as Father. This experience is available if they "see" the "way" that Jesus relates to God, and God relates to Jesus. I think it is also this intimate way of experiencing God, and knowing that God is constantly experiencing us, that Paul wants for his readers: "You have come to know God, or rather to be known by God" (Gal 4:9). It is an even deeper experience of this intimacy that he longs for in the future when "I shall know fully even as I am fully known" (1 Cor 13:12).

Jesus Is the Expression of the Character of God.

The centuries, and our overemphasis on Jesus as God, have caused us to lose some of the edginess of the New Testament writers' claim that, as a genuine human, Jesus fully expressed the character of God in purpose, desires, words, and actions. You feel the edginess return when Martin Luther King Jr. says it this way: "Christ is not only God-like, but God is Christ-like."[9] Think about how you would react to such a claim if it were made about anyone else. You might grant seeing God's character in an act, or a trait, or a relationship, but you—like some of Jesus's contemporaries—would find many claims credited to Jesus audacious and probably scandalous.

As examples, both "The Son can do nothing by himself; he can do only what he sees his Father doing, because whatever the Father does the Son also does" (John 5:19), or, "If you have seen me, you have seen the Father," are audacious and probably scandalous (John 14:9). Nevertheless, New Testament writers express such exalted sentiments concerning Jesus in a variety of ways. Here are a few more:

> For God, who said, "Let light shine out of darkness," made his light shine in our hearts *to give us the light of the knowledge of the glory of God in the face of Christ* (2 Cor 4:6, *emphasis mine*).

> The Son is *the radiance of God's glory and the exact representation of his being*, sustaining all things by his powerful word (Heb 1:3, *emphasis mine*).

> [28] And we know that *in all things God works for* [*eis* = "toward"] *the good* of those who love him, who have been called according to his purpose. [29] For those God foreknew he also predestined to be *conformed to the likeness of his Son*, that he might be the *firstborn among many brothers* [and sisters] (Rom 8:28–29, *emphasis mine*).

Passages such as the last-quoted one are often interpreted to mean that it is "good" that believers are persecuted for their faith, or that it was "good" that people connived to get Jesus unjustly executed (citing Rom 3 and 5), or that it was a "good" thing that the political and religious leaders of Jesus's time rejected him and his claims (citing Rom 9–11). But the New Testament claim about God's character is not that God demands that we call "evil" acts "good."

The promise is that God's character is such that even the most evil and most destructive situations that lovers of God find themselves in cannot keep God from working "toward good" for us. God wastes nothing experienced by those who love God. God might at times even "will" to intentionally lead us into a very "bad" situation (examples—Jesus's initial temptation in the wilderness and Jesus's execution), fully intending to bring "good" consequences from this very "bad" situation.

God does not want people to do evil. God does, however, plan for the evil choices people might or will make. And God is always prepared to catch those choices up into

---

9. King, *Strength to Love*.

God's goals and purposes. No situation need ever be wasted! That is God's character in action, and Jesus lived accordingly. Now that this character of God has been fully completed in Jesus, the "firstborn," Paul trusts that it will be God's gift to many of Jesus's "brothers and sisters" as well.

Another passage that I think is a claim that the relationship between Jesus and God was, and is, a revelation of the character of God is often interpreted very differently.

> [5] Thomas said to him, "Lord, we don't know where you are going, so how can we know the way?" [6] Jesus answered, "*I am the way and the truth and the life. No one comes to the Father except through me.* [7] If you really knew me, you would know my Father as well. From now on, you do know him and have seen him." [8] Philip said, "Lord, *show us the Father*, and that will be enough for us." [9] Jesus answered: "Don't you know me, Philip, even after I have been among you such a long time? *Anyone who has seen me has seen the Father*. How can you say, 'Show us the Father'? [10] Don't you believe *that I am in the Father, and that the Father is in me*? The words I say to you are not just my own. Rather, it is the *Father, living in me*, who is doing his work (John 14:5–10, *emphasis mine*).

We looked at this passage briefly in relationship to "knowing" God, but it is especially relevant to the question of how God's character is revealed through Jesus. It is Jesus's character as a human, relating faithfully to God, that uniquely reflects God's character and allows God to more fully reveal God's character as "Father." God's relationship with Jesus reveals what an incredibly faithful Father God is to us humans, when we allow it. John 14 certainly is not a discussion of Christianity compared to world religions. It is a condemned man's last supper with his closest allies. He assures them that, although all hell is about to break loose, they will soon see that living the *way* Jesus lives leads to seeing the *truth* concerning what a faithful Father (Abba) God is—a Father who works toward good for God's faithful child who loves God, even in the worst possible situations. In fact, they are about to see that the relationship Jesus has with God reveals *life*, even in the face of horrendous death.

Romans 6–8 extends to believers the claim of John 14:10, "I am in the Father, and the Father in me," by claiming that "you are in the Messiah," and "the Messiah is in you." John 17:21 made a similar assertion: "As you, Father, are in me, and I am in you, may they also be in us, so that the world may believe that you have sent me." 1 John 3:24 and 4:12–16 explicitly claims incarnation for Jesus's followers in a manner very similar to how Jesus claimed it for himself in the Gospel of John—we live in God, and God lives in us. If—a huge *if* given Christian history—we follow Jesus in daily living, we too will become more and more the incarnation of the character of God.

The way these declarations about what God has done through Jesus are extended to Jesus's followers shows that they are fully embedded in Jesus's humanness. That does not mean these claims are diminished; rather, it means that humanness in full relationship with God has far more potential than we can imagine. As "the firstborn," Jesus is the fully unique expression of what it means for a human to be "in the image of God." In imaging God, Jesus expresses fully the character of God in purpose, desires, words, actions, and relationships. In short, Jesus is God's first completed human, who lived all of life as an expression of the presence of God in human life. "*Therefore*, God has *highly exalted* him" (Phil 2:9, *emphasis mine*).

I love experiencing humans responding to other humans with the character of God. Years ago, my fellow pastor left our Fellowship to pursue a Harvard law degree. Then he used that law degree to work for human rights and justice, first in Ecuador and then in Washington, DC. As another pastor in town joked, "He is the only person I know who pursued a Harvard law degree so he could make even less money than he did as a pastor." It was true, and our pastoral salaries at the time were very small.

Recently, another member of our Fellowship left her teaching job to become a mentor for prisoners. She is determined to help these prisoners discover the wonderful gifts that they do not yet know they have. Ellen is concerned about the extent of our current mass incarceration and about the racial bias involved. She contextualizes her choice with these words:

> As a white person, I live with privileges that I didn't earn; my friends who are people of color deal with pain that they didn't earn either. If we act like these unearned privileges and pains aren't circulating in our world, we're at best naïve and at worst complicit in their continuance. And whether we're receiving the privileges or the pain, we're still part of a system that clearly is not God's will. (Used by permission.)

Another delightful young sister gives five years of her life teaching in North Korea because, even though she cannot mention God, she can attempt to show the Jesus-Way-of-life-and-love to young North Koreans. A recently married couple adopts two children from a home that is destroying them. A young mother with deadly cancer holds on through several years of excruciating pain, determined to see her children through their teens and to be sure that, before she dies, they will clearly hear how much Jesus loves them. Friends and family who have been blessed with more resources than they ever expected to steward see these resources as a God-given opportunity to incarnate the wonderful song by Caedmon's Call and "*Share the Well*" with others.

Another couple decides that, rather than the new "empty nest" and children's college graduations being an opportunity to add a second salary, it is an opportunity to use this new gift of time and resources to work for racial equality in our society, which is permeated with systems that protect and promote White supremacy and White privilege. Many very busy friends took time every day to pray for my wife as she journeyed through illness and toward her death.

Undoubtedly, many of you could add numerous stories of your own. My point here is that when Jesus imaged God's character in the way he treated other humans, he was expressing God's goal for how to be human. He was living as God's first completed human. His "God-likeness" was being expressed, not through being something other than human, but by being really and truly human. Jesus is one of us. The way he lived (and now lives) is how one lives who knows that God is our Father. Living this way is the way we humans can experience God as our Abba. When we let Jesus be our model for expressing that character in our relationships with others, we too are expressing tastes of what it means to become more completely human—more in the image and likeness of God.

Jesus Is the Expression of the Mission of God in Human History.

Throughout the New Testament, the writers present Jesus as God's ambassador, whom God sent on a mission on behalf of "the kingdom of God." The following are only a few of many possible examples.

Jesus says in Matthew 15:24–26 that he has been "sent" to the house of Israel, and that it would not be "good" to forget this God-ordained priority. Soon in this emotion-packed event, Jesus begins to be torn between the wisely limited mission to Israel that God has assigned him—no human can do everything he or she would like to do—and his compassion for others created in God's image who are outside the house of Israel.

True, the ultimate purpose of that mission is God's love for the world (Matt 28:18–20; John 3:16). However, unlike many of us, Jesus is clear that attempting to try to do everything that sounds good is to fail to accomplish what is necessary. But this time, Jesus chooses not "the good" (Matt 15:26) of his general assignment, but a response to the specific and overwhelmingly passionate love this Canaanite mother exudes for her daughter. I love this passage that shows Jesus wrestling with God's mission to Israel in tension with God's mission to love the world, which meant deciding how best to love this desperate mother without destroying his God-given ministry.

Another claim that Jesus is enacting God's mission occurs in John 5:17, when Jesus heals on the Sabbath. He summarizes his life of faithfulness as watching and listening to see what the Father is doing, and then getting involved. He then relates this way of living to carrying out the Father's mission—"For the very work that the Father has *given me to finish*, and which *I am doing*, testifies that *the Father has sent me*" (John 5:36, *emphasis mine*). Doing the work and mission of God is also the reason Jesus gives for healing on the Sabbath in Mark 3:1–6. Importantly, both the event in John and the one in Mark describe Jesus as prophetically participating in God's caring for the hungry, sick, disabled, and oppressed (Luke 4:17–21).

Hebrews 13:11 identifies Jesus as God's faithful "apostle," which could also be translated *ambassador*. Again, Jesus is said to share this mission by delegating this "sending by God" to others (Matt 10:40–42, 28:18–20; John 20:21; Acts 1:8; 2 Cor 3:3–11, 5:17–21; 1 Thess 1:7–10).

Jesus Is "the Way" to "Walk" into More of God's Presence Now and into God's Future.

Jesus saw life as a journey, so choosing to *walk* the right road was important. This had to be a meaningful metaphor in a world where a very large percentage of all travel involved walking. Responding to the challenging "follow me" means to choose to see Jesus for who he is and to walk the same road. Jesus is someone who *knows the way to live* that leads to God, reveals God as a Father to other humans by living this way, and fulfills God's purpose for humanity. He embodies this "way" of life in his very being. He is "the way" (John 14:6).

This journey imagery, as applied to and taught by Jesus, has a rich Old Testament background. In the Old Testament, God's presence leads God's people along the "way" as they "walk" through life's various situations (for a few examples see Exod 13:21; Pss 1:1–6, 18:30–32; Prov 2:8, 20). Israel is to *follow the cloud* of God's presence, as they journey in the wilderness. God's people are *to walk in the way that brings life,* or conversely, *not to walk the paths that bring death.* This type of instruction as a guide for practical living appears more than 30 times in the book of Proverbs alone.

When we move into the New Testament, the journey language is often emphasized by the invitation/command to "follow," or "follow me." Matthew seems almost to define being a "disciple" as "following" Jesus.[10]

Perhaps less well-recognized than "follow me," yet very significant in this context of journeying with Jesus, are the uses of "the way," "the walk," "the road," and "the path." Each of these images stresses Jesus's pioneering and trailblazing humanity. He is God's revelation of who we humans were created to be, how we are meant to live, and where God's future humanity is headed.

Jesus does not just teach "the way"; he *is* the embodiment of the journey into God's presence and God's future for humanity. He *is* the embodiment of "the new and living way" into God's holiest presence; his faithful life is our way to go there without fear (Heb 10:19–22). The teaching and the person, the words and the actions, the following and the relationship all blend into one. Jesus is the way. To follow his teachings is to be with him in person. To live Jesus's "way" as a trusting and obedient human is to open yourself to life as a journey toward experiencing more and more of God, as the "Father" who loves Jesus and loves you.

Jesus's teaching, and his living example, showing "the way," are filled with the dynamic tension that is so much a part of all of his life. On the one hand, journeying through life with Jesus is the way for the weary and worn out to find real "rest." It is a way to live that is lighter and less burdensome than any other way to journey through life (Matt 11:28–30).

On the other hand, following almost any other road might at first seem much easier than following the Jesus road. Jesus, following Old Testament precedent,

---

10. Franzmann, *Follow Me*, v.

describes the road, or way, that God wants humans to follow as one that a person does not just happen upon, nor is it one that God forces us to take; rather, "the road less-traveled" is one that demands choices, focus, and intention.

> [13] Enter through the narrow gate. For wide is the gate and *broad is the road* that leads to destruction, and many enter through it. [14] But small is the gate and *narrow the road* that leads to life, and only a few find it (Matt 7:13–14, *emphasis mine*).

Prophetically, Zechariah proclaimed Jesus's coming as the way God would "guide our feet into the path of peace" (Luke 1:79), but, with equal prophetic force, Jesus warned that following him could often bring rejection in our relationships, rather than the peace we long for (Matt 10:34–39). Obviously, a follower of Jesus makes a big mistake to think that Jesus means the journey will be easy or that experiences of grace will always come cheaply. Still, the relationship God and Jesus share is the life-journey the rest of us humans are being called to participate in, and it is the way of life, peace, mercy, grace, and redemption.

(For a few of the many other possible examples of the New Testament emphasis on Jesus as the "way" to "walk," *see* Mark 1:2–3, 7:31, 8:27; John 8:12, 12:35, 14:4–6; Acts 9:1–2, 16:7, 18:25–26; 19:8–9, 23, 22:4, 14, 22; Rom 6:4, 8:4; Eph 2:2, 2:10, 4:1, 4:17, 5:2, 8, 15; Jas 5:20; and 1 John 1:7, 2:6.)

Jesus Is the "Word of God," "the Light of God," and the "Life of God."

Various New Testament writers speak of the scriptures, as well as the orally preached Good News, as "the word of God." Hebrews 1:1–3 and the Johannine writings are emphatic about presenting Jesus himself as the incarnation of "the word of God." In fact, the prologue to John's Gospel is built around describing God's revelation as "word," "light," and "life."

The letter of 1 John continues to emphasize these same gifts that God gives humans through Jesus. In fact, all three descriptions of what God has given us through Jesus appear in the opening of the letter.

> [1] That which was from the beginning, which we have heard, which we have seen with our eyes, which we have looked at and our hands have touched— this we proclaim concerning the *Word* of *life*. [2] The *life* appeared; we have seen it and testify to it, and we proclaim to you the eternal *life*, which was with the Father and has appeared to us. . . . [5] This is the message we have heard from him and declare to you: God is *light*; in him there is *no darkness* at all (1 John 1:1–2, 5, *emphasis mine*).

The description of Jesus as "the word of God" continues into the book of Revelation, where Jesus is described as God's final communication concerning this age of human history and the judgment it is under. He is God's word, which will end the rule of the rebelling and demonic institutions and begin the rule of God in God's new age of human history: "He is clothed in a robe dipped in blood, and *his name is called The Word of God*. The armies of heaven were following him. . . ." (Rev 19:13-14, *emphasis mine*). And although Revelation does not emphasize light and life as often, Jesus is also the source of life for other humans in Revelation (2:10), and the source of God's light for us as well (21:23-24).

These themes of Jesus as the source of God's "word," "light," and "life" appear in various ways throughout the New Testament. And, as we find again and again in the New Testament, because of their relationship with Jesus, his followers also become the source of God's word (2 Cor 3:3, 5:19-20), God's light, (Matt 5:14-16; John 1:9; 2 Cor 4:6), and God's life for others (1 John 4:12, 15).

Jesus Is God's Revelation of the Meaning of Human History.

In a variety of ways, the New Testament writers claim that the "ages" of human history are to be understood in the light of what God has done in human history through Jesus. In Jesus, God begins to end the old age of human history, and in Jesus, God starts to begin the new age of human history.

The writer of Hebrews starts his letter emphasizing this claim. Hebrews identifies Jesus as the beginning of the end of the old age that cannot last, and as the beginning of the new age that *will* last. The "last days" of the old age begin with Jesus, and God "*made the ages (aiōnas* in Greek)" through Jesus by beginning the new age in him as well (Heb 1:2, *see* 9:26). This break in God's history with us humans is so dramatic that even the heroes and heroines of faithfulness prior to Jesus had to wait for the renewal and completion/perfection of humanity that God brought through Jesus before they could be brought fully into the presence of God. The fullness of the meaning of their own faithfulness at their time in history could not be revealed to them until God's response to Jesus's faithfulness revealed the full meaning.

> [39]These were all commended for their faith [and/or faithfulness], yet *none of them received what had been promised.* [40]God had planned something better for us so that *only together with us would they be made perfect* [or, "complete," *teleiōthōsin* in Greek] (*emphasis mine*, Heb 11:39-40).

When Paul wishes to outline human history from its beginning to its final goal, he outlines it in terms of what God intended to do through Jesus, and then what God has done through Jesus (Rom 5:12-21). Each of these stages of human history finds its meaning in what God has now revealed in Jesus.

Revelation 5 describes Jesus as the "lion" who is a "lamb." Only this lion–lamb can open the sealed scroll that resides in the hand of God. This imagery is another dramatic way of claiming that human history can make sense only in the light of God's revelation through Jesus. The *telos* (end goal) of a history that turns a human like Jesus into a sacrificial lamb has been revealed. It reveals both the brokenness and the wonder of being human. God accepts the human sacrificial lamb, not because of the evil intent of those humans who gladly sacrificed him, but because of the faithfulness of the human who offers himself as the sacrifice on their behalf. In response, God exalts the sacrificed Lamb as the victorious Lion of Judah, who begins a new age in human history.

All of these different ways of describing what the relationship between God and Jesus has brought about in human history share the paradigm of the new crashing into the old in the middle of history. Jesus's relationship with God is the pivotal point in human history that reveals God's purpose in what went before and what comes after. Beginning with Jesus, we are now living in the *last days* of this age, as well as in the beginning stage of *the life of the age to come*. And, be clear, says Jesus: the old wineskins cannot possibly contain the new wine that flows from Jesus (Luke 5:37–39).

Jesus Is the Fulfillment of God's Incarnation of Both Israel and "Adam/Humanity."

Another way Jesus is exalted in the New Testament writings involves the claim that Jesus is God's "new Adam/Human" and God's new Israel as well. The New Testament writers do not see Jesus as evidence of God's rejection of Israel, but rather as God's sustained choice of "Israel." Similarly, Jesus is not God's rejection of sinful humanity, but rather God's on-going creation of "humanity/Adam" through the "last Adam," who is the "new Adam." As William F. Albright and C. S. Mann maintained, the recapitulation of Israel's history and mission is an important interpretive paradigm for understanding Jesus in the Gospel of Matthew.[11]

N. T. Wright maintains much the same thing concerning the Gospel of John when he points out that Jesus fulfills the temple, the Jewish festivals, and "the entire story of Israel."[12] I think seeing Jesus as the "fulfillment" of Old Testament patterns is also an important interpretive key for several other New Testament books. We will explore that possibility in several upcoming chapters. In this section, the emphasis is on the fact that one of the reasons given for God's exaltation of Jesus is that Jesus fulfills, renews more than replaces, what is lacking in Adam and in Israel.

The following are just a few of the many New Testament passages that build on the understanding that God's relationship with humanity and with Israel has been drawn to a single focal point in God's relationship with Jesus. As we will examine more extensively in a later chapter, this is one of the main points of the designation *Messiah*—the one anointed by God to represent the rest of us humans in the presence of God and to represent God in the presence of us humans. Kings, prophets, and

---

11. Albright and Mann, *Matthew*, LV, 8.
12. Wright, *Broken Signposts*, 115.

priests were anointed as God's agents to stand before God on behalf of humans, and before humans on behalf of God. This anointing for service to God is brought to astounding fulfillment in *Jesus the Messiah* [anointed one]. Jesus is an ambassador from humanity before God and an ambassador from God among humans.

The following quotations are explicit claims that Jesus is the fulfillment of God's goal in choosing the people of Israel, who were often identified as "sons" or as "son" of God in the Old Testament.

> [26] You are *all sons of God* through faith in [or, through the faithfulness of] Jesus Christ, [27] for all of you who were baptized into Christ have clothed yourselves with Christ. [28] There is neither Jew nor Greek, slave nor free, male nor [Greek *kai* = "and"] female, for *you are all one in Jesus Christ.* [29] If you belong to Christ, then *you are Abraham's seed*, and heirs according to the promise. . . . (Gal 3:26–29, *emphasis mine*).
>
> 6 *Because you are sons* [children], God sent the Spirit of his Son into our hearts, the Spirit who calls out, *"Abba*, Father." [7] So you are no longer a slave, but a son [child]; and since you are a son [child], *God has made you also an heir* (Gal 4:6–7, *emphasis mine*).

Paul believed that the relationship between God and Jesus allowed God to create a new humanity and a new family of Israel in which neither ethnicity, nor gender, nor social status markers were our primary identity. Our primary identity is determined by "adoption" into the family relationship shared by Jesus and God.

In the passage from Romans that follows, Paul maintains that the way to understand what God has done through Jesus is to understand it as a recapitulation and renewal of the relationship between God and Adam ("humanity"). The emphatic relatedness of Adam and Jesus as fellow humans is as stark as is the difference. Each of them is related to us, and each became capable of passing his life on to the rest of us humans. In God's relationship with Jesus, God has given humanity a new start, a new age, a renewal. *Not only is Jesus God's antidote for what has happened to us humans, he is also the embodiment of the renewal of humanity.* Although Paul often uses masculine language in ways that bother our feminist instincts, it is worth noting that, in 5:19, Paul assigns the initiation of the human descent into alienation from God not to "the woman," but to "the one man."

> [17] For *if, by the trespass of the one* [human], death reigned through that *one*, how much more will those who receive *God's abundant provision of grace and of the gift of righteousness reign in life through the one human* [*anthrōpos*], *Jesus Christ*]. [18] Consequently, just as the result of one trespass was condemnation *for all men* [*anthrōpous*], so also the result of one act of righteousness was justification that *brings life for all men* [*anthrōpous*]. [19] For just as through the disobedience of the *one* the many were made sinners, *so also through the*

> obedience of the one man [*anthrōpos*] *the many* will be made righteous (Rom 5:17–19, *emphasis mine*).

The writer of Hebrews also thought Jesus's covenant relationship with God, and his full membership in humanity, made sense of God's original purpose for humanity. Now we can see God's one completed human, but he is the first of many more. In Jesus, God's creation of humanity is renewed through God's human agent Jesus—firstborn among many "brothers and sisters," who "all share one Father" with him. Through him, they too will be "crowned with glory and honor" that God always intended to give to humans, as the meditation on Genesis 1 in Psalm 8 had declared. The writer's exegesis of Psalm 8 makes it clear that he understood Psalm 8 not to be a unique prophecy applying only to Jesus, but a prophetic promise concerning God's intentions for many humans. Jesus is both God's means and God's model for others, but by no means the only human to whom this promise was given.

> ⁶ But there is a place where someone has testified: "What is man that you are mindful of him, the son of man that you care for him? ⁷ You made him a little lower than the angels; *you crowned him with glory and honor* ⁸ and put everything *under his feet.*" In putting everything under him, God left nothing that is not subject to him. Yet *at present we do not see everything subject to him.* ⁹ *But we see Jesus,* who was made a little lower than the angels, *now crowned with glory and honor* because he suffered death, so that by the grace of God he might taste death *for everyone* (Heb 2:6–9, *emphasis mine*).

The writer continues in Hebrews 2:10–18 to make it clear that this glory of God was always intended for many other humans, not only for Jesus. In fact, he wants the reader to understand that Jesus is the first perfected (completed) human (2:10). Then he stresses that Jesus is also the means by whom God will incorporate many brothers and sisters into salvation, glory, and the holy family of God. Jesus is not ashamed of us, because we share the same Father (2:11), and, in fact, Jesus is so embedded in our humanity that he is "like us in every way" (2:17). Jesus's exaltation is not because he is other than human, but rather he is the fulfillment of everything "Adam" and "Israel" could potentially become. He is both God's means and God's model for what God intends *human* to finally mean—the exalted one who comes before God "with the children God has given me" (Heb 2:13).

NEVER TO BE DIMINISHED

Living day to day desiring to thankfully honor and exalt Jesus as he deserves is fundamental to what it means to long for continued growth as a follower of Jesus. My emphasis throughout this book flows from my personal experience that the more I come to understand Jesus as genuinely one of us, as God's firstborn human in God's forever human family, the more I come to love and honor him. The closer Jesus becomes to me; the freer I am to experience his presence in daily life. It is the world he lived in as well.

The New Testament tells us that the One God over all of humanity, the God of Abraham, Moses, Ruth, and Mary, who is also "the God and Father of our Lord Jesus the Messiah," wants the following list of blessings—and more—for each of us.

1. We can see the character, the mission, and the goal God has for humans when we see Jesus for who he really is as one of us.

2. We can understand, and begin to experience, what humanity is intended to be by seeing Jesus.

3. We are free to accept God's gift of forgiveness of our sins because of the relationship between God and Jesus and the relationship between Jesus and the rest of us humans.

4. When we bow before Jesus as the one God has exalted to share God's reign, we please God.

5. When we trust and obey Jesus, we are also trusting and obeying his God and Father.

6. When we follow Jesus, listen to Jesus, and live like Jesus, we are on the path God desires for us.

7. What we receive from Jesus, we receive as a gift from God.

8. We are called to continue God's mission with Jesus's presence among us through the work of the Holy Spirit.

9. We are called to wait with expectation for the day when the inauguration of Jesus as our King, who is our Firstborn Brother of God's renewed humanity, is brought to completion, never again to be diminished by anyone.

10. We are to long for our own journey into completed humanness to be brought to fruition when we will be fully included in Jesus's exalted relationship with God forever as God's forever human family, made up of humans in the image of God.

It is my intention that everything in this book would provide an encouragement to you (and to me) to continue looking for more and more ways to exalt Jesus as God intends. That is clearly the will of "the God and Father of our Lord Jesus the Messiah."

My prayer: Jesus, it is true that we will never be able to say enough wonderful things about you! Thank you for your faithfulness as God's means and God's model for saving us from our individual and corporate self-destruction. I love you. More importantly, thank you for loving us, including me.

7

Personal Trust and Debt to Jesus

Context is always important to understanding, and like everyone else's, my background and my experiences in life influence my understanding of both God and Jesus. In fact, our backgrounds and later experiences influence how we perceive almost everything in our lives. I wish all authors of nonfiction books, no matter the topic, would tell the readers some of their personal experiences that led them to write. Writing about God, Jesus, Scripture, and life has never exempted anyone from the fact that we see through a lens at least partially constructed by the roads we have walked. The following is an attempt to make transparent to you a bit of my background and experience that colors everything I have written to this point and everything that will follow.

WHY I DO NOT TRUST THE LABELS WE CHRISTIANS USE

I was raised in a relatively conservative Protestant denomination that claimed to be nondenominational. Long before my time, what had begun in the 1800s as a *Christians-only* movement had in many local churches morphed into a stance closer to "We are the only Christians." Or at minimum, "We are the only Christians who have it right." Thankfully, most of the professors in the college and seminary I attended were not bound by that narrow exclusivism.

    The foundation of my love for the Bible I owe to my family and my denominational background. I completely rejected that background as a teenager and continued to do so as a young electrical engineering student at the University of Tennessee. However, when I began my search to see whether I could believe in God, I turned to the only source I knew at the time. Because the Christian college I was familiar with required that all males who enrolled desire to be pastors, I signed a document stating that I wanted to be a pastor. I remember praying: "God, if you are real, I think you will understand." I followed that prayer with the thought, "And if there is no God, it won't matter that I lied anyway." I certainly did not wish to be a pastor.

I graduated from the college, a fairly legalistic Christian, tempered somewhat by my much more loving young wife, who played a major part in drawing me toward God and toward Jesus. Both the way I treated her and the way I thought about God showed that I still had a lot to learn about "God is love" and "love your neighbor as yourself." To be honest, so did many of my professors and fellow students. Most were good people, but there was often a narrowness about how God's grace and mercy were understood.

By the time I graduated from seminary with two graduate degrees, I was what I would now label a somewhat openminded, conservative Christian. I had also become a protégé of one of my professors, who had hopes that I would join him as a professor in his department after I finished a doctorate. At that point, it seemed very important to me to find out whether my faith was genuine enough to survive in the *real world*. I didn't yet understand that the university world was often no more, or less, *real world* than the Christian school world.

Studying, living, and ultimately pastoring in an elite Big Ten University community soon taught me a new lesson. I found some of the more liberal and progressive Christian leaders in the community to be a breath of fresh air concerning how they viewed other humans who were not Christian, systemic social justice issues, and the theological and historical developments within the Bible. On the other hand, I was astounded by how closedminded and rigid many of those *open-minded* Christian leaders could be about their low views of God's presence, God revealing God's-self through the Scriptures, Jesus's resurrection, and Jesus actually being alive now. Several of my fellow book-study pastors loved the writings of Bishop Shelby Spong. I appreciated Spong's desire to move away from anti-Semitism and closedmindedness. On the other hand, I found myself asking, "Why be Christian at all if you believe, and do not believe, what Christians like Bishop Spong believe and do not believe?"[1]

Simultaneously with these experiences, I was also finding a great deal of both joy and challenge in my relationships with people who were influenced by the *Jesus People* movement, the Charismatic movement, and the Counterculture movement. In these contacts, I experienced important new ways of seeing God at work, side by side with attitudes and actions I thought were quite off base.

After a decade or so of wrestling, I arrived at what I now think should have been obvious to me from the beginning of my search. There are people in every nook and cranny of Christian circles who care deeply about trusting God's grace through Jesus and about following Jesus's way of daily living. There are also people in every one of those same nooks and crannies who call themselves Christian for some other reason. My search also brought me into contact with quite a few people who, for various reasons, do not want anything to do with Jesus. Sometimes these reasons are quite understandable and even caused by us Christians. To my continuing amazement,

---

1. Spong, *New Christianity*.

some of these folks live more Jesus-like lives than most of us who claim to follow Jesus. Only God will ever be able to sort things out. I know I cannot. Thankfully, I do not need to do so.

I TRUST THE EVIDENCE, BUT I KNOW I CANNOT PROVE THAT JESUS LIVES.

I have come to trust that the New Testament claims we have been, and will be, examining in this book concerning Jesus are genuinely embedded in the real history of God with humanity. I trust these claims more than I trust any other claims about the real meaning of human history or the purpose for creation.

Can I, or anyone else, prove conclusively beyond any doubt that these events really occurred in human history? No. Neither can anyone prove conclusively beyond any doubt that the many events that they believe have occurred without God, or without Jesus, in human history or in "natural" history occurred in precisely the way they think they did. To our chagrin, when we search for "proof beyond doubt," we find that we cannot rerun history with video.

And, perhaps more to our chagrin, we are finding out that even video evidence is characterized by the limitations of when it starts, where it is stopped, what context is included and not included, where the camera was relative to the events, and even whether or not the video record has been tampered with and doctored. Similar issues obtain with all historical records. That does not mean that genuine historical memories do not exist. My philosophy professor who began the graduate class on the philosophy of history with the comment, "There is no such thing as history," was wrong. The corporate and individual memories from the past are not all manufactured, nor are they all garbled beyond usefulness. Many reflect reality; however, *unquestionable proof of authenticity is never attainable.*

All humans must finally take a step of faith, and live, trusting a master story they cannot "prove beyond any reasonable doubt." The big picture narrative of those who report history, and of those of us who attempt to decipher it now, is never *provable* beyond doubt. Let's be clear: none of the issues I am mentioning are relegated only to religion, not even only to the specific religions that are more dependent upon historical claims. Everyone's master paradigms, including the most skeptical, the most religious, the most atheistic, the most cynical, or the one claiming to be the most scientific, are based on faith—trust that cannot be proven beyond doubt. Of course, we all want as much certainty as possible in the areas of life that matter most to us. That is a proper goal. Trying to develop proofs that are beyond questioning is a foolish goal.

I believe that God intentionally created the world so that trust is not optional—everyone must have faith. The only choice I have is who I will choose to trust. Will I put my most fundamental trust in my personal interpretation of my individual experiences, my culture's interpretation, my mentor's interpretation, my leader's interpretation, my subculture's interpretation—or God's revealed interpretation? Of course, "God's revealed interpretation" must humbly include: "as I understand and trust God" and "as I understand and trust revelation." You have the same options. Everyone makes the choice about what is the most basic master story about reality. The New Testament writers invite us to choose to place our trust in "the God and Father of our Lord Jesus the Messiah."

The Old Testament comes to us as a record of the relationship between God and Israelite/Jewish people. Everything in the New Testament claims to be built on that Old Testament background and then to flow from the relationship shared by God and Jesus. It is the depth and breadth of their relationship that led to God raising Jesus of Nazareth from death and exalting Jesus to Lordship over this age of history. Do I find it to be an audacious claim? Certainly. But do I find it to be an impossible claim? No! I even find it to be coherent and consistent within its own context, but that is not the same as being beyond questioning.

The same issues confront us when we focus on the New Testament claims about Jesus and his resurrection. The work and lives of three brilliant scholars provide an illustration of how this works. Each scholar responds intelligently to the claim that God raised Jesus from death into continuing human life. Each of their responses shows us that something is at work beyond the raw data. The lens of the master story of reality each author holds to be true is always at work as they process claims about Jesus's resurrection. That lens will continue to dominate the work of each scholar, unless some experience leads him to entertain the possibility that a new master story of reality is more trustworthy.

Before looking further at the conflicting conclusions these three scholars reach, I need to be clear about what I am not saying. Some readers might be worried that I am maintaining that everything is relative and there is no absolute truth. Others might be celebrating that I am saying everything is relative and there is no absolute truth. You would both be wrong about what I am attempting to express.

I am maintaining that God's revelation of truth is, above all else, a human person—Jesus, who he is, and how he lived. Instructions, doctrines, commandments, and reasons are all important, but God's truth is ultimately revealed in God's relationship with a human person—Jesus. The rest of these truths are completely true only when they are properly related to what God has revealed in that person (John 1:14–17, 3:16–21, 6:32, 7:18, 14:6, 15:1; Eph 4:21; 1 John 5:20; Rev 19:11). What God revealed in Jesus is the Truth about why we humans are here and where God is going with human history. That is the Truth to which God has related all other truths that have been, are being, and will be revealed.

I am saying that in a very important sense, but not the way that it is often meant by those who espouse relativism or those who oppose it, all truths are relative—relative to the True God. It is only when truths are in a proper relationship to God that they are true truths. Otherwise, all of the truths we learn, discover, or even have revealed to us are only partially true. In fact, they are always partially broken truths.

Only when what we know to be true is in a proper relationship with the Living God is it truth that is being brought toward truth that is completely true. True truth is always relative—to God—absolutely! And, because I am never completely related to God in all my thoughts and actions, I never experience absolute truth. But, thank God, we can be on the way!

An example of relating a truth to God so that it becomes a bigger truth is adaptation (evolution). When Darwin first started describing the process as likely, some influential Christians were excited. Then Thomas Huxley and others began to herald evolution as proof that we do not need God. Soon, many Christians reacted and began saying one cannot believe evolution is true and be faithful to God. This was such a sad move. Just think of the truths we learn about God when we see the amazing abilities to adapt that God built into the creation.

We learn that God is an amazing artist, craftsperson, animal lover, plant lover, and engineer. We learn that God, like many creative humans, loves each step of the process of creating, not just the completed work. In fact, the creation process is still ongoing, and the Creator must still be enjoying the process. Of course, there is still so much to learn about the creation. Let's look forward to seeing how what we learn teaches us more about the Creator. I trust that nothing we learn will ultimately prove to be either unrelated to the One True God or unrelated to what God has done through Jesus. To be clear, I am not encouraging the big mistake Christians often make in attempting to use the latest discoveries to *prove* God's existence. I am encouraging a patient excitement about allowing the creation to teach us how it reflects the glory of God (Ps 19:1-6).

Truth is defined in the New Testament as the *way* of life Jesus lived. For us that means a way of living daily—loving God, Jesus, and other humans. Of course, this includes responding to Jesus's teachings and humbly honoring God, but in action, not just as ideas. In the New Testament Truth is, above all, a way of life that models the way Jesus lived and taught us to live. (*See* for some examples: 1 John 1:6-8, 2:4, 3:18-23; 2 John 4-6; 1 Cor 13:1-13; Gal 5:6-14; Rom 13:8-10; Eph 5:9; 1 Tim 3:15; Titus 1:1; 1 Pet 1:22; John 4:23-24, 14:6, 14:15-18, 15:9-17.) Incarnating the truth God is revealing is always in process. None of us humans have arrived at complete, truthful living yet, except Jesus.

Finally, I am saying that because you and I are in a less-than-fully completed relationship with God, what we know is always partial, always partly broken, and always "a poor reflection in a mirror" (1 Cor 13:12). How we live is at best on the way toward the true purpose God has for us. Both the truth we know and the truth we live will always be partial until Jesus returns to make all things new. Again, not because there is no truth, but because truth is God's reality that draws us toward fully knowing God and loving God.

Knowing these truths about what we think we know to be truth, we should always be humble. We should always be busy seeking for more truth and for how to properly relate it to God. For a follower of Jesus, this means relating truth to what God has revealed through God's relationship with Jesus. We will not finish this task until finally we know fully as we are now fully known by God (1 Cor 13:12).

Now, back to the three scholars who look at the same data and reach entirely different conclusions. The Biblical scholar Bart Ehrman maintains that taking history seriously means that any other hypothesis concerning what happened after Jesus's death, no matter how improbable that hypothesis seems, is "more probable" than the "impossible" claim that God raised Jesus from the dead and exalted him to live and rule at the right hand of God.[2] I highly respect Ehrman's scholarship, and I do not think he is being illogical. His logic flows from the master story of reality he has chosen.

When Ehrman rejected his previous conservative Christian faith as untenable, he chose a new master story—a new faith. I appreciate his many insights, but I find his new master paradigm of reality far from compelling because of my own experiences. I assume that if the two of us were sitting here talking, he would maintain that I am misinterpreting the source of my experiences. I disagree about that, but I deeply appreciate his transparency about why he began looking for a new master story of reality. It is an honesty quite often lacking in both Christian and non-Christian scholars. Having said all of that, Ehrman's choice of a non-Christian master story that describes what he now concludes is possible, and not possible, demands a leap of trust. So does mine. So does yours.

My agnostic philosophy professor, who had agreed to become my advisor at the University of Illinois (a role neither of us stayed around to fulfill) used to remind us, "Whether there is a God or not, many really strange and seemingly impossible things have happened in human history." He said that he personally believed historical evidence favored the claim that Jesus somehow rose from death. He also thought that a god probably had nothing whatsoever to do with it. That discussion was long ago. I do not know what he would say now. My point is that I have no reason to think he was being illogical. He was processing the historical claims from the master story of reality and meaning that he had come to trust. So do I. So do you.

N. T. Wright published over 800 pages delineating why it is intellectually coherent and historically viable to trust that God *did* raise Jesus from death.[3] I agree with Wright's conclusions far more than I do with the other two examples I just referenced, but I do not claim that he is the only one of these three brilliant scholars who is logical. I know, as he does, that he has not proven beyond the possibility of doubt that God raised Jesus from death. Wright's personal experiences, and the master story of reality he has chosen to trust, deeply influence how he sees the very same data that Ehrman sees and that my grad professor saw. So do mine. So do yours.

Although I think all three scholars are pursuing logical validity, I am not arguing that all three perspectives are equally true, or that all three are equally false. I am,

2. Ehrman, *How Jesus Became God*, 173.
3. Wright, *Resurrection of the Son*.

however, facing the fact that we all operate from our trust in a master story of reality that we cannot prove beyond doubt. Ehrman, my graduate professor, and Wright are three very smart and well-read scholars, looking at more or less the same large data bank. Each sees the claim that God raised Jesus from death to live forever through a different master story, reflecting the faith paradigm of reality through which he interprets this historical data.

Given the perspective that I have just been describing, I have come to be at peace with having to give up my once deeply held desire to prove beyond a shadow of a doubt that my understanding of what God has done through Jesus was the only logical way to understand the data. In the long run, only God will be able to prove or disprove the claims made in the New Testament. Likewise, only God will be able to prove or disprove the validity of the experiences claimed by followers of Jesus since that time. On the other hand, it is important to acknowledge that these claims are coherent and consistent within the very long biblical narrative of God's involvement with humanity and with the Jewish people prior to Jesus's time. Within this master story, I have had enough experiences of that same God at work to cast my lot with that understanding of reality.

Because so often people claim otherwise, let me say this clearly again: It is not just religious people, but every human, who must choose some master story and live out of that master story, trusting and hoping that it is their best choice. There are no exceptions. Some would say we are "to freedom condemned."[4] I would say rather that God has given us the privilege of choosing who and what we will trust.

SOME SPECIFICS OF MY JOURNEY MIGHT HELP YOU UNDERSTAND MY FAITH.

God Holds It All Together.

After graduating with two seminary degrees, I decided (many years ago) to enter a university PhD program in philosophy. I wanted to see whether my trust in what God did through Jesus would survive the questions that I knew I would face. I focused my studies in epistemology (theories of knowing) in an atmosphere that rejected almost entirely what I believed to be true.

Of course, my naïve desire to have a wonderful and final answer for every important doubt and question was soon appropriately abandoned. However, I did leave the program, thinking at the time that I was headed for a PhD program in theology, and quite certain—with some new and important convictions—that not even God could get me to spend my life as a pastor *or* in the Midwest. I was now convinced that the most fundamental things I trusted to be true could never be *proven* with complete and final certainty.

---

4 Sartre, *Condemned*, 29–36.

On the other hand, it seemed clear to me that things I trusted to be true were no less, often far more, consistent and coherent than the answers and inferences I was being asked to trust as *certain*, or at least as *best guesses*, by some philosophers, scientists, ethicists, sociologists, and historians. Please note that I said "some." There are people in every discipline who believe in God, and there are people in every discipline who have chosen to follow Jesus. However, at the time, they were not welcome as professors in my department.

Many years later, I am only more convinced from experience that Jesus is alive and real. I am willing to bet my life on that reality, but I do know that it is a bet. I find trusting that the "One God" is Creator and Redeemer and is determined to bring God's "New Age" is, in my opinion, more consistent and more coherent than any other claim about reality. I think it makes sense of the world we live in better than any other understanding of why things are as they are. Having said that, I also understand why many others disagree.

Because this is a get-to-know-the-author chapter, I will share a strange personal experience. One day during that period, while I was doing graduate work in philosophy, I experienced the only waking vision of my entire life. Oddly enough, it occurred while I was looking out the window, waiting for a class lecture to begin. As I waited for a class on ethics to begin, I stood at the classroom window looking out across the quad toward the Foreign Language building. Some students were walking and others lounging in the sunshine. I thought, "OK, so what would be the difference if God really exists, or if I only think that God really exists?"

Before relating what happened next, I want to say clearly that I was not feeling anxiety, and I was not experiencing a psychological, spiritual, or rational crisis. No mental or emotional breakdown was imminent or even on the far horizon. You might choose to believe that I am not being honest about what I am about to relate, or you might choose to believe that even though I really did have the experience, God had nothing to do with it. But please don't play pop psychologist and relegate it to an anxiety attack or a faith crisis. It was not.

I was just doing what I came to the U of I to do—thinking about epistemological questions concerning why we think we know what we think we know. At that time in my life, reflecting my particular brand of conservative seminary training, I had serious doubts that people today still had God-given visions. In my theology at the time, those kinds of experiences were relegated to a few long-ago prophets. Honestly, I still find myself skeptical of many claims like the one I am about to make, but, nonetheless, onward I go with my story.

As I stood there musing over the very legitimate philosophical question that I was posing for myself, suddenly a vision was superimposed over my sight. I saw the Foreign Language building across the quad crack up and begin to disintegrate, then the quad and all the students cracked and began to disintegrate, then the window pane I was looking through began to crack and disintegrate, then I saw my mind begin to crack and disintegrate. Finally, I heard a clear voice say matter-of-factly, "That is the difference!"

I would like to say my entire life and relationship with God changed at that moment. That would have seemed a fitting follow-up. My actual response probably says more about me than I really want to know. I hope I have grown some since then. I thought, "That sure was strange." Then I found a seat and prepared to take notes.

For several years, I didn't tell my wife or anyone else about the experience. I continued with all my questions, doubts, faith, and searching with no noticeable impact caused by my experience at the window. Only several years later did I revisit that moment with some deeper realization that, as best I know—God both gave me a vision and spoke a very large truth to me. God really does hold everything together, and without that patience and grace, the cracks we see in this broken creation, in our nations and cultures, in our religions, in all of our systems, and in our individual personalities would soon result in complete disintegration.

If There Is a God, I Hope God Leaves Me Alone.

A decade prior to the experience I just recounted, I had not been not interested in God. If God existed, I saw God as a bother. Basketball, baseball, fast cars, money, girlfriends, and working just-hard-enough at school were my reality. Despite my minimal commitment to school, the University of Tennessee provided a scholarship and a coop position as an electrical engineering student. I worked every other term with the Tennessee Valley Authority, and the salary paid my school bills with some left over. One evening after work, a co-worker—in between dealing the cards and getting another beer—asked several of us "Do you believe there is, or is not, a God?" I responded, "There probably is, but if there is, I sure as hell hope he leaves me alone." Why did that conversation stick with me? Probably because no one had ever asked me that question so directly before.

About a year after my, "I sure as hell hope he leaves me alone," which I am very thankful God did not take too seriously, I began taking steps toward God. Up to that point, all of my steps since the age of twelve had been away from God. One major reason for beginning to ask myself new questions occurred as I sat in the offices of the TVA watching and listening to those much higher up the ladder than I was. They had everything I was aiming for in life, and most of them seemed bored with their lives, both at work and outside of work. I will note some of the other reasons for beginning my search in the following sections.

God Did "Save" Me Through the Human Jesus, and Some Other Humans as Well.

The phrase "Jesus saves" has been terribly misused by Christians in ways that are arrogant, judgmental, and provincial, as well as blatantly sinful and destructive at times. I have read the phrase in books on doctrine by authors who seem to think they know for certain whom God is going to be able to save and who cannot be saved. I have heard the phrase used in preaching with finger-pointing and a harsh voice. It appears on billboards, with nails in the hands of a very white Jesus, looking to me like the advertisements by lawyers offering to sue people on your behalf.

"Jesus saves!" appears on signs in front of church buildings where it will be followed the next week with another sign, damning people to hell—often with the implication "good for us; too bad about you!" Once I saw two signs hanging on a chain over the driveway leading up to a church building, one said, "Jesus saves." The other read, "Do Not Enter." That experience seemed to capture all of my worst experiences with the phrase. For these reasons, I find it difficult to use the phrase. However, I would be dishonest not to say that I personally trust and experience that "Jesus saves."

And, I would be totally dishonest not to acknowledge that my background and my personal experiences are reflected in that claim.

Would I be making that claim and writing this book if I had been born in Libya? Not impossible, but not very likely either, is it? Would I be making these claims and writing this book if my parents had been deeply hypocritical Christians, rather than for real? Not impossible, but not as likely either, is it? My background did not guarantee that I would be saying "Jesus saves," but it certainly gave me advantages that many others in the world do not have. I trust God will work that out graciously and justly for all.

God had many co-workers in God's outreach into my life. I have no way to prove it, but I have little doubt that it mattered that my parents started praying for me daily before I was born and continued to do so until the day each of them died. Similarly, the fact that through all their strengths and weaknesses each of them modeled an authentic life of seeking and serving God made them co-workers with God in influencing my life.

Carlos, a fellow basketball player, challenged me when I was a 19-year-old college student to "quit running away from God." That made me angry. I remember standing there with the basketball under my arm thinking, "Who does he think he is? I have a car; he doesn't. I have a girlfriend; he doesn't. I have a job that pays well; he doesn't." But I could not escape the truth of his words: I really didn't want to even think about God. Carlos was a part of God saving me through humans. My college basketball coach supported, encouraged, and loved me, despite my arrogance. He, too, modelled a Jesus-like love for a young man who certainly wasn't easy to love at that time. The fascination many of us Americans have with sports might not be at the top of God's agenda, but God does show up there.

On the other hand, my college coach, my fellow basketball player, some delightful aunts, and my parents were among the few bright lights in what was otherwise a deeply frustrating process of growing up around churches and Christians. With great frequency, I saw far too little love and far too much blatant hypocrisy in the Christian circles I grew up in. Often, God not only saves us *through* the influence of fellow humans, but must also save us *from* the influence of humans who claim to speak and act for God. That was definitely true in my case. I despised church and disliked most of the Christians that I knew growing up.

Most powerfully, God worked through my wife Donna again and again to save me from myself. This began when I first met her and continued throughout our more than 57 years of marriage. I have often said, "God saves me; Jesus saves me; Donna saves me! God saved me through the humanity of Jesus, and God saved me through the humanity of Donna." If the conversation continues, I make it clear that Donna could never have been God's way of saving me if it were not for her own constantly renewed relationship with God through Jesus.

She continued growing in that relationship until she died, and I trust continues now. Perhaps you can now understand a bit of why I cannot be honest except to say that my personal experience is "Jesus saves." Yes, the way "Jesus saves" has come to be used by many Christians makes me ashamed of their arrogance and lack of grace. It is repulsive. Nonetheless, the only truthful way I know to describe my life is that Jesus *saved* me, Jesus *is saving* me, and I trust that Jesus *will save* me, as well.

I am clear: none of the human saviors that God has used to help save me were substitutes for Jesus. All of them were who they were because of Jesus. It was through their humanity that I was enticed to consider, and then pursue, a relationship with the human Jesus whom the New Testament describes. For me, it was Jesus, and people who represented Jesus well, who led me toward an interest in God. It was, and is, through focusing on Jesus's relationship with God that I learned to love God—as well as I can. I admit that, all too often, I do not do so very well, but I do want to keep learning to do better.

At this point, I want to jump many years ahead. My experience over five decades now is that God almost always works through other humans to reach (*save*) us. So, it seems totally consistent with that experience to hear the New Testament authors describe Jesus as God's human Savior par excellence. In my years as pastor—yes, that was a big jump forward—many people have recounted to me how God saved them, and almost all of these stories have included God saving them through the influence of God's human agents. Some friends and acquaintances have included me in their story of how God used human co-workers in saving them from a loss of all meaning and hope in life. Knowing myself as I do, that is a clear indication to me of how amazing God is and how very human God's agents are. If *Jesus saves* includes saving others partly through me, Jesus truly is a wonder-worker.

Jesus Is the Only Hope I Have of Standing Before God with Peace and Joy.

I hope it is clear that I do not wish to stand before God and attempt to justify *on my own recognizance* how I have spent the many hours of the life that God has given me to steward. That statement includes my life as a follower of Jesus. And, it includes my decades as a pastor. Sometimes being a pastor helped in pursuing a deeper relationship with "The God and Father of Our Lord Jesus the Messiah." Just as often, it made it more difficult for me.

I have no wish to be my own advocate against the many human beings in my close circles or across the world who can justly say that I failed them. Some can point to what I did, or, perhaps even more often, can point to what I did not do. Some can point to my interpersonal failures. Some can point to my participation in and enjoyment of the many benefits derived from a nation that exploited them for military and economic reasons. Others can draw attention to my participation—sometimes naïvely, and sometimes not so naïvely—in the damaging of the God-given environment we are leaving to future generations. Still others can accuse me because sometimes naïvely, and sometimes not so naïvely, I benefitted at their expense from being a privileged White Male Christian American who is married, heterosexual, university-educated, and seminary-educated. My *IOUs* of privilege, advantage, responsibility, and personal failure are just far too many. I count on God saving my humanity through the faithfulness of the human Jesus. I do not count on myself. Nevertheless, God calls me to participate in the saving relationship between God and Jesus through which I am saved. I am even allowed to be God's agent in offering that relationship to other humans on God's behalf.

I am more than delighted to hope that, when I stand before God, it will be the grace of being incorporated into the relationship between Jesus and God that will *save* me from my own self-destructiveness. Likewise, it is being invited into their relationship that I trust will save me from the consequences of the hurt and destruction I have both knowingly and unknowingly brought upon others. I have this expectation only because of God's faithfulness and Jesus's faithfulness. I am trying to keep learning to be more faithful, but I never get it all right.

This seems like a good point to confess that the night before I wrote an earlier draft of this chapter, I finally completed a process of forgiving a person who hurt someone I love very much. At least I hope I have now completed the process of forgiving him. It took me almost a decade longer than it should have. I am a stubborn soul, but God is a patient God!

I often say, "When I find myself standing before God face to face, what I long to see is Jesus walking toward me with a smile on his face. Then I will know it's all right."

My wife often put it this way: "I just want Jesus to give me a hug; then whatever else happens will be fine." I trust that she has now had that experience, and I look forward to the smile I hope for. It is clear to me that I could never justify being allowed to live forever based on my own goodness, and I have learned to be a somewhat decent guy as far as we humans go.

All of this talk about personally being saved by Jesus is certainly not me groveling in some negative view of what it means to be human or what it means to be me. Surely you have gathered that truth from what you have read so far. I have been described as arrogant (so many times that I quit counting long ago) far more often than I have been described as wallowing in self-pity (zero times as far as I know, by anyone who knows me personally). It is the fact that we humans have so much potential—much of it unrealized and much of it wasted—that makes it quite clear to me that we need to be saved by someone who knows how to live the human life God has so graciously granted us. His name is Jesus.

Through My Growing Love for Jesus, God Tricked Me into Becoming a Pastor.

If you are tempted to think that my insistence on focusing on Jesus is because I spent 50 years as a pastor, I want to disabuse you of the thought. A better question would be how did someone who never wanted to be a pastor, someone who also lied about wanting to be a pastor in order to get into college, someone who promised his fiancée he would never consider being a pastor, end up being a pastor?

I did become a pastor because of my growing love for Jesus, but not the way many of my pastor friends became pastors. People often ask me, "When and how did God *call* you to be a pastor?" I respond by saying that I never experienced a call from God to be a minister. I did however experience being tricked by God.

Having grown up in a minister's home, I never glamorized the pastoral role. Not only did I have zero desire to be a pastor, my wife also had no wish to be a pastor's wife. Other than "faithful until death," the only other promise we made one another when we began talking about marrying was, "We will learn what we can about God at this church school we are attending, but we definitely won't go into the ministry." I had every intention of becoming a professor, either in a secular school or a seminary. She had zero intention of becoming a pastor's wife.

We kept the "faithful until death" promise through the wonderful times, and the difficult times, but we both felt as if God tricked us into a life as pastor and pastor's wife. We began a Bible study in our home while I was in the graduate philosophy program. We wanted to explore what it could be like to be in a community that genuinely encouraged and supported one another to take Jesus more seriously in daily living. We had no interest in starting a *church*.

We had both found most churches we had experienced—there had been several for each of us—to be startling failures when it came to loving other people, and when it came to encouraging one another to take Jesus seriously in the real world of daily living. We had also found that these churches consistently taught and lived the early church heresy of belittling Jews and Judaism,[5] and the original American church heresy of systemic racism.[6] We both longed for something different, something that involved the real presence of Jesus among us, and something that did not continue these tragic heresies.

The growing community that began in our living room became so exciting that I turned down what had been my dream opportunity to become a seminary professor. The president of the seminary from which I had received two graduate degrees promised the school would pay for anywhere in the world I wished to go to complete a PhD in theology if I would promise the seminary at least five years afterward. To my surprise, the vibrant small community meeting in our living room seemed more compelling to my wife and me than the generous offer.

As the Bible study became a church, we still agreed that I should not become a salaried staff member. We did not want to be pastor and pastor's wife. I continued in another position, and volunteered my time to the church. Finally, we were pressured to at least be willing to pray about being willing. We spent the rest of our adult lives in the ups and downs of my role as one of the pastors of that faith community. Even now, after retirement, it is still the community that provides spiritual support in my walk with God. In official documents, I am "Pastor Emeritus." In community life, I am "Ron," who still teaches and preaches occasionally and loves being loved by these sisters and brothers.

I love God, I love Jesus, and I love studying the Bible—even the parts I find very frustrating. I delight in learning all I can about its original cultural contexts. I love encouraging others to explore the possibility that they might also come to love God and Jesus. I also love watching people grow in their lives with God and community. I love being honored with the phrase "genuinely wants to be a follower of Jesus." I never really learned to love, though I did learn to accept, being called a "minister" or a "pastor."

I did manage to mostly put a stop to the use of "Reverend" being applied to me, because it seems clear to me that revering people like me is quite misguided. I have also learned to be at peace with the fact that many wonderful pastors and priests disagree with me on that and find the title "Reverend" to be helpful and meaningful. It took Jesus a while, too long I am sure, to teach me that I didn't always have to be right. I learned that I wasn't always right, even when I was sure I was right. Just as importantly, maybe more importantly, I learned that even when I am pretty sure I am right, I don't have to *be right* about other people's choices.

5. Simkins, *Truth, Tears*, 25–35.
6. Gushee, "White American Christianity," 3.

I Identify Far More with Following Jesus than with Being Christian.

As I mentioned in the introduction, I honestly do not know how to label myself with the current labels that tend to be used to describe where someone fits theologically. That does not derive from thinking that I am *better than* the people who identify with these different labels. I have met, heard about, and read works by many wearing these different labels who are more Christ-like than I am. I just honestly do not know which label fits me. Having said that, I have no hesitation to self-identify as someone who has been *saved by Jesus* from a life that would have otherwise been filled with destructive actions and attitudes toward others, as well as with self-destruction. Jesus *saved* me is not a religious cliché; it is just a fact of my life.

For me personally, Jesus was and still is my only path to a caring and involved God. I realize that other people seem to find other ways to God. Those experiences and claims are for God, not me, to sort out. What I do know is that I could never have turned toward God apart from Jesus. I trust God is caring and involved because I have come to trust that God is sovereign over the crosses and the resurrections of human history—and specifically over the lynching-like execution of Jesus and the resurrection that followed. For me this is what gives both history and my personal life meaning. It is also what allows me to hope expectantly that God will address and overcome all of the injustices that haunt so much of our history as humans, including the history of the church.

That is enough about me, but it did seem like a bit of personal context might help orient what you have already read and what you will read as you continue in this book. If you sense that I am not a very religious person by nature, you are definitely correct. If you trust that I am being as honest as I know how to be as I write, then you will be right in judging that, with all my failures and blind spots, with all my questions that still are not answered, I really do want to keep learning to honor and exalt Jesus better.

I want each year God continues to give me during this age of human history to be a year in which I come to know Jesus more effectively, and through him to know God better. When I have no more years left to live in this realm, I hope to honor and exalt Jesus even more, while I wait for God's future age to begin. And, when that resurrection day comes, I expect to have the opportunity to praise and honor God by honoring Jesus still more.

8

Jesus's Role as Messiah

Jesus Is Not the Only "Lord and Christ" in the Bible.

Did you know that someone other than Jesus is identified in the Bible as "My Lord and the Christ?" In 1 Samuel 24:6, David calls Saul "Lord" and "Christ." In Hebrew this was "*adoniah*" (Lord) and then twice YHWH's "*mashiach*" (messiah/christ/anointed one). In the Greek translation of the Old Testament, Saul is *kurios* and *christos* (Lord and Christ), the very same titles used in tandem to describe Jesus throughout the New Testament. Obviously, David was not identifying King Saul, who was attempting to kill David at the time, as "God," but he does see Saul as God's agent whom only God can judge.

A parallel passage occurs in 1 Samuel 26:16, where David reprimands Abner and the elite guard Abner heads for their shoddy work in guarding "their lord" and "YHWH's messiah/anointed one" (*adoniah/kurion* who is YHWH's *mashiach/kriston*). Because even an agent of God falling rapidly into a dark spiritual pit can be identified as "lord and christ," it should be clear that the background for the role "messiah/christ" fully embedded Jesus in our humanity. To a writer in New Testament times, calling Jesus "Lord and Christ/*adoniah* and *mashiach*/*kurios* and *christos*" would include as background these roles as they are applied to various agents of God in the Old Testament literature.

The Power of Roles Is Amazing.

Roles are a strange thing. Someone who has been "Barack" or "Donald" all his life is suddenly "Mr. President" to many long-time acquaintances. Some of my graduate school professors at the University of Illinois and in seminary had to be addressed as

"Doctor" and others said, "Just call me 'Roger' or 'Jack.'" (I graduated in an era when no "Rosas" or "Jills" were wanted as professors in my departments.)

A repairman would be cussing a blue streak, and then a co-worker would whisper, "He's a pastor," and immediately I would hear "Oh, sorry, Pastor." When it seemed right to do, I would respond with a smile saying that God was listening to how he treated his fellow-workers, whether I was or not, and that my role was rather secondary. Still, to the repairman, my role as pastor seemed to trump God's role as God when it came to worrying about who heard his curses.

So what are we to make of the various roles assigned to Jesus in the New Testament? Many of us have been taught to reflexively view most of the exalted roles assigned to Jesus as if they belonged only to Jesus. We tend to think that these roles separate him from our humanness. This causes some of us to diminish his humanity, and others of us to doubt that any human could actually fill the roles Jesus is credited with filling.

I maintain that a careful rereading of the biblical materials makes it clear that the uniqueness claimed concerning Jesus is his completely faithful and obedient fulfillment of these roles as a fellow human. The roles God assigned to Jesus are *uniquely fulfilled*, but they *are not unique roles* in our human history with God. In fact, they embed Jesus in our humanity and in our history as humans. This is certainly true when it comes to the role of "Messiah/Christ."

THE OLD TESTAMENT PROVIDES THE PATTERN FOR THE ROLE OF GOD'S MESSIAH—THE ANOINTED ONE.

King Saul is certainly not the only "messiah/christ" we meet in the pages of the Old Testament. The role of "messiah" is a transliteration from the Hebrew root *mashach* (anointed one). A "messiah" ("anointed one") was a relatively common agent in God's relationship with other humans in the Old Testament. Some, like Aaron and Josiah, were decent models as agents of God most of the time (Exod 30:30; 2 Kgs 23); others, such as Jehu (1 Kgs 19:16), some of Aaron's descendants (1 Sam 2), and Cyrus (Isa 45:1) were shady characters.[1]

Many, actually most, fall somewhere in between. David, the messiah king par excellence in Jewish history was anointed (made "messiah") at least three separate times to serve as God's agent king (1 Sam 16:13; 2 Sam 2:4, 5:3). David was at times a man seeking God's heart (1 Sam 13:14). At other times, he was a man who justifiably feared that God would take God's anointing spirit from him (Ps 51:11; 1 Sam 16:14). He had seen the results. What allowed him to continue to be a man seeking the heart of God (1 Sam 13:14) was not his very mixed record, but the fact that he kept turning

---

1. The "Cyrus Cylinder," discovered in the late nineteenth century, maintains in Cyrus's own words that the god Marduk made him "king of the world." Cyrus and Isaiah did not see eye to eye on this.

back to God. He did so even when it meant humbling himself in front of the world (2 Sam 12, 24; 1 Chron 28).

In addition to Aaron and his descendants, Cyrus, Josiah, Jehu, and David already mentioned, there are quite a few other "anointed ones" in the Old Testament. These "anointed ones" are human agents of God, not divine humans. "Anointing" implies that God has chosen an agent and promised to empower that agent for service to God and service to other humans on God's behalf. Many of these "messiahs" failed miserably in their God-appointed roles; others were quite faithful as agents of God.

Occasionally, an Old Testament writer spoke of future "anointed ones"—in some instances of the coming of "*the* Anointed One"—who would be filled with the Spirit of God in prophetic, kingship, and priestly roles. Far more often, the Old Testament writers used the term "anointed one" as a title for contemporary servants who had been "anointed" as agents of God—especially prophets, priests, and kings. The verbal form of the word was also used to describe the act of anointing for healing, good health, and skin care in a dry climate.

Various forms of the Hebrew word *mashach* (anoint) occur more than 100 times in the Hebrew Bible. All 39 uses of the noun *mashiach* (messiah/anointed) were translated into Greek as "*christos*." The "christ" was at times the "christ" who was a priest offering a bull in the tabernacle (Lev 4:50), the new High Priest who was the "christ on whose head the oil was poured" (Lev 21:10), or the foreign King Cyrus to whom Isaiah was to proclaim that he was God's "christ" (Isa 45:1).

Obviously, applying "Christ" to Jesus is far from unique. The title describes a longstanding pattern of roles God assigned to various humans prior to Jesus. In Jesus, God fills this role full (fulfills) of new depth and meaning. The title embeds Jesus in God's early history with humans. It does not separate him from humanity. Here are a few further examples out of many uses of "anointing" and "anointed one" as they are recorded in the Old Testament.

Priests

Exodus 28:41 Aaronic priesthood. "You shall put them on your brother Aaron, and on his sons with him, *and shall anoint them and ordain them and consecrate them, so that they may serve me as priests*" (*emphasis mine*). Psalm 133, which celebrates the oneness and unity of God's human family, does so by comparing that joy to the joy experienced when Aaron was anointed high priest to represent all of Israel before God.

Kings and Rulers

Judges 9:8 indicates that very early in Israel's history, tribal chieftains were expected to be God's "anointed ones." That role also seems to have been a mark of identity, not only for kings like Saul, David, and Solomon, but for all of the kings of Judah and Israel. The narrative concerning Jehu (2 Kgs 9–10) and the poetry about Judah's kings (Ps 89:38–39) indicate that God was often furious with the failures of God's messiahs (anointed ones). At other times, the "anointed one" is to be honored and celebrated: "He [YHWH] gives his king great victories; he shows unfailing kindness *to his anointed, to David and his descendants forever* (Ps 18:50, *emphasis mine*).

Elisha was even sent by God to anoint (declare as God's messiah) the Syrian Hazael to be the next king of Syria and to serve as an instrument of God's judgment against Israel (1 Kgs 19:15–17). As mentioned earlier, perhaps most surprising, the Persian empire-builder Cyrus the Great, who identifies himself in the *Cyrus Cylinder* as a "worshiper of Marduk" (the Babylonian god condemned in Jeremiah 50:2), is identified in Isaiah by God as "my anointed one" (Isa 45:1). This translated into the Greek Old Testament that most of the New Testament writers seem to have used as *tō christōmou*—"my Christ." This pagan, idolatrous, and arrogant king is to be God's agent (messiah) in God's renewal of Israel as a nation.

Prophets

Psalm 105:15 identifies prophets as God's messiahs (anointed ones) and scolds kings who were also God's anointed ones for despising and harming God's anointed prophets. God's prophets in general could be described as "my anointed ones" (1 Chron 16:22). A section of Isaiah begins by prophesying concerning an "anointed" servant of God who sometimes seems to be all of Israel, and sometimes one faithful agent of God who somehow embodies all of Israel (Isa 61:1). Throughout the section, God's anointed servant carries out God's mission to the oppressed and hopeless. At the beginning of his ministry and mission for God, Jesus reads from the Isaiah 61 passage and then applies it self-referentially by saying that it is "fulfilled today in your hearing" (Luke 4:16–21).

Any Faithful Servant of God

Psalm 23:5 symbolically describes God's presence and caring as "the Lord anoints my head with oil," a very important act of health care in an arid land. The Psalm speaks of God's relationship to humans, and this verse encourages all God-seeking people to see YHWH as a caregiver who "anoints" them with loving concern and protection, even when they are moving through very difficult situations.

Israel

In Ezekiel 16:9, the Prophet described God as "anointing" Israel with oil in preparation for the marriage ceremony between God and Israel. Although the "anointed one" of Habakkuk 3:13 applies to "Israel's king," the context seems to also indicate that the people of Israel are included. Warnings not to mistreat God's anointed ones appear in various parts of the Old Testament. In the passage noted earlier, David forbids his soldiers to harm King Saul because he is YHWH's anointed one (1 Sam 24:6–10). "Do *not touch my anointed ones*; do *my prophets* no harm" is a general warning about harming God's messiahs (1 Chron 16:22, *emphasis mine*).

Being "God's anointed" describes a special relationship with God and with God's mission among humans. It is also clear that the word describes titles and actions deeply embedded in the relationship various humans can have, and have had, with God. Even Saul, who ultimately fails in the role God assigned him, can still be identified as "my lord" who is "YHWH's christ." collectively as God's "messiah/christ" (anointed one).

JESUS IS GOD'S UNIQUE, AND NOT SO UNIQUE, MESSIAH.

A Translation Issue Hides Much of the Continuity in Jesus's Role as Messiah.

We all owe a lot to the good translators of the Hebrew, Aramaic, and *Koine* Greek texts of the Bible. I was once much more fluent in reading these texts in the original languages than I am now, but I still retain enough to know how thankful I am for the men and women who have dedicated their lives and talents to the work of translating the Bible well. It is a very difficult task.

Having said that, I think it is very sad that most of our English translations do not translate the various forms of the New Testament *Koine* Greek noun *christos* with various forms of the English "anointed" instead of "Christ." Doing so would make the relationship between the various forms of the verb *chriō* translated as "anoint" and "anointed," and the noun *christos* much clearer. At minimum, it would be wonderful if all the translations of the Greek *christos* were translated as "Messiah" instead of the common transliteration as "Christ."

The choice to transliterate rather than to translate usually hides some controversial issue, and in this case, it hides some of the deep connections Jesus's role as Messiah has to other agents of God designated messiah/christ in the Old Testament. It hides how deeply the title "christ" was originally embedded in humanity. Just as important, it hides how deeply Jesus is rooted in the Jewish world in which he lived.[2]

I believe this to be so important that my earlier drafts of this book changed every Scripture reference to the word *Christ* to *Messiah*. Due to copyright issues, the change needed to be noted each time, and it became too cumbersome and distracting. But please know that if I had my way, every English translation would translate *mashiach* and *christos* as Messiah—unless the translators took the even better step and always translated both as "anointed one."

---

2. Simkins, *Truth, Tears*, 1–8.

When we see that "Christ" means "Anointed One," we see plainly that assigning Jesus the role of Anointed One (Messiah/Christ) is a claim that his relationship with God allows him to completely fulfill a role God had assigned to many humans prior to Jesus. We also find that it is a role Jesus passed on to his followers.

Jesus Fulfills the Established Pattern of God's Anointed Ones as a Faithful Human, Not as Something Other Than Human.

Jesus is unique in that he fulfills and completes his role as God's anointed agent in complete trustworthiness/faithfulness. He is also unique in that Jesus is God's means of opening this role of "anointed ones" to the rest of us in new ways. He is not so unique in that this role is the fulfillment of a pattern already established in God's relationship with humans over the centuries prior to Jesus's birth. As I will illustrate in the following section, Jesus is also not unique because this role is extended in new ways through Jesus to Jesus's followers in the New Testament, who are "anointed ones" too.

The uniqueness of Jesus as "Anointed One" is the filling-full of the pattern describing a relationship between human agents of God and God; it is not in being something more than human. Richard Rohr and Marcus Borg argue that "the post-Easter Jesus"[3] or the "Universal Christ"[4] is quite separate from the human Jesus. Though I often find both Rohr and Borg to be delightful, gracious, caring, and inspiring writers, both of whom help me reflect in very meaningful ways on what God has done for us in Jesus, I think their argument does not at all reflect the New Testament claims concerning the role of "Messiah/Christ." Such a division between Jesus and the Christ is exactly the opposite of the New Testament understanding. As I hope became clear in chapter 5, several New Testament writers explicitly indicate that they understand Jesus to be human now and forever. "Messiah/Christ" is a role that continues to be fully embedded in humanity.

Not only did the Old Testament designate agents of God as "messiah," other Jewish leaders also claimed to be "messiah." In fact, Mark 13:21 says that Jesus predicted that people after him would claim, "Look, here is the Messiah," and we know they did. Although there seem to have been several others, both before and after Jesus's ministry, the most notable example, and the easiest to document with certainty, occurred when the prominent (and still highly respected) Rabbi Akiba recognized Bar Kokhba (who led the Third Jewish Revolt around 130 AD), saying "he is the king messiah."[5]

Akiba clearly did not intend to separate Bar Kokhba from being fully human; nor did Akiba believe that Bar Kokhba was somehow "God." Akiba believed that God had appointed Bar Kokhba to be God's agent in the renewal of Israel as a nation. It

---

3. Borg, *Meeting Jesus*, 15–17.
4. Rohr, Richard. *The Universal Christ*, 3–7.
5. Schama, *Story of the Jews*, 166–170.

was a sad mistake by a great Rabbi that involved him in the loss of many thousands of Jewish lives.

New Testament writers designate Jesus as "the Anointed One" more than 450 times in the New Testament writings. Only a few of these identifications of Jesus with the Greek *christos* occur in the Gospel narratives. Scholars have argued for centuries about exactly why this is so. Some call it "the messianic secret." The Gospel writers seem to indicate that Jesus wisely chose not to use the term *Messiah* early in his ministry to give himself more time to complete his *kingdom mission for God*. If it is true that Jesus did not use the term so as to give himself more time, this is one more indication that everyone in his time understood the term to embed him deeply in humanity.

The Romans were not at all concerned about executing someone whose claim to kingship had no bearing on current politics. Near the end of his ministry, being identified as a Messiah was not good for Jesus's physical health. Rome, the high priestly clan, and quite a few of the ruling elite in Jerusalem saw his role as God's "Anointed One" as a threat to the systems and structures through which they sustained their power and wealth.

After Jesus's execution and resurrection, the term "Messiah" was used freely to describe Jesus's role as God's agent. Acts and the New Testament letters use it to capture both the continuity and the discontinuity of what God was doing in God's relationship with Jesus. Jesus is one of many of God's Messiahs; he is also uniquely God's Messiah! In fact, Paul uses the term so frequently that many scholars now treat it as if it had become just a part of Jesus's name. I do not think this is true. It is almost inconceivable that someone living under Roman rule and trained as a first century Jewish rabbi could have used the term *Messiah* casually. It labeled a politically and theologically loaded role.

Every time the word was used in the New Testament, it was a claim concerning God's purpose in history and a claim that God was fulfilling the relationship God had established with various agents of God in the Old Testament. It was also a direct confrontation with the Roman Emperors who allowed no one anywhere in the Empire to be designated as "king" who was not under their direct authority. Each use was likewise a confrontation with every Jewish person who did not agree with the predominantly Jewish writers of the New Testament that Jesus was God's "Anointed One."

The following are four of the 468 references that stress the importance of the role in the New Testament claims about Jesus. Each embeds Jesus deeply in his own humanity and in ours:

> A record of the genealogy of *Jesus Christ* [the Messiah] *the son of David, the son of Abraham*: (Matt 1:1, *emphasis mine*).

The New Testament canon begins by claiming that Jesus fulfills a long-established pattern in God's history with humans. This statement also loads the phrase "Jesus the Anointed One" with political and theological meaning and controversy by identifying

Jesus as the descendant of King David, who was Israel's most successful and famous warrior king. The ante is raised even higher by the fact that it was God's covenant with David that promised that a "son of David" would forever be king over Israel and over everyone else as well (for example, see Isa 9:6–7). Imagine the reaction to that concept of a Caesar who claimed to be a son of god and the rightful ruler and lord of the world, as well as king-maker and king-breaker!

The confrontation with the current powers-that-be is clear throughout Acts. The praying community sees a sharp division between the Jews and Gentiles who violently oppose Jesus and the Jews (no Gentiles yet; they will come later in Acts) who are following Jesus, whom they believe to be the promised Jewish Messiah. They see their current struggle as in continuity with the promise in Psalm 2 that God's Anointed King would be victorious in the end. (Please note that in contrast to a lot of later Christian theology, Peter sees Gentiles as just as responsible as any Jews for the unjust execution of Jesus.)

> [25] You spoke by the Holy Spirit through the mouth of your servant, our father David: Why do the nations rage and the peoples plot in vain? [26] The kings of the earth take their stand and the rulers gather together *against the Lord and against his Anointed One*. [27] Indeed Herod and Pontius Pilate met together with the Gentiles and the people of Israel in this city to conspire against *your holy servant Jesus, whom you anointed* (Acts 4:25–27, *emphasis mine*).

Paul is so adamant that Jesus's role *as resurrected Messiah* fully embeds Jesus in our humanity that he concludes that if God does not intend to raise other humans, then God did not raise Jesus the Messiah, either.

> [13] *If* there is no resurrection of the dead, *then* not even Christ [the Messiah] has been raised.... [16] For *if* the dead are not raised, *then* Christ [the Messiah] has not been raised either (1 Cor 15:13, 16, *emphasis mine*).

The logic of Paul's two if–then statements is this: if humans cannot be raised as humans from death, then neither could Jesus the Messiah have been raised from death, because he is human. Later in the same chapter, this logic leads to identifying the risen and ruling Jesus as "the last Adam" through whom God now renews the humanity of many humans as *humans of heaven*. These *humans of heaven* are, through their relationship with Jesus "the last Human (Adam)," who is also *the human of heaven*, destined to bear the image of God forever (1 Cor 15:47–49).

The letter to the seven churches in the book of Revelation asserts that Jesus's continuing role as God's Anointed One is an ongoing ministry to "his God" and has placed him in continuity with, and fulfilment of, the faithful witnesses of the past. (Compare Heb 11:1–12:4 for an extended presentation of this same thought.) God has installed this "Anointed One" as the ruling firstborn human in God's renewed forever human family.

> [5] ... and from *Jesus Christ* [the Anointed One], who is *the faithful* witness, *the firstborn from the dead*, and the ruler of the kings *of the earth*. To him who loves us and has freed us from our sins by his blood, [6] and has made us to be a kingdom and priests *to serve his God and Father*—to him be glory and power for ever and ever! Amen. (Rev 1:5-6, *emphasis mine*).

This understanding of who the risen and exalted Messiah is fully roots Jesus as continuing in our humanity. As we note next, so does the fact that his followers come to be identified as "anointed."

JESUS'S ANOINTING IS EXTENDED BY GOD TO JESUS'S HUMAN FOLLOWERS.

One of the clearest indications that the New Testament writers saw Jesus's Messiahship as fully embedding him in our humanity is evident in their extension of that "anointing" to Jesus's followers. This extension of "the anointing" is a central point in the lengthy description of the experience of Jesus's outpouring of the Holy Spirit as recorded in Acts 2. Luke reports that Peter saw the *pouring out* of the Spirit as a fulfillment of the prophetic expectation that had appeared centuries earlier in the writing of the prophet Joel. God's promise to "pour out"—a description of anointing throughout Leviticus—God's Holy Spirit widely, with no limitations caused by gender, age, or social status, is now being fulfilled because of Jesus's relationship with God.

> [32] God has raised *this Jesus* to life, and we are all witnesses of the fact. [33] Exalted to the *right hand of God*, he has *received* from the Father the promised Holy Spirit, and he [Jesus] *has poured out* what you now see and hear. (Acts 2:32–33, *emphasis mine*).

Although Peter does not use the word *anoint*, it is this "pouring out of the Spirit" promised by Joel that Peter uses to describe what will then come to be described as the extension of God's "anointing" to the followers of Jesus throughout Acts and the rest of the New Testament. A few examples follow:

> [21] Now it is God who makes both us and you stand firm *in Christ* [the Anointed One]. He [God] *anointed us*, [22] set his seal of ownership on us, and put his Spirit in our hearts as a deposit, guaranteeing what is to come. (2 Cor 1:21–22, *emphasis mine*).

Unfortunately, the transliteration as "Christ" causes us to miss the wordplay in most English translations of the passage just quoted. Paul directly claims Jesus's anointing as the source for God's anointing of Jesus's followers with the same Spirit of God.

Jesus's success in faithfully filling the role God gave him is now demonstrated in the roles of service God is giving Jesus's followers. No one who reads the

Corinthian letters would imagine that Paul thought the Corinthians were divine beings, yet through Jesus's anointing, they too were participating in an extension of God's gift—the anointing of human agents with God's Spirit. They too, through their relationship with Jesus, were empowered by the anointing of the Spirit in their service to God and their service to other humans on God's behalf.

The writer of 1 John also describes followers of Jesus as people who have been anointed by God—"But you have an anointing from the Holy One" (1 John 2:20). Even the word *Christian* deeply embeds the Messiah or Anointed One in our humanity because his followers are called what perhaps should be translated as "the little anointed ones."

> [25] Then Barnabas went to Tarsus to look for Saul, [26] and when he found him, he brought him to Antioch. So for a whole year Barnabas and Saul met with the church and taught great numbers of people. The disciples were *called Christians* first at Antioch (Acts 11:25–26, *emphasis mine*).

It is not clear who began using the word "Christian" to identify the followers of Jesus. Perhaps its initial appearance in Acts 11:25–26 is a pejorative used by locals, or perhaps not. Either way, Jesus's title and function as "the Anointed One/Messiah" was being extended to his followers. In Acts 26:28, King Agrippa uses the term in what is probably an ironic statement, but perhaps not. Either way, it indicates that, at this point in time, it had come to be used to describe Jesus's follower by someone who was not a follower.

The only clearly positive use of "Christian" in the entire New Testament occurs in 1 Peter—that is, if you consider being told we should suffer as Jesus suffered to be a positive statement! This passage links Jesus's anointing with the anointing of his followers as God's way of empowering us humans to live faithfully and victoriously in a world filled with suffering, injustice, and evil.

> [13] But rejoice that *you participate* in the *sufferings of Christ* [the Anointed One], so that you may be overjoyed when his glory is revealed. [14] If you are insulted because of the *name of Christ* [the Anointed One], you are *blessed, for the Spirit of glory and of God rests on you*. . . . [16] However, *if you suffer as a Christian* [little *anointed one*, or *little messiah*], do not be ashamed, but praise God that you *bear that name* (1 Pet 4:13–14, 16, *emphasis mine*).

These rare uses of *Christian* in the New Testament make it obvious that the term did not become a popular designation for followers of Jesus until after the New Testament was written. Nevertheless, its usage places Jesus's followers in direct continuity with Jesus's *Messiahship/Anointing*.

Finally, note that both 1 John 2:20–27 and 4:2–3 use various forms of "anoint" and "anti-anoint" to designate Jesus, to designate Jesus's gifts to his followers, and to designate the spirit that empowers those who are fervently anti-Jesus. For our purposes, it is important to note that those who are claiming to be a part of the community of faith, but who are denying that "Jesus the Messiah has come in the flesh" (i.e., was deeply embedded in humanity) are the antichrists.

It would be difficult to imagine a statement that more deeply roots Jesus fully in our humanity than the author maintaining that *proclaiming or denying that the "Anointed One has come in the flesh" is the litmus test for whether one is "from God" or not.* Jesus's experiences of being anointed by God, and our experiences of being anointed by God because of Jesus, are not only in continuity, but anyone who denies the human continuity is actually "anti–the-Anointed-One" and "not from God" (1 John 4:2–3).

Rather than seeing the term "Messiah" as something that separates Jesus from our humanity, we should see it as a challenge to allow God to make us more like Jesus. We should also see it as the fulfillment of a pattern that God established among humans long before Jesus, a pattern that God filled full of new depth and meaning in Jesus, and a pattern that continues to be extended to Jesus's followers. Surely this comes to us today as an exciting promise and challenge. Are we presenting ourselves daily before God, ready to share in this gift of being God's anointed human agents who are empowered by the Spirit of the Messiah?

9

Jesus's Role as Son of God

Quite often, a sister or brother will say to me, "They called him 'the Son of God.' Doesn't that make it clear that they saw Jesus as something more than human?" Not really! Few descriptions of Jesus more clearly embed Jesus in our humanity than the title "Son of God." My guess is that most readers treasure relating to God as *daughter* or *son*. We are grateful this role and title did not end with Jesus. And, as is the case with most and perhaps with all of Jesus's roles and titles, this designation did not begin with him either.

THE OLD TESTAMENT PROVIDES THE PATTERN FOR SON(S) OF GOD.

Many scholars point out that the role *Son of God* embeds Jesus deeply in a relationship with God that was already established as a pattern in the Old Testament. Below are a few examples indicating that humans as *sons* of God comprise an Old Testament pattern for describing God's covenant relationships with human beings.

Israel Is the "Son of God."

Israel is sometimes identified as God's son or as the "children" God fathered.

> [22] Then say to Pharaoh, "This is what the LORD says: '*Israel is my firstborn son*, [23] and I told you, *Let my son go*, so he may worship me.' But you refused to let him go; so I will kill your firstborn son" (Exod 4:22–23, *emphasis mine*).

The following poignant introduction to the book of Isaiah is dependent for its emotional power on the understanding just noted in Exodus. YHWH relates to all Israelites of Isaiah's time as "sons of God." Although I usually appreciate the attempts by various translators to be more gender neutral by using "children" instead of "sons," here it can cause us to miss an important point. When Jesus is later designated as "God's Son," the role is the faithful fulfillment of a long-established pattern in God's relationship with Israel.

> ² Hear, O heavens! Listen, O earth! For the LORD has spoken: "*I reared children* [*benim*, "sons" in Hebrew] and brought them up, but they have rebelled against me. ³ The ox knows his master, the donkey his owner's manger, but Israel does not know, my people do not understand." ⁴ᵃ Ah, sinful nation, a people loaded with guilt, a brood of evildoers, *children* [*benim*, "sons"] given to corruption! They have forsaken the LORD (Isa 1:2–4a, *emphasis mine*).

Hosea 1:10 identifies redeemed Israel as "sons of the living God" (Hos 1:10) and as "My [YHWH's] son" (Hos 11:1). An additional example occurs in the practical wisdom literature of Proverbs. Throughout the book there is an intentional blending of the teaching role in a human father-son relationship and the teaching role God has as Father to Israel.

Specific Human Leaders and Angelic Cultural Spirits Are Called "Sons of God."

Angels or despotic kings, or both simultaneously, are designated as "sons of God" in some Old Testament writings and throughout the ancient world. Many ancient kings from various ancient cultures demanded to be designated as "God" or "son of God" and claimed to be "born of a god." The Old Testament recognizes this reality, and it rejects the idolatry associated with these claims. Nevertheless, it uses the phrase "son of God" to describe a covenant relationship that God establishes with people who are very human.

The following are examples of passages that refer to son(s) of God:

> ¹ When men began to increase in number on the earth and daughters were born to them, ²*the sons of God* saw that the daughters of men were beautiful, and they married any of them they chose (Gen 6:1–2, *emphasis mine*).

I am aware that many scholars think the "sons of God" in Genesis 6 are a part of ancient mythology, and the reference is to angelic beings who have intercourse with human women and breed superhumans. The Jewish writer of 1 Enoch (II, 6–7) interpreted and embellished the passage much that way, just before or after Jesus's ministry. I lean toward the scholars who see the designation "sons of God" to be the writer's way of describing despotic tribal chieftains who illustrate the trajectory of growing evil described throughout Genesis 3–6. This interpretation says that the degeneration in human relationships had finally reached a point so unredeemable that God would no longer tolerate it.

The example given is the action of despotic tribal chieftains who took any woman they wished as personal property for their harems. Understood this way, the text describes an early manifestation of what later became common practice among kings and despots who also often claimed the designation "sons of the gods." They saw beautiful women as available property to be seized and discarded when desired (*see* Esth 1–2). However, if, as many scholars and historians believe, the Genesis writer meant angelic beings when he used the phrase "sons of God," my main point remains. The phrase "sons of God" (or perhaps "sons of the gods") still designates powerful beings who are not God.

A psalm describes kings, the angelic cultural spirits that empower the kings and kingdoms of the world, or both as "sons of the Most High" and as "gods [*elohim*]. . .all of you" (Ps 82:1, 6–8, *see also* Dan 10; Isa 13–14; Ezek 28).[1] Clearly the psalmist does not mean to designate these kings as what we mean by "God" when we spell it with a capital "G." It is important to note that throughout the psalm the same Hebrew *elohim* is used to designate "God," which we choose to translate with a capital "G," and "gods," which we never translate with a capital G. So the distinction between "sons of the Most High" who were "gods, all of you," though they would die like any mortal, and the One God (*elohim*) who ruled over all history including over these "gods" (*elohim*) was made by context, not by the word *elohim*.

In John 10, Jesus refers to this section of Psalm 82 in his refutation of his enemies' claim that he is out of line in claiming an authoritative role in God's mission. Jesus argues that he is only claiming a role already established in the Old Testament as a description for authoritative agents of God—some of whom were pretty good and some of whom were awful. He identifies himself with those in the psalm whom God called "gods" (which we spell with a small g). Any other way of interpreting John 10:32–38 makes Jesus's use of the reference to Psalm 82 in John 10 almost incomprehensible.

Genesis 6 and Psalm 82 may designate humans or angelic beings as "sons of God." I favor powerful humans in both cases. On the other hand, there are references in Job that clearly designate angelic beings as "sons of God" (Job 1:6, 2:1, 38:7).

King David's Son(s) Are Designated by God as God's Son(s).

The use of "son(s) of God" that serves as a clear pattern for understanding the title as fully rooted in our humanity is its usage to describe God's covenant promise to King David. Future kings in David's dynasty are designated as the "son(s) of God" by both prophets and psalmists. There is however a significant difference from the usage in the Gentile world around them. "Sons of God" in the covenant with "David's sons" was not a claim that they were free to usurp God's rightful reign among humans; instead, it meant they were bound to honor a righteous covenant relationship with God. They

---

1. Zorn, *Psalms*, vol 2, 110–12.

were to be humble servants of God as corulers in God's reign among the people of God descended from Abraham and Sarah. When the "sons of David" forgot this part of their role, as many did, they were in big trouble with YHWH.

> [12] When your days [David] are over and you rest with your fathers, I will raise up *your offspring* to succeed you, who will come from your own body, and I will establish his kingdom. [13] He is the one who will build a house for my Name, and I will establish the throne of his kingdom forever. [14] *I will be his father, and he will be my son. When he does wrong, I will punish him* with the rod of men, with floggings inflicted by men (2 Sam 7:12–14, *emphasis mine*).

It is not legitimate to apply the first half of verse 14 only to Jesus and the last half only to Solomon and his descendants as some Christians do. Avoiding that mistake, we have a promise from God that David's dynasty—for good or ill—will be in the role of "son of God." Ironically, Jesus, as "Son of David," did suffer the punishment of human rods and flogging referred to in this passage.

We have here the dynamic tension that so often occurs in the Bible. Jesus suffered the punishment because the Empire and the Church decided his faithfulness to God was "wrong."

But, from the point of view of Jesus and his followers, Jesus suffered the rods and the flogging for choosing God's will and choosing *not to do* "wrong." Who was right? I would argue that if God did not intervene to raise Jesus from the death the Empire and State sentenced him to, then they were all wrong—Jesus for trusting God would honor his choice, and those in power for executing a man innocent of their charges. If, as I trust, God did intervene to raise Jesus from death, then the God of Abraham vindicated Jesus as truly "the Son of God" who is the Son of David (Rom 1:2–4).

The following are a few of the many Old Testament passages that describe God's relationship with human kings who are designated as "son of God" and "son of David."

Psalm 2 might have been used in ancient Israel as part of an installation ceremony for new kings. Whether it was or not, it is a use of "Son" that the New Testament writers aptly saw as especially applicable to the event when Jesus as "the Son of David" and "the Son of God" ascended into heaven and was exalted to the right hand of God.

> [6] "I have installed my King on Zion, my holy hill." [7] I will proclaim the decree of the LORD: he said to me, "*You are my Son*; today I have *become your Father*. [8] Ask of me, and I will make the nations your inheritance, the ends of the earth your possession (Ps 2:6–8, *emphasis mine*).

In Psalm 89:26–27, we have a prophetic promise that God will make one of David's future sons into "God's firstborn son." This son of David is to be exalted over all kings from all nations on earth. Clearly, the hope that God would someday begin God's reign and God's human family anew through God's "firstborn son" did not begin in New Testament times.

In Psalm 72, a celebration of the covenant relationship between God and "the king's son" described an agent of God whose job is to bless and raise up the "needy," the "poor," and the "weak" (Ps 72:13–14).

The references just mentioned, along with many others, indicate that Old Testament writers considered "David's son" and "God's son" to be appropriately applied to the same agents of God. Several of these psalms celebrate a world-wide sovereignty God plans to share with a coming son of David who is also a son of God.

Isaiah gives us one of the most quoted, and perhaps most often misinterpreted, instances of a prophet describing a "son of David" in exalted terms:

> [6] For to us a child is born, *to us a son is given*, and the government will be on his shoulders. And *he* [his name] *will be called* Wonderful Counselor, *Mighty God, Everlasting Father*, Prince of Peace. [7] Of the increase of his government and peace there will be no end. *He will reign on David's throne* and over his kingdom, establishing and upholding it with justice and righteousness from that time on and forever. *The zeal of the LORD Almighty will accomplish this* (Isa 9:6–7, *emphasis mine*).

Although this soaring passage clearly promises a future son of David who will be a very unique and exceptional human, does it really predict someone who will be "God?" Questioning that interpretation is definitely controversial. Many of us are so immersed in the interpretation of these verses presented to us in Handel's *Messiah*—as well as in many other books, sermons, and hymns—that we find it almost impossible to hear the passage any other way. But, does this passage really intend to predict that a coming son of David would be divine in the "big G" sense? The answer depends upon what Isaiah intended the names this son would be "called" to convey.

The two chapters of Isaiah that precede this very elevated promise—and it is an elevated promise—describe Isaiah's dealings with King Ahaz, the current "son of David." Ahaz was a "son of David" who was supposed to be acting like "God's son." Instead he regularly chose to be a hindrance to God's purpose (Isa 8–9, *see* 2 Kg 16). Isaiah tells him that God's patience is wearing out, and that God is about to bring destruction on Israel. Then, despite the failures of the current son of David and his opposition to Isaiah, the text records the thrilling promise that God will pursue an even greater fulfillment of God's covenant with David than anyone had previously imagined.

As wonderful as this coming son of David is predicted to be, if we are searching for an Old Testament passage that intended to describe a coming servant of God as something more than, or other than, human, consistency indicates that we should look somewhere other than Isaiah 9. Almost no one would insist on the name "Everlasting Father" as a name describing who Jesus is. This would fly in the face of all Trinitarian doctrine. But, insisting that some of these descriptors mean "like" and others mean "is" strains the language to the breaking point.

Just how problematic that approach is becomes quite clear in the dance that commentator E. J. Young, who was usually far more consistent, performed in attempting to explain that "Mighty God" means "*is* the Mighty God," but "Everlasting Father" should be translated "*like* an everlasting father" (*emphasis mine*).[2] There are several ways these names could legitimately be translated, but nothing in the Hebrew justifies inserting "is" for translating one phrase and "like" for the other. That translation comes from wanting the Bible to say what we have already decided it should say, rather than allowing it to say what it says.

It is much more consistent to see each of these descriptors in Isaiah 9:6–7 as "names" that celebrate a faithful human's relationship with God.[3] The Old Testament is filled with examples of the Jewish tradition of using names that include both *El* and *YHWH*. In fact, Isaiah's use of "*Immanuel*" (God with us) in the two sections that precede this passage illustrates the custom of naming humans with God's name (Isa 7:14, 8:8–10). So does Isaiah's own name (*yshayahu*) which means "YHWH saves" or "YHWH is salvation." A few, out of many possible, examples of this common pattern throughout the Old Testament include: "Who is Like YHWH" (Micah), "YHWH judges" (Jehosophat), "YHWH is Savior" (Joshua), "YHWH is my God" (Elijah) or "My God helps" (Eliezer). All of these names include names for God, but none of them imply that the person so named actually is God.

And, if you are thinking that a person can only have one name, remember that Solomon is also Jedidiah, Hadassah is also Esther, Gideon is also Jerubbaal, Peter (Greek for "rock") is also Cephas (Aramaic for "rock") as well as Simon or Simeon (his Hebrew heritage), and Saul is also Paul. Several of these double names occurred because of something unique God was doing in human history through their lives. The future person Isaiah is predicting is no exception. God is going to be doing many important things in human history through this coming Son of David who turns out to be Jesus. And, directly connected to my claim that all of the names in Isaiah are "names" Jesus can be "called" is the angel's directive involving two names: "Give him the name Jesus[4]" and "he will be called *Immanuel*" (Matt 1:21–23).

In short, Isaiah 9:6–7 promises a future son of David who will be in a relationship with God, serving as an agent of God, such that each of these descriptions of his relationship with God will be an appropriate name for him (*see also* Jer 23:5–6 for yet another "name" for the future "righteous branch of David"). These names embed this coming one fully in our human history as God's designated future human authority governing "on David's throne" and bringing the reign of "justice and righteousness" among humans forever—a promise yet to be completely fulfilled.

---

2. Young, *Isaiah,* vol 1, 338–339.

3. Freehof, *Isaiah,* 65.

4. Actually, his name should always have been translated as "Joshua" in English because we arrived at "Jesus" only by going from Greek to Latin to English. God told Joseph to name him after the ancient warrior-leader "Joshua" (Matt 1:21).

Jesus Is One of Us

JESUS FULFILLS THE ESTABLISHED PATTERN OF SON(S) OF GOD.

Jesus is designated as "the Son of God" more than 40 times in the New Testament literature. The uniqueness and discontinuity with the Old Testament patterns are in his "fulfilment" of the call for humans to be righteous and faithful in our relationship to God. It is this complete faithfulness that leads to God placing the resurrected Jesus "on David's throne . . . from that time on and forever" while governing with a peace of which "there will be no end" (Isa 9:6–7). What is not so unique is the relationship of "sonship" which is shared with the other human sons and daughters of God. Still he is a unique "Son."

> [32] He will be great and will be *called the Son of the Most High*. The Lord God will give him the *throne of his father David* . . . . [35] The angel answered, "The Holy Spirit will come upon you, and the power of the Most High will overshadow you. So the holy one to be born *will be called the Son of God*" (Luke 1:32, 35, *emphasis mine*).

Many read this passage from Luke and immediately conclude that the intent of the claim that Jesus is conceived without the involvement of a human father is to separate Jesus from the rest of humanity. I think it is important to remind ourselves that in the biblical paradigm, being born by a direct act of God establishes Jesus as a new Adam, a new beginning for humanity, not as something other than or more than human. "Adam" (Gen 2:7) and "Eve" (Gen 2:21–24) are the other humans in the Scriptures who become human by an act of God without the involvement of human sexual intercourse. Being brought to life by "the spirit/breath" of God and by a direct act of God did not make either Adam or Eve *divine* from a biblical perspective. It made them different from the animals, and the author of Genesis seems to see it as differentiating them from those designated by "whoever finds me" in Genesis 4:14–17. This "breath of God" allowed them to begin God's human family with a life that was meant to reflect the "image of God."

I think Luke, like his traveling partner Paul, sees God's act in Jesus's conception as the origin of renewed humanity. Jesus is "the second Adam/human" or "the last Adam/human" who is "firstborn" and thus the origin of God's renewed humanity. God is providing a restart for the human race. Both Luke's genealogy (Luke 3) and his temptation narrative (Luke 4) support this understanding because both situate Jesus firmly in our humanity. In his role as the new Adam and the new Israel, Jesus is the first human to be fully what God intends humans to be.

I also find the reversal in the narrative of Luke as compared with the Genesis 2 narrative to be fascinating. Did Luke think about it as a reverse parallel as I find myself doing? I would love to know. In Genesis, God acts to create the male and then acts to create the female from the male. In Luke 2, God calls the female, and God then acts to create the male from the female.

JESUS'S ROLE AS SON OF GOD

Luke soon moves from the conception narrative to a focus on sonship in both baptism and genealogy. God directly confirms Jesus's special relationship as God's "son" following his baptism.

> ^{21} When all the people were being baptized, Jesus was baptized too. And as he was praying, heaven was opened ^{22} and *the Holy Spirit descended on him* in bodily form like a dove. And a voice came from heaven: "*You are my Son, whom I love;* with you I am well pleased" (Luke 3:21–22, *emphasis mine*).

Luke then progresses from this identification of Jesus as God's Son to also identifying "Adam" as God's son.

> ^{23}Now Jesus himself was about thirty years old when he began his ministry. *He was the son*, so it was thought, of Joseph, *the son* of Heli, . . . ^{31b} the son of Nathan, *the son of David*, ^{32} the son of Jesse, the son of Obed, . . . ^{33b} *the son of Judah*, ^{34} the son of Jacob, the son of Isaac, *the son of Abraham*, . . . ^{38} the son of Enosh, the son of Seth, *the son of Adam, the son of God* (Luke 3:21–37, *emphasis mine*).

Luke uses "'son' [*huios* in Greek] of" only once in the genealogy (3:23)—to designate Jesus's presumed and probably legal relationship to Joseph. Subsequently he uses the shorthand "of" that almost all scholars agree clearly implies "son" throughout the genealogy. Powerfully, this includes the final phrase "Adam [son] of God." Luke identifies Jesus with "Adam" ("human") as the "son of God." Without doubt, Luke's Gospel goes on to claim overwhelming uniqueness in Jesus's sonship, distinguishing it from Adam's sonship, but the uniqueness is always in the context of a common humanity with a common source in God.

Luke next connects this affirmation of Jesus and Adam both as "son of God" by paralleling the fact that both were tempted to misuse this status.

> ^{9} The devil led him to Jerusalem and had him stand on the highest point of the temple. "*If you are the Son of God*," he said, "throw yourself down from here. ^{10} For it is written: "'He will command his angels concerning you to guard you carefully; ^{11} they will lift you up in their hands, so that you will not strike your foot against a stone.'" ^{12} Jesus answered, "It says: 'Do not put the *Lord your God* to the test.'" (Luke 4:9–12, *emphasis mine*).

Jesus's response to this temptation involves Jesus accepting his duty to be a faithful Jew who obeys the commandments God gave Israel through Moses in Deuteronomy 6. Jesus offers as his evidence of proof that he is truly "the Son of God" the fact that he honors God as every human should by not testing God. Likewise, he proves he is truly God's son by choosing to worship God only, as every human should. Further, he *proves* that he is truly God's son by *not doing a miracle*, just as in his response to the first temptation to turn the rock into bread.

Two of the three recorded temptations begin with "*If* you are the Son of God." And, the one that does not begin with "if you are the son" tempts Jesus to fail exactly as Adam and Eve failed. They failed by attempting to seize for themselves the very gift that God intended ultimately to give them—the gift of becoming more and more in the image and likeness of God. Jesus does not fail because he does not attempt to seize the gift, but waits for God to give it freely when appropriate. Two of the three temptations are resisted by choosing not to do a miracle. Of course, this was far from the last time that Jesus had to resist the temptation to attempt to find a shortcut to God's future and to avoid the suffering that came with taking the long road.[5]

Throughout the narrative of Luke 4:1–12, both the continuity and the discontinuity with other humans in Jesus's relationship with God is underscored. The continuity is the certainty that humans will be tempted to damage their relationship with God by usurping control of events in an arrogant and selfish manner. The discontinuity is Jesus's faithfulness, even as the intensity of the temptations far exceeds those experienced by "Adam son of God." Jesus remains faithful in his relationship with God and does what all other humans should do, but none of the rest of us consistently do.

The temptation accounts in Matthew and Luke present Jesus as faithfully reliving the pattern of Israel in the wilderness as it is recorded in Deuteronomy. Simultaneously, they both present Jesus as faithfully reliving the pattern of "Adam's" history with God recorded in Genesis. Jesus fills both patterns with a new depth of human faithfulness. Mark records a much briefer account of the temptations, but he adds the striking detail of Jesus experiencing a renewal of the peaceful relationship with animals and angels that had once been true for Adam and Eve in the Garden (Mark 1:13).

In John's Gospel, the powerful designation of Jesus as "the Son of God" not only draws much of its content from the creation narrative, from the wilderness narrative, and from the promise to King David, it also parallels God's relationship to Jesus with Abraham's relationship to Isaac. Jesus and Isaac are both described "as the loved only son" who as the "firstborn" is the provided "sacrifice" that initiates a "new covenant" intended to "bless all nations."

"For *God so loved* the world that he *gave his only Son*, so that everyone who believes [trusts] in him may *not perish* but may *have eternal life*" (John 3:16, *emphasis mine*) seems to echo Genesis 22:2 and 22:12. God now fulfills the role of Abraham, and Jesus is God's Isaac. Like Isaac, Jesus is the uniquely beloved only son who becomes the sacrifice and the channel through whom all future sons and daughters of the covenant will be born. Of course, in one sense neither Isaac nor Jesus is the "only son," nor the only "loved son," nor even the "firstborn son." Both God and Abraham have earlier sons (and daughters) who precede Isaac and Jesus and who are loved by their father. On the other hand, both Isaac and Jesus are the unique only sons in that each of these sons is the "only" son and the "firstborn" son of a new covenant.[6] It is

---

5. I think this is the constant "emptying" of himself that Paul says led to his exaltation (Phil 2:1–13).

6. Jesus is also the unique son in that he is the *monogenē* ("the only begotten").

in this sense that each is the only and the most loved son. Each son is the son who embodies the covenant that is another step toward creating God's forever future human family, a new era in human history.

"SON(S) OF GOD" IS A RELATIONSHIP EXTENDED BY GOD TO JESUS'S HUMAN FOLLOWERS.

Below are a few of the many references that indicate God is extending Jesus's sonship relationship with God to Jesus's followers. This usage seems to make it obvious that New Testament writers did not think the phrase "son of God" refers to something that separates one from humanness. Though each of the following texts extends Jesus's sonship relationship with God to his followers, none are claiming that Jesus's followers are other than fully human. Being sons and daughters of God does not make us God; rather, it identifies the relationship God wants to establish with humans. In fact, in Acts 17:26–29, Paul finds his connecting point with the Athenian philosophers by arguing that, not just followers of Jesus, but all humans are "God's offspring." He then tells them that God will judge how they have lived as God's offspring someday through *the human Jesus* (Acts 17:31).

However, most uses of "sons of God" in the New Testament describe the new covenant-relationship God has established with humans through God's relationship with Jesus.

> [14] . . . because those who are *led by the Spirit of God are sons of God*. [15] For you did not receive a spirit that makes you a slave again to fear, but you received the *Spirit of sonship*. And by him we cry, "*Abba*, Father." [16] The Spirit himself testifies with our spirit that we are *God's children* . . . . [19] The creation waits in eager expectation *for the sons of God to be revealed* (Rom 8:14–19, *emphasis mine*).

> [10] In bringing *many sons to glory*, it was fitting that God, for whom and through whom everything exists, should make the author of their salvation perfect through suffering. [11] Both the one who makes men [humans] holy and those who are made holy are *of the same family*. So Jesus is not ashamed to call them brothers [and sisters] . . . . [13] And again, "*I will put my trust in him.*" And again he says, "Here am I, and the children God has given me." (Heb 2:10–13, *emphasis mine*).

> [2:29] If you know that he is righteous, you know that *everyone who does what is right has been born of him*. [3:1] How great is the love the Father has lavished on us, *that we should be called children of God*! And that is *what we are*! The reason the world does not know us is that it did not know him. [2] Dear friends, *now we are children of God*, and what we will be has not yet been made known. But we know that when he appears, *we shall be like him*, for we shall see him as he is. [3] *Everyone* who has this hope in him purifies himself, just *as he is* pure (1 John 2:29–3:3, *emphasis mine*).

> *You are all sons of God* through faith in [or, the faithfulness of] Christ Jesus (Gal 3:26, *emphasis mine*).

In each of the preceding passages, Jesus's sonship is extended to other humans. Because of Jesus's relationship with God and their relationship with Jesus, other humans too are "born of God" and are called "children of God." They are moving toward purity as Jesus is currently pure, and they will someday "be like him." The extension of each of these descriptors from Jesus to Jesus's followers does not imply that we have become "God." Rather, they all emphasize how deeply Jesus is embedded with us in the family relationship God is establishing with humans. When it is used of Jesus, just as when it is used of others of us humans, "Son of God" does not separate him from our humanity; it embeds Jesus, and us, deeply in our calling. That calling is to allow God to be our "Father" and to bring us to completion as children of God. Jesus's "sonship" is both unique and not so unique in this regard.

Abba (Father/Parent) is who God is. "Daughters and sons of God" is who we are by God's grace! This great grace is extended to us through God's relationship with Jesus "the Son of God" who is also the "Son of David," "the seed of Abraham," and the "Son of Adam (Man)." In short, one of us!

10

Jesus's Role as Savior

I suspect some readers may immediately respond to the terms *savior*, *salvation*, and *save* as terms intended to identify Jesus as someone more than human. The terms do often relate to God, but in the Scriptures, they also describe how God is at work through God's human agents. God acts through human agents to bring about rescue, liberation, healing, or wholeness—all dimensions of God's salvation.

Once again, we have a very important title and role assigned to Jesus, which flows from a long history of recorded relationships between God and humans. As is true of so many roles assigned to Jesus, this role is fulfilled in God's relationship with Jesus and then extended to Jesus's followers as well.

In chapter 7, I shared a bit of why I am often repelled by the way the phrase "Jesus saves" is frequently used arrogantly by Christians, who then denigrate the value of other humans. I also shared a bit about why, nonetheless, I can be honest and transparent only if I acknowledge that Jesus did save me and is saving me from myself, and, as importantly, is saving me from hurting others much worse than I do.

In this chapter, the goal is to see how deeply rooted in humanity Jesus's role as *Savior* is throughout the New Testament. Once again, that means beginning with the Old Testament background to the New Testament claims.

THE OLD TESTAMENT PRESENTS HUMAN SAVIORS AS GOD'S AGENTS.

The connection between Jesus's humanity and God's desire to save (rescue, heal, liberate, and make whole) humans is much stronger in the New Testament than is often recognized. We see just how true this is when we understand the Old Testament background for these claims. Not only does the title *savior* apply to God in the Old Testament, it is also used of kings, judges, and warriors who are God's human agents.

In the Old Testament, humans often colabor with God as God works to *save* other humans. The verb *save/saved* appears 17 times in the book of Judges, and 15 of those occurrences describe God saving people through the colaboring of a human *judge*. Several of these judges through whom God *saved* God's people were of highly questionable character. The book of Judges gives us a clear example of the dynamic between God saving and God's human agents saving. The very same event is described in Judges 2:16 as human judges saving God's people and in 2:18 as God saving God's people.

The story of Jonathan describes the pattern succinctly. If he hadn't taken the risk of going to battle as God's agent against the invading Philistines, there would have been no salvation for Israel. On the other hand, if God hadn't acted on their behalf, Israel wouldn't have been saved (1 Sam 14:6). In the Old Testament, the most important kinds of *salvation* came to humans only as a gift from God; this salvation, however, usually came by God acting through human co-workers. Moses could never liberate Israel from Egypt without God's activity—he tried and failed. On the other hand, God chose not to do it without Moses. Only God could save Israel and bring the people back from captivity, but Esther, Mordecai, Nehemiah, Ezra, Zechariah, Haggai, Zerubbabel, Cyrus, and Artaxerxes were all agents through whom God worked in accomplishing that promise.

(Other examples that specifically speak of God saving people through the work of human agents include: Gen 45:5, 7; 2 Kg 14:24, 27; Ps 21:31; Prov 21:5, 23:14; Isa 19:20, 49:5–8; Ezek 3:18–21, 14:14, 20, 18:27.)

Given this dynamic understanding of God's salvation as both by God and by God's human agents, it is not surprising that promises recorded in the Old Testament led to an expectation among many in the Jewish faith community that God would save God's people through a future human who would also be the source of God's salvation for others. Isaiah 53 describes a peaceful sin-bearer who is coming as one of God's people to save God's people. Psalm 2 describes a future son of David who will be seated with God to reign over all nations of the world. Isaiah describes this coming one as properly named God's "Prince of Peace," who will rule on David's throne forever—a very earth-centered promise (Isa 9:6–7; Jer 23:5–6).

JESUS'S HUMANITY IS CENTRAL TO THE NEW TESTAMENT UNDERSTANDING OF SALVATION.

The New Testament writers claim the Old Testament hopes and promises are being filled full of new and deeper content through God's relationship with Jesus. He is the fulfillment, the overwhelming new step, in God's desire to rescue humans, heal humans, liberate humans, and make humans whole. They believed God is saving us from self-destruction, destruction of others, and ultimate destruction by others through the humanity Jesus shares with the rest of us. Once again, on a level far deeper than ever before, the salvation that can come only from God comes to us humans through a human co-worker with God.

This does not seem strange to me because my own personal experience has been that I have most often encountered God through God's presence in my fellow humans. In my 50 years of pastoring, I have heard hundreds of others say the same thing. My guess is that most if not all of you reading this have had some similar experiences.

Sometimes friends have first encountered Jesus through the most unlikely agents of God. One liberal Jewish friend of mine first encountered Jesus through the agency of a young, blond-headed, blue-eyed, very conservative Christian woman. How could a woman who fit the stereotype most difficult for a liberal Jewish person to deal with become the messenger God sent to bring grace and hope? It is beyond my comprehension why she would be the one to pick up the phone and respond to my friend's call. But she said exactly what needed to be said about Jesus's love for my friend. I am quite aware that, had I been there, I probably would not have said the right things for that moment. I am not even certain that she would have on any other day. More than four decades later, the grace and hope first inspired that day through hearing of God's unwavering love, grace, and forgiveness through Jesus is still being experienced by my still liberal, still deeply Jewish, friend. She loves and follows Jesus into God's presence as intimately as anyone I know.

Every person who has encountered Jesus through my agency as a pastor has encountered Jesus through an unlikely colaborer in God's desire to *save* us humans from ourselves and from one another. I find it comforting that Paul thought that this is what we should expect, because we humans can be "letters from the Messiah" to the world (2 Cor 3:3). As unlikely a colaborer as I am, I am no more so than the Jesus followers at Corinth or the leaders who taught them! They were a motley crew. Nevertheless, by God's choice, "God makes God's appeal through us" who are God's ambassadors of reconciliation to the world around us (2 Cor 5:20). Like Paul, who definitely did not suffer from low self-esteem, many of us know we are unfit for the roles God assigns us, and yet God chooses to work through us (1 Cor 15:9; Phil 3:12–14; 1 Tim 1:15).

Interestingly, the writer of Hebrews did not think it sacrilegious, bad theology, or poor doctrine to maintain that *God saved Jesus*. God responded to Jesus's faithfulness throughout his life and to Jesus's prayers by "*saving* him from death." The author says it was this faithfulness in all situations, right up to and including a horrible death, that allowed God to "complete" or "perfect" Jesus so that Jesus could become the source of God's eternal salvation for the rest of us humans: God saved Jesus so that Jesus could save the rest of us (Heb 5:7–9; 2:9–10).

In addition to Hebrews 5, there are other passages in the letter of Hebrews that explicitly state the connection between Jesus's humanity and the salvation God brings for other humans through him. As I noted earlier, Hebrews 2:5–18 claims that Jesus is the first, but far from the only, fulfillment of God's desire to crown humans with God's "glory and honor." Other humans will arrive at God's goal because of what God has done through God's first completed human! This same section of Hebrews also indicates that "it was fitting" that God save the rest of God's children through one who shares the same humanity and the same Father with the rest of us.

As the following references indicate, the theme of God saving us through Jesus's participation in our humanity continues to run throughout Hebrews.

> [14] Therefore, since we have a great high priest who has gone through the heavens, Jesus the Son of God, let us hold firmly to the faith we profess. [15] For we do not have a high priest who is unable to *sympathize with our weaknesses*, but we have one who has been *tempted in every way, just as we are*—yet was without sin. [16] Let us then approach the throne of grace with confidence, so that we may *receive mercy and find grace to help* us in our time of need (Heb 4:14–16, *emphasis mine*).

Hebrews 10:10 emphasizes *the importance of Jesus's bodily* (soma) *existence in God's salvation project for other humans.* Hebrews 10:19–20 stresses the physicality of Jesus as God's means of salvation, with the very earthy claim that the new way through which God allows the rest of us humans to enter the Holy of Holies (the direct presence of God) is through Jesus's lifeblood and Jesus's torn "flesh" (*sarkos*). The writer is not at all reticent to depict God's salvation of a self-destructive human race as necessarily brought about by Jesus's sharing (and risking!) our human dependence on "flesh" and "life that is in the blood" (*See* Lev 17:11, 14; Deut 12:23; then Heb 7:26–8:6, 9:11–17, 9:23, 10: 19–20; for examples of how this Old Testament theme continues throughout Hebrews).

It is not only the letter of Hebrews that stresses that God saves us through Jesus's humanity. In a very different context, the letter of Romans makes a similar point. Romans 3:24–27 maintains that God's redemption and atonement come through Jesus's willingness to pour out his lifeblood as the cost of faithfulness to God. In Romans 5:9–10, Paul returns to a connection between God's gift of salvation and Jesus's offering of his human lifeblood on our behalf. Paul then proceeds to a direct claim that it is through the "one human Jesus the Messiah" that God is offering to graciously save the rest of us humans by renewing the human (Adamic) race (Rom 5:15, my translation). It would be difficult to imagine a clearer statement connecting Jesus's humanity with God's way of saving humans than his claim that it is through the "obedience of the one [human]" that God is renewing the human race (Rom 5:19).

But Paul is rarely satisfied with making a key point only once, so he returns at least two more times in Romans to the emphasis on Jesus's humanity as the vehicle of God's salvation.

> [2] For the law of the Spirit of life in Christ Jesus has set you free from the law of sin and of death. [3] For God has done what the law, weakened by the flesh, could not do: *by sending his own Son in the likeness of sinful flesh*, and to deal with sin, he condemned sin *in the flesh*, [4] so that the just requirement of the law

Jesus's Role as Savior

might be *fulfilled in us*, who walk *not according to the flesh but according to the Spirit* (Rom 8:2–4, *emphasis mine*).

When Paul returns yet again to this emphasis on Jesus's humanity as essential to God's way of saving other humans, he becomes quite graphic about the physicality involved.

> [8] For I tell you that Christ has become *a servant of the Jews* [literally, "of the circumcision"] on behalf of God's truth, to confirm the promises made to the patriarchs [9] *so that the Gentiles may glorify God*. . . . (Rom 15:8–9, *emphasis mine*).

Apparently, Paul was sure that God's salvation not only had to come through a human sharing our "flesh," but also through a human sharing in the "circumcision" of the male penis that identifies participation in the covenant with Abraham. This is a very earthy embedding of Jesus's relationship with humanity and with God in Jewish humanness!

It is clear that the author of Ephesians thought that it was through Jesus's humanity that God was able to bring salvation that could even unite Jews and Gentiles in the family of God. After spending all of chapters 1 and 2 praising the grandeur of the salvation God has brought to us through Jesus, the author suddenly makes a very earthy claim about this great salvation as coming through Jesus's "flesh."

> [14] For he himself is our peace, who has made the two one and has destroyed the barrier, the dividing wall of hostility, [15] *by abolishing in his flesh* the law with its commandments and regulations. His purpose was to create in himself one new man out of the two, thus making peace, [16] and in this one body to *reconcile both of them to God through the cross*, by which he put to death their hostility (Eph 2:14–16, *emphasis mine*).

John's Gospel (1:1–18) emphasizes that God's *logos* (word) through which the entire creation came into being, and by which the history of Israel and the words of Israel's prophets were empowered, had to become fully incarnated in a human "Son" before God could bring the saving fullness of mercy and grace that God intended for the rest of us humans. Though it is true that no human has ever "seen God," we have seen God revealed as fully as we are able to see God's "grace," God's "glory," and God's "truth" through the incarnation of God's creative word.

Perhaps the rite of citizenship in the kingdom of God that every person who follows Jesus participates in provides the most direct connection between Jesus's humanity and God's gift of salvation.

> [23] For I received from the Lord what I also passed on to you: The Lord Jesus, on the night he was betrayed, took bread, [24] and when he had *given thanks*, he broke it and said, "This is *my body*, which is for you; do this in remembrance of me." [25] In the same way, after supper he took the cup, saying, "This cup is the

> *new covenant in my blood*; do this, whenever you drink it, in remembrance of me." ²⁶ For whenever you eat this bread and drink this cup, you proclaim the Lord's death until he comes (1 Cor 11:23–26, *emphasis mine*).

Jesus added a new dimension to the rite of citizenship that God gave the Jewish people as they left Egypt. He now says God's great Passover event of salvation—of liberation, freedom, forgiveness, and mutual covenanted relationships—is directly connected to his own physical being. You cannot describe being human in any more earthy terms than *body* and *blood*, nor was there anything more human and physical in Jesus's time than table fellowship around *bread* and *wine*.

Remember that *remembrance* in the biblical paradigm means *act on it*. For example, you were not only *to think* it was the Sabbath, you were *to act on the fact* that it was the Sabbath. The same was true with the annual Passover celebration. Jews were to remember by acting like a people liberated by God. In this light, partaking of the Eucharist with sisters and brothers in the presence of Jesus is a very earthy participation together in gratitude for Jesus's humanity through which God's salvation comes to us. "Do this in remembrance of me" means *to act like* you are part of a New Covenant people God is creating right now through God's relationship with Jesus.

I find it extremely important to understand that God always purposed to bring redemption, reconciliation, justification, glory, mercy, and salvation to the rest of us humans through a fellow human. I think if we took this reality more seriously, we could quit arguing about transubstantiation, consubstantiation, or symbolism, and instead celebrate in the presence of the firstborn son, who is present with us in his now glorified body as God's exalted human Savior. Communion/Eucharist then is a participation of gratitude and humility in God's amazing grace that has moved God's desire to save us humans forward toward completion through the human faithfulness of Jesus.

It is this glorified human who now mediates this saving process for us on God's behalf (1 Tim 2:3–5). In fact, "It was fitting" that God would save us in this way because Jesus and the rest of us are part of the same family (Heb 2:10–11). In fact, it is only because of Jesus's human faithfulness that extended even to offering his very human lifeblood that God can both be righteous (in a right relationship with humans) and make us righteous (put us in a right and just relationship with God) according to Paul (Rom 3:22–26).

God's salvation through Jesus did not come because of sin; God's salvation through Jesus came because God had always planned to bring humans into the image of God as the culture (kingdom) of God's future. Sin had to be dealt with in order for God to reach that ultimate goal. Sin did not cause salvation, but salvation dealt with sin, and God did this through a human who consistently chose not to sin—not to distrust God.

Some Western Christians have become squeamish concerning the biblical emphasis on the very earthy description of Jesus spilling his human lifeblood to save us humans. I find this somewhat ironic because we rightly make heroes of citizens, soldiers, firemen, policemen, doctors, nurses, and mothers who spill their lifeblood in daring rescues to *save* family, friends, and strangers. What is the disconnect?

Given the fact that we celebrate many people giving their lives to save others, why do we find it so difficult to comprehend that God sent his courageous warrior to *give* his life on our behalf, rather than to *take* lives on our behalf. Doesn't our sad reality need a salvation that includes the gift of a "peace that passes understanding?" And, why is it so easy for us to claim that other humans *save* us by giving their lifeblood for us, and so difficult for some of us to acknowledge that God can save us through Jesus giving his lifeblood for us?

It was (and is) in this brutal reality of our world systems that often demand blood that Jesus is God's warrior, but also God's antiwarrior *par excellence*. He rejected using war and weapons to save us. He poured out his lifeblood for us on the cross in the ultimate *sacred act* of one human giving his lifeblood to *save* the life of other humans. His saving acts were (and are) fully embedded in the all-too-familiar realm of human brutality, but also in his deep human trust that God's reign ultimately wins, even in that arena.

JESUS'S HUMANITY IS GOD'S MEANS AND MODEL FOR SAVING AND TRANSFORMING OUR HUMAN BODIES.

I have never been *me* apart from embodiment. You have never been *you* apart from embodiment. As the journey toward becoming you began, your initial cells began to create your body. If you and I are to be *saved* as humans, rather than saved from being human, that saving must include embodiment. I find it exciting that what God did in saving Jesus from death as an embodied human is destined to be God's way of fulfilling God's desire and promise to do the same for the rest of us humans—if we will allow it.

Throughout the New Testament canon, Jesus is seen as the Savior of our human bodies, not only of our *souls* or our *spirits*. The Greek intellectuals of the time thought (as have many others in human history, including many Christians) that the best hope was for humans to become eternal, disembodied souls or minds. In contrast, God not only *saved* Jesus's human body from death (Heb 5:7); God also *glorified* Jesus's body when Jesus ascended into God's presence after the resurrection (Phil 3:20–21).

This *salvation of the whole human is a gift God gave Jesus* when God raised him from death and exalted him with a "glorious body." Through Jesus, God is extending this promise to other humans. Jesus is both God's means and God's model for how God wants to *completely* save us too. Jesus is God's first, but is not to be God's only, completed human—a completion that includes glorifying our bodies so that our bodies "will be like his glorious body" (Phil 3:21). Apparently, Paul believed that Jesus, and other humans because of Jesus, are meant to remain humans with bodies forever, in God's forever family.

In addition to the Philippians 3 passage, Paul notes a connection between Jesus's fulfilled humanity and God's desire to complete our humanity expressed in other letters as well. Earlier I mentioned how in 1 Corinthians 15:13–20, Paul insisted that if God did not intend to raise many humans from death, then God didn't raise Jesus either. Later in the same chapter, he returns to emphasizing the connection between Jesus's resurrection and the resurrection God intends for others. After insisting that Jesus is a *human of heaven* and that God is making us *humans of heaven* as well (1 Cor 15:47–49; see also Phil 3:20), Paul further defines this gift that comes from God to Jesus as one that includes clothing our entire being in God's gift of immortality.

> [51] Listen, I tell you a mystery: We will not all sleep, but *we will all be changed.* . . . [53] For *the perishable must clothe itself with the imperishable, and the mortal with immortality* (1 Cor 15:51, 53, *emphasis mine*).

Other passages by Paul are even clearer in terms of emphasizing that our becoming like the exalted Jesus includes embodiment both for Jesus and for us.

> [18] I consider that our present sufferings are not worth comparing with *the glory that will be revealed in us.* . . . [22] We know that the whole creation has been groaning as in the pains of childbirth, right up to the present time. [23] Not only so, but we ourselves, who have the firstfruits of the Spirit, groan inwardly as we wait eagerly for our *adoption as sons, the redemption of our bodies* (Rom 8:18, 22–23, *emphasis mine*).

> [23] May God himself, the God of peace, *sanctify you through and through.* May your *whole spirit, soul, and body* be kept blameless at the coming of our Lord Jesus Christ. [24] The one who calls you is faithful, and he [God] *will do it* (1 Thess 5:23–24, *emphasis mine*).

With so many statements in the New Testament that connect Jesus's very physical and continuing embodiment as a human with our continuing embodiment in God's future for us, I confess that it somewhat eludes me why there is so little emphasis in Christian thought and doctrine on this exciting connection. Jesus's continuing glorified human embodiment is the model and the means of God's salvation for us—the same forever gift God has already given Jesus.

BEING GOD'S AGENTS OF SALVATION IS EXTENDED TO OTHER HUMANS.

You might, or might not, be comfortable with the idea, but if you are a follower of Jesus, the New Testament writers include you as a potential human agent of God's salvation. It is important to be clear that the saving (i.e. rescuing, liberating, healing, forgiving, completing) work that God has done in Jesus is unique. Having said that, it is also important to recognize that being God's agents of salvation is a mission that God extends to Jesus's followers. Jesus as God's human agent of salvation for other humans is both unique and not unique. Being God's Savior does not separate Jesus from humanity; it embeds Jesus in God's human project.

The following passages are examples of the New Testament paradigm that presents Jesus as God's unique source of God's salvation, and at the same time calls the rest of us to take up our God-given role as humans who colabor with Jesus as God's agents in God's gracious saving activity among us.

> ^{13b} I glorify my ministry ^{14} in order to make my own people jealous, *and thus save some of them* (Rom 11:13b–14, *emphasis mine*).

> ^{15b} It is to peace that God has called you. ^{16} Wife, for all you know, *you might save your husband*. Husband, for all you know, *you might save your wife* (1 Cor 7:15b–16, *emphasis mine*).

> ^{22} I have become all things to all people *that I might by all means save some.* ^{23} I do it all for the sake of the gospel, so that I may share in its blessings (1 Cor 9:22–23, *emphasis mine*).

> ^{19} My brothers and sisters, if one of you should wander from the truth and someone should bring him back, ^{20} remember this: *Whoever turns a sinner from the error of his way will save him from death and cover over a multitude of sins* (Jas 5:19–20, *emphasis mine*).

> And he testified with many other arguments and exhorted them, saying, "*Save yourselves* from this corrupt generation" (Acts 2:40, *emphasis mine*).

> For so the Lord has *commanded us*, saying, "I have set you to be a light for the Gentiles, *so that you may bring salvation* to the ends of the earth" (Acts 13:47, *emphasis mine*).

Comfortable with it or not, we are called to be human agents of God's salvation in a world that deeply needs healing, rescue, liberation, and wholeness. We are called to colabor with God and Jesus in the work of *salvation*.

Individually and corporately, we need to be *saved* from ourselves and from one another. We need a different kind of leader from those we continue to choose—when we are fortunate enough to live in nations where we have choices about who leads us. I find it easy to believe the New Testament claim that if the Messiah whom God raised from death is not the one to lead us toward a fulfillment of human potential, it is obvious no one else can. Thank God, because of Jesus, we can celebrate human potential without pretending. In God's great adventure with us humans, Jesus is the unique human agent of God's salvation. He is also not unique because God worked through saviors prior to Jesus and intends to continue the great work of salvation through those humans who serve "the God and Father of our Lord Jesus the Messiah."

SUMMARY

God saves us humans from our propensity toward self-destruction and the destruction of others. Likewise, Jesus is God's co-worker saving us fellow humans on God's behalf. In doing this, Jesus is the fulfillment of God's long-established pattern of saving humans through God's human agents. Human agency in God's saving other humans also often requires sharing in God's burden-bearing as we will explore in the next chapter.

11

Jesus's Role as Burden-bearer

GOD'S SALVATION THROUGH JESUS INVOLVES THE COSTLY BURDEN-BEARING OF FORGIVING.

Many of us have been burden-bearers without being forgivers, but no one is a forgiver without being a burden-bearer. Because I trust that God is the forgiver par excellence, I also believe that God is the burden-bearer *par excellence*. Human sharing in the cost of God's forgiving did not start with Jesus, and it did not stop with Jesus. He is the unique human burden-bearer on God's behalf, but many humans have shared in this way of imaging God.

Being a burden-bearer is to carry the hurts and consequences of other people's sins, mistakes, ignorance, arrogance, and failures. Sustaining intimate relationships always demands burden-bearing. Burden-bearing is often what it takes to make healing, rescue, liberation, and wholeness available to others. We will explore the meanings of the cross more fully in a later chapter. Here, it is important to note that when New Testament authors claim Jesus died for us, they often use burden-bearing imagery, and even more, they often use imagery that describes the cost of forgiving.

Forgiving as bearing other people's burdens is evident in Jesus's words at the Last Supper: "This is *my blood* of the covenant, which is *poured out for many for the forgiveness of sins*" (Matt 26:28, *emphasis mine*). Peter describes Jesus's burden-bearing in the following words: "He himself *bore our sins in his body* on the tree, so that we might die to sins and live for righteousness; *by his wounds you have been healed*" (1 Pet 2:24, *emphasis mine*).

Jesus's Burden-bearing Fulfills an Old Testament Pattern.

Being the burden-bearer of the consequences of the sins of others certainly expresses Jesus's imaging of God. But it does not separate Jesus from our humanity. In being the burden-bearer of our sins, Jesus is fulfilling a pattern established by other servants of God throughout the history recorded in the Old Testament. Jesus bears the burdens laid upon him by others with a fullness that others only incarnated in bits and pieces. Still, the pattern was established long before Jesus in the lives of people such as Leah, Rachel, Isaac, Jeremiah, Joseph, Isaiah, Hagar, Esther, Hosea, Ruth, Rizpah, and Ezekiel—to name only a few of the Old Testament burden-bearers. Sometimes, as it does with Hosea, the burden-bearing also demonstrates an incredible act of forgiveness. Sometimes as with David (1 Kgs 2:1–9), or Mordecai and Esther (Esth 9), or a psalmist (Ps 137:7–9), perhaps not so much.

The prophets knew God was, in some important sense, the one who "bore" our sins and was weighed down by our failures. They also knew that their faithfulness to God included joining God in bearing the burden of the brokenness of God's people. The message of the great prophetic writers of Israel, such as Hosea, Jeremiah, Samuel, Isaiah, the writer of Genesis, and the writer of Chronicles was that God has been forgiving human beings ever since we first alienated ourselves from God's presence. God has chosen to willingly absorb the unjust hurt, suffering, and insults that we have inflicted upon God, pleading with us to allow a restored authentic relationship. For example, Isaiah 1:14 says of the worship of those who praise God, yet hurt their brothers and sisters, "Your new moons and your appointed festivals my soul hates; they *have become a burden to me, I am weary of bearing them*" (*emphasis mine*).

Isaiah (or "Second Isaiah" as most scholars designate the source of the following quotation) also reflects a strong prophetic knowledge that God was going to need, and provide, a unique human burden-bearer to forgive and completely heal the relationship between God and God's people.

> [4] Surely he *took up our* infirmities and *carried our* sorrows, yet we considered him stricken by God, smitten by him, and afflicted. [5] But he was *pierced for our* transgressions, he was *crushed for our* iniquities; the punishment that brought us peace was *upon him*, and by his wounds *we are healed* (Isa 53:5–6, *emphasis mine*).

Hosea provides an awesome demonstration of how much burden-bearing and forgiving can cost. He bears the hurt of loving and then forgiving a prostituted wife. She is described as an incarnation of the practices of an entire culture. The heartrending narrative describing the relationship between Hosea and Gomer concludes with *God telling Hosea that Hosea now knows through personal experience how much hurt God bears and how costly it is to love and to forgive* "my people" (Hos 3:1)

Forgiving Is Costly.

The burden-bearing of forgiving is a part of all genuine relationships when (not *if*) they need mending and healing. We all need forgiveness for many of the ways we relate to God and to one another. Forgiveness is never the goal of a good relationship, but it is always a necessary means to maintaining a good relationship.

Forgiving us costs God just as it costs you when you forgive someone. Forgiving is an act of burden-bearing for others. In fact, the most basic meaning of the Hebrew word *nagah* (forgive) seems to have been "lift a burden up," and a basic meaning of the Greek word *aphiemi* (forgive) is to bear the cost of someone else's debt. Both words translated "forgiveness" are filled with "burden-bearing" content.

What are the *costs to the burden-bearer who forgives*? First, *a willingness to absorb pain, suffering, hurt, and disappointment that you do not deserve* to spare others from experiencing what they *do* deserve. It is very costly to love people who intentionally and unintentionally hurt us and disappoint us. If God is like Jesus, then like Jesus, God has long been willing to suffer a tremendous amount of pain and hurt that we humans inflict upon God. God forgives to free us from the debt/load we deserve to carry for so many of our attitudes and actions.

I think it is a tragic heresy when Christians claim that God is passionless and exists beyond the emotional change that suffering and hurt bring in each of us. Many Christians have come to believe that the very definition of the word *God* excludes any genuine experience of hurt and suffering. They think that God cannot really hurt because God is "unchangeable," "immutable," "without passion," and "foreknows all." This seems strange, because the traditional English translation of the Ten Commandments includes "I, the LORD your God, am a jealous God" (Exod 20:5).

As any of us who have ever experienced jealousy know, that is a statement of deep passionate feeling. Several scholars think a better translation of the Hebrew *kana* is *zealous* which indicates it is an even broader word about deep feelings. The New Jewish Publication Society translation of the two uses of *kana* in God's response to Moses is "the LORD, whose *name is Impassioned*, is an *impassioned God*" (Exod 34:14).[1] Now that is a deeply passionate self-description by God! Whatever translation of *kana* (in Exodus) you decide is best, they all describe YHWH telling Israel that *passion* is very much a characteristic of God's relationship with the people of God. Rather obviously, the "passionless God" of theology and philosophy does not share much in common with YHWH, who is the "One God" of weeping prophets like Hosea and Jeremiah and the zealous, impassioned God of Exodus.

If God does not hurt, then Jesus does not reflect the image of God in circumstances where he seems to reflect God most deeply—in his genuine passionate responses to our wounds and suffering. How can we possibly argue that Jesus's execution should be

---

1. Sarna, *Exodus*, 218.

designated "the Passion," and then argue that God is passionless? Isn't this where Jesus most clearly images God's love for us?

Another cost of forgiving is that we must decide to *give up our right to what seems to be a fundamental need for immediate "justice."* We decide to absorb the injustices perpetrated upon us rather than demand retribution, revenge, and an equal balancing of accounts. How can there be justice if things are not balanced out evenly? There are probably many other costs, but the cost of leaving justice for God to decide causes most of us to find the burdensome cost of forgiving to be formidable. This is true especially when the hurt caused by injustice runs very deep. Perhaps the only way the cost of forgiving can be justified is by understanding that the cost of not forgiving is even higher. It imprisons us, and others, in our need for revenge, and it ends the possibility of deep and intimate relationships.

On the other hand, most of us are quite aware of *the cost of being willing to be forgiven*—even if we seldom acknowledge it. It costs us the difficult step of *being truthful about our own sins, wrongs, failures, and mistakes without attempting to justify them.* If we are honest, most of us humans despise being forgiven. Why? Because being forgiven means admitting we really blew it, and it means acknowledging that someone else is bearing the burden for our failure. Most of us would rather avoid the pain that the path to being forgiven involves. We need to be *forgiven*, not *excused*. Quite often, we prefer to be excused, not forgiven!

Some Evangelicals tend to emphasize forgiveness as though it were God's final goal for humans, rather than God's means to God's ultimate goal. God's ultimate goal is to create a deep forever relationship with humans as God's daughters and sons in God's forever human culture ("the kingdom of God"). Others seem even to deny that God truly forgave people throughout Israel's history prior to Jesus, despite dozens of statements to the contrary in the Hebrew Bible—not one of which Jesus ever contradicts. Others claim to know for certain that God will not forgive anyone who does not know that Jesus is God's Messiah before she or he dies, even though every faithful person who lived prior to Jesus is said to have received God's gift of salvation through Jesus long after they died (Heb 11:39; 1 Pet 3:18–20, 4:6).

That forgiveness is not God's ultimate goal, but rather God's *means* to God's ultimate goal, is not so difficult to understand. God did not create us to be able to forgive us, any more than my wife Donna entered the marriage covenant with me to have lots of opportunities to forgive me. However, she did enter a covenant that would be sustained only if she chose to forgive me—more often than she could have imagined. She forgave me again and again because she valued our covenant relationship of marriage.

Likewise, God did not create humans so God could practice forgiving us, but God did choose to enter covenant relationships with us that could be sustained only if God chose to bear the burdens involved in forgiving us. God pays an incredible cost to forgive us—because God values a relationship that can lead to God's forever human family. Jesus faithfully pursued God's goal, not because Jesus enjoyed the cost of forgiving, but because Jesus loves God and loves us fellow humans. The burden-bearing of forgiveness is a necessary means to a much higher end—the renewing and sustaining of real relationships.

At the other extreme, some modern Christians are embarrassed by the fact that the Bible often states that we all need forgiveness and that offering forgiveness costs God dearly. If any of us carry that wrong attitude into the rest of our intimate relationships, we are headed for shipwreck. Forgiving means shouldering a burden we do not deserve, and it is costly. It is also the only way relationships can survive and continue to deepen.

This forgiveness comes at great cost to God because God's relationship to us is one of *stubbornly and graciously wanting and acting toward good* for us humans—the content definition of *love* in the *chesed* (Old Testament) and *agape* (New Testament) sense. God wants this relationship whether we as God's children want God's love or not. Such love is an experience that God shares with many a good parent. It is an experience my own parents shared with God when they decided to continue loving me, even though I was a very ungrateful and rebellious teenager who hurt them, hurt my siblings, hurt my friends, hurt the girls imprudent enough to want me for a boyfriend, and hurt my church.

There were no excuses, though I am still tempted to look for them. But forgiveness is what I needed, not excuses. Both then and now, like most humans, I find it much easier and less immediately costly, though not nearly as healing, to be excused rather than forgiven. Excusing myself leads to entrenchment in my sins; accepting forgiveness is my only hope of transformation.

My wife seemed to understand the importance of costly burden-bearing and forgiveness, even when we were young. This was true even though she was always a woman with a strong personality and a deep sense of the importance of fairness and justice. For any reader who might be tempted by my praise of Donna in this book to think either that I am exaggerating or that I have her on an unrealistic pedestal, be assured that is not true. Like me, she was a naturally stubborn person. She was always very aware of her personal weaknesses. It is because, like me and everyone I know, she was a very real human with strengths and weaknesses, that I am so overwhelmed with the way the image of God often shone through her.

I still remember vividly an event that occurred almost fifty years ago. I made a major life decision, buying a new car that cost much more than we could afford. I did this while ignoring her request that I come home and pray with her before finalizing the decision. During the two-hour drive home in *our* new car, purchased from the car dealership owned by a family friend, I carefully arranged my long string of very logical excuses. I was prepared!

When I arrived home late that night, Donna awoke and delivered this bit of wisdom. "Don't start trying to explain why you ignored me; it will just make it hurt worse. I forgive you. Let's leave it there. I love you." She then rolled over and went back to sleep, and I stood there speechless with my well-prepared excuses unspoken. That was the first time in my life that I began to understand what real forgiveness is and how much it costs. It was the beginning of a major change concerning decision-making in my life! Forgiving can lead to transformation in relationships. *Transformation is the goal; forgiving is a costly, burden-bearing, means toward that relational goal.*

It is not just in marriage and parenting, but in all our relationships, that we see the importance of the burden-bearing of costly forgiveness as a means of maintaining good relationships and of encouraging possible transformation. Some of us seem to learn this lesson quickly; others definitely take our time.

Before continuing, there is an important caveat. The biblical challenge to be a burden-bearer who forgives has been tragically misused in some church and counseling settings. What I am describing as choosing to be a burden-bearer for God is not to be laid upon people who are being degraded and abused by spouses, pastors, parents, children, or employers. The burden-bearing of forgiving is a choice made from a position of strength, not a passive submission to abuse. People who are being abused should be protected and encouraged to exit the relationship as quickly and safely as possible.

The burden-bearing Jesus, encouraged and modeled, represents a decision made to bless others, as well as to confront them with another way of life. Jesus said he could call 10,000 angels to deliver him—a position of strength that I cannot fathom—but he chose instead to bear the burden of systemic and individual sins. The same is true in Jesus's teachings that are sometimes presented as passively accepting injustice. When Jesus commanded turning the other cheek, giving more clothing than was required, and going the extra mile, he was counseling actions designed to shift the balance of power away from the socially powerful into the hands of the person suffering injustice (Matt 5:38–41).

The hope is that the shocking action will lead to repentance and redemption for the perpetrator. Sometimes it works; sometimes it does not. These actions are very much in line with Jesus's responses to Pilate—first silence, where pleading or venom was expected, and then "You would have no power if my Father weren't allowing you to briefly exercise it" (my paraphrase). A modern example would be the crowd kneeling in prayer at the Selma bridge as the racist police force came with their dogs, clubs, and guns. Who was in the most powerful and history changing role in that event? I think it was those who actively chose to express inner strength as the "burden- bearers" publicly confronting generations of injustice!

Let's Not Cheapen the Costly Grace of Forgiveness.

My wife illustrated forgiveness as costly burden-bearing. The question becomes this: Is that kind of forgiveness real between us humans and God as well? Is forgiving even more costly to God than it is to us?

The brilliant, influential (and highly anti-Semitic) atheist Voltaire famously captured the cheap view of God's grace and forgiveness when he ironically commented "*God* forgives because it's his business." Of course, Voltaire thought we humans (especially Jews and Christians) created this kind of God to have "someone" to forgive us for the things we do not know how to face about ourselves.

A century and a half later, Ludwig Feuerbach[2] and Sigmund Freud[3] attempted to prove through their philosophical and psychological theories that we humans invented a forgiving God as a projection of our fears, wishes, and weaknesses. More recently, Richard Dawkins has attempted to use his scientific credentials to give credence to his philosophical belief that belief in God is not only improbable, but also dangerous.[4]

Many Christians do understand that forgiveness is not God's "business"; instead, God is stubbornly committed to bringing good to us humans, if we will allow it. That means God's "business," if we want to use the term, is transforming us humans fully into the image of God—completing us. How dare we view this graciousness as not very costly and painful to God?

Forgiveness that is not costly actually subverts rather than cements relationships. It is a form of what Bonhoeffer termed "cheap grace."[5] Let me illustrate from my experience as a pastor for over five decades. I have counseled quite a number of marriage relationships having to deal with marital infidelity. It might seem counterintuitive, but I have observed that the relationships that most often survived were those in which the partner who was wronged and the partner who committed the breach of trust both realized that forgiving was going to be very costly and would probably take time.

When the partner who breached trust just wants things to get back to normal as quickly as possible—in other words wants the forgiveness to be easy and not very costly—the relationship is unlikely to survive. If it does, it is likely to remain shallow. Perhaps more surprising, when the partner who was wronged forgives too easily and feels very godly in doing so, the relationship is also unlikely to survive. If it does, it is likely to remain shallow. Why? Because either consciously or unconsciously, the person in need of being forgiven realizes that if forgiveness comes that easily, something isn't right. If forgiveness comes that easily, it is because the partner does not care enough to be hurt very deeply. There was no burden to be borne.

If easy forgiveness among humans is a sign of shallow relationships, then easy forgiveness by God would mean God's relationship with us isn't deep and caring. Why can't we see this? If forgiving doesn't cost God, then God doesn't really care very much about us humans or about the ways we hurt God, hurt one another, and hurt ourselves. If God isn't broken-hearted when we waste ourselves and all of our God-given

---

2. Feuerbach, *Essence of Christianity*.
3. Freud, *Future of Illusion*.
4. Dawkins, *God Delusion*.
5. Bonhoeffer, *Cost of Discipleship*, 45–47.

potential, then God isn't the God of Hosea, Jeremiah, and Isaiah—or the "jealous" God of the Ten Commandments.

The unhurt God we've imagined bears no resemblance to the Father-figure that Jesus describes in the parable of the father and two sons, usually called the parable of the Prodigal Son. The father who stands in the role of God longs for and watches for his boy to come home every day. It is costly to care deeply because it means hurting deeply. He then embarrasses himself in front of the entire town by going out and begging his older son to come into the house—offering costly forgiveness again.[6] Costly forgiveness is the only way forward in a meaningful relationship. Cheap grace and forgiveness imply cheap relationships.

God is good, and God does love us. God is stubbornly committed to grace and good toward us—that is covenant love. God considers our relationships valuable and does not, for the many ways we fall short with God and fall short with each other, offer cheap or easy forgiveness. God does not want our excuses for the inexcusable, nor does God excuse us.

Rather, in Jesus's life and death, God demonstrates experientially just how costly our sinfulness is to the God who dearly loves this faithful Son. We also see how costly forgiveness is to the most faithful and righteous human ever to live. And, if we are really seeing and listening, we see how costly it is to the rest of us humans—each and all of whom have helped construct this warped world. This is a world that is willing to execute the clearest reflection of God in the flesh ever to live, as soon as we can get our hands on him. God takes us very seriously indeed, and it often hurts a lot! God and Jesus bear the burdens that come with desiring a relationship with people like us!

Jesus Fully, and Uniquely, Incarnates God's Costly Burden-Bearing.

How does Jesus fit into God's burden-bearing? He is God's dearly beloved Son, whom God sent "into harm's way," in order to be the "doctor without borders" who can heal the lives of God's other sons and daughters. Many servants of God might have incarnated some of the burden-bearing described in Isaiah 53, but it was and is Jesus who fulfilled it. Does this somehow separate Jesus from our humanity or does it fully embed Jesus in our humanity?

I find it strange that so many moderns find this "substitution out of love" so distasteful in the theology of the Bible, though the same paradigm is the underlying theme in so many of our most loved secular books and movies. As the World War II purple heart hero who was the father of a good friend of mine once reported, "You risk dying the first three days for the abstract patriotic ideal of a nation; then for the next three years, you risk your life daily to keep your buddies alive and your family back home safe. It is the relationships that drive you."

---

6. Bailey, *Poet and Peasant*, 200–206.

Courage and risk might flow from many causes, but they most often come from relationships! Isn't this the essence of substitutionary love as it is expressed in the relationship between God and Jesus? We matter as individual humans, and Jesus gave his life so his friends, and those who might yet choose to be his friends, could live (John 17:20–21). This, expressed more fully than we can comfortably handle, is the character of the God of the universe. God is like Jesus. Jesus is like God.

Great literature, great news stories, and great movies are filled with stories of humans who give their lives to save the lives of other humans. We love to write stories and make movies in which people pay huge personal prices to "save" others from various bad situations. Often these bad situations have been caused by foolish choices on the part of the person who needs to be saved.

Even not-so-great movies can touch us with this theme. Not too long ago, I watched the not-so-great and very violent movie *3:10 to Yuma*—some readers are probably thinking I need forgiveness for watching it! Perhaps so, but it is touching to see a father and husband grow into the love and courage required to give his life for his wife and son, and then to see his son also risk his life for his father. Even the bad guy finally risks, and maybe even gives, his life so that another man can die honorably, and so that the other man's son can live honorably.

It is not just in literature. but in real life that we honor such sacrificial burden-bearing. The U.S. Medal of Honor exists to honor people who courageously risked their lives to save others. Not long ago, many of us were glued to the real-life events as people from all over the world risked their lives, and one gave his life, hoping to rescue the Thai boys stranded in a cave.

Often parents bless and support their sons and daughters as they go to be missionaries or Peace Corps workers in a dangerous land, even though the parents know their child might be imprisoned or killed. Many other parents proudly *send off* their sons and daughters to be soldiers in what our government considers to be a *necessary* war, or to work in the field for Doctors without Borders, hoping their cost—and ours—can save others. Every year on 9/11, we remember the heroic people who gave their lives by taking down their passenger plane to save the people in the Capitol.

I watched as parents in our small group risked supporting one of their children who decided to risk her personal health to *save* someone's life. They asked us to pray and to support their daughter's decision to donate a kidney to save the life of a stranger she had just met. Similarly, we hear the news of a child who risked her life to save her sister who stepped in front of a car—whether successful or not, we celebrate the love and courage.

As another specific, real-life example, friends of mine supported and blessed their son when he decided to serve in the Peace Corps in West Africa. They knew he was placing himself in a situation where he might die; they had earlier risked their own lives in this same war-torn area. The parents certainly did not want other humans to kill their son unjustly for attempting to do good; nevertheless, both the son and the parents believed the risk was worth it. He died at the hands of sons of the local tribal chieftains. The parents and the tribal chiefs later made peace together by partaking in a *communion* meal that acknowledged, rather than denied, the horrendous hurt.

Why is the willingness to support and bless a child who is willing to give his life for the good of others seen as a risky good, even a loving act when we do it, but seen as a weakness when the New Testament claims this is exactly the route God had to take in order to demonstrate God's love for us (Rom 5:8)? Why is giving one's life for others such a glorious, dramatic theme in so many stories in Hollywood, literature, and real-life heroics, then looked upon as something evil or unloving by many when it occurs in the relationship among God, Jesus, and us?

God and Jesus Bear the Burden of Our Sins Because We Are So Valuable to Them.

Jesus is the human through whom God has provided a way to save humans—to rescue us, to heal us, to liberate us, to make us whole beings "in the image of God," and to make us "brothers and sisters" in the family of God. The New Testament writers present Jesus as the necessary completion of God's costly burden-bearing forgiveness being incarnated.

God wants to save us because we are so valuable (the first word of the good news as noted in chapter 2), not because we are worthless. We might trash ourselves, but God never wants us to be trash. God wants us to be God's greatest treasure! Humans are creatures with amazing God-given potential, yet we somehow bend these wonderful capacities back upon themselves individually and corporately. Nations, cultures, ethnic groups, and individuals live before God without excuse for the ways we violate and damage one another, destroy the creation, debase ourselves, and dishonor God. Still, God wants to move beyond our failures and move forward with the great goal of making us "into the image and likeness of God" as the forever family/ kingdom of God.

The following passages connect Jesus's humanity with his willingness to take our place as God's unique burden-bearer for other humans. Each of these passages stresses the reality that the burden-bearing of forgiveness is because of the value of real relationships.

> In *bringing many sons* [and daughters] *to glory, it was fitting* that God, for whom and through whom everything exists, should make the *author of their salvation perfect through suffering* (Heb 2:10, *emphasis mine*).
>
> [7] During the days of Jesus's life on earth, he offered up prayers and petitions with loud cries and tears *to the one who could save him* from death, and *he was heard because* of his *reverent submission.* [8] Although he was a son, he *learned obedience from what he suffered* [9] and, once made perfect [complete], he *became*

> *the source of eternal salvation for all who obey* him [10] and was *designated by God* to be high priest in the order of Melchizedek (Heb 5:7–10, *emphasis mine*).

> [26] While they were eating, Jesus took bread, gave thanks and *broke it*, and gave it to his disciples, saying, "Take and eat; this is *my body*." [27] Then he took the cup, gave thanks and offered it to them, saying, "Drink from it, all of you. [28] This is *my blood* of the covenant, which is *poured out for many for the forgiveness of sins* (Matt 26:26–28, *emphasis mine*).

The role of High Priest is that of being a human who is the mediating burden-bearer between God and humans. It is Jesus's very human "body" and "blood" that allow Jesus to bear the burden of the of the rest of us humans (Heb 2:14, 10:10, 20).

If you wonder how Jesus's willingness to shed his lifeblood can cover over your brokenness and sinfulness, I encourage you to spend less worry on how it works and more energy on trusting the God who says it will work. It seems to me that the pattern is the same as when God passed over all houses that had the blood of the Passover Lamb on the doorposts (Ex 12:13). It did not matter whether those preparing for the Exodus from Egypt understood how it worked—apparently no one did. What mattered was choosing to trust that, if God said through God's agent Moses that it would work, it would! Just so, you do not need to understand how Jesus's pouring out his lifeblood allows God to forgive and cover over your brokenness and sins; so long as you trust that if God says it will work, it will work!

There are actually a lot of experiences in my life that work well without me understanding how they work. From the mundane—the computer I am typing on and the Internet I will use tonight are beyond my understanding, to the profound—the love my family has for me is totally beyond my understanding, but I love how it works!

Having said that, I confess that I could easily have been among those who stood outside looking at the doorpost and wondering how it could work, or if the angel of death really was going to come passing by. I also used to spend a lot of time trying to sort out all the various doctrinal theories of atonement, although even the best never seemed to be as vibrant as the reality, and the worst are horrendous. I continue to think about those things and still wonder *how* and *why*. That is a good thing. But it is also a good thing that now my trust is *not* in my understanding of *why* it works or *how* it works, but in trusting the one *Who* promises it will be effective.

> [16] *For God so loved the world that God gave his* [God's] *one and only Son*, that whoever believes [trusts] in him shall not perish but may have eternal life. [17] For God did *not* send his Son into the world *to condemn the world, but to save the world* through him (John 3:16–17, *emphasis mine*).

The Who is the God who loves each person in the entire "world" and the God who has no desire to condemn anyone or to have anyone's humanity finally destroyed. This God wants no human to miss being made whole (*see also* 1 Tim 2:4; Rom 5:1–10; 2 Cor 5:19; 1 John 2:2, 4:14). Passages that make a connection between God's love for the entire world and Jesus's willingness to bear our burdens to save us from ourselves are spread throughout the New Testament.

God's love for God's son Jesus, and God's love for God's other human sons and daughters, is central to the relationship shared by God and Jesus. Jesus responds to the sins of both friend and foe by choosing to absorb the hurt, pain, suffering, and injustices that are inflicted upon him. Thus he demonstrates that love and mercy are at the core of what we need if we are to have an authentic relationship with him. In responding as he does, Jesus also reveals what God has been choosing for millennia—to bear the burdensome cost of forgiveness that makes loving relationships possible.

(*See* also Matt 20:28, 26:26–30; Mark 10:43–45; Luke 5:24, 22:19–22, 23:34; John 1:29, 36, 11:51–52; Acts 20:28; Rom 3:26, 4:25; 1 Cor 5:7, 6:20, 7:23, 8:11; Col 2:13–14; 1 Thess 5:9–10; Titus 2:14; Heb 9:12–15, 9:26, 10:12–14; 1 Pet 2:21–25, 3:18; 2 Pet 2:1; 1 John 2:2, 4:10–12; Rev 1:5–6, 5:9–14.)

Jesus's Costly Burden-Bearing on God's Behalf Is Extended to Jesus's Followers.

Jesus's dying "for us" in a costly act of burden-bearing leads to forgiveness that makes possible a renewed and deepened relationship with God. God is a burden-bearer. Jesus is uniquely a burden-bearer on God's behalf. Perhaps most of us would like to stop the process at this point if we have managed to get this far comfortably, but . . .

Not only were great heroes of the faith prior to Jesus, such as Jeremiah, Elijah, and Hosea, God's burden-bearers; if you are a follower of Jesus, you too are called to be a fellow-burden-bearer with Jesus. Follower of Jesus or not, I hope you have learned that relating to people you love often includes being a burden-bearer and that this burden-bearing often means costly forgiveness as well. If we understand that being fully human means burden-bearing, then we can see that Jesus's burden-bearing is embedded in his humanity.

The following three New Testament examples indicate that the New Testament writers see Jesus's burden-bearing as a human act that other humans are called to emulate.

> [1] Brothers, if someone is caught in a sin, you who are spiritual should restore him gently. But watch yourself, or you also may be tempted. *2 Carry each other's burdens, and in this way you will fulfill the law of Christ* (Gal 6:1–2, *emphasis mine*).

> [21] To this you were called, because Christ suffered for you, *leaving you an example, that you should follow in his steps. . . . 24a Christ himself bore our sins in his body* on the tree, so that we might die to sins and live for righteousness (1 Pet 2:21, 24a, *emphasis mine*).

> Now I rejoice in *what was suffered for you*, and *I fill up in my flesh what is still lacking in regard to Christ's afflictions*, for the sake of his body, which is the church (Col 1:24, *emphasis mine*).

Like Jesus's closest disciples, who ran and hid when they realized that Jesus was allowing himself to be arrested, we do not easily connect *choosing to suffer for other people's mistakes* with the journey toward *being made "in the image of God."* Nevertheless, each of the passages above maintains that the burden-bearing of forgiveness is deeply embedded, not only in Jesus's humanity, but also in ours—if we follow him.

Actually, we do understand; we just resist the implications. We understand that the young Ruby Bridges paid the cost of integrating American schools on behalf of tens of thousands of others. We also understand that Ruby's parents were not cruel or uncaring parents when they encouraged their daughter to walk into mockery and possible death—a scapegoat for white racists to jeer at, but a burden-bearer for millions of disenfranchised non-White children in the United States.

We understand that the Ten Boom family and the village of Le Chambon, unlike most other people of the time (including most Christians all across the world), decided to share in bearing the horrendous burden the Nazi system was heaping upon the Jewish people of Europe. These folks chose to risk their lives and freedoms, not because they had to do so, but because they could not bring themselves to leave others to bear their burdens alone. They chose to become burden-bearers for God and for the good of others.

We understand that John Lewis crossed the bridge at Selma and took the beating by White policemen acting on behalf of a racist culture because he was willing to "suffer on behalf of many" for the sins of American racism. Lewis was no more a masochist than Jesus was. Lewis's willingness to forgive was amazing, as throughout his political career he used his power not in attempting to get even with racists, not in trying to be sure the racists who hurt him most directly had to "pay up," but rather as an encourager and model of how a different kind of relationship is possible. This is burden-bearing that expresses an authentic willingness to forgiveness anyone who will accept that forgiveness. Most in the Amish community of Nickel Mine, PA, chose to forgive the shooter who entered their school and killed their children. Most of the members of Emanuel AME Church in Charleston, SC chose to forgive the shooter who allowed them to pray for him and then shot members of the prayer group in cold blood. These are powerful examples of the choice to be burden-bearers through forgiveness.

If we can understand, or at least attempt to understand, Ruby Bridges's parents, the Ten Boom family, the residents of Le Chambon, John Lewis, the Pennsylvania Amish, and the Charleston Christians, perhaps we can understand, or at least attempt to understand, that God was not cruel or uncaring when he supported his Son as he walked into mockery and certain death! Of course, they would all have preferred another way. They did not want a world in which others had to risk life and limb as they did. Jesus too would have loved for the world to be different, even as he prayed, "If it is possible, let this cup pass" (Matt 26:39). Still, he encouraged his followers to follow in his steps, whatever the cost. Sometimes choosing to bear the burden for others is the only way forward toward the possibility of healthier relationships in the future.

As unsettling as it is, not only did the human Jesus enact God's burden-bearing for the sake of relationships, he also asks us to be willing to do the same. It would be difficult to even imagine a more direct and terrifying invitation to join Jesus in being a burden-bearer than the one he gives—take up your cross daily and follow me (Luke 9:23). And yet, it is also honoring, isn't it? We are invited to be like him—burden-bearers through whom God might bring healing to other humans. This is the central role that Jesus plays in God's great human project that always demands burden-bearing that forgives others. It fully embeds Jesus in his own humanity—and in ours.

12

Jesus's Faith and Faithfulness

Wrestling with whether God was really faithful or not was one of the primary themes in the Old Testament prophetic literature and in dozens of psalms. In many ways, trust (faith) and trustworthiness (faithfulness) are among the primary themes and questions in the New Testament, too. As N. T. Wright demonstrates, the faithfulness of God is a central theme for Paul, and it is *the* primary question in Romans.[1] It must be one of the main things Paul wrestled with during that time he spent alone after he met Jesus face to face.

In addition, the faithfulness of Jesus is a central theme in the New Testament.[2] In Romans, Jesus's faithfulness is God's means for saving us (Romans 3:23–31). The faithfulness of Jesus, along with the faithfulness of Abraham, also provides the model for the rest of us (Romans 3–4).

The letter of Hebrews features Jesus's faithfulness throughout by doing these things:

1. Comparing Jesus's faithfulness with Moses's faithfulness (Heb 3:1–6)
2. Creating a roll call of the faithful from the Old Testament, with a special emphasis on the faithfulness of Abraham and Moses (Heb 11)
3. Including what seems to be a reference to the mother and brothers executed by Antiochus, as told in 2 Maccabees 7 (Heb 11:35)
4. Telling us that everyone before Jesus still needed what God did for them through Jesus's faithfulness, just as those of us coming after Jesus do (Heb 11:39—12:12).

Jesus's faithfulness is often described with the word group *pistis*, Hebrews also emphasizes Jesus's faithfulness with other words. The writer says that God heard and responded to Jesus's fervent prayers because of Jesus's "reverence" and "obedience

---

1. Wright, *Faithfulness of God*.
2. Zorn, *Faithfulness of Jesus*.

(Heb 5:7–8). He also tells his readers to respond to God with this same reverence and obedience (Heb 5:9, 12:28). Throughout the letter, the writer emphasizes God's faithfulness in fulfilling for Jesus, and then through Jesus for others, many of the promises and patterns God had prepared throughout God's history with Israel.

It is important to grasp the broad perspective the biblical writers had concerning faith (trust) and faithfulness (trustworthiness), if we wish to understand how deeply our trusting God, and being trustworthy before God, embeds Jesus in our humanity.

THE BIBLICAL UNDERSTANDING OF "FAITH" INCLUDES RELATIONAL FAITHFULNESS.

Trust and Trustworthiness Are Primarily Relational.

I think Gabriel Marcel is correct in maintaining that it is a big mistake to think of what he calls "fidelity" as static. Genuine faithfulness flows from faith, and it demands constant creativity. In a living, vibrant relationship, neither party stands still. So, maintaining trust, and expressing that trust in a trustworthy manner, means being willing to constantly reevaluate what will express love and trust to the other person in his or her current situation.

In a genuinely two-sided relationship, this means creative engagement is a must. It also means that we always experience faithfulness as having the potential to deteriorate from either side of the relationship. The real world is filled with many possible twists and turns; therefore, acting in a trustworthy manner involves many choices to be made with imagination and inventiveness.[3] The dynamic is clear. Trust leads to acting trustworthily; acting trustworthily leads to deepening trust.

Why would we think it would be any different in our relationship with God? Why would we think that it would be any different in Jesus's relationship with God? The tendency to degrade the deeply personal, responsive, creative, and risky nature of the relationship between God and Jesus—and the relationship God wants with the rest of us—is furthered by our English translations of the New Testament Greek word group *pistis*. "Belief" and "faith" capture a part of the content of the *pistis* word group. However, as these words are currently used in English, they are far too narrow. Neither "belief" nor "faith" emphasizes the primary relational meaning of *pistis*. "Trust" and "Trustworthiness" come much closer to expressing the relational breadth and depth involved in *pistis*. As we will explore shortly, the *pistis* word group has several important dimensions, but *mutual relational trust is primary*.

To make matters worse, the English word "*believe*" is now often heard as primarily signifying assent to intellectual content or to right thinking. For example, "I believe in the Ten Commandments" is not heard primarily as *I trust God and attempt to live these instructions in a trustworthy manner*, but rather as *I affirm their content*. Still

---

3. Marcel, *Homo Viator*, 90–91.

worse, in many other instances "belief" and "faith" are often used in current English as the opposite of having substantial evidence, and therefore are heard primarily as unsubstantiated wishful thinking. To many, "believing" and "having faith" have come to mean being irrationally emotional, rather than facing reality.

Humans have known for millennia the importance of the trust–trustworthiness dynamic in relationships. Modern studies of child-parent relationships underscore how important this is in human character formation. Long before a child can formulate a verbal description of what she or he has learned, that child will have already learned whether the world as she or he experiences it is a trustworthy place, or is not. At a very young age, the child is already responding to life either with peaceful trust or with increasing fear, anxiety, and distrust.

Similarly, marriages and friendships that are healthy relationships are founded in mutual trust, not in control. Surely if God's relationship with us is a real, interpersonal relationship, it must be the same. Otherwise, it is not an interpersonal, shared relationship, but rather a transactional contract enforced by law and domination or continued only so long as there is perceived mutual usefulness.

Of course, there are friendships and marriages based only on contractual usefulness. In such relationships, we remain trustworthy only as long as the other person is useful to our goals. There are also relationships sustained only by the dominating power of one of the persons involved. In such relationships, there is no trust involved. And the disempowered person remains in the relationship only until she or he dares to risk escape. Most of us do not long for such relationships with other humans. Why would we want such a relationship with God? Why would we think God would want such a relationship with us?

Trust that flows into trustworthiness is essential in healthy, intimate human relationships. The Scriptures claim that God desires that type of mutual relationship with us humans. Trust is, above all, a willingness to risk entrusting the core of my being—my "heart"—into someone else's hands. Isn't that what God wants to give to us and to receive from us? But, as we all know, this kind of trusting relationship is always risky. It has the potential to provide the wondrous gifts of shared love and joy, but it also has the potential to permit deep wounds and terrible suffering. If the relationship between Jesus and God is a real relationship involving mutual trust and mutual trustworthiness, it must be a relationship with the potential for great mutual joy and great mutual hurt.

Relationships of Trust and Trustworthiness Involve Mutual Shared Risk.

Before exploring the various dimensions of faith, it is important to emphasize that New Testament writers were convinced that Jesus was fully committed to a risky, adventurous human relationship with God. Faith does not rule out risk. In fact, faith (trust) is always a risk. I am amazed that so many Christians seem determined to find ways of explaining Jesus's interactions with God in Gethsemane as though it were risk-free (Mark 14:33–36). More controversially, and I admit less explicitly, I think the Gospels also portray God as on a risky adventure of mutual trust with Jesus. That would be an understanding of the event in harmony with how so many of the Old Testament interactions between God and humans are described. The relationship God and Jesus share is mutual, rather than a relationship of domination that results in lack of real choice. This means the relationship involves mutual risk.

Isn't this the *stuff* of all real relationships? Like all other relationships that are genuine, the human relationship with God has as its only ultimate guarantee God's loving and trustworthy character. Will God keep God's word? For example, all the legal, familial, and financial intertwining did not guarantee that my wife would be faithful in our relationship for over 57 years; only her trustworthy character did. I trusted her because she was trustworthy. If I had attempted to make her be faithful by controlling and dominating her, at best we would been living an enforced contract, not a loving relationship based in a covenant of mutual trust.

The relationship between Jesus and God was a genuine relationship, they chose to trust one another, and they chose to respond in a trustworthy manner to one another. The guarantee was not dominating control; the guarantee was God's character and Jesus's human character, which reflected and imaged God's character.

C. S. Lewis wrestled with how we can know whether a relationship is serious, and he concluded that we cannot know whether our relationship is truly filled with trust and love unless it is a relationship in which we are risking high stakes.[4] And it is when everything is at stake, when instead of trusting a rope to pull a wagon, we trust it to swing us over an abyss, that we know we are really trusting and believe the rope to be trustworthy.[5] Jesus's faithfulness to God, no matter the cost, was a swing out over the great abyss facing every human—death.

This is the main point of Hebrews 11:1–12:12, a section of the letter that initially emphasizes many human responses to God's trustworthiness (faithfulness). Each responded "by faith [trust]" or "faithfulness [trustworthiness]" (chapter 11). Then, in chapter 12, the writer emphasizes Jesus's trust in God, and Jesus's trustworthiness toward God, as the overwhelming fulfillment of the pattern first seen in the lives of the heroes and heroines of faith. The writer next asserts that it is this kind of trust and trustworthiness that is required of those of us who want to follow Jesus who *trailblazed* and *completed* human trust/trustworthiness.

A similar challenge is expressed in Romans 3:21–4:25, as the reader is called to faithfully follow in the footsteps of Jesus and Abraham—both of whom risked trusting God to be trustworthy, when many of the surrounding circumstances provided plenty of reasons to question God's faithfulness. As several scholars have pointed out, the replicated Greek phrasing in Romans 3:26 and 4:16 clearly parallels the trust Jesus and

---

4. Lewis, *Grief*, 36.
5. Lewis, *Grief*, 21.

Abraham each placed in God. Paul stresses the uniqueness that is so overwhelming in Jesus's complete faithfulness to God. Simultaneously, he also emphasizes its continuity with the model Abraham provided for Jesus and for us.[6]

When we insist that there was no risk for either God or Jesus, based on our definition of God's sovereignty, and when we then add to that an insistence that Jesus could not fail because, after all, he was "God," we remove their relationship from the realm of genuine, shared interpersonal relationships between God and humans. Even worse, we rob both God and Jesus of so much of the honor each is due.

How can there be a real relationship—a real covenant relationship—in this world that is filled with contingencies, without risk on both sides? Isn't the very essence of genuine trusting relationships of love the mutual risk that knows that the responsiveness of the partner in the relationship cannot be coerced or guaranteed, except by the partner's character and choice?[7] And isn't the essence of covenant-making seen in the fact that the participants promise to be faithful, even if future circumstances bring unwanted and difficult changes—"for better or for worse, for richer or for poorer, in sickness and in health?" Has there ever been a truly loving relationship that did not involve both risk and adventure?

This is not to say that God would not have found another way to fulfill God's purpose and promises to humans if Jesus had failed; it is to say God would have been brokenhearted if Jesus had failed to remain faithful—to act trustworthily toward God. In fact, we are told that is exactly what occurred when Saul failed as God's chosen, and David was chosen to carry out the role God had intended for Saul (1 Sam 13:13–14). The author of Exodus tells us that another example almost occurred. Only Moses's passionate prayer averted God's plan to restart God's promise to Abraham through Moses's lineage (Ex 32:1–14, 33:1–33).

I am not sure whether Ellen Davis would apply her insight concerning the relationship between God and Abraham to the relationship between Jesus and God, but I think we should. She maintains Genesis 22 indicates that God's heart and hopes were as much at risk as were Abraham's and Isaac's.[8] How much greater, then, is God's risk in God's relationship with the human Jesus? Jesus is at the center of God's purpose for humans. Will Jesus be faithful "even unto death," or will God have to start all over in this great next step of salvation, much as God was prepared to start over with Moses and did start over with David? When you read the Gospel narratives through that lens, the power of Jesus's faithfulness is breathtaking!

---

6. Wright, *Paul and Faithfulness*, 844–847.
7. Witherington, "God Is Love," 60–61.
8. Davis, *Getting Involved*, 59–62.

BIBLICAL FAITH/TRUST HAS SEVERAL IMPORTANT DIMENSIONS.

New Testament literature describes human faithfulness (trust and trustworthiness) toward God in several different dimensions, each being important to the overall broad meaning of "faith" or "trust." Each of these categories of trust (faith) and trustworthiness (faithfulness) is a part of Jesus's life as it is described throughout the New Testament. Each is also a part of how the rest of us humans are challenged to respond to God if we wish to follow Jesus.

Pistis (Trust/Faith) Is, above All, a Matter of Who One Believes: Trusting In.

The primary personal and relational dimension of trust begins with *Who* we trust. As far as Jesus is concerned, the *Who* he trusted is the One God of Israel who is also the Creator. Jesus trusted the God who interacted in very special ways with Abraham, Sarah, Moses, Rahab, Ruth, David, and the great prophets of Israel. Jesus trusted the God whose master story was enacted in a special way in the individual and corporate lives of the Jewish people, as narrated in the Hebrew Bible. To be clear, I am not maintaining that there was not more to Jesus's relationship with God than knowledge and application of the Hebrew Bible; I am maintaining that the experiences with God recorded in the Hebrew Bible were always a central part of that relationship. It was the "God of Abraham" whom Jesus trusted as his "Father."

The Gospels present Jesus as a *very faithful Jew*, who worships God by regularly attending the synagogue, going to the Temple in Jerusalem, wearing fringes on his garments, as the Torah commanded (the "edge" or "hem" of Luke 8:44), and praying daily. Always in the specific context of being a faithful Jew, Jesus is also presented as *the faithful human*, the one human, whether Jew or Gentile, who lives faithfully without transgression before the One God of all humanity. Overemphasis on "Jesus is God," as well as theologies that define God's sovereignty as "no risk," have tended to greatly demean the level of trust and trustworthiness involved in the relationship between Jesus and God as his Abba. This diminishing of Jesus's trust tends to then diminish our understanding that Jesus is God's first completed human.

Given how widespread the use of the Greek word group *pistis* ("trust," "faith," "belief") is in most of the rest of the New Testament, it is somewhat surprising that the Gospel writers use different words to describe this dimension of Jesus's relationship with God. The only times in the Gospels that Jesus is described with the *pistis* word group is in his statements concerning how every human should relate to God. Before making too much of this, we should note that, unlike John, the synoptic gospels do not use the word *agape* (love) to describe Jesus's relationship with God, except in instances that involve what all humans should do. Few of us would maintain that Matthew, Mark, and Luke did not think that Jesus loved God. They just use different words.

Clearly, when Jesus quotes, "Man does not live on bread alone, but on every word that comes from the mouth of God" (Matt 4:4; Deut 8:3), he is including himself. In fact, the quotation is his response to why he will be faithful and not give in to the temptation. Context indicates that several passages using the *pistis* word group apply specifically to Jesus's own actions, as well as to his challenge to others.

Walter Zorn points out that Mark gives us several examples of Jesus using this everyone-so-also-me device. In Mark 5:36 Jesus says, "Do not fear, only believe," implying that he himself does trust that God will overcome the young girl's death. Jesus's explains to a terrified father why his disciples had failed in their attempts to heal his boy, and why Jesus will not fail—"All things are possible for one who believes" (Mark 9:23, *see* also 9:29, 11:23).[9] Finally, having just acknowledged to his disciples that he is "overwhelmed" (Mark 14:34), Jesus then prays using the intimate "Abba" to tell God that he would like for God to "Take this cup from me. Yet not what I will, but what you will" (Mark 14:36). It would be difficult to imagine a more vivid description of ultimate interpersonal trust. *Jesus risked all on Who he trusted.*

The fact that Jesus not only taught with wise words, but actually lived to the fullest what he taught, was what impressed people the most. He called people to a faithfulness that he modeled for them, and for us. It is what still impresses me the most about Jesus. I learned long ago that talking about faith is so much easier than walking the talk. And, once we begin to think of Jesus as faithfully living his faith, we begin to realize just how many times he challenged the people around him, both to "believe" and "trust," just as they saw him doing.

It is no wonder that the writers of the New Testament letters felt free to describe Jesus as trusting/faithful—as the one who expressed in its fullness the right human relationship with God. In fact, the faithfulness Jesus expressed was so profound that they began to identify God as "The God and Father of our Lord Jesus the Messiah." Jesus's willingness to be faithful and trustworthy, even through the execution event, is Paul's example for how we should model Jesus in our lives (Phil 2:1–15). Revelation 19:11 gives Jesus the title "the Faithful and True," or perhaps even better translated "Trustworthy and True." As noted earlier, the entire letter of Hebrews and an entire section of Romans are testimonies to this trustworthiness of Jesus.

Recently, several scholars have begun to maintain that there are quite a few other passages in the letters that should be translated as "Jesus's faith/faithfulness." My first exposure to the insight occurred in the mid-1970s when Walter Zorn, now a Lincoln Christian University professor emeritus, told me that he was convinced several New Testament passages would be better translated, not as "faith in Jesus Christ" (the dominant English tradition), but as "the faith of Jesus Christ," or "Jesus the Messiah's faithfulness." It is primarily Jesus's faith and faithfulness that saves us, not ours. He convinced me that this was true in Romans 3:21–26 and probably in several other passages as well.

9. Zorn, *Faithfulness of Jesus*, 191–194.

As for technical linguistic issues concerning the translation choice, the question revolves around whether a Greek phrase should be translated as an objective genitive or as a subjective genitive—is Jesus the object of faith/trust or the subject of faith/trust in these statements? Does the phrase "faith of Jesus" mean someone's faith in Jesus, or Jesus's faith in God? Only context can determine, because the same wording can mean either.

This translation issue does not occur because there is something esoteric about *Koine* Greek; we sometimes face the same problem in English. When we say, "the love of God," do we mean God's love for us, or do we mean our love for God? The right choice must come from the context because the phrase itself can mean either. To give one further example, if I write "This is the history of the Native Americans," do I mean this is how some Caucasian scholar has recorded history about Native Americans, or do I mean history as told by Native Americans?

You could not know without a context that, when I wrote "the history of the Native Americans," I was thinking of how the Native Americans tell the history of what has often been called "Custer's Last Stand" in history books written by White Americans. It is quite clear from the Native American versions of the same event that "Custer's Last Arrogant Mistake" or "Custer's Last Vicious Assault" would be more appropriate descriptions of the event.

Zorn sent me an unpublished article in the early 1990s, which articulates some of his reasons for his claims.[10] One of the most important is that the Greek phrase in Romans 3:26 (*ek pisteōs iēsou*) speaking of Jesus's faithfulness is exactly paralleled in Romans 4:16 (*ek pisteōs abraam*) regarding Abram's faithfulness, and no translator translates 4:16 as "our faith in Abraham"—the meaning is clearly "Abraham's faithfulness." Another reason he gave was that, using the meaning "Jesus's faithfulness" removes the awkward redundancy in speaking of our faith in Jesus twice in 3:22. He also noted that the emphasis in 3:25 on Jesus's faithfulness saving us, rather than our own faith saving us, is in better theological harmony with Paul's overall theology, which views Jesus's faithfulness as the primary source of our salvation, whereas our faithful response, though essential, is secondary in this process.

In 2002, Richard Hays of Yale and Duke wrote of the faith of Jesus as described in Galatians.[11] In his recent book on Paul's theology, N. T. Wright states that he, too, has believed for some time now that the best translation of several passages in Paul's letters describes the faithfulness of Jesus as Israel's Messiah, not the faith of Jesus's followers.[12] Scot McKnight has recently made the same point concerning Romans 3:26.[13] The Common English Bible has provided us with an English translation of the New

---

10. Zorn, "Faith of Jesus: New Perspectives."
11. Hays, *Faith of Jesus Christ*, 141–162.
12. Wright, *Faithfulness of God*, 844–847.
13. McKnight, *Romans Backward*, 123.

Testament that reflects this scholarship in some passages. Here are two of those passages from the Common English Bible.

> [21] But now God's righteousness has been revealed apart from the Law, which is confirmed by the Law and the Prophets. [22] *God's righteousness comes through the faithfulness of Jesus Christ* for all who have faith in him. There's no distinction. [23] All have sinned and fall short of God's glory, [24] but all are treated as righteous freely by his grace because of a ransom that was paid by Jesus Christ. [25] *Through his* [Jesus's] *faithfulness, God displayed Jesus as the place of sacrifice where mercy is found* by means of his blood (Rom 3:21–25, Common English Bible, *emphasis mine*).

> [16] However, we know that a person isn't made righteous by the works of the Law, *but rather through the faithfulness of Jesus Christ*. We ourselves believed in Jesus Christ *so that we could be made righteous by the faithfulness of Christ* and not by the works of the Law—because no one will be made righteous by the works of the Law.... [20] I have been crucified with Christ, and I no longer live, but Christ lives in me. And the life that I now live in my body, *I live by faith, indeed, by the faithfulness of God's Son, who loved me and gave himself for me.* (Gal 2:16, 20, Common English Bible, *emphasis mine*).

In his recent book, in addition to Romans 3:22, 26 and Galatians 2:16a, 16b, 20, Zorn notes Galatians 3:22, 26 (the papyrus 46 reading), Philippians 3:9, and Ephesians 3:12 as passages where Paul's Greek phrasing should be read as Jesus's faith/faithfulness, rather than as his readers' faith in Jesus. He also adds Revelation 14:12 as a Johannine example of the subjective genitive phrase that should be translated "the faithfulness of Jesus," and he gives solid grammatical and contextual reasons for doing so.[14] He further notes that the author of Revelation uses a different phrase to designate the risen and exalted Jesus as continuing to be "the faithful witness, the firstborn from the dead" (Rev. 1:5).

Zorn not only gives solid reasons why the Greek subjective genitive phrasing should be translated as "the faith/faithfulness of Jesus," but throughout the book he shows how this fits the overall theology of the New Testament far better than alternative translations. He also provides helpful insights into why this translation has been resisted by many, even though it fits much better the claim that we are saved by Jesus's righteous actions, not by our own. I for one find it incredibly freeing to rely on Jesus's faithfulness and righteousness, rather than my faithfulness and righteousness, as the primary basis upon which I dare stand before God without fear.

If we take the subjective genitive translation, then each of the Scriptures from the list above is added to those in the Gospels that narrate Jesus's obedience to God and to those in Hebrews that celebrate Jesus as the model of faithfulness. Above all else, these

---

14. Zorn, *Faithfulness of Jesus*, 74.

point to Jesus's faith and faithfulness in terms of *Who* Jesus trusted—Jesus's response to the relationship he shared with the God *Who* is his Father.

And, as we have seen in so many other instances, and will continue to see throughout this book, what God asked of Jesus is what Jesus asks of those of us who follow him.

[15] . . . that *everyone who believes in him* [trusts in him] may have eternal life. [16] For God so loved the world that *God* gave *God's* one and only Son, that *whoever believes* [trusts] in him shall not perish but have eternal life (John 3:15–16, *emphasis mine*).

[43] All the prophets testify about him that *everyone who believes* [trusts] *in him* receives forgiveness of sins through his name (Acts 10:43, *emphasis mine*).

[42] And if anyone causes *one of these little ones who believe* [trust] *in me to sin* [stumble], it would be better for him to be thrown into the sea with a large millstone tied around his neck (Mark 9:42, *emphasis mine*).

Sometimes good writing means breaking the normal rules; so in Romans 4, Paul intentionally overuses the word group *pistis* in order to emphasize the primacy of trusting—especially of Who we trust. In the relatively short section of Romans 4:11–25, as Paul parallels the faith of Abraham and the faith of Jesus, he uses various forms of the Greek word group *pistis* thirteen times. The emphasis throughout this section is on *Who* Abraham decided to trust, even when situations were such that there were plenty of reasons and emotions pushing him in other directions. As followers of Jesus, we are called to the same journey. *It is all about Who Jesus trusted, Who Abraham trusted, and Who we trust.*

Pistis (Trust/Faith) Includes How Intensely One Believes at the Core: Trusting Deeply.

Other than *who* we trust, *how deeply* we trust might be the most important aspect of trust. To use a common biblical term, does my trust go all the way to my *heart*—reside in my core? The heart is the place where our true meaning in life resides, the place from which our deepest desires and passions flow, and the place where our primary master story of reality resides. It is where our deepest fears, dislikes, loves, motives, and hopes reside, and it is where they are often hidden away, even from ourselves (Pss 19:12–14, 51:10, 17; Gen 6:5–6; Deut 8:2, 10:12; Prov 3:5, 4:23; Matt 5:8, 6:21, 12:34, 13:15, 15:18–19). As the prophets proclaimed, God wants human hearts turned toward God in trust (Jer 3:10, 17:10, 24:7, 29:13, 31:33), so God can then relate to us humans with God's whole heart as well (Jer 30:24, 31:20).

It seems to me that who we trust—God, god, culture, subculture, or self—is exhibited in a dynamic interplay that occurs in every human's life. This constantly developing dynamic is what forms each person's heart. Our developing character is expressed in our choices. Our repeated choices become our customs (habits). Our customs then become the next development in our character. The dynamic interplay of *Character-Choice-Custom-Character* continues until we take our last breath.

Jesus's entire life, as well as the entirety of his teaching, emphasizes the importance of choosing to be "all in" with "all your heart." He lived with a fierce, fiery, gentle, and patient faithfulness that is overwhelming. He claimed that we can trust him to relate to us in kindness and grace—because his heart is tamed and humble (Matt 11:29). He quotes "with all your heart" from the *Shema* as the central commandment from God, and he demands a willingness to "lose your life for my sake." These were all teachings that describe his own relationship with God.

Importantly, Jesus enacts these teachings, even in the most difficult times of his life. Jesus passionately acknowledges what he desires—"Let this cup pass." Then he focuses on a deeper desire—"Yet, not as I will, but as you will." "Overwhelmed" and "in anguish," Jesus openly reveals the tension of two deep desires in his heart as he works his way through the deeply emotional decision (Mark 14:32–36).

Jesus not only lived from the heart, he also taught that all of us should live out of the depths of our hearts, focused on God. In addition to summarizing the Torah as loving God with all our hearts, he said, "*the pure in heart* will see God" (Matt 5:8). He also taught that we can discern what is in our hearts by noting what "treasure" dominates our thoughts and actions (Matt 6:21).

As noted earlier, C. S. Lewis learned that, though he still believed what he had written concerning the rationality of faith and love, that part of his faith alone could not carry him when faced with the abyss—faith now clearly included a sense of great risk. Some historians believe that Thomas Aquinas experienced a vision near the end of his life that made it plain to him that all of his rational writings fell short of capturing the fullness of faith and faithfulness.[15] Blaise Pascal wrote powerfully of the rationality of faith in God, then concluded that we all still have to wager our lives on God or on something else.[16] Each of these writers who highly valued the rational wanted us to understand that even more important is the inner core that lies underneath our reason—the heart!

If we avoid the reductionism that sometimes defines faith as nothing but an inner stance, we can learn a lot from such existentialists of past generations as Sartre, Camus, Kierkegaard, and Marcel. From a wide variety of worldviews, these writers demonstrated how important our inner stance and passion are in determining how we humans live our lives. Trust is a matter of the heart—a matter of intensity and authenticity at the core of one's being. Trust is an inner stance toward reality. As much as some of us (and I confess this is my own tendency) might like for faith to be "a cool matter of intellect," trusting God and what God has done through Jesus can never be

---

15. "Aquinas," *Christian History Magazine*, #73.
16. Pascal, *Pensées* 233, "Infinite—Nothing," 213–216.

cool. It sometimes demands a *hot* and *all-in* willingness to "sweat blood" and take the "leap of faith" that risks everything. As the risen Jesus said to a community of Jesus followers, If you won't be hot, please just be cold; neutral and lukewarm are completely unacceptable (Rev 3:15–17).

(Other New Testament passages that emphasize this inner and passionate dimension of trust that expresses what we really desire in life include Mark 7:19, 11:22–24, 12:29–31; Luke 6:45, 8:15; Acts 8:13–22; Rom 10:9–10; 2 Cor 11:21–12:10.)

Pistis (Trust/Faith) Includes Deeds and Actions that Express Trust In God: Doing Trust.

Jesus's trust is expressed as *trusting behavior—trustworthy responses* to God. Jesus's faith is faith in action. The Gospel writers often use words such as "do," "doing," "works," "working," "serving," "receiving (from God)," "listening to (hearing) God," "obeying," "being thankful," "he went into the synagogue as was his custom," and "keeping the commandments" to describe Jesus's faithfulness in action. They tell us that Jesus lived day by day as a faithful and observant Jewish believer. We hear him praying under great duress, "Not my will, but your will be done." When you read the Gospels, it would be difficult to think of a better summary of how Jesus responded to God than the words from an old hymn, "Trust and obey, for there's no other way."

Much as other rabbis taught, based on God's covenant with Noah, Jesus teaches that caring and uncaring human actions toward other humans will be the basis for judging all nations (Matt 25:31–48, *see* Rom 2:7–11). Perhaps above all else, he both lives and teaches that "loving God" means putting our *love* for our fellow humans into action (Luke 10:25–37; John 15:13–15). Philippians 2:1–13 challenges readers to think and act as Jesus did toward his fellow humans, as the way to please God. In fact, Jesus is seen as still acting faithfully on our behalf before God as Mediator, Priest, Lord, and Savior in various parts of the New Testament.

Finally, Jesus's call to "follow me" is a call to emulate his faithful covenant relationship with God. We too are to express our faith in action. *His way* of living is "the way" for us humans to see God as our Father, just as it has been for him (John 14:1–10, which begins "Trust in God; trust also in me.") Never is the demand for costly action more intense than "Anyone who does not *take his cross and follow me* is not worthy of me" (Matt 10:38, *emphasis mine*).

Even the risen and exalted Jesus is described in terms of faithful actions toward God. Jesus is called the faithful witness to God (Rev 1:5–6, 3:14) using the same phrase that identifies another faithful human prophet who was executed (Rev 2:13). Jesus serves God as God's faithful High Priest mediating between God and the rest of us humans (Heb 2:17), and he is God's faithful firstborn son over God's household of human believers (Heb 3:6).

Although it is wrong-headed to define faith apart from faithful actions, it is equally wrong-headed to define faith only in terms of observance and obedience. This was the context for Paul's arguments concerning "works of the law" versus "trust" in Romans and Galatians. Nevertheless, there have always been groups of Christians who have tended to define faith in a very legalistic manner. The chasm is not between *trusting God* and *acting trustworthily in response to God*. The chasm is between *trying to be obedient in order to earn God's love and acceptance,* and *being obedient as our thankful response because we are loved and accepted by God.*

(There are many other examples demanding that our faith be expressed as "doing" and "acting." *See* for examples: Matt 25:31–46; Luke 18:20–23; John 15:9–14; Rom 1:1–6, 16:25–27; Gal 5:6, 13–14; Heb 12:1–2; Jas 2:17–24; 1 Pet 4:8–11; 1 John 3:16–18.)

Pistis (Trust/Faith) Includes What One Believes: Trusting That.

Just as what we do reflects what resides at our core and impacts what we think, what we think impacts what we do. The interplay is constant. So, the *content of our trust* is very important in the biblical definition of faith. Shared content was important to Jesus. He showed up regularly to worship at the Synagogue and Temple, and he knew, taught, and lived the Old Testament scriptures.

Among other reasons, this emphasis on rational content is an important check on the individualistic tendencies of American Christians. It is one way to emphasize the community nature of faith. Though it is sometimes necessary to question the handed-down content of church history, of scholarship, and of our specific Christian groups, the content of trusting also needs to be grounded in shared reasons for trusting/believing.

Throughout the Gospels, Jesus is portrayed as trusting the God who had revealed God's-self through the Hebrew Scriptures and through genuine relationships with real people in real history. He teaches the Scriptures and lives them. Jesus makes decisions to reenact Old Testament patterns revealing God's ways of relating to humans because he trusts that God will honor this way of living. He believes that God is the source of food, and his way of thankfully blessing God for giving food becomes a hallmark of his character. Jesus's trust was expressed in specific content and was fully embedded in human actions that worshiped, honored, and served God.

The New Testament writers clearly understood that trusting/faith also *includes specific content*. Here are a few examples of such specific content:

- that Jesus died for us (1 Cor 1:17–25)
- that God raised Jesus from death and will raise us (1 Cor 15:1–17)
- that Jesus came from God (John 16:27)
- that the claims written in the Gospel are true (John 21:24–25)

- that the eyewitness experiences of the disciples are empirical truth (1 John 1:1–3)
- that Jesus was "flesh" (1 John 4:1–4)
- that the apostles' teaching is essential (Acts 2:42; 1 Cor 15:3)
- that remaining faithful in hard times is crucial (Acts 14:22–23)
- that the disciples fearlessly confessed Jesus's Lordship and encouraged others to do the same (Acts 2:22–36, 4:18–19; Rom 10:8–10)
- that suffering is a part of following Jesus (1 Pet 5:8–9).

The New Testament insists on more content to faith and faithfulness than some of us are comfortable with. It is wrong-headed to define faith mainly in terms of intellectual content, including creeds, doctrines, and theologies, as some of us Christians are prone to do, but it is equally off base to define faith as without rational content, as others of us Christians are prone to do.

Pistis (Trust/Faith) Includes Why One Believes: Trusting Because.

Jesus's faith and faithfulness included *becauses* in his relationship with God. An intense example occurs in Jesus's desperate cry, "My God, My God, why have you forsaken me," as he struggles for his final breaths on the cross. The prayer, which is from Psalm 22, is filled with heartrending expressions of the anguish and anxiety faithful humans experience when God seems to be inexcusably absent in the present (22:1–2, 6–8). Despite this reality, and prior to God acting in the present, the psalmist still encourages himself to trust God. Why? *Because* God has acted to save God's people in the past (22:3–6), and *because* God has been with him personally in the past (22:9–10). With his anguished cry, Jesus places himself right with the psalmist, experiencing apparent abandonment, while crying out to the God who has been there for him, and for his people, in the past.

Hebrews 5:7 indicates that Jesus prayed fervently because he believed that God was the only one who could save him from the death that he faced. Then the writer maintains that God honored this passionate expression of Jesus's faithfulness.

The rest of us are also challenged to trust *because*. Sadly, quite a few Christians who recognize the importance of *becauses*, have attempted to make them carry a weight they cannot carry. When we attempt to turn the *trust because* into rational arguments that are supposedly "indubitable proofs," we make a huge mistake. Ironically, this approach attempts to make faith require no real faith, just knowledge. New Testament writers never thought evidence or reason alone could be enough to *prove* beyond doubt or question that biblical claims are *the truth*.

Though some modern Christians seem to think based on "creation science" or "archaeology" or claims of "biblical inerrancy" or "rational philosophical argumentation" they can place their faith beyond questions or doubts, the Gospel writers did not think it could happen. It is true that James encouraged his readers to pray without doubting, but the *because* he gives for not doubting is not a series of evidences, but the challenge to remember Who we are dealing with (Jas 1:6–18).

The three following examples indicate the Gospel writers did not see faith as immune to doubting, no matter how strong the evidence.

1. Matthew concluded his gospel by maintaining that several of the disciples who were about to be commissioned to "go into all the world" stood in the presence of the risen Jesus and yet "doubted" (Matt 28:16–20). Obviously, the writer did not think any act of God was beyond questioning, even by "disciples."

2. John 6 begins with Jesus pronouncing a blessing prayer and then feeding 5,000+ people with five loaves and two fish, but it ends with many of Jesus's "disciples" leaving him because of his confusing words. They had followed him, believed his teachings, and participated in his miraculous feeding of thousands, but, at least for the moment, their doubts, fears, and confusions won out, and they abandoned Jesus. (*See also* John 12:37.)

3. In a parable, Jesus teaches that, no matter how strong the evidence, it cannot compel us if we are determined not to trust—"If they do not listen to Moses and the prophets, neither will they be convinced, even if someone rises from the dead" (Luke 16:31).

Recognizing the danger of attempting to make evidences carry too much weight, it is still true that the New Testament writers never attempted to separate "faith" from the evidence that supports faith/trust. New Testament trust is not defined as believing with no evidence or despite all evidence to the contrary. Though acknowledging that at any given moment there can seem to be little or no evidence that God is real or faithful, the Bible never indicates that trust exists without foundation. Trusting someone includes reasons for trusting, even though genuine trust always demands going beyond our *becauses* to the *Who*.

There are many New Testament passages demonstrating various author's view that faith includes the *because* content of trust. I think all of the writers agree that we should "Always be prepared to give an answer to everyone who asks you to give the reason for the hope that you have" (1 Pet 3:15). (*See also* John 1:50, 2:11, 2:23, 4:41–42, 4:53, 7:31, 10:37–39, 20:29, 21:24–25; Rom 10:14; 1 John 1:1–4.) In addition to many obvious examples, I think Paul's use of four "because/for" (Greek *gar*) statements concerning why he is "not ashamed of the good news" in Romans 1:15–18 is a strong statement of the importance of content in Paul's own faith.

My wife was not belittling our love when she would respond to my "I love you so much" with "*Why?*" She wanted to hear that my saying I loved her was not just mushy fluff. She wanted it to have *becauses*. And my love did have content. I would enumerate some of the many ways she was such a wonderful wife, mother, friend, support, and lover in our relationship. Was there more to our relationship than these *becauses*? Yes! But our trust in one another always included these *becauses*. They are a part of a trusting relationship with a mate, a child, a parent, and a friend.

It can be no less so if we want our relationship with God through Jesus to image the trusting relationship Jesus has with God. The *Whys* are important. To say that trust/faith must go beyond our rationality and beyond our *becauses* is not to say that it is either irrational or nonrational. Rather, it is more than rational.

Our faith cannot be protected from the need to wrestle with the doubts brought on by life in the modern world. Biblical faith and faithfulness cannot legitimately be redefined as only "existential"—as only the inner dimension of faith. The *why* and *what* dimensions of trust are an essential part of trust. Some of us might wish to protect our faith in God, or even think we are protecting God, by eliminating the *becauses* of faith, but what is left is certainly not the faith that is encouraged by Jesus and his early followers. Truly, neither God, Jesus, nor the Scriptures need our protection. They will all be here long after the doubts are resolved. Granting that the *becauses* of trust are never fully self-authenticating apart from an interpersonal stance of trust, it is also true that *there are some very good reasons to trust God.*

Pistis (Trust/Faith) Includes a Shared Community: Trusting With.

Having been intricately involved in churches and church ministries from my birth to the present, I am in no danger of seeing the Church or Christian Community through rose-tinted glasses. Sometimes I find it difficult to live with the church community, but it is even more difficult to live faithfully without it. I have no doubt that many in my various church communities through the years found plenty of reasons not to be thrilled to be in community with me, as well. Nonetheless, we humans are conceived in community, and we live in a network of community all our lives. It is not surprising that God intends for us to pursue our faith in community, too.

Just as important, we cannot image Jesus if we try to make our faith primarily individualistic. Jesus very intentionally chose to live out his trust in God in community. He first spent about thirty years as a "firstborn" son and brother to four brothers and at least two sisters in his family of origin (Mark 6:3). Apparently during that time, he learned from his father Joseph and his mother Mary, and then took his place as eldest son overseeing provision for the family when his father passed away. His custom was to worship God in community (Luke 4:16).

As he began his ministry, Jesus prayerfully chose a group of disciples and demanded that they learn to live in community with himself and with one another—no small challenge, given their various backgrounds and personalities! In Mark 3:34–35, Jesus claimed (and promised) that those who seek to do God's will are his family—"my brothers and my sisters." In Luke 22:15, the account of Jesus's last supper with his disciples begins with him saying, "I have eagerly desired to eat this Passover with you before I suffer."

During that same Passover event, Jesus said he entrusted his followers with the future of his mission (John 14:12–18), and that he loved them as dear friends (John 15:9, 14–16). His need for community was further expressed by the fact that he took his closest friends with him as he retreated to the Garden of Gethsemane to pray for the strength to be faithful to God when everything was at stake. Though recognizing that they were exhausted, Jesus was still clearly hurt that they did not muster the energy to pray with him when he wanted and needed their support (Mark 14:32–37). With one of his last breaths, he uttered his dependence upon community as he asked a disciple to take care of his mother (John 19:26–27).

Throughout Jesus's life, his trust matured as he was tested by new situations. Both Jesus and God proved trustworthy toward one another (Luke 2:50–52, Heb 5:7–9). Jesus enacts this mutual covenant relationship of trust in God in the community of God's people. The relationship with the community of faith is filled with intensity, passion, disappointment, and many joyful moments. Jesus can say: "As the Father has loved me; so I have loved you" (John 15:9). During a situation that caused Thomas to have very reasonable fears that Jesus was making a major mistake that might cost them all their lives, Thomas could still say: "Let us also go, that we may die with him" (John 11:16). Such statements describe a deep mutual love!

Throughout the Bible, faith includes a shared community dimension. The modern tendency is to hear the biblical promises and demands very individualistically and, therefore, to think of "faith" individualistically. This is true despite the fact that the entire Bible is written to humans, primarily in their corporate settings. Individual challenges and promises are embedded within community settings. This was not to diminish the importance of the individual, but to recognize that every human is a relational being, embedded in community.

Our modern Western tendency is to read the approximately sixty (the Greek has more) "you/your" statements in most English translations of Ephesians as though they were singular, even though they are all plural except for a couple quotations (*see* Eph 5:14, 6:2–3). This confusion is understandably encouraged by a peculiarity of the modern English language, which does not distinguish between "you" as plural and "you" as singular.

After Jesus's resurrection, the initial responses of trust in him are recorded in terms that were extremely corporate in nature, even though they had to be chosen and enacted by each individual.

> [44] *All the believers were together and had everything in common.* [45] Selling their possessions and goods, they gave to anyone as he had need. [46] Every day they *continued to meet together* in the temple courts. They broke bread *in their homes and ate together* with glad and sincere hearts (Acts 2:44–46, *emphasis mine*).

In Galatians, Paul is so concerned about the potential disruption of Jesus's open table that he embarrasses Peter and Barnabas in front of the entire community. He argues that, although he, they, and their fellow "Jews" are observant in many ways, they cannot be fully observant and follow the faithful and crucified Jesus (Gal 2:12–21). Paul argues throughout Galatians that it is important to be incorporated into the relationship God offers for all to share, to belong to the *one family* of the *One God*. He maintains that this means crossing many seemingly insurmountable social boundaries, but he insists that God is creating exactly that kind of extended family, where the members find their primary identity in their shared trust (Gal 3:26–4:7). The plural "you" includes them all as a community of faith and faithfulness.

> [26] You *are all sons of God* through faith in Jesus Christ [or better, through the faithfulness of Jesus the Messiah], [27] for *all of you* who were baptized into Christ have clothed yourselves with Christ. [28] There is neither Jew nor Greek, slave nor free, male nor [*kai* in Greek = "and"] female, for *you are all one in Jesus Christ* (Gal 3:26–28, *emphasis mine*).

In 1 Corinthians, it is the imagery of "the body of Christ" and the plea for *oneness* that emphasize community throughout the letter including the reprimand concerning their fellowship meals (1 Cor 11:17–34). In James 2:1–13, it is the plea for the socially empowered not to shame those who are socially disempowered because Jesus has fully empowered them as equals. Ephesians proclaims "the dividing wall of hostility" dividing ethnicities and cultures has been broken down, and God has created "one new humanity" through Jesus (Eph 2:14–18). Ephesians 4:11–13 describes the community as increasingly "one" as it matures in relationship to Jesus. 1 Peter 2:4–7 proclaims that all followers of Jesus are one priesthood and one chosen people—the "you" is plural in both cases.

There are many other passages in the New Testament emphasizing community as a part of genuine faith. There have been a few groups throughout Church history that have defined faith only in terms of belonging to their specific community, which is devastating, but the much more dangerous definition in modern Western Christianity is the tendency to define faith as though it were only an individual matter with no community content.

SUMMARY

When we are asked and commanded to "have faith," we are being invited into the relationship of trust and trustworthiness that is shared by God and Jesus. This trusting relationship is multidimensional, but for us, as for Jesus, it is always grounded in the interpersonal trust and trustworthiness—the *Who*. When we make the *Who* primary in our trust, we allow the relationship between God and humans to flourish and to move toward maturity and completion. Our relationships with fellow humans function as an analogy to this relationship with God because they, too, are multi-dimensional, but they can continue to deepen only if they are grounded in mutual interpersonal trust and trustworthiness. The more trustworthy we become in our relationships with God and other humans, while living in this world filled with many temptations and much suffering, the more we allow God to complete (mature) us as humans (Jas 1:2–4).

As we will explore further in the next chapter, this trusting and trustworthiness between God and Jesus is put to the ultimate test when Jesus is led into a situation that means execution by church and state, abandonment by friends, and the experience of apparent abandonment by God.

13

Jesus's Cross and Resurrection

JESUS'S CRUCIFIXION AND RESURRECTION ARE FULLY EMBEDDED IN THE QUESTION OF GOD'S FAITHFULNESS AND HUMAN FAITHFULNESS.

Jesus's crucifixion and resurrection are a full participation in the dilemma that puts both God and humans to the test. How can God be trusted, and how can God be truly good, when so much bad, so much evil, and so much injustice is allowed to occur? Will humans ever consistently trust God with all their heart, mind, and strength in this wonderful, precious, yet bent and broken world? Will even one human do so? Can the brokenness of humans ever be addressed in a manner that brings genuine transformation?

The New Testament writers present the cross–resurrection event as the climactic test of Jesus's faithfulness to God and God's faithfulness to Jesus. They also maintain that this event is an expression of God's faithfulness to Abraham, David, Israel, and all humanity. Would Jesus be trustworthy toward God at all costs? Could God possibly be trustworthy if God allowed Jesus, who entrusted his entire life to God, to be unjustly executed by both church and state? Is God trustworthy in the real world and not just in wishful religious thinking?

The cross and resurrection are the theme of a myriad of books, but their power and meaning are never exhausted. My goal is to stress how deeply the cross and resurrection are embedded in issues of human trust and in the completion of God's creation purpose for humans, as it is understood in the New Testament.

Jesus's Cross and Resurrection

Neither the Cross nor the Resurrection Can Stand Alone in Exploring Faithfulness.

If we wish to be true to the "old, old story" as a song writer of a previous generation summarized the "good news," we need to understand the crucifixion and resurrection as one event. To say it a different way, the cross means something different concerning God's faithfulness and Jesus's faithfulness in the light of the resurrection, from what it would mean standing alone. Likewise, the resurrection means something different concerning God's faithfulness and Jesus's faithfulness in the light of the cross, from what it would mean standing alone. Also, both the execution and the resurrection mean something different in the context of God's ongoing story of Creation, Covenant, Israel, Exile, Grace, and Judgment from what they would mean if they were not embedded in the revelatory patterns of God's history with humanity and with Israel.

Standing alone, the cross is just one more example in human history that indicates that brute power wins over love. The cross is also one more example of the fact that we humans tend to kill those who seem to threaten the systems, while they are still young. (What does that say about me at 78 years of age?) As a young adult in the 1960s, because of my own political ultraconservatism at the time, I was not particularly concerned when John F. Kennedy, Martin Luther King Jr., Malcom X, Bobby Kennedy, and Fred Hampton were assassinated. In fact, I thought it might not have been such a bad thing for them to be gone. What ignorance and arrogance on my part! I now wonder how many people in occupied Israel felt that same way when they heard that the trouble-maker Jesus was gone.

Several of those assassinated in the 1960s were apparently eliminated with the approval of FBI Director J. Edgar Hoover. Pretty clearly, Hampton was assassinated with the approval of the Illinois Attorney General and Mayor Daley of Chicago. I am not saying I think each of these victims was faultless. I am saying that each was assassinated because powerful people who profited from the system staying as it was considered him a threat. Each was assassinated prior to reaching the age of 50; Hampton was only 21. Jesus, too, was seen as a threat by powerful people who profited by things remaining as they were. Standing alone, the cross makes it clear that being like Jesus means you might not make it to your 35th birthday.

Standing alone, the resurrection would be another odd claim concerning one of those weird events in a world where occasionally strange things really do happen. I mentioned my agnostic graduate school philosophy advisor in chapter 7. I do not know what he would say today, but at that time he believed the evidence that Jesus's resurrection really occurred in space and time (history) was compelling. He said to me, "Ron, occasionally strange things happen. I think the historical evidence is that Jesus's resurrection occurred, but strange occurrences don't *mean* anything. They just happen. We humans make up the meanings. I don't think God has anything to do with it."

Obviously, the writers of the Gospels claim that the cross and resurrection together are an event that does *mean* a lot, and they insist they were not making up the meanings. Each of the Gospel writers, in his own way, points out the importance of seeing the cross and resurrection as one event in the middle of God's great master story with humans. The cross–resurrection event finds its primary meaning in God's faithfulness to God's purpose for humanity, and in human faithfulness to God—as well as in human unfaithfulness.

There Is A Tension That the Biblical Writers Freely Acknowledge.

There is a legitimate question that has always haunted those who seek (and are sought by) the One God of the Bible. The question is real for most of us: Can God be trusted to be good, purposeful, trustworthy, and loving toward humans, given that we also experience a world filled with many evils and horrors? For many of us, that question stands in tension with another question: Where could all the wonder, beauty, intelligence, love, meaning, and good gifts of creation come from if there were no good God?

Thankfully, the biblical materials are honest about this tension. We hear the near-despairing cries expressed by such prophets as Jeremiah, Habakkuk, Hosea, and Ezekiel, as well as the wistful "We used to hope he was the one to redeem Israel," voiced by two followers of Jesus after the execution (Luke 24:21). Some psalms are filled with wonder and praise, but others are filled with pain, frustration, and unanswered questions. The New Testament canon ends with a book filled with descriptions and images of the ongoing tensions experienced by followers of Jesus.

Perhaps less in the forefront of many of our minds, but equally important, are these questions: Can God find a way to entrust humans with the good blessings and the good future God wishes to give us? Is there any human who can be entrusted to lead a renewed community of God that will not descend yet again into the temptations of fear, need, power, wealth, and fame?

The writers of the New Testament literature claim that both questions have received a new answer with a new clarity through the relationship shared by God and Jesus. They also see the results of this relationship, which was first revealed at a moment in human history, as spreading out into the future of creation and the future of humanity. Some even maintain that the consequences of the relationship between God and Jesus will fill our known universe with God's purpose and presence. God's plans include creation, character, and community—all of which are fully embedded in God's purpose for creating humans (Eph 1:3–2:21; Rom 8:18–39).

The Cross is Central, but It is Not the Entire Story about Jesus's Faithfulness.

Sometimes, we Christians seem to present the "good news" as though the "cross" were the entire story. Of course, we can quote Paul's "I resolved to know nothing while I was with you except Jesus Christ and him crucified" to justify this stance (1 Cor 2:2). But, in doing so, we ignore the fact that the same letter continues by addressing several other issues without mentioning the cross. Then there is a pause in the middle of the letter to remind the readers in soaring poetry that, without love for their fellow humans, their lives amount to nothing. Finally, the letter concludes with a section just as passionate as the section on the cross. There, Paul stresses that all would be vain and empty, if not for the resurrection.

The cross and crucifixion are mentioned directly 73 times in the New Testament, of which 46 times are in the Gospels and 27 in the rest of the New Testament writings. If we add in other references such as "lamb," "slain," and "lifted up," we increase that total by at least 38 additional references. If we add in direct and indirect passages saying Jesus would be, or was, "killed," we find another 15 or so references.

There are other major themes in the New Testament. Forms of the word "righteous" appear over 130 times, forms of the word "love" over 280 times, forms of the word "trust (believe/faith/faithfulness) over 400 times, and forms of the word "hope" 77 times. "Resurrection" and "raised" are mentioned 123 times. Jesus is referred to as the "Messiah" (Christ) 477 times. Jesus is mentioned by name 992 times, and God is mentioned 1,253 times.

Having once loved math, I am quite aware that statistics can be made to say almost anything, but I do think it is good to remind ourselves that the writers had a lot to talk about in addition to the cross. This includes the fact that each of the four Gospels spends three-fourths of its material on Jesus's life of healing, caring, teaching, obeying, confronting, and loving—and only the last fourth of its material on the cross. It is the first three fourths that gives the last fourth of each Gospel its meaning. On the other hand, it is the last fourth of each Gospel that interprets the earlier material in a new light. All of this is to say that the New Testament speaks of many topics other than the cross, but none of these topics falls outside the shadow cast by the execution of Jesus and Jesus's faithfulness in facing it.

The Cross Need Not be Fully Understood to be Effective.

Perhaps, before or after reading this chapter, you find yourself saying, "But I still don't fully understand why God couldn't, or didn't, choose some way other than execution as a salvation event. Why did Jesus have to die?" If so, give yourself the slack that Brian McLaren's friend recommended—realize you are struggling with the same issue Jesus was struggling with in the Garden of Gethsemane.[1] Why this way? Isn't there another way?

---

1. McLaren, *More Ready*, 81.

Jesus had seen the cross as a *necessary* outcome of his faithful living for quite a while (Matt 16:21; *see also* Luke 24:26). He acted in ways that pushed the issue farther in that direction when he began to increase the number of his public challenges to the political and religious power-brokers. Nevertheless, Jesus's prayer in Gethsemane indicates that he thought it possible God might have an "Abraham and Isaac" type of answer in mind (Gen 22). What we are told about his intense prayer isn't a "Now, I fully understand that it is necessary" response of cool reasoning; instead, his passionate heart-rending response was "If it is possible let this pass . . . Not my will, but your will be done." At least at that moment, Jesus doesn't seem to be sure it has to be that way, and he prays it does not.

Struggling with "Why the cross?" is also struggling with the reality that turned the world of Saul of Tarsus upside-down. It impacted him so strongly that he went into seclusion for three years to work through its implications, once he was persuaded that the person he had been certain was a blasphemer turned out instead to be God's crucified and resurrected Messiah (Gal 1:17–18).

Even after Saul came to peace with God, Jesus, Israel, and Gentiles, it seems to have taken the church nearly a decade before one local community, Antioch, was willing to risk trusting that the power of the cross–resurrection event might have genuinely transformed Saul of Tarsus into a trustworthy brother (Acts 11:23–26, 13:1–3). Apparently, the full meaning and power of the cross wasn't readily apparent to them either, at least not when it came to trusting that an enemy had been transformed into a friend.

My personal experience has been that I continue to learn and grow as I explore all the meanings of the cross–resurrection event. And, I especially find it important to accept and trust that Jesus died for us, for me. It is fine to attempt to understand why, but what is most important is to trust that God knows what God is doing. Just like a Hebrew slave who put the blood on the doorpost of his slave dwelling that night in Egypt long ago, I don't have to fully understand how it works or why it works. I do need to respond as God asks me to and trust God to be faithful. It is God's actions and my trust, not my complete understanding, that allow the cross to work for me and in me—for us and in us.

THE NEW TESTAMENT GIVES US SEVERAL MEANINGS OF THE CROSS–RESURRECTION EVENT.

It Is Important to Explore the Various Meanings of the Cross and Resurrection.

The New Testament presents several meanings for the cross–resurrection event. Each meaning we are about to explore involves issues of faithfulness on God's part, on Jesus's part, and on the part of other humans, as well. I think two things are critical: First, we should not move to the meanings of the resurrection before we face the meanings of the cross. Second, we should not become stuck at the cross and never move on to the resurrection. We have at times developed theologies that make each of these mistakes. In both cases, we miss so much of what God is attempting to reveal to us about God, about Jesus, and about ourselves. Most of this revelation becomes much clearer when we see the cross and resurrection as one event, with each of the two parts helping interpret the other.

I struggle with some of the meanings of the cross more than I do with others. You likely do as well. My experience has been that my more progressive brothers and sisters tend to struggle with one group of the meanings of the cross–resurrection event, whereas my more conservative brothers and sisters tend to struggle with a different group of these meanings. I encourage you to wrestle with all of the New Testament claims concerning the meanings of this pivotal event—both the ones you find comforting and those you find unnerving.

I think each meaning is connected to the other meanings, so that nothing stands alone. The overall revelation and its meanings for us should be pictured much more like the intertwining strands of a rope, rather than as links in a chain. Just because one or the other strand gets frayed or confused for us at times, the rope need not give way.

1. Before Exploring What the Cross Is, We must be Clear on What the Cross Is Not.

The cross is not Jesus paying a dishonored God off, nor is it Jesus appeasing an angry God who couldn't stand being near us sinners. These views became common among Christians from the eleventh to the sixteenth centuries. They still are common, but there are many reasons why they are terribly misguided.

First, the cross is an event meant to transform us, not to transform God. I am the party who needs to be changed, not God. From beginning to end, the Old Testament presents God as the God who continues to faithfully love us humans, despite our horrible record of not faithfully loving God. God has always sought a relationship with us far more than we have sought a relationship with God. God did not need to be convinced to love us. The New Testament affirms this theme throughout: "For God so loved *the world*."

Second, someone will say, "But the Bible does often talk about God's wrath toward humans." True, but it is an anger that comes from loving. It is the loving that cries out to a loved child, "Adam [human] where are you? What have you done?" Any loving parent becomes angry when a loved child hurts other loved children, or trashes herself, or devalues himself. But it is not an anger for which the parent needs to be properly paid; it is rather the anger of a loving, broken heart. I hear, "But didn't the cross 'pay the debt?'" Yes, but it is not Jesus paying God off. It is God and Jesus bearing the cost of our sins and the myriad kinds of death those sins have brought upon us humans. The debt that is forgiven costs God and Jesus as they pay for a transformation and renewal of our humanity that we desperately need, but do not ourselves have the resources to resolve.

Third, the theology that teaches that the cross was about God being so legalistic that Jesus had to change God's angry mind, or at least, the legalistic half of God's mind—the angry half—presents a God that Jesus certainly did not know or serve. God did not have a split personality that needed Jesus's execution so God could be healed and love us again. Neither did Jesus serve a God who was so hung up on exacting punishment for law-breaking that the law preempted loving. Jesus served the God who loves humans so much that any cost was worth paying to give us an opportunity to quit destroying ourselves and come home.

Fourth, the New Testament never talks about God needing to be reconciled to us, but it stresses that we desperately needed to be reconciled to God. God was not our enemy; we were the enemies of God and of God's loving purposes for us humans. Only by being included in God's new creation that has begun in Jesus can we make this desperately needed and transformative change (Rom 5:10–11; 1 Cor 5:17–21; Col 1:20–22). And, of course, when we allow ourselves to be reconciled to God, we begin the much-needed process of learning to be reconciled to our sisters and brothers (Matt 5:24; 1 Cor 11:20–29; Eph 2:16–18; Phil 4:2–3).

Shortly, we will look at the challenging possibility that a loving God could lead a loved Son to choose a life that ended in an unjust execution. Here, let's be clear. If divorce, or choosing to leave the family, are the right metaphors, they occurred because we left God to pursue our own illicit affairs (Hos 1–3; Luke 15:11–31). If reconciliation is the right metaphor, it is we humans who keep breaking the relationship and need to be reconciled to a God who loves us, waits for us to come home, and is ready to include us as family (Hos 1–3; Luke 15:11–31). The purpose of the execution of Jesus was to make changing *us* possible. It was not to change an unreconcilable turmoil inside of God, nor did God need to be convinced that reconciliation would be a good thing.

So, what are some of the meanings of the cross? There may be more meanings to the cross-resurrection event than what follows, but I do not think there are fewer.

2. The Cross is Jesus's Faithful Participation in the Common Human Experience of God's Apparent Absence.

Many of us have experienced the apparent absence of God during human suffering that cries out for God to show up. Isn't this when we feel the need more than any other time for a clear sense of "I am with you?" Two of the four Gospel writers tell us that Jesus, too, suffered this horrific experience of abandonment—"My God, My God, Why Have you forsaken me" (Mark 15:34; Matt 27:46)? For me personally, this is one of the most gut-wrenching meanings of Jesus's crucifixion. I find this statement to be among the most abhorrent, and at the same time, most consoling, in the Gospel accounts.

I abhor the experience of God's apparent absence when it happens to those I personally know and love. I also feel sad when I read about it in the life of Jeremiah, Job, and the author of Psalm 22. I hate experiencing this absence of God myself. But, most of all, I find it almost inconceivable when I focus on Jesus experiencing God's apparent absence right at the moment when he most wanted to experience God's presence. If it can happen to the most faithful and righteous human who ever lived, it can happen to any of us. That is not a happy thought!

Not long ago, I spent four years praying that God would heal the young mother of two teenagers. I prayed for her as regularly as I have ever prayed for anyone or anything in my life. She died a brutal death brought on by cancer. Where was God when this young woman and her family so needed him? Where was God, as I daily begged for her life and healing, my frustration not even to be compared with her pain and that of her family? Yes, there were days when this young, dying friend did experience God's presence and the consoling closeness of Jesus, but those days did not take away the times she sensed only absence and excruciating pain.

This common, but devastating, experiencing of God as absent, when we most want God to show us that God is present, fully embeds Jesus in our humanity. I am quite certain that Jesus knew that Psalm 22 ended with a wonderful celebration of the victory of God in the life of a faithful, suffering human servant. However, the psalm begins with the psalmist describing a time when the experience of God's absence overwhelmed him, and Jesus is described as fully immersed in that same overwhelming reality.

It might even be that the Gospel writers are implying that this was the first time Jesus had ever experienced this sense of God's complete absence in his relationship with God. If so, that makes the experience even more profound for him. He was risking all, and in the midst of this act of ultimate faithfulness, he hung over the abyss, experiencing no relief and no intuitive sense of God's presence. He still chose to trust in God, but like the psalmist before him, he was going through a time with no immediate, experiential reinforcement for that trust. Like his faithful forefather, all Jesus had was the memory that God had acted before in the corporate history of his people and in his own personal life.

However you work out the theological arguments concerning the manner in which Jesus is related to humanity and to divinity, you must not let your theology water down the cry, "My God, My God, why have you forsaken me!" There certainly does not seem to be any "I am God" consciousness on Jesus's part going on here. Jesus just wept and cried out to "the one who could save him from death" (Heb 5:7). Still, with his last breath "Jesus, crying with a loud voice, said, 'Father, into your hands I commend my spirit.' Having said this, he breathed his last" (Luke 23:46). The cross is vividly portrayed in the synoptic Gospels as the faithfulness of a human who is experiencing the apparent absence of the God he has trusted all his life. Jesus is deeply embedded in one of the most frightening and demoralizing experiences a human can have.

Yes, there is another way to retell the story after the resurrection, but we dare not allow that narrative to diminish the way the reality was experienced as it occurred.

Both ways of living the story must be given equal weight. One of the meanings of the cross is that sometimes even the most faithful humans experience life as the absence of God. If we do not allow this event to be fully embedded in the human experience as the New Testament records of the event do, we do not see that the resurrection that follows is also fully embedded in Jesus's human experience of God's faithfulness.

Why then do I say that this abhorrent reality is also comforting? Because many of us experience that apparent absence of God at times when we most want to experience God's presence. I am deeply comforted by the fact that this did not separate the human Jesus from God, and it will not separate us from God, either (Rom 8:26–27, 38–39). God was there preparing to act more powerfully than anyone could imagine when current experience, and felt need, cried out that God was not there at all! That, too, is a meaning of the cross.

3. *The Crucifixion of the Messiah is Reasonable Only from One Paradigm—God's Foolish Wisdom.*

Paul seems to have reflected more on the theological/philosophical meanings of the cross than most of the other New Testament writers. If you take seriously the claims in his letters (and in Acts) that he was a conscientious, serious, and zealous Pharisee, who had become convinced that people following Jesus were a danger to Israel's covenant relationship with God, then it is not difficult to imagine that he would also be the apostle who would be most intense about working through the meanings of Jesus's execution. The person he had once believed to be a justly executed blasphemer was the person God had raised from the dead and exalted as Lord—so much to work through!

In the early chapters of 1 Corinthians, Paul notes that one of the main things we learn about God from Jesus's execution on a Roman cross is that the way God has chosen to express God's faithfulness to humanity is reasonable according to only one paradigm of reality—God's viewpoint. That paradigm includes God's desire to show us humans conclusively the failure of all our false gods. Our false gods include the people, positions, reputations, armies, nations, economies, legal systems, policies, and institutions, as well as the personal talents, we humans tend to trust for our *salvation*. This is a challenge that most of us Christians—conservative, evangelical, moderate, liberal, progressive, or any other branding name we choose—need to take far more seriously.

The very idea of an executed Messiah was not only unexpected, it makes no sense from any other paradigm than God's need to confront us with the "foolishness" of each of our attempts to save ourselves. God allowed—*led*—Jesus to fully participate from the side of the used and abused in the chronic exploitation of power that has haunted all human societies. This abuse usually includes the threat of imprisonment and death as the trump card used by power brokers in their attempts to control other humans.

In the cross–resurrection event, God showed the impotence of *the powers that be*, because the brutal and unjust execution that was supposed to guarantee Jesus's powerlessness became, instead, God's way of exposing the ultimate powerlessness of the abusers of power (1 Cor 2:8). In the cross–resurrection event, God and Jesus moved the great covenant relationship with Adam (humanity) and Abraham (Israel) forward in a manner that exceeded everyone's wildest expectations. The event makes sense in only this one paradigm of reality. N. T. Wright rightly describes this perspective with the title of his book *Jesus and the Victory of God*.[2]

In 1 Corinthians, this "reasonable" and "wise," yet "not reasonable" and "not wise," claim is expounded dramatically. Paul argues that we must see the cross as a profound expression of God's "foolishness"—foolishness from every perspective other than God's. Who would have ever dreamed that sin and death would be defeated, not from outside, but by a faithful human confronting directly, headlong, an all-out attempt by the power brokers of the greatest empire and the best religion of the day to control him and render him impotent? No one but God! Even Jesus prayed right up to the last minute that God might provide a different way.

This "foolish" way of addressing our idolatry and self-sufficiency was God's wisdom. Paul claims that the *privileged* status Jews had enjoyed in relationship to God, and the privileged status Greeks had enjoyed philosophically in their world, had both been removed by "God's foolishness." That "foolishness" was allowing the Jewish Messiah to be executed in shame on a cross (1 Cor 1:18–25, *compare* Gal 3:26–4:7). Paul knew from his own experience how difficult it is for us humans to relinquish these status privileges, no matter what God does. Who would choose such a way of *saving* humans from our own self-destruction and others' destruction? No one but God!

Next, Paul argues that God chose to even further heighten the contrast between how we humans design success and express wisdom and how God designs success and expresses wisdom (1 Cor 1:26–31). Not only did God choose the foolishness of the cross as God's source of political and religious power, God also "foolishly" chose a community of people like the Corinthian followers of Jesus as God's means of moving human history forward. Paul demands that they take a good long look at themselves so that they will understand just how "foolish" God's "wise" plan really is. Do you and I, Paul asks, really dare to claim that God's forward movement in human history, not only takes place through a Messiah, crucified by Rome and Jerusalem, but is actually being moved forward through a community made up of people like you? Is God foolish enough to choose, not the courts of Rome, not the high-powered business deals of the Corinthian agora, but communities of people like you? Yes! Talk about God's foolishness! Who would have ever imagined it? No one but God!

Then, sounding completely like an antisalesman trying to make his point, Paul carries his theme of "God's foolishness" one step further (1 Cor 2:1–5). God was foolish enough to choose me as one of his messengers. You Corinthians claim that I am

---

2. Wright, *Victory of God*.

not a very polished speaker. You are right! Isn't it incredibly foolish (wise?) that God picked a person like me to tell people like you about what God has done through Jesus the crucified Messiah! But don't you see? That means the powerful transformations you have experienced really are the work of God's Spirit, not something brought about by great powers of leadership or oratory persuasion.

Paul certainly agrees with Abraham Joshua Heschel that God is far more committed to searching for an intimate relationship with us humans than we are to searching for God.[3] But Paul also wants to emphasize that God nonetheless "foolishly" chose people like Paul, and other leaders of the early church that the Corinthians know, to be God's colaborers and ambassadors of God's good news. This choice is a key theme of 1 Corinthians 1–4, 9 and 2 Corinthians 5. Paul is clear that picking people like him to lead a movement to transform the world is foolishness. Who would do such a thing? No one but God!

Finally, Paul summarizes his assertions concerning God's foolish wisdom as it is seen in the cross by noting that it is true that no one, regardless of how smart, how powerful, or how religious, would have ever imagined that God would choose such foolish ways to pursue God's purposes (1 Cor 2:6–16). Who would have ever dreamed that God would have been so foolish as to reveal God's purpose in our world through an executed Messiah, messy communities, and less-than-eloquent spokespersons? No one but God!

And that is why God planned from the beginning of time to do it exactly this way (1 Cor 2:7). God always knew that God's purpose could be moved forward only by directly confronting the false gods that we construct and trust to save us. The beginning of the final exodus of God's people, like the first one, would have to include allowing arrogant rulers (this time both Gentile and Jewish) to do their best to prevent the liberation in order to maintain their own power. What would the outcome of exerting all this power be? It would be the revelation of how futile their power was when attempting to thwart God's ultimate purpose.

Paul concludes his argument that the cross is foolish from every perspective except God's perspective, with this challenge to his readers:

> [14]The man without the Spirit does not accept the *things that come from the Spirit of God, for they are foolishness to him*, and he cannot understand them, because they are spiritually discerned. . . . [16] "For who has known the mind of the Lord that he may instruct him?" *But we have the mind of Christ* (1 Cor 2:14–16, *emphasis mine*.)

Not only does crucifixion embed Jesus deeply in the deadly nature of the dark side of human wisdom and human righteousness (1 Cor 1:22–23), it also embeds followers of Jesus in "the mind of the Messiah." The rest of the letter makes it clear that

---

3. Heschel, *God in Search*.

this means Jesus is still deeply involved in very human lives, with all their potentials and all their weaknesses.

This "foolish wisdom" of God is one of the key meanings of the cross, and it is fully embedded in Jesus's participation in our humanity. It makes sense only if we are willing to see it from God's perspective. Revelation 13:1–18:24 uses strong political cartoon-like imagery to assure the readers that the powerful dark side of empire, religion, and economics will not defeat the child from God, whom the dragon-inspired powers wish to destroy. (For other examples of the way God's foolishness disarms the powers that be and the idols we trust, *see* Col 2:8–17; Gal 4:7–9; Eph 6:10–18.)

4. The Cross is Deeply Embedded in a Sad Universal Truth—When Someone Sins, Someone Pays.

To claim that Jesus "paid for our sins" is not to maintain that God is doing something weird through Jesus. Someone or something pays for everyone's sins. Paying for the sins of others roots Jesus's crucifixion deeply in a built-in-law of the universe—actions have consequences, and often the consequences fall heavily on someone other than the person doing the action. When someone sins, someone pays. Although the language I am using might be different, there are many studies and experiences that demonstrate the validity of this claim.

I say the reality is obvious, and it is for those "who have eyes to see and ears to hear," but it is a reality we often prefer to repress. Given how often we humans fail to be who we could be, and should be, it is tempting to ignore the fact that someone always gets hurt by our failures.

Perhaps the most widely acknowledged, and most widely studied, experience of this universal truth is evidenced in the way children pay for the errors, failures, abuses, mistakes, and omissions of parents in the parent–child relationship. It is so universal that many counselors begin their counseling sessions by exploring the parent–child relationship, even when the counselee's stated reason for making an appointment is something entirely different. Children are debtors because of the failures of their parents. To the chagrin of most of us parents, there is no escaping this reality.

My children carry scars and wounds for my weaknesses and failures as a parent. This truth is captured in the Ten Commandments, one of which states that this experience is so powerful that the results impact the next three or four future generations. Jeremiah promised that God's future covenant renewal would intervene in this reality with a new, more powerful, transformative experience of God's grace: "The fathers have eaten sour grapes, and the children's teeth are set on edge" would no longer be the last word (Jer 31:29). The New Testament claims that the crucifixion of Jesus is part of God keeping that prophetic promise.

The expression of this universal law—someone sins, someone pays—can be brutal. We see how brutal when we discover that so many who physically abuse others were first abused. We also observe this law at work when we learn that a very high percentage of male and female prostitutes were themselves sexually abused as children. Recently, we have been confronted with how deeply people pay for the sins of sexual predators in the Me Too movement. Someone sins, someone pays.

The power of this law of the universe is played out in the corporate sphere, too. Many studies indicate that the sins of White Privilege and White Supremacy built into the fabric of American society pile up debts that are then often collected in the bodies, minds, and hearts of Black, Hispanic, Asian, and Native Americans. In the United States, each of these minority ethnicities has a life expectancy shorter by about a decade than that of Whites. Tests even indicate that marginalized people themselves tend to be prejudiced in favor of Whites—a fact they hate and certainly do not deserve. That is how deeply the "someone sins, someone pays" consequences run.

We who are White Americans often dispose of our debts by excusing ourselves and blaming the *other* for wounds they did not earn. At the same time, we remain part of the group experiencing advantages we did not earn. To see who pays, we need to listen to our black and brown sisters and brothers as they tell us what it means to be black and brown in our society. The Me Too movement is not just about individual acts; it is also an exposure of the power of cultural sin that can easily prime males to assume male privilege, and from that privilege to think that rape can be justified by saying, "she wanted it" or "she asked for it."

The debt-collecting for the sins of others is everywhere. One little phrase in the Thirteenth Amendment to the U.S. Constitution allowed the very slavery the amendment was supposed to address to later become a constitutional justification for continuing to enslave Blacks and Hispanics through "mass incarceration." The Clinton administration made this debt-collecting far worse by deciding thousands more should go to prison for very small repeat infractions. Hundreds of thousands of Iraqis have died or been displaced as "debtors" for the sins of the Saudis who orchestrated the 9/11 attack on the United States, and by the attempt of the United States to collect the debt of these Saudi terrorists by bombing Iraq. In so many different ways, we corporately attempt to place others in a debtors' prison to make them pay for sins that were not their own.

The built-in *debt-collecting* that flows from the consequences of our actions is not always collected in the bodies, minds, and spirits of the *other*. Sometimes we collect the debts for our own sins in our own bodies, minds, and spirits. We have many different methods for becoming do-it-yourself disposals for our own unpaid debts or even for debts we suppose are ours. Some of us carry around dozens of *oughts* that control our lives. Many of them can even be *oughts* that cannot possibly be achieved in the real world. Perhaps it is insightful that the English words *ought* and *owe* come from the same root. Many *oughts* that go unfulfilled become unpayable debts that we believe we *owe*.

Jesus's Cross and Resurrection

Here are a few examples of the way debt-collecting can be expressed when it is internalized. Our body becomes a debt-collector, as expressed in such things as colitis, stooped shoulders, headaches, overeating, refusing to eat, and high blood pressure. Our emotions become debt-collectors through anxieties, fears, obsessions, rage, or even cold detachment that reflects the walls we have built.

Our interpersonal relationships become debt-collectors through excessive demanding, abusive rage, playing the victim, detached isolation, or the passivity of playing the doormat for others. Our choices become our debt-collectors as we insist upon consistently making choices that are going to fail, to cause us to be rejected, to cause us to be hurt, or to ensure the fulfillment of our felt need to be victims.

I have been saying that, if someone sins, someone pays, but there is often an intermediate step in this debt-collection process. Often when we humans sin, the creation pays. I have always found it fascinating that Genesis 3 describes the consequences of sin not only as impacting our relationship with God, others, and self, but also as having a powerful impact upon the entire creation. The claim throughout the Old Testament is that the creation absorbs our sinfulness as debts, and then, at some point, demands that we repay those debts. Almost every nature documentary I watch includes a warning that we are dumping our debts upon "nature," and nature is responding with consequences directly tied to our sinful actions. We dump our sins of greed and carelessness on the creation—and the creation pays, but then it begins to collect the debts from us, our neighbors, and future generations of humans.

Finally, I have known many people in my lifetime who dump the IOU's of life on God. I know that I (and most Christians I know) spend far too little time crediting God for the thousands of daily gifts we receive, while being quick to blame God for even one bad thing occurring. Still, I am not unsympathetic with the frustration most of us feel when we find ourselves and others suffering unjustly. Like many of the prophets and psalmists, I often ask God "Why?" I am comforted by the fact that Jesus did too—"My God, my God, why . . . ?"

However, honesty requires me to face the fact that, even when I cannot understand why God allows the horrible ways the law of *someone sins and someone pays* to work out so unjustly, it is still true that in almost every situation I can see how humans have contributed to the horror. Think about Jesus's execution as an example. No doubt it was confusing to attempt to figure out what God was doing or why God allowed this horror. On the other hand, there is no confusion about the fact that Jesus, who did not deserve this horror, was collecting in his mind and body the consequences of the cruelty of Pilate, Herod, Caiaphas, and Roman soldiers. There is also no confusion about the fact that Jesus hung on that cross feeling emotionally abandoned by most of his closest circle of friends and confidants. His debt-collecting of the IOU's of others is aptly described in the following passage.

> ⁴Surely he took up our infirmities and carried our sorrows, yet we considered him stricken by God, smitten by him, and afflicted. ⁵But he was pierced for our transgressions, he was crushed for our iniquities; the punishment that brought us peace was upon him, and by his wounds we are healed (Isa 53:4–5).

One meaning of the cross is that God is fulfilling the promise made long ago through the prophet Jeremiah. It no longer needs to be true that the debt-collecting just keeps being passed on from one of us humans to another, from one generation to the next. It no longer needs to be true that (as biographer Fischer attributed to Ghandi) "It is an eye for an eye until the whole world is blind." If we allow God to give us the gift God wishes to give us, we can allow our debts to be nailed to Jesus's cross. When we do so, we can be freed from the IOU's our own lives have generated and from the IOU's others claim we owe them (Col 2:13–15; Gal 2:15–21; Rom 6:1–7).

Just as importantly, we no longer need to attempt to collect the debts we think others owe us (Matt 6:12–14). We are offered the gift of belonging to the debt-free human society of God's future kingdom—the Jubilee finally fulfilled. If we do not let Jesus carry our IOU's for us, we will construct some elaborate collection system that will leave either other people, self, and/or God in our own personal debtor's prison.

In the face of the suffering of this world, especially the suffering of a loved one, many of us find ourselves saying, "If only I could take your suffering for you." As C. S. Lewis observed, we don't really know whether we would, because we cannot. The world just doesn't work that way. But one meaning of the cross is that one time someone did take our place.

> It was allowed to One, and I find that I can now believe again, that He has done vicariously whatever can be done. He replies to our babble, "You cannot, and you dare not. I could, and I dared."[4]

This reality embeds Jesus deeply in our human dilemmas and our need for someone who can do what the rest of us cannot do—end the indebtedness and the debt-collecting that goes with it. We all sinned, and Jesus paid the consequences.

5. The Cross Is a Participation in the Use of Arrest and Torture to Secure Systemic Domination.

One key meaning of the cross is that it embeds Jesus in the common human experience of people in power using threats, torture, abuse, and execution to maintain their systems of domination. One way of looking at the scriptural storyline is to follow the concept of human alienation from God, others, self, and creation as a narrative of the human determination to dominate. Cain fears losing his dominating position as honored firstborn, so he kills his brother. Lamech constructs a poem/song for his two

---

4. Lewis, *A Grief*, 36–37.

wives celebrating his past dominance over a fellow human and promising to do more dominating in the future. By the time we arrive at Genesis 6, we see dominating men "taking" whatever women they want. The relationship between Jacob's sons is a saga of who will dominate who.

Exodus describes the growth of a system of domination. The current Pharaoh is determined to continue to exercise that domination. Soon, in the book of Joshua, we have the question of how a nation can be created without dominating and killing the people previously on the land? Or is it even a question? Once the earth was populated, has any nation ever been created without pushing someone else off the land? Israel is warned that wanting a "king like the nations" is asking to be dominated. Nonetheless, God gets involved in setting up the system of domination called kingship. Then we have God blessing the reigns of David and Solomon as they become a wealthy dominating power in the region. Then both David and Solomon show us that, even with God involved, humans cannot handle the power and prestige. Both "successful" kings and their advisors bring hurt and evil, not only to their enemies, but also to their wives, children, loyal supporters, and nation. Perhaps most of all, they bring hurt and disappointment to God (Ps 51:4).

I understand why many brothers and sisters decide that a good God could not have been involved in any way in the tragic horrors that accompanied the fulfillment of the promises that Israel would be a nation, have a land, and prosper as a people. On the other hand, I am intrigued that, as far as we know, Jesus never intimated that now God refused to be involved with these tragic realities. Instead, Jesus taught that what we should have learned is that, even when God is with those involved, the domination-system doesn't save us. He says we should have learned from God's history with us that, when we live by the sword, we will die by the sword (or, as it may be, by guns and bombs). He didn't only teach these truths; he lived them and died trusting them to be true.

We should see that emphasizing domination doesn't create humans in the image of God. Being a servant who expresses authority by taking the lowest servant's role and washing the feet of our fellow humans is what really allows God to move God's goal forward. Jesus consistently rejected the temptation either to join the systems of domination or to run and hide from them. Instead, he chose to confront them, along with the rulers' unwillingness to see the evil that undergirded their claims to rightful domination over both empire and church, over both politics and religion. He saw God's willingness to be involved with humans who seek God (at whatever point in history) as real and important, but also as an education in what would never bring the kingdom of God to fruition.

Jesus made a severe choice. He chose the path that led to execution, rather than the path of exercising domination over others. The one who walks that path almost invariably becomes the abuser, the torturer, or even the executioner of someone else.

Throughout history, imprisonment, abuse, and execution have been, and still are today, consistently presented as the rational way to end threats to our power, our peace, our security, and our way of life. I love the America many of us aspire to be, but I am horrified at how often we have used our legal system to legitimize torture and abuse. Here is just one of many examples. Even before we were officially a country that legally endorsed slavery in our Constitution, the Virginia Slave Codes of 1705 legislated that a slave master or someone acting as his emissary could give "correction" to a slave without fearing any legal liability, even if the slave was maimed or died in the process.[5] Attempts to protect systems by legalizing domination has written much of human history, including our American history. Sadly, and even more inexcusably, it has written far too much church history as well. Jesus rejected that approach. He paid the cost of confronting it with his life.

Jesus experienced this common practice, but he did so from the side of the victims. In fact, much of Jesus's participation in our humanity was, and is, from the side of the abused, the misunderstood, and those unjustly imprisoned and executed as victims of our misuse of power. He was born into an occupied nation dominated by a rising Empire, into a people often despised by other cultures, into a family dealing with pregnancy prior to marriage, and into a family that had to flee their country due to persecution by their king. He apparently lost his father at a rather young age, and he finally became a rabbi without the proper academic credentials. Thus, the cross is the ultimate experience of a life-long pattern of participating in humanity from the side of the vulnerable, marginalized and dominated.

James Carroll offers compelling evidence that the "cross" was not the dominant symbol Christians used to identify themselves until Constantine's reign in the fourth century AD.[6] Other than a graffiti that mocks Christians by showing a crucified human with the head of an ass, there is no known art emphasizing the crucifixion of Jesus until the fourth century. Constantine turned the cross into the major symbol of Christianity by redefining the cross as "the sword" of his empire. For this reason, until medieval times, art still did not show a suffering and dying Jesus on the cross, but rather a victorious and glorious conqueror destroying all his enemies.[7]

Christendom turning the cross into a conquering sword of Rome's Empire is one of history's greatest ironies. When Jesus was executed, every follower of Jesus saw the cross as the symbol of imperial injustice in the name of justice, of abuse in the name of protection, of torture in the name of peace, of a plethora of illegalities in the name of law and order, and of arrogant power destroying godly humility. From Constantine forward, the cross becomes the symbol of the right for Christians to attack, crusade, invade, kill, oppress, hate, torture, execute and destroy in order to preserve the "peace."

---

5. "An Act Concerning Servants and Slaves," sec 34.
6. Carroll, *Constantine's Sword*, 175.
7 Jefferson, "Jesus the Magician," 41–42.

Prior to that point, few if any followers of Jesus would have thought of using the cross as a decoration, a piece of jewelry, an image identifying a place of worship, or as a symbol on a political flag. Of course, the cross was a central part of their trust in what God had done for them through Jesus, but they fully understood what the cross meant. Until Constantine made the cross a symbol of imperial power, it was recognized for what it actually was—a symbol of the torture and dominance widely used by the Roman Empire. God's victory in the cross of Jesus is God's victory through the lynching noose and the electric chair of the modern world. An astounding victory, but one unlikely to be worn as artful jewelry or symbolized on a flag.

Simultaneously with choosing the cross as the new symbol of "Christian Roman Imperialism," apparently the Romans also stopped using the cross as the preferred method of torturing their enemies. This further enabled a transition toward a new meaning of "the cross." No longer was the cross evidence that the "victory of God" came through the choice to faithfully serve God, even when it meant absorbing the abuse of imperial and religious power. Instead, it became the symbol used to justify the imperial and religious power that often conquers, uses, and abuses others. To use the imagery of Revelation—the lion that was a sacrificed lamb (Rev 5) was swapped for the two beasts of imperial and religious power that use threats to coerce the allegiance of all (Rev 13).

I am not saying that everything that occurred around the time of Constantine was evil and destructive, nor in the paragraph that follows do I mean to claim that everything in the current American church is negative. Both times in history include people seeking good and truth. What I am saying is that the times of Constantine began to legitimize a very antigospel identification of the cross of Jesus with imperialism, nationalism, and the destruction of enemies. And I am saying that it is very sad that this sin has been repeated again and again by "Christians" with power over the past 1,700 years. We need, not only truthful recognition, but also repentance, for turning the symbol of abuse and torture into a symbol that legitimizes abuse and torture. We continue this practice every time we justify torturing captives or bombing thousands of civilians as necessary to protect "our Christian nation."

This seems like a good point in my writing to be very clear. I love being a part of the church. I love being American. Both systems have been channels of blessings in my life. Gratitude for blessings does not, however, justify our sins. I hate the sinful arrogance, self-justification, and willful blindness that we Christians often bring to the table. I also hate the sinful arrogance, self-justification, and willful blindness that we Americans often bring to the table. I am not considering changing religions, nor am I considering changing nationalities. I am not anti-institutional, and I am not unpatriotic. Neither am I placing myself outside the sins of these two systems that have been the water I have swum in from the day I was born. Fellow Christians and fellow Americans who hear such critiques as I am making often say that they prove that someone like me is anti-Christian and a heretic, or anti-American and unpatriotic. They are just flat out wrong.

I am heart-broken about how the White Church in America has been warped by the lust for privilege, power, self-preservation, greed, and self-justification. I am heart-broken to see the ways I have participated in these sins in the past and to know that I am probably blindly—I hope not willfully blindly—participating in them right this moment. We need to quit excusing ourselves, name our sins truthfully, lament our failures, turn from our wicked ways, and trust that God will respond with grace and mercy.

I am heart-broken that my nation continues to refuse to openly acknowledge and find meaningful ways to make reparations for the past abusive treatment within our national boundaries—often including various forms of false arrests and torture—of Chinese, Japanese, Jews, and especially Mexicans, Native Americans, and African Americans. How I wish such abuses were only in the past! We are far from *"exceptional"* when it comes to the determination to dominate and control by using torture, abuse, and execution—and Jesus chose to actively identify with the dominated and victimized.

This need for repentance is very clear when it comes to followers of Jesus supporting torturing other humans. It seems that we insist on being blind to where Jesus faithfully cast his lot in this paradigm of domination. According to several polls, a very high percentage of American Christians favor torturing people who might be terrorists or traitors that threaten "national security" and "our way of life." In other words, many of us favor doing to others exactly what was done to Jesus—and for the same reasons that Jesus was tortured. Many justify this stance as a legitimate way of sustaining, protecting, and even "saving Christianity" and what they view as "a Christian nation." These attitudes and words reflect the logic of the High Priest, who wanted Jesus dead in order to protect the faith and the nation (John 11:49–50). Is there no limit to the "rational" ironies we Christians perpetrate?

Because I grew up in the American South, I am quite aware that you should not feature a hangman's noose anywhere without presenting a very clear explanation of why you are doing so. I am also aware that lynchings *made sense* to many "good" people of the South and the North, who often identified as Christian. They saw lynching as the "rational" means of protecting and saving the society and the economy they valued highly. Apparently, my grandfather, who was at various stages of his life a county sheriff, a chief of police, and an elder in the church, wore the white sheets meant to sustain such a society. It is difficult to imagine what else it meant to find the KKK sheet in his belongings when he died. And we know for certain that many "White Christians" attended the "legal" lynching of African Americans and Mexican Americans—many of whom were fellow Christians—after they attended Sunday church services. Pictures and written descriptions of those gatherings exist!

Jesus, too, participates in the kind of violence represented by crosses and lynching nooses, but from the side of those who have been and are being abused and mistreated in order to "protect the stability" of societies and religions. It is very telling that the New Testament writers recorded Jesus's crucifixion, not just as the torture used to stabilize the empire and the church, but also as an execution on a cross that rightfully belonged to a man named Barabbas, who was seen as a "terrorist" by some and a "patriotic revolutionary" by others. Barabbas's goal in life was to torture and abuse those who wanted to torture and abuse him. Jesus died while participating as one of the used and abused humans in an all-too-familiar human scenario in which those grasping for power are willing to torture those on the other side from theirs—if it seems helpful in gaining or retaining power.

Torture and abuse exist, and they have existed for millennia, all over the world. Thousands of other Jewish people died, as Jesus died, on Roman crosses. Millions of humans have been tortured and abused by various political and religious powers and by those revolting against them throughout recorded human history, and no one can even guess how many more we do not know about. In the six centuries spanning the Crusades through the Inquisition, torture and abuse were done under the symbol of the cross, sometimes "to destroy the infidel" and sometimes supposedly "to save the soul by destroying the body."

We know of thousands of African Americans and Mexican Americans who were lynched and millions of Native Americans who were annihilated in the name of the "White" right to power. Often this occurred with the explicit claim that it was happening in order to build a "Christian nation." Of course, these atrocities are not limited to the religious, to Christians, or to Americans.

In the twentieth century alone, we have many examples of mass torture and abuse, supported and perpetrated by the religious, the superstitious, the atheists, the capitalists, the socialists, the totalitarians, and the communists. The Holocaust was the most notorious, and, sadly, far more Christians supported or were silent about what the Nazis were doing than ever openly opposed it. The Siberian torture chambers of Stalin's Communism tortured many and often targeted Jews and Christians. Torture and slaughter were perpetrated by the people's revolution led by Mao, the mass exterminations by Idi Amin of Uganda, the policies of Nicolae Ceausescu of Romania, the Rwandan genocide, and Bashar al-Assad's torture of fellow Syrians. Each of these horrors reminds us that Jesus was participating in something very much a part of humanity. And he chose to engage it from the side of the tortured and abused.

Although many Christians seem to want to present "the Passion of Christ" as though it were unusual and even the worst torture anyone has ever experienced, it should be obvious that this is not true. Jesus's experience of false imprisonment, crooked judgments, torture, and execution all lasted less than 48 hours. For many throughout history, these experiences have gone on for months, years, and lifetimes. More importantly, such claims to *"uniqueness"* miss the real point, which is that Jesus's unjust torture and execution is *a participation in the all-too-common* reality of state, religious, and church "justice" used to protect systems of domination. The only things uncommon about this entire scenario were Jesus's unique relationship with God and his relentless determination to remain faithful in every way.

Growing up in his hometown of Nazareth guaranteed that Jesus knew he was positioning himself in opposition to powers of domination in a manner that had very predictable consequences. There was nothing uncommon about the expected outcome. Historians note that Jesus would have grown up in a town that had experienced more than 2,000 Jewish males from the area being crucified by the Romans not long before Jesus was born. These thousands were crucified, not because they were guilty, but as symbols of domination. A small band of terrorists had ambushed a few Roman soldiers. No Galilean Jews would turn in the names of these terrorists. So Roman soldiers randomly rounded up 2,000 men to execute by crucifixion all along the roadsides of that part of Galilee. This was meant to be a clear sign of who was in charge—massive random retaliatory terror to deal with terrorists.

This event was probably viewed by the Romans very much as many Americans viewed the retaliatory bombing of Iraq because of the horrible destruction of the twin towers carried out by predominantly Saudi terrorists. Likewise, the event was probably viewed by the people of Jesus's hometown much as the modern event is viewed by war-torn Iraqis—or as many inner-city black citizens view their interactions with the policing system. The retelling of the event of random retaliatory executions had to be rampant in the streets and homes of Nazareth as Jesus grew up. Jesus knowingly confronted the powers that pervert justice in the name of justice, that murder in the name of peace, and that pervert righteousness in the name of righteousness. Hometown stories made it clear that, if he rattled the *powers that be*, he would pay for it. He needed no special revelation to know that crossing the High Priestly clan would cause him to be branded a heretical danger in the name of God. What was unique and special was his unwavering trust that his relationship with God was more powerful than all the misused powers of church and state combined.

Two final clarifications are in order here: First, my critique is not a critique of America as a Christian nation. The United States is, and has always been, a pagan nation, just as all of the other so-called Christian nations and empires of the past have really been pagan nations and empires. No nation other than ancient Israel has ever been "chosen" by God for a special covenant role in God's historical purpose. This does not, however, excuse our nation's sins. As an American follower of Jesus, I believe that America is, as all nations are, dependent upon the goodness, mercy, and grace of the One God. Paul saw world history through this lens (Acts 17:26–28), as had Amos, Jonah, and Isaiah before him. Like all Empires, from Nineveh to New York, we are called to repent for our violence, abuse, and torture toward the "others" of our world.

Second, a meaning of the cross that I think should be clear to those of us who are followers of Jesus and also citizens of this very blessed nation of the United States, is that we must place our relationship with Jesus far above national security or national loyalty. Early followers of Jesus had to do this; we do as well. If we fail to do so, we will end up supporting the very attitudes and behaviors that caused Jesus to be tortured and executed as an innocent human.

Every time we vote for "security" at the price of the abuse, torture, and death of unknown innocents, we should hear Jesus saying, "When you did it to the least of these my brothers and sisters, you did it to me" (Matt 25:40). That is how deeply Jesus saw himself embedded in the human dilemmas created by human history. That is how desperately we all need God's forgiveness for what we do to one another. That is how deeply embedded in our human reality this man Jesus was and is. Can his faithfulness to God, even in the face of condemnation and torture by empire and church, at least challenge us to more reflection and prayerfulness than we often show?

I am not parroting some easy, naïve answer to these horrible dilemmas of human history. I am not a pacifist by temperament, nor am I a consistent pacifist by theology. I watch the news and find myself angry and wanting to get even with and destroy those who abuse others: in our nation, around the world, and especially those I know and love. I find that I can begin to move from bitter hatred toward mercy and intercession only if I am surrounded by a praying community that keeps reminding me that hating enemies and destroying them with the same powers of domination with which they wish to destroy us, is not Jesus's way of saving the world. He had a difficult time convincing his closest disciples of this 2000 years ago, and, obviously, he has a difficult time convincing people who want to follow him today.

But, let's at least be honest. Jesus knew that these same political, economic, and religious solutions that require the tools of domination all seem so reasonable, so wise, and so necessary—but he rejected them as the way to "save the world." Audre Lorde captured this reality in American colonial plantation terms:

> For *the master's tools will never dismantle the master's house.* They may allow us temporarily to beat him at his own game, but they will never enable us to bring about genuine change (*emphasis mine*).[8]

The risk is great in this step of trust. Like all of us, Jesus had friends and family at risk in a world dominated by systems of empire and church that often turn to abuse, torture, and execution. It might leave me feeling uneasy, but his clarity that *defeating the dominating powers with the same means they use cannot save the world* is one of the meanings of the cross.

6. The Cross is Jesus's Experience of How Costly Human Faithfulness Can Be and How Little It Seems to Be Accomplishing at the Moment.

People often say to me that Jesus's death is a great model for human faithfulness, courage, and goodness, even if he was not raised from the dead. I always respond along the following lines. No! Apart from an intervention by God, what I learn from Jesus's

---

8. Lorde, Sister Outsider, 111.

model is that, if you are good enough and courageous enough to speak truth to power in a manner that threatens that power, they will kill you. Then this crazy, mixed-up world will go right on acting as if nothing much happened. They might later turn you into an honored, dead hero, but not much will really change.

Jesus summarized this common historical process quite succinctly in Luke 11:49–52—we humans build tombs to honor the prophets of the past, swear that we would never have abused and executed them, and continue to abuse and kill those prophets God is currently sending. Hasn't our society done the same for people currently recognized as heroes? Martin Luther King Jr., Chief Joseph, Harriet Tubman, and Abraham Lincoln were hated, criticized, and ostracized while they were living. The scapegoating of the current perceived "threats" to national, cultural, and religious stability is always alive and well, side by side with the honoring of those who no longer threaten us. A vivid current example occurred when Fox News began to quote MLK favorably, while critiquing Black Lives Matter as a terrorist organization.

Many liberal senators openly praised those who courageously protested the bombing and use of Agent Orange during the Vietnam War. How many of these same senators simultaneously voted for destroying the infrastructure of Iraq to get even for a terrorist attack by Saudis? As I mentioned in the Introduction, many of us think ourselves righteous enough to throw stones at our evangelical fundamentalist Christian brothers and sisters for blatant support of systemic racism and nationalistic arrogance, but we refuse to acknowledge how unwilling we are to listen to our black and brown sisters and brothers ourselves. Progressive Christian brothers and sisters have a particularly difficult time listening when African American brothers and sisters say Progressives have often hurt them more deeply, and disappointed them more profoundly, than conservative Christians ever have!

Far too often, we relate to Jesus, not as to a living presence and a living model of how to be human, but as another dead hero. Simultaneously, we ignore anyone who is currently challenging the way our world works as Jesus did. Why? Because his way of living seems to cost so much and accomplish so little.

The cross is Jesus's participation in this difficult path of faithfulness that often seems to achieve so little in a lifetime. Jesus's faithfulness to God at all costs is amazing, but unless God truly did intervene at a point beyond Jesus's death, his faithfulness to God was not matched by God's faithfulness to Jesus. Far from providing a model of hope, the crucifixion, left to stand apart from the resurrection, provides a clear picture of the ultimate futility of human goodness and faithfulness.

But let's not skip to the resurrection part of this event too quickly or too easily. All four Gospels record that the most righteous person who ever lived was unjustly executed by what was arguably the best church and the best state of his time, and the appropriate conclusion was drawn by his followers who went away in despair. Two are quoted in Luke 24:21 as saying, "We *had hoped* [not now] that he *was* the one who *was* going to redeem Israel. . . ." (*emphasis mine*).

They also tell this *"stranger"* their other devastating conclusion from the events of the past few days—our church leaders instigated this travesty of justice, so there is little left to do but go home and try to figure out some other meaning for our lives, if that is even possible. Their hopeless despair is the realistic meaning of the cross. Isn't that the realism that tempted Jesus when Peter encouraged him not to foolishly go to Jerusalem and push the buttons of dominating institutional power? He could have stayed in Galilee away from their spotlight and continued a very productive ministry. Jesus told Peter that, though his counsel was filled with earthly political wisdom, it was in fact a temptation from Satan (Matt 16:21–23).

So Jesus resisted the temptation and chose to head directly into a situation guaranteed to end up with him looking a failure whose entire life and ministry accomplished almost nothing of lasting value. Do you ever think about how little it appeared that Jesus had really accomplished as he hung there on that Roman cross? His church and country had rejected him. Even his closest friends and followers had abandoned him and run away in fear. We are told that the multitudes of people who had at one time or another followed him dwindled to a few women and "the loved disciple" at the execution site. It becomes clear that not even the closest family and friends really believed God would deliver Jesus from the tomb. And the new community after the resurrection begins with a gathering of only 120 people (Acts 1:15).

Surely, one meaning of the cross is that you might well die having to trust that God accomplished more through your life than you or anyone else can see at the time. In fact, you might do everything God is asking of you, and you still might die looking as if you had failed at what you were attempting to do. Jesus did! And, like Jesus, if you have high goals for serving God in life, you will definitely die before they are all brought to completion. As we noted in chapter 2, no human gets finished or completed this side of death, not even Jesus.

7. Apart from the Resurrection, the Cross Is a Horrible and Terrifying Event. Where Is the Love?

Perhaps the most controversial claim in the New Testament writings is the claim that the crucifixion took place in the presence (active though not felt at that moment) of a loving God, who faithfully loves "the Son," as well as loving the "sons and daughters" cooperating in the execution of "the Son." Although there are many words and phrases that describe God's covenant love for humans, two key words are the Hebrew *chesed* and the Greek *agape*, both of which stress God's stubborn, committed, faithful covenant-love.

For the rest of this section to make sense, it is important to remember that *agape* (love) in New Testament usage has far less to do with nice feelings than it does with a stubborn desire and commitment to act for the ultimate good of the other person in a relationship. This is easy to see when you think about how many commands there are in the Bible to "love God" and to "love" other humans, even enemies. You cannot command warm fuzzy feelings when they are not there, but you can choose to act "for the good" of the other. So, as you read the following paragraphs wrestling with God's love, and it is a wrestling, please don't be thinking "warm fuzzies." Be thinking "love" is "stubbornly committed to the other person's ultimate good." And, don't forget that this kind of "loving" is almost always risky and costly. Remember also that all four Gospels state clearly that Jesus died because of his "love" for God, and all four clearly describe his mental and emotional state during the crucifixion as not feeling many "warm fuzzies" toward God.

It cannot be accidental that the two principal figures through whom God initiates the two central covenant relationships recorded in the Bible are both involved in an event that most of us find it difficult to imagine God was genuinely present for—Abraham offering Isaac, and Jesus being crucified. That either of these events should be referred to as events flowing from God's stubborn love both awes and terrifies us, yet they are both presented as events that initiate a new covenant relationship between God and humans. Is the Bible covertly telling us that God is really an ogre, an abusive father who defines abuse as love? Or . . . ?

I believe the afterstory to the Abraham and Isaac narrative is a clear statement that God is not like the other gods who demand that we sacrifice our children in the fires. YHWH is not like that, and that means that the God and Father of Our Lord Jesus the Messiah is not like that. However, the prestory to the event is that God cannot create a covenant that will drive all of human history toward God's goal for us without a person who is willing to be faithful, no matter how great the cost. In Abraham, God had that faithful human, a human who had heard the voice of God before and was sadly certain that he was hearing it again. In Jesus, God had an even more faithful human, and God was free to inaugurate an even greater covenant through Jesus's faithfulness. The afterstory is that God exalts Jesus to reign with God at God's right hand, but the prestory is that Jesus has to risk everything, while trusting that God was trustworthy. He had to make this choice when it did not look or feel as if God were trustworthy.

Though the afterstory is wonderful, I would still argue that there is no way to justify God's participation in these events, unless (1) God has at least as much at risk personally as each of the humans, Abraham, Isaac, and Jesus do; (2) the suffering of God, Abraham, Isaac, and Jesus are real; (3) God's suffering is at least as profound and deep as that of Abraham, Isaac, and Jesus; and (4) the very real cost paid by all of the participants opened up a future for the human community—including Abraham, Isaac, and Jesus—that God knows is more than worth the cost paid by everyone involved.

We must not deny or tone down implications of the biblical narratives, as fatalistic theologians who define God's sovereignty as total domination tend to do. We need to let the quotations in the texts that narrate these two key interactions between God and humans have their full weight, not explain them away.

> Do not lay a hand on the boy," he said. "Do not do anything to him. *Now I know that you fear God, because you* have not withheld from me *your son, your only son.*" (Gen 22:12, *emphasis mine*).

"*Abba*, Father," he said, *"everything is possible for you. Take this cup* from me. *Yet not what I will*, but what you will" (Mark 14:36, *emphasis mine*).

> ⁷ During the days of Jesus's life on earth, he offered up prayers and petitions with *loud cries and tears to the one who could save him from death*, and he was *heard because* of his reverent submission. ⁸Although he was a son, *he learned obedience* from what he suffered ⁹ and, *once made perfect*, he became the source of eternal salvation for all who obey him (Heb 5:7–9, *emphasis mine*).

Genesis indicates that God, Abraham, and Isaac are at risk in that event. I think both God and Jesus are at risk in the crucifixion because it is the test of faithfulness on both sides. Mercy is often *hard mercy*. When we begin to understand this, we begin to understand more fully one of the *"meanings"* the New Testament writers see in the crucifixion-resurrection event.

In both Old and New Testaments, Abraham is known as the special "friend of God" (2 Chr 20:7; Jas 2:23), and we may be tempted to quote the old saying, "With friends like this, who needs enemies!" Abraham was told, *"Offer your son, your only son, the one you love."* Abraham responded by deciding to trust the voice of the God who had led him to this point in his journey of faith. And God responded by entrusting Abraham with the renewal and expansion of their covenant relationship because *"Now I know* that you fear God" (Gen 22:2, 12, *emphasis mine*).

In Romans 3 and 4, Paul portrays Jesus's faithfulness as the fulfillment of Abraham's faithfulness, and he uses the same Greek phrase to make his point. In Romans 4:16, the blessings of the first covenant flow from God to other humans "out of the faith of Abraham [*ek pisteōs abraam* in Greek]," and in Romans 3:26, the blessings of the new covenant flow from God through Jesus to other humans "out of the faith of Jesus [*ek pisteōs iēsou* in Greek]."

As difficult as it is to grasp the level of trust that both Abraham and Jesus expressed in their relationship with God, it seems to be even more difficult for us to wrap our minds and hearts around God taking on the role of Abraham. This is the after-the-afterstory of Genesis 22—that is, the third way of telling the story of the Binding of Isaac. "For God *so loved the world* that *God gave his one and only son*" (John 3:16, *emphasis mine*), and *"God proves his love for us in that* while we were still sinners, *Christ died for us"* (Rom 5:8, *emphasis mine*).

Whether we like it or not, whether we agree with it or not, the biblical storyline concerns a God whose stubborn love for us is often most active in events that push human trust to the limits of our imagination. At those limits, we find the God revealed to us to be so unlike our other gods that we are often not sure how to cope with this God. But this is the God who is often identified in the New Testament as "the God and Father of our Lord Jesus the Messiah."

If the New Testament writers' claim—that the cross event took place within a relationship of love between God and Jesus—is not true, then most of their other claims are either false or relatively unimportant. On the other hand, if it is true, it says things about us humans and about God that we would often rather not know. If we are going to get our story straight concerning the covenant relationship of mutual love between God and Jesus, then, like it or not, we must face the fact that God's love for Jesus, and God's willingness to allow Jesus to be executed at the hands of other "children of God," are both an integral part of God's self-revelation.

It is not too difficult to imagine that Jesus might have given his life because he saw what he was doing as an act of love toward other humans. People do give their lives out of love for other humans. It is also not too difficult to imagine that Jesus might somehow see his choice as an expression of faithfulness and love toward God. People do give their lives for God. Some people even give their lives for their false gods.

It is much more difficult to see how an all-powerful God can be loving while allowing a beloved Jesus to be executed. Do loving parents do this? Even worse, God leads and guides Jesus toward choices that guarantee that the powers that be will respond with violence, as they almost always do when they feel threatened. Can this be an expression of God's love for humanity, of God's love for Jesus?

Nevertheless, that is the perspective that pervades the New Testament writings. In the writers' view, it is this event that completed Jesus's faithful life before God, and it is this faithfulness that led directly to God's exaltation of Jesus to the "right hand" of God. And God's exaltation of Jesus is certainly viewed as the fulfillment of God's love for Jesus in action. Further, they see the cross-resurrection event as wrapped up in God's love, not just for Jesus, but for the rest of humanity as well. Given that so many moderns see the crucifixion as described in the New Testament as representing either a wrathful God (quite a few fundamentalists and conservatives), or a horrible God who defines abuse as love (quite a few liberals and progressives), how could the New Testament writers, who were extremely familiar with abuse by the Romans and hated it, see this event as an expression of overwhelming love?

I find that I can trust and love this God if I trust that God is a passion-filled Father who hurt terribly when his "deeply loved" and "only begotten" Son suffered at the hands of many of God's other loved sons and daughters. I can trust this God if God was as at risk as Jesus was and suffered at least as much as Jesus did. Ellen Davis describes God's risky involvement in human history when she speaks of God's relationship to the prophets of Old: "Intense involvement with the world and with humankind . . . As the combined witness of the two Testaments shows, *for God it is costly beyond calculation*" (*emphasis mine*).⁹ I think her comment applies most fully to God's loving relationship with Jesus.

The cross is either an awesome expression of God's faithful love—a stubborn commitment to act for the good of the others involved—that can give us hope in all circumstances, or it is a vivid expression of the tragic reality that God allows horrors and does nothing about them. If the cross of Jesus was not an event, and a relationship, caught up in God's *chesed/agape*, there was no God present at the cross, not in the sense of the Old Testament phrase, "the God of Abraham." Similarly, if it was not such an event and relationship, there was no God present in the sense that the Jewish Christians who wrote the New Testament meant when they spoke of "the God and Father of our Lord Jesus the Messiah." Only if this event was the only way toward God's wondrous future for Jesus, and God's wondrous future for the rest of us humans, can this possibly be an event occurring within a relationship of mutual love and faithfulness.

As can be seen in the following quotations, the New Testament writers insist the meaning of the cross definitely is to be found in God's love for Jesus and for the rest of humanity.

> ¹⁶ *For God so loved the world that he gave his one and only Son*, that whoever believes in him shall not perish but have eternal life. ¹⁷ For God did not send his Son into the world to condemn the world, but *to save the world through him* (John 3:16–17, *emphasis mine*).

> ⁸ *But God demonstrates his own love for us* in this: While we were still sinners, Christ died for us . . . .¹⁰ . . . when we were God's enemies, *we were reconciled to him through the death of his Son*. (Rom 5:8, 10, *emphasis mine*).

> ⁷ Dear friends, let us love one another, for *love comes from God*. Everyone who loves has been born of God and knows God. ⁸ Whoever does not love does not know God, because God is love. 9 *This is how God showed his love among us: He sent his one and only Son into the world that we might live through him.* ¹⁰ *This is love*: not that we loved God, but that he loved us and *sent his Son as an atoning sacrifice for our sins* (1 John 4:7-10, *emphasis mine*)

(For further examples maintaining that we can see God's love in the crucifixion, *see*: John 15:12–13; Acts 2:32–36; Phil 2:4–11; Heb 5:4–10; 1 John 3:16–18; Rev 5:4–10.)

Whether we modern Christians are comfortable with it or not, our original story is a story in which the relationship of love—stubborn commitment toward good for one another—between God and Jesus leads to the crucifixion. We are asked to trust that, in this horrendous event, extreme faithfulness is being expressed on God's part and on Jesus's part. We are being asked to trust they were both expressing their love for one another and for the rest of us. Wrestle with this claim? Sure. How can we not? But let's not try to change or evade the master story the entire New Testament is founded on!

---

9. Davis, *Biblical Prophecy*, 16.

I think I was able to grasp a little bit more clearly how this claim concerning the relationship between God and Jesus might be understood a couple of decades ago. Some friends in our Bible study small group supported their son who went to serve in the Peace Corps as an expression of his compassion for the hurting people in a part of Africa. He was a pilot who could have earned much more money and enjoyed a lot more prestige, but his concern was for a war-torn region near where he had grown up.

His parents supported him because they, too, cared about the welfare of the people in that part of Africa. Neither the parents, nor the son, were naïve, as Christians who send their children on dangerous missions sometimes are. As a family they had lived through several uprisings and revolutions in the area. The mother had been captured and mistreated by terrorists while the family thought she was likely dead. The parents had also lost many of their closest friends and co-workers in the various tribal wars.

The son was killed by the children of some of the very tribal elders he was there to serve and help. His parents were heartbroken, but never once did I hear them question their love for their son, nor his love for them. This was true even though they had supported and encouraged him, as well as warned and cautioned him, in his choice to serve in a very dangerous area. The analogy was pushed even one step further when, still suffering intense grief at the unjust death of their son, these parents met with the tribal elders to enact a covenant of reconciliation by sharing a meal together. If we can love our children and yet send them to serve in harm's way as they express love—a stubborn commitment to do good—for other people, perhaps God can do so as well. Perhaps it is in these times that God's love is most active. Perhaps it is these times that are also most costly to God.

Only if God hurts at least as much as Jesus does on the cross, only if God hurts at least as much as his children who have been suffering all over the world throughout history, does the relationship between God and Jesus survive the cross as love. Only then can it be both God's love for the world and God's love for God's only begotten Son (John 3:16).

The power of this event as an event of love is greatly lessened when we diminish Jesus's humanity as a faithful Jew. It is in emphasizing Jesus's genuine humanity that we see the trust he had to have in God, and the risk he was taking when he said to God, "Not my will, but your will be done," just hours before his execution. The is also greatly diminished if we emphasize that "Jesus is God" as a way of meaning that there was no risk for God or for Jesus.

Both Mark and Luke indicate this event pushed Jesus to near the breaking point as he was "overwhelmed" and in "anguish." Only if Jesus could have failed does the risky love of God, and the risky love of Jesus, reach the heights and the depths that the New Testament writers claim they reached. Only then do we understand how deep the "faithfulness" and "love" of both the human Jesus, and the God he trusted, runs. This is one of the meanings of the cross.

8. The Cross Faces Jesus with the Two Ultimate Tests of Faithfulness Necessary to His "Completion" as a Faithful Human.

The offer of power, success, and fame (or our fear of losing them) has a magnetic attraction for most humans, and it did for Jesus. The cross embodied the opposite—public shame and apparent failure. The other great temptation to fail in our faithfulness to God is suffering (or our fear of suffering). (Perhaps for some of us—myself included—you could add boredom/ennui as another great temptation, but it doesn't seem to have plagued Jesus very much.) The New Testament writers saw the temptation to avoid social, spiritual, psychological, and physical suffering as a powerful temptation for Jesus. They also saw facing it as an important part of his faithfulness to God and to the rest of us humans.

Not only is the last quarter of every Gospel focused on the last week of Jesus's life and ministry, it is also true that those parts contain very explicit statements about the necessity of going through the suffering Jesus endured during that last week. Here are a few examples.

> From that time on, Jesus began to explain to his disciples that he must go to Jerusalem and suffer many things. . . . (Matt 16:21).
>
> Did not the Christ *have to suffer these things* and then enter his glory? (Luke 24:26, *emphasis mine*).
>
> ² . . . he reasoned with them from the Scriptures, ³ explaining and proving that *the Christ had to suffer* and rise from the dead (Acts 17:2–3, *emphasis mine*).
>
> In bringing many sons to glory, *it was fitting that God*, for whom and through whom everything exists, *should make the author of their salvation perfect through suffering* (Heb 2:10, *emphasis mine*).

It is wrong to think that Jesus's crucifixion somehow separates him from our humanity. Not only were many other Jews and people of other ethnicities crucified by the Romans, we who follow Jesus are also called to "take up our cross and follow" Jesus (Matt 10:38, 16:24, and parallels). There was a clear expectation in the various letters that Jesus's followers would find it necessary to emulate Jesus's decision to be obedient and faithful even at great cost. In fact, Paul summarizes what it means to follow Jesus in these words:

> "*I have been crucified with Christ* and I no longer live, but Christ lives in me. The life I live in the body, I live by faith in the Son of God [or, *I live within the faithfulness of the Son of God*], who loved me and *gave himself for me*" (Gal 2:20, *emphasis mine*).

The expectation runs through the New Testament that, in following Jesus, we enter not only into the joy and success of his resurrection, but also into his sufferings that culminated on the cross. Here are a few examples out of many possible ones:

> Now if we are children, then we are heirs—heirs of God and co-heirs with Christ, *if indeed we share in his sufferings* in order that we may also *share in his glory* (Rom 8:17 and see 6:1–6, *emphasis mine*).
>
> [20] But if *you suffer for doing good and you endure* it, this is commendable before God. [21] To this you were called, *because Christ suffered for you*, leaving you an example, that you should *follow in his steps* (1 Pet 2:20–21, *emphasis mine*, and *see* 4:13).
>
> Now I rejoice in what *was suffered for you*, and I *fill up in my flesh what is still lacking in regard to Christ's afflictions*, for the sake of his body, which is the church (Col 1:24, *emphasis mine*).
>
> I, John, your brother and *companion in the suffering* and kingdom and patient endurance that are *ours in Jesus*, was on the island of Patmos because of the word of God and the testimony of Jesus (Rev 1:9, *emphasis mine*, see 1 Thess 1:5).
>
> [2] Consider it pure joy, my brothers, *whenever you face trials* of many kinds, [3] *because* you know that the testing of your faith *develops perseverance*. [4] Perseverance must finish its work *so that you may be mature and complete*, not lacking anything (Jas 1:2–4, *emphasis mine*).

Jesus's crucifixion does not separate Jesus from our humanity, but rather invites us to join him in his human faithfulness to God, whatever the cost to us might be. According to James this is the route toward becoming "mature" and "complete" humans. Paul maintains that this is the route that allows God to make us "glorified" humans. According to the author of Hebrews, it is how we too become "perfected/completed" by God. If it sounds as if I am saying this lightly, God forbid. I do not like suffering; I like joy and delight. However, I have seen that when I have allowed it, God has often used the times that I have suffered pain, loss, and disappointment to lead me into new heights and depths in my relationship with God. This seems to be one of the meanings of the cross for Jesus, because it was through this suffering caused by faithful obedience that Jesus was completed/matured/perfected. That "completion" then allowed God to entrust Jesus with new levels of ministry, authority, and responsibility (Heb 5:7–10).

9. Jesus's Death on the Cross Is the Continuation of the Pattern of Hard-Mercy.

The theme of God's *hard-mercy* is related to other themes treated throughout this chapter. Jesus's experience faces us with a truth most of us do not like. From Genesis 3 forward in our Bibles, we are told and shown that God's mercy often comes as *hard-mercy*. We are told that not only did the original distrust in God cause dire consequences, it was also met with God's merciful presence, provision, care, and promises of ultimate victory. But these new circumstances are fraught with a difficult new reality—a *hard-mercy*.

Cain received a "mark" to protect him, but he became a wanderer. Jacob did receive the blessing he was supposed to have, but what a hard-mercy route! The once arrogant young Joseph's prophetic dreams were fulfilled, but what a hard-mercy route he and his brothers caused! Israel was saved from the famine, and then finally from the slavery that ultimately developed out of being saved from the famine, but what a hard-mercy! The wilderness journey to the "promised land" was a journey of hard-mercy. King David was mercifully spared the dethroning and execution he deserved for stealing the wife of a loyal soldier who was willing to die for him, but what a hard-mercy road now lay ahead for David and his family!

Jesus' crucifixion is presented to us in the New Testament as the new and deepest source of God's mercy being offered to us humans as *hard-mercy*. Jesus's resurrection is clearly an enactment of God's grace and mercy to Jesus personally. Apparent abandonment and apparent defeat are turned into overwhelming presence and amazing victory, but what a hard-mercy road Jesus lived through on his way to exaltation! Moreover, he had already been preparing his disciples for the fact that his resurrection would not mean the end of difficult times for them. He told them that they would be misunderstood, persecuted, made to suffer, and sometimes even be imprisoned and killed, as they lived in the light of his cross and resurrection. God's mercy for them? Yes! But a *hard mercy* that would be their form of taking up Jesus's cross in their own life.

I have seen in the lives of others, and experienced enough in my own life, to find that I need to say, God is mercifully present, but sometimes it is a hard-mercy. What else should I expect? I am attempting to follow the most faithful person who ever lived, knowing that his faithfulness led him to a completely unjust execution at the hands of his church and his nation. This theme of mercy, but hard-mercy, while living faithfully in a broken world, is a meaning of the cross.

10. Jesus's Cross Is the Death of the First Humanity (Adam) and Opens the Way for the Second Humanity (Adam).

The New Testament emphasizes that God had planned for a needed re-creation of the human race even prior to the beginning of the initial creation (2 Cor 5:5; Eph 1:4; 2 Tim 1:9; Heb 4:3; Rev 13:8, 17:8). No one really saw it coming, although various prophets caught glimpses of the need. This re-creation could be accomplished only from within by a faithful human—the Second Adam.

The writers don't just emphasize that Jesus was truly human, they also emphasize that Jesus lived within our broken and bent humanity—he was "flesh." Jesus did not live a life above temptation, anxiety, weakness, horror, or desire (Mark 1:13; 14:34; Heb 4:15). He lived faithfully, always trusting God as a part of our broken reality. He lived as Adam (human) with all of the temptations, weaknesses, and vulnerabilities that come with being genuinely human. He did this while always choosing to be faithful to God and to other humans. For providing this gift to God and to us, God exalted him as the "Second Adam"—the beginning of a new human society, a new family of God that can be eternal. This faithfulness of Jesus led to both death and life: death in the realm of our bent and broken age, and life as the beginning of God's creation of the humanity of God's future. Death and Sin are conquered from within the systems where they have reigned since we humans first became alienated from God, others, self, and creation. They are conquered by the one human who refused to let them reign over his relationship with God, others, self, or creation. The resurrection is not so much a great miracle as it is the expression of the unrelenting love God has for humanity, a love that is at work to reclaim God's purpose for creating us.

As the following passages show, Jesus shared the wounded inheritance handed down to us from the "First Adam," and at the resurrection he began a new stage for humanity as the "Last Adam."

> [19] For through the law *I died to the law so that I might live for God.* 20 *I have been crucified with Christ and I no longer live*, but Christ lives in me. The life I live in the body, I live by faith in the Son of God [*I live by the faithfulness of the Son of God*[10]]], who loved me and gave himself for me (Gal 2:19–20, *emphasis mine, see also* Rom 6:2–6)!

> [14] For Christ's love compels us, because we are convinced that *one died for all, and therefore all died*. . . . [17] Therefore, if anyone is in Christ, *he is a new creation; the old has gone, the new has come* (2 Cor 5:14, 17, *emphasis mine, see* 1 Cor 15:22, Heb 1:1–2, Rev 21:4–5)!

> [44] If there is a natural body, there is also a spiritual body. [45] So it is written: "*The first man Adam became a living being*"; *the last Adam, a life-giving spirit*. [46] The spiritual did not come first, but the natural, and after that the spiritual. [47] The first man was of the dust of the earth, the *second man* from heaven. [48] As was the earthly man, so are those who are of the earth; and *as is the man from heaven, so also are those who are of heaven*. 49 And just as we have borne the likeness of the earthly man, so shall we bear the likeness of the man from heaven (1 Cor 15:44–49, *emphasis mine*).

> [19] Therefore, brothers, since we have *confidence to enter* the Most Holy Place by the blood of Jesus, [20] by a new and living way *opened for us through* the curtain, that is, his *body* [*sarkos* = "flesh" in Greek] (Heb 10:19–20, *emphasis mine, see* Phil 3:20–21).

This cross event was not God's emergency response to human sin; it was something God knew from the beginning would be needed. God planned for a way to have an eternal kingdom, society, household, and family. But it would take an educational process for the children of God. God knew that giving us the ability to choose—an ability that being in the image of God demands—meant that a re-creation would be needed. God planned for it before the beginning of creation.

---

10. *See* chapter 12.

> ⁸ All inhabitants of the earth will worship the beast—all whose names have not been written in the book of life belonging to *the Lamb that was slain from the creation of the world* (Rev 13:8, *emphasis mine; see also* 2 Tim 1:8–10; Eph 1:4–7).¹¹
>
> ²³ *This man* was handed over to you *by God's set purpose and foreknowledge*; and you, with the help of wicked men, put him to death by nailing him to the cross (Acts 2:23, *emphasis mine, see* Heb 6:17).
>
> ⁴ For while we are in this tent, we groan and are burdened, because we do not wish to be unclothed but to be clothed with our heavenly dwelling, so that what is *mortal may be swallowed up by life*. ⁵ Now it is *God who has made us for this very purpose* and has given us the Spirit as a deposit, guaranteeing what is to come. . . . ¹⁷ Therefore, if anyone is *in Christ, he is a new creation; the old has gone, the new has come!* (2 Cor 5:4–5, 17, *emphasis mine*).

However difficult it might be for us to accept, the reality is that God's choice to create us, male and female, in the image of God ensured from the beginning that suffering and death would occur. God knew that giving us choices meant that someone would choose wrongly. So God has always planned to overcome death by renewing the human race through a completely faithful human life. Death had to be overcome from within. Jesus "poured out his life unto death," trusting that a faithful and loving God was already prepared to let life and love be victorious in human history.

11. Jesus's Death on the Cross Is a Kingly Act by an Anti-king, a Warrior's Victory by an Antiwarrior.

The Gospels say that Jesus died as "King of the Jews." However, anyone looking on at the time, if they saw Jesus as a potential king at all, would have seen him as a failed potential king. In the ancient world, kings who lost the wars with more powerful kings were the kings who died on crosses, had their heads put on poles, were led down main street in chains, or had their eyes gouged out.

The intentional irony of John 3:14–17 is noted by many commentators. John presents Jesus's "lifting up" both as an exaltation and as a crucifixion.¹² The dynamic tension in the paradox is awesome, and we still all struggle with it. What an *unkingly* kingly act Jesus endures under the death sentence nailed to his cross—"King of the Jews."

In a similar manner, Jesus is presented in the Gospels and in the letters as a warrior and yet as an antiwarrior. This tension comes into bold relief in their descriptions of the cross. The cross is where Rome put the losers, and crucifixion was designed to make a clear statement that Rome—and no one else—was in charge of the world. The same cross is where God and God's human son Jesus fought a victorious battle that

---

11. Other translations apply "from the creation" to the "book of life," which still supports the point.
12. *See* chapter 6.

began to once and for all disarm evil, sin, and death. This event is God's statement: "No, I am in charge!"

Jesus was executed as a treasonous pretender king, even though the New Testament writings are filled with claims that Jesus always rejected such treasonous actions (John 6:14–15, 18:36; Mark 11:1–11). This does not mean, however, that Jesus rejected identification as God's warrior king.

Jesus taught constantly of "the kingdom of God," and he clearly related it to his own actions. There is also a strong kingly–warrior emphasis in the Gospels. When Jesus entered Jerusalem on Palm Sunday, he was consciously reenacting King Solomon's triumphal coronation march into Jerusalem centuries earlier (1 Kgs 1:32–40; Mark 11:1–11). Luke's Gospel presents Jesus's garden of Gethsemane experience as *agonia*, a Greek word we translate as "agony" or "anguish," but one that could also be used of the single-minded focus needed by a gladiator preparing for a contest or by an athlete preparing by "getting in the zone," as we would say (Luke 22:44). However, Jesus's preparation for the contest is preparation for *not* taking up the sword and for *not* going to war with weapons of political and military power.

It is the preparation of a warrior who rejects war as we humans know it in favor of allowing God to win a victory of an entirely different sort. God's victory is over the wiles of the Roman Caesar, Caesar's surrogates Pilate and Herod, and the cooperating High Priests Annas and Caiaphas. It is also over the spiritual powers that incarnate so much of our human attempts to dominate one another. It seems likely that Luke 23:46–47 indicates that the Roman centurion overseeing the crucifixion recognized Jesus's last loud cry—"Father, into your hands I commend my spirit," as the victory cry of a successful warrior.

It is not just the Gospels that emphasize Jesus's kingship. The use of the title "Messiah," translated as "Christ" in most English translations of the New Testament, occurs 468 times in the New Testament writings, mostly outside the Gospels. In my opinion, every use is a claim that a crucified human is king! This was always a direct confrontation with Rome's Caesars and with Israel's Herodian Kings.

In one way or another, every writer of the New Testament expresses the conviction that this same Jesus, who was "lifted up" as though under a curse (Gal 3:13; Deut 21:23), was also in the same event being "lifted up" toward future exaltation by the God. This defeat that births victory is an expression of the covenant relationship they shared with one another. Jesus's faithfulness "even unto death" became the beginning of God's final victory over the sin and death that haunt the humans God loves. It began the re-creation of the human race in which life, not death, has ultimate reign. What strange and ironic good news—Jesus's road to coruling with God is execution!

Peter preached it this way:

> [30] *The God of our fathers raised Jesus from the dead—whom you had killed* by hanging him on a tree. [31] *God exalted him to his own right hand as Prince and*

Savior that he might give repentance and forgiveness of sins to Israel (Acts 5:30–31, *emphasis mine*).

Revelation 5 captures the same ironic dynamic in describing Jesus with two Old Testament symbols. In the same act of faithfulness, Jesus becomes the sacrificed Passover Lamb of God and the promised kingly Lion of the tribe of Judah.

Throughout the New Testament, Jesus the Messiah is the king who was victorious in the warfare with sin and death, by rejecting warfare as we other humans practice war, and by rejecting kingship as we other humans practice kingship. This warrior-king won the kind of victory for God that our wars never do. Choosing to "lay down one's life for friends and enemies" proves to be more powerful than taking lives. God leads a triumphal procession through the streets of the world as the result of what God has done through Jesus's faithfulness that led him to a cross. This victorious procession smells like the very fragrance of God to those who accept that this is the way of God, but it smells like death itself to those who reject this as reflecting the character of God (2 Cor 2:14–16).

Paul tells us that, when we follow King Jesus, we join a kind of warfare (2 Cor 10; Eph 6), but it is also a matter of joining a way of life that is antiwarfare in terms of the way world powers fight wars. The new "Joshua" and his followers "take the promised land," not by taking the lives of others, but by giving their lives for others. God "disarmed the powers" and "triumphed over them" through Jesus's execution (Col 2:13–15).

To say the least, following this crucified king is a calling most of us still find daunting. Sadly, during the past 2,000 years, the church has rejected Jesus's call to follow him in being antiwarriors more often than it has accepted this call. Thankfully, there are shining examples to the contrary. This way of doing battle with evil through stubborn, faithful, loving, nonviolent resistance is one of the meanings of the cross.

12. The Cross and the Resurrection Vindicate God's Faithfulness and Vindicate the Faithfulness of God's Faithful Human.

Only when we have allowed the perspectives noted above to have their full weight should we move on to the more joyous and celebratory meanings of the cross–resurrection event. The "good news" is not a "prosperity gospel." It is "good news" that says the way to God's blessings is often straight through the hurt and suffering that so often fills this broken world. It is a mistake to jump to God's vindication of Jesus without allowing the other meanings of the cross to really sink in. The New Testament writers were not wearing gold chains with crosses or purchasing stained glass windows with halo-encircled crosses. They were followers of a Messiah executed for treason by the state and executed for blasphemy against God by the church.

They understood the same accusations could be leveled at them at any time. They knew, and taught those who joined them, that a Roman cross accompanied with the usual torture of shaming, mocking, physical pain, social isolation, and mental/spiritual pain might well be in their own future as well. For them to nonetheless be willing to risk their lives and ask others to do the same by following this crucified Messiah makes sense only when we understand that *they knew that Jesus is one of us humans*. Only then do the faithfulness of God and the vindication by God of this faithful human, translate into a promise that applies to the rest of us humans as well. Even lynching cannot trump God's love and God's future for God's faithful humans. We, too, can risk faithfulness because God faithfully risks loving us. That is the meaning of the cross, and *that is why the promised participation as completed humans in Jesus's resurrection was a nonnegotiable part of their "good news."*

It is in that light that the New Testament writers use the grand words that describe what God has done through the cross-resurrection event. This is the event of God's "salvation" being unleashed in human history at an entirely new level. Salvation is rescue from what really destroys us—fear, sin, and death. Salvation is liberation from what really enslaves us—fear, sin, and death. Salvation is healing from what makes us "*sick*" as a species. Salvation is the outpouring of a new *"wholeness"* that lets us see Jesus as the human who fully expresses what it means to be the humans God wants—humans in the image of God.

This does include imaging God's faithfulness and God's suffering, but it also includes *sharing God's life and joy as well*. Salvation incorporates us into the vindication of humanity we see when God's faithfulness results in eternal life for Jesus. Salvation is life, life that conquers the many dimensions of death. It is about this reality that we can say with Paul, "Rejoice in the Lord always. I will say it again: Rejoice!" without being foolishly Pollyannaish (Phil 4:4). This life to which Jesus was raised is a goal worth the journey; it is worth all the hurt that has occurred, and is still occurring, to both God and humans, along the way. There is great joy in the journey.

In God's faithfulness and God's vindication of the human Jesus, we see *justification* (being put into a right and just relationship with God) that deals with both our brokenness and God's grace and love. Justification expresses both God's angry judgment on what we do to one another, and God's love goes far deeper. Justification vindicates God's responsibility for allowing such a broken world to exist—as Mother Teresa is reported to have said, "God, you have a lot to answer for." God answers by showing us the "firstborn" human of God's future. God demonstrates for us where creation, character, and community is all headed for humans who seek God. Through grace and love, we are adopted into this great renewal of the human family. Jesus's current status as "Firstborn" human of a glorious future human society justifies the journey.

In God's faithfulness and God's vindication of the human Jesus, we see *reconciliation* that is not cheap. This reconciliation squarely faces the distance between God and humans. It also deals with the distance between what we humans could be and what we are. This is reconciliation that crosses the divide between us humans and God, by means of Jesus's faithfulness to God and God's faithfulness to Jesus. A reconciliation that includes God's offer to incorporate us into the covenant relationship shared between God and Jesus, and thus to give humanity a restart in our relationship with God.

The following are just three of the many passages in which New Testament writers rejoice about God making possible a new level of reconciliation, justification, and salvation through the relationship between God and Jesus that culminated in the cross–resurrection event.

> [17] Therefore, if anyone is in Christ, he is *a new creation* [or as several others translate—there is a new creation]; the old has gone, the new has come! [18] All this is from *God, who reconciled us to himself through Christ* and gave us the ministry of *reconciliation*: [19] that *God was reconciling the world to himself in Christ*, not counting men's sins against them. And *God* has *committed to us the message of reconciliation*. [20] We are therefore Christ's ambassadors, as though God were making his appeal through us. We implore you on Christ's behalf: Be reconciled to God. [21] God made him who had no sin to be sin for us, so that in him we might become the righteousness of God (2 Cor 5:17–21, *emphasis mine*).

> He is *the atoning sacrifice* for our sins, and not only for ours, but also *for the sins of the whole world* (1 John 2:2, *emphasis mine*).

> [29] For those God foreknew he also predestined to be *conformed to the likeness of his Son, that he might be the firstborn among many* brothers. [30] And those he predestined, he also called; those he called, he also justified; *those he justified, he also glorified* (Rom 8:29–30, *emphasis mine*).

One meaning of the cross and resurrection is the vindication of both God's faithfulness and Jesus's faithfulness. They both endured the cross as the *"necessary"* path toward God's desired future for humans (Luke 24:26): a future of life, wholeness, and reconciled relationships.

13. God Raising Jesus Is the Down Payment on God's Faithfulness Regarding God's Purpose for Creating Humans.

The cross–resurrection event is seen by the New Testament writers as God's guarantee that God will complete God's purpose for creating us humans. This down payment on the promise includes:

1. God showing us that sin and death are not the final powers over human life.
2. God showing us through the glorified and completed Jesus that the future of human life—in the hands of God—is filled with potential beyond our wildest imagining.

3. God showing us that humans from all tribes, ethnicities, eras, and backgrounds can be "*one*" family of God.

4. God showing us through the current workings of the Holy Spirit that this intrusion of the new age into the old age is already in process for us.

In the cross and resurrection, the covenant relationship between Jesus and God was brought to a climax that helps us interpret the whole of human history both before and after. God is giving us a new way to see and tell the human story. Jesus, as God's representative to us, and as our representative before God, takes upon himself the injustice and violence so commonly chosen by other children of God. The brute power we so often use to sustain for a bit longer our place in this dying creation does not prevail; instead, God's gift of life prevails.

The very act that seems to guarantee the power of death—the cross—becomes a part of God's amazing next step in fulfilling all of God's covenant promises. The New Testament writers see the cross–resurrection event as the fulfillment of the covenant promises to all humanity: to Abraham and Sarah, to Israel and Moses, and to David and his descendants. The covenant relationship between God and humans had been "renewed" or "made anew" through the dynamic tension in the cross–resurrection event. Jesus, as the representative of God, the representative of humanity, and the representative of Israel, has faithfully taken on himself the inevitable death (and the sin/alienation that sustains it) that haunts everything in "this age" of creation. But the astounding result is that God is now free to move history forward toward God's desire to glorify, exalt, and complete humans. Not only does human life win; the life that wins is human life as we would never have dared imagine it!

Right in the middle of human history, the future age begins. The glorified, exalted, and completed Jesus is God's guarantee for the rest of us; the workings of the Holy Spirit are the down payments (Eph 1:14; 2 Cor 1:22, 5:5). When we allow both the horror and the wonder of the cross–resurrection event to equally dominate the narrative, we begin to understand why it is "good news." As one of us, Jesus fully participates in the results of our brokenness and in the fulfillment of our potential—a potential that we can now see and experience—as guaranteed by God. This is one of the meanings of the cross–resurrection event.

14. God Raising Jesus from Death Gives Us a New Way to Understand the Old Testament Experiences.

For a follower of the risen Jesus, the Old Testament can be comprehended only if it is read in two equally important ways. Richard Hays is correct in maintaining that followers of Jesus must reread the Old Testament through the lens of the cross–resurrection event. We interpret Scriptures correctly only when we read them in light of the resurrection, and we begin to comprehend the resurrection only when we see it as the climax of the scriptural story of God's gracious deliverance of Israel.[13]

Sometimes, however, we Christians have forgotten that the Old Testament must also be read as it was written—the experiences of faithful and unfaithful humans prior to the cross–resurrection event. The New Testament writers do begin to reread their Scriptures in the light of God's relationship with Jesus, but they also honor the Hebrew Bible as the experiences of people prior to Jesus. It was not first a narrative about Jesus; it was rather first a narrative about God's faithfulness, human faithfulness, and human unfaithfulness in the centuries prior to Jesus (Heb 11).

God loved, spoke to, forgave, cared about, and responded to faithful people in the past, but now we can see that God was also always moving toward something new as well. Isaiah, more clearly than most, seems to have seen his present reality with wide open eyes, while also glimpsing that God was preparing a future that stretched the imagination. Jeremiah called this future the coming "new covenant."

God's willingness to be involved with people who were far from perfect in their faithfulness, and in their understanding of their culture's brokenness, is a powerful message throughout the Old Testament. However, seeing Jesus and God relate to one another also gives us a way of reading the Old Testament as an educational process. With all of the grace and wonder of God's involvement with Abraham's and Sarah's faithfulness, with Jacob's family, with the Exodus, with Moses and Torah, with David and Solomon as successful empire builders, we can now also see that none of these structures was enough to save us from ourselves.

Church history has definitely added another sad and frightful chapter to this saga of failed structures of domination, even in the midst of God's gracious willingness to be with us humans. Both the Old Testament narratives and the history of the church are evidence that "God with us" is not enough. The power of dominating systems that crush others needs to be brought into subjection to God. If we are not being transformed, the default is that we will be conformed to the dominating influence of these broken systems (Rom 12:1–2).

This way of reading the Old Testament from both directions permeates the New Testament revelation concerning what God has done through God's relationship with Jesus. "In the past *God spoke* to our forefathers through the prophets at *many times and in various ways*" (Heb 1:1, *emphasis mine*). I have read that the Old Testament in various forms maintains that "God said" over 3800 times. And that would not count all the times that it says that God acted in various ways. The New Testament writers never deny God's activity in this important revelatory narrative that we call the Old Testament.

What they do claim is that the cross–resurrection event gives us a second way to tell the same story. The same story can now be told from the other side of the cross–resurrection event— "But in these *last days God has spoken* to us by a Son" (Heb 1:2,

---

13 Hays, *Art of Reading*, 216.

emphasis mine). This way of viewing the Old Testament as able to be seen from two perspectives dominates the New Testament. For example, the sermons in Acts honor what God has done before Jesus as valid and important, while also claiming it should now be seen from a newly revealed perspective as well. For example, David was a prophet of God, but God has raised Jesus, not David, from the dead (Acts 2:25–31).

Galatians and Romans are all about the validity of the previous way of telling the story, paired with the necessity of retelling it in the light of what God has done for us through Jesus. Matthew's Gospel is from beginning to end about this *fulfillment* perspective. I think the entire New Testament reflects this perspective of two ways to tell the story—tell the story the way it was first lived *and* tell the story the way it looks after God reveals (completes) more of God's purpose through God's relationship with Jesus.

I also think that much of our history as Christians and Church since Jesus has reflected that we are still trying to live the story without facing fully the new way of telling the story that God is trying to show us. We still think that having God with us as we try to manipulate the broken structures of domination and control can save us. As the Old Testament narratives reveal, it wasn't enough. We were supposed to learn this (Gal 2:11–21, 4:1–6; Col 2:13–15; Eph 6:10–18). Church history, including that of the current American church, makes it clear that God's education process is still not completed. The Jesus Way is a different way, and God raising Jesus from the death caused by the dominating systems was God's vindication of the Jesus Way. This is a meaning of the resurrection.

15. The Resurrection of Jesus is the First Step in God's Plan to Give Humans Immortality.

The new way to tell God's story provides a new understanding of what human life is intended to be. And it shows us the only way we can arrive at that goal—a gift from God. The hope that some kind of afterlife was possible seems to go back about as far as our records about humans go; but even when humans had this hope, the content never came close to what God has actually done for Jesus.

It probably says a lot about my personality that I love Stephen Wright's humor when so much of it has the ironic ring of gallows humor. When he said, "I intend to live forever; so far, so good," he was being ironic, and I can easily feel the same. There is a lot going on in the world that seems to justify a cynical and ironic gallows humor view of reality. But in my better moments, I place my full trust in the New Testament writers' master story that can be summarized by this rephrasing of Wright: By the grace of God, through the risen and exalted Jesus, we will continue living together forever, along with many human sisters and brothers; so far, so good. This is a claim that the grave has been overcome from within by God's gift of life to Jesus, and that, through God's relationship with Jesus, that gift has been offered to the rest of us humans as well.

Many Christians maintain that God raising Jesus from death was primarily meant to give us evidence that "Jesus is God." In contrast, the New Testament presents the resurrection as definitive evidence of God's value of our humanness (1 Cor 15:12–16). It was a bodily resurrection that firmly embedded Jesus's ongoing life in the realm of the human and clearly demonstrates God's desire to be with humans forever.

As N. T. Wright argues masterfully, the New Testament writers are clear that, by choosing the word *resurrection*, they mean the ongoing life of the whole person, including the renewal of the body.[14] As Larry Hurtado maintained, this bodily resurrection of Jesus allows these writers to present us with a Jesus who was, is, and always will be human.[15] It is in this context that Jesus can serve as God's means and model for us to understand the future God wants for the rest of us humans—a new way of telling the story of God's creation purpose.

The New Testament writers also believed that the first way of telling the story of God's self-revelation to the people of old included hints that God was moving in this direction. Many scholars have pointed out that the resurrection hope is not a central feature of the Old Testament literature—but it is not totally absent either. Sometimes implicitly, and occasionally explicitly, some writers of the Old Testament glimpsed a future that needed to include resurrection. The most explicit statements are in Isaiah 25:6–9, 53:8–13, and Daniel 12. Perhaps also Isaiah 26:14–19 and Ezekiel 37 qualify.

At least in some key circles, Jewish hope for a general resurrection preceded Jesus's ministry. How else could God's promises and God's justice be fulfilled for those who had gone before? How else for those still living under severe oppression? Not only the few explicit and implicit references in the Old Testament, but also rabbinic sources, Josephus, other Second Temple literature, and various New Testament writings indicate this hope was widespread by Jesus's time. The Pharisees (and other Jewish groups of the time) had come to the conclusion that the God of Israel had always intended a final resurrection as the event that would allow many of God's promises to be faithfully kept by God.

Nowhere before Jesus' time is the hope of a general resurrection of humans clearer than in the book of 2 Maccabees, which presents a full-blown faith in the resurrection. This book, which most scholars are certain predates Jesus, describes a deep faith in God's plan to raise faithful humans from death. The Seleucid king Antiochus IV Epiphanes demands that this faithful family—a mother and her seven sons—break the Torah by eating pork. The mother encourages her sons not to give in, and one by one Antiochus has them brutally tortured and then killed before their mother's—and still living brothers'—eyes. As the brutality increases, the mother encourages each remaining son to trust in God and God's future intention to raise them from death. Finally, after each son is tortured and killed before her eyes, the angry king has the mother killed as well, and she too dies trusting that God will raise the faithful from

---

14. Wright, *Resurrection of Son*, 129–138.
15. Hurtado, *God in New Testament*, 113.

death.[16] Regardless of how you view the historicity of the events recorded in 2 Maccabees, it is a witness to the resurrection hope among Jewish people prior to Jesus.

We are told that when Paul was on trial, he was able to create a partially successful defense by claiming his belief in resurrection aligned him with fellow Pharisees over against the Sadducees. He presents his trust that Jesus was raised from death by God as an extension of the faith he shared with his "brothers"—the Pharisees (Acts 23:6–10).

Certainly, we would love to discover more ancient writings that clarify exactly how and when this development came about. Perhaps that will occur at some point. In the meantime, modern writings by faithful Jewish exegetes of the Old Testament such as Jon Levenson[17] and Pinchas Lapide[18] give us some hints as to what might have been going on in first century Jewish thinking. They were obviously wrestling with the continuing tension between the reality of the great promises of Torah and Prophets and the reality of Jewish corporate life under Babylon, Persia, Greece, the Seleucids, and then Rome.

Though we do have to do some guessing as to how the Pharisees and others came to such a clear hope in resurrection by the first centuries BC and AD, we do not have to guess concerning the fact that the writers of the New Testament saw the event of God raising Jesus from death as embedding Jesus deeply in our humanity. Many of the passages that show this perspective have been referenced earlier in this book, but at least some of those passages need to be revisited because they so clearly maintain that Jesus's resurrection gives us a new way to understand human life.

The writer of Hebrews embeds Jesus's resurrection fully within God's plan for the future of other humans, as well:

> [9] But *we see Jesus*, who was made a little lower than the angels, *now crowned with glory and honor because he suffered death*, so that by the grace of God he might taste death for everyone. [10] In *bringing many sons* [and daughters] *to glory*, it was fitting that God, for whom and through whom everything exists, should make the author of their salvation perfect through suffering. [11] Both the one who makes men [humans] holy and those who are made holy *are of the same family. So Jesus is not ashamed to call them brothers* [and sisters] . . . [17] *For this reason he had to be made like his brothers* [and sisters] *in every way*, in order that he might *become a merciful and faithful high priest* in service to God, and that he might make atonement for the sins of the people. [18] *Because he himself suffered when he was tempted, he is able to help* those who are being tempted. (Heb 2:9–11, 17–18, *emphasis mine*).

---

16. *Second Maccabees*, ch. 7. Heb 11:35 might refer to this event.
17. Levenson, *Resurrection and Restoration*.
18. Lapide, *Resurrection of Jesus*.

Paul, too, sees God raising Jesus from death as an event fully embedded in God's new revelation about human life. Human life is not immortal. If we are to be immortal, it will be by God's intervention with a gift. Although much of the content of 1 Corinthians 15 argues that our future hope for resurrection depends upon and is guaranteed by Jesus being raised, Paul begins his presentation from a different perspective. Jesus's resurrection depended upon God's long-standing intention to raise humans from death. It is only if God has always intended to raise humans from death that Jesus the Messiah has been raised. If that has not always been God's intention, then the human Jesus has not been raised either!

> [12] But if it is preached that Christ has been raised from the dead, how can some of you say that there is no resurrection of the dead? [13] *If there is no resurrection of the dead, then not even Christ has been raised* (1 Cor 15:12–13, emphasis mine).

Paul then moves on to say that, in raising Jesus from death, God has revealed something new about human life:

1. He claims that Jesus is the "second human" who is "from heaven" and that through Jesus, God is making other humans "*humans of heaven,*" as well (1 Cor 15:47–48).

2. He then maintains that no part of human life in this age is immortal. We do not have immortal souls; we are perishable beings. What God has shown about human life through Jesus's resurrection is that *God can give the gift of immortality* and imperishability to humans, *when God chooses to do so*. We do not have it now, but God does intend to give it because of what God has done in Jesus (1 Cor 15:50–54).

3. It is not some inherent immortality in humanity that has been revealed in Jesus's resurrection, but rather God's desire to give humans immortality. God has demonstrated through Jesus what the victory of human life over human death looks like. We now have a new way to understand human life because we can see it in God raising Jesus from death. Life that defeats death is a gift of grace that God offers the rest of us because of God's relationship with the "last Adam/human" (1 Cor 15:45–58).

I find that many of us Christians are still resistant to what both Paul and the writer of Hebrews see as God's new revelation about human life. No part of our humanity is currently immortal—God alone is immortal. However, God is capable of giving humans the gift of immortality. The first human to be gifted with that fullness of immortality is the risen Jesus, and what was thereby revealed about human potential in the hands of God exceeded our wildest imagination.

Anyone who rejects the New Testament story should do so, not because it presents us with a low view of humanity, but because it presents us with a God-ordained outcome for human potential that is so rich that it strains our imagination far beyond the wildest science fiction presentations of a human future in the universe. It is this paradigm, this retelling of the creation story, that makes sense of the claim that God's faithfulness will be expressed when God acts, *not to save us from our humanity, but to save us into wholeness* as *"humans of heaven"* (1 Cor 15:48–49). Paul expected this outcome as this Jewish blessing makes clear:

> [23] May God, the God of peace, *sanctify you through and through. May your whole spirit, soul and body be kept blameless* at the coming of our Lord Jesus Christ. [24] The one who calls you is faithful and he [God] will do it (1 Thess 5:23–24, *emphasis mine*).

One meaning of the cross and resurrection event is that human faithfulness has become the means by which God has moved toward God's future for humanity. This is a future that has always been God's purpose for creating us humans. Through Jesus, the first glorified and completed human, God intends to glorify many more humans and bring them to completion as children of God in the family of God created in the image of God.

16. The Resurrection Allows the Human Jesus to Continue Being Faithful toward God and toward Other Humans, as Well.

No human ever completes all that he or she wanted to do before dying. Jesus did not either. In honoring Jesus's faithfulness by raising him from death, God allows Jesus to continue to faithfully minister to both God and his fellow humans on God's behalf. This understanding runs throughout Hebrews, with its stress on Jesus's role as the faithful High Priest who understands and empathizes with our humanity—because he shares it. But this understanding of Jesus's continuing role as our faithful human mediator is not limited to Hebrews. As we just saw, it underlies Paul's great exposition of the resurrection in 1 Corinthians 15. This understanding of Jesus's continuing identification with us humans is also apparent in the following passage:

> [20] But our citizenship is in heaven. And we eagerly await a Savior from there, the *Lord Jesus Christ,* [21] who, *by the power that enables him* to bring everything under his control, *will transform our lowly bodies so that they will be like his glorious body* (Philippians 3:20–21, *emphasis mine*).

This final inclusion of others in the great victory of God's faithfulness enacted in raising the faithful human Jesus from death is also celebrated in Paul's portrayal of the risen Jesus as firmly within humanity in Romans.

> [28] And we know that in all things God works for [*eis* in Greek = "toward"] the good of those who love him, who have been *called according to his purpose.* [29] For those God foreknew he also predestined to be *conformed to the likeness of his Son,* that he might be the *firstborn among many brothers.* [30] And those he

predestined, he also called; those he called, he also justified; those he justified, he also *glorified*. ³¹ What, then, shall we say in response to this? If God is for us, who can be against us? ³² He who did not spare his own Son, but gave him up for us all—how will he not also, *along with him, graciously give us all things* (Rom 8:28–32, *emphasis mine*)?

What does Paul think God's *purpose* is? It is that we become humans formed in *the likeness of God's Son*. Many theological issues that have been argued throughout the centuries are raised in this passage, but for our purposes here, the main point is that the "good" toward which God is working, the purpose God decided about humans from the beginning, is that, "along with him (Jesus the firstborn)," other humans would become "glorified" brothers and sisters, formed to be with, and to be like, Jesus in God's forever family.

This is not just a future that Jesus's faithful mediation guarantees; like the writer of Hebrews, the writer of 1 Timothy says that it is a current reality as well. The resurrection has made it possible for the *human Messiah Jesus* to mediate faithfully at this very moment between other humans and God:

> ³ This is good, and pleases God our Savior, ⁴ who wants *all men [anthrōpous] to be saved* and to come to a knowledge of the truth. ⁵ For there is one God and *one mediator between God and men [anthrōpon], the man [anthrōpos]* Christ Jesus, ⁶ who gave himself as a ransom *for all men* [men/humans is implied]— the testimony given in its proper time (1 Tim 2:3–4, 6; *emphasis mine*).

This faithful mediation between the resurrected human Jesus and the rest of us will allow Jesus to mediate God's final judgment (Acts 17:30–31). I think Paul even sees Jesus as our human mediator when, on our behalf, he presents the entire creation back to God as a gift from us.

> ²⁰ But *Christ has indeed been raised* from the dead, *the firstfruits of those who have fallen asleep*. ²¹ For since death came *through a human [anthrōpou], the resurrection of the dead comes also through a human [anthrōpou]*. ²² For as in Adam all die, so in Christ all will be made alive. ²³ But each in his own turn: *Christ, the firstfruits; then, when he comes, those who belong to him*. ²⁴ Then the end will come, *when he hands over the kingdom to God the Father* after he has destroyed all dominion, authority and power. ²⁵ For he must reign until he has put all his enemies under his feet. ²⁶ The last enemy to be destroyed is death. ²⁷ For he "has put everything under his feet." *Now when it says that "everything" has been put under him, it is clear that this does not include God himself, who put everything under Christ*. ²⁸ When he has done this, *then the Son himself will be made subject to him* [God] who put everything under him, so that God may be all in all (1 Cor 15:20–28, *emphasis mine*).

In this part of Paul's discussion of the centrality of the resurrection, he sees Jesus's final act in ending the old age and fully initiating God's future age as Jesus doing what we humans were always supposed to do—but have never fully done. Jesus will lead us in offering back to God our gift that now includes what we have added as cocreators. But even the opportunity to add to the gift is itself a wonderous gift from God to us. As David asked long ago, what do we have to give that God hasn't first given us (1 Chron 29:16)?

Finally, once and for all, the systems of domination are destroyed. Where we humans have so often seized and abused the authority we have been given, Jesus, as our King and Firstborn Brother, submits it all to God on our behalf. The human who has been granted far more authority and power by God than any other human responds with open-handed gratitude, rather than grasping and seizing. Finally, a human will demonstrate in action that we can be cocreators and corulers with God without attempting to usurp God's rightful place and authority.

Finally, we will no longer be a community integrated into the longstanding failures of humanity, but humans integrated into the community formed through Jesus, the Second Adam. Jesus will have faithfully mediated between God and humans so that God's purpose is fulfilled. This too is a meaning of the cross-resurrection event!

17. The Cross-Resurrection Event Addresses the Hungers We Experience.

As I was finishing this book, my friend Walt Zorn recommended N. T. Wright's new book *Broken Signposts*. I highly recommend it, too. Among the many wonderful insights throughout the book, the main theme is that our current structures show us both what we were created for and our inability to get there on our own. We hunger for justice, truth, and love, as well as for power that is used only for good. And, we constantly come up far short. But this hunger points us toward what we were created for.

On the other hand, our failures in each area make it clear that a re-creation is needed. As Wright says,

> But the way in which each of the signposts "fails"—justice denied, love trampled upon, power abused, and so on—corresponds in an almost eerie fashion to the way in which, in all four gospels and particularly in John's majestic account, Jesus of Nazareth went to his death, with a kangaroo trial, friends betraying and denying, truth sneered at, and all the rest.[19]

Humanity was created needing these structures and institutions, and yet their dark side continues to crucify and oppress—in the imagery of Revelation, to be horribly beastly. We do not have the solution, but God has planned for the solution from the beginning.

What has always been God's plan? The kingdom of this world will become the kingdom of God (Rev 11:15, 12:10). The church will become an assembly of the faithful from all nations, tribes, and times (Rev 7:9–10). Trustworthiness, truth, and justice

---

19 Wright, *Broken Signposts*, 190.

will reign throughout human society (Rev 19:11; Acts 17:31). The family will become Jesus's sisters and brothers in the eternal family of God (Rom 8:28–30). Human authority will be submitted forever to God, as we cocreate God's future with God (1 Cor 15:24–28). And these structures that we were created to work through in serving and cocreating with God will no longer be the structures that kill Jesus; instead, their beastliness will be publicly humiliated, and our systems and institutions will be reconciled to God forever (Col 1:20, 2:13–15; Rev 13, 17–19, 21:24–26). The glorified and completed Jesus will be the first, but by no means the only, human to arrive at the goal. God is addressing our best longings and our deepest frustrations. This, too, is a meaning of the cross-resurrection event.

18. The Cross-resurrection Event Addresses the Unsustainability of Our Age, as Does Current Scientific Understanding.

The New Testament master story presents "this present age" as unsustainable. The writers believed that, apart from what occurred in the cross–resurrection event, both humanity and our world would inevitably be conquered by death, destruction, and chaos. Our attempts to dominate one another and to dominate the creation will inevitably lead to destruction.

They saw the cross–resurrection event as a necessary and decisive intervention by God, and they believed that we humans have proven conclusively that, left to our own solutions, we are incapable of fixing what is wrong in our relationship with God, one another, self, and the creation. God's intervention, made possible by the relationship between Jesus and God, is the beginning of the end of the "old age" and the beginning of the beginning of the "new age to come." Peter described the current unsustainability this way: "But the day of the Lord will come like a thief. *The heavens will disappear with a roar; the elements will be destroyed by fire,* and the earth and everything in it will be laid bare" (2 Pet 3:10, *emphasis mine*). Another writer speaks more positively of the unsustainability of the present systems, God "made the ages [*aiōnas* in Greek]" through the newness God brings in the Son (Heb 1:2).[20]

What the New Testament writers concluded for theological reasons, our current scientific theory concludes from empirical observation. It seems increasingly clear that neither the current earth, nor current humanity, can ultimately survive the day when everything, or at least our part of everything as we know it, either implodes or explodes in complete destruction.

Our current scientific master story concerning the earth is uncertain about just how it will happen, but is rather certain that the earth will end. This may be by the sun exploding into a supernova, a huge asteroid hitting the earth, making human life impossible, a black hole imploding and taking our earth with it, the available resources of the earth needed for human life being exhausted beyond sustainability, the death of

---

20. The word often translated *world* is better translated *ages*, describing a new stage in history.

the seas and thus the planet in a "red ocean," a level of human population that is unstainable, a nuclear holocaust, climate change that destroys too much of the environment to allow recovery, a runaway bacterial experiment, a new supervirus for which we find no cure, the pollution of the water or air beyond reclaiming, or yet another among many possible last gasps. Increasingly, even our technological breakthroughs create more unsustainability. For example, we create new compounds and radioactive material that we cannot get rid of. It's like the Midas touch in reverse. Everything we touch becomes unsustainable.

I love our space exploration discoveries, but I doubt that they will solve the unsustainable nature of our current reality, any more than the discovery of new oil or new Higgs boson particles did. The New Testament writers believed that "futility" (Rom 8:20–25) is built into the current age of creation and can be changed only by a gracious intervention by God. God may allow us to be important colaborers in bringing about God's planned future, but only the promised intervention by God will allow humans to be the heirs of God's future. Only God's planned intervention will allow us humans to become fully the image and likeness of God, and thus to become the successful corulers of the creation, as God has always intended for us to be. As Queen Latifah sings so beautifully, our prayer should be, "Fix me, Lord," but we should also be praying, "Fix us and the entire creation, Lord." One wonderful meaning of the cross–resurrection event is God's guarantee that God is able and willing to give us humans a sustainable future (Rom 8:18–39; Rev 21–22).

SUMMARY

All the meanings of the cross–resurrection event are embedded in issues of faithfulness—God's faithfulness, and human faithfulness. For God and for Jesus, the cross–resurrection event was the test of God's faithfulness to humans and human faithfulness toward God. Not only did God prove faithful to Jesus, the "God and Father of our Lord Jesus the Messiah" will also include many other human "sons and daughters" in that covenant relationship (Heb 2:10). This has been God's purpose from the beginning: a purpose God has pursued, is pursuing, and will faithfully pursue until it is completed. When we understand the cross and resurrection as one event, we see Jesus is fully embedded in our humanity and in God's ongoing goal for humans.

A MEDITATION ON THE MEANINGS OF THE CROSS AND THE RESURRECTION.

I am sure that, from God's viewpoint, things always look different from the way they look to us. However, we humans who are following Jesus are always looking at things from the disciples' viewpoint—at best!

Jesus's Cross and Resurrection

As the Passover–Easter season of 2020 passed, I found myself thinking a lot about the meaning of Jesus's cross and resurrection from our place in history as disciples, 2000 years later. Obviously, "Take up your cross daily and follow me" is a meaningful way to meditate on Resurrection Sunday. However, as I wrote during this first season of Covid-19—we all hope the only season, but we have little reason to expect it to be so—food was dying in the fields because we didn't want immigrant workers. Meanwhile, other "unwanted" immigrant workers, side by side with American citizens paid $7.25 per hour, risked their lives and freedom as "essentials," packaging the meat and other groceries so many of us think we cannot live without. Milk was being poured down the drain, while poor malnourished children hungered. Blacks, Latinx, Asians, and Native Americans were dying from Covid-19 at far greater rates than Whites, as they do from so many other diseases and inequities. Our political system was dysfunctional, and our scientific community was clearly in over its head.

Almost nightly on the news, we were being faced more clearly than ever before with the inherent racism of our American health system, our policing system, and our economic system. Every day that went by appeared to bring more economic chaos, with no end in sight. And, our country seemed as politically divided as it had been during pre–Civil War days. As all of this was going on outside my home, inside my home my wife of 57 years was moving toward a brutal, final few weeks, despite the gracious care of her hospice workers.

I found myself reflecting on discipleship in ways I had not before. I thought about "Good Friday," "Somber Saturday," and "Resurrection Sunday." I also found myself adding, "What do we do now that it's Monday?" to my Friday-through-Sunday discipleship calendar. I think most of us who are honest about our journey together with Jesus live in the dynamic tension symbolized by these four long-ago days.

Sometimes it's still Friday, and all hell seems to be breaking loose. We follow Jesus, but we seem to be following him into one cross, one injustice, one broken and unfair world-system after another. We don't understand any better than Peter or Thomas did why Jesus insists on diving headlong into spiritual and political battles sure to cause rejection and pain, or why he seems to expect us to follow him there. The innocent and poor are still bludgeoned by the systems, and the most powerful are often still soulless in response. As some of my Jewish friends tell me I should, I find myself wondering "If Jesus is really God's Messiah and Savior, why hasn't the world changed for the better?" Like Peter, I just want to get angry and cut off someone's head (he missed almost entirely, but got an ear), but also like Peter, I am tempted to end up running and hiding from the tragedies all around me. And Jesus just seems to get crushed and executed again and again by my world. Heartbreak and crushed expectations seem to be the norm.

Sometimes it's still Saturday. Everything seems bleak and hopeless. Better to just disengage and be silent. Others have the power; what can we do? I feel guilty for not doing more, but I have no idea what to do because, though "we used to hope" things would be different (Luke 24:21), many of the leaders of the American church seem to be among those destroying the Jesus Way. Like Jesus's wonderful women friends of old, some good-hearted people still prepare sweet smelling words and actions, hoping to add some spice in this realm of death. But now as then, it seems rather futile, as death still reigns. The broken, bent systems go on their merry way, continuing to post guards to be sure nothing about Jesus gets out of hand and threatens things as they are. We disciples just don't know what else to do, so we talk in whispers to one another and hope *they* don't find us.

Sometimes it's Sunday! There are rumors of life; I have been told of Jesus's resurrection. Then I even experience him popping through some of my walls and touching my life. I experience joy, wonder, hope, and peace in his presence and through his promises. I am thrilled. But I don't fully understand why he keeps saying, "But you can't hold on to me." Why, when I become overwhelmingly excited with his presence, does he keep disappearing from my sight again? But he lives! So life seems to have potentials and options that draw me onward. I trust that God can bring life from death, justice can overcome injustice, and love is deeper than hate-filled power. God has a future for us humans, and I want to join Jesus, our "firstborn from the dead" brother in God's new coming age. I love those Sundays!

Most often, as a disciple who follows the risen Jesus, it is "What do we do now that it's Monday?" Some of us keep getting glimpses of the living Lord. He is with us. Some of us, like Thomas, understandably say, "I can't take your word for it; I need to see him for myself." (I pray that you receive Thomas's needed touch from Jesus.) Others, like Mary, have no doubts—he is risen! Some find the time between appearances to be terribly frustrating; so we go back to fishing as several of the apostles did—or back to whatever seemed to give our lives meaning before we met Jesus. Some wait around for his next appearance, or for the next Pentecost outpouring. Some hear Jesus say, "You talk big, but do you really still love me? Then feed my sheep!"

Some "go into all the world," confident that Jesus is with us; we see him at work on some days, and we wish for more of him on many other days.

I think if you take the time to reread the New Testament; you will find that the writers honestly describe themselves and their fellow disciples as living in this Friday-through-Monday dynamic, too. That is what it means to trust Jesus's faithfulness and to learn to live faithfully ourselves.

I thank God, and I thank Jesus, that the disciples who wrote the New Testament were honest about this reality. It allows me to trust that I, too—even when I am living on another Friday or Saturday—or even on a Monday—can "hope against hope," "take up my cross daily," and "follow Jesus," while saying, "rejoice, and again I say, rejoice." Someday, it will always be Resurrection Sunday. Keep pressing on. That is what the cross and resurrection mean!

14

Jesus: Spirit-filled and Spirit-led Human

"But doesn't the fact that Jesus is born of the Holy Spirit and filled with the Holy Spirit mean that Jesus was something more than human?" This is another of those questions I am often asked that usually isn't a question. It is meant to remind me of the *obvious*: Jesus is actually an entirely different variety from the rest of us humans. This question—that is really a comment—reflects once again how difficult it is for us to allow the New Testament writers and their Old Testament background to inform the way we view Jesus's humanity. In the New Testament literature, Jesus's incarnation with the Spirit of God overwhelmingly stresses Jesus's uniqueness, and just as overwhelmingly embeds him in God's venture in creating humans to be in the image of God. The uniqueness is the faithfulness that flowed from always living daily human life out of the empowering fullness of the Spirit of God.

THE SPIRIT OF GOD WAS AT WORK IN OLD TESTAMENT ACCOUNTS.

In the Old Testament, the Breath of Human Life Originates from God.

As noted in chapter 2, Genesis identifies humans as chemical (dirt) and as animal ("living souls"), then proceeds to make an audacious claim. This bundle of dust and animal life is also given the gift of "the breath of God" and is intended to be a creation in "the image and likeness of God" (Gen 1:26–27, 2:7).

In biblical accounts, only three humans are created by a direct action of God without a human sexual encounter involved—Adam, Eve, and Jesus. God's goal from the initial creation forward was to relate to humans in a manner that allows humans to be filled with the breath–spirit of God. The Hebrew word *ruah* is translated into English sometimes as "wind," sometimes as "spirit," and sometimes as "breath."

The same phenomenon occurs in New Testament English translations of the Greek *pneuma*. To be human is to somehow share the image and likeness of God, the very breath-spirit of God.

Ecclesiastes 8:8 challenges the reader to face the fact that we humans cannot gain control over this gift of God's spirit-wind or over our certain death when that breath is drawn one final time. Having just watched my wonderful wife take her last breath, it is quite clear to me that any opportunity for life after death is completely out of our control and is not caused by anything inherent within us. The *qoheleth* (lecturer, teacher) wanted his hearers to be clear that the most righteous of us is no more in control of our lives than is an animal or a very evil human. Death is a power larger than any of us, and it reigns equally over the lives of both the best and the worst humans—as unjust as that often seems to us.

Ezekiel indicates that only the Spirit of God can bring a dead culture and community—perhaps including dead individuals—back to *life* (Ezek 37:5). Isaiah made it clear that the same reality applies to individual humans from all cultures of the world (Isaiah 25:6–9). Similar statements appear in a few psalms.

Humans Are Spirit-empowered Agents of God in the Old Testament.

The history of Israel in the Old Testament tells us that quite a few priests, kings, and prophets were "anointed" (messiahs) to serve as God's agents with an extra measure of God's Spirit at work through them. A few of many possible examples of this anointed Spirit-empowered human agency for God include these:

1. The head craftsman and artist for building God's tabernacle (Exod 31:3).
2. The men appointed to help Moses as judges among God's people (Num 11:25).
3. Joshua as Moses's successor (Deut 34:9).
4. Saul, briefly, as a prophet (1 Sam 10:6).
5. David as a future king (1 Sam 16:13).

It was also seen as a very sad thing to have God's Spirit withdrawn from the life of someone whom God had anointed as God's human agent (1 Sam 16:14; Ps 51:10–11).

The prophet Joel claimed that God was promising a time in the future when the anointing Spirit of God would be poured out in a manner no longer restricted by ethnicity, gender, age, or social status. In modern language, we might say Joel promised that someday God would be seen at work far more broadly and across all of the social boundaries that so often separate us humans. A time would come when every citizen under God's reign would have some spiritual agency for God (Joel 2:28–29).

JESUS IS THE COMPLETELY SPIRIT-FILLED AND SPIRIT-LED HUMAN.

The Old Testament maintained that what is unique about human life originates from the breath of God. It then narrates a long history describing agents of God, specially anointed and empowered by the Spirit of God. That background is the context for the New Testament presentation of Jesus as a fully Spirit-filled human. In addition to the implications of *Anointed One/Messiah/Christ*, which often points to the work of God's Spirit in a human agent,[1] there are many other ways in which the New Testament writers speak of Jesus as Spirit-filled and Spirit-led.

The records of his birth, life, ministry, death, and resurrection are described in terms of the Spirit of God at work. Once again, Jesus's life is in discontinuity with that of other humans by the overwhelming overabundance of the Spirit at work in Jesus, not by the presence of an entirely different essence. The work of God's Spirit embeds Jesus in our humanity.

Jesus Was Conceived by the Spirit of God in an Environment of New Activity of the Holy Spirit.

As we see especially in Luke's Gospel, acts of the Holy Spirit surrounded Jesus's birth through the lives of Zechariah, Elizabeth, and Simeon. We are told that Jesus was conceived in Mary by the work of the Holy Spirit of God (Luke 1:35; Matt 1:18–20; John 3:16). This is a claim that Jesus ("the second Adam") is the first human since the initial humans (Adam and Eve) to be given human life by a direct act of God, rather than as a gift from God via intercourse between two sexual partners. In fact, though nothing further is made of it, two accounts present an inversion of the initial creation narrative. In the creation account, God works through the living male to create the female without intercourse. In Matthew and Luke, God works through the living female to create the male without intercourse.

Because so many Christian theologians and preachers have taken the accounts of virgin conception as evidence that human sexuality was viewed negatively, let's be clear that Gospel writers, like other biblical writers, viewed sexuality, rightly expressed, as a wonderful gift from God. Mary and Joseph would be sexually involved partners as soon as this special act of God reached completion, and Mary was purified for sexual activity (Matt 1:25; Mark 6:3; Luke 2:22). Paul is the most negative writer in either the Old Testament or the New Testament on the topic of sexual expression in general, but he is clear that his hesitancy is for what he considers practical reasons. He, too, says that sexual expression is God's gift to most of us (1 Cor 7:7), and he acknowledges that all the other apostles were examples of married life in service to the Messiah (1

---

1. *See* chapter 8.

Cor 9:5). One passage even goes so far as to say that forbidding people to marry as a doctrine of necessary abstinence will be a demonic teaching (1 Tim 4:1–4).

The manner of Jesus's conception was not to prevent him being contaminated by sexual intercourse. Biblically, it functions as *the fulfillment of a pattern.* God created the first Adam without sexual intercourse, and now God renewed God's human family through the life-giving role of the "second Adam," or the "last Adam"—again without sexual intercourse. The purpose of this miraculous conception was *not* to keep Jesus from inheriting our "fallen nature." Mary is not sinless (Mark 3:21, 31), and Jesus inherits her biological humanness just as much as he would have if he had been Joseph's child too. He is "flesh"—a description that includes all of the realities and temptations that come with being genuinely human; no part of Jesus is immune to these human realities. Part of what Jesus's life makes uncomfortably clear to us is that *"flesh"* with all of its weaknesses, vulnerability, and temptations is *not sinful until* we make choices that cause it to be enslaved by the powers of sin (1 John 4:1–4; Heb 4:14–16).

In the interest of transparency, I do not think the virgin birth—actually described as a virgin conception in the Gospels with the nine-month gestation and the birth occurring quite normally—is a key New Testament emphasis. Perhaps surprisingly, 25 of the 27 books of the New Testament never refer to it directly. Other than the accounts in Matthew and Luke, two or three other books might, or might not, obliquely allude to it. Mark, which most scholars think is the earliest of the Gospels, gives no hint of the virgin conception.

Surely this is an indication that most of the writers did not see it as essential to the "good news" they pressed their hearers to trust in and live by. In this light, I take issue with Christians who claim believing in the "virgin birth" is central to being a "faithful" or "real" follower of Jesus. My personal experience has included quite a few deeply committed and faithful followers of Jesus who bet their life on Jesus's relationship with God and risk a lot to follow him, but do not think a virgin conception is likely to have occurred. My personal experience has also included far too many Christians who insist that everyone must believe in the virgin birth, though their lives show little that resembles living the Jesus Way of love and peace.

Further transparency—perhaps frustrating some who found the previous paragraph to be a delightful acknowledgment—means affirming that I believe that Mary conceived Jesus while she was a virgin. I personally have no difficulty in believing that a virgin conception occurred. It seems to be a very easy accomplishment for the God who created the universe, created the earth, created animal life, created human life, and transforms the lives of people who like myself were not able to learn to love on their own. All of those are unique, unrepeatable, onetime events as well—yet here we are! If God exists and is the ultimate source of human life, I see no reason to think that implanting a life in an already existing life is more difficult than creating life when it did not exist on earth.

I remember decades ago reading Philip Roth's delightful, humor-filled fictional short story "The Conversion of the Jews" and thinking that his precocious boy Ozzie had it right when he argued along similar lines with his rabbi and his mother. I am pretty sure that Roth saw the implications of his humor as evidence for a conclusion 180 degrees opposite mine, but the logic seems right—either God can intervene as God chooses, or God cannot intervene at all. And if God is an active, communicating, intervening God, then the virgin conception is pretty small potatoes compared to some other biblical claims about the acts of God.

Jesus's Life and Ministry are Empowered by the Holy Spirit of God.

Jesus needed to be filled with and empowered by the Holy Spirit, as the rest of us humans do. Unlike the rest of us, he lived faithfully in a manner that allowed this to always be true for him. This new level of empowerment by the Holy Spirit is God's next step in God's purpose for humanity. It is the reason for calling Jesus "the Messiah" ("the Anointed One"). All four Gospels are clear that the Spirit of God is the source of empowerment in Jesus's ministry. Perhaps Mark is the least emphatic, but he still is quite clear. Mark's prologue introduces the theme as essential to who Jesus is (Mark 1:12), and Jesus's confrontation with the principalities and powers is a matter of "tying up the strong man" through the power of the Holy Spirit (Mark 3:27–29).

In the interest of space, the following illustrations of this emphasis on the empowering of the Spirit in Jesus's ministry in the Gospels are limited to Luke.

> [21] When all the people were being baptized, Jesus was baptized too. And as he was praying, heaven was opened [22] *and the Holy Spirit descended on* [epi *in Greek*] *him* in bodily form like a dove. And a voice came from heaven: "*You are my Son, whom I love*; *with you I am well pleased*" (Luke 3:21–22, *emphasis mine*).

Jesus's obedient response to John's anointed ministry is affirmed by an outpouring of the Holy Spirit upon Jesus, by a voice from heaven, and by identifying Jesus with the great Old Testament promises to kings and prophets. Although unique in its purpose, this descent of the Spirit upon Jesus does not separate Jesus from humanity. In fact, Luke uses the same Greek *epi* ("upon") to describe the Spirit coming "upon" the prophet Simeon that he uses to describe the spirit descending as a dove "upon" Jesus (Luke 2:25, 3:22).

Given the mostly silent approach the Gospels have to Jesus's early life, other than to note that he always chose to be faithful to God, it seems likely that they see this moment of his baptism as the moment when God empowers Jesus with new gifts for his upcoming ministry. Jesus's relationship with God and with other humans (Luke 2:52) has matured sufficiently for him to move forward in serving God and his fellow humans in a new way.

If it is true that Luke is presenting this event as the first time Jesus is overwhelmingly empowered with new gifts for new ministry and mission, then the temptation "*if* you are the Son of God," prove it, becomes even more poignant. Isn't this temptation a very human one? All of us find it extremely difficult to resist the goading to do something we know we are empowered to do, even if we sense that the circumstances, the timing, and the methods are not right. The temptation intensifies if we are newly empowered in a given area. Sometimes it takes a lot of confidence, trust, and restraint *not* to act, and that kind of restraint is often identified with the work of the Holy Spirit.

> ¹ *Jesus, full of the Holy Spirit*, returned from the Jordan and was *led by* [or "in" = *en* in Greek] *the Spirit* in [*en* in Greek] the wilderness, ² where for forty days he was tempted by the devil (Luke 4:1–2, *emphasis mine*).

Jesus's relationship with God was empowered by the Holy Spirit, but this reality did not somehow spare Jesus from the temptations common to us humans. Jesus was both "in the Spirit" and "in the wilderness." Empowerment by the Spirit prepared him for temptations and even led him into them. Had Jesus already developed the practice of praying daily "lead us not into temptation?" If so, God, at this point, answered the prayer with a "No," as occurred again when Jesus later prayed "If possible, let this cup pass."

This new empowering does seem to prepare Jesus in new ways to be God's channel for blessing other humans. A new ministry is now ready to begin in his life before God. I believe that the sisters and brothers who have for several decades been calling us back to an expectation of powerful "charismatic" works of the Holy Spirit have performed an important prophetic ministry for the worldwide church. I have been privileged to see special gifts of healing prayer, prophetic pronouncements, teaching, preaching, generosity, and inspired counsel expressed through sisters and brothers in ways that brought gifts of great grace to other sisters and brothers.

However, given the huge number of scandals, deceptions, and immoralities that have accompanied these ministries worldwide, it would have been prudent to stress with equal power the intense temptations that go with such gifts and ministries. Some of the most gifted have done the most to diminish what could have blessed the church with renewed empowerment. It would be wonderful if many more of these gifted sisters and brothers displayed the accompanying personal humility, and the awareness of needing others, displayed by Willie James Jennings when he speaks of the gifts of the Spirit.²

Luke tells us that, at the beginning of his ministry, Jesus faced the temptations that would follow him throughout his ministry. The more God empowers you, the more insidious will be the temptations to misuse the empowerment. This was neither the only, nor the last, time Jesus was tempted, but it is evidence that he began his ministry with a firm decision about how he would respond to the temptations all humans

---

2. Jennings, *After Whiteness*, 135–155.

face in our quest to be faithful and obedient to God. Having seen the shipwrecks caused in the lives of many highly gifted fellow pastors, church leaders, and seminary professors, as well as the destruction brought into the lives of those around them, I find Jesus's determination to depend upon the Giver, and not just the gifts, to be a very important human response to the gifts God was unleashing through him.

Jesus began his first sermon in his hometown synagogue by identifying himself with a relationship to God described in Isaiah (Isaiah 61:1–2; Luke 4:17–21). Jesus claimed that "the Spirit of the Lord was on him," and he claimed that he was "anointed" by that Spirit to "preach good news to the poor"—along with other Jubilee themes. He then added: "Today, this scripture is fulfilled." God had anointed prophets before, but now the pattern of God's relationship with God's agents of the past was being filled full of new meaning and new power. This theme of Spirit-empowered ministry continues throughout Luke.

> One day as he was teaching, Pharisees and teachers of the law, who had come from every village of Galilee and from Judea and Jerusalem, were sitting there. *And the power of the Lord was present for him to heal the sick* (Luke 5:17, emphasis mine).
>
> . . . and the people all *tried to touch him, because power was coming from him and healing them all* (Luke 6:19, emphasis mine).

Luke's statements indicate there were times when Jesus knew he was more empowered to heal than at other times. Sometimes this was so obvious to others, they felt they needed only to touch him for healing to occur. Apparently, at other times this was not true. Luke's paradigm is that the One God empowers Jesus, and Jesus responds by blessing others freely with what he receives from God.

> [45] "*Who touched me?*" Jesus asked. When they all denied it, Peter said, "Master, the people are crowding and pressing against you." [46] But Jesus said, "*Someone touched me; I know that power has gone out* from me (Luke 8:45–46, emphasis mine).

Here Jesus is presented as experiencing an event that is unprecedented in the records we have. God chose to respond to an unnamed woman's courage and faith, without Jesus knowing exactly what was occurring until the physical part of the healing process was already completed (8:47). Jesus had his mind focused on quickly making his way through a crowd in response to the pleas of a terrified father whose daughter was dying. Then suddenly, Jesus knew God had already done something through him. He was caught by surprise and wanted to know more about what had just occurred. Then Jesus intentionally completed another step in the healing process by making sure this woman, who had been ostracized for twelve years, was publicly pronounced clean and able to reenter community life (Luke 8:48).

Thankfully, Jesus is the kind of human who, when he sees God working, is willing to make the *important* people wait while he deals with those ostracized, oppressed, and defrauded people who always seem to remain unnamed—often even in the Bible. As he often does, Luke shows us that Jesus confronted the powerful social systems that treat some people as more important and more deserving of the minister's time than others. This is as much a work of the Holy Spirit in Jesus as is his ability to do the healings.

In trying to picture this event in which God's power flowed through Jesus before he really knew what was happening, I am reminded of the many times someone has come to me after a class, sermon, or counseling session (sometimes almost immediately, and sometimes years later), to tell me that some phrase or point had been used by God to change her or his life. Often, I was unaware this specific touch of God's Holy Spirit was occurring in that person's life. Other times, I have had a sense during preparation, or even on the spot, that I should include a specific challenge or comfort, even though it was not the primary focus of the sermon or class. Similarly, I am reminded of the many times I have been deeply touched, enlightened, challenged, or comforted by a stray sentence in someone else's personal sharing, teaching, or writing that was clearly not the point that person was focused on.

This passage describing Jesus as an agent of God's gift of healing, without too much effort on Jesus's part, also reminds me of one of the four most impressive healings that I personally ever participated in. A fellow seminary graduate heard me speak about the importance of calling church leaders to anoint with oil and pray for healing as James 5:13–16 instructs. When his wife became completely paralyzed from toes to neck, he called me, even though we hardly knew one another, to ask if I would come and anoint her with oil. I first visited with his wife and told her that she needed to confess any sins that were standing between her and God as James instructed, and then I would return to anoint her with oil. To my surprise, she and her husband told me that this led to a very powerful evening together clearing the air between them at many levels. The following day they asked me to return.

With almost no faith that God would act, I recruited two friends to go with me, and we prayerfully anointed the paralyzed woman with oil and prayed for healing. To my complete surprise, I received a call the next morning from the husband, "Ron, we are on our way home with my wife walking out of the hospital. The doctors don't know how this happened!"

Can I prove beyond doubt that God healed her? No. Can I prove that whatever explanation the doctor decided to put in the files isn't the complete explanation? No. But the best I can tell, the three of us who prayed for this woman (a stranger to us) experienced "the power of God" moving through us to respond to this couple's major step of faith. God moved despite our minimal efforts, and minimal faith, as the prayer team. Unlike Jesus, who always trusted that God could do more, we had little faith in what God could do through us; yet like Jesus, we were God's human agents through whom the Holy Spirit's healing power flowed before we became aware of it.

In the interest of transparency, I should admit that this event did not lead me into new spiritual heights. It actually made me quite angry with God because, just a week earlier, I had prayed fervently for healing for my sick son. As I waited—somewhat expectantly—for this healing, nothing happened except that my son grew more feverish. The waiting cost us an extra after-midnight emergency room fee at a time in our family life when dollars were quite scarce. More importantly, it cost my son several more hours of discomfort. Above all, I was frustrated because God choosing not to heal my son through prayer cost my young son an opportunity to experience a clear intervention by God. I was thankful for the gift of God's healing through the doctor, but I did not receive what I was asking for.

Why would God use my prayers in healing a total stranger one week, but not say "yes" to my much more fervent prayers for my dearly loved son the week before? Still today, I have no idea. It did make me much more empathetic with how, around the same period of time, my wise young daughter used to respond when I would ask her if she wanted us to pray for her to be healed from various illnesses. "No!" Of course, I would ask, "Why?" To which this insightful middle schooler profoundly and honestly answered, "Because if God says 'No,' I will be furious at God!" A sentiment many of us share, but that only a few of us are honest enough to admit. My guess is that we have no idea how often this fear on our part—this very understandable fear of risk and disappointment—is an impediment to the working of God's Spirit in our lives.

I mentioned that this was one of the four most impressive healings I have personally been involved in. The other three involved the disappearance of a definitive diagnosis of cancer, the sudden disappearance of a diagnosed clot, and the sudden disappearance of six months of intense back pain. Prayers for the cancer were by a congregation my wife and I participated in. Prayer for the clot was my prayer for a good friend while we sat in the library of our church building. Prayer for the back pain was the prayer of a Jewish follower of Jesus for my back pain. I had tried medicine, massage, and physical therapy exercises for six months. The pain continued to be intense. My friend insisted on praying for my back. She is a firm believer in praying for healing. I said, "Why not?" That question reflects accurately the level of my expectation! She prayed with her hands lying on my back. She experienced nothing. I experienced an electric shock running through my back. A few hours later, the intense pain was gone.

I will make two further personal observations about how *I think* the Holy Spirit tends to work when it comes to healings. It appears to me that physical healings are most often given when people are first having opportunities to meet Jesus or when major life-transforming renewals are occurring in various church communities. I do not think the same is true of the Spirit-empowered healings of relationships, mental issues, and emotional issues. These healings that are often called *inner healings* seem to occur most often in faithful, loving community relationships.

The second observation is that it always proves to be a mistake when followers of Jesus make experiences of healing their main emphasis when praying for more of the Holy Spirit. One reason is that the fruit of the Spirit is far more important and lasting—love, joy, peace, patience (Gal.5:23–24). Another reason is that the physical healings, unlike the healings of mind and spirit, are always temporary down payments on a future wholeness that comes only at the resurrection. Everyone Jesus healed during his ministry likely experienced other later illnesses, and certainly each one deteriorated physically and died at some point. Physical healings just don't last. They are pointers to a glorious future.

The point of all of these observations in this chapter is to remind us that Jesus was Spirit-filled and Spirit-empowered, and that he passed this ministry on to his followers. We definitely need to make ourselves more available to Jesus in these areas. Jesus's healings are not weird events. They are fully embedded in humanity and are meant to point us toward God's presence and God's love for us.

In the next passage, Luke also sees Jesus's joy resulting from the work of the Holy Spirit in Jesus's life, much as Paul does for the rest of us humans (Gal 5:22).

> At that time Jesus, *full of joy through the Holy Spirit*, said, "I praise you, Father, Lord of heaven and earth, because you have hidden these things from the wise and learned, and revealed them to little children. Yes, Father, for this was your good pleasure" (Luke 10:21, *emphasis mine*).

Jesus is also quoted as encouraging his hearers to ask for more of the Holy Spirit in their lives. Is he speaking from his personal experience in his own prayer life when he tells us that, if we ask for more of the Holy Spirit, we will receive more abundant life for ourselves and more empowering to bless others?

> If you then, though you are evil, know how to give good gifts to your children, *how much more will your Father in heaven give the Holy Spirit to those who ask him*" (Luke 11:13, *emphasis mine*)!

Because it seems clear to me that all of Jesus's actions are the living out of what he taught about God and about how we humans should relate to God, I trust that he was regularly among "those who ask" the Father for more.

Later, when Peter wanted to summarize Jesus's ministry in a way that Cornelius, the Roman centurion, would understand, he summarized it as a ministry that God anointed with the Holy Spirit.

> . . . *God anointed Jesus of Nazareth with the Holy Spirit and power*, and how he went around doing good and healing all who were under the power of the devil, because God was with him (Acts 10:38, *emphasis mine*).

Jesus is Empowered by the Holy Spirit during the Crucifixion and Resurrection Events.

Perhaps somewhat surprisingly to many of us, Jesus's execution and resurrection are both presented as events involving special empowering by the Spirit of God.

> How much more, then, will the blood of Christ, *who through the eternal Spirit offered himself unblemished to God,* cleanse our consciences from acts that lead to death, so that we may serve the living God (Heb 9:14, *emphasis mine*)!

Whether or not the author of Hebrews has in mind here some of the last words of Jesus as recorded in Luke 23:46—"Father into your hands I commend my spirit"—he definitely presents Jesus as able to offer his life-blood for us *through the empowering of the Spirit of God.*

The resurrection too is a Spirit-empowered event. It was certainly not something Jesus could do for himself. Only God could save him from death (Heb 5:7–10). Paul seems to have the same reality in mind when he speaks of the cross as Jesus's participation in human weakness and the resurrection as God's power overcoming this weakness (2 Cor 13:4). Even a rare statement where Jesus says he can lay down his life, and he has the authority to pick it up again, is immediately qualified. He states "This command I received from my Father" indicating complete dependence on God's authority and faithfulness (John 10:18).

Paul sees Jesus's entire life prior to the resurrection as empowered by the "Spirit of holiness." He also sees Jesus's resurrection as a Spirit-filled and Spirit-empowered experience, and he sees that same Spirit-filled life as available to us because it is the same Spirit that empowered Jesus's resurrection.

> ³ . . . [*the good news*] regarding his Son, who as to his human nature was a descendant of David, ⁴ and *who through the Spirit of holiness was declared with power to be the Son of God by his resurrection* from the dead: Jesus Christ our Lord (Rom 1:3–4, *emphasis mine*).

> ⁹ You, however, are controlled not by the sinful nature but by the Spirit, if the Spirit of God lives in you. And if anyone does not have the Spirit of Christ, he does not belong to Christ. ¹⁰ But if Christ is in you, your body is dead because of sin, yet your spirit is alive because of righteousness. ¹¹ And if *the Spirit of him [God] who raised Jesus from the dead* is living in you, he who raised Christ from the dead will also give life to your mortal bodies through his Spirit, who lives in you (Rom 8:9–11, *emphasis mine*).

In Acts, the teaching of the resurrected, but not yet ascended, Jesus, is described as empowered by the Holy Spirit. So also will be the mission of his disciples.

> ¹ In my former book, Theophilus, I wrote about all that Jesus began to do and to teach ² until the day he was taken up to heaven, *after giving instructions*

through the Holy Spirit to the apostles he had chosen. ⁴ᵇ "Do not leave Jerusalem, but *wait for the gift my Father promised*, which you have heard me speak about. ⁵ For John baptized with water, but in a few days *you will be baptized with the Holy Spirit*" (Acts 1:1–2, 4b–5, *emphasis mine*).

Peter speaks of God giving Jesus victory over death as Jesus being "made alive by the Spirit" (1 Pet 3:18). Paul sees the resurrection of other humans in the future as a Spirit-filled event as well (1 Cor 15:42–45). Once again, Jesus's experiences with the Holy Spirit of God connect Jesus with the rest of humanity, rather than separate him from us. This is true even of his resurrection life.

God Has Put Jesus in Charge of the Way God's Spirit Works among Humans during This Period of Human History.

What follows will probably seem strange to some and controversial to others, but it does appear to be a part of the paradigm of at least some of the New Testament authors. Without claiming that I know all they had in mind, there are several passages that seem to indicate that the work of the Holy Spirit is now under Jesus's authority, and/or is Jesus's presence with us and in us.

John the Baptist predicted that Jesus "*is he who will baptize* with the Holy Spirit" (John 1:33, *emphasis mine*). In a small way, when Jesus empowered his apostles to minister in his name, he was already being presented as in charge of the work of the Holy Spirit (Mark 9:41; John 15:26, 16:7). The resurrected Jesus could "breathe" the Holy Spirit into the lives of his apostles as he prepared them for ministry on his behalf (John 20:22).

After Jesus's ascension and exaltation, Peter says that the Pentecost outpouring of the Holy Spirit is an act of Jesus. Jesus who has now been exalted to the right hand of God "*has received from the Father* the promised Holy Spirit and [Jesus—implied] *has poured out what you now see and hear* (Acts 2:33, *emphasis mine*).

In fact, in the passage (Romans 8:9–11) quoted in the previous section, the Spirit of God, the Spirit of the Messiah, and the Messiah all are "in" the followers of Jesus. All three designations seem to refer to the same empowering that those who follow Jesus are experiencing and should count on. It seems to me that Paul here, and other New Testament writers in other letters, understand the "Holy Spirit" to be how God works in us humans. And, this work in us is now in some sense being determined or overseen by Jesus as the exalted human colaborer with God, who has been given that authority and promises to be with us at all times in all places (Matt 28:18–20).

The context of 2 Corinthians 3:17 rather clearly identifies Jesus, into whose image we are being transformed, with the work of the Spirit: "*Now the Lord is the Spirit, and where the Spirit of the Lord is, there is freedom*" (*emphasis mine*). We are also told that Jesus "allots" how the gifts of the Holy Spirit are experienced, and the goal of all of this is that the community of faith should become like a "complete human," reflecting the Messiah himself (Eph 4:7–8, 4:12–13). Finally, throughout Revelation, the words of the exalted Jesus and the words of the Spirit are equated (*see* for example Rev 2:1–2, 7).

If you disagree with how I have just described what I understand to be the current relationship between Jesus and the Holy Spirit, please do not let that divert you from the main point of this chapter: Jesus is the completely Spirit-led and Spirit-filled human into whose image God wishes to transform us.

On the other hand, if you are following the strand of New Testament scriptures that see the work of the Holy Spirit today as Jesus's work in us as he colabors with God, you will then likely relate this to the other topics we have explored, such as Jesus's role as "Messiah" and "Savior," in which he is also presented as the human colaborer mediating our relationship with God. Other roles and functions could also be added, such as "Shepherd," and "Giver of Life." Each of these is a work of God in which Jesus is now a colaborer, according to the New Testament writers.

Does Jesus use his authority to sometimes choose to work with spiritual power through the lives of people who do not acknowledge him as Savior, Lord, and Messiah? I leave it entirely to God and Jesus—as if I had a choice in the matter—to determine how they work in the lives of people who do not trust in what God has done through Jesus. It appears to me that God finds, and has found, many ways to do so throughout history. I think this opinion is in line with Biblical examples such as Jethro the priest of Midian, who was a spiritual blessing to God's people, but who never joined them (Ex 18). It also seems to fit Jesus's words about "other sheep that are not of this sheep pen" (John 10:16). It corresponds with the description of Cornelius in Acts 10 as a devout, God-fearing, prayerful, and generous human—even before he encounters Jesus. It also fits what I see of godly, caring, generous, courageous God-seeking people today who do not follow Jesus—often because those of us who say we do follow Jesus do so very badly at times.

JESUS'S FOLLOWERS ARE ALSO TO BE SPIRIT-LED AND SPIRIT-FILLED HUMANS.

We Are to Expect the Holy Spirit to Be at Work in Our Lives as the Holy Spirit Was at Work in Jesus's Life.

The writers of the New Testament leave no doubt that they believe Jesus was uniquely filled with the Holy Spirit of God in a manner that dwarfs both the experience of God's agents recorded in the Old Testament and the experience of Jesus's followers after Pentecost. They unhesitatingly include themselves among those who are delighted to receive the gifts, but who know that their experience is far short of Jesus's.

Although Old Testament writers tell us that God's Holy Spirit was at work in some prophets, some kings, and some other humans as well, the New Testament writers maintain that being filled with the Holy Spirit as a gift from God is now available to anyone who asks for it "in Jesus's name." Being Spirit-led and Spirit-filled is a potential experience for all seeking humans, according to Jesus (Luke 11:9–13). This reality is taken for granted in the New Testament, but it is most explicitly described in Acts, 1 Corinthians, Galatians, and Ephesians.

Few followers of Jesus are more naturally skeptical of other human beings than I am. Having grown up around churches, church schools, and seminaries, and then having pastored for five decades, I have seen plenty to fuel that skepticism. I have seen people pretending that God did things that were intentionally being faked. I have observed people convincing themselves that what they were wishing God would do had actually occurred, when time revealed it definitely had not. Even as I write, I see people claiming that God is giving them revelations about the president of our country that they think justify the insurrection that just occurred at the Capitol building in Washington. Clearly, claiming a connection with God's Spirit can be fraught with delusion.

On the other hand, I have also seen many changes in peoples' lives that seem best explained as the transforming action of the Spirit of God. In fact, sometimes I see no other plausible explanation. What appeared to be impossible occurred. Although I have seen many prayers for healing go unanswered—some breaking my heart—I have also seen seemingly *impossible* physical, psychological, and relational healings that flowed directly from prayer and trust. I have observed people empowered to live and minister in ways that once they could not. I have seen people given intuitions that empowered choices they had no ability to carry out apart from God's Spirit. Most important of all, I have experienced people being empowered to risk loving and caring in ways that they could not before, and I have seen lives filled with joy and peace that cannot be explained any other way than as a gift of God's Spirit.

Knowing that skeptics will doubt me, as I often doubt others, I still find it important to say that the promises that we humans can be empowered and led by the Spirit of God are true and real. We do in fact experience *tastes* and *down payments* that serve as God's guarantee of God's promise that someday we will be completed as humans (Eph 1:13–14).

We previously explored the challenge in Ephesians 4:7–16, encouraging followers of Jesus to become a completed community, incarnated with the Spirit that incarnated the Messiah. The following passages are a few more of the many possible examples of the New Testament claim that we humans are called to share through the power of the Holy Spirit in what God has done in God's relationship with the human Jesus.

Because I focused on Luke's Gospel earlier, I will begin here by concentrating on the approach John's Gospel takes to include us in the way God's Spirit was and is working through Jesus's life.

> ⁵ Jesus answered, "I tell you the truth, no one can enter the kingdom of God *unless he is born of water and the Spirit* [*pneuma* in Greek]. ⁶ Flesh gives birth to flesh, but the Spirit gives birth to spirit [*pneuma*]. ⁷ You should not be surprised at my saying, '*You must be born again.*' ⁸ The wind [*pneuma*—spirit/wind] *blows wherever it pleases.* You hear its sound, but you cannot tell where it comes from or where it is going. So it is with *everyone born of the Spirit* [*pneuma*]" (John 3:5–8, *emphasis mine*).

The paradigm of this Gospel is that Jesus is filled with the Spirit of God, and that, through Jesus, God wishes to share that gift with many other humans who can also be "born of the Spirit" and "born from above."

> ³⁷ On the last and greatest day of the Feast, Jesus stood and said in a loud voice, "*If anyone is thirsty*, let him *come to me* and drink. ³⁸ *Whoever* believes in me, as the Scripture has said, *streams of living water will flow from within him.*" ³⁹ By this *he meant the Spirit*, whom those who believed in him were later to receive. *Up to that time the Spirit had not been given, since Jesus had not yet been glorified* (John 7:37–39, *emphasis mine*; see also John 14:25–27, 15:26, and Luke 11:9–13; Matt 10:20; Mark 13:11).

In addition to John's Gospel, I think that most of Jesus's teachings—the Sermon on the Mount is a great example—were based on his own experiences of how God responds and teaches us when we choose to be trusting, faithful, and obedient humans. Jesus was the ultimate model of a good teacher who can say, "I have lived it; I know it works!" So, when Jesus said that if we seek, we will find that God will give us more of the Holy Spirit, I am sure Jesus spoke from the experiences born of his own relationship with God (Luke 11:9–13). The working of the Holy Spirit in Jesus's followers is to be a replication of the Spirit-empowered ministry throughout Jesus's life. Are we looking for evidence that this promise is actually being incarnated in followers today? Are we asking for it in our own lives?

Jesus said the Holy Spirit caused him to care about the poor and oppressed (Luke 4:18). I have seen that same Spirit energize people in the congregation I love, to give freely of time and money that did not come easily, to bless those disinherited by our society. Jesus said being anointed by the Spirit of God meant that he cared about the captives. Where else could the amazing, calm, positive, selfless energy of the Harvard-educated lawyer Bryan Stevenson of the Equal Justice Initiative come from, as he works on behalf of those wrongly incarcerated? Why are people I know who live many states away stirred to support his work, even though they do not know him or those he so deeply cares about, who have been imprisoned because of racial injustice? Isaiah 11:2 said that God's Spirit gives wisdom and understanding. Not only did Jesus display this gift, I have also observed other counselors provided with amazing healing insights that they credit to the inner stirrings of God's Spirit.

Recently, I observed a marriage that had fallen apart for a decade reach the point where no one thought a healing was possible—although my wife never quit praying for that healing to occur; so apparently one person did think it possible with God's help. Certainly, no one else, including the couple involved, thought reconciliation was possible any longer. Suddenly the Holy Spirit began to move in both parties, and one of the greater miracles I have ever experienced in a relationship began occurring. An *impossible* reconciliation is now a year in the making, and they report that joy and love abound. I know that no counselor or friend had any answers. I do not know of any honest way to describe what occurred other than as a major work of the Holy Spirit in the lives of this couple.

I would be hesitant to claim that any personal experience of mine has ever been "*filled* with the Holy Spirit," but I have certainly experienced, and seen in others, the nudges and guidance that bring good gifts from God into our lives and into the lives of others. As far short of fully emulating Jesus as my life is, it is clear to me that only the empowering presence of God could have brought my life from the self-centered place my journey with Jesus began to the place where now, at least occasionally, I act somewhat Jesus-like. My personal transformation is far from *completed*, but it is real. As I often say, "I am not what I should be or want to be, but I definitely am not what I used to be." I have seen that same transformation in many other lives as well.

The Work of the Spirit in Jesus's Followers Is to Bring about a Oneness with Jesus and with One Another.

Part of what is to occur in the lives of followers of Jesus is a relational *oneness* between our spirit and Jesus: "But *whoever* unites himself with the Lord *is one with him in spirit*" (1 Cor 6:17, emphasis mine). This Jesus-empowered, Spirit-empowered, community life is also the focus of large sections of Paul's letters (1 Cor 12–14; Rom 8, 12–15; Gal 5; Eph 4–5).

The identification between the fullness of God's Spirit in Jesus, and then because of Jesus, the same experience in other humans, is quite clear in the following statement by Paul. The "all" is not applied to the rest of us, at least not now, but the "fullness" is:

> [9] "*For in Christ all the fullness of the Deity lives in bodily form,* [10] and *you have been given fullness in Christ*, who is the head over every power and authority" (Col 2:9–10, *emphasis mine; compare* Eph 4:13).

John 20:21–23 is particularly graphic because Jesus enacts with physical breath his God-given role as supplier of the Spirit of God to other humans. In fact, Jesus explicitly entrusts his disciples to act as God's (and Jesus's) agents, who are also being empowered by the Spirit to share God's forgiveness with others (*see* a similar promise in Matt 18:18–20)—a promise and a challenge that Catholics have explored more fully than Protestants.

Wouldn't it be wonderful if all of us who are a part of the community of Jesus followers took seriously our role as Spirit-filled mediators of forgiveness, rather than our all-too-common propensity to take on the role of "accuser of our brothers and sisters" (Rev 12:10)? Being determined accusers is supposed to be Satan's role, not that of fellow Christians! In my 50-plus years as a pastor, and during my youth as a pastor's son, I have seen so many people hurt, even destroyed, by fellow Christians choosing to be accusers rather than forgivers. How do we who call ourselves followers of Jesus so easily forget one of the primary works Jesus wants the Holy Spirit to do in our lives—teach and empower us to forgive as Jesus forgives?

Once as a young teen, I told my mother I never wanted anything to do with Christians or church again because I had just watched a rather petty church quarrel destroy a close friendship three families had maintained for decades. A friendship they had enjoyed for years without the church had now been trashed through their participation in a church! Even now I find it heartbreaking to remember how these amazing families that I enjoyed and respected so much blew apart. Thankfully, they later experienced some healing and forgiveness, but the scars remained. I saw almost exactly the same thing occur after I left the first church I pastored. Even though I had warned the elders not to return to bickering with one another after I left, they did. And most of the newer believers soon left the church. It was heartbreaking to hear the sad news.

Just a few years ago, I experienced a similar blow-up in the church community I had pastored for years. Again, it was heartbreaking to experience brothers and sisters exhibiting stubborn accusations toward one another, rather than stubborn commitment to grace and good for "the others." This time it was around an inability to even talk and pray together as brothers and sisters around the issues of gay and lesbian marriage. Soon people on each side of the arguments became "the others," those "others" who Jesus says are not "other," but rather our "brothers and sisters." Obviously, we who wish to follow Jesus desperately need more of the Holy Spirit that filled Jesus in our lives as his followers!

We can be thankful that, unlike those of us who sporadically follow him, Jesus consistently sees his role in terms of sympathizing and empathizing with those of us who are fellow humans (Heb 4:14–18). Each time I have experienced the wonders God enacts when communities choose to be communities of forgiveness and support, rather than communities of accusations and criticisms, I realize yet again the importance of Jesus's promise. He promised that in forgiving others, we will be able to experience forgiveness ourselves (Matt 6:12–15). This interpersonal healing is one of the great works of the Holy Spirit in our lives.

Of course, there are many other works of the Spirit beyond the examples I have been focusing on—forgiving one another, caring for the poor and oppressed, and relational oneness. Most of us humans have not even begun to imagine how much positive empowering can be unleashed in a genuinely human life through a trusting relationship with God. The New Testament tells us to allow that imagination to be renewed by looking at the trust and the actions of the Spirit-empowered human Jesus.

Being Filled with the Spirit Did Not Mean an Escape from Human Limitations and Errors.

As I mentioned earlier, in the New Testament the work of the Holy Spirit seems to describe God at work in us humans, with our limitations and finitude. With all of his strong talk, Paul was quite ready to acknowledge that he was finite and limited in allowing the Holy Spirit to work through him (1 Cor 7:40, 13:12; Phil 3:12–14). These are personal admissions that many of us who read his letters seem to forget—both many conservatives and many progressives—for opposite reasons. The Holy Spirit worked in real humans with real feelings, real thoughts, and real concerns. This work of God did not produce a nonhuman inerrancy, but rather an amazing empowering of real people with the Spirit of God.

The following chain of events illustrates both the amazing empowerment and the limitations that are involved in the Holy Spirit's work in us humans and the community of faith to which we belong. In Acts 19:21, we are told that Paul decided to go to Jerusalem and that he thought he "must" soon visit Rome as well. By Acts 20:22, Paul is saying he must go to Jerusalem because of the Spirit, even though "in every city the Holy Spirit warns me that prison and hardships are facing me." However, in Acts 21:4, we are told, "Through the Spirit they [disciples at Tyre] urged Paul not to go on to Jerusalem." So far, we have had the Spirit working in people to say, "go" and working in people to say, "do not go."

Then in Acts 21:11, Agabus, one of the most trusted of the early church prophets, takes Paul's belt and ties up his own hands and feet, then tells Paul "The Holy Spirit says, 'In this way the Jews [the power elite] of Jerusalem will bind the owner of this belt and will hand him over to the Gentiles.'" The people do not respond to Agabus's prophecy with a sense of finality or fatalism; instead, they immediately begin begging Paul not to go (Acts 21:12–14). But Paul maintains he must go. Paul does arrive in Jerusalem, and together he and James attempt to devise a plan that will keep Agabus's prophetic word about Paul being arrested and handed over to Gentiles from coming true (Acts 21:20–24). Somewhat ironically, it is the failure of their plan that causes Paul to end up in Rome, where he thought he "must" go.

This same understanding of the empowering of the Holy Spirit as God really at work through real humans with real limitations underlies all of Paul's instructions. In 1 Corinthians 14, both the real presence and the real limitations are obvious: "Two or three prophets should speak, and the *others should weigh carefully what is said*"(1 Cor 14:29). The Holy Spirit's work in the midst of human limitation is also clear in the dynamic tension portrayed in the following instructions: [19]"Do not put out the *Spirit's fire*; [20] do not treat *prophecies with contempt*. [21] *Test everything*. Hold on to the *good*. [22] Avoid every kind of *evil*" (1 Thess 5:19–22, *emphasis mine*).

I think the same recognition of the work of the Spirit through human limitations is also evident in the humility of the letter sent out by the leaders of the Jerusalem church, after a lengthy and argumentative leadership meeting when they say: "It *seemed* good to the *Holy Spirit and to us* not to burden you with anything beyond the following requirements. . . ." (Acts 15:29, *emphasis mine*).

Please do not take my insistence that the guidance of the Holy Spirit in our lives has limitations as a demeaning of the importance of this work of God. If we wish to follow Jesus, this work is imperative in our personal lives and in human history. Modern discoveries about how the human brain works indicate that we are extremely susceptible to being nudged toward decisions. The one who nudges does not need to exert any direct control over us at all in order to nudge us in the direction she or he wants us to go. Almost all advertising depends upon our susceptibility to being nudged by suggestive possibilities. So does almost all political campaigning. Why would we think God cannot also nudge without controlling?

The interference in American elections by foreign powers using social media was based on the knowledge that a percentage of those who read the propaganda were likely to be influenced toward the goals the originators had in mind. Importantly, the goals toward which we were being nudged were often not even the ones that appeared to be the *obvious* goals of the originators. These nudges can also be used for good. Studies show that seeing someone giving makes us more likely to give—and seeing someone acting courageously makes us more likely to act courageously. It is equally true, as we have often seen throughout the Covid-19 pandemic, that seeing someone hoarding makes us more likely to hoard and seeing someone being fearful makes us more likely to be fearful. If we know how to nudge people without controlling them, surely God can do so. In fact, God does do so!

All of this to say that being Spirit-filled and Spirit-led does not separate us from our humanity. Neither did the work of the Spirit separate Jesus from being human; it is rather God's way of working through our humanity to bring about God's purposes in the world. *Jesus fulfilled and completed the goal as none before or since have done, but he did it as one of us.*

SUMMARY

From conception through ascension and current reign, Jesus is described by various New Testament writers as empowered by God's Holy Spirit. Although Jesus's experience is overwhelmingly beyond their experiences, his experiences are still in continuity with those of the great prophets, kings, and priests who are also described as anointed with the Spirit of God in the Old Testament narratives. The New Testament sees Jesus as now in charge of the work of the Holy Spirit among his followers. In every respect, this is seen as a gift from God that fills Jesus's human potential to the maximum, and then is a "down payment" to the rest of us, designed to move us toward becoming completed humans in God's future society. Far from separating Jesus from our humanity, the Spirit-filled and Spirit-led experiences of Jesus overwhelmingly embed him in God's purpose for humans.

My own experience has been that only through Jesus could God ever have saved me from myself and from destructive actions toward others. Further, it is clear to me that whenever more of the character of God is reflected in my actions, it is an empowering that I did not have prior to my relationship with God through Jesus. So, without question, I do trust that the promises are true. God empowers our human lives with the Spirit of God when we trust what God has done through the faithfulness of the human Jesus.

So, I challenge you: Draw nearer to Jesus from wherever you are in your process of life. You will experience more longing for the character of God in your life and more empowering of the Spirit of God in your actions.

15

Jesus's Jewishness

A PLEA FOR TRUTH, TEARS, TURNING, AND TRUSTING IS NECESSARY.

Jesus was Jewish. For many this is an inconvenient truth. But Howard Thurman was correct:

> It is impossible for Jesus to be understood outside of the sense of community that Israel held with God. This does not take anything away from him; rather does it heighten the challenge his life presents, for such reflection reveals him as the product of the constant working of the creative mind of God upon the life, thought, and character of a race of men. . . . How different might have been the story of the last two thousand years on this planet, grown old from suffering, if the link between Jesus and Israel had never been severed.[1]

Thurman wanted those of us currently advantaged by our cultural systems to see that Jesus lived among the disinherited. Even more strongly, he encouraged those currently disenfranchised due to ethnicity, lack of resources, or legal oppression to see that Jesus lived among those disinherited by his church, his nation, and the laws of the empire. He lived as a noncitizen in an empire that saw people like him mostly as a source of cheap resources for the Empire, but a bother. Jews wanted too much and caused too many disturbances.

By the second century AD, many church leaders were already working hard to hold on to the part of Jesus they honored and loved, but to legitimate continuing to disinherit his Jewish people. The logic is ironic; the results have been catastrophic in world history.

---

1. Thurman, *Jesus and Disinherited*, 5–6.

Jesus Is One of Us

It is not too difficult to draw a straight line from the early church heresy of anti-Semitism and anti-Judaism[2], through the church's growing lust for domination,[3] through the church's decision to baptize European lust for power and money,[4] through the legitimization by the Papal "Doctrine of Discovery" of a theologically privileged status for White European Christians who were deemed as serving God when they forced conversions, seized property, killed non-Europeans, and destroyed non-Christian cultures.[5]

The consequences came to America as the church legitimizing the invasion of Native American lands. Most churches in America continued the heresy by privileging Whiteness and legitimizing seeing nonwhite people as unworthy of the same advantages and privileges they wanted for themselves. The majority of the White Christian church in the USA supported the legalization of slavery, the continued anti-Semitic interpretation of the New Testament, the development of the most racist legal system in human history up to that time, and the confiscation of land based on the ""Doctrine of Discovery."

The heresy that began taking root in church leadership at least by the second century AD still "legitimizes" many American Christians in their support of systemic racism, anti-Semitism, and mistreatment of immigrants. What for centuries had been a wedding of anti-Judaism and a lust for Roman Imperial power in church history was fully racialized in sixteenth century Europe as a theological legitimization for the economic exploitation of non-Europeans. If it weren't a tragedy of epic proportions, the irony would be humorous. A church claiming to follow a dark-skinned Jew who was executed by Rome, legitimizes in the name of Rome, and of the the now-Whitened European *Jesus* of the church, the right to torture, enslave, and abuse people who are Jewish and/or dark skinned. What a horror early Christian anti-Semitism had unleashed upon the world!

Without denying that the early church fathers gave us some important gifts, and that some of them took courageous stands against their culture in other ways, it is important to note how rapidly the movement from being a predominantly Jewish movement to becoming a predominantly Gentile movement came to include Gentile anti-Semitism and Gentile anti-Judaism. Rather than allowing God to transform this cultural prejudice, most of the church fathers allowed the culture to conform their teaching and doctrine to the culture and adopted a heresy that Paul had warned against early on (Rom 11:25–32).

"Jesus wept" over the pain death caused a family of close friends as well as over the coming pain of Jerusalem, the city he loved so much (John 11:34; Luke 13:34). I have no doubt Jesus is still weeping over the way people who claim to be following him

---

2. Simkins, *Truth, Tears*.
3. MacCulloch, *Christianity*, 189–228.
4. Kendi, *Stamped*, 22–28.
5. Charles and Rah, *Unsettling Truths*.

have treated Jesus's sisters and brothers by blood during the past 19 centuries. Church history is filled with horrendous attitudes and actions toward the Jewish people. As members of the community called "the church" we need desperately to follow the biblical pattern of truth, tears, turning, and trusting. Using the terms more commonly used in English translations of the Bible, we all need to confess, lament, repent, and trust (have faith that God will respond).

In my 50 years of experience as a pastor, I have found that whatever label we wear, very few of us who are called "Christian" can rightly claim to be free of anti-Semitism or anti-Judaism. It is built into our systems and our privileges, just as the ideology of White supremacy and White privilege is built into the systems of the White American church. David Gushee credits theologian J. Kameron Carter for connecting early anti-Semitism and later racism in his thinking,[6] and I credit my father for doing the same in my thinking. Independently of either of these sources, David Swanson also connects the American White Church's systemic prejudice against nonwhite ethnicities to the church's failure to emphasize the particularity of Jesus as Jewish.[7]

CHURCH HISTORY TOWARD THE JEWS IS MOSTLY ATROCIOUS.

Very Early in Church History, Jesus's Jewishness Became an Inconvenient Truth.

Two changes that moved away from the New Testament's descriptions of Jesus began to occur very early in church history. One move was a change of emphasis away from the New Testament's stress on the faithful relationship between the human Jesus and the God he worshiped, served, loved, and revealed. This change involved a growing (until almost exclusive) emphasis on "Jesus is God." True, a nod was always made toward Jesus as "made man." But neither the Creeds, nor everyday practice, put any emphasis there. The emphasis and the arguments were about divinity.

The other major change was away from the very faithful, observant Jewish Jesus of the Gospels toward presenting Jesus as a more universal and somewhat abstract human. There were probably other reasons this occurred, but here are some of the most salient.

1. Many of the early church leaders were schooled in Greek Platonic philosophy, which glamorized the *ideal* and downplayed the importance of the material, historical, and earthy. For this reason, a more abstract and universal Jesus was preferable to an earthy and uniquely individual Jesus.

2. Even though, and perhaps partly because, Jews had been given some unique exemptions from the laws of the Roman Empire, anti-Semitism—ethnic

---

6. Gushee, "White American Christianity," 3.
7. Swanson, *Rediscipling White Church*, 140–142.

prejudice—was widespread in the Empire. Although the writings he refers to as examples have not yet been found, Josephus responds to several different anti-Semitic authors of his era in "Against Apion."[8]

3. A disdain for Jewish worship and cleanliness customs fueled an anti-Judaism—religious prejudice—throughout the Empire as well. Pompey voiced his disdain of the Jewish Temple and Jewish God when he entered the Holy of Holies and found it empty. The famous Roman orator Cicero proclaimed that the Jewish people did not really fit in the Empire and seems to view them as almost traitors to Rome because of their worship and cultural practices.[9] Seneca, the playwright Martial, the satirist Juvenal, and the Roman historian Tacitus all degraded Jewish customs, worship, and people.[10]

4. The earthiness, ethnicity, and specific historical claims of the Old Testament bothered most of these early theologians. They much preferred seeing the Old Testament as an instructive metaphor for living—usually a big stretch in terms of interpretation—or as somehow really about the coming divine Jesus.

Given all these contextual realities, it is not difficult to see why many of the church fathers found Jesus's historical Jewishness to be at best irrelevant, and more often a very inconvenient truth. It would have taken a major transformational work of the Spirit of Jesus to change their hearts and minds. Sadly, in this area of their thought and actions it did not occur.

Examples of anti-Semitism and anti-Judaism permeating the teachings of the church fathers are easy to find. Examples to the contrary are very difficult to find. Although he was later repudiated by some Church leaders for other reasons, Tertullian, who was very influential in the second and third century as a theologian, was virulently anti-Semitic and a lethal misogynist. Neither of those hate-filled teachings was why he was later repudiated.

By the late fourth and early fifth century, Chrysostom, who was *sainted* by the church, and who is still heralded in many Christian history books as one of the greatest Christian preachers of all time, was fueling anti-Semitism. He preached eight sermons that, among other even more horrendously anti-Semitic statements, damns "the Jews" as well as any Christian who would celebrate the Passover Seder with Jewish people. The flagrant irony, given that Jesus's "last supper" was a Jewish Passover celebrated with fellow Jews, should be obvious. Sadly, these sermons have stoked the fires of anti-Semitism and anti-Judaism for centuries.

Slightly later in the early fifth century, Augustine—deemed the patron saint of theologians by many—also taught a deeply anti-Semitic and anti-Judaism way of understanding what it meant to be Jewish. He described the Jews as those with the "mark

8. Josephus, "Against Apion," 151–238.
9. Grant, *Jews in Roman World*, 55–56, 62.
10. Schama, *Story of Jews*, 156–157.

of Cain," who continued to exist as unwilling witnesses to God's judgment on their rejection of Jesus. Apparently, Augustine's approach was meant to stop Christians in the fifth century from killing Jews in retaliation for Jesus's execution in the first century. Augustine labeled Jews as the ongoing witnesses to God's permanent rejection of Judaism. This new label meant that murdering Jews was no longer appropriate Christian action. God needed Jews as foils. What a sad example of the old adage "With friends like this, who needs enemies!"

Whatever the reasons for each individual church father, the overall tenor of their developing theology was anti-Semitic and anti-Judaism. It was quite inconvenient for them to dwell on Jesus as Jewish—so they did not.

Their influence continued to fuel the fires of anti-Semitism and anti-Judaism. The following are just a few of the many possible examples from church history of this virulent plague continuing to emanate from a church that supposedly honors "Jesus the King of the Jews."

1. In 1096 AD, the Pope (Urban II) inaugurated a (first) Crusade to free the Holy Land from the Infidels. The Crusaders were sent to fight the Muslims for control of the Holy Land, but they decided it was "better" (easier?) to stop off in Germany and rob and kill as many Jews as possible in "the name of the cross of Christ." When they arrived in Jerusalem, they decided again that it was better to first burn the synagogues and kill the Jews—"in the name of the cross of Christ."

2. European Christian rulers periodically expelled Jews from their empires, accusing them falsely and allowing them to be robbed of their possessions. This was especially likely to occur when a ruler had borrowed money from Jewish people and did not want to pay it back.

3. Although the Inquisition was instituted to ferret out Christian heretics, it moved toward a focus on finding out who was Jewish at heart while pretending to be Christian as a survival strategy. Finally, in 1483, Spanish Queen Isabella's personal confessor, the Dominican priest Tomas de Torquemada (with some Jewish ancestry), was appointed head of the Inquisition. Torquemada was considered an incorruptible monk; he was also a fanatic hater of Jewish people. At this point, the Spanish Inquisition morphed toward a greater focus on expelling or torturing Jews—all in the name of the cross. Perhaps Jesus had a different definition of "incorruptible" than the church did?

4. Horrible false stories about Jewish habits and beliefs were circulated throughout the European churches and beyond. They were often carried by missionaries to every continent on earth, where they continue to be repeated at this moment.

5. Lest those of us who are Protestant start to excuse ourselves, please remember that one of the great heroes of Protestantism made it worse, not better for the Jewish people. After failing in his attempt to convert the German Jews to Christianity,

Martin Luther encouraged the Duke of Saxony to expel the Jews from Saxony, Later he wrote his horrible pamphlet—"On the Jews and their lies"—in which he encouraged almost every mistreatment of Jews that he could think of. He even states that murdering a Jewish person should not be considered a sin or fault. It is not an accident that this pamphlet was widely distributed in Nazi Germany.

6. In AD 1747, Hungarian Empress Maria Theresa instituted the "toleration tax," which taxed the Jews for the "privilege" of remaining in the country as unwanted immigrants—regardless of how long they and their ancestors had lived there. This seems to have been a harsher version of the earlier Islamic tax on Christians and Jews.

7. The Nazi Holocaust of the mid-twentieth century was publicly initiated with Kristallnacht (night of broken glass), which included reprinting and widely distributing Luther's pamphlet. We are currently learning through the identification of more and more previously unidentified mass graves throughout Europe that probably far more than 6,000,000 Jewish people were annihilated during this time. Yes, there were a few Christian heroes; however, more than 90% of Christians in Europe and worldwide either supported, accommodated, pretended not to know about, or ignored the attempt to annihilate the Jewish people from the face of the earth.

Interpreting and Applying the New Testament Critiques Rightly Is Important.

In what follows, I am not denying that the Jewish Jesus and some very important Jewish leaders of his time ended up in intense conflict with one another. There is nothing strange about that. Think of all of the conflicts between Christians during the past two millennia.

Jesus spoke very unwelcome truth to power. Of course, it caused conflict with other Jews. The power roles and the income derived from them in Temple or Synagogue—Jesus's church—were all filled by Jewish people. Rome had installed a Governor over Judea in Jesus's time, and the Jewish High Priestly clan worked closely with him to preserve *peace* as well as their huge income. In addition, the Herodian family, who were converts to Judaism and ruled at the pleasure of Roman Caesars, found Jesus a threat from his birth until his death. In short, almost every main character in Jesus's daily life, and every main character in Jesus's church-life and national-life were Jewish people. So, yes, the New Testament writers do claim that some Jewish leaders were deeply involved in the intrigue that led to rejection and ultimately to torture and death as an expression of Roman justice.

They also claim that thousands of Jewish people "believed" in Jesus and followed him at different times in his ministry, especially in the Galilean part of the country. They claim that some members of the Sanhedrin and some Pharisees became followers of Jesus. And they make it clear that for several decades almost every key leader of the expanding communities of Jesus followers were Jewish.

Denying that some Jewish people hated or feared Jesus would be as silly as denying that almost all of the followers and friends of Jesus were Jewish. I am denying that the right way to hear and apply the critiques Jesus and New Testament writers made of some Jewish people in the first century would be to apply them to "the Jews" today. Neither is it right to apply them to most Jews in New Testament times. Sadly, this is still being done daily in churches, mission stations, and even in many seminaries. I am confident that neither Jesus, nor the writers of the New Testament, would be making such a tragic exegetical and theological error if they were teaching and writing among us today.

The only correct way for a Christian today to apply any criticism of "some" Jewish leaders or of "some" Jewish people written in the New Testament is to apply the criticism to those of us who at present claim to be Christians. When we do that, we always quickly add "some," and we wish our critics would do the same. Our failure to understand that this is the only godly way to apply statements in the New Testament has led to sin upon sin in church history.

I see no reason to think that the Temple and Synagogue leaders of Jesus's day were any better, or any worse, than the Church leaders of Christian history or Christian leaders today. Did some Synagogue and Temple leaders of Jesus's day steal the resources of widows as Jesus claimed? We know for certain that some of today's Christian televangelists have done so, as have a number of pastors!

I imagine that some of the leaders in the time of Jesus were no better than the high priest during Jeremiah's time. Jeremiah blasted that high priest without being anti-Semitic. What I am positive of is that the Jewish leaders in Jeremiah's, and in Jesus's, time who were corrupted by political power were no worse than those popes, cardinals, Protestant theologians, and Protestant pastors who have been blatantly corrupted by the lure of political power, prestige, sexual abuse, and wealth through the centuries—not to mention the current sexual abuses and disastrous political messages of many American church leaders. Did some Pharisees use, abuse, and discard their wives as Jesus seems to accuse them of? What I know for sure from both pastoral counseling and court records is that many preachers and priests have abused and discarded women, boys, and girls, while using God's name and clergy prestige as cover for their lies.

Pastors, writers, and teachers need to again and again make it clear that the only proper way for a Christian today to read the criticisms in the New Testament of "the scribes and Pharisees" and "the High Priests" and "the Synagogue" and "the Jews" is to see that they speak to us Christians, not to modern Judaism. Written today, these texts would read "seminary professors," "Christian theologians," "pastors," "parish priests," "popes," "preachers," "denominational leaders," "the church," "Christians,"—and without question would be especially focused on the arrogance of some very serious and very observant Christians.

If we consistently took this step, we would undoubtedly understand it means "some" when we read the New Testament, just as we do when we speak about the current realities in the leadership of churches. When I say, "Priests and pastors have abused many boys and girls," you know I mean, "*Some* priests and *some* pastors have abused many boys and girls." I do not mean "all" or even "most" priests or pastors, I mean "some." The same is true when the New Testament writers spoke negatively of Pharisees, priests, and Jews, as the rest of their writings, the makeup of their communities of faith, and their own ethnicity make clear.

A Caveat Is Necessary.

Jesus was and is deeply embedded in his Jewishness; Jesus was and is deeply embedded in his humanness. Church history is replete with our ungodly treatment of his fellow Jewish humans. However, before continuing, it seems important to say that I am certain Jesus has been, and is, weeping about many other realities in church history in addition to our anti-Judaism and anti-Semitism.

Our misapplication of scriptures, and our insistence that our misapplications represent God and Jesus, has been and is heartbreaking, atrocious, and completely inexcusable. The church structures have repressed women, defended and supported racism, defended ruthless rulers of both empire and church, supported brutal slavery and ruthless imprisonments, excused genocides including that of Native Americans, debased the humanity of the LGBTQ community, supported ruthless treatment of immigrants who are the "sojourners" and "aliens" of the Bible, and inflamed prejudices against Muslims. Many of our structures still support these sins, and this list of our sins is greatly abbreviated!

And, no, we who follow Jesus cannot begin by saying "Those were not 'real' Christians," or, "That was them, not us." Perhaps many were not genuine followers of Jesus, but we must begin by praying as Jesus taught us to pray: "*Our Father* in Heaven, . . *Forgive us our sins* as we forgive those who sin against us." Only after truth, tears and turning can we begin a more trustworthy journey of following Jesus.

Jesus's Jewishness Still Seems to Be an Inconvenient Truth for Many Christians Today.

The widely used Bible I appreciate and have relied upon for years has editorial section headings to help the reader. In the Gospel of John these *helpful* headings include "Unbelief of the Jewish Leaders" and "The Unbelief of the Jews."

However, even though John specifically notes several times that *many of the "Jews" put their faith in Jesus* (John 2:23, 7:31, 8:30, 10:42, 11:45, 12;11, 12:42), there are *no helpful* editorial captions on these paragraphs noting "the believing Jews." Neither are there any helpful captions noting that everyone in the Gospel of John who follows Jesus (depending on how you identify the Samaritans of John 4) were by ethnicity and by faith "Jewish" as we use the term today. Why? And to my shame, why did it take me 30 years of using my Bible to even notice this glaring inconsistency in the *helps* despite my concern about Christian anti-Semitism?

Obviously, as I hold my Bible with its helpful headings in my hands, I must confess that this is not an issue of the past. Neither is it an issue confined to conservative Christian practices. As the Jewish New Testament scholar Amy-Jill Levine points out, Christians who are more conservative and Christians who are more liberal both tend to spread anti-Judaism and anti-Semitism all over the world. They just do so to support different agendas.[11]

Many conservatives promote anti-Judaism and anti-Semitism as a way of claiming that God chose Christians instead of Jews because we are "better," "right," and "chosen instead of the Jews." It is impossible to square those attitudes with the Jesus described in the New Testament.

Many more liberal Christians love to present Jesus as the heroic champion who rebelled against the legalistic, rule-oriented tendencies of the Jewish religion, while ignoring the many ways Jesus worshiped and served "within the system." Jesus also often taught what other Jewish rabbis taught. Yes, Jesus took issue with the church leaders of his day who were using doctrine, theology, and practice to oppress the poor, the disabled, the diseased, and women. We should be doing the same today. But Jesus also honored, practiced, and reapplied the guidelines that came to him through God's history with the Jewish people. We should be doing the same.

The Jesus of the New Testament also lived a life guided by Torah righteousness. He worshiped in synagogue and temple. He observed the Sabbath. He quoted from and alluded to the Old Testament constantly. He wore the fringes on his garments commanded by Torah as a way of remembering God's presence and promises (Luke 8:44—almost certainly the meaning of the word often translated "hem" or "edge"). Jesus definitely confronted the institutional powerbrokers and their oppression of their fellow Jews, but he did so as a faithful, practicing Jew.

In short, many of us who identify as Christians are reenforcing for yet another generation the horrors of Christian history toward Jewish people all over the world. Tragically, we are at the same time once again diminishing the importance of Jesus's Jewishness and Jesus's humanity.

We will never change if we do not truthfully confess and lament this history. I am convinced that part of confessing, lamenting, and turning from this horrid history is realizing clearly that we who follow Jesus owe the Jewish people so much! Turning

---

11. Levine, *Misunderstood Jew*, 157–190.

from is always turning toward. We should turn toward thanking God for the Jewish people, past and present.

We Who Follow Jesus Owe the Jewish People for Jesus and for Much More.

There are many important aspects of our faith for which we who follow Jesus owe the Jewish people. The following is a list of the topics that I discuss at length in my book *Truth, Tears, Turning, and Trusting*.

1. We owe the Jews for the revealed experiences that show God is "One," as well as complex, deeply involved, good, caring, communicating, responsive, and relational.

2. We owe the Jewish people for teaching us to experience history as purposeful and as ultimately climaxing where God intended it would from the beginning.

3. We owe the Jews for the content of all the roles assigned to Jesus. Each of these roles was filled with content in the Old Testament narratives.

4. We owe the Jews for our Bible. Both the Old Testament and the New Testament were written primarily by Jewish authors. The Hebrew Bible was also preserved for us by Jewish people down through the ages, often at great risk and cost to themselves.

5. We owe the Jews for the language through which God speaks to us today in the New Testament records concerning Jesus. It is the Old Testament that gives us the unique historical background content of "sacrifice," "redemption," "forgiveness," "righteousness," "sin," "salvation," "the wilderness," "the promised land," and "liberation." I am *not* saying somewhat comparable concepts never appeared anywhere else; I *am* saying that it was from the Old Testament that the unique content in Jesus's life, and in the community he founded, comes.

6. We owe the Jews for the patterns that are "fulfilled" (filled-full) in Jesus's life and ministry. Jesus did not replace the patterns through which God had related to the Jewish people for centuries; rather, he filled them full of new and deeper meaning. This fulfillment is built upon, not a replacement for, all that God had prepared prior to Jesus. Neither Jesus, nor the church, was meant to replace Jewish experience with God. It was instead God's next step in revealing the depths these experiences with God could have.

7. We owe the Jewish people for modeling centuries of faithfulness. As the writer of Hebrews 11 makes clear, we owe the Jewish people and their records in the Old Testament for our understanding of what it means to trust God. That model continued in the New Testament, where we again see Jewish people taking courageous risks because of their faith in God—remember almost every early follower of Jesus was Jewish. Jewish modelling of risky and courageous faithfulness did

not end with the New Testament either. There have been faithful Jewish people, who have often put Christians to shame, throughout the centuries since Jesus—some of those Jewish people have been heroes and martyrs, others have been wise and steady everyday people who trust God with their lives. If you want to be touched by the faithfulness and wisdom of one of those everyday Jewish people, read Naomi Rachel Remen's celebration of her grandfather's wisdom and faith.[12]

8. We owe the Jews for Jesus. Because Jesus's Jewishness has become such an inconvenient truth, I want to elaborate a bit more on this last point. We owe the Jewish people for giving us Jesus—genetically, historically, and in every other way. The Jesus described in the New Testament is completely unintelligible apart from his Jewish roots. When we who are Christians do not recognize that truth, it is because we have become so accustomed to crediting ourselves with what were Jewish values, patterns, history, and teachings that we ignore the fact that they were uniquely Jewish in Jesus's time. We even tend to think of the obviously Jewish Jesus as the Christian Jesus, even though such an identification makes no sense in the New Testament context. In fact, it is more accurate to maintain that two forms of Judaism survived the final Roman conquest of Israel—Rabbinic Judaism and the Followers of Jesus.

The New Testament Presents Jesus's Jewishness as an Essential Part of the Good News.

According to New Testament writers, the Messiah and Savior from God could not have been born in any other than the Jewish culture because he incarnates God's promises made to people including Abraham, Sarah, Moses, David, and Isaiah (2 Cor 1:19–20). The writer of Hebrews believed that the Messiah had to be Jewish, or God would have been a liar (Heb 6:13–20). Paul makes pretty much the same point (Rom 9–11).

Jesus is described in the Gospels as Jewish through and through. He is introduced as "son of David," who will fulfill the promises God made to David (Luke 1:27, 32–33). As noted earlier, he worshiped in synagogues, kept Sabbath, kept Passover, and traveled to Temple during the high holy days. He knew, loved, and lived the Hebrew Bible. He was executed as "King of the Jews" by Pilate, who hung this reason for execution over his head. In the New Testament, Jesus's appearances after the resurrection were all observed only by Jewish people. In short, Jesus was a very Jewish person, born into a long history that formed and informed his teachings, his actions, and his relationship with God.

Jesus's faith, teachings, and actions flowed directly out of his trust that the God who was revealed in the experiences recorded in the Old Testament narratives was the God he was experiencing as *Abba*. Jesus never rejected the earlier experiences of

12. Remen, *Grandfather's Blessings*.

God as they were recorded in the Old Testament. He always claimed to be revealing more of who that God is, *not a different God.* Jesus responded to those Scriptural texts as God-given guides for his life and growth as a faithful human, and the writers of the New Testament encouraged their readers to do the same.

Yes, there is a new way of telling the Old Testament story in the light of what God is revealing about God's-self through God's relationship with Jesus. This new way of telling the story does not replace either the Hebrew Bible or the revelations of the God recorded there; it fulfills them. The retelling is truthful and genuine only if it is based fully in the first telling of the story God had been writing for millennia prior to Jesus. That is certainly how the New Testament presents Jesus as living into the ancient narrative.

My wife and I shared an experience that helped illustrate for us these two ways to tell the same story. My wife endured 18 months of increasing pain in her leg, hip, knee, and back. Professionals took two MRIs and several x-rays. A Harvard-educated surgeon told her she did not need a hip replacement, while insulting her by suggesting she was exaggerating her pain in order to have surgery—he certainly did not know Donna! A doctor skilled at injecting cortisone into "just the right spot" tried to help, and nothing positive occurred. Our concerned Parkinson's doctor picked up the phone and asked, as a special favor to him, a highly skilled physical rehab doctor to examine Donna immediately (the expected wait was 6 months).

That kind and skilled rehab doctor spent far more time and effort than we expected, attempting to ascertain the cause of all the pain. Finally, and with an honest sadness, he said, "Mrs. Simkins, I just don't know what is causing all your pain." An amazingly skilled deep massage therapist relieved the pain for a short time on several occasions, but the relief didn't last beyond a few hours. Many friends, some in medical fields, made other suggestions, but eventually, everyone shrugged their shoulders and said, "It is a mystery; I cannot figure it out." Of all the people involved, only the initial surgeon was wrong; the rest were just working with an incomplete picture. I have told our story in one true and accurate way.

There is another way to tell the same story that began when, after more than a year of increasing pain, our family physician told my wife, "I think you should get a second opinion from a different surgeon." This new surgeon looked over all the past notes, had my wife turn in a different direction while keeping her weight fully on the painful leg, and took a new x-ray. A few minutes later, he walked into the room, flashed the picture up on the screen, and said, "Mystery revealed. The bone that is pressing down on your hip socket has no more left of it than the tip of a ballpoint pen. No wonder you hurt! But I can fix it! A hip replacement is the only thing that will help. None of the things you have been doing could have ever been enough. It isn't that these people were wrong, but they didn't have the whole picture." And, thank God, he did fix it. A few months later she was walking the trails in the Rocky Mountains with me.

We now had a second story to tell, but it was completely embedded in the first story. The *before* story is a story of historical process involving one event after another, all moving us forward and providing important information, but none of which shone a clear light on the bigger picture. Often, the story seemed to be going nowhere fast, and at other times it was very confusing. Trying to make sense of what had been revealed seemed much like people attempting to figure out the prophecies of old concerning God's coming salvation. Things had been revealed in bits and pieces, but no one could fit them into a clear big picture because a key part was yet to be revealed.

Our second story is the story of *after* that "aha" moment, when something no one could figure out was suddenly revealed from an entirely different perspective. Suddenly the unclear was clarified. The key had been uncovered. Nevertheless, his moment of revelation was an amazing moment for us, as we experienced the uncovering of what was previously a mystery, but which now suddenly became a "now you can see it" moment of revelation. But it is important to remember that the new way of telling the story is completely embedded in the first story and flows directly from the way we experienced the first story. Without the first way of telling the story, the second way of telling the story loses so much of its power!

At least for us, this experience helps a bit in understanding the *aha* moments the followers of Jesus experienced when the risen Jesus first appeared to them. These were followed by other "aha" moments over the next decade. Perhaps none were more surprising than the day Peter and his friends experienced the Spirit of God being poured out right in front of their eyes on a Gentile Roman officer of the occupying military forces (Acts 10–11). However, the New Testament's way of telling the second story, makes sense and maintains its fullness only if the first story is allowed to be told as it was experienced prior to the second story being revealed. The events of Jesus's life were fully embedded in the covenant with Abraham and Sarah that was to bless all nations for all time, but who could have guessed what was coming? No one! Nevertheless, the story makes sense only as embedded in the original story.

As we have explored, and will further explore, every claim concerning Jesus's roles and titles derives its primary content from his Jewish context. Jesus as Prophet, High Priest, King, Messiah, Savior, Suffering Servant, and Lord are fully informed by Jesus as Jewish. Many of these roles and titles existed in other cultures, but it was Jewish history with God that gave them the content that Jesus fills with new and renewed meaning. Those stories of experiences with God are meaningful on their own and should be told that way. They were also first told in a manner that often made it clear that a new story was needed that would reveal how all the pieces fit together.

For example, Jesus's role as prophet brings something new, but ignoring the meaning of the role of Jesus as grounded in the long history of Jewish prophets has reenforced some of the horrible anti-Semitism and anti-Judaism of church history. Jesus did criticize some of the Jewish Temple leaders, some of the Pharisees who were popular teachers, and some of the attitudes of some of the everyday Jewish people. He did this just as Isaiah did, just as Ezekiel, Hosea, and Jeremiah did. In fact, he often did so by using their words. The role of the Jewish prophet was to call the Jewish people back to the relationship with God and with their fellow humans that God intended for them. There was nothing anti-Semitic or anti-Judaism in the Jewish prophetic history that severely critiqued what some Jewish people had done, or had not done.

Failure to see Jesus as in the line of these Jewish Prophets has led to loading his words with anti-Semitic and anti-Judaism content. Why does it never occur to us to make that claim about the words of the Prophets of old? Because we have come to think that Jesus was speaking from outside as a Christian, whereas we know the Prophets before him spoke as Jews to fellow Jews. What keeps us from seeing the New Testament critiques of those who rejected Jesus were of specific types of leaders, just as critiques of Jewish leaders in the book of Tobit were of specific types of leaders?

Why are the fiery critiques in the *War Scroll*, one of the Dead Sea Scrolls, that describe fellow Jews as "the sons of darkness" and as "the army of Belial (demon-god)" soon to be destroyed by God never seen as anti-Semitic or anti-Judaism? Why are the tamer words of Jesus and his disciples in the New Testament considered to be anti-Semitic and anti-Judaism? We never think of the Dead Sea Scrolls as anti-Jewish because we know they are in-family critiques, not "us" versus "them" critiques. Despite this being just as true of the New Testament, we Christians have spent over 1,800 years training ourselves to read the primarily Jewish literature of the New Testament as though it was not Jewish.

If we understood Jesus's role as Jewish prophet, we would understand that his critiques, and those made by his Jewish followers, were in-the-family critiques modeled on the role filled earlier by Hosea, Isaiah, Jeremiah, Ezekiel, and John the Baptizer. They are no more anti-Jewish than the searing critiques of many of us Christians by Christian writers like Bonhoeffer, Dostoevsky, Kierkegaard, and Martin Luther King Jr. are anti-Christian.

Pope Francis regularly and vehemently criticizes Christians. Is Pope Francis anti-Christian? Of course not: he is pleading with fellow Christians. Not long before I finished this book, a friend introduced me to two critiques by David Gushee. In one, he evaluates American Christianity as heretical about race from its beginnings.[13] His other critique is an assessment of American Evangelicalism as increasingly sold out to American cultural domination.[14] Is David Gushee anti-Christian or anti-American? Of course not: he is pleading with us, his fellow Christians, who are also American citizens, to turn away from our heresy before it is too late.

---

13. Gushee, "White American Christianity."
14. Gushee, *After Evangelicalism*.

WE ARE UNLIKELY TO FULLY EMBRACE THE CLAIM THAT JESUS IS GOD'S FIRST COMPLETED HUMAN UNTIL WE EMBRACE JESUS'S JEWISH HUMANITY.

There is so much to look at in the New Testament that relates to Jesus's Jewishness and the Jewishness of the New Testament writings. I attempted to look primarily at those issues in *Truth, Tears, Turning and Trusting*, but there is so much more that we need to face squarely. For our purposes here, let's not forget that the authors of the New Testament (excepting Luke) were Jewish, continued to be Jewish, and were proud of it. They expected Jews and Judaism to go on until after the "times of the Gentiles is fulfilled," and the promises to Jewish people would be brought to completion as "the kingdom of God draws near" (Luke 21:24–31).

They never saw God as rejecting the Jews or as choosing "Christians" in place of God's covenant with Jews—"I ask then: *Did God reject* his people? *By no means*! I *am* [not "was"] an Israelite myself, a descendant of Abraham, from the tribe of Benjamin" (Rom 11:1, *emphasis mine*). The New Testament never identifies Jesus as "the first Christian," but it often identifies him as thoroughly Jewish. The writers do maintain that God's relationship with Jesus created a "before and after" in God's movement toward God's goal for human history. They do not see this new step of "fulfillment" as "replacement" or "abandonment" of the Jewish people.

This new covenant made some things "obsolete," but only because these patterns were now being fulfilled with something deeper, not because they were being rejected, and certainly not because the Jewish people were being rejected. In fact, the Pharisees of Jesus's time and shortly after also believed that God was moving in ways that made it possible to be thoroughly Jewish without a Temple, without animal sacrifices, without an active Levitical priesthood, and without being centered in the Land of Israel. This certainly did not mean that they were rejecting Judaism.

I emphasize again, when the writers were critiquing other Jewish people who rejected Jesus, they were engaging in an intrafamily argument. They were not presenting themselves as a new religion. In doing this type of arguing, they were no more anti-Semitic than were Hosea, Jeremiah, Ezekiel, and Isaiah, when they made the same kinds of critiques—often using the very same words.

There is so much more to say, but for now, my point is this: we are not likely to reclaim the New Testament paradigm that presents Jesus as the next step in fulfillment of God's goal for humanity, and of God's goal for Jewish humanity within that larger goal for all humanity, so long as we continue to de-emphasize Jesus's Jewishness and Jesus's continuing humanity. And sadly, we are unlikely to end our "us and them" sins against the Jews until we take this step back into the New Testament master story on a much broader scale.

I conclude with this question to my fellow Jesus followers: how many Jewish people do you know personally or Jewish authors do you read? It should probably be more. Having said that, I also challenge you to be clear in your own mind and with your fellow Christians about the following reality. If you are a follower of Jesus, you should be hanging out with at least one Jewish person every day—Jesus, a Jewish human, whom Peter continued to identify as "this same Jesus of Nazareth," after his exaltation by God (Acts 2:22, 32, 36). Please don't forget this when you speak of Jewish people or when you interact with Jewish people. I feel sure that Jesus of Nazareth, God's first completed human, does not forget where he came from.

16

Jesus's Other Roles

Do Jesus's Other Roles Embed Jesus in Our Humanity?

A few chapters in this book are somewhat controversial. For some readers this chapter might be the most so. Though acknowledging there are some legitimate questions, I think overall, the New Testament writers see every role and relationship ascribed to Jesus as fully rooted in our humanity. That is a reality I find very exciting and very challenging.

In addition to the roles of Messiah, Son of God, Savior, and Spirit-Filled that describe Jesus's relationship with humans and with God, there are numerous other roles, descriptions, and relationships attributed to Jesus in the New Testament.[1] I think these, too, fully root Jesus in our humanity. The references noted in the following sections can easily be expanded with other New Testament passages, but the results are the same. New Testament writers again and again link Jesus with us humans. They do not see his roles and functions as separating him from humanity.

The roles and relationships ascribed to Jesus reflect patterns through which God worked in human history prior to Jesus, and these patterns continue to be how God works in the human followers of Jesus—when we allow God to do so. The discontinuity is in the overwhelming and astounding way each is filled full of new depth in the relationship between God and Jesus.

SOME ROLES RELATING JESUS FULLY TO OUR HUMANITY.

It does not take long in pursuing modern scholarship or the doctrines of various churches to realize that very few things are noncontroversial. For each opinion

---

1. In addition to this chapter, *see* chapters 6 and 8–11 for other roles Jesus filled.

someone champions, there seems to always be someone with a divergent opinion. Nevertheless, relating Jesus's roles and functions as Prophet, King, Priestly mediator, last Adam, and Keeper of God's commandments to his humanity is not overly controversial. Seeing his role and function as Miracle-worker and Judge as fully human might be a bit more controversial.

The Prophetic Role Is Rooted in Human Experience with God.

Jesus was brought into the world by a mother with a prophetic voice (Luke 1:46–55). His uncle and aunt both spoke with prophetic power (Luke 1:42–45, 1:67–79). He was welcomed as a baby at God's Temple by the prophets Simeon and Anna (Luke 2:25–38). Sometime before Jesus reached two years of age, Magi from a non-Jewish culture arrived with an amazing prophetic insight, having discerned that the God of the heavens was at work in the birth of a Jewish baby boy (Matt 2:1–12). All the Gospels agree that Jesus's ministry was prepared for by the powerful prophetic ministry of John the Baptizer.

Jesus's first sermon in the book of Luke involved a self-identification with an anointed prophetic ministry described by the prophet Isaiah. Jesus claimed that the description was being "fulfilled" as he spoke (Luke 4:18–21). Throughout his ministry, Jesus was identified by many as a prophet (Matt 21:11, 46). Even in their deep disappointment at his death, his disciples saw him as a prophet "in the sight of God" (Luke 24:19). Jesus also identified himself as a prophet in a long line of human prophets (Matt 23:34–35; Luke 13:33). After Jesus was raised from death by God and exalted to the "right hand of God," those witnessing to his relationship with God continued to identify him as embedded in the line of God's great Jewish prophets of old (Acts 3:22, 7:37).

Passages such as Matthew's "Sermon on the Mount" also indicate that Jesus saw himself as the fulfillment of Moses's prophetic promise—"The LORD your God will raise up for you a prophet like me from among your own brothers. You must listen to him" (Deut 18:15). "You have heard that it was said . . . but I tell you . . ." is the strong voice of a prophet of God interpreting Scriptures and announcing God's intentions (six times in Matt 5:21–48). Most of Jesus's prophetic teaching, like that of the other prophets, was prescriptive and interpretive rather than predictive of the future.

However, like Jewish prophets of old, sometimes Jesus did make predictions and fulfill predictions that flowed from his relationship with God. He showed foreknowledge of coming events in predictions about his betrayal, his execution, the future persecution of his followers, and the coming fall of Jerusalem, including the dismantling of the Temple. When he made longer-range predictions, like those in the Old Testament, they tended to be somewhat vague. There is a little specificity but quite a bit of vagueness in the prediction that there would be an "end of the time of the Gentiles" (Luke 21:24). The same combination of certainty and vagueness occurs when he states unequivocally that God will bring a time of justice for those who are oppressed by injustice, but he follows that with the question "When the Son of Man comes, will he find faith [or, faithfulness] on the earth" (Luke 18:8)?

This prophetic combination of ready-to-occur specifics and long range-vagueness about distant outcomes had been a part of his birth as well. Think about the specific details of the ready-to-occur announcement that Mary would bear a child without a male involved in the conception, and the specificity of the information that her cousin Elizabeth was already unexpectedly pregnant. Then contrast the rest of the prophetic announcement that this baby would sit on the throne of David and rule over a kingdom forever (Luke 1:26–38). Mary was almost guaranteed to misunderstand the long-range part of this prophecy. She could not help but think it meant the Romans were about to be thrown out by a movement led by her son. Only the cross–resurrection event could have reoriented this thinking. And we are still trying to figure out what the final fulfillment of the prophecy will finally look like!

All of this indicates that Jesus's role as a prophet and as the fulfillment of prophecy was fully embedded in his humanity. He is the prophet Moses promised would come someday—a someday that turned out to be much farther away than Moses could ever have imagined.

As with other roles, Jesus's fulfillment of the prophetic role did not mean the prophetic role ended with Jesus. Various writers see it as extended to many of Jesus's followers—both male and female (Matt 10:40–42; Acts 2:17–18, 11:27–28, 21:8–9; 1 Cor 14:5–6; 1 Thess 5:19–21; 2 Pet 3:15–16; Rev 1:3, 11:3). We have also seen that Spirit-empowered role exercised in our time. Martin Luther King Jr., Billy Graham, and Jim Wallis have all exercised roles with prophetic dimensions. This does not mean they were exempt from personal and theological weaknesses; it means God challenged large numbers of people through each of them.

I have seen, as I am sure you have, many portraying themselves as prophetic voices who were charlatans and others who were terribly misguided. But I have also occasionally seen God-led prophetic words change lives in everyday congregational life through counseling, songwriting, sermons, choice of readings, comfort, and compassion. The role of speaking and acting as agents, speaking God's word into specific situations, is a role that embeds Jesus in our humanity.

King, Throne, Ruler, Power, and Authority Are Human Roles Ordained by God.

Because I have seen a lot of abuse, I sometimes need to remind myself that power and authority are not bad words. Humans were created to have power and to exert authority in the creation. Having said that, both the Bible and all other human history are filled with examples of the brokenness with which we humans often exert our power. The only example in human history of someone who consistently in every situation saw power and authority as needing to be paired with vulnerability and servanthood is Jesus. Some humans have been faithful some of the time with power and authority; a few have been faithful much of the time. Jesus was without exception faithful in using his power and authority to bless others, often simultaneously making himself vulnerable to being hurt, misunderstood, and demeaned.

The pairing of authority and vulnerability came to an amazing crescendo in two events recorded in Jesus's last night before the cross. He did a show-and-tell expression of Lordship. He took the role of the lowest and most vulnerable servant by washing his disciples' feet. Then he powerfully ordered Peter to allow his feet to be washed—or else. He followed this by using his role as "Lord" to order his disciples to model his actions as servant (John 13:4–17). A few hours later, he gave Peter another specific order—put the sword away! In the midst of this crisis, he took a moment to explain to Peter that if he, Jesus, wished to exert power instead of vulnerability at this moment, he would ask God for the help of legions of angels, not Peter's puny sword (Matt 26:52–54).

Although Americans have no experience of being ruled over by a king or queen since 1776, many humans have had that experience throughout world history. Living under kingship was the experience of most of the writers of both the Old Testament and the New Testament. On the one hand, the books of 1 and 2 Kings are an extended rehearsal of the tragic results of kings grasping for, then abusing, then losing power. On the other hand, one of the most often referred to covenant promises of God involved human kingship—the covenant promise to David that a son of David would sit on God's throne forever, beginning with Solomon (2 Sam 7).

Mary was challenged to accept the role of mothering a future king. Her son would be the coming "son of David," whose "kingdom will never end" (Luke 1:33; Isa 9:7). Herod's response to the Magi was a clear understanding that the coming king was a human and therefore a threat to the Herodian dynasty (Matt 2:1–12). Jesus was executed with the accusation of treason: "This is Jesus: The King of the Jews" (Matt 27:37). The New Testament canon ends with an exiled prisoner making the treasonous claim that God has designated Jesus, not the Roman Caesars, to rule the kingdoms of the world as "King of kings and Lord of lords" (Rev 19:16, *see* also 11:15).

From beginning to end, the New Testament canon claims that Jesus is the fulfillment of God's promise in Isaiah 9:6–7 that a son of David is coming, and that "the government will be upon his shoulders" forever in a reign of "endless peace." We will discuss the title "Lord" later. Note here, though, that finalizing Jesus's title as "king" and "lord" does not separate him from human history, but rather places him directly in the line of human kings and human governments. As their ruler, Jesus will finally bring the proper fulfillment of governing human society. Finally, the kingdom of heaven will belong to "the poor in spirit," and "the meek [the tamed] will inherit the earth" (Matt 5:3, 5).

There is no question that Jesus is seen as the person to whom God has given extraordinary authority, power, and rule (the throne). The risen Jesus is even called "the ruler of God's creation" (Rev 3:14). Having said that, it is important to remember that throughout the Old Testament, humans were understood to be agents of God, entrusted with authority, power, and rule (thrones). And in the New Testament, followers of Jesus were to acknowledge this role, even when the world rulers were not good rulers (John 19:11; Acts 4:8, 4:17–21, 23:2–5; Rom 13:1–2; 1 Pet 2:17).

Understanding that Jesus's authoritative roles did not separate Jesus from our humanity is clarified further by the promise that followers of Jesus will continue to speak and act with God-given authority. They will also continue to share the reign of God on earth (Matt 5:3–5, 19:28; Mark 6:7; Luke 22:30; John 20:21–23; Acts 1:8, 4:33; 2 Cor 10:8, 13:10; 2 Tim 2:12; Titus 2:5; Heb 13:17; Rev 2:26, 4:4, 5:10, 20:4, 22:5). Sharing in the reign of God, with God-granted authority, is a gift and responsibility that Jesus fulfills with unique faithfulness, but it is one he shares with other humans who lived before, and who live after, his ministry in Israel.

Priestly Mediator Is a God-given Role, Fulfilled by Humans.

Jesus's role as high priest also deeply embeds Jesus in humanity. The priests, and especially the high priests, were human agents appointed by God to stand as mediators between God and other humans. Melchizedek was the mediator between God and Abram who accepted Abram's offerings on God's behalf while serving Abram at God's table (Gen 14:18–20). Aaron and his descendants were to be the mediating priests between God and Israel (Exod 28). The entire nation of Israel was to be God's priesthood mediating God's presence among and for the nations (Exod 19:6).

Jesus is given this role in a manner that uniquely fulfills it in a deeper way, but his role is still embedded in his humanity. The writer of Hebrews explicitly relates this role to Jesus's humanity:

> For we do not *have* [present tense] a high priest who is unable to sympathize with our weaknesses, but we have one who *has been tempted* [Greek perfect tense usually emphasizes "with continuing results"] *in every way, just as we are—yet was without sin* (Heb 4:15, *emphasis mine*).

Some take the discussion in Hebrews 5–8 that compares Jesus's priesthood to that of Melchizedek as a hint that Melchizedek was "the preexistent Christ." The author's point seems instead to be that both Jesus and Melchizedek served as God's high priest because of their relationship with God. Neither had a priestly genealogy, but both could mediate God's presence because of their unique relationship with God. The author even says that prior to his exaltation Jesus could not have served as High Priest because of his lack of genealogy, but now he can because of his continuing faithfulness in his relationship with God (Heb 7:14, 8:4–6).

Jesus's relationship with God and his continuing identification with our humanity are explicitly stated as the bases for his role as God's new high priestly mediator in the following passage: "For there is one God and *one mediator between God and men* [*anthrōpōn* = humans], *the man* [*anthrōpos* = human] *Jesus* Christ . . . ." (1 Tim 2:5, emphasis mine).

Perhaps not so surprisingly, Jesus passes this mediating role on to his very human followers who are to serve as "priests" (1 Pet 2:5, 9; Rev 1:6, 5:10, 20:6). Because of their relationship with God through Jesus, these followers are designated as mediators of God's forgiveness (Matt 18:15–20; John 20:21–23; Jas 5:14–20; 1 John 5:16).

Jesus's priesthood and mediating role continues to embed him, and us, in our humanity. As I mentioned in the previous chapter, it would be wonderful if we took this mediating role far more seriously, as Jesus's earliest followers did. Following Jesus means avoiding the role of accusers and condemners while embracing the role of God's human priestly mediators of grace, mercy, and forgiveness.

Jesus as Miracle Worker Is an Expression of His Humanity.

Occasionally, I hear someone speak of the New Testament claims that Jesus enacted miracles, signs, and wonders as evidence of Jesus's divinity as opposed to his humanity. I always find this strange because so many of Jesus's miraculous acts are modeled after the earlier acts of Moses, Elijah, and Elisha. Once again, we have Jesus fulfilling a pattern established much earlier in God's relationship with other human agents of God. And once again, we find Jesus passing this agency on to his followers (John 14:12; Acts 2:43, 8:6; Gal 3:5; 1 Cor 12:10).

Accounts of Jesus working signs, wonders, and miracles appear in each of the Gospels, and the claim is a part of several sermons in Acts. Probably Jesus's acts of healing were seen as the most important miracles by people of his time. They were very important for at least four reasons.

1. They connected him to the miraculous healings by prophets such as Elijah, Elisha, and Isaiah.

2. They were evidence that God was at work in a powerful way through Jesus. Sickness and death have always caused some of humans' deepest fears and most clearly revealed our limitations. Isaiah 53 had promised a future human agent of God would be God's suffering servant who brought new healing to the people of God.

3. Many illnesses in Jesus's time led to death or drastic physical limitation because medical science was very limited at the time—of course, it is still more limited today than we like to acknowledge.

4. Most of the medical cures available at the time were *not* available to the poor, just as most of the current cutting-edge medical technology today is available only to the wealthy and well-connected.

Jesus's ability to bring healing of all kinds—spiritual, emotional, social, psychological, mental, and physical—was amazing. There are some great differences in how we moderns make the creation submit to our will and how Jesus did so. He did so without the brokenness that often accompanies our attempts to force the creation to submit to us. Jesus's miracles lacked the "side effects" and "unintended consequences" that attend so many of our "modern miracles."

1. Jesus did miracles of feeding and healing people instantaneously with a word, touch, or prayer. Most of our amazing medical feats are extended processes. Jesus's way would still impress most of us today. In fact, though I tend to be skeptical, the one time I was involved in a prayer time in Jesus's name that ended with a person paralyzed from the neck down walking out of the hospital the next morning, I was quite impressed.

2. Jesus's healings did not involve the cruel torture of millions of test animals, followed by the horrible suffering often experienced by many humans in the early stages of medical experimentation (cancer research for example).

3. Except for one fig tree, Jesus's miracles did not have the unintended consequences of devastating the environment—God's gift of creation—as ours so often do. All too often, we strip, pollute, and litter as we go.

4. Perhaps most amazing, Jesus's miracles often led people to thank God—not always; sometimes they angered religious people—although we moderns often seem to think our breakthroughs prove that we no longer need God. We express hubris right at the point where we should be thanking God for the gifts God built into the creation for us.

On the other hand, we should not be afraid to note that there are reasons why modern human breakthroughs in working with *nature* to override "natural laws" have made many of Jesus's miracles not quite as striking today as they were in his time. The following are a few examples of what I mean:

1. Jesus walks on water for a little while—a feat geckos and some swans do fairly well—however, we put a crew of 100 men and women under water in a submarine for a year. They often travel 25,000 miles or more under and on the water during that year. One might also argue that astronauts walking on the moon reflects overcoming natural obstacles in a manner that is a bit more impressive than a short walk on the Sea of Galilee.

2. As for healing and curing, many of our current medical advances seemed "impossible" only a century or two ago, and some of them seemed impossible only a

decade or two ago. We transplant hearts, lungs, valves, and kidneys—not without lifelong costs to the recipient, but often with a decent prolonging of life. We treat mental illnesses with drugs somewhat successfully—though not without very real side effects at times. We are working on altering DNA and RNA coding to prevent genetic illnesses and seem to be close to some important breakthroughs leading to amazing healings—and probably leading to some horrible temptations to misuse this power. Any description of these cures two centuries ago would have been a claim that "miracles" were going to occur. Through these gifts of modern science, my wife and I both lived many extra years that would not have been possible a century ago.

I am attempting to make two points: First, for those of us who think Jesus's miracles somehow signify that he is something more than or other than human, do we think our modern miracles in the same areas mean we are more than or other than human? No! From the beginning God designed the creation to respond to human interactions with the creation.

Second, for those of us who think Jesus's miracles were impossible and therefore did not occur, let's face the fact that what we are really saying is that we modern day people can learn how to work with nature in order to override nature, but Jesus—and other miracle workers throughout history—could not have. Just because these people, who are witnessed to as healers in almost every culture in human history, "knew" how to heal with methods different from those our science "knows," does this mean only ours are real? Why?

If, as you are reading, you find yourself discounting all records of miracle-working throughout human history because many claims prove to be false or exaggerated, I remind you that many of our medical and technological claims have also proven to be false or exaggerated—sometimes even deadly. I just found out that a medicine I took for ten years, which was touted as miraculous and harmless, is now said to cause cancer. I have also gone back and forth half-a-dozen times on the "latest" medical advice about taking a small dose of aspirin every day for my heart. These false and exaggerated claims have not caused me to reject the positive results of medicines that have saved my health and my life. Neither do the false and exaggerated claims about miracles given in response to prayers and spiritual gifts need to cause us to reject grace that God might wish to give us at times.

Even the rabbis of later centuries, although rejecting all claims that Jesus was God's Messiah, acknowledged that he was a miracle worker and a healer. There was too much historical evidence for them to deny it; they just did not think the power came from God. Only our modern tendency to see the "laws of nature" as binding to everyone and everything—except our scientific and technological expertise in manipulating them—would see Jesus's miracle working as something that separates him from our humanity. This gift did not separate him from our humanity, it roots him in humanity.

Jesus's Role as Firstborn, Son of Man, Last Adam (Human), and Second Adam (Human) Embed Jesus in Our Humanity.

The title for this section would seem to so clearly embed Jesus in humanity one would think there might be no controversy. However, it is amazing how often the implications of Jesus's role as "firstborn" of God's future human family are ignored. Paul claims that God decided ahead of time to complete God's creation venture by making other humans into the image of the Messiah "that he might be the *firstborn among many brothers*" (Rom 8:29–30, *emphasis mine*). He also identifies Jesus as the "firstborn from the dead" and as God's firstborn human to be placed over the entire creation (Col 1:15–18). In the ancient world, "firstborn" was a role that identified the firstborn son as deeply embedded with the rest of the family. At the same time, the role of the firstborn son placed the rest of the family in a dependent relationship with him.

Although the phrase "son of man" seems to root Jesus clearly in humanity, this too is not without some controversy. In fact, some scholars respond to the phrase almost as if it read "son of God." The phrase "son of man" appears earliest in the Old Testament canon in Numbers 23:19, where it contrasts God with humans who are the "son of man." In Psalm 8:4–8 "the son of man" (*ben adam*—son of Adam—in Hebrew) is a poetic parallel to "man/humanity" (*enosh* in Hebrew). The psalmist sees all humans as "son of Adam" and promises that someday God will complete God's creation project and humanity (son of Adam) really will be crowned with the glory and honor of God. Ezekiel uses the phrase over and over to designate himself as humbly human in contrast to God. Daniel promises that the day is coming when "one like the son of man" will come into God's presence to receive all authority and honor—a gift he will then share with other humans who are "the holy ones of the Most High" (Dan 7:13–18, 22).

Literary developments involving the Daniel passage near the time of Jesus have led to some questioning whether Jesus's usage really embedded him in our humanity. However, I agree with R. T. France, who presents a strong case for Jesus's usual application of the Daniel passage as a promise of the exaltation he would receive as he ascended into the presence of the Father to receive authority over the nations. This application fits the wording in Daniel because the one to be exalted is coming *into* God's presence, *not* coming *from* God's presence.[2] Jesus ascends into God's presence as the first human, but not the last, to be included in God's future reign.

The phrase "son of man" became one of Jesus's favorite ways of identifying himself. Given that Jesus probably spoke more often in Aramaic (and maybe some Hebrew, especially in quotations) than in Greek, it is likely that he was constantly identifying himself as *ben-adam* (in Hebrew) or *bar-adam* (in Aramaic). Both the Aramaic and the Hebrew translate into English as "son of Adam." There is every reason to see this choice as Jesus's self-conscious identification with all of the meanings of "son of man"

---

2. France, *Mark*, 342–343.

noted above—human in contrast to God, but empowered by God with great authority in God's creation which is then to be shared with other humans ("saints").

Although it is unclear whether it will catch on, I appreciate the choice the translators of the Common English Bible (as well as Ched Myers in his *Binding the Strong Man*[3]) made in translating the Greek *ho huois tou anthrōpou* as "the human one." Maybe "son of Adam" would be even more preferable in reflecting the Hebrew and Aramaic backgrounds. C. S. Lewis used "son of Adam" in his Narnia tales with good effect. Either "human one" or "son of Adam" catches a lot of the nuance in the Old Testament usage. The phrase deeply embeds Jesus in our humanity.

Jesus claims that it is his humanity—his identity and role as "son of Adam"—that gives him the freedom to "forgive sins" (Mark 2:10). It is also as "son of Adam" that God grants him Lordship over the Sabbath (Mark 2:28–29). Jesus even claims that it is "*because* he is the Son of Man [Adam]"—fully embedded in our humanity—that God will give him the authority to be our judge and to finally bring justice to this broken world (John 5:27, *emphasis mine*).

Outside of the Gospels, only Acts, Hebrews, and Revelation identify Jesus as "the Son of Man." The Acts reference is important for our emphasis on Jesus's continuing humanity. Praying as he is being executed, Stephen sees the risen, exalted, and reigning Jesus, and identifies him as still the "Son of Man/Adam" (Acts 7:56).

Paul does not use the phrase "Son of Man [Adam]." However, like the authors just cited, Paul too sees Jesus's continuing humanity—relationship with "Adam/Human"—as fully embedding him in our humanity. Paul contrasts the impact that "one Adam's [human's]" sin had on his fellow humans with the impact that another "one Adam's [human's]" righteousness has on his fellow humans (Rom 5:12–21). Just prior to that contrast of the two "Adams," Paul speaks of how God's love for Jesus, and God's love for the rest of us humans, led God to reveal God's love through Jesus's faithfulness to God and to us (Rom 5:1–11).

In 1 Corinthians 15, Paul identifies the risen Jesus as the Messiah who is "the last Adam [the last restart of humanity]," and he is clear that it is Jesus's relationship with God as "the last Adam" that qualifies Jesus to bring other humans into God's forever family. Only in God's relationship with this "last human" will death be defeated for the rest of us humans. As previously noted in 1 Timothy 2:3–5, Paul (or a "Pauline" author, as many scholars maintain) asserts that it is Jesus's continuing humanity that allows God to give the human Jesus the mediating role between God and the rest of us humans.

The New Testament often declares the wonder of Jesus's humanity is that now God can extend the results of Jesus's faithful human relationship with God to other humans as well. The following are two powerful examples of the claim that Jesus's glorified humanity as God's child is being passed on to other humans:

---

3. Myers, *Binding*.

> ²⁹ For *those* God foreknew he also predestined to be *conformed to the likeness of his Son*, that he might be *the firstborn among many brothers*. ³⁰ And *those* he predestined, he also called; those he called, he also justified; those he justified, *he also glorified* (Rom 8:29–30, *emphasis mine*).

As noted previously in chapter 1, I think the plurals in Paul's language make it clear that he is speaking of God predeciding to have a forever righteous human family, not God predeciding which individuals would be saved and which would be rejected by God. This is more consistent with other New Testament themes such as "For God so loved the world" (John 3:16, *see* also 1 John 2:2) and God "not wanting anyone to perish," but rather "all men to be saved" (2 Pet 3:9; 1 Tim 2:4). And as noted in chapter 2, God's creation project has always been to "glorify" humans, so God "glorifying" Jesus, and through Jesus glorifying other humans, fully embeds Jesus in God's creation project. It is within this paradigm that Paul claims that what God has done for the human Jesus, God will now, because of God's relationship with Jesus and our relationship with Jesus, do for other humans also.

The writer of Hebrews uses the phrase "son of man" and does so in a manner that directly links Jesus and other humans in the same phrase. The risen Jesus is the first—but by no means the last—fulfillment and completion of God's intention to crown humans with the glory and honor of God.

> ⁶ But there is a place where someone has testified: "What is man that you are mindful of him, *the son of man* that you care for him? ⁷ You made him a little lower than the angels; you crowned him with glory and honor ⁸ and put everything under his feet." In putting everything under him, God left nothing that is not subject to him. Yet at present we do *not see everything subject to him*. ⁹ But *we see Jesus,* who was made a little lower than the angels, now crowned with glory and honor because he suffered death, so that by the grace of God he might taste death for everyone.
>
> ¹⁰ In bringing *many sons* [and daughters] *to glory*, it was fitting that God, for whom and through whom everything exists, should make *the author* of their salvation *perfect* [complete] through suffering. ¹¹ Both the one who *makes men* [humans] *holy* and those who are *made holy are of the same family*. So Jesus is *not ashamed to call them brothers* [and sisters] (Heb 2:6–11, *emphasis mine*; a meditation on Ps 8 which is itself a meditation on Gen 1).

The writer of Hebrews, like Paul in Romans and 1 Corinthians, sees Jesus as the fulfillment of God's creation goal. He is the first human "crowned with the glory and honor of God." The "Son of Man [Adam]" is "the Son of God." He is God's means and God's model for completing the goal so other "sons [and daughters] of Man [Adam]" can be glorified as the "children of God."

Jesus Is One of Us

Jesus as Judge Is an Expression of His Role as God's Human Agent.

It is important to remember that the words *justice*, *judge*, and *judgment* were not negative words in the Bible. Today, if we go before a judge in a legal trial, the best "judgment" we can hope for is for nothing to happen to us—"not guilty!" The judgment/justice word group was far more positive in biblical usage. "Judgment" meant above all else the righteous reordering of society so that it functioned more equitably. Judgment was a negative concept only for those who resisted these righteous transformations. So, when the New Testament writers claim God has appointed Jesus to be "Judge," they are claiming he will be God's agent who finally sets the human social order right.

Most Christians acknowledge the New Testament writers believed God has given Jesus the role of "Judge" over humanity. It seems many of us are less aware that several writers explicitly described this future role as an expression of Jesus's continuing humanity.

Paul is quoted in Acts as telling the philosophers in Athens Jesus will be "the human" to whom God will assign the role of judging all other humans.

> For he [God] has set a day when he *will judge* the world with justice *by the man* he has *appointed*. He has given proof of this to all men by raising him from the dead (Acts 17:31, *emphasis mine*).

Paul here seems to reflect a claim John attributes to Jesus. Jesus maintains that it is "*because* he is the son of man" that God has given him God's role of judging other humans (John 5:22–27, *emphasis mine*). Peter too is quoted as confident that, after raising Jesus from the dead, God "appointed" Jesus to be the judge of all other humans, whether currently dead or alive (Acts 10:41–42; *see also* Rom 2:16; 2 Cor 5:20; 2 Tim 4:1, 8). It is also likely that the logic of Romans 3:25–26 is—as more and more scholars including the Common English Bible are translating the passage—a claim that God can be "just" as God and also "justifier" of us sinful humans because of "the faithfulness of Jesus"[4] who shared our humanity, but who did not share our falling short when it comes to trusting God.

Throughout the New Testament, the final judgment of humans is still God's rightful role. However, God has made Jesus his agent for carrying out this judgment *because* Jesus remains embedded in our humanity. Perhaps the importance of this choice is somewhat reflected in the modern development of the ideal that justice should involve being judged by a jury of our peers who live in our own home district.[5]

Another indication that this role embeds Jesus in our humanity is that the role is extended to Jesus's followers. Jesus promised his followers that they would somehow be included with him when he exercises the role of judge to finally bring complete justice into human history (*see* Matt 19:28; Luke 22:30). Paul and John of the Apocalypse

---

4. *See* chapter 12.
5. U. S. Constitution, 6th Amendment.

both maintain that Jesus's faithful followers will join him in exercising this future role (1 Cor 6:2–5; Rev 20:4). The title and role of "Judge" is yet another role that deeply embeds Jesus in humanity, rather than separating him from our humanity. He will be the source of our deep longing for a just society.

Anyone who has served in leadership roles in church communities knows the dynamic tension that Paul's letters to the Corinthians reflect concerning community life. Sometimes we should not judge others or even ourselves, and at other times, we should make godly judgments about what is going on in our community and act accordingly. This same dynamic tension is reflected in many of Jesus's statements recorded in the Gospel of John as he sometimes claims the God-given role of judge, and a few paragraphs later is found saying "I do not judge," or I was sent to save, not to judge (often translated "condemn").

Nonetheless, though acknowledging the dynamic tension created by the various ways the Greek word group *krino* is used in the New Testament, there is no question that the general paradigm in the New Testament is that the human Jesus, along with other humans included in Jesus's relationship with God, will be God's agents in God's final judgments. Jesus explicitly says that he, instead of the Father, will be the judge concerning other humans (John 5:22). God's plan to bring the justice (righteous ordering) human society so desperately needs will be brought to completion through Jesus's agency. The "final judgment" is not something to be feared; it is the making right of all things!

Jesus Is the Human Keeper of God's Commandments—Obedient Whatever the Cost.

Jesus claims to be the keeper of God's commandments (John 15:10). In that same sentence, he compares his commandment-keeping to what he wants from his followers. Jesus also claims that he would never abrogate any of the Torah, but that he will fulfill it through proper responses (Matt 5:17–19). He further states that if he, or anyone else, taught people to break even the least commandment, that person would be "least in the kingdom of heaven"—certainly not the ranking God awarded Jesus (Phil 2:9–11)! He also taught that the way "to enter life" is to obey God's commandments (Matt 19:17; Luke 11:28). Jesus claims to be the commandment keeper par excellence, and he demands that others follow his example.

Other concepts related to commandment-keeping include the times Jesus is described as "obedient" (Phil 2:8; Heb 5:8–9) and as in "submission" to God (Heb 5:7; 1 Cor 15:28; 1 Pet 2:13–25). I would also include all the references we noted in the two chapters on Jesus's faithfulness. In fact, you can make a strong case that in the first century Jewish milieu, every description of Jesus as "righteous" is also a claim that he was an obedient keeper of God's commandments.

DO OTHER ROLES AND RELATIONSHIPS ALSO ROOT JESUS IN OUR HUMANITY?

The following assertions are more controversial than those we have just explored. If I lose you in what follows, please do not forget the rest of the book—Jesus was, is, and always will be one of us. I think the roles, titles, functions, and characteristics describing Jesus's relationship with God that follow also present him as our fellow human.

Jesus is Lord, We Pray to Him, and We Bow before Him, but These Roles Do Not Separate Him from Our Humanity.

1. Jesus's Lordship Is Unique.

Recently, several scholars have argued that the New Testament writers' designation of Jesus as "Lord," especially the passages in which they designate Jesus as Lord using Old Testament language describing the roles and functions of YHWH (Lord), are clear examples of language that separate Jesus from the rest of us humans. It is also often argued that the passages that speak of "bowing before Jesus" make his separation from our humanness quite clear. I am now making the obviously controversial claim that the title and role of "Lord" does not separate Jesus from our humanity. Neither do our proper responses to his Lordship.

Having said that, I do want to emphasize that Jesus's Lordship is overwhelmingly and astoundingly unique as the following scriptures illustrate.

> [8] And when he had taken the scroll, the four living creatures and the twenty-four elders *fell down before the Lamb*. Each one had a harp, and they were holding golden bowls full of incense, which are the prayers of the saints. [9a] And they sang a new song: "*You are worthy to take the scroll*. . . ." [14] The four living creatures said, "Amen," *and the elders fell down and worshiped* (Rev 5:8–9a, 14, emphasis mine).

It is not only in the highly symbolic book of Revelation but also in the very down-to-earth letters from Paul that we are told that the One God wants humans to honor and bow before the newly exalted Jesus.

> [9] *Therefore God exalted him to the highest place and gave him the name* that is above every name, [10] *that at the name of Jesus every knee should bow*, in heaven and on earth and under the earth, [11] and every tongue confess that *Jesus Christ is Lord, to the glory of God the Father* (Phil 2:9–11, emphasis mine).

The uniqueness is stated strongly and is presented as overwhelmingly awesome!

2. Jesus's Unique Lordship Does Not Separate Jesus from Our Humanness.

I mentioned earlier that the Greek Old Testament has David twice referring to King Saul as "Lord and Christ" (1 Sam 24:6, 26.16). Quite obviously the writer of 1 Samuel did not think that these roles separated Saul from our humanity. Almost everyone agrees that the term "lord" (*kurios* in Greek) is used in the New Testament to describe many differing levels of authority.

On the one hand, there are quite a few uses of the Greek words *kurios* and *kurie* ("lord" in direct address) in the New Testament that are clearly not intended to communicate divinity. Often these are translated into English as "lord" in lowercase or as "sir." The *koine* Greek of the New Testament uses forms of *kurios* for God, Jesus, kings, masters, and other socially prominent people *(see* Matt 21:29–30, 25:11, 27:63, John 4:11, 1 Pet 3:6, Rev 7:14). On the other hand, New Testament writers do use words and phrases to describe Jesus's roles and functions that were reserved for YHWH in the Old Testament. This includes their use of *kurios* to translate *YHWH* in a manner similar to what seems to have been the most commonly used Greek translation of the Hebrew Bible in their day.

Such varied usage of *kurios* means that overall theology and context, not word usage, is how we must attempt to determine what level of authority is being described. When it is used of Jesus, is it always, sometimes, or never claiming that he is something other than, or more than, human?

If you are convinced that when applied to Jesus, *kurios* always, or almost always, is intended to emphasize Jesus's divinity as something more than human, you will find many passages that describe Jesus as somehow separate from the humanity the rest of us share. On the other hand, if Jesus's Lordship is an agency God gave to Jesus as God's firstborn of God's future human society, you will see these descriptions as the righteous fulfillment of the Genesis mandate for humans to subdue the creation. If this is the correct understanding of "Jesus is Lord," then Jesus's Lordship is deeply embedded in humanity. To make it about something other than Jesus's humanity seems to leave unfulfilled forever the Genesis 1 mandate for humans to bring the entire creation into submission before God. At least, I see no indication that the rest of us humans can do it without Jesus as our human representative.

It would take a separate book to pursue the many ramifications of this question concerning Lordship. In my first thousand-page draft of this book, I attempted to address many more of the issues than I will here, and even then, I realized there were many more issues to be addressed. Acknowledging the sparseness of this section, here are a few more reasons I think *Lord* was being used to describe Jesus's ongoing role as God's completed human. If you wish to read the works of scholars who answer this question very differently from the way I do, I refer you to two authors whose works I highly respect—Richard Bauckham[6] and N. T. Wright[7].

Does "Jesus is Lord" separate Jesus from humanness? There are two related questions. Do various New Testament authors present Jesus's Lordship as a role gifted from God to Jesus as God's human agent? Do they see this gift as a process involving different degrees of authority as the relationship between Jesus and God develops and matures to new levels? What follows are a few of the many reasons I think various New Testament writers see Jesus's Lordship as progressively granted to him by God in a manner that fully embeds Jesus in his humanity and in ours.

The use of words and phrases such as God *has made* Jesus Lord (Acts 2:36), Jesus *became* superior to the angels (Heb 1:4), *once made perfect* [complete], he *became* the source of eternal salvation (Heb 5:9), and *therefore* God exalted him to the highest place (Phil 2:9–11), all indicate that the writers saw Jesus's Lordship as a process of increasing authority. Each new degree of authority is granted by God as a gift in response to different stages of Jesus's faithfulness—completed as Paul says when "He humbled himself and became obedient to death— even death on a cross! Therefore . . ." (Phil 2:8–9).

The Gospel writers indicate that Peter, and many others, had addressed Jesus as "Lord" for several years. Nevertheless, in Acts 2:36, Peter claims that Jesus of Nazareth has been given a new level of lordship by God because of Jesus's faithfulness throughout his life and during his execution—"God *has made* this Jesus, whom you crucified, both Lord and Christ" (*emphasis mine*).

Mark's Gospel maintains that Jesus saw his Lordship as deeply embedded in his humanity and in our humanity. Jesus speaks of the way he obeys the commandment to keep the Sabbath holy by embedding himself and the Sabbath in God's creation project.

> [27] Then he [Jesus] said to them, "*The Sabbath was made for man [humans]*, not man [humans] for the Sabbath. [28] *So* [*hoste* in Greek] *the Son of Man [Humanity] is Lord* even of the Sabbath" (Mark 2:27–28, *emphasis mine*).

According to Greek scholars, *hoste* means "consequently" or "resulting in." Mark maintains that Jesus sees his Lordship over the Sabbath as derived from his fulfillment of God's original intentions for the relationship between humans and the rest of Creation. Even the Sabbath was to be "subject" to humans as was everything else God created. We were to subject the creation as faithful stewards of God's gracious gifts. That is part of what it means to be "in the image of God." The Sabbath is God's gift to humans to be celebrated as we celebrate the gift of the entire creation. It was never meant to be a burden imposed by religious leaders in ways that oppressed the poor and women. Many Rabbinic Pharisees agreed with Jesus, but some Pharisees used the Sabbath rules as a way of stroking their own egos and social status at the expense of

---

6. Bauckham, *Jesus and God*, and "Orthodoxy."
7. Wright. *Faithfulness of God*. Vol 2. Ch 9.

the poorer working class—just as some Christian leaders today teach guidelines that elevate the clergy and priesthood in a manner that oppresses and degrades "ordinary" or "lay" Christians.

Here in Mark's Gospel, Jesus claims that God shares God's authority and Lordship with the human Jesus as God always intended to share it with humans. Perhaps Jesus has in mind the same "everything subject to him" passages that the writer of Hebrews uses later in making the same point (Heb 2; Ps 8; Gen 1:26–31).

One of the key examples of an author using words describing Jesus that were previously reserved in the Old Testament only for YHWH occurs in Philippians 2:9–11. Many see this passage as clearly maintaining that Jesus is something more than human. However, when we read these words in their context, Jesus's Lordship is being celebrated *as God's reward to Jesus for his faithfulness and as a model for our faithfulness.* Far from separating Jesus from our humanity, the context embeds our humanity in Jesus's humanity.

> [1] *If you have any encouragement from being united with Christ,* if any comfort from his love, if any fellowship with the Spirit, if any tenderness and compassion, [2] then make my joy complete *by being like-minded, having the same love, being one in spirit and purpose.* . . .
>
> [5] *Your attitude should be the same as that of Christ Jesus:* [6] Who, being in very nature [*en morphē* in Greek = in the form] God, did *not consider equality with God something to be grasped* [exploited], [7] but made himself nothing, taking the very nature of a servant, being made in *human* [*anthrōpos*] *likeness*. [8] And being found in *appearance as a human* [*anthrōpos*], he humbled [root *kenaō* in Greek = empty or make void] himself and *became obedient* to death—even death on a cross!
>
> [9] *Therefore God exalted him* to the highest place and *gave him* the name that is above every name, [10] that at the name of Jesus every knee should bow, in heaven and on earth and under the earth, [11] and every tongue confess that *Jesus Christ is Lord, to the glory of God the Father.*
>
> [12] *Therefore,* my dear friends, as you have *always obeyed*—not only in my presence, but now much more in my absence—continue to *work out* your salvation with fear and trembling, [13] for it is *God who works in you to will and to act* according to his good purpose (Phil 2:1–2, 5–13, *emphasis mine*).

This passage by Paul is one of the most argued about among scholars. Some think this passage stresses that "Jesus is God," and that this is what separates him from our ordinary humanness. Other scholars think this section was intended to embed Jesus deeply within our humanity. Both sides of the argument tend to be focused on various Greek words.

Those who think Paul is stressing Jesus's "two natures" as both human and divine point out that the Greek *morphē* in verse 6 is not the word commonly used to speak of "Adam/human" being in the "image" of God. They say this change of wording suggests that Paul's use of "form" is his way of saying that "Jesus was God," and then became also human.

These commentators also argue that "equality" with God is something describing "the Son" prior to incarnation. The Son didn't selfishly "grasp" this status. In this paradigm, "emptying himself" describes "the preexisting Son's" choice to become human, and becoming human is the same as "taking the form of a slave." It is also claimed that "the name" above all others must be "God" or "YHWH." Finally, it is correctly pointed out that 2:9–11 is filled with language that the Old Testament reserved for YHWH (*see* Isa 45:2).

On the other side, scholars argue that when Paul wrote, he had Genesis 1–3 in mind, rather than a preexistent scene in heaven. This would mean that Jesus's human connection with Adam and Eve is in mind, rather than Jesus as a preexistent part of the Godhead. They also stress that the context is all about Jesus's faithfulness and the challenge for other humans to "have this same mind" that Jesus had when he humbly and faithfully obeyed God. In other words, unlike Adam and Eve, Jesus did live "in the image and likeness of God."

Those who think this passage is primarily about Jesus's humanity also focus on different nuances in the Greek wording. When the text is understood within the paradigm of God's relationship with humans, "in the form of God" in verse 6 is understood as a reference to the creation of humans in the image and likeness of God.

Some of these scholars point out that Greek words related to *morphē* are used in other Pauline letters in a manner that clearly means "similar" or "like," not "the same as" (Gal 4:19; 2 Tim 3:5). That meaning of *morphē* fits more easily into the Genesis 1–2 context than into a focus on preexistent divinity. Others point out that if Paul had really wanted to say that the reason God exalted Jesus so highly is because Jesus is God, Paul could have just said, "because Jesus is God." It is a phrase that was as easy to write in Greek as it was for me to write just now in English. For some reason, Paul chose not to say that here.[8]

Also, Genesis 3:5 indicates that "equality with God" is what Adam and Eve "grasped" for in response to the explicit temptation to "*become like God.*" Unlike them, Jesus did not "grasp" for "being equal with God" when he was tempted by the evil one. The first humans chose not to wait for God to give them the gift of a new depth and maturity as humans "in the image of God;" Jesus chose to wait for God to give him this gift, rather than attempting to "seize" it as they did. In contrast to other humans, Jesus consistently chose to empty and humble himself in favor of God and other humans. "Taking the form of a servant" refers to the way of life Jesus chose day by day, not to his choosing to leave heaven and become human (Mark 10:42–45; John 13:2–17). It was his way of living life vulnerably and faithfully before God no matter what it cost him. That is his uniqueness!

---

8. Scholars and translators debate fiercely whether Paul's Greek says "Jesus is God" in Rom 9:5 and Titus 2:13.

Jesus's Other Roles

I do not read German, but I assume Bart Ehrman is correct in maintaining that the German scholar Vollenweider's work shows that the Greek verb translated "grasped" (*arpagmon*) was used by several Jewish authors to refer to a person grasping for something they did not have, not for attempting to hold on to something they already had. He further maintains that *arpagmon* (grasp/seize) usually characterizes people who are arrogant and trying to seem to be more than they really are.[9] All of this would indicate to me that Paul is emphasizing Jesus's human experience, not his preexistence. Ehrman concludes that Paul's emphasis is on Jesus's lower level of divinity, not as "God" but as "god." In contrast to Ehrman, I hear Paul speaking of Jesus as the firstborn of God's future human family, the new Adam, and as the model for the rest of us. These are themes that run all through Paul's letters.

There are other phrases and words that favor seeing the focus throughout this section as Jesus's humanity. The statement that Jesus "*became obedient* to death—even death on a cross" (2:8) stresses Jesus's decisive human faithfulness in the direst of situations. "*Therefore* God exalted him" indicates that God exalted Jesus to something new *because of* his human faithfulness (2:9). God "*gave* him the name" indicates that Jesus's new level of authority as "Lord" is a new gift from God to Jesus because of his human faithfulness to God.

The ancient world was familiar with people who were "given" the authority to speak and write with the "name" and "full authority" of the ruler who appointed them. Such a person was a coruling agent of the throne, the ruler's "right-hand man." Old Testament examples include Joseph to Pharaoh (Gen 41:39–44), and first Haman (Esth 3:10–11) and then Mordecai to the Persian King (Esth 8:10). Jesus lauds a Roman centurion for his understanding of this kind of delegated power and authority. The centurion paralleled his own delegated Roman authority over others to Jesus's relationship to God and God's authority. Jesus responds by saying that this pagan military occupier is the first person he has met who "really trusts [has such great faith]" in Jesus's relationship to God (Matt 8:5–10). As a further example in Jesus's time, most Jews in the first century world would have experienced life under Roman provincial rulers who operated with a great deal of autonomy "in the name of" Caesar. Paul was held in prison and then sent to Rome as prisoner, based on a ruler's authority granted to him as an agent of Caesar.

Deciding whether the primary emphasis in Philippians 2 is on Jesus's divinity or on Jesus's humanity seems to be decided usually by whether one thinks the stress of the passage is on how Jesus differs from the rest of us or on how the rest of us are called to become more and more like Jesus. I think the larger context should be the deciding factor. And, that larger context is all about embedding Jesus in our humanity and embedding us in Jesus's faithful humanness (2:1–5, 12–13). Paul surrounds the beautiful poetic exaltation of Jesus with a challenge that his human readers become more and more like the obedient human Jesus (2:1–5) by allowing God to work in us (2:12–13).

---

9. Ehrman, *Jesus Became God*, 263.

This challenge, at least for me personally, loses much of its power if we understand 2:6–11 as a claim that Jesus was able to live this way only because of his divinity.

Space does not allow pursuing this topic further, but I think Colossians 1:15–22 and 1 Corinthians 8:5–6, which are two of the other key passages that ascribe to Jesus words previously only used for YHWH, should also be understood similarly to Philippians 2. Though many scholars that I highly respect disagree, I think these passages are best seen through the overall New Testament lens that views Jesus's new level of Lordship as the role God "gives" the "completed" human Jesus as a reward for his unrelenting faithfulness in his relationship with God—a faithfulness that allows God to exalt and enthrone Jesus as the firstborn of God's future human society.

Regardless of how you understand Colossians 1:15–22 in terms of divinity, the risen and exalted Jesus is still embedded in our ongoing humanity in Colossians. Jesus is "Firstborn from the dead" in order that we too can live beyond death as glorified humans (Col 1:19, 3:3–4). Jesus is filled with all the fullness of God—so that we too can be filled with the fullness of God (Col 1:19, 2:9–10). Likewise, however you understand 1 Corinthians 8 concerning Jesus and divinity, it is abundantly clear in chapter 15 of the same letter that Paul considered Jesus to still be human. He identifies the risen and exalted Jesus as the "the last Adam/Human" and "the human of heaven" through whom God would make Jesus's followers "humans of heaven" as well (1 Cor 15:45–49).

Describing Jesus as "Lord of lords and King of kings" (Rev 17:14)—a title previously reserved for God alone in the Bible (1 Tim 6:15; Deut 10:17; Ps 136:3)—does not separate Jesus from humanity either. Although the title "Lord of lords and King of kings" was reserved for God in the Old Testament, similar wording was often used in the Middle Eastern world to describe ancient human rulers. Using it of God was a direct rebuttal to the claims made by these dictatorial monarchs. And, the way the writer of Revelation uses it, is likewise a direct rebuttal to the claims of the Roman Empire, as well as the religious and economic institutions that sell their souls to support Empire. It is Jesus, not Caesar, who will be revealed as installed by God as Messiah (king) over of all the kingdom of the world as it becomes the kingdom of the Lord (God) and of the Lord's Messiah (Rev 11:15). This will be the beginning of a new level of the reign of God on earth, and the end of the reigns of those who have been destroying God's wonderful earth (Rev 11:17–18, 5:9–10, 21:1–4).

But, does this separate Jesus from the rest of us humans? Various New Testament writers say that God intends his future forever family of humans to "rule," "sit on thrones," and "have dominion" in the renewed creation. They saw Jesus as God's means and God's model for other humans, not as the only human to receive authority from God. Jesus is the first and the "way" for other humans to be brought into sharing this authority from God.

3. Does Praying to the Lord Jesus Separate Jesus from Our Humanity?

The uniqueness of Jesus's role led some followers of Jesus in New Testament times to not only "pray in Jesus's name" but, at least sometimes, to pray to Jesus. Does praying to Jesus mean that he is no longer embedded in our humanity? I do not think so. It does mean that God has given this firstborn completed human a new role as our King, our Lord, and our Mediator, whom we can properly approach with our entreaties, desires, needs, and hopes.

Although the "ask me" of John 14:14 is somewhat disputed as original text, the passage seems to indicate that Jesus told his followers to keep praying–talking to him after he was no longer with them. Whether that text originally instructed disciples to pray to Jesus or not, some of them did so.

Acts records the following prayer to Jesus as Stephen models Jesus's prayer on the cross:

> [59] While they were stoning him, *Stephen prayed, "Lord Jesus, receive my spirit."* [60] Then he fell on his knees and cried out, "*Lord*, do not hold this sin against them." When he had said this, he fell asleep. (Acts 7:59–60, *emphasis mine*).

I am never quite sure where the line between talking with Jesus and praying to Jesus is, or even if there is a line that differentiates. Both Paul and Ananias are described as having conversations with Jesus at least part of which seem to be prayers (Acts 9:1–18).

Other prayers to Jesus in the New Testament include these:

> "Come O Lord"—the translation of the Aramaic *marana tha*—is a prayerful request to Jesus (1 Cor 16:22).

> [8] Three times *I pleaded with the Lord* [seems to refer to Jesus] to take it away from me. [9] But he said to me, "My grace is sufficient for you, for my power is made perfect in weakness." Therefore I will boast all the more gladly about my weaknesses, *so that Christ's power* may rest on me (2 Cor 12:8–9, *emphasis mine*).

> [11] Now may our God and Father himself and our Lord Jesus clear the way for us to come to you. [12] *May the Lord make your love increase and overflow for each other and for everyone else, just as ours does for you.* [13] *May he strengthen your hearts* so that you will be blameless and holy in the presence of our God and Father when our Lord Jesus comes with all his holy ones (1 Thess 3:11–13, *emphasis mine*).

Because both verse 11 and 13 in the preceding quotation identify Jesus as "Lord," it is likely that verses 12–13a record a prayer to Jesus as Lord in the form of a typical Jewish blessing. The following is a prayer addressed to both Jesus the Messiah and to God the Father.

> [16] *May our Lord Jesus Christ himself* and God our Father, who loved us and by his grace gave us eternal encouragement and good hope, [17] *encourage your hearts and strengthen you in every good deed and word* (2 Thess 2:16–17, emphasis mine).

In addition to receiving visionary words from Jesus throughout the book, the author of Revelation pens a final prayer to Jesus: "He who testifies to these things says, 'Yes, I am coming soon.' *Amen. Come, Lord Jesus*" (Rev 22:20, *emphasis mine*).

To summarize, we are instructed to pray to and through Jesus because he is still embedded in our humanity, not because he is something other than human: "There *is* one God and *one mediator* between God and man [humans], *the man Jesus Christ* [*the human Jesus the Messiah*]" (1 Tim 2:1–5, *emphasis mine*). We are also told that Jesus can serve as the mediator of our prayers because having been "tempted in every way" like the rest of us, he *is* still empathetically embedded in our humanity (Heb 4:14–16). As his "bride," we await Jesus our human bridegroom and the ensuing celebration of the renewed creation of God's forever human family.

Personally, I most often pray to the Father in Jesus's name (faithful character and authority). However, at times, especially when I am focused on the dilemmas of daily human life that I, my family, my friends, and my fellow humans often experience, I talk to Jesus. It is a great comfort to know that the one I am talking to is a fellow human who went through the same kinds of experiences embedded in our "flesh" (Heb 2:14; 1 John 4:2).

4. Does Bowing Before and Worshiping Jesus Separate Him from Humanity?

Did bowing before Jesus mean that Jesus was, and should be, seen as something other than human, or is it an acknowledgment of his unique relationship with God and his role as God's human agent? The primary words translated as "worship" in both the Old Testament and the New Testament actually describe the act of "bowing down." Because, as I hope I have shown throughout this book, the New Testament writers believed that Jesus continues to be human now, it cannot be assumed without further evidence that they thought bowing before a human was anathema.

Several of my favorite New Testament scholars claim that observant first century Jews would never have "worshiped/bowed before" Jesus unless they were primarily focused on his divinity rather than on his faithful humanity. I do not think that this claim turns out to be conclusive for several reasons.

First, throughout the Old Testament, humans bowed before other humans without thinking they were insulting God by doing so. *Chavah* is the most common Hebrew word for "bowing in honor," and there are other, even more humbling, forms of honor that translate in phrases such as "lay prostrate before," "fell on his face," and "put his face to the earth." All are used to describe humans responding to other humans in

JESUS'S OTHER ROLES

an honoring manner. These are the same Hebrew words and phrases used to describe honoring God.

In fact, it would have been insulting not to bow before kings, fathers, and other people in roles of honor. It was only when bowing before someone, or a representation of someone, was an act of idolatry that faithful Jews refused to bow down to dignitaries. There are dozens of positive references to people bowing before other humans in the Old Testament, so many it does not seem necessary to innumerate them here. There are also a few instances of people refusing to bow before humans or their representation when it was considered idolatrous to do so. Examples include Shadrach, Meshach, and Abednego, in Daniel 3, and Mordecai, in Esther 3. Although the New Testament records events that include apostles and angels forbidding others to bow before them (Acts 14:14–15; Rev 19:10), this definitely was not true of God's agents in Old Testament times. Various writers record positively that people bowed down before Jonathan, David, Bathsheba, Elijah, and Elisha.

Second, the behaviors among the Jewish people of Jesus's time seem to have been very much like those described in the Old Testament. When it was a proper and respectful way of honoring of a person's role before God, it was fine to bow before someone; but when it was in any way idolatrous, it was forbidden.

Like the Hebrew (*chavah* = *bow down* in honor and often *worship*), the Greek *proskuneō*, which was usually used in the Greek Old Testament to translate *chavah*, is used in the New Testament literature to describe the very concrete action of bowing before someone. Although our English word *worship* is amorphous and ambiguous, most of the biblical words involved in *worship* originally described very specific physical behaviors. This certainly true of *proskuneō*.

Given the first century Jewish context, it might well have been an astounding development for people to bow before a commoner from Nazareth, who was not even a well-credentialed rabbi from Jerusalem or Babylon. It certainly would have been more astounding to find people still bowing before this person after he was executed on a Roman cross as a blasphemer of God and a traitor to Rome. Still, there is nothing in the New Testament that indicates that bowing before Jesus, then or now, inherently separates him from being fully rooted in our humanity. Matthew often records people bowing before Jesus. At least some, perhaps all, of these recorded events are the actions of people who did not think they were bowing before God, but rather before an amazing teacher and healer who came from God. Here is one example:

> Then *those who were in the boat worshiped* [*prosekunasan* = *bowed before*] *him*, saying, "Truly you are the Son of God" (Matt 14:33, *emphasis mine*).

Perhaps you are thinking that I just chose as my first example one that proves me wrong. I suggest that the narrative context in Matthew proves my point. Rather than an awesome response such as "Now we know Jesus is God," this passage is followed by the kinds of responses one would expect from disciples of a highly respected *man of God*. They respond to him as a master teacher, whose followers considered him to be wonderful, and hopefully their future king who would sit on the throne as David's son, who was also God's son (2 Samuel 7). Nevertheless, they also see their beloved friend and Rabbi as a little erratic and far from infallible. Only a few paragraphs later, Matthew includes the following much less respectful interaction between Jesus and his disciples. These disciples are tired and harried; so, they command (not ask) Jesus to get with the program in order that they might experience the restful vacation they all traveled so far to enjoy.

> Jesus did not answer a word. *So* his disciples came to him and *urged* [Greek imperfect = *kept urging*] him, "*Send* [Greek imperative] *her away*, for she keeps crying out after us" (Matt 15:23, *emphasis mine*).

"Send her away" is as blunt a confrontation with Jesus by his disciples as any I ever experienced as a fallible pastor when congregational members were frustrated with my slowness to act. The disciples were very frustrated with Jesus's lack of action, they told him so, and they told him what to do to make things right. He had assigned them the ministry of protecting his boundaries, and now he was ignoring their attempts to do so. They told him off!

In fact, the disciples regularly reprimanded and corrected Jesus, even as they also bowed before him. The following passage occurs just a bit later in Matthew's Gospel. Peter lauded Jesus's uniqueness and immediately followed this with the disrespectful, though passionately loving, accusation that Jesus had just expressed both very bad theology and very bad intentions. At that moment, Peter did not seem to think Jesus understood God's way very well, and he certainly didn't think Jesus was showing much wisdom. Jesus had just made it plain that he was heading straight into the domain of his powerful enemies, and it would cost him his life. Peter tried to straighten Jesus out, saying in essence, "We have a good thing going up here in Galilee, and God is blessing us. Why ruin a good thing?" Clearly, the Gospel writer thought one could bow before Jesus without implying that you thought Jesus was standing before you as the infallible God.

> [15] "But what about you?" he asked. "Who do you say I am?" [16] Simon Peter answered, "*You are the Christ, the Son of the living God.*" [17] Jesus replied, "Blessed are you, Simon son of Jonah, for this was not revealed to you by man, but by my Father in heaven. [21] From that time on Jesus began to explain to his disciples that *he must go to Jerusalem and suffer many things* at the hands of the elders, chief priests and teachers of the law, and that he must be killed and on the third day be raised to life. [22] Peter took him aside and *began to rebuke him*. "Never, Lord!" he said. "This shall never happen to you!" (Matt 16:15–17, 21–22, *emphasis mine*).

Neither literarily nor historically is there reason to think Matthew's use of "bowing before" Jesus in any of the following instances implies Jesus is seen as something other than, or more than, a highly honored human. The Greek *proskuneō* word group, sometimes translated "worship" and sometimes "bow before," is used often in Matthew with no indication of divinity (Matt 2:11, 8:2, 9:18, 15:25, and 17:14). Matthew also uses the Greek *gonupeteō* (worship/bow) with no indication that it always implies divinity (Matt 20:20, 27:29, 28:9, 28:17). It describes both the action of mockingly honoring Jesus as King of the Jews by Roman soldiers, as well as the awe-filled honor of disciples bowing before the risen Jesus. Fascinatingly, it even describes disciples bowing before the risen Jesus while simultaneously "many" of these same disciples "doubted" (Matt 28:17).

I think the same honoring of a fellow human is reflected in the usage of *proskuneō* (honor, bow before, worship) in John. It can describe a direct response to Jesus's challenge to a man just healed from blindness to "*trust* in the Son of *Man* (John 9:38, *emphasis mine*)." John also describes Jesus's good friend Mary as "falling to the ground [*piptō* in Greek]" before Jesus. Mary honors Jesus as a person with exceptional God-granted authority. Frustrated and fearless, she simultaneously reprimands him for failing to be the friend she hoped for (John 11:32).

Mark and Luke also use these same Greek words *proskuneō* (bowed before), *prospiptō* (fall down before), and *gonupeteō* (Mark 1:40, 5:6, 7:25, 10:17; Luke 5:12, 24:5, 24:52). Of these passages, Luke 24:52 would be the one most reasonably interpreted as a response implying, "Now we know 'Jesus is God,' and we are worshiping him as God." However, Luke's other uses of the word make this unlikely.

Third, there are two other passages that indicate the words "bowing before/worshiping" in the New Testament did not separate Jesus from our humanity. Jesus tells a parable that assumes his Jewish audience would expect servants to bow before a human master (Matt 18:26–27 using *prosekunei*—"fell on his knees"). It is not idolatry in the parable; it is begging. The servant is appropriately bowing/worshiping before someone who is not God.

Revelation gives us a clear indication that "worship" does not separate Jesus from our humanity. On the one hand, there is a passage that clearly describes honoring the risen and exalted Jesus by bowing before him—"The four living creatures said, 'Amen,' and the elders *fell down and worshiped* [*prosekunēsan* in Greek]" (Rev 5:14, *emphasis mine*). On the other hand, the same author uses the same familiar Greek word to describe *how God wants some humans to be honored by other humans.*

> I will make those of the synagogue of Satan who say that they are Jews and are not, but are lying—I will make them *come and bow down* [*proskunēsousin*] before your feet, and *they will learn that I have loved you* (Rev 3:9, *emphasis mine*).

I am always a bit hesitant to refer to this passage that critiques some Jewish people of the first century, because Christians have frequently used such passages to justify their anti-Semitic heresy, but it is enlightening for our current topic. As we read the passage, we need to remember that many Christians have similarly criticized fellow Christians through the centuries, and that many Jews during the writer's time critiqued fellow Jews with similar wording. It is also important to note that other New Testament writers use the noun and verb forms of the word translated *synagogue* to describe gatherings of Jesus's followers.[10]

With those realities in mind, we see the very frustrated Jewish author of Revelation saying that the risen Jesus's critique of some of the author's Jewish peers includes a promise that they will have to bow before Jesus's followers (Jews and Gentiles). This promise seems to be a loose allusion to several passages (Gen 27:29; Isa 45:14, 49:23, 60:14; Pss 45:11, 72:9; Prov 14:19; Zech 8:22–23), some of which explicitly promise that at some future time, the gentiles of the world will bow before faithful Jews, honoring their covenant relationship with YHWH. These are hardly anti-Semitic sources for the promise! The Jewish writer repurposes the promise. The attackers, though ethnically Jewish, are acting like the gentiles referred to in the Old Testament. So, like the gentiles in those promises, they will someday have to "worship/bow down" before the Jewish and gentile followers of Jesus in the church at Philadelphia, humans who definitely are not God.

To summarize, the act of "worshiping/bowing before" is an act that can honor God *and* an act that can honor God's human agents. In Jesus's world, it was also a word describing the act of honoring someone of higher social status. There is no compelling reason to think that when it is used of honoring Jesus it somehow separates him from his, or our, humanity.

Jesus Says, "I Am." Isn't He Saying He Is God?

"I am." This is a rather common statement in most languages throughout history including ours. And yet, sometimes it does seem to be loaded with extra weight when Jesus uses the phrase. That is especially true in the Gospel of John. The questions surrounding Jesus's "I am" statements are related to his "Lordship," but because these words are often used to separate Jesus from our humanity, it is important to treat them separately. It seems to be true, though not without some controversy, that the name YHWH, which God gives as God's new name in Exodus 3 and 6, reflects the Hebrew words that could be translated either as "I am who I am" or "I will be who I will be." It is also true that Isaiah (example Isa 48:12) emphasizes YHWH as speaking powerfully with the Hebrew words *ani hou* ("I he" or "I am"), which were translated in the Greek Old Testament as *ego eimi* ("I am").

Jesus makes some very powerful "I am" statements that the Gospel of John translated with the Greek phrase *ego eimi*. Whatever words Jesus had used in Aramaic, they must have been edgy given the contexts in which John records them. However, as I will note shortly, the phrase was also in common everyday use in New Testament *Koine* Greek.

---

10. Simkins. *Truth, Tears*, 76

At least two of the quotations seem to indicate Jesus is claiming some type of undefined preexistence in God's covenant purpose. However, as Raymond Brown, who thinks John's Gospel is definitely focused on Jesus's divinity, made clear with his usual candor, it is not true the Greek *ego eimi* ("I am") would necessarily have been understood as a claim to be "God" or "Yahweh." He notes that *ego eimi* appears in the New Testament, and in the Greek translation of the Old Testament, as "a phrase of common speech, equivalent to 'it is I' or 'I am the one.'"

Brown thought several passages (John 8:24, 28, 48, 13:19) were especially likely to imply "I am God"; yet he also acknowledges that other scholars disagree. He even presents the evidence indicating the edgy use of *ego eimi* might have been commonly understood as implying "I am the Messiah." Jesus used *ego eimi* as the false claim of Messiahship (Mark 13:6; Luke 21:8). The parallel in Matthew uses "Messiah/Christ" instead of "I am" (Matt 24:23–25) to be sure the reader understands. Bolstering this argument even further, Jesus's answer to the High Priest's question "Are you the Messiah?" is *ego eimi* (Mark 14:62).[11]

There are also passages in the New Testament that record people other than Jesus using *ego eimi* of themselves with no additional predicate. Perhaps the most important, because it occurs right in the middle of Jesus's most powerful uses of the *ego eimi* phrase in John 7–10, is when a blind beggar uses the same phrase with no predicate just as Jesus had a few paragraphs earlier in John.

> [8] His neighbors and those who had formerly seen him begging asked, "Isn't this the same man who used to sit and beg?" [9] Some claimed that he was. Others said, "No, he only looks like him." But he himself insisted, "*I am [ego eimi]* . . . " (John 9:8–9, *emphasis mine*).

Although it is often supplied in English translations, there is no word for "the man" in Greek. The phrase stands alone, and the beggar says, as Jesus had just said, "*ego eimi* [I am]!"

Here are two other examples: (1) Paul is quoted as using the phrase of himself in Acts 22:3 and 26:29, and (2) each of the Apostles uses the *ego eimi*, with no predicate, of himself at the Last Supper (Matt 26:22, 25), though including a negative in the phrase. Each disciple is hoping Jesus will respond "Of course not you!" But Jesus doesn't. It seems clear to me that the various writers of these New Testament books would never have used "I am" in their records of other people's conversations if Jesus had used it to mean "I am God." That would be especially true of the beggar in John 9:9. Why cloud the issue by telling us other people used the same phrase when referring to themselves?

Jesus uses the phrase "I am" while claiming to be "the shepherd," "the light," "the truth," and "the life," all of which are phrases sometimes used to refer to God in the Old Testament. We also have Jesus saying "I am" and claiming to be "the way," "the

---

11. Brown, *John*, vol 1, 533–538.

vine," and "the gate," all of which speak of a pathway to reach God. "Light," "truth," and "life" are also used of God's words in the Old Testament, as well as of God. "Shepherd" is used, not only of God, but also of God's human agents in both testaments. So, the overall New Testament context has to help us determine whether Jesus was implying "I am God" or "I am the unique agent of God's revelation."

Finally, what puzzles me most about many who claim that some of the *ego eimi* passages indicate that Jesus was consciously claiming to be God is that these same theologians and pastors often interpret numerous other New Testament passages as though Jesus had been "emptied" of any self-consciousness of being God. Surely, we cannot claim that the use of the *ego eimi* statements indicate that Jesus is clearly conscious of a second nature as God (*YHWH*) on some days, although on other days he is not conscious of being God or even of experiencing God's presence. By no means the only instances, but the most powerful instances portraying a lack of "I am God" consciousness are the prayers, "Not my will, but your will," and, "My God, my God, why have you forsaken me?"

My point here is that Jesus's use of *ego eimi* does not provide us with an obvious claim that Jesus was separating himself from the rest of us humans. Whether "Jesus is God" or not must be decided from other passages. Meanwhile, we should be able to agree that he cannot be aware of a second nature on some days and not on other days. And perhaps we can agree that if he was always aware that he "is God," many passages are very difficult to make sense of. And, whether we say so or not, I would argue that most of us find Jesus a less meaningful model for how to live a faithful human life if we allow ourselves to qualify his faithfulness with "But he was God! How can I be expected to act like that? I am not God!"

Finally, if Jesus was not consciously aware of a "second nature" as "God," and was therefore experiencing being human as the rest of us do, then we need to understand the *ego eimi* passages within that paradigm. It seems to me that the clearest way through this interpretive dilemma is to remember that the writers were not focused on issues of essence, substance, and second nature, but rather were focused on the amazing relationship shared between the faithful human Jesus and the faithful Abba who was always with the human Jesus.

JESUS IS THE WORD OF GOD.

As noted in chapter 6, Jesus is celebrated as the new and deeper form of the "word of God" in the New Testament. What had once been identified with Torah, and with the words and actions of the great prophets, now becomes incarnate in a human named Jesus. This way of identifying Jesus introduces Hebrews (1:1–3), and most famously introduces the Gospel of John. Speaking of Jesus as God's "word" is clearly one of the ways of exalting him and his role in God's self-revelation. I definitely do not question that! It is also often presented as a claim that Jesus is something in addition to being human. That move I do question.

Because God's revelation of Jesus as "Word" is most often focused on John's prologue, let's look at that together. I would argue that the tendency of many commentators and translations to import "Jesus" or "the Son" back into the entire prologue beginning with verse 1 is quite arbitrary. John's soaring poetic introduction uses the Greek word *logos* ("word") only two times (1:1, 14). I am going to use my own translation of the prologue in order to reflect the use of *logos* (word) and *phos* (light) as the referents of the many pronouns used throughout the prologue. I am not attempting to bias the translation. I am attempting to provide a neutral or unbiased translation. To translate these pronouns as "he" is to bias the translation just as much as it would be to translate them all as "it." Both are viable translation choices, but each biases the translation beginning with the second verse.

To avoid this interpretive choice, I note the words the pronouns refer back to in the text—"word/*logos*" and "light/*phos*" and "John." To be certain that I was being as neutral and accurate as possible, I asked a good friend who works regularly in New Testament Greek to check the translation carefully for me and to offer any needed improvements. There are a few verses where it isn't clear, at least to me, whether the pronoun refers to "word" or "light;" so I attempted to show that as well. Again, as you read, note that the word *logos* ("word") appears only in 1:1, 14.

> [1] In the beginning was the word [*logos*], and the word [*logos*] continued to be with God, and the word [*logos*] continued to be God. [2] The word [*outos*] was with God in the beginning. [3] Through the word [*autou*] *all things were made*; without the word [*autou*] nothing was made that has been made. [4] In the word [*auto*] was life, and that life was *the light of humans.* [5] The light continually shines in the darkness, and the darkness never destroys the light [*auto*].
>
> [6] A man came—he was sent by God—his [*auto*] name was John. [7] He [*outos*] came as a witness to testify to the light, so that all might trust through the light [*autos*]. [8] That one was not the light, but he came to testify to the light.
>
> [9] The authentic light that enlightens every human was coming into the world. [10] The light/word [*autou*] was in the world, and though the world was made through the light/word [*auton*], the world did not recognize the light/word [*auton*]. [11] The light/word ("he" or "it" contained in the verb) came to what he/it owned, but the [light's or word's] own did not receive the light/word [*auton*].
>
> [12] But to all who received the light/word [*auton*], to those the light/word ["he" or "it" contained in the verb] gave the authority to become children of God—those trusting in the name of the light/word [*auton*]. [13] These were not children because of blood, or because of the will of the flesh, or because of the will of a male, but because they were *born of God.*
>
> [14] And the word [*logos*] became flesh, and he [contained in the verb] made his tent among us. We have seen the glory of the word [*autou*], the glory of

the *only-born* who came from the Father, full of grace and truth. [16] From the fullness of his [*autou*] grace we have all received grace piled upon grace. [17] For the law was given through Moses; grace and truth came through Jesus the Messiah (translation by the author) (John 1:1–14, 16–17).

I have two further notes concerning my admittedly rough translation:

1. I am using "born" and "only-born" because alternatives such as begotten, sired, caused, or engendered didn't seem any better. More importantly for our purposes, it needs to be clear that the same Greek word group is represented in the translation of John 1:13, referring to other children "born of God" as in 1:14, referring to Jesus with the addition of "only. All of God's children must be "born of God," and yet Jesus is the "only-born" (*see* the same progression in John 3:3–6, 16). This seems to be similar to designating Jesus as the "firstborn." Like Isaac was described as Abraham's "only son," even though in other ways he was one of several sons, John describes Jesus as the "only-born," while also telling us that there were humans prior to and after Jesus who are "born of God." Being God's child and born of God stresses that Jesus is unique, and also not so unique, in his relationship to the rest of us humans.

2. I am not omitting 1:18 because it does not fit my point. Some translations fit my point quite well and others not as well. However, the last half of the verse is textually uncertain, and both text and translation are the source of much scholarly disagreement. It seems clear that the original ending of 1:18 emphasized the uniqueness of Jesus's relationship with God and the revelation that came from that relationship; it just isn't clear with our current textual knowledge exactly what was being said about it. Some texts indicate it is a claim Jesus is "God" in some sense, others do not. Fascinatingly, the part of 1:18 that is textually certain and is almost always translated similarly is "No person has ever seen God . . ." This is a very strange way to begin this last sentence of the prologue if the author's main point was to tell us that "Jesus is God."

At this point, I will no longer attempt to remain neutral. It seems to me that the beautiful and poetic prologue did not intend for the reader to immediately insert Jesus as the "Word." Reading the prologue as I am suggesting, allows John 1:1–3, including its leading phrase "in the beginning," to remind the reader that passages such as Genesis 1 ("And God said"), Proverbs 3:19–20, and Psalm 19 all present the creation as an expressive revelation of a communicating God. In fact, Genesis 1 is saturated with the Hebrew *dbr*, which is the source throughout the Old Testament of both the verb translated "said" and the noun translated "word."

As I read it, John's prologue then continues in 1:4–5 by reminding the reader that throughout the history that prepared for the coming of "the Son," God the Communicator par Excellence communicated "God's word" in various ways by various means. This claim would parallel the way Hebrews begins: "In the past God spoke to our forefathers through the prophets at many times and in various ways" (Heb 1:1).

I am told (I did not count myself) that the Old Testament writers claim over 3000 times some form of "the Lord says" and "God has spoken." The "Word of God" in the Old Testament is also a phrase often applied to the Torah. Proverbs 2–8 reminds us that Torah, morality, and right relationships all flow from hearing and obeying the instructions God communicates to a willing listener. A psalmist proclaims "Your (Yahweh's) *word* is a *lamp* to my feet and a *light* to my path" (Ps 119:105, *emphasis mine*), and then witnesses to the power of God's revelation with the words "by them [God's precepts or communications] you have *preserved my life*" (Ps 119:93, *emphasis mine*). These themes of "light" and "life" and "word" run throughout the Old Testament as descriptions of God's revelatory actions. I think it is that background that the prologue is referring to.

John 1:6–8 introduces God's next preparatory communication—John the Baptist who is the most recent prophetic voice calling upon God's children to hear God as God speaks to them through his agent. He is not the full incarnation of God's "light," but he is commissioned by God to proclaim that what has long been prepared for is now about to occur.

Then John 1:9–13 continues the transition from the past into the present by reiterating themes that were true in the Old Testament times and have recently been brought to a new level of fulfillment. Proverbs 2–8 insists, as do Amos 1–5 and Psalm 19 from different perspectives, that God's revelatory light and God's revelatory word have been coming to humans throughout history. Sadly, God's communication has been ignored more often than it has been heeded.

This part of the prologue that emphasizes the tendency to reject God's revelation is preparing us for the rest of John's Gospel, which claims that this sad pattern has happened again. Although many see God's revelation in Jesus, many also reject God's revelation just as the Old Testament narrates so often concerning God's earlier "words." However, God's word has also always been able to create "children of God." First, when at creation God spoke, and humans were created as children of God (Luke 3:38; Ps 8). Later, God spoke the words of the covenant with Abraham and created Israel as God's unique children (Ps 82:6; Exod 4:22–23; Isa 1:2–4; Hos 1:10).

Although it is somewhat rare, there are scholars who think that Jesus as the Son begins to be referred to only in 1:14, whereas others think the reference begins in 1:10 or 1:12.[12] These scholars think everything earlier is a reference to God's preparation for the Son, but does not refer to the Son himself. Again, this way of understanding the prologue would parallel Hebrews: "But in these last days he has spoken to us by his Son, whom he appointed heir of all things, and through whom he made the universe [ages]" (Heb 1:2).

---

12 Dodd, *Fourth Gospel*, 263–285.

Now, in John 1:14–18, all of this preparation has come to a new level of fulfillment—a new level of truth, glory, grace, life, light, and word (communication). It has all been embodied in human flesh, in a Son who never fails to be faithful to God. Now the God who came to dwell in the midst of his people in the tent in the wilderness has come to dwell in the midst of his people in the human Jesus who is the new Tabernacle/Temple of God's Presence (1:14).

Whether you think 1 John is by the same author as John's Gospel as I tend to, or by a different "John" as many scholars argue, almost everyone agrees that 1 John has the Gospel in mind. I think the author of 1 John understood John's prologue to emphasize the way God reveals God's-self is through God's relationship with the human Jesus. That is how God is revealed more clearly than ever before as "Father." However, we also find the parallel emphases on the fact that no human has ever seen God, while many humans have seen, touched, and heard Jesus the Son. As in the Gospel, also in the letter, Jesus is the way that God reveals more life, more light, and more love so we can become more and more like Jesus—the Jesus whom humans have seen even though we cannot see God.

> ¹ That which was *from the beginning*, which we have *heard*, which we have *seen* with our *eyes*, which we have *looked* at and our *hands* have t*ouched*—this we proclaim concerning the *Word* of *life*. ² The *life appeared*; we have *seen* it and testify to it, and we proclaim to you the eternal *life*, which was with the Father and has *appeared to us* (1 John 1:1–2, *emphasis mine*)

The incarnated word of God was not just a verbal message, but a human whom other humans could encounter empirically in the space-and-time world, where he could be touched and seen. Nevertheless, although some of us humans have now been privileged to see with our eyes and touch with our hands the very life of God as it was expressed in Jesus's relationship with God, it is still true that "*no human has ever seen God*" (1 John 4:12, 4:20, *emphasis mine*). Thankfully, in 1 John, as in other passages (2 Cor 4:5–6; 2 Pet 1:16–18; John 20:21), we are assured that though many of us have not been privileged to touch and gaze upon Jesus, this self-revelation of life from God, and light from God, can still be experienced in our relationship with God through Jesus. "Anyone who has seen me has seen the Father" (John 14:9).

Taking nothing away from the exaltation that accompanies the New Testament descriptions of Jesus as "word," "light," and "life," it does seem to me that none of these descriptions of Jesus's identity and role in God's revelation in any way separate Jesus from our humanity or serve to describe Jesus as something more than human. They fit within the same paradigm as the occasional New Testament emphasis on Jesus as the incarnation of the "wisdom of God," and the more common emphasis on Jesus as the human who is completely filled with—incarnates—the "Spirit of God." Once again, we have a claim that the relationship between the human Jesus and God is one that leads to the first completed human and the first step in fulfilling God's creation project for humanity—the venture God began by speaking "in the beginning." When we see this self-revelation of God in God's relationship with Jesus, we see far more of who God is and who we are than is available to us by any other means.

Finally, just as the revelation that humans can be the incarnation of communications from God did not begin with Jesus, it does not end with Jesus either. As Jesus is God's word incarnate, his followers can now be the Messiah's *word* incarnate.

> ³You show that *you are a letter from Christ,* the result of our ministry, *written not with ink but with the Spirit of the living God,* not on tablets of stone but *on tablets of human hearts.* (2 Cor 3:3, *emphasis mine*).

Paul even claims that God is "exhorting/calling/appealing to" (*parakalountos*) other humans to be reconciled to God through Jesus's followers (2 Cor 5:20). We too are called to be the Father's communication to the world around us (Matt 10:20).

As followers of Jesus we are to be the "*light* of the world" (Matt 5:14–16) as Jesus is. Our relationship with Jesus is to make us "sons of light" (John 12:36; Eph 5:8; 1 Thess 5:5). In fact, Paul and Barnabas apply to their ministry the same reference from Isaiah that the angel told Mary would apply to Jesus—"a light to the Gentiles" (Isa 49:6; Acts 13:47; Luke 2:32).

Followers of Jesus are also to be the source of *life* for others. Streams of living water are to flow from Jesus through us out into the world around us (John 7:37–39). We are "the fragrance of life" as we follow Jesus through this age (2 Cor 2:16), and God has made us ministers of life (2 Cor 3:6). We are even told that our prayers can open the channels for God to give other humans life, and save them from death (1 John 5:16; Jas 5:20).

Perhaps most astounding of all is the claim that through our *love*, people can see God incarnate. "No one has ever seen God; but if we love one another, *God lives in us*, and *his love is made complete* in us" (1 John 4:12, *emphasis mine*).

In short, there is nothing inherent in the New Testament use of "word," "light," or "life" that separates Jesus from humanity—not from those who preceded him and not from those of us who come after him. Uniquely human? Yes! But really one of us!

JESUS IS: BORN OF GOD, FROM GOD, SENT BY GOD, BORN FROM ABOVE, AND THE HUMAN-OF-HEAVEN. GOD LIVES IN (INCARNATES) JESUS.

Often, the descriptions of Jesus as "from above," "of heaven," "from God," "sent from God," and "born of God" are read as though they somehow separate Jesus from our humanity. On the other hand, when the same phrases are applied to Jesus's followers, we never think of reading them in that manner.

Jesus Is One of Us

Jesus "Came from God," and Is "from God," "out of God," and "Sent from God."

Jesus is often described in these and similar terms. The following passages from John are only a few of many possible examples.

> He [Nicodemus] came to Jesus at night and said, "Rabbi, we know you are a teacher who *has come from* [*apo* in Greek] *God*. For no one could perform the miraculous signs you are doing if God were not with him" (John 3:2, *emphasis mine*).

> "My food," said Jesus, "is to do the will of him *who sent me* and to finish his work. (John 4:34, *emphasis mine*).

> Not that anyone has seen the Father *except the one who is from* [*para* in Greek] *God*; he has seen the Father (John 6:46, *emphasis mine*).

> Anyone who resolves to do the will of God will know whether the *teaching is from* [*ek* in Greek] *God* or whether I am speaking on my own (John 7:17, *emphasis mine*).

> But now you are trying to kill me, a man who has told you *the truth that I heard from* [*para* in Greek] *God* (John 8:40, *emphasis mine*).

> Jesus, knowing that the Father had given all things into his hands, and that *he had come from* [*ek* in Greek] *God* and was going to God . . ." (John 13:3, *emphasis mine*).

> The Word became flesh and made his dwelling among us. We have seen his glory, the glory of the One and Only, who *came from* [*para* in Greek] *the Father*, full of grace and truth (John 1:14, *emphasis mine*).

Other Humans, too, "Came from God," and Are "from God," "out of God," and "Sent from God."

Perhaps surprisingly to some of us, these same phrases that refer to Jesus are also used to describe other humans in the New Testament. The following citations are a few examples that ascribe these same descriptions, used of Jesus, to his followers as well. If they apply to our humanity, there are strong reasons to see them as applying to Jesus's humanity as well.

John the Baptist, who precedes Jesus, is "a man *sent* from God" (John 1:6). Followers of Jesus are identified by the phrases heading this section as the following examples indicate.

> For we are not peddlers of God's word like so many; but in Christ we speak as persons of sincerity, *as persons sent from* [*ek* in Greek] *God and standing in God's presence* (2 Cor 2:17, *emphasis mine*).

> [4] Little *children, you are from* [*ek* in Greek] *God*, and have conquered them; for the One *who is in you* is greater than the one who is in the world . . . [6a] *We are from* [*ek*] *God* (1 John 4:4, 6a, emphasis mine).

> Unlike so many, we do not peddle the word of God for profit. On the contrary, in Christ we speak before God with sincerity, *like men sent from God* (2 Cor 2:17, emphasis mine; see John 20:21).

Jesus Is the "Human of Heaven."

Jesus is identified as a "human of heaven" and as one who "came down from heaven."

> [38] For I have *come down from heaven*, not to do my own will, but the will of him who sent me. [41] "I am the bread which *came down from heaven.*" (John 6:38, 41, emphasis mine).

> The first man [human] was *from* [*ek* in Greek] *the dust of the earth, the second man* [human] *is from* [*ek* in Greek] *heaven* (1 Cor 15:47, emphasis mine).

Others, too, Are "Humans of Heaven."

Not only Jesus, but because of their relationship with Jesus, Jesus's followers are also described by Paul as "humans of heaven," who are and will be like Jesus in this respect.

> [47] The first man [human] was of the dust of the earth, the second *man* [*human*] *from heaven.* [48] As was the earthly man, so are those who are of the earth; and *as is the man* [human] *from heaven, so also are those who are of heaven.* [49] And just as we have borne the likeness of the earthly man [human], *so shall we bear the likeness of the man* [human] *from heaven* (1 Cor 15:47–49, emphasis mine; see also 1 John 3:1–3).

Jesus Is Born of the Spirit of God.

In various ways, the Gospel writers tell us that Jesus is a human, born of the Spirit of God. Here are two well-known claims:

> The angel answered, "*The Holy Spirit will come upon you*, and the power of the Most High will overshadow you. So the holy one *to be born will be called the Son of God* (Luke 1:35, emphasis mine).

> The *Word became flesh* and made his *dwelling among us*. We have seen his glory, *the glory of the One and Only,* who *came from the Father*, full of grace and truth. (John 1:14, emphasis mine).

Others, too, Are Born of the Spirit of God.

Once again, this relationship of being born of God is reflected not only in the Old Testament passages that speak of Israel as God's firstborn and as God's "sons," but the role is also a status held by the followers of Jesus.

> [12] Yet *to all who received him*, to those who believed in his name, he gave the right to *become children of God*—[13] children *born not* of natural descent, nor of human decision or a husband's will, but *born of God* (John 1:12–13, *emphasis mine*).

> In reply Jesus declared, "I tell you the truth, no one can see the kingdom of God *unless he is born again*" (John 3:3, *emphasis mine*; NIV footnote reads "Or, 'born from above'").

John's prologue is often described as a section of the New Testament that most clearly separates Jesus from other humans, yet John immediately introduces the dynamic tension that runs all through the New Testament. Jesus is truly one of us, "flesh" (1:14), and Jesus is truly unique. Jesus comes from the Father and is "Son" in a unique sense, and through the relationship Jesus shares with God, we too can be "born of God" and "become children of God" (John 1:12–13).

This dynamic tension between uniqueness and sameness carries over in the letter of 1 John.

> [1] Everyone who believes that Jesus is the Christ *is born of God*, and *everyone who loves the father loves his child* as well. . . . [4] for *everyone born of God* overcomes the world (1 John 5:1, 4, *emphasis mine*; *see* also John 3:5; 1 John 3:9; 1 Pet 1:23).

The New Testament writers use phrases such as "from God" or "out of God," or "of heaven," and "born of God" to describe the uniqueness in the covenant-relationship between God and Jesus. They also use these same phrases to describe what God has made possible through Jesus for Jesus's followers. The descriptions do not separate Jesus from our humanity, but rather embed us in Jesus's humanity and in his relationship with God.

God Incarnates (Lives In) Jesus.

That Jesus is the incarnation of God's Word and of God's Spirit is basic to almost all Christian teaching. Not only does John's beautiful prologue tell us that the creative word of God came to tabernacle among us in Jesus (John 1:14), Paul too, proclaims that "in Christ all the fullness of the Deity lives in bodily form" (Col 2:9, and see 1:19).

God Incarnates (Lives in) Other Humans, Too.

Although the claim that Jesus is a human in whom God lives is often understood to separate Jesus from our humanity, this claim embeds him in our humanity. One way we see this is through the many times the New Testament speaks of the Messiah "living in us" and the Holy Spirit being given to live in us.

John specifically includes followers of Jesus as incarnated by God: "No one has ever seen God; but if we love one another, *God lives in us* and his love is made complete in us" (1 John 4:12, *emphasis mine*). To make sure we understand that we are included in "incarnation" by God, the author says it again a few sentences later: "God is love. Whoever lives in love lives in God, and *God in him*" (1 John 4:16, *emphasis mine*). The author also describes followers of Jesus in a manner quite reminiscent of the description of Jesus's incarnation by God's *logos* (word) in John's Gospel: "the word [*logos*] of God *lives in you*" (1 John 2:14, *emphasis mine*).

Paul is also quite specific. In a context filled with encouragement to think and behave like Jesus, Paul says, "For it is *God who works in you* to will and to act according to his good purpose" (Phil 2:13). In a less specific, but important, incarnational statement, Paul reminds his readers that the fullness of God that currently dwells in the Messiah (Col 1:19) is also currently dwelling in his followers (Col 2:9–10, *see* also Rom 8:9; 1 Cor 6:19; Eph 2:22).

A parallel to Paul's assertion that other humans can participate in "the fullness of God" occurs in another letter, as well. Followers of Jesus are told that through this relationship with Jesus "you may *participate in the divine nature*" (2 Pet 1:4, *emphasis mine*).

JESUS'S PRAYER FOR HIS FOLLOWERS EMBEDS HIM IN OUR HUMANITY.

Jesus's prayer as recorded in John 17 includes a strong emphasis on Jesus being "in God" and God being "in Jesus." It is easy to read these statements as though they are separating Jesus from the rest of us humans. However, Jesus's prayer states exactly the opposite. He prays that his followers too may share the same relationship with God: "That all of them may be one, Father, *just as you are in me and I am in you. May they also be in us* so that the world may believe that you have sent me (John 17:21, *emphasis mine*). Jesus goes on to pray that those of us who will come along much later will also see what God revealed through Jesus—we are loved by God with the same love that God has for Jesus (John 17:26).

Twice during this prayer, Jesus promises to "*be in*" his disciples just as God is "in" Jesus. He also asks God to give his fellow human followers the same "*glory*" from God, the same "*love*" from God, the same being "*in God*," and the same *oneness* Jesus shares with God.

These themes continue in various parts of the New Testament writings. Paul often writes to his listeners as people who are people "in the Messiah" (1 Cor 1:30) and who "the Messiah is in" (Rom 8:10; Gal 2:20; Col 1:27). Another letter identifies the new followers of Jesus in Thessalonica as an "assembly *in* God" (1 Thess 1:1). And, though many might think what separates Jesus from our humanity is that God lives in (incarnates) Jesus, as mentioned earlier, the writer of 1 John tells his readers that "*God lives in us* and *his love is made complete in us*" (4:12. *emphasis mine*; *see* also 4:16; Eph 2:22). I cannot think of a stronger way of embedding us in the same incarnational relationship Jesus had and has with the Father.

There do not seem to be any ways that Jesus's relationship with God separates Jesus from our humanity except—a huge exception—that he was the human uniquely faithful to God in every great success, every bitter trial, and every uneventful day, without sinning.

JESUS IS ONE WITH GOD.

Although "one" is often used in the New Testament as the cardinal number "1," there is also a very strong theological focus on "one" as a relational description. It is used quite often to describe interpersonal human relationships. I think it is clear that "one" is also used to describe the relationship between Jesus and God. This relational emphasis fully embeds Jesus in our humanity and in the relationship God wishes to have with the rest of us humans.

Interpersonal covenant relationships, in contrast to contracts, always involve us in something deeper than our reason can fully comprehend. That does not mean they are "irrational." We Western Christians need to learn that *more than rational is not the same as irrational*! This type of relational *oneness* was celebrated by the ancient Psalmist who wrote: "How good and pleasant it is when *brothers live together in unity*" (Ps 133:1, *emphasis mine*). It is a *oneness* that is both rational and more than rational, but it is far from irrational.

In the New Testament, an even deeper level of relational *oneness* with God and with one another is celebrated. This *oneness* with God includes not only the human Jesus, but is extended to the relationship God desires to have with other humans as well. The New Testament books that especially emphasize this relational *oneness* include Ephesians, 1 Corinthians, John's Gospel, and Acts. Although passages using "one" when applied to Jesus are often quoted as evidence that the writers were describing Jesus as of "one" essence or substance with God, the language they use, and the contexts in which they use this language, demonstrate that they were instead describing a relational *oneness*. That seems obvious once we note that they use the same language to talk about the relationships that the rest of us can have with God, with Jesus, and with one another.

In the letter to the Ephesians, there is a biblical example of the "mystery" of relational *oneness*. The writer compares the *oneness* spoken of in the biblical description of sexual *oneness* in marriage with the *oneness* Jesus shares with the church. Clearly the *oneness* the writer of Ephesians is describing in the following quotations is the relational *oneness* possible in a covenant relationship, not numerical identity of substance or essence. It is not because two people become one essence, but because two people enter the covenant relationship of marriage that they are "one." The writer also claims a similar *oneness* of relationship can be experienced as followers of Jesus become one with Jesus the Messiah and with the rest of his followers.

> [30] . . .for we are *members of his body*. [31] "For this reason a man will leave his father and mother and *be united* to his wife, and the *two will become one* flesh." [32] This is a profound mystery—but I am talking about *Christ and the church*. [33] However, *each one of you also* must love his wife as he loves himself, and the wife must respect her husband (Eph 5:30–33, *emphasis mine*).

As is easily seen in the next quotation, the writer of Ephesians not only believed that relationally two can be one, but also that x^n (any number) can become "one" when God's spiritual power is at work in covenant relationships. Relational *oneness* is described in terms first century Jews and Gentiles found almost unthinkable prior to what God accomplished through Jesus. Jews and Gentiles are seeing and experiencing one another as complete equals, as sisters and brothers, in the "one" family "household" of God. Psalm 133:1, quoted previously, is now being fulfilled in a manner that exceeds everyone's prior imaginings.

> [13] But now in Jesus Christ you who once were far away have been brought near through the blood of Christ. [14] For he himself is our peace, *who has made the two one and has destroyed the barrier*, the dividing wall of hostility, [15] by abolishing in his flesh the law with its commandments and regulations. *His purpose was to create in himself one new man [humanity] out of the two*, thus making peace, [16] and *in this one body* to reconcile both of them to God through the cross, by which he put to death their hostility (Eph 2:13–16, *emphasis mine*).

John's gospel also describes relational *oneness* ($1 = x^n$) between Jesus and the broader human family of God. Jesus's use of "one" with God in John is often interpreted and preached in ways that intend to separate him from humanity. In contrast, John maintains that Jesus believed the *oneness* occurring in the relationship he and God shared was what God wanted for other humans as well. There is no grammatical or theological reason to think that the use of "one" in the verses below refers to a shared "essence" when applied to Jesus, but only to a shared relationship when applied to the rest of us humans. This is true especially when the same word is used in the very same sentences. Surely, it is the shared relationship that is emphasized in both cases.

> [11] I will remain in the world no longer, but they are still in the world, and I am coming to you. Holy Father, protect them by the power of your name—the name you gave me—*so that they may be one as we are one.* [20] My prayer is not for them alone. I pray also for those who will believe in me through their message, [21] *that all of them may be one, Father, just as you are in me and I am in you.* May they also *be in us* so that the world may believe that you have sent me. (John 17:11, 20–21, *emphasis mine*).

Paul used the concept of relational *oneness* throughout 1 Corinthians in what he called "the *oneness* of the body of Messiah." In fact, one of the main emphases of 1 Corinthians is Paul's insistence that the "One God" wants "One Family" ($x^n = 1$). He pleads with the Corinthian community of Jesus followers to behave accordingly toward one another. Here are two examples:

> Because there is one loaf, *we who are many are one body, for we all partake of the one loaf* (1 Cor 10:17, *emphasis mine*).

> [12] *The body is a unit,* though it is made up of many parts; and though all its parts are many, they *form one body.* So it is with Christ. [13] For we were *all baptized by one Spirit into one body*—whether Jews or Greeks, slave or free—and we were all *given the one Spirit to drink.* [14] Now the body is not made up of one part but of many. . . . [20] As it is, there are *many parts, but one body* (1 Cor 12:12–14, 20, *emphasis mine*).

The relationship among the growing number of followers of Jesus is also described as a deep bond of relational *oneness* in Acts.

> [32] All the believers *were one in heart and mind.* No one claimed that any of his *possessions* was his own, but they *shared everything* they had. (Acts 4:32, *emphasis mine*; compare Acts 2:44–47.)

A *oneness* that touches our core as well as our thinking, and certainly one that touches our bank account and property, is a very deep "family" relationship indeed.

When we are included in Jesus's relationship with God, we are included in a *oneness* that is deeper than even the most intimate of other relationships. Our relationship with God is destined to become more intimate than the best parent-child relationship, more profound than the closest friendship, deeper than the best wife-husband relationship, and closer than closest community relationship. In the words of the Seer, "Now the *dwelling of God is with men* [humans], and He *will live with them*" (Rev 21:3, *emphasis mine*). In Paul's words, "Then we shall *see face to face.* Now I know in part; then *I shall know* [God] *fully, even as I am fully known* [by God]" (1 Cor 13:12, *emphasis mine*). This *oneness* with God does not separate Jesus or his followers from humanness; rather, it allows God to complete our humanness into its intended full potential which includes relational *oneness* forever.

(For further examples of *oneness* as relational, *see* John 10:16, 30, 11:52; Gal 3:20; Phil 1:27, 2:2. Also, *see* the parallel emphasis on having the "same" mind, heart, faith, and behavior in various letters, as well as the focus on "with one accord" and "all things in common" in Acts.)

Oneness with God is demonstrated in Jesus's actions and should be demonstrated in our actions as well. The relational nature of Jesus's *oneness* with God was demonstrated in Jesus's acts of healing and forgiveness. When Jesus healed on the Sabbath, he justified his actions by saying that he could see his Father working and he joined in (John 5:17).

I love being around followers of Jesus who see their calling not primarily in terms of rules and regulations, nor institutional maintenance, nor personal license, but in terms of acting with God on behalf of the people God is wishing to bless. Don't you? When a Fellowship attends to God's commandments as guides for living in a manner that brings grace and good to others, we are obeying in a manner that expresses *oneness* with God and with God's purposes, just as Jesus did.

Jesus saw his concern for the poor, the incarcerated, the physically challenged, and the oppressed as an expression of his *oneness* with God, empowered by the Spirit of God.

> [18] The *Spirit of the Lord is on me*, because *He* [*the Lord*] *has anointed me* to preach good news to *the poor*. He has sent me to proclaim freedom for *the prisoners* and recovery of sight for *the blind*, to release *the oppressed*, [19] to proclaim the year of the Lord's favor (Luke 4:18–19, *emphasis mine*).

Jesus passed this *oneness* with God, and with God's concerns, on to his followers as well. Throughout the New Testament, we are urged to allow the Spirit of God to empower us to bring grace and blessings to the least empowered in our cultures. Church communities are most expressive of *oneness* with God when we are acting in that manner, just as Jesus did.

I watched the completely unexpected results when a sister took a meal to the home of an older woman who had just broken her leg. This older woman and her husband were hurt, bitter, and deeply entrenched in atheism. Much of this had occurred in reaction to the horrendous attitudes and actions of Christian family members. Of course there were several steps along the way, but the meal ultimately led to an openness to Jesus in the lives of this couple and then in the lives of their adult children as well. Not only did they experience a new *oneness* with God, but also a new *oneness* with one another, a new *oneness* with their adult children, and a new *oneness* with a community of people attempting to follow Jesus's way.

Not too long ago, a former prison inmate spoke in our church about being introduced to Jesus when each of his parents, who at that time were not even speaking to one another, independently contacted him on the same day. Each parent told him that the only way his life would change would be to open up to a relationship with Jesus.

Not only did the life of this prisoner change, but that change brought about a healing that allowed the parents to begin treating one another with civility as well. *Oneness* occurred at several levels in this Spirit-empowered process.

When Jesus forgave sins, he did so out of the *oneness* that flowed from his relationship with God (Mark 2:5–17). When he passed this mission on to his followers, he promised them that they could carry it out successfully because they could count on a *oneness* in their relationship with him, as they forgave the sins of others (Matt 18:15–20; John 20:21–23).

Don't you love it when members of a community demonstrate the presence of God's grace and forgiveness, rather than the all too familiar blaming that further entrenches divisions? Most likely you, too, have seen friendships, marriages, parent-child relationships, and church communities healed when *oneness* with God leads to truth, tears, forgiveness, and reconciliation. Most likely, you have also seen the potential *oneness* in each of these relationships shattered when the empowering grace of truth and forgiveness is ignored in favor of getting even.

All relational *oneness* is an amazing gift from God, and each experience of this gift in our various relationships is meant to point us to the greatest possible relational *oneness*—the *oneness* God has made possible between the Messiah and God's people (John 17:22–23; Eph 5:28–33). *Oneness* in relationships is one of those ways in which we are an analogy into which God can speak and reveal to us who God is. The human Jesus lived in a *oneness* with God that we who share his humanity are now invited to share.

Transparency requires me to add, not only have powerful experiences of the *oneness* that our relationship with Jesus can create been the source of some of my greatest joys, it is equally true that some of my greatest heartbreaks and disappointments have been experiencing our failures in this area. I have watched recent followers of Jesus driven away by the divisions among those they looked to as "mature." I have watched entire thriving communities be blown apart over failures to handle differences about the gifts of the Holy Spirit, differences flowing from ethnic and racial backgrounds, differences in understanding exactly how the Bible is "inspired," differences in understandings about what it means to include believers from the LGBTQ community, and differences over preferred worship style. Church history gives us hundreds of other examples of our failures to be the "one" people who Jesus promised could be a powerful witness of God's presence in the world.

Still, I love every experience that allows God to answer Jesus's heartfelt prayer for *oneness* among his followers with "Yes!" As we become more like the human Jesus, we become more available for this great miracle God loves to work among the human children of God.

JESUS IS IMMANUEL—GOD WITH US.

I have always found Jacob's response to his vision of God's angels descending and ascending to be very powerful, challenging, and comforting: "Surely the LORD is in this place, and I was not aware of it" (Gen 28:16). I cannot imagine how many times God has been where I am, and I have been oblivious. Like Jacob, I am glad this has not kept God from trying again to get my attention.

God's presence with God's people is a persistent theme throughout the Old Testament. The cloud of God's presence led Israel in the wilderness. Phrases such as "God with us," "God is with you," "God will be with you," "God was with him," "God was with her," and "God was with them" appear hundreds of times in the Old Testament and the New Testament. Since this description of the relationship between God and humans is one of the most common in the entire Bible, I will not take the space to enumerate examples.

Immanuel—no description of the relationship between God and Jesus could be more indicative of the fact that the New Testament is focused on the relationship between the human Jesus and God. Joseph being told that Jesus will be *Immanuel* (Hebrew for "God-with-us") fulfilled a long-standing pattern. It was also the re-enactment of a specific event with even deeper content (Matt 1:23; Isa 7:14, 8:8–10). Centuries before Jesus was born, another young mother, who lived during the reign of another bad king and during times of foreign oppression, expressed her faith by naming her child "God-with-us" (*Immanuel*). Obviously, that young Israelite mother who named her child "God-with-us" did not mean that her child was God. Even a cursory reading of Isaiah 7:15–17 makes it clear that Isaiah's predictions were to come to fruition within 30 years at most. So this young woman's child was born somewhere around 720 BC, and his mother trusted that, even though the social, political, and religious realities looked dire, "God-is-with-us."

Matthew was claiming the renewal and fulfillment of a pattern in which a faithful God and a faithful young woman interact faithfully toward one another. I do not think Matthew was claiming that the original context predicted Jesus's birth. I think Albright and Mann were correct in maintaining that "fulfillment" in Matthew does not mean prediction, but rather means re-enactment of a pattern by deepening its content.[13]

Ahaz was a bad king; Herod was worse. Oppression by outside Empires made life fearful in both contexts. In both situations, in contrast to a faithless leader, a young maiden trusts that "God is with us!" Both young women take their conception and pregnancy as an opportunity to trust God in very difficult circumstances.[14] The nameless woman of Isaiah's time is amazing; Mary's faithfulness is even more

---

13. Albright and Mann, *Matthew*, LV, 8.

14. The first to marry and then conceive in difficult times, the latter to conceive as an unwed virgin, which just added to her many difficulties during her time.

astounding. And both babies are a sign that God is bigger than the foreign oppressors or the faithless kings who rule God's people—"God is with us."

Far from being limited to the relationship between Jesus and God, the description of God's desired relationship with us humans as "God with us" (in a wide variety of wordings) spans Genesis to Revelation in our Scriptures. In various forms, it appears many times in the New Testament, describing the lives of followers of Jesus. "God with us" does not separate Jesus from our humanity; it roots him deeply in humanity lived in the presence of God.

SUMMARY

This chapter could be extended with further illustrations under each topic, as well as by introducing other topics included in the New Testament writings. Hopefully these examples, along with those of Messiah, Son of God, Savior, and Spirit-filled from previous chapters, provide enough illustrations to indicate the New Testament writers were able to exalt Jesus to the heavens, while also seeing Jesus as fully rooted and embedded in our humanity. His roles were not roles that separated him from humanity; they were roles that fulfilled God's longstanding intentions for what humans in the image of God can be. Jesus is God's first completed human. He was human, is human, and will be human forever.

17

The God and Father of Our Lord Jesus the Messiah: Revisited

As we began this journey together, I stressed that the New Testament writers understood Jesus's life as a revelation of the relationship God has been pursuing with humans since the beginning of Creation. In Jesus, we see God's "firstborn" among many brothers and sisters. The relationship between God and Jesus is God's renewal of humanity. Jesus is God's next step in the creation of humans, male and female, in the image of God. As such, Jesus is God's first "completed" human. That means he is also God's definition of human potential.

What are some additional things we have seen along the way about the character of "The God and Father of our Lord Jesus the Messiah?"[1]

JESUS'S GOD HAS AN INCLUSIVE HEART AND AN EXCLUSIVE PURPOSE.

It is a question as relevant today as it was in first-century Palestine: "Is the relationship 'the God and Father of Our Lord Jesus the Messiah' has with humans exclusive or inclusive?" I propose that Jesus's answer is "Yes! Both!"

God's Inclusive Heart Thrills Some and Creates Frustration in Others.

God's inclusive heart has never been popular with those who find their identify in exclusivity and exceptionalism. When Jesus preached his first sermon, he did not create tension in the room when he claimed to be fulling the long-awaited prophetic

---

1. The new name for God, describing God's covenant-relationship with Jesus as "the God of Abraham," was used in the Old Testament (*see* chapter 1).

promises given to Israel. In fact, "all spoke well of him and were amazed at the gracious words" (Luke 4:22). The words that almost got him killed tell us a lot about the sinful side of human nature and about the sinful side of church history.

When Jesus finished his comments on the Isaiah prophecy with two further references from the Scriptures, the good feelings of the people assembled in the name of God turned to anger. Why? Because Jesus reminded them that God sometimes found more open hearts among their enemies than in the church. For one example, Jesus reminded them that, during a severe famine, God miraculously fed a widow from the region of the Canaanites, but not anyone in Israel. For his second example, Jesus demonstrated God's inclusive heart by calling to mind the miraculous healing God gave Naaman the elite pagan general of an enemy army (Luke 4:24–29).

Jesus could have used many other examples from the Old Testament to make his point. Jethro, priest of Midian and Moses's father-in-law, provided great wisdom and comfort to Moses, but he declined to go with Moses when he left for the land of Israel. Nineveh repented, but did Jonah? Job seems to have been a non-Jewish Middle Eastern patriarch, known for his God-fearing wisdom and faithfulness. The Egyptian midwives Shiphrah and Puah were the God-fearing women through whom God saved the lives of many Jewish boys. Isaiah prophesies that God's highway will run through Assyria and Egypt, as well as Jerusalem (Isa 19:23–25). And, perhaps most important of all, from the beginning the covenant with Abraham, and the Temple in Jerusalem, were intended to be a blessing for all the ethnicities and cultures of the world (Gen 12:3; 1 Kgs 8:41–43; Isa 56:7; Mark 11:17).

As always, Jesus lived what he taught. He consistently brought touches of God's grace, mercy, forgiveness, and acceptance to people the more elite church leaders disdained. Lepers, the disabled, a "woman of the streets," Samaritans, one of the terrorists (*lāstās* in Greek) beside him on the cross, and a Roman centurion, to name a few. He spoke of having (present tense) sheep who were his, but not a part of the Israel of God (John 10:16). He told a parable, illustrating how he, as God's agent, would carry out God's judgment among the people of "all the nations" by looking for those who cared about the hurting people around them. He indicated that when these good-hearted people from every culture of the world stand before him, they will be totally surprised to find out that all along he had identified with the hurting of the world they had cared about (Matt 25:31–46). In another parable, he answered the question of a Bible scholar: "Who is my neighbor?" The answer had a Samaritan merchant (heretic and political enemy) showing godly compassion to a Jew that fellow Jewish religious leaders dared not risk. Jesus identified a Roman Centurion as having more faith and understanding of Jesus's authority than anyone in the Israel of God. And he crossed his own God-given ministry boundaries to heal the daughter of a Canaanite mother, whose love for her daughter, and whose willingness to take the crumbs of grace, was too strong for Jesus to ignore.

We are then told that the risen Jesus sent his followers into all the world. The rest of the New Testament is filled with their attempts to work out what it means that "the God and Father of our Lord Jesus the Messiah" has an inclusive heart and an exclusive purpose.

God's Exclusive Purpose Thrills Some and Creates Frustration in Others.

God's exclusive purpose has never been popular with those who find their identity in being accepting, open-minded, and pluralistic. Early in his reign, King Solomon seems to have held God's exclusive purpose and God's inclusive heart in dynamic tension (1 Kgs 8:22–30). Soon the lure of belonging to, and being accepted by, the world of power, fame, and money diminished the importance of God's exclusive purpose. Without that side of the dynamic tension, he soon was immersed in the idolatry of unbridled inclusivism (1 Kgs 11:3–8). This kind of inclusivism had previously led to the golden calf in the wilderness. Fighting against that kind of inclusivism would become the mantra of many of the prophets of Israel. It also seems to have been one of the reasons for the lack of respect for King Herod shown by Jesus and his followers, as well as by many other Jews of the time (Mark 8:15; Luke 23:8–9; Acts 4:27, 12:19–23).

Today, many who find it important to emphasize God's inclusive heart find the obvious exclusiveness in many parts of the Bible to be frustrating. I do not think God has ever worried too much about whether God frustrates us, but I do think it is important to realize that the exclusiveness is about God's ultimate purpose in history, not about who God seeks and loves.

Jesus always related to "The God and Father of our Lord Jesus the Messiah" as having a very exclusive purpose in history. That purpose is to bring humans into the "kingdom of God." All of Jesus's teachings and actions indicate that he saw this purpose as being moved forward in history through God's covenant with Abraham and through the history of Israel that flowed from that covenant. He did not see himself as starting a new and more universal Christian religion, but rather saw himself as God's agent for fulfilling the original historical purpose of God that flowed from the covenant with Abraham—"all peoples on earth will be blessed through you" (Gen 12:3). This was certainly not an "all religions are seeking the same God and the same goal" approach to understanding God's involvement in the direction and purpose of human history.

As the "son of man/Adam," Jesus fulfilled not only God's covenant with Abraham, but also God's original purpose for creating humans (Adam = humanity). As we have seen throughout this book, that purpose is ultimately to create a new human community (kingdom/church/nation/people/family) made up of individuals who are Jesus's brothers and sisters, humans in the image of God. This exclusive purpose of God is the constant theme of the New Testament's understanding of who "the God and Father of our Lord Jesus the Messiah" is, and of what is being ultimately accomplished in human history. It is why we are here.

Perhaps only the continuing work of the Spirit of God can empower any of us to live faithfully with the dynamic tension caused by holding tightly to both God's inclusive heart and God's exclusive purpose. In our time, when many Christians define their identity by only one of the prongs of this dynamic reality, we should be praying for the empowering to incarnate both.

JESUS'S GOD IS NOT TAMABLE, AND THAT CREATES TENSION IN US.

I think our journey through the New Testament's records describing the relationship between God, Jesus, and other humans makes it very clear that the God Jesus worshiped and served is not tame or tamable. Many of Jesus's critiques of the religious leaders of his day involved their attempts to domesticate God. According to the rest of the New Testament, a large part of the work of the Holy Spirit among Jesus's followers was a constant push away from attempts by some followers of Jesus to domesticate God and Jesus.

Attempts to control and domesticate God were, and are, at the heart of human sinfulness and idolatry. Jesus worshiped the God who sometimes roars like a lion (Amos 3:8), sometimes shakes the earth (Ps 18:7), sometimes offers to reason with us humans concerning our sinfulness (Isa 1:18), and sometimes rejoices and sings with delight about the relationship shared with humans (Zeph 3:17). This God chose the name YHWH, which seems to reflect the Hebrew for "I am who I am" or "I will be who I will be" (Exod 3:14)—a name that serves as an ongoing warning against our attempts to control and tame the Living God. God might graciously choose to reveal more and more of who God is to us, but that never means we can tame God.

Two events—one recorded in the Old Testament and one in the New—show us in ways most of us find uncomfortable just how untamable our God is. Moses attempted to coerce God to allow him to see God face to face. God said "No" to this person who had often been touched with "the glory of God" so powerfully his face shone. Jesus prayed, "If possible let this cup pass," and the God who loved him beyond all imagining said "No" (in the short run) to this man who would, and did, do anything for God.

Given God's response to the pleas of Moses and Jesus, I find it incomprehensible that followers of Jesus develop theologies that imply that we can coerce and domesticate God by praying hard enough, giving enough, praying exactly the right prayer, or enacting some specific ritual. It is equally beyond me how others of us can think that the God of Jesus is a permissive and nondemanding God who wants only a *cheap grace* relationship with us. Not that I too do not wish to tame God: of course I do at times. But our efforts are clearly doomed to failure. If God would not be tamed when relating to Abraham, Jacob, Moses, Naomi, Mary, or Jesus, why fool ourselves?

The book of Revelation is filled with claims that through God's relationship with Jesus, the revelations of God in the Old Testament have been brought to new and deeper fulfillment. In this context of fulfillment, the risen and exalted Jesus continues to be the faithful witness for this untamable God (Rev 1:5). As you read Revelation, surely you are impressed with the fact that the New Testament canon comes to completion with multiple images of an untamable God who works toward God's ultimate human project, despite all human attempts to systemically bring God under control. Both humans, and the evil spirits that often inhabit our political, religious, and economic structures, are pictured as attempting to manage and control God. Of course, these dark powers will ultimately fail.

The God Jesus loves and serves will *not* be tamed, but Jesus witnesses to the reality that this God is good, loving, faithful, truthful, just, merciful, compassionate, responsive—and will prevail. Neither our doubts, our attempts to control God, nor our many attempts to redefine God will ever change who God is. God is who God chooses to be, and God will be who God will choose to be. This untamable God has chosen to move the adventure begun at creation forward through God's relationship with a Jewish human named Jesus who was executed 2000 years ago.

A RELATIONAL AND INVOLVED GOD CREATES TENSION IN US.

The Relationship with an Involved and Loving God Often Frustrates and Confuses Us.

Unlike believing that God is distant, and everything is already predestined by a detailed blueprint, understanding that God is good and powerful, as well as a personal and responsive communicator, often leaves us humans confused, frustrated, and angry with God. I believe frustration, confusion, and anger are not only understandable, but probably necessary for any honest and thoughtful God-seeker. Necessary or not, they are reactions that many of us share with Moses, Jeremiah, Naomi, Peter, John, Martha, Mary, and Thomas. I certainly do.

Before looking at the Scriptures, let me illustrate the tension that is created in my own life right now by trusting that God is good, caring, responsive, personal, and present. Just as she entered her long-anticipated retirement years, my wife found out that she had Parkinson's brain disease. I know many far less godly, far less prayerful, humans who have the privilege of enjoying years of healthy retirement. But this woman, who had rarely taken a sick day in her life, was suddenly faced with limitations that grew more severe each passing year.

Do I believe that God allowed sickness and death because that is the only way God could deal with our alienated world and move toward God's final wonderful goal for humans? Yes. Do I believe that, just like the rain that falls on the just and unjust alike, so also do pain and sickness? Yes. Do I think God decided to pick out my wife and give her Parkinson's disease? No. Do I believe that God could have prevented the Parkinson's or could have healed it? Yes. But God did not! Did God show us that God was still present and blessing us in many ways during the ten years after her diagnosis up to the day she passed? Absolutely! Does this mean that I need to thank God that she had Parkinson's because it was God's will? No—why would anyone be thankful for a brokenness that ravaged body and mind until she finally looked like a victim of the Holocaust?

Does this mean that even though I am sure that this is not God's ideal world, God will still use even this sad situation that led to her death to work toward God's ultimate will? Yes, I trust that when resurrection day comes God will complete the promise that my wife will be fully "female in the image of God" as a part of God's forever human family. As much as I know how, I *trust* that to be true with my entire life. Does it *feel* like it right now, after I just watched brain disease disintegrate this delightful human's gifts and abilities? Not at all! This is the tension we face every day by trusting God in the real world. I cannot tame God to fit my wishes. Any attempt to do so belittles God. It also belittles the faithfulness my wife showed in God until the day she passed.

Recently, my delightful, healthy great-grandson suddenly died in his sleep. God gave us this wonderful boy. We live in a world filled with accidents and brokenness. I understand that every day, hundreds of six-month-old boys and girls die in war-torn, bombed-out lands, in displaced persons camps from malnutrition, and on the southern border of the United States in the arms of broken-hearted parents. That does not assuage my tensions with God over the death of my great-grandson. It just increases the tension I feel in relating to the God who allows this kind of world to exist and is the God of love, good, and justice whom Jesus served and worshiped.

All God had to do to allow us to keep this wonderful little boy in our family was to wake someone up early, have someone ring the phone, or whisper "go check" in someone's ear. Am I frustrated, confused, and angry that God did not choose to do so? Certainly. How could I not be if I truly believe that God is present and involved in human realities? How could I not be if I love his adoring and broken-hearted father, mother, and big sister? Do I understand why God allowed this tragic accident? Absolutely not! Do I resonate with the people who say "It was God's will that he died?" Honestly, they drive me crazy.

I picture someone at the foot of Jesus's cross saying, "Don't ask why God has forsaken you! It is a good thing that is happening to you. You will be better off. We'll all be better off! Don't cry! You will see someday; it will work out good in the long run." The only proper response at these moments of horror is tears of sadness and dismay at the evil and brokenness of our world! The women around the cross had it right and expressed genuine faithfulness when they stood in abject silence filled with tears, while the best person they had ever known was unjustly and brutally executed. God could not be tamed to fit their immediate heart-felt wishes; nor will God be tamed to always fit into yours or mine. This produces a lot of unwanted tension in most of us.

One final personal example, one I mentioned earlier. The daughter of our very close friends passed a few years ago leaving two teen age boys, a heart-broken husband, and a crushed extended family. Many people had prayed fervently that the cancer that ravaged this young woman's body would be healed. For more than four years, I prayed every day for her healing—probably more consistently than I have prayed for anyone or anything else in my entire life. She died a very painful death. Yes, I am frustrated with God about this. What caring and honest person wouldn't be? This God and Father of the Lord Jesus our Messiah who keeps showing up just will not be tamed by me—no matter how much I wish I could.

Yes, I do trust that even though all of this brokenness, bentness, and outright evil in our world is allowed by God as the only world that can lead to God's future age, that does not mean these tragic events are God's ideal will. As Leslie Weatherhead said years ago, let's be clear that God's contingent will in this bent and broken world is neither God's ideal will nor God's ultimate will. Weatherhead even provides an unambivalent New Testament text that should at least give pause to those who argue everything that happens is God's will. Jesus makes it clear that events God very much does not want to happen, do happen—"Your Father in heaven is not willing that any of these little ones should be lost" (Matt 18:14).[2] Another time, Jesus says that Judas would have been better off to have never been born (Matt 26:24). Clearly Jesus did not think that God's ideal desires always occur in this broken and bent world.

It cannot be God's ideal will that a few years ago a depressed man got roaring drunk, sped away in his car, and killed a young teenage girl innocently riding her bike down the bike path two miles from my home. If that had been God's will, the legal system would have no right to put the man in jail for manslaughter.

Do I trust that if we allow God to do so, God will still be present and work toward various good outcomes in our lives, even as we go through tragedies? Yes. Do I trust that God's ultimate will includes grace and justice for our little great-grandson and for our dear friends' daughter? Yes. Do I believe that God's will ordains that 1000's of innocent children across the world will die today because of sexual exploitation, broken genetics, our senseless wars, and our unwillingness to provide food and medicines from our plenty? No! Do I believe it is God's will that the infant mortality rate for American children of color is more than double that of White Americans because many of us are too greedy to provide equal health care resources for these new born children—even though many of us White Christians claim to highly value the lives of these same children six months before they were born, when it didn't cost us anything? No way!

Do I have to grapple with the reality that, nonetheless, the God who "is with us" allowed all these adults and children including my great-grandson to die? Yes. And I am both horrified and comforted by the fact that God allowed it to happen to his most "beloved Son" Jesus as well. Further, I am both horrified and comforted by the

2. Weatherhead, *Will of God*, 11.

fact that as Jesus's crucifixion occurred, God was experienced as completely absent by the most righteous human who ever lived. But the after story is that as Jesus experienced the absence that led to the cry "My God, My God why have you forsaken me, God turned out to be more present than anyone could imagine. That is the tension of trusting an active and personally involved God in the real world. Thankfully, the Bible taken as a whole does not attempt to hide from this tension—but portrays it vividly for us to wrestle with.

The Relationship with Us often Frustrates God as Well.

Before pursuing further how frustrating a relationship with "The God and Father of our Lord Jesus the Messiah" can be for us at times, it seems important to note that relating to us is very frustrating for God at times, probably more often than we can imagine! Many prophetic messages in both the Old and New Testaments describe how frustrated God can be with entire communities at times (*see* for examples: Exod 32–34; Isa 1; Ezek 14:14-20; Hos 1–3; Luke 20:9-16).

We also have many examples of how frustrated God sometimes becomes with individuals, even those we call heroes of the faith. The same David who sometimes radically pleased God, also sometimes radically displeased God (2 Sam 12:1-12). In fact, David was aware that he had so deeply displeased God that he feared God would abandon their relationship altogether, and David understood that God would be fully justified in doing so (Ps 51). David had seen this happen to King Saul. If you have any doubts about the claim that the biblical writers believed relating to us often frustrates God, use your concordance to trace the many times God is said to be angry, displeased, distressed, hurt, sad, or grieved.

I have no doubt God has been frustrated with me at times in our relationship. Sometimes this may have been for repeating an inexcusable generational pattern such as being far too busy and away from home when my children were young, and my wife was carrying too much of the load. Sometimes I have failed to act righteously when I did not have the courage to obey the inner light of God's Spirit because I didn't know how to reasonably justify my choices and actions to others. Sadly, others and I paid for some of these failures. I am incredibly grateful God has never completely abandoned me to my own self-will, nor to my lack of righteous will.

Still, once we acknowledge that God often has good reasons to be frustrated with us, both corporately and individually, we are nevertheless faced with the many times that we find ourselves frustrated with God for allowing things that we find almost incomprehensible. Thankfully, many of the writers of Scriptures also found such events almost incomprehensible. They never pretend that God can be tamed, but they consistently find that this same God does not abandon us.

Biblical Materials are Filled with Expressions of the Tension the Writers Experienced.

Knowing God is a communicating God creates deep frustration when there seems to be a dearth of communication coming our way. The psalms that Walter Brueggemann aptly named "Psalms of Disorientation" are filled with frustration and confusion about God's absences and silences.[3] Here are a few examples:

> *Why*, O LORD, do you stand far off? *Why* do you hide yourself in times of trouble? (Ps 10:1, *emphasis mine*).

> [23] *Awake, O Lord! Why do you sleep? Rouse yourself!* Do not reject us forever. [24] *Why do you hide your face and forget* our misery and oppression? (Ps 44:23–24, *emphasis mine*).

> [1] My God, my God, *why have you forsaken me? Why are you so far* from saving me, so far from the words of my groaning? [2] O my God, *I cry* out by day, but *you do not answer*.... (Ps 22:1–2, *emphasis mine*).

Jeremiah is clear that God's promises recorded in the Bible can be very frustrating at times. Jeremiah seems to be quoting Psalm 1 back at the LORD and saying to God that the promises do not at all describe the way reality is working:

> [1] You are always righteous, O LORD, when I bring a case before you. *Yet* I would speak with you about your justice: *Why* does the way of the *wicked prosper*? *Why* do all the faithless live at ease? [2] *You have planted them*, and they have *taken root*; they *grow and bear fruit*. You are always on their lips, but far from their hearts. (Jer 12:1–2, *emphasis mine*).

I find it comforting that God doesn't tell Jeremiah he is wrong in maintaining that Psalm 1 isn't proving to be experientially true in Jeremiah's current context. Instead, God tells Jeremiah to hang in there until this difficult and hurtful season passes. God will still be there. This response from God to Jeremiah concerning Psalm 1 should be a clear hermeneutical warning against absolutizing any promise in Scripture apart from its proper context in real life. It is also a warning against thinking faithfulness can tame God or will always make life easier.

Obviously, the creation that Genesis deems to have once been "very good" can be now also described as a place filled with deserved and undeserved experiences of calamity, illness, death, and suffering. Equally obvious is the reality that humans whose creation was once deemed "very good" are now inflicting horrendous injustices upon one another—that was Jeremiah's frustration. Worse for the faithful, all of this can be accompanied by silences and apparent abandonment, right at the times we most wish to hear clearly from God. That frustration is voiced in several psalms, but never more clearly than in the psalm Jesus quotes as he is executed: "My God, My God, why have

---

3. Brueggemann, *Message of Psalms*, 51–122.

you forsaken me" (Ps 22:1). To push the point a bit further, Jeremiah's exasperation was that even when we are hearing from God, reality can still be terribly frustrating and filled with injustice.

Experiences of injustice and calamity should never be designated as "good." The biblical writers challenge us to trust that, in the long run, God promises to work "toward good" in every situation (Rom 8:28, throughout the Old Testament prophets, and the cross–resurrection event). There is deep and genuine comfort in that promise when we trust it is true. However, our daily experience as humans is not "in the long run;" we live in the now, and we cannot honestly let God off the hook for allowing a world filled with injustice and horror to exist. Just as we should not take for granted the many good gifts for which God deserves thanksgiving, we cannot explain away the pain we humans suffer in situations when the God who is supposed to be personal and responsive seems to act—or not act—in a manner that we experience as not good, not personal, and not responsive. Neither can we rest easy in the times when we long for some word from God, some sense of God's presence, and when we instead feel the horror of God's absence (Ps 22:1, Mark 15:34).

Like their Old Testament heroes of the faith, New Testament writers also acknowledge the tension created by claiming that God is personal and responsive. This confusion concerning God, and Jesus as well, is reflected throughout the Gospel of John. This tension is blatant in the descriptions of Thomas's relationship with Jesus. Every narrative that mentions Thomas includes both his honest doubts and his risky love for Jesus (John 11:16, 14:5, 20:25) The same confusion is evident in the responses of both Martha and Mary at the death of their brother. Why would God allow Lazarus to die? Why didn't Jesus come and do something when they asked him to come (John 11:17–37)?

Luke records the same kind of questioning of Jesus, as well as of God, in the following narration:

> [19] "What things?" he asked. "About Jesus of Nazareth," they replied. "*He was a prophet, powerful in word and deed before God and all the people.* [20] The chief priests and our rulers handed him over to be sentenced to death, and they crucified him; [21] *but we had hoped* that he was the one who was going to redeem Israel (Luke 24:19–21, *emphasis mine*).

Matthew also illustrates this tension in Jesus's own relationship with God. At one point, Jesus experiences God's closeness so powerfully that Jesus dramatically "lights up" from the experience.

> [2] There he was transfigured before them. *His face shone like the sun*, and his clothes became as white as the light.... [5] While he was still speaking, a bright cloud enveloped them, and *a voice from the cloud said, "This is my Son, whom I love; with him I am well pleased. Listen to him!"* (Matt 17:2, 5, *emphasis mine*).

The same writer tells us that Jesus also experienced the deep hurt and frustration that sometimes comes in a genuinely human relationship with God. For example, about 3:00 p.m. one afternoon, he prayed these words of frustration, pain, and disappointment, first prayed by one of his forefathers in the faith: "'*Eloi, Eloi, lama sabachthani*' which means, *My God, my God, why have you forsaken me*?" (Matt 27:46).

Apparently, relating to the God of the Bible means one should expect delight, wonder, adventure, risk, stretching, confusion, frustration, and anger. Jesus was one of us, and he too experienced the tensions and the risks of trusting this God who communicates "God's word" to us. It seems strange, given this biblical view of the relationship between God and humans, to find that a lot of what passes as biblical teaching, biblical preaching, and biblical scholarship presents a much more "Isn't life always wonderful with God!" view of God. I have talked with many people raised in the church who have walked away from their early faith because this sanitized view of who God is and how God works did not at all match the reality they were experiencing in life.

Not surprisingly, questions are being raised in many corners concerning this widespread tendency to present cleaned up *Sunday School* versions of the relationship between God and humans. However, agreement in churches or in scholarship about how to respond to the questions that a straightforward reading of the Bible often raises concerning God's relationship with humans is not easy to come by. Some want to smooth out what cannot be made smooth. Others decide it is all so inconsistent that it cannot be a true picture. I think neither of those approaches does justice to God or to how God speaks through the Bible. There is a difficult dynamic tension in relating to the God and Father of Our Lord Jesus the Messiah. Because Jesus is one of us, he shared in that difficult real-life tension. Acknowledging that truth is a big step toward allowing God to be with us as we move through the difficult and tension-filled situations of life. Thankfully, the biblical writers make plenty of room for that honesty.

THE GOD WHO IS CONSTANTLY EXPERIENCING US CAUSES TENSION IN US.

It is not only God's apparent absence, but also God's constant presence that sometimes causes a lot of tension in us humans. I remember when my children were around three years old, they thought if they covered their eyes so they could not see me, then I could not see them. Many of us seem to be a lot like that when it comes to relating to God. We want to be aware of God's presence when we want God to be present. We also want God to not be present when we wish to cover our eyes and hide our thoughts, attitudes, fears, prejudices, and actions. We think—remember your actions speak much louder than your words—God doesn't see what we are trying to hide from ourselves and from others.

A frequently quoted Psalm meditates on the reassuring—and frightening—knowledge that there is nowhere to hide from God's constant presence.

> ⁵ You *hem me in* . . . ⁶ Such knowledge is too wonderful for me; it is too lofty for me to attain. ⁷ *Where can I go* from your Spirit? *Where can I flee* from your presence? Where can I go from your Spirit (Ps 139:5–7, *emphasis mine*).

It seems clear to me that our only hope for life to have any ultimate meaning comes from this awe-inspiring, but fearsome thought—the God who is both Creator and Savior is always experiencing each of us. God knows—not as an intellectual, abstract omniscience, but as a personal experience—us as us, you as you, and me as me.

In Galatians, after speaking at length about the great forever family of children and heirs that God is creating, Paul pled with his readers to never forget that God is constantly experiencing us. He used the Greek word group *ginoskō* to say we know God experientially, and God knows us experientially as well.

> . . . you have come to know [experience = *ginotes*] God, or *rather to be known* [experienced = *gnōsthentes*] *by God*, how can you turn back again to the weak and beggarly elemental spirits? How can you want to be enslaved to them again? (Gal 4:9, *emphasis mine*).

Although it is awesomely scary to think that God experiences my every thought and action, why would I want to hide from the only hope there is of me being transformed into the person I was created to be? Why hide my eyes and pretend, given that doing so immediately makes me vulnerable to all the other "gods" of culture and self? Only if we present ourselves daily to live in God's relational presence can we be transformed toward the completed humans God intends us to be. Romans 12:1–2 tells us this is the only way to avoid the default of being conformed by our cultures, and then the rest of the letter tells us what transformation should begin to look like in our daily lives.

Isn't it amazingly strange that the same reality—God knows and experiences us at all times—is the source of my greatest fears and my only hope? Our fear: how can we stand before the God who really knows us inside and out? Our only security: Who else can save us from ourselves and from one another?

LET'S LEARN TO LIVE WITH, NOT HIDE FROM, THE TENSIONS CREATED BY LIVING IN THE PRESENCE OF A PURPOSEFUL, PRESENT, PERSONAL GOD.

The Biblical Claims about God's Self-revelation and God's Relationship with Humans Are Messy.

We who follow Jesus would be much better off if we quit attempting to do away with the messiness of God's self-revelation as it is described in the Bible. Our failed attempts to iron out all of the messy wrinkles include theologies of permissive universalism, absolute sovereignty, rigid biblical inerrancy, a New Testament God who is different from the God of the Old Testament, and a God who is omnipotent, omniscient, omnipresent, changeless, passionless, and essentially unknowable. None of these attempts to get rid of the messiness in God's relationship with us humans does justice to the experiences humans have in relating to God, as they are described in the Bible. We might think we are safer with the relatively neat views of the God we construct, but we are not. It didn't work when I tried to make my wife fit my fabricated images of what she should be; why would I think it would work with God?

Why doesn't it work? Because real, growing, loving relationships are always messy. I have never seen a parent-child relationship that was not messy in various ways. I have never seen a sibling relationship that did not have its messy side at times. I have never seen a husband–wife relationship that did not have some very messy aspects. I have never seen a church with relationships that were not far messier than many of us like to acknowledge. The relationships between nations are extremely messy. The current relationships between citizens of the United States are very messy, even as we all claim to be patriots who love our country. The relationship we humans have with creation is messy, as is our scientific understanding of this relationship. All of these relationships can be wonderful and beautiful at their best, but they are always challenging and always risky.

I am very grateful that the biblical writers describe messy, un-ironed out, tension filled, real and genuine relationships between the God who created our world and we humans who are at the center of God's purpose in this world. Most of the loose ends and the dynamic tensions never get completely ironed out in the narratives. Just as in our lives, so also in the lives described in the Bible, if the messiness and tensions are ever to be fully resolved, it will be in God's age to come. If the questions that go unanswered in our lives—and there are many, and the questions that went unanswered in the relationships described in the Bible—and there are many, are to be ironed out completely, it will be when "we shall see face to face."

But until then, "Now I know in part; then I shall know fully, even as I am fully known" (1 Cor 13:12). Between now and then, our relationships with God and one another will continue to be about as messy and have about as many loose ends as the relationships described in that letter to Corinth. However, such a messy account of our relationship with God is precisely what we should expect if the relationship being described is a genuine interpersonal relationship. All of our other real and growing relationships are messy!

God's Relational Purpose is Risky for God and for Us Humans.

There is a level of riskiness in all real and growing relationships. Let's follow Jesus's model and learn to live with that reality in our relationship with God. Doesn't the very nature of a deepening and growing interpersonal, loving relationship always involve the relinquishing of the fear that tempts us to try to take the risk out of trusting?

I hope it has been clear, as we have examined the relationship between God and Jesus, that God is willing to be at risk in order to love us and allow us to choose whether or not we want to love God back. God chooses to relinquish much of the control that God's awesome power could demand because God wants real maturing relationships. This means God chooses, as Jesus does in imaging God, to pair authority with vulnerability. If the primary relationship Jesus reveals is that God is Father, and we are sons and daughters, then God is choosing to be vulnerable. No parent who wishes his or her child to grow and mature can insist on absolute control. Demanding absolute control seems to some parents to be the way to avoid risk to themselves and their children, but it destroys the relationship and severely damages the child. The relationship between God and Jesus shows us that this is not God's way. God's way is the way filled with the risk, the messiness, and the accompanying tensions that always occur in real maturing relationships.

Amazingly, "The God and Father of our Lord Jesus the Messiah" is a faithful, caring, responsive, and committed God, who is willing to take the risk, and endure the accompanying hurt, of relating to us humans with care and love. It is overwhelming to seriously engage the audacious claim that the One God who created the universe has as God's primary purpose in this creation a whole and enduring relationship with a righteous community of humans. Equally audacious is the promise that individual humans will finally express the God-given potential of being "in the image and likeness of God." All of this is overwhelming, but wonderfully assuring and challenging.

How differently I see Jesus when I see him as one of us in this risky and messy God project—a human brought step by step, fully and forever, into the image of God. As noted earlier, the writer of Hebrews likes to describe Jesus as the first human who has been "made complete/perfected" by God (Heb 2:10, 5:9, 7:8), but Jesus won't be the last (Heb 6:1, 10:1, 10:14, 11:40, 12:23). How differently I see my neighbor, myself, and even my enemy when I live in this great God-given narrative! I never know which of the enemies Jesus calls me to love might suddenly, like the thief on the cross hanging next to Jesus, move from enemy to friend—a friend who will be with God and God's people forever in God's future society. I pray and trust that transformation includes me! What I know is that I am not to attempt to destroy an enemy, but rather to live in peace, as much as I am able, and to love (be stubbornly committed to his or her good) the best I can. At the same time, I am to continue asking God to forgive my own many failures so that I may live in a manner that images Jesus's faithful covenant relationship with God. This is the risky calling of being in a relationship with the Living God.

God's Choice to Be in Real Relationships is Why History Is Filled with Messy Contingencies.

Healthy and deep relationships include risky promises to respond to one another and to adjust to one another in future realities that can unfold in as-yet-undetermined directions. The biblical writers believed the covenant relationship God wants to have with humans included this kind of reciprocal interaction. The Old Testament writers tell us God turned from God's intended directions in response to the deeply emotional and deeply personal prayers of Moses (Exod 32:9–14) and Hezekiah (Isa 38:1–8). The prophet Joel followed his pronouncement that under current circumstances destruction was inevitable with this plea:

> [13] Rend your heart and not your garments. *Return* [*shuv* in Hebrew] *to the LORD* your God, for *the LORD* is gracious and compassionate, slow to anger and abounding in love, and *the LORD* relents from sending calamity. [14] *Who knows? The LORD may turn* [*shuv* in Hebrew] *and have pity and leave behind a blessing* (Joel 2:13–14, *emphasis mine*).

Not only did Moses, Hezekiah, Isaiah, and Joel view God's plans as contingent at times, it is difficult to imagine a more contingency oriented description of the relationship between God and humans than the one recorded in Jonah. Nineveh's experience with God turns out to be contingent, just as Jonah feared. Jonah is sent with a message containing "no ifs" and "no maybes:" "Forty more days, and Nineveh *will be* overturned" (Jon 3:1–3, *emphasis mine*). Despite what the text plainly says—and does not say—I thought for years that the message was "Unless Nineveh repents within forty days, Nineveh will be destroyed."

My understanding reflected the fact that my Sunday school teachers, and one of my Bible College professors, did not really believe God sometimes changes God's mind when we humans change our minds and our actions. The Ninevites, whom Jonah understandably hates because of the brutality of their Empire, repent. It turns out that God's relationship with the enemies of God's people is also a mutually responsive relationship. Jonah had feared that might be so! The repentant Ninevites hoped God would repent and not destroy them, and God did compassionately change God's mind—to Jonah's chagrin (Jon 3:9–10).

I have no problem understanding why Jonah would rather die than be faced with returning home and explaining to his fellow Israelites that he was the channel God used to save their tyrannical Assyrian enemies. How would you as an American Christian like to come back home and explain to the rest of us how God used you to bring about several more decades of the current brutal Putin-run Russian government?

Abstract and noncontingent sovereignty is not the New Testament paradigm for Jesus's relationship with God, either. The relationship between Jesus and God is a relationship between Jesus and the God revealed in the Old Testament. Jesus prays a very contingency-laden prayer: "*If* possible, let this cup pass." That prayer is filled with the same personal passion and angst that filled the prayers of Moses, Hezekiah, and Joel. Jesus clearly believes there might be contingencies in this time of trial; but this time, God answers differently from God's answer to the prayers of Moses, Hezekiah, and Nineveh. God's "No" to Jesus creates deep tension for us, so deep that many today say that a God who leads Jesus into a situation guaranteeing execution cannot be a loving God—a denial of everything the New Testament claims about God. Others attempt to explain how Jesus as God knew that he would have to die, but as a human he had to pray this prayer—a view I can find no way to reconcile with the biblical accounts of Jesus's relationship with God.

Jesus seems to have taken for granted that there were contingencies in his relationship with God. True, the New Testament writers claim that God finally resolved the tension in God's relationship with Jesus through the resurrection and the following exaltation, but they never skip Jesus's agony or the brutal injustice that overwhelmed Jesus as he prayed in the Garden. Instead of a predetermined blueprint, we are told of a real drama playing out in the relationship. On Jesus's part, there were choices to be made between waiting and grasping, between trust and temptation. These risks are paralleled with God choosing to allow Jesus to have to make these choices under the most trying of circumstances as the necessary way for Jesus to become completely mature as a faithful human (Heb 5:7–10, 2:10). The risk for both God and Jesus was high. The only guarantee Jesus had was a promise—a promise that seemed far distant from the realities he was currently experiencing. The only guarantee God had was Jesus's faithfulness—a faithfulness that was put to an excruciating test by God's choice to be silent when Jesus most wished to hear God speak; by being experientially absent when Jesus most wished to feel God's presence.

The following quotation (which we have noted before in other contexts) presents the relationship between God and Jesus in terms impossible to harmonize with an underemphasis on Jesus's full humanity and the contingencies that involves.

> [7] During the days of Jesus's life on earth, he offered up prayers and petitions with loud cries and tears *to the one who could save him* from death, and he was *heard because of* his reverent submission. [8] Although he was a son, *he learned obedience from* what he suffered and, [9] once *made perfect [complete]*, *Jesus became the source* of eternal salvation. . . ." (Heb 5:7–9, *emphasis mine*).

Jesus really was and is one of us humans. God is sovereign in Jesus's life, but it is a sovereignty that operates within the larger framework of God's desire to relate purposefully, relationally, responsively, and lovingly toward humans. God wants real, healthy, relationships with us—relationships we choose. Jesus's relationship with God is just such a real, healthy relationship.

As I read the New Testament, I see Jesus choosing to trust God in a manner that says, "I have no claim on you except your choice to love me, and your word that you will continue to love me, regardless of the cost to both of us." This relational security sees that nothing is guaranteed except by God's character, faithfulness, promises, and love. This is what covenant relationships are about. It is not a security founded in a view of God's sovereignty as noncontingent and nonresponsive. It is a relational security that led Jesus to offer "up prayers and petitions with loud cries, and tears *to the one who could save him* from death," and be "*heard because of his reverent submission*" (Heb 5:7, *emphasis mine*). The opposite of fear is not trust that God controls every circumstance and every choice; rather, the opposite of living fearfully is living out a mature trust in God's love for us that allows us to mature in loving others (1 John 4:17–20).

That choice to trust God's love is the choice Jesus made many times in his life, and the choice he made once again in prayer as he chose to trust God's (Abba's) love and faithfulness over his own distress, anxiety, and grief.

> [32] They went to a place called Gethsemane, and Jesus said to his disciples, "Sit here *while I pray*." [33] He took Peter, James and John along with him, and *he began to be deeply distressed and troubled*. [34] "My soul is *overwhelmed* with sorrow to the point of death," he said to them. "Stay here and keep watch." [35] Going a little farther, he fell to the ground and prayed that *if possible the hour might pass from him*. [36] "*Abba*, Father," he said, "*everything is possible for you. Take this cup from me*. Yet *not what I will, but what you will. . . .*" [39] *Once more he went away and prayed the same thing* (Mark 14:32–36, 39, *emphasis mine*).

All three Synoptic Gospels record a version of this event in the garden. Jesus acted upon God's leading and publicly confronted those determined to dominate and retain their power. He knew this meant they would try to arrest and execute him. Still, all three Gospels tell us Jesus prayed, hoping there still might be a contingency in God's purpose. Was Jesus thinking of Abraham and Isaac (Gen 22)? Long ago, at the last possible moment, God had decided that a willingness to sacrifice Isaac's life was enough; the willingness need not be brought to fruition. Jesus seemed to think it was "possible" that God's purpose might be accomplished if Jesus were genuinely willing to face this agonizing situation head on. Jesus prayed to God hoping for contingency ("if" and "possible"). Might God still choose to "remove this cup?" Any other understanding of these prayers that were offered three times in the midst of overwhelming distress and sorrow seems to make them a sham.

Even though Jesus begged three times for God to "let this pass," the Gospel writers do not see this as a lack of faithfulness on Jesus's part. In fact, they present this interaction as an example of Jesus's deep trust in his relationship with a responsive and personal God. They do not think Jesus was misunderstanding the sovereignty of God when Jesus assumed that God would be responsive to his prayers and might even allow for a drastic and surprising contingency in the next steps of their covenant relationship. Neither is there any indication the writers thought this was all a charade by Jesus, who is aware of his "second nature" as "God" and is praying these prayers only as a model for the rest of us humans. Nor do they indicate that Jesus's choice was not really a choice because God causes everything that happens to happen the way it does. Jesus prayed these prayers, hoping to be surprised by God saying to Jesus what God said to Abraham—we need not go through with this because your genuine willingness makes it clear that you fear God to your core.

Ellen Davis describes God's waiting with bated breath as God watched and hoped Abraham would be faithful at all costs—a faithfulness at which Abraham had sometimes failed and sometimes succeeded.

> The binding of Isaac shows us a God who is vulnerable, terribly and terrifyingly so, in the context of covenant relationships. We are more comfortable using the *omni* words—omnipotent, omniscient—to describe God. Yet if we properly understand the dynamics of covenant relationship, then we are confronted with a God who is vulnerable.[4]

Isn't Davis correct that this is the most obvious way to understand God's response?

> "Do not lay a hand on the boy," he (the angel of YHWH) said. "Do not do anything to him. *Now I know that you fear God, because* you have not withheld from me your son, your only son" (Gen 22:12, *emphasis mine*).

Now God could move history forward as God wished to do through the faithfulness Abraham showed in his relationship with God. If this view of the relationship between God and humans presented in the Old Testament is correct, and if Jesus is really human, how much more deeply must God have felt the risk as the "deeply distressed and troubled" Jesus bowed, "overwhelmed with sorrow," before God in the Garden of Gethsemane (Mark 14:33–34)? Would God finally have the *Adam/human* God needed, the *Israelite* God needed, the *King* God needed, the *faithful child* God needed to move history to the next stage of God's covenant relationship with humanity? Or when the chips were down, would Jesus, as so many decent and faithful people before him, prove to be faithful sometimes and quite unfaithful at other times? Would Jesus complete the risk of trusting God as the God who would be faithful no matter what—faithfulness guaranteed only by God's character and not by some inflexible blueprint that brooks no contingency?

To his very core, the fully human Jesus wanted to fully please his Father. *Jesus was not a human who could not fail to trust; Jesus was a human who willed not to fail to trust.* This New Testament picture is a very different one from the one I heard from a recent Bible study group: "Of course Jesus couldn't fail, he was God."

What made my relationship with my wife so meaningful was that I knew she did not *have to* keep choosing to love me and be faithful to me, instead, she *wanted* to. It was risking her choice, and her risking my choice, that filled the relationship with such gratitude and depth. If she could not have done otherwise, the meaningfulness of our

---

4. Davis, *Involved with God*, 62.

relationship would have been greatly diminished. It is God's risky faithfulness, and our risky human faithfulness, including Jesus's risky human faithfulness, that makes the relationship so meaningful. God takes the risk of loving humans, which is also the risk of having God's heart broken. God takes the risk of being in a genuine relationship with humans (and real relationships are messy) and continues even when the situation is less than ideal. We are asked to take the risk of loving both God and other humans. We are asked to take the risk of being in genuine relationships with God and one another. God's relationship with the human Jesus demonstrates the outcome God desires for us humans.

That is our story! This relational and responsive understanding of God's nature is the New Testament writers' understanding of what it means that "the God and Father of our Lord Jesus the Messiah" is faithful and loving! Because of Jesus's faithfulness, we all can be included in God's great renewal of God's purpose for humans—"male and female in the image of God."

What a difference it makes in our day-to-day living when we remember that in every situation, we can bless and please God, and we can hurt and disappoint God. What we do, and what we do not do, always changes history, even if only a little bit, so our choices genuinely matter and the One God of all responds to them. I have a very different view of both God and Jesus when I see the risks they took in faithfully loving one another in this world, filled with temptations to destroy their relational oneness. Do you?

Jesus's God Is Often Deeply Hurt.

Another reason we tend to downplay the risks, contingencies, and messiness revealed in the relationships humans have with God as they are described in the Bible is the tension caused by knowing God can be deeply hurt. Do you like to think that your thoughts, your actions, and your nonactions hurt people? Even more overwhelming, do you like to think that your thoughts, your actions, and your nonactions hurt the loving God who knows you can be so much more than you are? What do we do with the God who loves those *others* we hurt as much as God loves us? What do we do with a God who is often disappointed in how we enact our relationship with God?

My guess is that one of the psychological realities underlying our desire to reconstruct the biblical God into a God who is abstract and totally sovereign over every choice is our desire to avoid the fact that a really involved and a genuinely good God is a God who is being hurt by each of us on a daily, often even an hourly, basis. We would rather hide than face this God with the shame we feel if we confront honestly how badly we hurt an involved and loving God.

Of course, as any good parent does, the God Jesus loves sees the mistakes and failures of God's children with empathy for the difficult process of growing up in a broken world. Despite the failures, God is delighted if the child is heading in the right direction overall. Such love and caring is costly to any parent—including God! Every good parent is a pain bearer for his or her children. In revealing God as "our Father," Jesus, like the prophets before him, show us that God is often hurt by us humans. This understanding of our relationship with God is both demanding and comforting, and it is very uncomfortable as well.

Several years ago, Bill and Gloria Gaither wrote a song celebrating the fact that, if we know God loves us, we are free to risk loving each other. The song ("I Am Loved") captures a truth about genuine loving relationships—they are always filled with risk. Because the biblical writers thought of, and claim to have experienced, God's relationship with us humans as a genuine relationship chosen by a loving God, they knew God was risking hurt and disappointment. Any genuine relationship that is really loving opens the participants to the possibility of equal amounts of joy and suffering, of thrill and pain.

How much it costs God to love us humans is the central message of the first section of Hosea, which concludes in Hosea 3:1–3 with God reminding Hosea that the pain he experiences in his relationship with his wife Gomer, who had been a prostitute and then returned to that lifestyle, is like the pain God experiences in his relationship with Israel.[5] Jeremiah's message about the tears and pain of God becomes so passion filled at times that the reader (even the best Hebrew scholars) cannot tell whether the fountain of tears, and the accompanying frustration and heartbreak, belong to God or Jeremiah, or both. The book is filled with descriptions of a grieving and broken-hearted God and a grieving and broken-hearted prophet of God, both of whom know that sometimes judgment is necessary when a culture becomes too broken and corrupted. Still, it hurts terribly to be involved and to care when that judgment occurs.

Genesis 6:6 puts it this way: "The LORD *was grieved* that he had made man on the earth, and *his heart was filled with pain.*" (*emphasis mine*). Ezekiel is certainly dark, at times almost hopeless, and he includes descriptions of God backing away from important relationships with God's people; yet even this distancing is not stoic on God's part; Ezekiel describes God's heartbreak this way: "Those who escape will remember me—*how I have been grieved by their adulterous hearts. . . .*" (Ezek 6:9, *emphasis mine*).

And that is how the biblical writers portrayed God again and again. As Ellen Davis says about God's pursuit of love and of justice in the world: "The divine *modus operandi* is impassioned and demanding *on both sides*. As the combined witness of the two Testaments shows, *for God it is costly beyond calculation*" (*emphasis mine*).[6]

When we come to the New Testament understanding of the relationship between God and Jesus, we find that it, too, is a relationship of mutual risk with the potential for mutual joy and mutual hurt. Jesus suffered deeply as he chose to risk continued faithfulness to the covenant relationship shared by God and Jesus. However, this event

---

5. Richter, *Epic*, 43–45
6. Davis, *Biblical Prophecy*, 16.

was the expression of a genuine two-way relationship and was loving and just only if God was suffering at least as much as Jesus was.

If God created this world and allowed it to proceed as it has, prophets such as Habakkuk, Jeremiah, Ezekiel, and the writers of several Psalms are right—God has a lot to answer for. The claim that God is good and loving, and yet has allowed human history to proceed as it has with all the pain and suffering even the best humans have endured, can be sustained only if two things are true. *First*, God has suffered at least as much as we humans have suffered. *Second*, God's future for humanity is so wonderful that it is worth all of that suffering both to God and to humans of the past and the present. Only if God truly turned Jesus's execution into Jesus's exaltation as a human, only if God was as thrilled and joyful as Jesus was when Jesus walked out of that tomb, knowing he had been faithful at all costs, only if humans can in fact be brought into the kingdom of God and into the image and likeness of God—only then has God begun to justify what God has allowed, and is allowing, to occur on our journey through human history.

We will return to the final-outcome theme shortly, but let's first pursue more deeply the importance of God's willingness to suffer. The New Testament claims that a God who deeply loved Jesus led Jesus on a path that increasingly moved toward execution on a Roman cross. *Only if God hurt as much as Jesus hurt was their relationship truly a two-way relationship.* If God is love, then God not only hurts because of our sins and failures, but also hurts when his faithful children pay such a high cost for faithfulness.

Only if God was also experiencing heartbreak and pain while Jesus was in agony, as other children of God tried Jesus as a blasphemer of God, gambled for Jesus's clothing, tortured him, sentenced Jesus to death (all the while knowing him to be innocent of the charges), wore the priestly robes of God's Temple as they mocked Jesus, and denied knowing their very best friend when the cost of friendship became too high— only then might God be good and loving. *How would you feel if one of your children was brutalized by your other children?* Do you think God cares less and hurts less than you would?

It must be true in God's relationship with Jesus that "in their distress, He [YHWH], too, was distressed (Isa 63:9). It must be true as Jesus died that "The death of the Lord's faithful is a costly loss in his [YHWH's] eyes" (Ps 116:15, Common English Bible). Isn't that the meaning of the darkness that came over the earth as Jesus breathed his last breath (Luke 23:44–45)?

Because the One God, who is YHWH and who is "The God and Father of Our Lord Jesus the Messiah," is a God who is genuinely relational, purposeful, responsive, and personal, the God of the Bible is always at great risk of being wounded and hurt *by* the humans God loves (Eph 4:30). Just as important, this God is always at risk of being wounded and hurt *for* the humans God loves. If Jesus was genuinely human as the New Testament clearly claims, then in loving Jesus, God risked great heartbreak in anticipation of even greater joy.

God Teaches and Educates Through a Messy Historical Process that Moves toward God's Goal for Creation.

To be very clear, I am not supporting the claim of inevitable progress in human history. Some philosophers, social Darwinists, and Christian theologians have taken that view,[7] but deterministic "inevitability" as an inherent universal process is rightly being abandoned by most people today. Such a view was certainly not the prophetic message of the Bible. God's ultimate goal is not inherent in the processes of creation or the processes of human history. God's goal comes as a promise of future intervention by "the God and Father of our Lord Jesus the Messiah."

Having said that, it is true that genuine relationships involve ongoing processes. They cannot be static if they are real relationships. It is also true that any real parent-child relationship involves an educational process. And, ask any parent or any school teacher: educational processes are always filled with messiness and contingencies.

Much of the teaching in both the Old and New Testaments includes reminders of what should have been learned from past interactions with God. This is especially true in Deuteronomy and the Prophets. In the same vein, when we translate *Torah* with its broader content of "instruction," rather than its limited application as "laws," we see more clearly that all of the narratives, as well as the commandments, are examples of God's educational process (2 Tim 3:15–16).

The New Testament writers understood the Old Testament as a record of a relational and educational process. The writer of Hebrews begins by establishing God's communication in history as a long educational process—"In the past God spoke to our forefathers through the prophets at many times and in various ways, but in these last days he has spoken to us by his Son" (Heb 1:1–2).

Paul outlines human history by describing God's process of step-by-step revelation, as he understood it to have been recorded in the Old Testament—(1) there was a time before sin and death, (2) there was a time including sin and death, but before Torah, (3) then there was a time with Torah, but before Jesus, and (4) finally there is a renewal of humanity in God's gracious restart of the human race through the human Jesus (Rom 5:12–21). This educational purpose is also central to Paul's imagery in describing the Torah as the schoolmaster (or the servant overseeing the student at school). Paul saw that one of the primary purposes of Torah was to prepare God's people for the revelation that would come through the Messiah (Gal 3:28—4:7).

Life with God as an educational process in practical wisdom is the perspective presented in the letter of James. That is why he instructs: "Not many of you should

---

7. Tielhard, *Phenomenon*.

presume to be teachers" (Jas 3:1). An educational process is also the perspective Jesus took in the Sermon on the Mount when he gave new instructions on how to apply the law: "You have heard it said, . . . but, I say. . . ." (Matt 5). Similarly, Jesus taught that an ongoing process of education would be necessary after his death and resurrection when he instructed his disciples with these words: "I have *much more to say to you, more than you can now bear*" (John 16:12, *emphasis mine; see* also 14:26).

Above all else, the entire New Testament sees God's self-revelation through God's relationship with Jesus as the creation of a new *before* and *after* in God's relationship with humans (for three examples out of many, *see* Heb 1:1–4; Rom 5:1–11; Acts 10:1–11:18).

But this new step in God's chosen relationship with humans does not diminish the risks God is taking or the risks demanded of us humans who want to relate to this God. Both love and freedom always involve risks. How do we humans deal with relating to the God who leads the risen Jesus to send us into all the world with very few specific guidelines other than "I will be with you" (Matt 28:18–20)? The risky ambiguity was heightened when the risen Jesus made it very clear that the Father wouldn't reveal to Jesus's followers exactly when or how this narrative God is creating would play out. To the chagrin of the disciples, Jesus answered their when and how questions with "It is not for you to know." What could they know? They could know that, as his followers, they would be empowered for the journey into the unknown by the same Holy Spirit who had empowered his life (Acts 1:2, 7–8). It would be a learning process.

How do you deal with an event that puts everything up for new understanding and new interpretation, and yet can be understood only as the continuation of God's work and purpose in creation and in Israel? How do you deal with standing in the presence of an obviously human friend and mentor who just went through an execution, but who stands before you exhibiting the next step toward an entirely new level of human life? How do you react to a God who risks placing the next steps in God's purpose for all of history in the hands of people who only a month before ran for their lives when Jesus was executed? How do you respond to a God who risks how everything God has done through Jesus will be presented to the world for years to come by entrusting the future of this treasure into the hands of people just like you and me?

You enter a steep learning curve. And, you find out that it is all still a rather messy process, even among the very blessed and the most faithful. You pray, keep learning, spend time together, and share your resources (Acts 2, 4). You try to figure out what to do with the poor who are outsiders socially (Acts 6:1–7), and what to do with those new brothers and sisters whose theology and politics you have never liked (Acts 8:4–17). You argue about how to best honor Jesus (Gal 2, Acts 11, 15). You reread your scriptures in a new light (Luke 24, Acts 15). You almost refuse to go talk to someone Jesus just appeared to (Acts 9), and you almost refuse to obey an explicit vision in which the voice of God tells you to go and share the table in a Gentile home (Acts 10–11).

You say that sometimes eating meat sacrificed to idols might be all right, and sometimes it certainly is not (1 Cor 8, 10; Acts 15; Rom 14; Rev 2:14). You receive Spirit-led prophetic input telling you to go to Jerusalem (Acts 19:21, 20:22), not to go to Jerusalem (Acts 21:4), and that you will be arrested if you go to Jerusalem (Acts 21:11). Then with all that Spirit-led input, you must prayerfully decide to go or not to go (Acts 20:21–22). Like the authors of Acts and 1 Corinthians, you write about these tensions without attempting to smooth them all out because you know that somehow God is working through it all and is moving history on toward God's ultimate reign.

Throughout the New Testament there are texts that make it clear that the writers believed God's self-revelation was still in process in a manner that involves many contingencies (Phil 3:12–14; 1 Cor 1:13–17, 7:12, 13:9–12; Acts 1:8; 1 John 1:8; Rev 2:5, 3:3). At the same time, these writers who freely admit there is so much they do not know, and so much yet to be revealed, also adamantly swear before God that they are truth-tellers embedded in a real historical process in which a real God is really "with us." They insist that they are neither mythmakers nor liars (Luke 1:1–4; John 21:24; 2 Pet 1:16; 1 Cor 15:1–8), but rather humans who touched the very presence of God among us when they touched the human Jesus through whom God was communicating life and love to the rest of us humans (1 John 1:1–3). So, keep learning and keep growing (Rom 12:1–2; Eph 4:15). That is what it means for God to be your Father and you to be God's child!

The God of Jesus Will Accommodate Humans, and Even Compromise God's Ideals, to Pursue God's Purpose for Us.

Some of you might find the use of the word *God* and the word *accommodate* in the same sentence theologically disturbing. However, failure to understand that God frequently chooses to prioritize a relationship with flawed persons in flawed cultures, rather than insisting that God's ideals be met, often leads to sad outcomes in our understanding of Jesus's God.

When those of us who call ourselves *progressive* Christians fail to see that the God of the Old Testament is a God willing to accommodate to the times, place, context, and personalities through whom God is acting, we often end up wanting to replace the God of the Old Testament with the Jesus we remake in our own progressive image. The author of the book from which the following quotation is taken ignores the fact that every New Testament record presents Jesus as claiming the God of the Old Testament as his "Father" for whom he lives and for whom he is willing to die. I do not think Jesus's view of the Old Testament, God, or himself is captured in the following:

> I want to suggest that if you want to know whom [sic] God is you, go to one name, the name of Jesus [not YHWH, El, Adonai, El-Shaddai, etc.]. . . . If in the Hebrew Bible God's holiness, God's otherness, God's inapproachability,

and God's majesty are God's *primary attributes*, in the New Testament it is quite otherwise.[8]

On the other hand, those of us who see ourselves as *conservative* Christians often fail to see that the God of the Old Testament is the God who often is willing to accommodate to the times, places, contexts, and personalities through whom God is acting. When we will not take this reality into account, we remake God in our own conservative image. The authors of the following extract use the person they quote to illustrate how this tragedy has haunted the church.

> If slavery were legal, I'd probably have two myself. That would not have made me a racist. . . . I have a big heart, but the law is the law. I would have slaves, but I wouldn't treat them harshly because, after all, we are all humans. Last time I checked, slavery was acceptable back in the Bible days. So if slavery is cool with God; it is cool with me.[9]

Of course, only a few twenty-first–century American Christians would be so flip as the person just quoted was on social media, but it was this type of understanding of the Bible and of God that led the congregation of the early Puritan leader Cotton Mather to buy a slave for him as a gift, and allowed the still-heralded intellectual preacher Jonathan Edwards to own several slaves and support American slavery as biblically warranted.

It was this same way of understanding that allowed Christian White Americans to participate in and to support slaughtering the Native American tribes because they were the "Canaanites" and it was our "Manifest Destiny" to take the "New Israel" as God's gift to the Exceptional American White Settlers. It is why quite a few popular Christian leaders today still support patriarchy in the church, in the home, and in their staffing choices, as well as opposing the ERA for women. If you do not see God as a God who educates us through the processes of history, and especially through God's relationship with Jesus, consistency in reading the Bible as static leads to views of God and of obedience that are time-bound by the ancient cultures into which God spoke and acted.

Jesus seems to have had no problem combining his trust that God is all loving and all powerful with his understanding that God has chosen to be in genuinely responsive relationships that lead God to (at least temporarily) accommodate and even compromise in order to relate to us humans. Like the writers of the Old Testament, Jesus understood that God speaks to us where we are in history, and *God being with us* does not rubber-stamp for all times the limited understandings of reality expressed by even the many faithful (and sometimes not so faithful) people in the biblical narratives.

Neither their cultural limitations, their faith limitations, nor their personality limitations were understood to be sacred. It is God's relationship with us humans that

---

8. Hardin, *Jesus Driven*, 94.
9. Charles and Rah, *Unsettling Truths*, 98.

makes things sacred. It is a sacred and holy event when God meets us where we are and graciously loves us in the broken lives and cultures we bring to God. However, this mercy and grace does not sacralize the personal and cultural weaknesses into which God chooses to be self-revealing. It did not in Abraham's life, Rachel's life, or David's life. It does not in yours or mine either.

Jesus refers to the ways God worked through Jonah, Abraham, the widow of Zarephath, Naaman, Elijah, Elisha, David, Jeremiah, wars, patriarchy, slavery, polygamy, and various other parts of the Torah, without absolutizing the accommodations God was making by relating to humans in these situations. Unlike many of us, Jesus seemed to have no problem relating to God as the God who was with David in David's wars, while being certain that God was leading him as the "Son of David" to refuse to take up the sword. He continued to refuse even when almost everyone around him thought that is what God would want him to do.

It is great to find a moderately conservative theologian like Sandra Richter, who takes the Bible seriously as God's word to us but sees clearly that we were never meant to "canonize" the personalities and the cultures God chooses to show up in.[10] I too am maintaining that seeing that God is accommodating and responsive allows us to trust that God was truly involved in both speaking to and acting through flawed individuals within very flawed ancient social structures. We can see God at work without assuming we are to see these personalities and social structures as God's ideals. God did not intend for them to be considered *sacred* and *holy*, but God did pursue a *sacred* and *holy* relationship with these flawed children of God.

Unlike many of us who today call ourselves conservatives, Jesus saw no need to clean up the Old Testament claims about God's involvement in less-than-ideal lives and circumstances, but unlike many of us who call ourselves progressives he also saw no need to deny that God was genuinely present in these less than ideal lives and circumstances. At the same time, Jesus knew that following God's guidance in his life and times meant not treating the earlier experiences with God as *absolutes* that Jesus must repeat. Jesus related to God as the "One God" who is willing to work in many structures, and in many personal lives, without justifying or sacralizing all the social structures, or all the words, or all the current scientific or cultural understandings, or all the acts of an individual who is genuinely a faithful agent of God's work in the world.

I think all the New Testament writers reflect the approach Jesus took (Mark 10:1–9—instructions for human realities). Some do so explicitly. James says the risky faithfulness of "Rahab the prostitute," was declared "righteous" by God for hiding the spies while she was still the Madame of her household (Jas 2:25). He compares her risky trusting response to God with that of Abraham. James is not encouraging prostitution as an Old Testament model for receiving God's grace. He is celebrating God's

---

10. Richter, *Epic*, 22–23.

gracious willingness to accommodate to where we are when we open ourselves to a relationship with God.

The letter of Hebrews is even clearer in espousing Jesus's approach to the Scriptures. He reminds the reader of narrative after narrative portraying the risky faithfulness of less than sterling characters whom God rewarded for seeking God (Heb 11:1—12:1). The tension in God's willingness to accommodate is then made clear. Because of their risky faithfulness the "world was not worthy of them," yet none of them arrived at God's goal for humans. "*God had planned something better* for us so that only together with us would they *be made perfect [complete]*" (Heb 11:38–40, *emphasis mine*). What is this something better, that makes sense of God's willingness to accommodate to our realities? It is Jesus who is *the trailblazer who has "completed/perfected" human faithfulness*. He is both the fulfillment of human faithfulness and the completion of a better relationship with God that no other human could complete without him (Heb 12:1–2).

God's educational process did not end with Jesus's ascension. It continued in the early church, just as Jesus said it would need to (John 14:26, 16:12–14). It wasn't easy, and it was sometimes messy. God is still presented as accommodating to where people are, as God slowly tries to move them forward in maturity.

I mentioned earlier how messy the prophetic messages were concerning Paul going to Jerusalem after his third missionary journey.[11] The following are two more examples of the New Testament's honesty about the messiness of the ongoing educational process that God accommodated to in working with humans who had real faith, wanted to be faithful, and had to negotiate the real world in which they were living.

There is honesty about the messy educational process involving the tensions between conservative Jewish followers of Jesus, more liberal Hellenized followers of Jesus, and Gentiles who were becoming followers of Jesus. The learning curve was steep and messy.

1. In Acts 6, we find out that the Hellenistic widows who would have reflected more Gentile influences were not being treated equally with the widows more fully identified with Jerusalem. Wisely, this was addressed by appointing seven more Hellenized Jewish leaders to oversee the ongoing ministry.

2. In Acts 8, a large group of Samaritans, who many in Jerusalem considered heretics, turned to Jesus through the ministry of Philip, one of the most culturally liberal and Hellenized leaders in the early church. It took a movement of God's Spirit to convince the Apostles to accept the Samaritans and to convince the Samaritans to accept the Apostles.

3. In Acts 10–11, Peter finds himself first in deep tension with the voice of heaven concerning eating nonkosher food and going to a Gentile's home. Then he finds himself in deep tension with his fellow church leaders because he relented and

11. *See* chapter 14.

went. It cannot have helped that the first Gentile household to experience the outpouring of God's Spirit was headed by a warrior of the occupying empire.

4. In Acts 15, the church leaders argued openly about the ramifications of Gentile incorporation into the Jesus Movement. When they finally came to an agreement, the letter they wrote was itself an accommodation. The letter indicates they would have loved to say more, but they knew they shouldn't.

5. In Galatians 2, we have two events narrated by Paul, describing some of the most influential leaders in the early church wrestling with the theological conundrums created by Gentile inclusion. In a behind-the-scenes event in Jerusalem, Paul describes a meeting that seems to have barely reached an agreement with no participant being overly happy. Then he describes a later public confrontation that began with some visitors from Jerusalem and then escalated into a showdown with Peter and Barnabas about the practical implications of Jewish and Gentile table fellowship.

6. By the time Paul wrote to the church at Rome, the shoe was beginning to be on the other foot. It was now necessary to instruct and challenge the attitude of Gentile followers of Jesus toward Jewish people. Like many Gentiles in the Roman Empire, some members of the Roman church were expressing anti-Semitism and anti-Judaism. Paul was extremely unhappy with them, and he warned them that their arrogance and lack of appreciation for what God had done through the Jewish people endangered their spiritual well-being (Rom 11:13–24).

7. Sometimes, in the midst of all of these messy tensions, God's ideals were written about in soaring rhetoric. Through God's relationship with Jesus, all the walls between Gentiles and Jews have been broken down, and the two have become one (Eph 2:11–22). In our mutual relationship with Jesus the Messiah, we stand equally, whether Jew or Gentile (Gal 3:28). People of every tribe on earth join with the tribes of Israel to praise God for what has been given to us through Jesus (Rev 7:4–10).

8. But, like us, those early followers of Jesus didn't always live out God's ideals. Still, God was with them, and God is with us. In the midst of the messy tensions between the followers of Jesus who were Gentiles and those who were Jews, we see James and Paul attempting to work out a Spirit-led response to a big problem. James says thousands of Jewish followers of Jesus have come to believe that Paul has himself basically become a Gentile and completely abandoned the Torah and the Temple. The two leaders agree to act on a solution James proposes. It seemed very wise, but it lands Paul in prison for several years (Acts 21:17–23:34). Of course, if that had not happened, we might not have several of the letters in our New Testament. God works in strange and messy ways indeed.

Various New Testament writers also provide us with glimpses into another tense, messy, and never completely resolved educational process. In a Gentile world where almost all meat was sacrificed to idols before being sold in the marketplace, what should followers of Jesus do about eating "meat sacrificed to idols?"

1. The apostles and the Jerusalem elders, with the consent of the whole church including Paul, sent a letter to the new mostly Gentile communities. The leaders' tone indicates that they thought they were asking little of these new converts. They gave only four brief instructional statements on how these Gentiles should behave in practicing their new relationship with Jesus. One of those was the unequivocally statement "abstain from what has been sacrificed to idols" (Acts 15:22–29).

2. By the time Paul wrote to the Corinthians, he had a lot more to say beyond the early agreements in Jerusalem. He is straightforward, but rather nuanced in his instructions. He says that it is alright to eat meat that has been sacrificed to idols, as long as you, and anyone else involved with the meal, know that idols are nothing. If there is no idolatry, and no fear of idols, feel free to eat if you wish. He even notes that at times it might be a better witness to eat than to insult a host by raising questions (1 Cor 8:4–13; 10:25–33).

3. Two other passages about eating, and not eating, certain foods seem to be abbreviated versions of the instructions to the Corinthians (Col 2:15–23; Romans 14:1–23).

4. Another letter addresses eating and not eating from a different perspective. Forbidding people to marry or forbidding the eating of certain foods can reflect the influence of "deceiving spirits." Sexual expression and foods are holy gifts from God when received with thanksgiving, scriptural authority, and prayer (1Tim 4:1–6).

5. Then in a letter likely written in a time of persecution, John tells the church at Pergamum to correct the members of their community who are eating meat sacrificed to idols and committing sexual immorality (Rev 2:13–20).

In some important situations, the agreement between leaders of the new community of followers of Jesus is, at best, quite tentative and meets with mixed consequences going forward. What the leaders all agreed on was that Jesus lived faithfully, gave his life out of love for God and the rest of us humans, was raised from the dead by God, lives as the first glorified human exalted to the right hand of God, is reigning now in God's kingdom, and will someday reign over all the kingdoms of the earth. Beyond that, these early leaders were trying to figure it all out as they went. Their differences showed in how they wrote and spoke. Various parts of the New Testament make it clear that some people in the early church accentuated these differences between gifted leaders into excuses for their own divisive goals. Do you follow James, Peter, or Paul? This became divisive for some in Galatia (Gal 2). Do you think James, Paul, Peter, or Apollos is a better leader? This question divided people at Corinth (1 Cor 3–4).

Then, as the years went by in Church history, Peter, despite his marital status, became the "first Pope." Just as difficult to fathom is the fact that the radical, liberal, Hellenistic Jew named Paul became the champion of legalistic Christians. I sometimes wonder whether, even right now, Jesus has to tell Peter and Paul to calm down and remember this always was a messy process.

Can you accept the dynamic tension in these five claims the New Testament presents us with as truths?

1. Our understanding of "the God and Father of our Lord Jesus the Messiah" and how we should respond to God in our culture and our subcultures is limited and filled with times when God chooses to accommodate to our limitations, just as God has so often done in the past.

2. God's self-revelation in the Bible provides us with equal opportunities to grow in truth and mature in life, or to misuse it by adding *authority* to our lies and our perversions of truth. If quotations from the Bible could be used to tempt Jesus as he began his ministry (Luke 4:10), we cannot expect that Scriptures will end the tensions and the messiness for us either. Nevertheless, the Scriptures are an important and necessary gift from God, without which we would know little of God's desire for covenant-relationships with humans, and nothing of God's first completed human, Jesus.

3. We are privileged to participate in cocreating with God the future that God is pursuing for humanity, and our choices and actions genuinely matter in this process. But we can never control the process, and our freedoms and choices can never thwart God's ultimate goal.

4. Jesus participated fully as one of us in this human reality before God, as he again and again chose to be faithful to God and incarnated the Spirit of God and the Word of God. Because of this submission and obedience to God, God saved him from death, completed him as a human, and is able to save the rest of us in relationship to Jesus (Heb 5:7–9).

5. Jesus is God's "better way" that justifies God's willingness to accommodate to our realities so long as we join in the risky choice to trust God in the real world. This allows God to keep moving us toward the "completion" of our humanity that Jesus has already attained.

In her poem *Farewell*, Emily Dickinson captured our need to take a risk by trusting that God will hold on to us and save us from death, even though we cannot save ourselves:

> Tie the strings to my Life, My Lord, Then I am ready to go! . . . Held fast in the Everlasting Race—By my own choice, and Thee.[12]

---

12. Dickinson, *Complete Poems*, 128.

I wish she had written "By Thee, and my own choice," but either way, her sentiment is similar to Paul's, "Not that I have already obtained all this, or have already been made perfect, but I press on to take hold of that for which Christ Jesus took hold of me" (Phil 3:12), or to his even more risky sounding "Run in such a way as to get the prize . . . I beat my body and make it my slave, so that after I have preached to others, I myself will not be disqualified for the prize" (1 Cor 9:24–27).

I can live with the risky reality that says our only claim on God is God's goodness, mercy, and love. That reality is how God takes hold of us and holds us tightly. God asks us to respond by being willing to keep returning to our trust in what God has done for us in God's relationship with Jesus. Are you willing to take this risk? Do we really have any other choice, if we wish to relate to "The God and Father of our Lord Jesus the Messiah?"

I find that "The God and Father of our Lord Jesus the Messiah" is willing to work in the world and to guide and speak to us through the Bible in a manner that is both non-absolutist and non-relativistic. The lives we offer God are lives that certainly have not arrived at the goal, but are securely held by God's love and our choice to love God back. God is willing to be present with whoever will allow it in a manner that is personal, loving, communicative, responsive—and therefore, sometimes tense, messy, and far less than ideal. This is a lot like all of our best relationships as humans in this world.

Don't you, too, depend on God to compromise God's ideals in order to be present in your far less than completely faithful daily life? I definitely do! Don't we all have to trust that God will accommodate to our many twenty-first–century cultural blind spots? None of us deserves this love and mercy, but God accommodates to where we are because we so desperately need what we do not deserve. Absolutely! And that is absolute love!

RESPONSIVENESS, ACCOMMODATION, AND CONTINGENCY ON GOD'S PART DO NOT JEOPARDIZE GOD'S ULTIMATE PURPOSE.

God's Character is Not Threatened by Contingency and Accommodation.

I am not demeaning God's character or Jesus's character when I say that Jesus saw God as willing to accommodate to human reality and to temporarily compromise God's ideals because of our sins and weaknesses. What else could forgiveness mean? What else could it mean that Jesus "died for us?"

However, Jesus, and the New Testament writers following him, were clear that God does not ever compromise God's character of love and goodness. This character is expressed in an unchanging stubborn commitment to work toward good for any human who will receive it (Jas 1:17;). Neither does God ever compromise God's ultimate purpose—a forever human family where God's love reigns and individuals are "in the image of God" forever (Rom 8:28–30).

It is not because God is weak, but because God is powerfully purposeful and powerfully loving that God accommodates. It is not because God cannot speak truth through the Bible that God chooses to communicate to us in human language, which can always be misquoted and distorted. It is because God wants real relationships with real humans. Communication, as difficult and fraught with possible misunderstanding as it always is in this broken world, is also central to any good relationship. All communication, even from God, is in danger of being misunderstood in our current brokenness—sometimes innocently, sometimes not at all innocently, and sometimes somewhere in between innocence and outright guilt.

God's relationship with Jesus is not embedded in a view of God's sovereignty and purpose that demands that, prior to human history, God laid out a detailed blueprint that was finished in every detail and could not be altered. It is not because God is weak that God allows humans to make choices that temporarily thwart God's will and desires. It is because God is so powerful that God does not need to control our choices in order to reach God's goals and ultimate purposes.

This God of the Bible allows cocreators to make real choices that change reality. Yet God never changes in character or in ultimate purpose. This describes a very powerful and active God. Much bigger than the God we Christians have sometimes constructed who must control everything in order to be God. The God of the Bible has an ultimate sovereign purpose that means God chooses to limit God's exercise of power in order to pursue God's desire to have genuine relationships with humans.

We humans cannot be "in the image of God" if our choices do not really matter, or are not really "our" choice. After all, "choosing" is an integral part of God's character. Jesus was truly one of us, only if his choices involved risks for him and brought about responsiveness to those risky choices on God's part. You do not sweat drops of blood if you are not really making meaningful and difficult choices that are yet to be completed faithfully. Our master story is a about the God who now has the Firstborn of the human cocreators who can work freely and powerfully with God to bring about God's future age for the rest of us humans.

A final biblical analogy—isn't it possible that God really is the leader of a group of very fallible humans who are on an adventure with God? We are being liberated from a broken world that enslaves us, and formed into God's promised kingdom of the future. We make many choices along the way. Not all will be the best choices. Some will even highly disappoint God and make God angry. But the "cloud of the presence" will lead us on, and we will arrive in the promised land—a completed humanity through God's relationship with Jesus. In some ways, it is a very risky adventure since it requires trusting God in the wildernesses of our lives and of our history. In another way, it is not risky at all. The character of the God and Father of Jesus the Messiah is complete trustworthiness.

God's Ultimate Goals are Not Threatened by Contingency and Accommodation.

God's Audacious Ultimate Goal is Secure.

Various letters in the New Testament affirm what the prophets in the Old Testament often proclaimed—despite human frailties and failures, God ultimately keeps the covenant-promises and reaches the goal God has for human history. God's character as a faithful God and Jesus's faithful relationship with God guarantee the outcome. Paul states his conviction that God will finally liberate us humans from our slavery to sin and death and bring us into the "glorious freedom of the children of God" (Rom 8:18–21)—a freedom that includes us being "glorified" into the likeness of God's Son which has always been God's ultimate "purpose" for humans (Rom 8:28–31). He follows this declaration with the soaring promise that nothing and no one can prevent this ultimate fulfilling of God's purpose.

> [35] Who shall separate us from the love of Christ? Shall trouble or hardship or persecution or famine or nakedness or danger or sword? [37] No, in all these things we are more than conquerors through him who loved us. [38] For I am convinced that neither death nor life, neither angels nor demons, neither the present nor the future, nor any powers, [39] neither height nor depth, nor anything else in all creation, will be able to separate us from the love of God that is in Christ Jesus our Lord (Rom 8:35, 37–38).

In an earlier letter, Paul encouraged new followers of Jesus with a similar understanding of what God's faithfulness guarantees as a final outcome of human history.

> [23] May God himself, the God of peace, sanctify you through and through. May your whole spirit, soul and body be kept blameless at the coming of our Lord Jesus Christ. [24] The one who calls you is faithful, and he will do it (1 Thess 5:23–24)!

Throughout the Bible, it is God's character that is at stake when it comes to God making certain that the promises of the covenant with humans comes to a complete fulfillment. In Genesis 15, Abraham had a vision of an ancient covenant-making ceremony. In those ceremonies, the human with the lesser social status guaranteed faithfulness to the covenant being made with the more powerful person by walking between two halves of a sacrificed animal. The ceremony meant, if I am not faithful to the covenant, I expect to be destroyed just like this animal has been. But, in Abraham's strange vision, it is a symbol of God's power, not Abraham, that passes through the halves of the sacrifice. It is God's guarantee to Abraham that God would sooner not exist than ultimately fail to keep the covenant they were making.

The writer of Hebrews sees this act as God doubling down on God's promise that nothing can keep God from God's ultimate goal. God cannot lie, and God made a binding covenant; then God doubled down by swearing an oath that the covenant would be kept. The writer then says that the new step in this guarantee by God is that Jesus stands in God's presence as one of us humans, mediating God's covenant with us. The hope that God's ultimate goal will be achieved is "firm and secure," not because we get everything right or deserve it, but because of Jesus's faithfulness to God and to us (Heb 6:16-20).

In chapters 2-5, we explored the audacious claims made in the New Testament concerning God's goal for humanity. At the individual level, God promises to completely fulfill all human potential so that we can be fully female and male in the image of God. Because of Jesus's relationship to God and to us, we will ultimately be like Jesus—completed and glorified humans.

At the corporate level, all of the gifts of all cultures of all time will be incorporated into the future human culture God is planning to give us and "the kingdom of the world will become the kingdom of our Lord and his Messiah" (Rev 11:15; Isa 61:11).

The contingencies of history, the brokenness of our lives and our cultures, the fact that we can make choices that are not in line with God's ultimate goal—none of this will stop God from fulfilling the covenant-relationship God has made with us through the faithful Jesus. Our firstborn brother is the first of God's glorified and completed humans, but he certainly will not be the last (Heb 2:5-18).

The "God and Father of our Lord Jesus the Messiah" has moved forward toward this ultimate goal, is adopting us into the relationship with Jesus, is willing to give us down payments on this promise, by touching us with God's Spirit now. God will not relent until everything in our universe can be filled with humans who are incarnated with the presence of God (Eph 1:3-23). God has guaranteed this outcome through the life, death, and renewed life of Jesus the first completed and glorified human. This is who "The God and Father of our Lord Jesus the Messiah" is (Eph 1:3, 17-19). And, because of who Jesus's God is, and because of the relationship between God and Jesus, you cannot find a higher view of what it means for you to be human!

We Are Familiar with Ultimate Goals and Short-range Contingencies.

The Scriptures are filled with claims that God can achieve God's ultimate purpose, while allowing humans to make real choices that meaningfully change history for either the good or the bad. Even though we often seem to have difficulty incorporating it into our theology, we are quite familiar with the dynamic of achieving ultimate goals, while dealing with short-range contingencies. Here are a few examples that help me better understand how God can take the great risks that God's purpose demands, without risking God's character or God's final goal for humans.

The God and Father of Our Lord Jesus the Messiah: Revisited

1. One of the biblical writers' favorite descriptions of God is as homebuilder and temple-builder.

Both Israel and the church are identified as "God's house" and "God's household." Over 20 years ago, my wife and I decided that it was time to leave our home near the campus of the University of Illinois, which we had enjoyed for almost 30 years. Our reasons included the fact that we wanted to live in a home that was accessible to our friends in wheelchairs, and the realization that someday our own aging might well make a one-story home without any outside or inside stairs much more practical. We decided to have a new home built. We sat on the lot we were thinking of choosing and prayed with dear friends with whom we have shared many of the major decisions in our lives through the years. Soon after that prayer time, we decided to move forward, while asking God to make what would be our new house also God's house.

Although the level of our sovereignty certainly does not approach the level of God's sovereignty, already owning a home in an area that had appreciated to approximately the same value as the house we wanted to build empowered us. Those resources made our purpose sensible and perhaps doable. As we pursued our goal, it is fascinating to note how many people made choices for their own personal reasons, with little to no concern about us and our desires.

Although we exerted very little control over anyone in the process, we reached our ultimate, predestined (predecided) goal of having an accessible home.

The following are just a few of the contingencies we did not control. The local contractor had his own personal goals for taking on the job, which included keeping his crews working, keeping his family's economic resources growing, and moving forward with a new subdivision in which he had heavily invested. The banker, a friend of the contractor, agreed to the bridge loan for her own reasons and those of her bank—money, and keeping the contractor happy. She probably could not remember our names two hours after we walked out of her office. On the first day when the "for sale" sign went up, a wonderful Jewish family approached us about buying our current home for the exact price we needed to pay for the new house. They chose to do this because they wanted to live in that specific neighborhood to be close to a parent and to a special school.

The contractor's primary crew of four craftsmen never really learned our names—and now I cannot remember theirs—though they spoke to us cordially when we showed up to see how things were progressing. Each had his own motives for spending hours on our home, and none of their motives directly involved our hopes and dreams. One needed a summer income before returning to the classroom. One needed money to start his own business.

Truckers brought in supplies and timber, timber that had been cut and milled by many others somewhere far away. One day, a crew of about 20 roofers showed up, and in less than two days, the house had a roof. None of the 20 knew us, nor did they care to know us. On and on the process went—drywall, carpets, plumbing, siding, cabinets, electrical. . . .

All in all, over 50 people were directly involved in building our home and hundreds more from all over the country indirectly provided energy and materials for the project. Most could not have cared less whether we reached our goal or not, so long as they reached their goals. Nonetheless, our home was completed within a few weeks of the original target date.

My point? People with power and resources as limited as ours can decide on an ultimate goal and see that goal achieved, even though we exerted no direct control over the contingencies in the lives of 50+ people who chose to work on our home for their own reasons. Our goal was also brought to fruition although we had no power over the hundreds, probably thousands, of people who indirectly provided energy and resources that allowed our goal to be reached. Given this experience, why would I think that God's allowing humans to make all kinds of contingencies, freedoms, and choices along the way will thwart God's ultimate goal?

God can easily be *in control of* human history without *controlling* our human decision-making. All God needs to do is be aware of all possible choices and be ready to respond to each as it is made. I think this is the view of most, if not all, of the biblical writers regarding God's sovereignty as it relates to God's covenant relationship with humans and God's determination to reach God's goal for human history. This understanding of God's covenant relationship with humans allows our relationship with God to be a real relationship, and it allows God to be unchanging in character and purpose.

2. Perhaps the single most salient description of God's relationship with humans in the Bible is the relationship of parent to children.

My wife and I have three children, with two more adopted into the family through marriage. We now have four grandchildren and, so far, five great-grandchildren, with four still living. If we learned anything along the way, it was that the goal of raising a child who reaches adulthood as a capable and mature person means responding to many contingencies and surprises along the way. It also means having guidelines that are real, but flexible. It even means parenting with a gradual changing of what the rules (commandments) and instructions (Torah) are throughout the maturation process. In short, without ever giving up the ultimate goal, there is a process that demands changing perspectives, sometimes even accommodating and compromising, but certainly a lot of reorienting along the way.

A parent who will not allow for a process of changing the rules along the way will not end up being a good parent. When the child is three or four years old and, for the first time, is allowed to play in the yard without hand holding by the parent, there is a clear admonition, "Never, ever, go into the street—or else!" At six years of age, the ultimate parental goal is the same—a safe and sound child—but the commandment changes a bit for this child who now walks three blocks to school, "Never go into the street without looking both ways, and if any cars are coming, wait until they pass. Then hurry across with no playing in the street."

At thirteen, the rule changes yet again, "When you ride your bicycle in the street, be careful and remember that the cars always have the right of way, even if they don't. Stay away from the cars in the street. We want you alive and healthy." At sixteen, it all changes again as parents instruct (and plead), "If you want to drive the car, please stay in the street and not on the sidewalk. You must be careful, follow the rules, stay alert, and be especially careful about children on bicycles and children crossing the street. Remember, pedestrians and bicycles always have the right of way, even if they don't."

Wouldn't it be sad if our definition of commandments, sovereignty, and truth-telling as parents were such that, when our children were sixteen, we were still insisting on being "changeless and sovereign" parents who were still demanding, "Never go into the street?" Perhaps this would be less "messy" when we attempt to explain it to our children, but it would not be loving, nor would it be a healthy relationship.

Sadly, isn't this exactly the approach that many Christians take in understanding God's sovereignty and God's revelation? We act as though every commandment and every instruction is unchangeable, unaccommodating, inflexible, and timelessly absolute, no matter what age of human history it addressed? We act like God is a parent who doesn't know times change at different stages of life. Of course, it is this same belief that all the commands and instructions in the Bible were intended to be timeless that causes others of us not to even entertain the possibility that the Bible might be giving us a true, big-picture story about God's involvement in human history.

As for accommodating, our children often broke our family rules, though never as often as I had broken my parents' rules. Sometimes this resulted in us increasing the strength of the teaching and disciplining. But sometimes the new situation meant we had to revise the parental guidelines to fit the new context. The Bible is clear that God did the same. One example occurred when God gave Israel a king, even though God did not want them to make this move at that time (1 Sam 8–12). God chose to bless the decision anyway. Then God's first choice for king turned from God's ways, and God chose David in his place in order to move things forward (1 Sam 13:13–14). Good parenting involves a lot of flexibility on the way to the final goals!

3. According to the New Testament master narrative, history is God's classroom.

The One God is the giver of Torah, who teaches God's people how to relate to God and to other humans. The history of Israel prior to Jesus is described by Paul as having served as "tutor" to bring human history to a "fullness of time." Jesus chooses "disciples/students" who often address him as "Teacher." Yet even this wonderful teacher must tell his disciples that they need to know a lot more than they are able to absorb right now; the rest will have to come later (John 16:12). Paul describes history after Jesus as a process that involves us "knowing God in part," while moving toward God's future in which "we will know God fully as we are fully known" (1 Cor 13:12).

Understanding history as an educational process with an ultimate goal, but with many accommodations and contingencies along the way, is very helpful. The human interactions with God in the biblical materials begin with real and intelligent, but very inexperienced, human relationships with God and with one another. The interactions between the early humans and God sound a great deal like the interactions between a kindergarten teacher and her students. Soon there are contingencies based on the different choices and on the different personalities of the "students," and even on different classroom settings. With all of these contingencies the overall goal remains the same. We want each student to learn to excel with her gifts and to use them to help make society a better place. A good teacher makes many responses to the different choices, different contingencies, and different personal needs of her students. Her short-term goals and purposes can be modified as needed, but the goal does not change. I think this is the correct way to understand the obvious changes in how God relates to humans in the extensive era covered in the Old Testament and even in the brief era that spans the New Testament writings.

The relationship between God and Jesus is presented by the New Testament writers as a huge next step in this great educational process that is preparing humanity for God's purpose and God's future. Jesus grew with God, learned obedience, was made perfect/complete as a fully obedient human (Heb 5:7–10; Luke 2:50–52). History prior to Jesus and ever since is God's educational preparation for our future with God.

4. There are other analogies that are not as solidly rooted in biblical imagery as the previous ones, but that also make a strong point concerning the viability of ultimate purposes paired with real choices on the part of others.

One is to compare God's sovereignty and the pursuit of God's ultimate purpose to that of a lead jazz musician, who is constantly accommodating and responding to other musicians, while sharing the goal of making good music.[13]

Another describes the "sovereignty" of a great chess master who begins the game without controlling even a single move that the other player will make, and who, every step of the way, adjusts to those contingencies, yet is always many steps ahead in terms of pursuing the goal of checkmate. This is like God, who is described in the Bible as planning far ahead for all possibilities and contingencies, and who has no need to exert absolute control over each move.

Another analogy notes the difference between a stage play or movie that is 100% scripted, with no allowed variations, and another in which the director allows a great deal of freedom of interpretation on the part of the actors. Perhaps a director even

---

13. Miller, *Like Jazz*, ix.

encourages improvisation and then adjusts the play or movie to the contingencies that arise in the process. This is all done without ever relinquishing the original plotline.

I personally love to envision God as our "worship team leader"—delighting in the new roll played by the drummer, being thrilled that the soprano and the alto sing different parts, and enjoying the new creative riff introduced by the bass guitarist, as well as the beautiful interlude the pianist has been perfecting. God allows all of this creative freedom; yet God always insists that we all sing and play God's song, and not wander off into something else.

SUMMARY

The "God and Father of our Lord Jesus the Messiah" might scare us, or comfort us, or both. Jesus's God is willing to take risks, be hurt, wait patiently, love fiercely, pursue relentlessly, be present, be absent, accommodate, compromise, demand, and forgive. Scary, comforting, or both, this is who Jesus's God was and is. And through this maze we call human history, Jesus's God presses on faithfully toward a goal so audacious that we would never have imagined it or believed it if we could not see that one of us humans is already there. For this reason, it seems appropriate to conclude with a passage I have referenced several times.

> [9] But we see Jesus, who was made a little lower than the angels, now crowned with glory and honor because he suffered death, so that by the grace of God he might taste death for everyone. [10] In bringing many sons [and daughters] to glory, it was fitting that God, for whom and through whom everything exists, should make the author of their salvation perfect [or, complete] through suffering. [11] Both the one who makes men [and women] holy and those who are made holy are of the same family. So, Jesus is not ashamed to call them brothers [and sisters] (Heb 2:9–11).

Conclusion

SO WHAT?

The theme of this entire book has been the claim that Jesus was, is, and always will be human. I trust that it has become clear that several New Testament writers make this claim explicitly, and others do so implicitly. I have asked you throughout to consider what might be for you a different lens through which to see Jesus in the New Testament. In addition to a new pair of glasses, there are many other good images describing a search for a better master story of reality.

Thomas Kuhn called it a "paradigm shift" as he evaluated scientific progress. He maintained that we tend to doggedly hold on to our old paradigms no matter how much data is being ignored. Only when we finally have so much data that our old paradigm begins to malfunction will we begin to search for a better lens.[1] Brian McLaren calls it locating our "framing story."[2] Vernard Eller described what we have been doing as "seesaw theology," in which we attempt to let God's purpose dominate our picture, rather than focusing only on how we have framed our faith.[3] Another way to look at our journey is as the New Testament's completion of the framework Sandra Richter gave for understanding God's revelation in the Old Testament. She says it is not a hodge-podge, but as a single epic with God as the main character.[4]

But there is a question that always remains after any claim—*so what?* This book is important to me if it accomplished at least one of the following goals for you as a reader.

1. If you are a follower of Jesus, I hope it has been helpful to you, as it has been to me, in honoring both Jesus and God more than ever. I want it to encourage you to value more than ever what it means to be human. I hope you find it exciting that we humans, who live in constant tension between what we are and what we

---

1. Kuhn, *Structure of Revolutions*, 91–109.
2. McLaren, *Everything Must Change*, 5–6.
3. Eller, *His End Up*, 9–16.
4. Richter, *Epic of Eden*, 15–20.

know we could be, can be "completed" both individually and corporately. I pray it also encourages you to desire to live more fully than ever in the direction Jesus points us—loving God and loving your neighbor as yourself. Why? Above all else because God loves both you and your neighbor more than you can imagine. Sound theology is important only if it frees us to experience more of God's love, and in doing so frees us to express more of God's love (commitment to enacting good) for others in very real and practical ways.

2. If you are not a follower of Jesus, but you are interested in what the New Testament writers had to say about the relationship Jesus and God shared, I hope the book intrigued you. In fact, I pray it has encouraged you to explore further the claim that God has defined human potential in the life of the risen, completed, and glorified Jesus—God's "firstborn" in the renewal of humanity. You too are a person God loves and wishes to "complete."

3. If you are neither a follower of Jesus nor very interested in the New Testament claims, I hope whatever led you to read this book has been rewarded. I also pray you can at least hear that some of us who are followers of Jesus do not share in the all-too-prevalent devaluing of your humanity by people claiming the name "Christian." I know this attitude has permeated far too much of Christian history and continues to be expressed by many who claim Jesus is their Lord. This devaluing of you does not represent Jesus, nor the God he serves. You and your gifts are valuable to the rest of us humans, and I deeply believe you are valuable to God as well. I hope you can see that followers of Jesus do not have to be arrogant, primitive, naïve, or gullible in order to trust that Jesus really might be God's Son, who was, is, and always will be human in the image of God.

4. I mentioned in the Introduction that I would not attempt to reconcile my understanding of the New Testament presentation of the relationship between God and Jesus with third- and fourth-century credal theology. My goal was to emphasize what I think has been a terribly underemphasized theme of the New Testament—Jesus was, is, and always will be one of us humans. If my avoidance of these ongoing debates has bothered you, allow me to point you to the words of someone who did attempt this reconciliation. Hear the words of the late Larry Hurtado, who was an astute biblical scholar and avowedly trinitarian:

> In particular, Jesus's resurrection constitutes the emphatic reaffirmation of Jesus (and *precisely as the embodied human figure*) as thereafter uniquely to be included in the understanding of divine purposes and even (per traditional Trinitarian faith) in what is meant by "God." To use Trinitarian language, "God the Son" is eternal, without beginning or end. But in the incarnation, "the Son" became genuinely an embodied human, and in Jesus's resurrection, this incarnate move was irrevocably reaffirmed by "God." *In short, from Jesus's*

resurrection onward, "God" in some profound way now includes a glorified human. That, I believe, represents quite a significant alteration (emphasis mine)![5]

So, however you sort out the relationship between the New Testament and the "Trinity," the thrust of this book still holds—the New Testament followers of Jesus followed a Jesus who they knew as still human then, now, and forever.

5. Whether you are a follower of Jesus or not, I hope you have seen that the writers of Scriptures thought it was alright to fuss at God about this messy, stormy, unjust, bent, and broken world we live in. Psalmists asked God to quit sleeping through the turmoil of their time (Pss 44:23, 7:6, 35:23). Job wanted to take God to court (Job 9:32–35). Jeremiah reminded God that the promises of Psalm 1 did not seem to be working. Even worse, the world seemed to be working as an exact reversal of those promises (Jer 12:1–4).

    Jesus's disciples did not mind questioning him either. They often did so. At one point they screamed at him to wake up as he slept through a raging storm. They feared it was going to take them, and him, down along with their boat. Jesus did calm that storm. Of course, another raging storm of a different kind met them as soon as they reached shore. Life with Jesus is often like that (Mark 5:2–9)! But he reminded them of what I hope is a message you take away from reading this book. Jesus said it was actually the disciples who needed to wake up. They needed to realize they could trust him. If he was in their boat, no raging storm could destroy them (Mark 4:36–41).

    My challenge to you is to bet your life on that truth! If Jesus is allowed to live in your lifeboat, you will live because he lives. The storms will rage, but death will not win. You mean that much to him. And you mean that much to "the God and Father of our Lord Jesus the Messiah."

6. No matter what you think of some of the claims in this book, please know the New Testament conviction is that God intends through the relationship God and Jesus share to renew *Creation*, to renew human *Community*, and to renew human *Character*. No higher view of human potential has ever been presented. An audacious claim? Absolutely! A claim worthy of a great God? No doubt! And, this ultimate renewal flows from the wondrous relationship between God and *Jesus, who was, is, and will always be human—one of us*!

Thanks to you for your time and thought in reading this book. Be blessed!

---

5. Hurtado. *God in Theology*, 113.

Bibliography

Albright, William and John Mann. *Matthew*, Anchor Bible 26. New York: Doubleday, 1982.
Alter, Robert. *Genesis: Translation and Commentary*. New York: W.W. Norton, 1966.
Bailey, Kenneth E. *Poet and Peasant*. Grand Rapids: Eerdmans, 1976.
Barclay, William. *Flesh and Spirit*. Nashville: Abingdon, 1962.
Barth, Markus. *Ephesians 1–3*, Anchor Bible 34. New York: Doubleday, 1974.
———. *Ephesians 4–6*, Anchor Bible 34A. New York: Doubleday, 1980.
Bauckham, Richard. *Jesus and the Eyewitnesses: The Gospels as Eyewitness Testimony*. Grand Rapids: Eerdmans, 2006.
———. *Jesus and the God of Israel: God Crucified and Other Studies on the New Testament's Christology of Divine Identity*. Grand Rapids: Eerdmans, 2009.
Bodo, Murray. *The Way of St. Francis: The Challenge of Franciscan Spirituality for Everyone*. Cincinnati: St, Anthony Messenger, 1995.
Bonhoeffer, Dietrich. *The Cost of Discipleship*. New York: Macmillan, 1977.
Borg, Marcus. *Meeting Jesus Again for the First Time*. San Francisco: HarperCollins, 1994.
Boyarin, Daniel. *The Jewish Gospels: The Story of the Jewish Christ*. New York: New Press, 2012.
Brown, Raymond. *The Gospel According to John*, Anchor Bible 29, volume 1. New York: Doubleday, 1984.
Brueggemann, Walter. *The Message of the Psalms*. Minneapolis: Augsburg, 1984.
Carroll, James. *Constantine's Sword: The Church and the Jews*. New York: Mariner Books, 2002.
Charles, Mark and Soong-Chan Rah. *Unsettling Truths: The Ongoing Dehumanizing Legacy of the Doctrine of Discovery*. Downers Grove: InterVarsity, 2019.
Claiborne, Shane. *Common Prayer: A Liturgy for Ordinary Radicals*. Grand Rapids: Zondervan, 2010.
Cone, James H. *The Cross and the Lynching Tree*. Maryknoll, NY: Orbis, 2018.
Courtney, Jeremy. *Love Anyway*. Grand Rapids: Zondervan, 2019.
Crossan, John Dominic. *Jesus: A Revolutionary Biography*. San Francisco: Harper, 1994.
Davis, Ellen. *Biblical Prophecy: Perspectives for Christian Theology, Discipleship, and Ministry in the Interpretation Series*. Louisville: Westminster, 2014.
———. "Take Your Son" in *Getting Involved with God*. Lanham: Rowman & Littlefield, 2001.
Dawkins, Richard. *The God Delusion*. New York: Mariner, 2008.
Dickinson, Emily. *The Complete Poems of Emily Dickinson*, #279, ed. Thomas H. Johnson. New York: Back Bay Books, 1976.
Dio Cassius, Lucius. *Roman History*, trans. Earnest Cary, Volume VIII, Books 61–70 (Loeb Classical Library No. 176). Cambridge: Harvard University Press, 1925.

Dodd, C. H. *The Interpretation of the Fourth Gospel.* Cambridge: Cambridge University Press, 1995.

Dunn, James D. G. *Did the First Christians Worship Jesus? The New Testament Evidence.* Louisville: Westminster, 2010.

Ehrman, Bart D. *How Jesus Became God: The Exaltation of a Jewish Preacher from Galilee.* New York: HarperCollins, 2015.

Eliade, Mircea. *The Sacred and the Profane: The Nature of Religion*, trans. Willard R. Trask. New York: Harcourt, Brace, and World, 1957.

Eller, Vernard. *His End Up: Getting God into the New Theology.* Nashville: Abingdon, 1969.

Evans, Rachel Held. *Inspired: Slaying Giants, Walking on Water, and Loving the Bible Again.* Nashville: Nelson, 2018.

Feuerbach, Ludwig. *The Essence of Christianity.* New York: Harper Torchbooks, 1957.

France, R. T. *The Gospel of Mark* in The New International Greek Commentary. Grand Rapids: Eerdmans, 2002.

———. *Jesus and The Old Testament.* London: Tyndale, 1971.

Franzmann, Martin H. *Follow Me: Discipleship According to Saint Matthew.* St. Louis: Concordia, 1961.

Freehof, Solomon B. *Book of Isaiah.* New York: Union of American Hebrew Congregations, 1972.

Freud, Sigmund. *The Future of an Illusion.* Garden City: Anchor, 1964.

Grant, Michael. *The Jews in the Roman World.* Dorchester: Dorsett, 1984.

Gushee, David P. *After Evangelicalism: The Path to a New Christianity.* Louisville: Westminster, 2020.

———. "White American Christianity Is Rooted in Colonial Empire-Building," https//sojo.net/magazine/septemberoctober-2020/white-american-christianity-rooted-colonial-empire-building.

Hardin, Michael. *The Jesus Driven Life.* Lancaster: JDL, 2013.

Hays, Richard B. *The Faith of Jesus Christ: The Narrative Substructure of Galatians 3:1-4:11.* Grand Rapids: Eerdmans, 2002.

———. "Reading Scripture in Light of the Resurrection" in *The Art of Reading Scripture*, ed. Ellen F. Davis & Richard B. Hays. Grand Rapids: Eerdmans, 2003.

Heschel, Abraham Joshua. *God in Search of Man: A Philosophy of Judaism.* New York: American Book–Stratford, 1955.

Hurtado, Larry. *God in New Testament Theology.* Nashville: Abingdon, 2010.

———. *How on Earth Did Jesus Become a God? Historical Questions about Earliest Devotion to Jesus.* Grand Rapids: Eerdmans, 2005.

Irenaeus. *Against Heresies*, book 4 in Ante-Nicene Fathers, Vol.1, ed. Roberts A. Donaldson, 1885.

Jefferson, Lee M. "Jesus the Magician?" *Biblical Archaeology Review*, vol. 46, no. 4.

Jennings, Willie James. *After Whiteness: An Education in Belonging*, Grand Rapids, Eerdmans, 2020.

Josephus, Flavius. "Against Apion" in *Antiquity of the Jews* in Works of Flavius Josephus, vol. IV, trans. William Whiston. Grand Rapids: Baker, 1974.

Kimmerer, Robin Wall. *Braiding Sweetgrass.* Minneapolis: Milkweed Editions, 2013.

Kindi, Ibrim X. *Stamped from the Beginning: The Definitive History of Racist Ideas in America.* New York: Nation Books, 2016.

King, Martin Luther, Jr. *Strength to Love.* Minneapolis: Fortress, 2010.

Kruger, C. Baxter. *Jesus and the Undoing of Adam*. Jackson: Perichoresis, 2003.
Lapide, Pinchas. *The Resurrection of Jesus: A Jewish Perspective*. Minneapolis: Augsburg, 1983.
Levenson, John D. *Resurrection and the Restoration of Israel: The Ultimate Victory of the God of Life*. New Haven: Yale University, 2006.
Levine, Amy-Jill. *The Misunderstood Jew: The Church and the Scandal of the Jewish Jesus*. New York: HarperOne, 2006.
Lewis, C. S. *A Grief Observed*. New York: Seabury, 1961.
———. *Miracles*. New York: Touchstone, 1996.
Lorde, Audre. *Sister Outsider: Essays and Speeches*. Trumansburg, NY: Crossing, 1984.
MacCulloch, Diarmaid. *Christianity: The First Three Thousand Years*. New York: Viking, 2010.
Marcel, Gabriel. *Homo Viator*. New York: Harper Torchbooks, 1962.
McKnight, Scot. *The Jesus Creed: Loving God, Loving Others*. Brewster: Paraclete, 2004.
———. *Reading Romans Backwards: A Gospel of Peace in the Midst of Empire* (Waco: Baylor University Press, 2019.
McLaren, Brian D. *Everything Must Change: Jesus, Global Crises, and a Revolution of Hope*. Nashville: Thomas Nelson, 2007.
———. *More Ready than You Realize*. Grand Rapids: Zondervan, 2002.
McNeil, Brenda Salter. Comment in Swanson *Rediscipling the White Church* Book Launch, May 21, 2020. https://www.facebook.com/PastorDavidWSwanson/videos/882397075569939/.
Meyers, Ched. *Binding the Strong Man: A Political Reading of Mark's Story of Jesus*. Maryknoll: Orbis, 2018.
Miles, Jack. *God: A Biography*. New York: Alfred P. Knopf, 1997.
Miller, Donald. *Blue like Jazz*. Nashville: Thomas Nelson, 2003.
Nietzsche, Fredrick. *Thus Spoke Zarathustra*, trans. Thomas Common. Ottawa: East India, 2019.
Pascal, Blaise. *Pensees*, trans. W. F. Trotter, #33 Pascal in Great Books of the Western World. London: Britannica, 1978.
Peterson, Eugene. *Reversed Thunder*. New York: HarperCollins, 1991.
Piper, John. *Coronavirus and Christ*. Wheaton: Crossway, 2020.
Pulkinghorne, John. *The God of Hope and the End of the World*. New Haven: Yale University, 2002.
Remen, Rachel Naomi, *My Grandfather's Blessings*. New York: Riverhead Books, 2000.
Richter, Sandra. *The Epic of Eden*: *A Christian Entry into the Old Testament*. Downers Grove: InterVarsity, 2008.
Robinson, Marilynne. *The Givenness of Things*. New York: Farrar, Straus and Giroux, 2015.
Rohr, Richard. *The Universal Christ*. New York: Convergent, 2019.
Sartre, Jean-Paul. *John-Paul Sartre: To Freedom Condemned—A Guide to His Philosophy*, ed. Justus Streller, trans. Wade Baskin. New York: Philosophical Library, 1960.
Schama, Simon. *The Story of the Jews: Finding the Words (1000 BC–1492 AD)*. New York: HarperCollins, 2013.
Second Macabees, ch 7.
Simkins, Ron. *Truth, Tears, Turning, and Trusting: A Pastor's Plea to End Our Ongoing Anti-Semitism and Anti-Judaism*. Eugene: Wipf and Stock, 2020.
"Spanish Massacre the French in Florida, 1565." http://www.eyewitnesstohistory.com/spanishmassacre.htm.

Bibliography

Spong, John Shelby. *A New Christianity for a New World: Why Traditional Faith is Dying and How a New Faith is Being Born*. New York: HarperCollins, 2002.

Stevenson, Bryan. *Just Mercy*. New York: Spiegel & Grau, 2015.

Swanson, David. *Rediscipling the White Church: From Cheap Diversity to True Solidarity*. Downers Grove: InterVarsity, 2020.

Thielicke, Helmut. *The Waiting Father*, trans. John Doberstein. New York: Harper & Row, 1957.

Thurman, Howard. *Jesus and the Disinherited*. Boston: Beacon, 1949.

Tielhard de Chardin, Pierre. *The Phenomenon of Man*. New York: Harper Perennial, 2008.

U. S. Constitution, 6th Amendment.

Walton, John. *The Lost World of Genesis One: Ancient Cosmology and the Origins Debate*. Downers Grove: InterVarsity, 2009.

Watterson, Bill. "Calvin and Hobbes," (Sunday comic strip), *The Chicago Tribune*, December 30, 1990.

Weatherhead, Leslie. *The Will of God*. Nashville: Abingdon, 1972.

Witherington, Ben III. "What 'God Is Love' Means," Biblical Archaeology Review, Vol 46, no. 4.

Wright, N. T. *Broken Signposts: How Christianity Makes Sense of the World*. New York: HarperOne, 2020.

———. *Paul and the Faithfulness Of God*. Minneapolis: Fortress, 2014.

———. *Jesus and the Victory of God*. Minneapolis: Fortress, 1996.

———. *The Resurrection of the Son of God*. Minneapolis: Fortress, 2003.

Young, Edward J. *The Book of Isaiah, Vol 1*. Grand Rapids: Eerdmans, 1965.

Zorn, Walter D. *Psalms*, Vol 2, in College Press NIV Series. Joplin: College Press, 2004.

———. "Segullah: A Word of Worth" in *Deuteronomy: The Prophets and the Life of the Church*, edited by Jason T. Lecureux, J. Blair Wilgus, and James Riley Estep, Jr. (Preston Vic: Australia, Mosaic Press, 2013): ch. 3, 36–54.

———. *The Faithfulness of Jesus the Messiah*. Eugene: Wipf and Stock, 2020.

Index

Abraham, 24, 29–30, 33, 36, 60, 64, 81, 105, 118, 123, 135, 157, 165, 169–70, 172, 177, 197, 200–02, 204, 206, 216, 220, 225–26, 240–41, 254, 297, 299, 333, 349, 363–64, 372, 379
Adam, 34, 40, 59, 68, 80, 85, 100–02, 132–34, 168–72, 247–48, 259, 267, 269, 278, 304, 311–13, 320, 349
After Evangelicalism: The Path to a New Christianity, by David P. Gushee, 300, 390
After Whiteness: An Education in Belonging, by Willie James Jennings, 7, 272, 390
"Against Apion," in *Antiquity of the Jews*, in Works of Flavius Josephus, vol. IV, 290, 390
Against Heresies, book 4, in Ante-Nicene Fathers, Vol.1, by Irenaeus, 47, 390
Albright, William F., 32, 132, 345, 389
Alter, Robert, 34, 389
American Civil War, 6
Anointed One, as title of Jesus, 13, 133, 151, 152–61, 169, 269, 271
Art of Reading Scripture, The, by Ellen F. Davis and Richard B. Hays, 255, 390

Bailey, Kenneth E., 190, 389
Barclay, William, 63, 189
Barth, Markus, 37, 389
  Ephesians 1–3, 37, 389
  Ephesians 4–6, 37, 389
Bauckham, Richard, 9, 10, 318, 389
becoming fully human as ultimate goal, 1, 9, 10, 16, 21, 22, 65–68, 71–75, 85, 95, 113, 157, 171, 194, 246, 286, 304, 364
Biblical Prophecy: Perspectives for Christian Theology, Discipleship, and Ministry, by Ellen Davis, 243, 366, 389
Binding the Strong Man: A Political Reading of Mark's Story of Jesus, by Ched Meyers, 84, 312, 391

Blue like Jazz, by Donald Miller, 384, 391
Bodo, Murray, 72, 389
Bonhoeffer, Dietrich, 189, 300, 389
Book of Isaiah, by Solomon B. Freehof, 167, 390
Borg, Marcus, *Meeting Jesus Again for the First Time*, 156, 389
Boyarin, Daniel, 9, 104, 389
Braiding Sweetgrass, by Robin Wall Kimmerer, 38, 78, 390
Broken Signposts, by N. T. Wright, 132, 262, 392
Brown, Austin Channing, 3, 27
Brown, Raymond, 329, 389
Bruce, F. F., 3
Brueggemann, Walter, 355, 389

"Calvin and Hobbes," (Sunday comic strip), by Bill Watterson, in *The Chicago Tribune*, 53, 392
Carroll, James, 232, 389
Carroll, Samuel, vii
Carter, J. Kameron, in "White American Christianity Is Rooted in
Cassius, Lucius Dio, 119, 390
Charles, Mark, 115, 288, 371, 389
Checker, Judy, vii
Christ Jesus, preexistence of, 8, 11, 321, 329
Christianity: The First Three Thousand Years, by Diarmaid MacCulloch, 288, 391
Christos as title of Jesus, 13, 119, 151, 153, 155–57
Civil War, American, 6
Claiborne, Shane, 112, 389
Common Prayer: A Liturgy for Ordinary Radicals, by Shane Claiborne, 112, 389
Complete Poems of Emily Dickinson, The, by Emily Dickinson, 376, 389
Cone, James H. *The Cross and the Lynching Tree*, 389
Constantine's Sword: The Church and the Jews, by James Carroll, 232, 389

Index

Cost of Discipleship, The, by Dietrich Bonhoeffer, 189, 300, 389
Coronavirus and Christ, by John Piper, 391
Courtney, Jeremy, 5, 389
Cross and the Lynching Tree, The, by James H. Cone, 389
Crossan, John Dominic, 71, 389

Daily Bread Meditations, 3
David (King David), 7, 25, 31, 80, 82, 97–98, 105–06, 110, 117–18, 151–58, 164–70, 174, 201, 231, 247, 256, 297, 305–06, 326, 354, 372
Davis, Ellen, 201, 242–43, 364, 366, 389, 390
Dawkins, Richard, 189, 389
Dickinson, Emily, 389
Did the First Christians Worship Jesus?, by James D. G. Dunn, 9–11, 85, 390
Dio Cassius, Lucius, 119, 389
Dodd, Charles Harold, 333, 390
Dunn, James Douglas Grant, 9–11, 85, 333, 390

Ehrman, Bart, D., 9, 41–42, 104, 105, 141, 321, 390
Eliade, Mircea, 74, 390
Eller, Vernard, 386, 390
Ellul, Jacques, 3
Elohim, 10, 27, 164,
Ephesians 1–3, by Markus Barth, 37, 389
Ephesians 4–6, by Markus Barth, 37, 389
Epic of Eden, The: A Christian Entry into the Old Testament, by Sandra Richter, 366, 372, 386, 391
Epistemology, 4, 142
Equal Justice Initiative, the, 53, 281
Essence of Christianity, The, by Ludwig Feuerbach, 57, 58, 189, 390
Evans, Rachel Held, 4, 389
Everything Must Change: Jesus, Global Crises, and a Revolution of Hope, by Brian D. McLaren, 386, 391
Ewald, Thomas, vii, 25, 103

Faith of Jesus Christ, The: The Narrative Substructure of Galatians 3:1–4:11, by Richard Bevin Hays, 204, 390
Father (God), v, 10, 21, 24, 94, 123, 128
Feuerbach, Ludwig, 57, 58, 189, 390
firstborn (Jesus and Israel), iii, iv, 1–2, 11, 12, 16, 17, 23, 25, 27, 29, 46, 57, 63, 66, 68, 73, 87, 90, 94–96, 100, 110, 125, 127, 134–35, 159, 162, 170, 178, 205, 212, 230, 252–53, 260–62, 266, 311, 313, 317, 321–23, 332, 338, 347, 378, 380, 387

Flesh and Spirit, by William Barclay, 63, 389
Follow Me: Discipleship According to Saint Matthew, by Martin H. Franzmann, 129, 390
Footnoting, 3
France, Richard Thomas, 129, 243, 311, 390
Franzmann, Martin H., 129, 390
Freehof, Solomon B., 167, 390
Freud, Sigmund, 189, 390
Future of an Illusion, The, by Sigmund Freud, 189, 390

Genesis: Translation and Commentary, by Robert Alter, 34, 389
Getting Involved with God: Rediscovering the Old Testament, by Ellen F. Davis, 201, 389
Giveness of Things, The, by Marilynne Robinson, 9, 10, 391
God
　as Father, v, 10, 21, 24, 94, 123, 128,
　future human family of, 1, 7, 9, 12, 16, 23, 26–28, 30–31, 39, 48–51, 54, 57, 59–64, 66, 68, 73, 78, 94–96, 110–11, 133, 134–35, 159, 165, 168, 171–72, 177, 180, 186, 192, 212, 214, 222–23, 232, 242, 252, 254, 258, 260–63, 270, 275, 288, 311–13, 321–24, 341–43, 349, 352, 358, 377
　my God and your God, 10, 24
　Son of, 11, 17, 48, 55, 82, 124, 125, 162, 165, 168–72, 176, 239, 245, 248, 261, 263, 272, 277, 313, 320, 325, 326, 331–34, 337, 387
　sovereignty of, 8, 11–12, 201–02, 240, 363, 378, 381–84
God: A Biography, by Jack Miles, 391
God Delusion, The, by Richard Dawkins, 189, 389
God in New Testament Theology, by Larry Weir Hurtado, 257, 387–88, 390
God in Search of Man: A Philosophy of Judaism, by Abraham Joshua Heschel, 40–42, 226, 390
God of Hope, The, and the End of the World, by John Pulkinghorne, 57, 391
Gospel According to John, The, by Raymond Brown, 329, 390
"Gospel of Mark, The," by Richard Thomas France, in *The New International Greek Commentary*, 243, 311, 390
Grant, Michael, 290, 390
Grief Observed, A, by Clive Staples Lewis, 200, 230, 390
Gushee, David P., 33, 149, 289, 300, 390

Hardin, Michael, 371, 390

INDEX

Hays, Richard Bevin, 204, 254–55, 390
hermeneutics, 4
Heschel, Abraham Joshua, 40–42, 226, 390
His End Up: Getting God into the New Theology, by Vernard Eller, 386, 390
Homo Viator, by Gabriel Marcel, 198, 207, 391
How Jesus Became God: The Exaltation of a Jewish Preacher from Galilee, by Bart D. Ehrman, 9, 41–42, 104, 141, 321, 390
How on Earth Did Jesus Become a God? Historical Questions about Earliest Devotion to Jesus, by Larry Weir Hurtado, 9, 17, 113, 390
Hunt, Karyn, vii
Hunt Wassink, Mari, vii
Hurtado, Larry Weir, 9, 17, 113–14, 257, 387–88, 390

Irenaeus, 47, 390
Inerrancy, 4, 210, 285, 359
Inspired: Slaying Giants, Walking on Water, and Loving the Bible Again, by Rachel Held, 4, 389
Interpretation of the Fourth Gospel, The, by Charles Herold Dodd, 333, 390
Iraq, 5, 228, 236, 238
Isaiah, Book of, by Solomon B. Freehof, 167, 390

James, 37, 47, 107, 211, 214, 246, 274, 284, 363, 368, 372, 374–75
  as conservative Galilean Jew, 7
Jean-Paul Sartre, To Freedom Condemned—A Guide to His Philosophy, ed. Justus Streller, 391
Jefferson, Lee M., 232, 390
Jennings, Willie James, 7, 272, 390
Jesus: A Revolutionary Biography, John Dominic Crossan, 71, 38
Jesus and the Disinherited, by Howard Thurman, 92, 287, 392
Jesus and the Eyewitnesses: The Gospels as Eyewitness Testimony, by Richard Bauckham, 389
Jesus and the God of Israel: God Crucified and Other Studies on the New Testament's Christology of Divine Identity, by Richard Bauckham, 9, 10, 318, 389
Jesus and The Old Testament, by R. T. France, 104, 390
Jesus and the Undoing of Adam, Kruger C. Baxter, 10, 390
Jesus and the Victory of God, by N. T. Wright, 4, 122, 225, 392
Jesus, as God, 10

Jesus Creed, The: Loving God, Loving Others, by McKnight, Scot, 75, 391
Jesus Driven Life, The: Reconnecting Humanity with Jesus, by Michael Hardin, 371, 390
Jesus, preexistence of, 8, 11, 321, 329
"Jesus the Magician?" *Biblical Archaeology Review*, vol. 46, no. 4, by Lee M. Jefferson, 323, 390
Jewish Gospels, The: The Story of the Jewish Christ, by Daniel Boyarin, 9, 104, 389
Jews in the Roman World, The, by Michael Grant, 290, 390
Josephus, Flavius, 257
Just Mercy, by Bryan Stevenson, 53, 39

Kierkegaard, Soren, 3, 38, 207, 300
King, Martin Luther, Jr., 217, 238, 300, 305
Kimmerer, Robin Wall, 38, 78, 390
Kendi, Ibrim Xolani., 288, 390
Kuhn, Thomas Samuel, 3, 386

Lapide, Pinchas, 258, 390
Levenson, John D., 58,
Levine, Amy-Jill, 295, 391
Lewis, Clive Staples, 3, 57, 200, 230, 390–91
Lewis, John, 76, 195
Lord, as title of Jesus, 11, 18, 22, 23, 68, 86, 106, 116, 119, 151, 210, 224, 306, 312, 316–24, 387
Lorde, Audre, 237, 391
Lost World of Genesis One, The: Ancient Cosmology and the Origins Debate, by John Walton, 18, 120, 392
Love Anyway, by Jeremy Courtney, 5, 389

Mann, John,
Maccabees, *see* Second Maccabees
MacCulloch, Diarmaid, 288, 391
Mann, John, 132, 389
Marcel, Gabriel, 198, 207, 391
Matthew, by William Albright and John Mann, 132, 389
McKnight, Scot, 75, 204, 391
McLaren, Brian D., 219, 386, 391
McNeil, Brenda Salter, 3, 65, 391
Meeting Jesus Again for the First Time, by Marcus Borg, 156, 389
Message of the Psalms, The, by Walter Brueggemann, 355, 389
Messiah, as title of Jesus, 11, 13,15, 19, 21–27, 31, 33, 35–37, 47, 58, 85, 97, 101–03, 109–10, 113–14, 117–19, 121, 126, 132–35, 139, 147, 151–61, 166, 175–76, 181–82, 186, 203–04, 214, 219–20, 224–26

Index

Messiah, as title of Jesus (continued), 240–43, 250–52, 259, 261, 264–65, 269–71, 278–80, 297, 299, 303, 310–12, 322–24, 329, 332, 339–68, 374, 389
Meyers, Ched, 84, 312, 391
Miles, Jack, 391
Miller, Donald, 384, 391
Miracles, by Clive Staples Lewis, Miracles, 391
Misunderstood Jew, The: The Church and the Scandal of the Jewish Jesus, by Amy-Jill Levine, 295, 391
More Ready than You Realize, by Brian D. McLaren, 219, 391
Miles, Jack, 391
My Grandfather's Blessings, by Rachel Naomi Remen, 297, 391

Nagasaki, Christians in, 6
Nietzsche, Fredrick, 38, 391
New Christianity for a New World, A: Why Traditional Faith is Dying and How a New Faith is Being Born, by John Shelby Spong, 137, 391

Pascal, Blaise, 207, 391
Paul and the Faithfulness of God, by N. T. Wright, 85, 197, 201, 204, 318, 392
Paul, as Hellenistic Jewish Roman citizen, 7
Pensées, by Blaise Pascal, 207, 391
Peter, 13, 14, 47, 86, 88, 97, 107, 123, 158–160, 167, 183, 214, 239, 250, 263, 265, 273, 276, 278, 299, 302, 306, 314, 318, 326, 351, 363, 373, 374–76
  As moderate Galilean Jew, 7
Peterson, Eugene, 57, 68, 391
Phenomenon of Man, The, by Pierre Tielhard de Chardin, 392
Philip, as Hellenistic Jewish Roman citizen, 7
Piper, John, 391
Poet and Peasant, by Kenneth E. Bailey, 190, 389
preexistence of Christ Jesus, 8, 11, 321, 329
Pulkinghorne, John, 57, 391

Rah, Soong-Chan, 115, 288, 371, 389
Remen, Rachel Naomi, 297, 391
Resurrection of Jesus, The: A Jewish Perspective, by Pinchas Lapide, 113, 258, 390
Richter, Sandra, 366, 372, 386, 391
Roman History, by Lucias Dio Cassius, 119, 389
Reading Romans Backwards: A Gospel of Peace in the Midst of Empire, by Scott McKnight, 204, 391

"Reading Scripture in Light of the Resurrection" in *The Art of Reading Scripture*, by Richard Bevin Hays, 255, 390
Rediscipling the White Church: From Cheap Diversity to True Solidarity, by David Swanson, 33, 289, 391
  Book Launch, 391
Remen, Rachel Naomi, 297, 391
Resurrection and the Restoration of Israel: The Ultimate Victory of the God of Life, by John D. Levenson, 258, 391
Resurrection of Jesus, The: A Jewish Perspective, by Pinchas Lapide, 113, 258, 390
Resurrection of the Son, by N. T. Wright, 141, 257, 392
Reversed Thunder, by Eugene Peterson, 57, 68, 391
Richter, Sandra, 366, 372, 386, 391
Robinson, Marilynne, 9, 10, 391
Rohr, Richard, 156, 391
Roman History, by Lucius Dio Cassius, 119, 390

Sacred and the Profane, The: The Nature of Religion, Mircea Eliade, 74, 390
Sartre, Jean-Paul, 142, 207, 391
Savior, as title of Jesus, 11, 92, 146, 173–82, 208, 265, 279, 297, 303
Schama, Simon, 156, 290, 391
Scriptures, and context, 4–5, 10, 19, 33–34, 44–45, 68–69, 76–77, 85, 124, 136–39, 155, 164, 203–04, 209, 269, 278, 317–21, 325, 330, 339, 351, 35, 370
Second Macabees, 197, 257–58
Shupack, Martin, vii
Siedenburg, Rob, vii
Simkins, Cyril, 19–20
Simkins, David, vii
Simkins, Donna, vii, 298
Simkins, Mary Ann, vii
Simkins, Ronald, 52, 149, 155, 288, 328, 391
Sister Outsider: Essays and Speeches, Audre Lorde, 237, 391
Sovereignty of God, 8, 11–12, 201–02, 240, 363, 378, 381–84
"Spanish Massacre the French in Florida, 1565," 115, 391
Spong, John Shelby, 137, 391
Stamped from the Beginning: The Definitive History of Racist Ideas in America, by Ibrim Xolani Kindi, 390
Story of the Jews, The: Finding the Words (1000 BC–1492 AD), Simon Schama, 156, 290, 391
Stevenson, Bryan, 53, 392

Streller, Jusus, 391
Strength to Love, by Martin Luther King, Jr., 125, 390
Structure of Scientific Revolutions, The, by Thomas Samuel Kuhn, 3, 386
Swanson, David, 33, 65, 289, 391, 392

teleioō (made perfect, made complete), 1, 36, 37, 38, 49, 65
theos, meaning, 10
Tielhard de Chardin, Pierre, 392
Thielicke (Pastor) Helmut, 44, 392
Thurman, Howard, 92, 287, 392
Thus Spoke Zarathustra, by Fredrick Nietzsche, 38, 391
Tournier, Paul, 3
translation issues, 10, 13–14, 46, 115, 151, 155–56, 167, 185, 204–05, 317, 323, 329, 331–32,
Tribble, Phyliss, 3
Trinity, 8–10, 388
Truth, Tears, Turning, and Trusting: A Pastor's Plea to End Our Ongoing Anti-Semitism and Anti-Judaism, by Ronald Simkins, 52, 149, 155, 287–89, 294, 296, 301, 328, 344, 391

Universal Christ, The, by Richard Rohr, 156, 391
Unsettling Truths: The Ongoing Dehumanizing Legacy of the Doctrine of Discovery, by Mark Charles and Soong-Chan Rah, 115, 288, 371, 389
U.S. Constitution, 6th Amendment, 314, 392
U.S. Constitution, 13th Amendment, 228

veterans, WWII, 6
Victory of God, Jesus and, The, by N. T. Wright, 4, 225, 392

Waiting Father, The, by Helmut Thielicke, 6, 44, 392
Walton, John, 18, 120, 392
Wassink, Adey, vii
Watterson, Bill, 53, 392
Way of St. Francis, The: The Challenge of Franciscan Spirituality for Everyone, by Murray Bodo, 72, 389
Weatherhead, Leslie, 392
"What 'God Is Love' Means," by Ben Witherington III, *Biblical Archaeology Review*, Vol 46, no. 4, 27, 201, 392
"White American Christianity Is Rooted in Colonial Empire-Building," by David P. Gushee, 3, 33, 149, 289, 300, 390
Will of God, The, by Leslie Weatherhead, 392
Witherington, Ben III, 27, 201, 392
Wright, N. T., 3, 4, 9, 10, 85, 122, 132, 141, 142, 197, 201, 204, 225, 226, 257, 262, 318, 392
Wright, Stephen, 256
WWII veterans, 6

YHWH, 11, 26, 27–28, 39, 58, 60, 74, 97, 122, 151–55, 162–63, 165, 167, 185, 240, 316–22, 328, 330, 350, 364, 367, 370

Zarathustra, Thus Spake, by Friederich Nietzsche, 38, 391
Zorn, Walter, vii, 35, 41, 47, 164, 197, 203–04, 205, 262, 392

www.ingramcontent.com/pod-product-compliance
Lightning Source LLC
Chambersburg PA
CBHW080934300426
44115CB00017B/2806